THE H.M. GOUSHA COMPANY
Managing Director: John Stephens

CARTOGRAPHY
Production Directors: Tim Carter, Cary Wilke
Map Design: Kristin Watson
Production Managers: James Craft, Tom Deiley, Karen Novian
Production Coordinators: Cindy Arhelger, Rebecca Bergmann, Pat Flach, Fran Hohman, Sherri Marcee, Lavonne Miller, Glen Pawelski, Evelyn Rolfe, Kate Smith

EDITORIAL
Senior Editor: Rosemarie Robotham
Senior Managing Editor: Brian Phair
Production Coordinator: Malya Alperin
Assistant Editor: Irene Milanos

BALLIETT & FITZGERALD, INC.
Managing Editor: Duncan Bock
Designer: Steven Johnson
Copy Editor: Susan Leopold
Layout Artist: Phil Chin
Assistant Editor: Rachel Florman

GOUSHA

SKI ATLAS

By
Balliett & Fitzgerald
and the USA TODAY Sports Staff

Text by Jordan Simon

Printed in America. First Edition
ISBN 0-671-89138-3

Published by
THE H.M. GOUSHA COMPANY
P.O. Box 98
Highway 87
Comfort, TX 78013

A Division of Simon & Schuster, Inc.

The USA SPORTS *Ski Atlas* is the first comprehensive, hands-on, geographical guide to ski areas, both Alpine and Nordic, across North America. Each area is highlighted on full-color road maps and described in the state-by-state, province-by-province text. The *Atlas*, which also locates major ski museums and halls of fame, provides general information about skiing in every U.S. state and Canadian province. For those "Low Snow" states that lack ski venues, the *Atlas* provides contact numbers for representative retail stores and ski clubs. Other elements include sidebar features on topics ranging from backcountry skiing to seasonal bargains, a glossary of ski terms, USA TODAY Snapshot graphics, and regionally appropriate photography.

We have created a structure to make all this information readily accessible, both on state and city maps and in the accompanying text. This introduction explains the text structure by carefully following the sequence you will find within each chapter and each individual listing. (For complete information on how to understand the maps, please see "How to Read Our Maps" on the inside front cover.)

Much of the text for each state and province is made up of alphabetical area listings. We have divided these into two main categories, **Alpine** and **Nordic**. For those Alpine (or downhill) areas that include Nordic facilities, they are listed together, not separately. Each area is open to the public; in those cases when an area is operated by a ski club, we have noted any restrictions. We list private areas whenever possible in the state or province introductions.

For each entry, whether downhill or cross-country, we include the **name of the facility**; the physical **address**; the general **phone number** and **snow condition hotline** (where available); and a **grid coordinate** (e.g., P. 9, C-3, #1) so you may easily locate a numbered icon for each ski area on the map. Only a handful of small Canadian areas not covered by available mapping lack a grid coordinate. For each **Alpine** area, the above information is followed by the **season** and days open (when it doesn't operate seven days a week). It is always advisable to call an area, since opening and closing dates, as well as hours of operation vary. In addition, smaller areas may close during poor snow periods. We also list **average annual snowfall**, and **terrain**. The latter consists of number of trails, skiable acreage, longest run and breakdown of difficulty— expert, advanced, intermediate and beginner—using the officially recognized symbols for each: double black diamond (♦♦), single black diamond (♦), blue square (■), and green circle (●). **Lifts** come next: number, breakdown (gondola, tram, high speed quad, quad, triple, double and surface lifts, which comprise platters, pomas, T- and J-bars, and rope tows) and uphill capacity per hour. **Summit** and **vertical** statistics follow. Other winter sports **activities** are next: snowboarding (half pipe or terrain park are mentioned in venue notes), ice skating, tubing, tobogganing, dog sledding, sleigh rides and night skiing are the most common. We do not list such indoor activities as a pool, mini-golf, or health club. Finally, the **features** line tells you what percent of snowmaking coverage (if any) the area has, whether there is a ski school, rental shop, restaurant (which may mean full-service, cafeteria, or snack bar), child care, and lodging. If an area also boasts Nordic facilities, these will be listed on the next line. Every area then includes detailed **venue notes** describing the ski experience, with tips on where to find the best runs for your level. For Canada, we have restricted these descriptions to the best known destination ski resorts: approximately one third of the total.

The only exceptions to the above format in the USA listings are "local favorites" or learning hills. These are smaller mountains that serve very well as an introduction to the sport and are predominantly frequented by locals. For our purposes, they might have five or fewer slopes, a vertical of under 500 feet, or only very short runs. (In the case of higher mountain ranges like the Rockies, these criteria shift upward.) For these local favorites we will list salient features on one line: number of trails, vertical, number of lifts, whether there is a half pipe or Nordic system. Though most of these areas offer rentals and instruction, we recommend that you call ahead to find out. A few local favorites may not include venue notes.

For **Nordic**-only areas, we list the physical address, phone, and grid coordinate, followed by a "facilities" line that details the number of groomed and ungroomed kilometers, presence of a skating lane, whether an area offers rentals, lessons, a restaurant or snack bar, lodging, and other winter sports activities similar to those under the Alpine headings. Venue notes here are restricted only to the most notable Nordic centers. Our criteria for inclusion are restricted to those venues that offer either rentals or lessons, as well as some form of central lodge or meeting place where snacks are available. The only listed venues that fail to meet these criteria are those offering something out of the ordinary. We suggest that you call the individual tourist boards listed in each state for information on the many national, state, and provincial forests and parks that offer groomed trails but no facilities.

Starting on page 181 are 14 full-color, trail maps drawn from available material. These illustrations were provided by a geographical range of top-rated ski areas, and are included here not for specific use, but to give skiers a preview of the fun to come. —J.S.

Preface *by Jordan Simon*

Few sports so thoroughly engage the senses as does skiing. The slap of the wind on your face; the whoosh of skis and scrape of snowboards; the panoramic, picture-postcard views—all these are an integral part of the ski experience. Regardless of ability, skiing is the great equalizer: ten-foot cornice or ten-degree bunny slope, the surge of adrenaline is the same.

Then there's the social aspect. While many sports breed their own camaraderie, no one speaks of après jogging. But for skiers, the taste and aroma of hot chocolate or wild game turkey at a mountaintop lodge is as exhilarating as mastering the snow. Everyone knows you're here because you love winter. And for earning that hot tub and hot toddy, nothing beats skiing.

Although I first put on skis at the age of six, I still freeze at the sight of an endless field of moguls, an unbroken sheet of shimmering blue ice, or rocks and stumps poking up from the ground like mischievous sprites. I freeze, but my heart races, my blood pounds, and slowly— because there is no other way that will save my pride—I ski off the lip and seek the fall line as if it were some holy grail. I may not look pretty, but I am a skier.

In the course of researching this atlas, I visited places I had never skied, like Michigan and West Virginia. I discovered the same joy, the same camaraderie wherever I went. I can honestly say you will, too. So go find your own ski adventures. And trust the USA SPORTS *Ski Atlas* to be your guide.

USA SPORTS SKI ATLAS

INDEX TO SKI AREAS

Alpine and Nordic ski areas are represented on the maps by numbered icons. In the index below, the ski area are listed alphabetically and by number within each state. Following the name of each ski area is a map-page number and coordinate, so that you can easily locate the corresponding icon on the maps.

8. Ski Mill Ridge (P. 42, B-3)
9. Sugar Mountain Resort (P. 42, B-3)
10. Wolf Laurel (P. 42, B-2)

NORTH DAKOTA

ALPINE

1. Bottineau Winter Park (P. 44, B-3)
2. Frostfire Mountain (P. 44, B-5)
3. Skyline Skiway (P. 44, B-4)

OHIO

ALPINE

1. Alpine Valley (P. 45, A-5)
2. Boston Mills/Brandywine Ski Resorts (P. 45, B-5)
3. Clear Fork Ski Area (P. 45, B-4)
4. Mad River Mountain (P. 45, C-2)
5. Snow Trails Ski Area (P. 45, C-2)

NORDIC

6. Bunker Hill Golf & Ski Center (P. 45, B-4)
7. Chapin Forest (P. 45, A-4)
8. Cross Country Ski Center (P. 45, D-2)
9. Edgewood Cross Country Ski Area (P. 45, B-4)
10. Highland Park Cross Country (P. 45, A-4)
11. Lake County YMCA (P. 45, A-4)
12. Northwest Ohio Nordic Ski Center (P. 45, A-2)
13. Punderson State Park (P. 45, A-4)
14. Quail Hollow Resort (P. 45, A-4)

OREGON

ALPINE

1. Anthony Lakes Mtn Resort (P. 47, B-5)
2. Cooper Spur Ski Area (P. 47, A-3)
3. Hoodoo Ski Bowl (P. 47, B-3)
4. Mount Ashland Ski Area (P. 47, D-2)
5. Mount Bachelor Ski Resort (P. 47, C-3)
6. Mount Hood Meadows Ski Resort (P. 47, A-3)
7. Mount Hood Ski Bowl (P. 47, B-3)
8. Spout Springs (P. 47, A-5)
9. Summit Ski Area (P. 47, B-3)
10. Timberline Lodge Ski Area (P. 47, B-3)
11. Warner Canyon (P. 47, D-4)
12. Willamette Pass (P. 47, C-3)

NORDIC

13. Black Butte Ranch (P. 47, B-3)
14. Blue Lake Nordic Center (P. 47, B-3)
15. Diamond Lake Ranch (P. 47, C-3)
16. Odell Lake Lodge (P. 47, C-3)

PENNSYLVANIA

ALPINE

1. Alpine Mountain Ski Area (P. 48, C-6)
2. Big Boulder Ski Area (P. 48, C-5)
3. Blue Knob Recreation (P. 48, D-3)
4. Blue Marsh Ski Area (P. 48, C-5)
5. Blue Mountain (P. 48, C-5)
6. Boyce Park Ski Area (P. 48, D-2)
7. Camelback Ski Area (P. 48, C-6)
8. Crystal Lake Ski Center (P. 48, C-4)
9. Doe Mountain Ski Area (P. 48, D-6)
10. Eagle Rock Ski Center (P. 48, C-5)
11. Edinboro Ski Area (P. 48, B-1)
12. Elk Mountain Ski Center (P. 48, B-6)
13. Fernwood Ski Area (P. 48, C-6)
14. Hidden Valley Ski Area (P. 48, D-2)
15. Jack Frost Mountain (P. 48, C-5)
16. Montage Ski Area (P. 48, B-5)
17. Mount Airy Lodge (P. 48, C-6)
18. Mount Pleasant Ski Area (P. 48, B-1)
19. Mount Tone Ski Resort (P. 48, B-6)
20. Seven Springs Mountain Resort (P. 48, D-2)
21. Shawnee Mountain (P. 48, C-6)
22. Ski Denton (P. 48, B-3)
23. Ski Liberty (P. 48, E-4)
24. Ski Roundtop (P. 48, C-4)
25. Ski Sawmill (P. 48, B-4)
26. Split Rock Ski Area (P. 48, C-5)
27. Spring Mountain Ski Area (P. 48, D-6)
28. Tamiment Ski Area (P. 48, C-6)
29. Tanglewood Ski Area (P. 48, B-6)
30. Tussey Mountain Ski Area (P. 48, C-3)
31. Whitetail Resort (P. 48, E-3)
32. Willowbrook Ski Area (P. 48, D-1)

NORDIC

33. Callender's Windy Acres Farm (P. 48, B-5)
34. Camp Spears Eljabar (P. 48, C-6)
35. Cherry Ridge Farm (P. 48, C-5)
36. Elk Valley Cross Country (P. 48, B-1)
37. Evergreen Park Cross Country Area (P. 48, C-6)
38. Gateway Lodge (P. 48, C-2)
39. Hanley's Happy Hill (P. 48, C-2)
40. Indian Head Nordic Center (P. 48, B-1)
41. Indian Mountain Inn (P. 48, B-5)
42. The Inn at Starlight Lake (P. 48, B-5)
43. Maple Hill Farm (P. 48, B-6)
44. Pack Shack Adventures (P. 48, C-6)
45. Penn Hills Lodge (P. 48, C-6)
46. Pocono Hershey Nordic Cen (P. 48, C-6)
47. Sterling Inn (P. 48, C-5)
48. Stone Valley Rec Cen (P. 48, C-3)
49. Wilderness Lodge (P. 48, B-1)

RHODE ISLAND

ALPINE

1. Yawgoo Valley (P. 30, D-4)

SOUTH DAKOTA

ALPINE

1. Deer Mountain Ski Area (P. 49, C-1)
2. Terry Peak Ski Area (P. 49, C-1)

NORDIC

3. Riverview Cross Country Ski Center (P. 49, D-6)
4. Ski Cross Country (P. 49, C-1)

TENNESSEE

ALPINE

1. Ober Gatlinburg (P. 27, D-8)

UTAH

ALPINE

1. Alta Ski Lifts (P. 52, B-3)
2. Beaver Mountain (P. 52, A-3)
3. Brian Head Ski Resort (P. 52, D-2)
4. Brighton Ski Resort (P. 52, B-3)
5. Deer Valley Resort (P. 52, B-3)
6. Elk Meadows Ski Resort (P. 52, D-2)
7. Nordic Valley (P. 52, B-3)
8. Park City Ski Area (P. 52, B-3)
9. Park West Ski Area (P. 52, B-3)
10. Powder Mountain Resort (P. 52, B-3)
11. Snowbasin (P. 52, B-3)
12. Snowbird Ski Resort (P. 52, B-3)
13. Solitude Ski Resort (P. 52, B-3)
14. Sundance Resort (P. 52, B-3)

NORDIC

15. Best Western Ruby's Inn (P. 52, E-3)
16. Homestead Cross-Country Ski Centers (P. 52, B-3)
17. Jeremy Ranch (P. 52, B-3)
18. Sherwood Hills Nordic Cen (P. 52, A-3)
19. Tag-A-Long Expeditions (P. 52, D-4)
20. White Pine Touring (P. 52, B-3)

VERMONT

ALPINE

1. Ascutney Mountain Resort (P. 38, D-2)
2. Bolton Valley Resort (P. 38, B-2)
3. Bromley Mountain (P. 38, E-1)
4. Burke Mountain (P. 38, A-3)
5. Cochran Ski Area (P. 38, B-1)
6. Jay Peak Resort (P. 38, A-2)
7. Killington Ski Resort (P. 38, D-2)
8. Lyndon Outing Club (P. 38, B-3)
9. Mad River Glen (P. 38, C-2)
10. Maple Valley Ski Area (P. 38, E-2)
11. Middlebury Coll Snow Bowl (P. 38, C-1)
12. Mt Snow/Haystack Resort (P. 38, E-2)
13. Northeast Slopes (P. 38, C-3)
14. Norwich Univ Ski Area (P. 38, C-2)
15. Okemo Resort (P. 38, D-2)
16. Pico Ski Area (P. 38, D-2)
17. Quechee Lakes (P. 38, D-2)
18. Smugglers' Notch Ski Area (P. 38, B-2)
19. Stowe Mountain Resort (P. 38, B-2)
20. Stratton Mountain Resort (P. 38, E-2)
21. Sugarbush Resort (P. 38, C-2)
22. Suicide Six Ski Area (P. 38, D-2)

NORDIC

23. Amiski Ski Area (P. 38, B-2)
24. Barrows House (P. 38, C-1)
25. Blueberry Lake Cross Country (P. 38, C-2)
26. Camel's Hump (P. 38, B-2)
27. Catamount Family Center (P. 38, B-1)
28. Craftsbury Nordic Center (P. 38, B-2)
29. Edson Hill (P. 38, B-2)
30. Fox Run Cross Country (P. 38, D-2)
31. Grafton Ponds (P. 38, E-2)
32. Green Mountain Lodge Touring Center (P. 38, C-2)
33. Green Trails (P. 38, C-2)
34. Hazen's Notch Cross Country (P. 38, A-2)
35. Hermitage Touring Center (P. 38, E-2)
36. Highland Lodge (P. 38, B-3)
37. Hildene (P. 38, E-1)
38. Lake Morey Inn Resort (P. 38, C-3)
39. Mountain Meadows (P. 38, D-2)
40. Mountain Top Cross Country (P. 38, D-1)
41. Nordic Inn Cross Country (P. 38, E-1)
42. Ole's Cross Country Center (P. 38, C-2)
43. Rikert's (P. 38, C-1)
44. Round Barn Farm (P. 38, C-2)
45. Sitzmark (P. 38, E-2)
46. Tater Hill Cross Country Cen (P. 38, E-2)
47. Timber Creek Cross Country (P. 38, E-2)
48. Topnotch (P. 38, B-2)
49. Trail Head Cross Country Ski Area (P. 38, D-2)
50. Trapp Family Lodge Cross Country (P. 38, B-2)
51. The Viking Ski Touring Cen (P. 38, E-2)
52. White House (P. 38, E-2)
53. Wild Wings Ski Touring Cen (P. 38, E-2)
54. Wilderness Trails (P. 38, D-2)
55. Windham Hill Inn (P. 38, E-2)

VIRGINIA

ALPINE

1. Bryce Resort (P. 17, C-7)
2. The Homestead Ski Area (P. 16, D-5)
3. Massanutten Resort (P. 17, D-6)
4. Wintergreen (P. 17, E-6)

NORDIC

5. Mountain Lake Resort (P. 17, E-4)

WASHINGTON

ALPINE

1. Alpental/Ski Acres/Snoqualmie/Hyak (P. 53, B-3)
2. Badger Mountain (P. 53, B-4)
3. Crystal Mountain (P. 53, C-3)
4. Echo Valley (P. 53, B-4)
5. 49 Degrees North Ski Resort (P. 53, B-5)
6. Hurricane Ridge Ski Area (P. 53, B-2)
7. Loup Loup Ski Bowl (P. 53, B-4)
8. Mission Ridge Ski Area (P. 53, B-4)
9. Mount Baker (P. 53, A-3)
10. Mount Spokane Ski Area (P. 53, B-5)
11. Sitzmark (P. 53, A-4)
12. Ski Bluewood (P. 53, C-5)
13. Stevens Pass Ski Area (P. 53, B-3)
14. White Pass Village Ski Area (P. 53, C-3)

NORDIC

15. Bear Mountain Ranch (P. 53, B-4)
16. Mazama Country Inn (P. 53, A-4)
17. Methow Valley Sport Trails Association (P. 53, A-4)
18. Nordic Way XC Ski Sch & Northwest Telemark Institute (P. 53, B-3)
19. Sun Mountain Lodge (P. 53, B-4)

WEST VIRGINIA

ALPINE

1. Alpine Lake Resort (P. 16, C-5)
2. Canaan Valley Resort (P. 17, C-6)
3. New Winter Place (P. 16, E-4)
4. Oglebay Park (P. 16, B-4)
5. Snowshoe Mountain Resort (P. 16, D-5)
6. Timberline Four Seasons Resort (P. 17, C-6)

NORDIC

7. Blackwater Nordic Center (P. 17, C-6)
8. Elk River Touring Center (P. 16, D-5)
9. White Grass Ski Touring Cen (P. 17, C-6)

WISCONSIN

ALPINE

1. Alpine Valley Resort (P. 54, E-4)
2. Americana Ski Area (P. 54, E-4)
3. Ausblick Ski Area (P. 54, D-4)
4. Bruce Mound Winter Sports Area (P. 54, C-3)
5. Calumet Ski Area (P. 54, D-4)
6. Camp Ten Ski Area (P. 54, C-3)
7. Cascade Mountain (P. 54, D-3)
8. Christie Mountain (P. 54, B-2)
9. Christmas Mountain (P. 54, D-3)
10. Crystal Ridge (P. 54, E-4)
11. Devil's Head Lodge (P. 54, D-3)
12. Hidden Valley Ski Area (P. 54, D-5)
13. Kettlebowl Hill (P. 54, C-4)
14. Keyes Peak Ski Hill (P. 54, B-4)
15. Little Switzerland (P. 54, B-2)
16. Mont Du Lac Ski Area (P. 54, B-2)
17. Mount Ashwabay (P. 54, A-3)
18. Mount La Crosse (P. 54, D-2)
19. Nordic Mountain (P. 54, D-3)
20. Olympia Village (P. 54, D-4)
21. Paul Bunyan Ski Hill (P. 54, C-4)
22. Potawatomi Park (P. 54, C-5)
23. Powers Bluff Winter Recreation Area (P. 54, C-3)
24. Rib Mountain Ski Area (P. 54, C-3)
25. Sky Line Area (P. 54, D-3)
26. Standing Rocks (P. 54, C-3)
27. Sunburst (P. 54, D-4)
28. Sylvan Ski Hill (P. 54, C-3)
29. Telemark Ski Area (P. 54, B-2)
30. Triangle Sports Area (P. 54, C-4)
31. Trollhaugen Ski Area (P. 54, C-2)
32. Tyrol Basin (P. 54, D-3)
33. Whitecap Mountain (P. 54, B-3)
34. White Tail Ridge (P. 54, D-3)
35. Wilmot Mountain (P. 54, E-5)
36. Woodside Ranch Resort (P. 54, D-3)

NORDIC

37. Abbey Springs (P. 54, E-4)
38. Camp Tapawingo (P. 54, C-5)
39. The "Club" at Eagle River Nordic (P. 54, B-4)
40. Crivitz Cross Country Ski Cen (P. 54, C-4)
41. Currie Park (P. 54, D-5)
42. Ft Wilderness Christian Camp (P. 54, B-3)
43. George Williams Ski Touring Center (P. 54, E-4)
44. Glacier Pines Outfitters (P. 54, B-2)
45. Goat Farm Trails (P. 54, D-4)
46. Hammond Golf Club (P. 54, C-2)
47. Hill Havens Ski & Golf (P. 54, C-4)
48. Holiday Acres' Holiday Trails (P. 54, B-4)
49. Interlaken Resort & Country Spa (P. 54, E-4)
50. Iola Winter Sports Complex (P. 54, C-4)
51. Johnson Park Winter Wonderland (P. 54, E-5)
52. Just-N-Trails (P. 54, D-3)
53. Lake Forest Recreation Area (P. 54, B-4)
54. Lake Lawn Lodge (P. 54, E-4)
55. Milwaukee County Zoo (P. 54, D-5)
56. Minocqua Winter Park (P. 54, B-3)
57. Mount Hardscrabble (P. 54, B-2)
58. Mountain-Nicolet (P. 54, C-4)
59. Nine Mile Country Forest/Sylvan Hill Park Ski Center (P. 54, C-3)
60. Old World Wisconsin (P. 54, E-4)
61. Palmquist's "The Farm" (P. 54, B-3)
62. Paust's Wood Lake Resort (P. 54, C-4)
63. Perkinstown Trail/Sitz Mark (P. 54, C-3)
64. Quit Qui OC Golf Course (P. 54, D-4)
65. The Springs Golf Club Resort (P. 54, D-3)
66. Trail Farm (P. 54, C-3)
67. Trees for Tomorrow Natural Resources Education Center (P. 54, B-4)
68. Wagon Trail Resort (P. 54, C-5)
69. Whitnall Park (P. 54, D-5)
70. Wild Wolf Inn Cross Country Trails (P. 54, C-4)
71. Willow Creek Parks (P. 54, D-4)
72. Woodland Dunes Nature Cen (P. 54, D-5)

WYOMING

ALPINE

1. Antelope Butte/Big Horn (P. 55, A-4)
2. Grand Targhee Resort (P. 55, B-2)
3. High Park Ski Area (P. 55, B-3)
4. Hogadon Ski Area (P. 55, C-4)
5. Jackson Hole/Teton Village (P. 55, B-2)
6. Pine Creek Ski Area (P. 55, C-2)
7. Sleeping Giant Ski Area (P. 55, A-2)
8. Snow King Resort (P. 55, B-2)
9. Snowshoe Hollow Ski Area (P. 55, C-2)
10. Snowy Range Ski Area (P. 55, D-4)

NORDIC

11. Big Horn Mountain Sports (P. 55, A-4)
12. Dornan's Spur Ranch (P. 55, B-2)
13. Pahaska Tepee Resort (P. 55, A-3)
14. Spring Creek Resort (P. 55, B-2)
15. Squaw Creek Ranch (P. 55, A-3)
16. Teton Pines Cross Country (P. 55, B-2)
17. Togwotee Mountain Lodge Touring Center (P. 55, B-2)
18. Wood River Valley Lodge (P. 55, B-3)
19. Yellowstone Park TW Recreational Services (P. 55, A-2)

ALBERTA

ALPINE

1. Canada Olympic Park (P. 59, E-9)
2. Canyon Ski Area (P. 59, D-9)
3. Edmonton Ski Club (P. 59, B-9)
4. Fortress Mountain (P. 59, E-8)
5. Kinosoo Ridge (P. 60, A-1)
6. Lake Louise Ski Area (P. 59, E-8)
7. Marmot Basin (P. 59, C-7)
8. Mount Norquay Ski Area (P. 59, D-8)
9. Nakiska (P. 59, E-8)
10. Nitehawk Ski Hill (P. 59, A-6)
11. Snow Valley Ski Club (P. 59, C-9)
12. Sunshine Village (P. 59, D-8)
13. Sunridge Ski Area (P. 59, C-9)
14. Westcastle Park (P. 59, F-9)
15. Wintergreen (P. 59, E-8)

NORDIC

16. Canmore Nordic Centre (P. 59, D-8)
17. Country Corral Lodge/Panther Valley Wilderness Retreat (P. 59, D-9)
18. Homeplace Ranch (P. 59, E-9)
19. Jasper Park Lodge (P. 59, C-6)
20. Lac La Biche Nordic (P. 59, B-10)
21. Lake O'Hara Lodge (P. 59, D-7)
22. Mount Assiniboine Lodge (P. 59, D-8)
23. Strathcona Wilderness (P. 59, C-9)
24. Tecumseh Mtn Guest Ranch (P. 59, F-8)

BRITISH COLUMBIA

ALPINE

1. Apex Alpine (P. 59, F-6)
2. Bear Mountain Ski Hill (P. 58, A-5)
3. Big Barn Ski Hill (P. 58, A-5)
4. Big White Ski Resort (P. 59, E-6)
5. Clearwater Ski Club (P. 58, D-5)
6. Crystal Mountain (P. 58, F-5)
7. Cypress Bowl (P. 58, F-3)
8. Fairmont Hot Springs Resort (P. 59, E-8)
9. Fernie Snow Valley (P. 59, F-8)
10. Forbidden Mountain (P. 58, E-3)
11. Grouse Mountain (P. 58, F-4)
12. Harper Mountain (P. 58, E-5)
13. Hemlock Resort (P. 58, F-4)
14. Kimberley Ski Resort (P. 59, F-8)
15. Manning Park Resort (P. 58, F-5)
16. Mount Arrowsmith (P. 58, F-3)
17. Mount Baldy Ski Area (P. 59, F-6)
18. Mount Cain (P. 58, E-1)
19. Mount Mackenzie (P. 59, E-7)
20. Mount Timothy Ski Hill (P. 58, D-5)
21. Mt Washington Ski Resort (P. 58, E-3)
22. Murray Ridge Ski Hill (P. 58, B-4)
23. Panorama Resort (P. 59, E-8)
24. Phoenix Mountain (P. 59, F-2)
25. Powder King (P. 58, A-4)
26. Purden Ski Village (P. 58, B-4)
27. Red Mountain Resort (P. 59, F-7)
28. Salmo Ski Area (P. 59, F-7)
29. Seymour Ski Country (P. 58, F-4)
30. Shames Mountain (P. 58, A-1)
31. Silver Star Mountain (P. 59, E-6)
32. Ski Smithers (P. 58, A-2)
33. Snowpatch Ski Hill (P. 58, F-5)
34. Summit Lake Ski Area (P. 59, E-7)
35. Sun Peaks at Tod Mountain (P. 58, E-5)
36. Tabor Mountain (P. 58, B-4)
37. Troll Ski Resort (P. 58, C-4)
38. Whistler/Blackcomb Ski Resort (P. 58, E-3)
39. Whitetooth Ski Area (P. 59, D-7)
40. Whitewater Ski Area (P. 59, F-7)

NORDIC

41. Big Bar Guest Ranch (P. 58, D-5)
42. Emerald Lake Lodge (P. 59, D-8)
43. Hamilton Falls Lodge (P. 58, D-5)
45. Larch Hills Ski Area (P. 59, E-6)
46. McBride Yellowhead Ski Club (P. 58, C-5)
47. Nature Hills Resort (P. 58, D-5)
48. 108 Resort (P. 58, D-5)

MANITOBA

ALPINE

1. Agassiz Ski Resort (P. 61, D-7)
2. Falcon Ski Area (P. 61, E-9)
3. Holiday Mountain (P. 61, E-7)
4. Mystery Mountain (P. 61, A-7)

NORDIC

5. Ski Valley (P. 61, E-7)
6. Springhill Winter Park (P. 61, E-8)
7. Thunder Hill Ski Club (P. 61, C-6)

NEW BRUNSWICK

ALPINE

1. Crabbe Mountain Winter Pk (P. 64, B-2)
2. Mont Farlagne (P. 64, B-1)
3. Poley Mountain (P. 64, C-3)
4. Silverwood Winter Park (P. 64, B-2)
5. Sugarloaf Provincial Park (P. 64, A-2)

NORDIC

6. Rockwood Park Golf Course (P. 64, C-2)

NEWFOUNDLAND (LABRADOR)

ALPINE

1. Marble Mountain (P. 64, A-4)
2. Ski White Hills (P. 64, A-5)

NORDIC

3. Clarenville Ski Center (P. 64, A-5)
4. Deep Cove (P. 64, A-4)
5. Notre Dame Ski Club (P. 64, A-4)
6. Whale Back Nordic (P. 64, A-4)

NOVA SCOTIA

ALPINE

1. Cape Smokey Ski Lodge (P. 64, B-4)
2. Ski Ben Eoin (P. 64, B-5)
3. Ski Martock (P. 64, C-3)
4. Ski Wentworth (P. 64, C-3)

NORDIC

5. Old Orchard Inn Nordic Cen (P. 64, C-3)

ONTARIO

ALPINE

1. Adanac Ski Centre (P. 62, D-4)
2. Alice Hill Park Ski Area (P. 62, B-6)
3. Atitokan Ski Club (P. 62, A-2)
4. Beaver Valley Ski Club (P. 63, G-4)
5. Big Ben Ski Centre (P. 62, B-6)
6. Big Thunder National Ski Training Centre (P. 62, A-3)
7. Blue Mountain Resorts (P. 63, F-4)
8. Buttermilk Alpine Ski Village (P. 62, C-1)
9. Caledon Ski Club (P. 63, G-4)
10. Candy Mountain Ski Area (P. 62, A-3)
11. Capreol Ski Club (P. 62, C-4)
12. Caribou Mountain Ski Club (P. 62, C-5)
13. Caswell Resort Hotel (P. 62, E-5)
14. Chapleau Ski Club (P. 62, A-4)
15. Chedoke Winter Sports Park (P. 63, H-5)
16. Chicopee Ski Club (P. 63, H-4)
17. Devil's Elbow Ski Area (P. 63, G-6)
18. Divine Lake Resort (P. 62, E-5)
19. Dryden Ski Club (P. 62, A-2)
20. Eagle Ridge (P. 62, A-2)
21. Espanola Ski Club (P. 62, D-3)
22. Etobicoke Centennial Park Ski Hill (P. 63, G-5)
23. Glen Eden Ski Area (P. 63, H-4)
24. Hidden Valley Highlands (P. 62, E-5)
25. Hockley Valley Resort (P. 63, G-4)
26. Horseshoe Resort (P. 63, F-5)
27. Kamiskotia Ski Resort (P. 62, A-4)
28. Kingston Ski Hills (P. 62, B-6)
29. Lakeridge Resort (P. 63, G-5)
30. Landslide Ski Hill (P. 62, C-1)
31. Larder Ski Club (P. 62, A-5)
32. Loch Lomond Ski Area (P. 62, A-3)
33. London Ski Club (P. 63, H-3)
34. London/Thamesford Cobble Hills Golf & Ski Club (P. 63, H-3)
35. Loretto Ski Resort (P. 63, G-4)
36. Mansfield Ski Club (P. 63, G-4)
37. Minto Glen Sports Centre (P. 63, G-4)
38. Mount Antoine-Mattawa (P. 62, D-5)
39. Mount Baldy (P. 62, A-3)
40. Mount Chinguacousy (P. 63, G-5)
41. Mount Madawaska (P. 62, B-5)
42. Mount Martin Ski Club (P. 62, B-5)
43. Mount Pakenham (P. 62, B-6)
44. Mount St. Louis/Moonstone (P. 63, F-5)
45. Mount Wawa Ski Hill (P. 62, A-4)
46. Mountain View Ski Hills (P. 63, F-5)
47. North Bay Laurentian Ski Club (P. 62, D-5)
48. North York Ski Centre (P. 63, G-5)
49. Onaping Ski Hills (P. 62, D-3)
50. Oshawa-Kirby Ski Club (P. 63, G-6)
51. Raven Mountain (P. 62, A-5)
52. Rene Brunelle Winter Recreation Area (P. 62, A-4)
53. Searchmont Resort (P. 62, C-1)
54. Silver Fox Ski Resort (P. 63, G-6)
55. Sir Sam's Ski Area (P. 63, F-5)
56. Ski Dagmar (P. 63, G-5)
57. Snow Valley Ski Resort (P. 63, G-5)
58. Superior Slopes (P. 58, A-3)
59. Talisman Mountain Resort (P. 63, F-4)
60. Tri-Town Ski Village (P. 62, A-5)

NORDIC

61. Albion Hills Conservation Area (P. 63, G-4)
62. Algonquin Cross Country Ski Centre (P. 62, E-6)
63. The Baldwins (P. 63, F-5)
64. Bayview-Wildwood Resorts (P. 63, F-5)
65. Beachwood Resort (P. 63, F-6)
66. Bear Trail Inn Resort (P. 62, E-6)
67. Bingeman Park (P. 63, H-4)
68. Blue Water Acres (P. 63, E-5)
69. The Briars Resort (P. 63, G-5)
70. Bruce's Mill Conservation Area (P. 63, G-5)
71. Circle R Ranch Touring Centre (P. 63, H-3)
72. Deer Lodge Resort (P. 63, F-6)
73. Deerhurst Resort Trail System (P. 62, E-5)
74. Domain of Killien Resort (P. 63, F-6)
75. Duntroon Highlands Resort (P. 63, G-4)
76. Elmhirst's Resort (P. 63, G-6)
77. Fern Resort (P. 63, F-5)
78. Georgian Ski & Canoe Club (P. 62, E-4)
79. Grandview Inn (P. 62, E-5)
80. Gravenhurst Nordic Trails (P. 63, F-5)
81. Halimar Lodge (P. 63, F-6)
82. Hardwood Hills (P. 63, F-5)
83. Hearst Cross Country Ski Club (P. 62, A-4)
84. Hiawatha Highlands (P. 62, C-1)
85. Irwin Inn (P. 63, F-6)
86. Kamview Nordic Centre (P. 62, A-3)
87. Laurentian Lodge and Outdoor Centre (P. 62, E-5)
88. Locarno Resort (P. 63, F-6)
89. Lochaven Inn (P. 63, F-6)
90. Mansfield Outdoor Centre (P. 63, G-4)
91. Maple Sands Resort (P. 63, F-6)
92. Mattawa Golf & Ski Resort (P. 62, D-6)
93. Mountsberg Conservation Area (P. 63, H-4)
94. Muskoka Flag Inn (P. 62, E-5)
95. Muskoka Sands Resort (P. 63, F-5)
96. Nangor Resort (P. 62, B-6)
97. Nottawasaga Inn (P. 63, G-4)
98. Pickerel Lake Lodge (P. 62, E-5)
99. Pine Stone Inn (P. 63, F-6)
100. Pleasure Valley (P. 63, G-5)
101. Pow-Wow Point Lodge (P. 62, E-5)
102. Red Bay Lodge (P. 63, F-3)
103. Rocky Crest Resort (P. 63, E-5)
104. Shamrock Lodge (P. 63, F-5)
105. Sherwood Inn (P. 63, F-5)
106. Silent Lake Provincial Park (P. 63, F-6)
107. Smoothwater Outdoor Centre (P. 62, C-5)
108. South Shore Rim Laurentian University Cross Country Trails (P. 62, D-4)
109. Sportsman's Lodge, Resort & Conference Centre (P. 62, D-4)
110. Stokely Lodge (P. 62, C-1)
111. Terra Cotta Conservation Area (P. 63, G-4)
112. Trillium Trails (P. 63, G-5)
113. Viamede Resort & Conference Center (P. 63, F-6)
114. Wasaga Beach Provincial Park (P. 63, F-4)
115. Westwind Inn (P. 63, F-6)
116. Whitefish Lodge (P. 63, A-4)
117. Wigamog Inn (P. 63, F-6)
118. Wye Marsh Wildlife Centre (P. 63, F-5)
119. Y.M.C.A. Geneva Park Vacation & Conference Center (P. 63, F-5)

PRINCE EDWARD ISLAND

ALPINE

1. Brookvale Provincial Park Ski Center (P. 64, B-4)

QUEBEC

ALPINE

1. Belle Neige (P. 64, D-4)
2. Bellevue Ski Center (P. 64, D-4)
3. Bromont (P. 64, E-5)
4. Camp Fortune (P. 64, D-1)
5. Club De Ski Mont Villa Saguenay (P. 65, A-6)
6. Club De Ski Plessis (P. 65, C-6)
7. Club Tobo-Ski (P. 65, A-5)
8. Cote Des Chats Centre De Plein Air (P. 65, B-8)
9. Cotes 40-80 (P. 64, D-4)
10. Edelwiss Valley Ski Centre (P. 64, D-2)
11. Grand Coulee (P. 65, C-7)
12. Gray Rocks (P. 64, D-4)
13. L'Avalanche (P. 64, D-4)
14. La Crapaudiere (P. 65, C-7)
15. La Tuque Centre De Ski (P. 65, B-5)
16. Le Massif (P. 65, B-7)
17. Le Relais Centre De Ski (P. 65, C-6)
18. Le Valinouet (P. 65, A-7)
19. Massif Du Sud (P. 65, C-7)
20. Mont-Alta (P. 64, D-4)
21. Mont Bechervaise (P. 64, A-3)
22. Mont Bellevue (P. 64, E-6)
23. Mont Belu Centre De Ski (P. 65, A-7)
24. Mont-Blanc Centre De Ski (P. 65, D-4)
25. Mont Castor (P. 64, A-2)
26. Mont-Christie Ski Area (P. 64, D-4)
27. Mont Citadelle (P. 65, B-7)
28. Mont Daniel (P. 64, D-3)
29. Mont Edouard (P. 65, A-7)
30. Mont Fortin Centre Du Ski (P. 65, A-6)
31. Mont Gabriel (P. 64, D-4)
32. Mont Garceau (P. 64, D-4)
33. Mont Grand Fonds (P. 65, B-7)
34. Mont Habitant (P. 65, D-4)
35. Mont Joye (P. 65, E-6)
36. Mont Labelle (P. 64, D-4)
37. Mont Lac Vert (P. 65, A-6)
38. Mont Olympia (P. 64, D-4)
39. Mont Orford International Tourist Area (P. 65, E-6)
40. Mont Orignal (P. 65, C-7)
41. Mont Pontbriand (P. 64, D-4)
42. Mont Rigaud (P. 64, E-4)
43. Mont St. Bruno (P. 65, A-6)
44. Mont St. Castin (P. 65, C-6)
45. Mont St. Sauveur/Avila (P. 65, D-4)
46. Mont-Ste.-Marie (P. 64, D-2)
47. Mont Sauvage (P. 64, D-4)
48. Mont Shefford (P. 64, E-5)
49. Mont Sutton (P. 65, E-6)
50. Mont Tibasse (P. 64, A-2)
51. Mont Tremblant Lodge (P. 64, D-4)
52. Owl's Head (P. 65, E-6)
53. Parc Du Mont Comi (P. 64, A-2)
54. Parc Du Mont-Ste.-Anne (P. 65, C-7)
55. St. Georges Centre De Ski (P. 65, D-7)
56. St. Mathieu (P. 64, C-5)
57. St. Raymond Centre De Ski (P. 65, C-6)
58. Ski Chantecler (P. 64, D-4)
59. Ski Mont Glen (P. 65, E-6)
60. Ski Mont-Cascades (P. 60, E-3)
61. Ski Montcalm (P. 64, D-5)
62. Ski Morin Heights (P. 64, D-4)
63. Ski Stoneham (P. 65, C-6)
64. Station De Ski Des Bois-Francs (P. 65, D-6)
65. Val D'Irene (P. 64, A-3)
66. Val Mauricie (P. 64, C-5)
67. Val Neigette Centre De Ski (P. 65, A-9)
68. Val St. Come (P. 64, D-4)
69. Vallee Bleue Ski Centre (P. 64, D-4)
70. Vallee Du Parc (P. 64, C-5)
71. Vorlage (P. 64, D-2)

NORDIC

72. Bec Scie Outdoor Centre (P. 65, A-7)
73. Camp Mercier (P. 65, C-7)
74. Centre De Neige (P. 65, C-7)
75. Cross Country Ski Centre (P. 65, C-7)
76. Cross Country Ski Trails (P. 65, E-6)
77. Far Hills (P. 64, D-4)
78. Farmer's Rest (P. 65, E-6)
79. Gatineau Park (P. 64, D-1)
80. Hotel La Sapiniere (P. 64, D-4)
81. Hotel L'Esterel (P. 64, D-4)
82. Hovey Manor (P. 65, E-6)
83. La Montagne Coupee (P. 64, D-5)
84. La Vigie Outdoor Center (P. 64, E-4)
85. Lac Bouchette Outdoor Centre (P. 64, D-2)
86. Le Chateau Montbello (P. 64, E-3)
87. Le Parc D'Oka (P. 64, E-4)
88. Le Petit Bonheur (P. 64, D-4)
89. Ripplecove Inn (P. 64, D-4)
90. Ste.-Anne-Des-Plaines Centre De Ski De Fond (P. 64, D-4)

SASKATCHEWAN

ALPINE

1. Mission Ridge (P. 65, D-5)
2. Ochapowace Ski Area (P. 60, E-5)
3. Table Mountain (P. 60, C-2)
4. Twin Towers Ski Resort (P. 60, C-2)

Correct at date of publication, but subject to change.

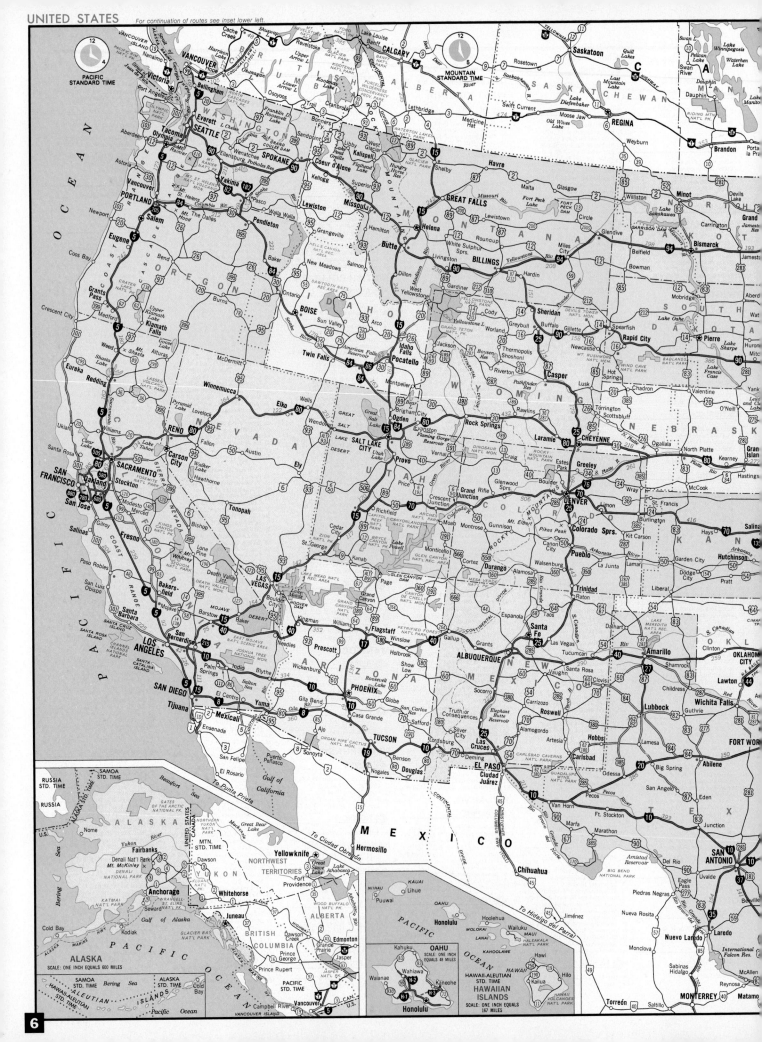

PACIFIC STANDARD TIME

MOUNTAIN STANDARD TIME

ALASKA
SCALE: ONE INCH EQUALS 600 MILES

OAHU
SCALE: ONE INCH EQUALS 48 MILES

HAWAIIAN ISLANDS
SCALE: ONE INCH EQUALS 167 MILES

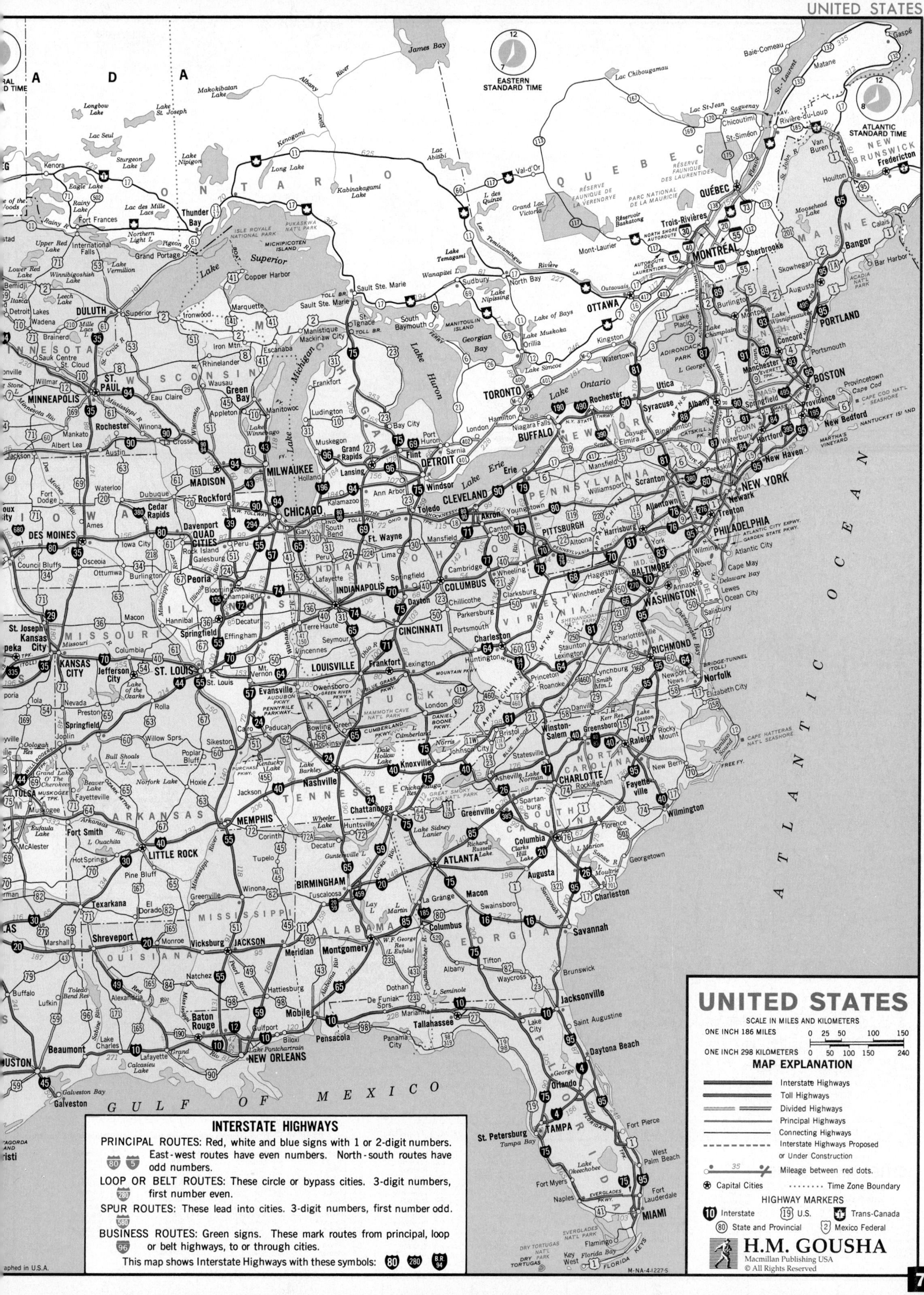

EASTERN STANDARD TIME

ATLANTIC STANDARD TIME

INTERSTATE HIGHWAYS

PRINCIPAL ROUTES: Red, white and blue signs with 1 or 2-digit numbers. East-west routes have even numbers. North-south routes have odd numbers.

LOOP OR BELT ROUTES: These circle or bypass cities. 3-digit numbers, first number even.

SPUR ROUTES: These lead into cities. 3-digit numbers, first number odd.

BUSINESS ROUTES: Green signs. These mark routes from principal, loop or belt highways, to or through cities.

This map shows Interstate Highways with these symbols: 80 280 B.R. 94

UNITED STATES

SCALE IN MILES AND KILOMETERS

ONE INCH 186 MILES 0 25 50 100 150

ONE INCH 298 KILOMETERS 0 50 100 150 240

MAP EXPLANATION

———— Interstate Highways
———— Toll Highways
———— Divided Highways
———— Principal Highways
———— Connecting Highways
– – – – Interstate Highways Proposed or Under Construction
○—35—○ Mileage between red dots.
✶ Capital Cities   · · · · · Time Zone Boundary

HIGHWAY MARKERS

10 Interstate   19 U.S.   Trans-Canada
80 State and Provincial   2 Mexico Federal

H.M. GOUSHA

Macmillan Publishing USA
© All Rights Reserved

M-NA-4-I227-S

7

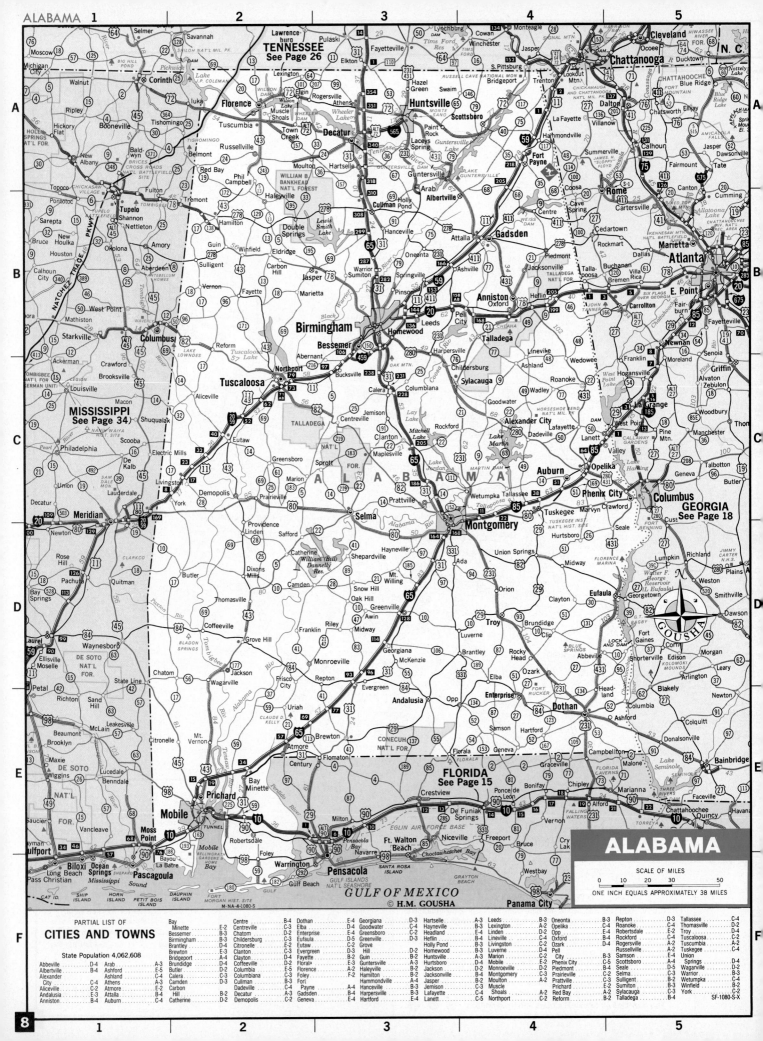

ALABAMA

SCALE OF MILES

0 10 20 30 50

ONE INCH EQUALS APPROXIMATELY 38 MILES

SF-1080-S-X

© H.M. GOUSHA

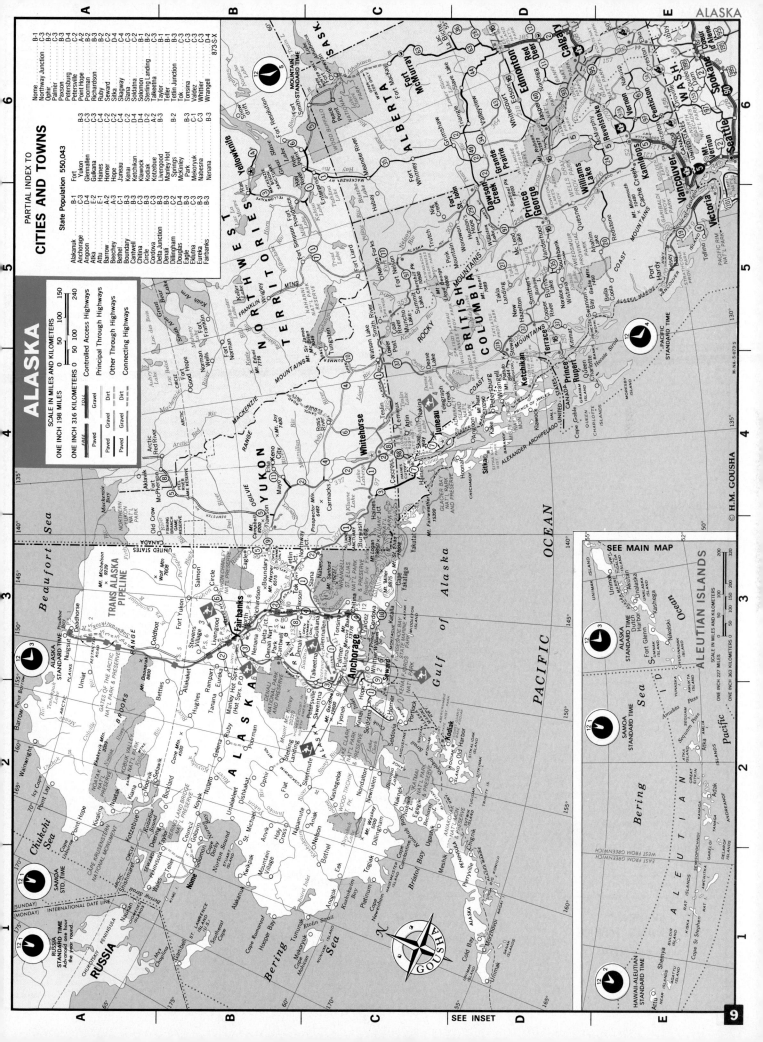

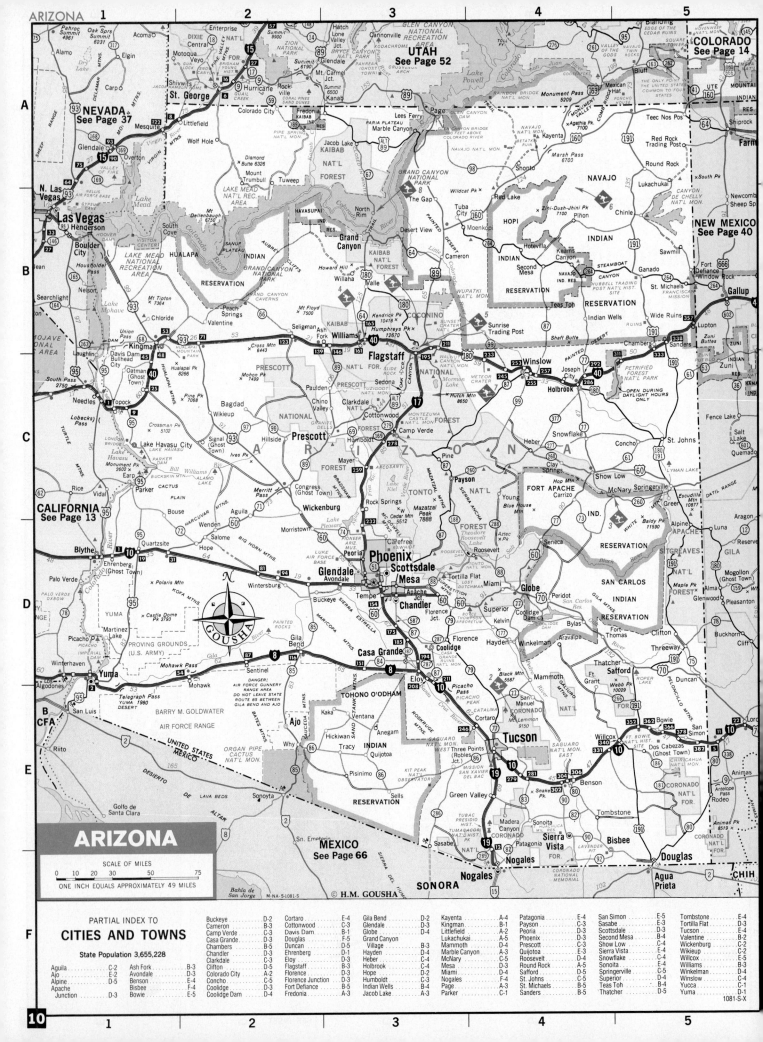

ARIZONA

SCALE OF MILES

0 10 20 30   50   75

ONE INCH EQUALS APPROXIMATELY 49 MILES

© H.M. GOUSHA

M-NA-5-1081-S

10

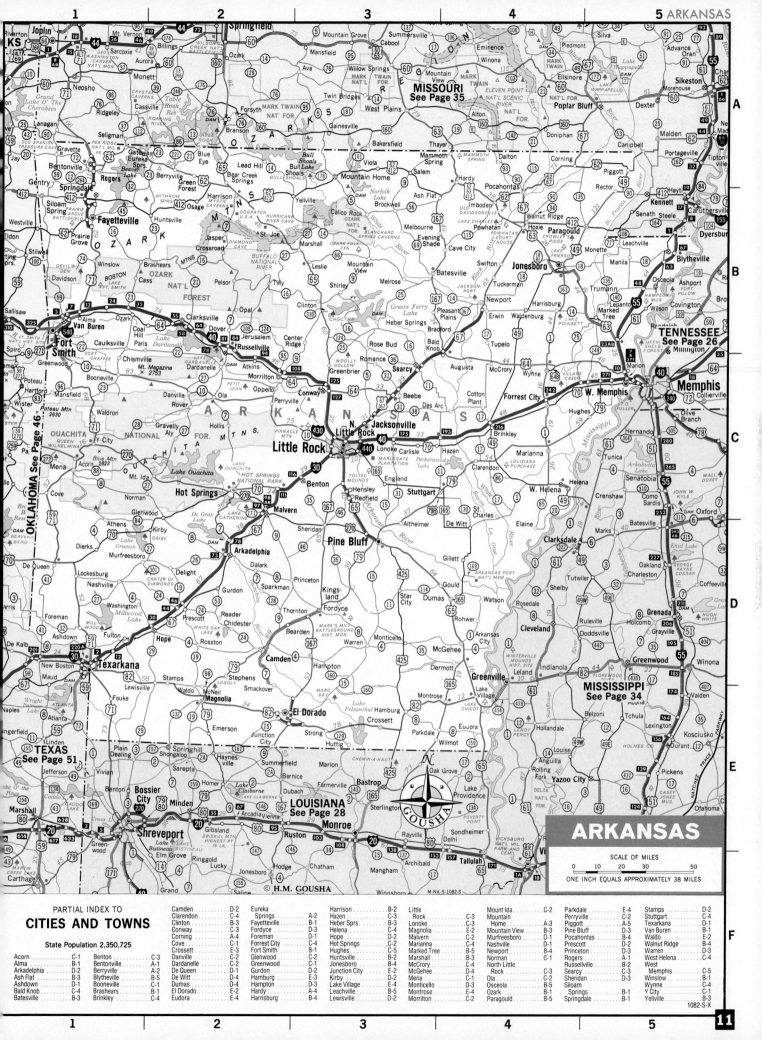

ARKANSAS

SCALE OF MILES

0 10 20 30   50

ONE INCH EQUALS APPROXIMATELY 38 MILES

© H.M. GOUSHA

M-NA-5-1082-S

1082-S-X

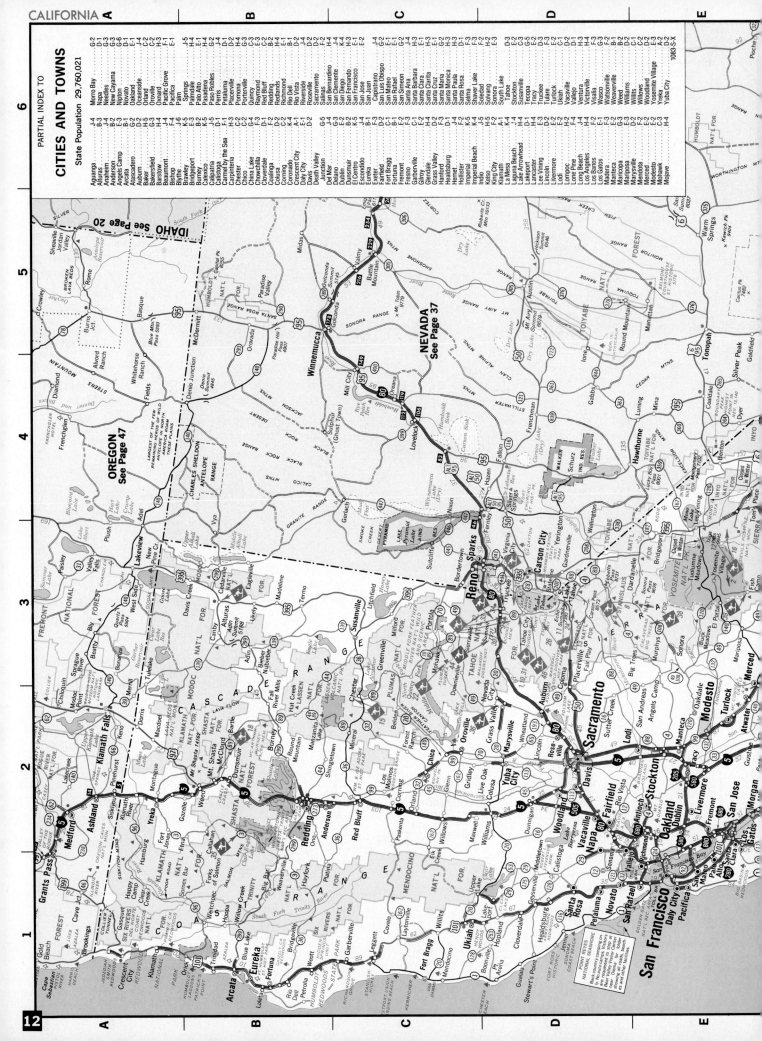

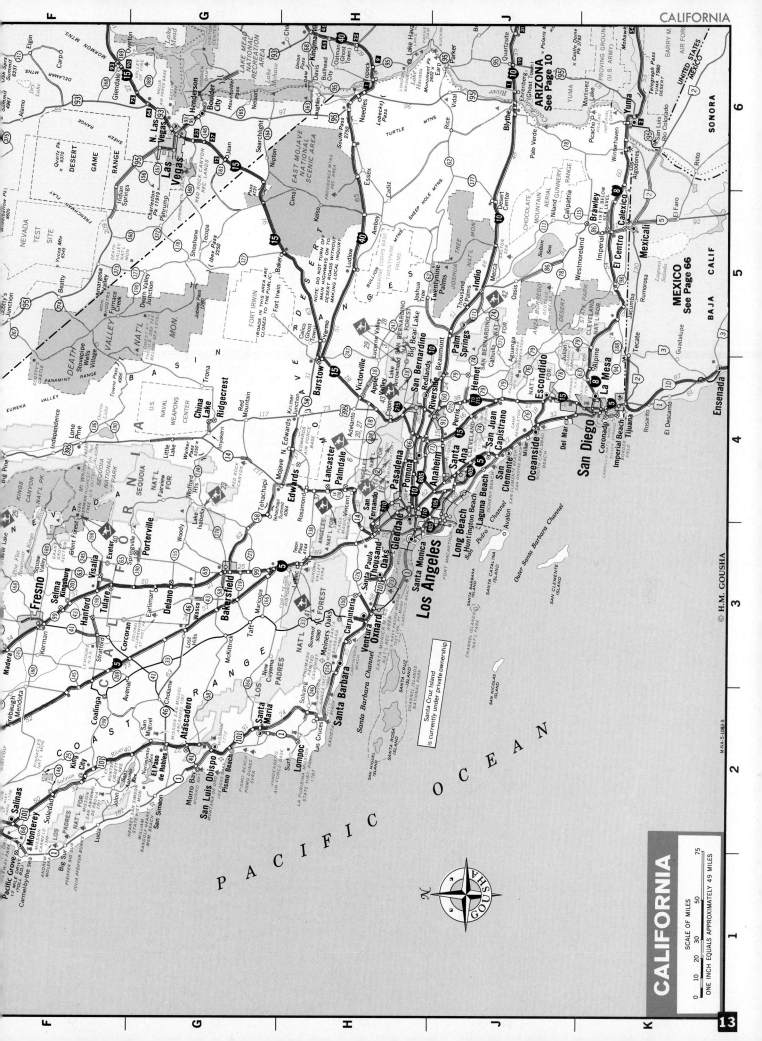

PACIFIC OCEAN

Santa Cruz Island
is currently under private ownership

NOTE: DO NOT TURN OFF
MAIN HIGHWAYS ON TO
DESERT ROADS WITHOUT
MAKING LOCAL INQUIRY.

EAST MOJAVE NATIONAL SCENIC AREA

DEATH VALLEY NAT'L MON.

ARIZONA
See Page 10

MEXICO
See Page 66

UNITED STATES
MEXICO

SONORA

BAJA CALIF

Los Angeles
San Diego
Las Vegas
N. Las Vegas
Bakersfield
Fresno
Salinas
Monterey
Santa Barbara
Ventura
Oxnard
San Luis Obispo
Santa Maria
Lompoc
Barstow
Victorville
Palmdale
Lancaster
Mojave
Ridgecrest
China Lake
Visalia
Tulare
Porterville
Delano
Hanford
Selma
Kingsburg
Madera
Coalinga
King City
Atascadero
El Paso de Robles
Pismo Beach
Morro Bay
Pacific Grove
Big Sur
Needles
Kingman
Blythe
Quartzite
Yuma
Calexico
Mexicali
El Centro
Brawley
Westmoreland
Indio
Palm Springs
San Bernardino
Riverside
Redlands
Beaumont
Hemet
Escondido
Oceanside
San Clemente
San Juan Capistrano
Santa Ana
Anaheim
Pomona
Pasadena
Glendale
Santa Monica
Long Beach
Huntington Beach
Laguna Beach
Del Mar
La Mesa
Coronado
Imperial Beach
Tijuana
Thousand Oaks
Santa Paula
Carpinteria
Avalon
Henderson
Boulder City
Searchlight
Baker
Shoshone
Tecopa
Stovepipe Wells Village
Furnace Creek
Beatty
Independence
Lone Pine
Big Pine
Bishop
Twentynine Palms
Yucca Valley
Big Bear Lake
Lake Arrowhead
Apple Valley
San Fernando
Tehachapi

SCALE OF MILES
0 10 20 30 50 75
ONE INCH EQUALS APPROXIMATELY 49 MILES

CALIFORNIA

13

M-NA-5-1063-S

PADRES NAT'L FOREST

LOS PADRES NAT'L FOREST

SEQUOIA NATIONAL PARK

KINGS CANYON NAT'L PK.

SEQUOIA NAT'L FOR.

ANGELES NAT'L FOREST

SAN BERNARDINO NAT'L FOREST

CLEVELAND NAT'L FOR.

ANZA-BORREGO DESERT STATE PARK

JOSHUA TREE NAT'L MON.

MOJAVE DESERT

COAST RANGE

SAN JOAQUIN VALLEY

NEVADA TEST SITE

CHANNEL ISLANDS NATIONAL PARK

Santa Catalina Island
San Clemente Island
San Nicolas Island
Santa Barbara Island
Santa Rosa Island
San Miguel Island
Santa Cruz Island

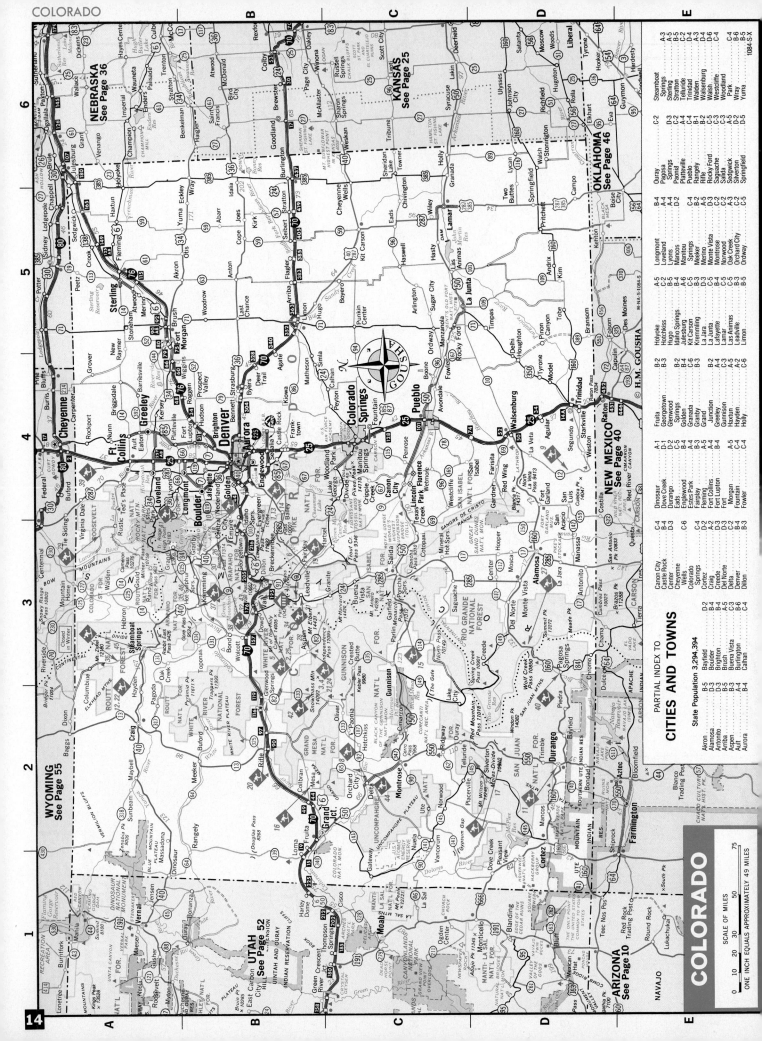

COLORADO

© H.M. GOUSHA

M-NA-S-1084-S

SCALE OF MILES

0 10 20 30 50 75

ONE INCH EQUALS APPROXIMATELY 49 MILES

14

NEBRASKA See Page 36

KANSAS See Page 25

OKLAHOMA See Page 46

NEW MEXICO See Page 40

ARIZONA See Page 10

UTAH See Page 52

WYOMING See Page 55

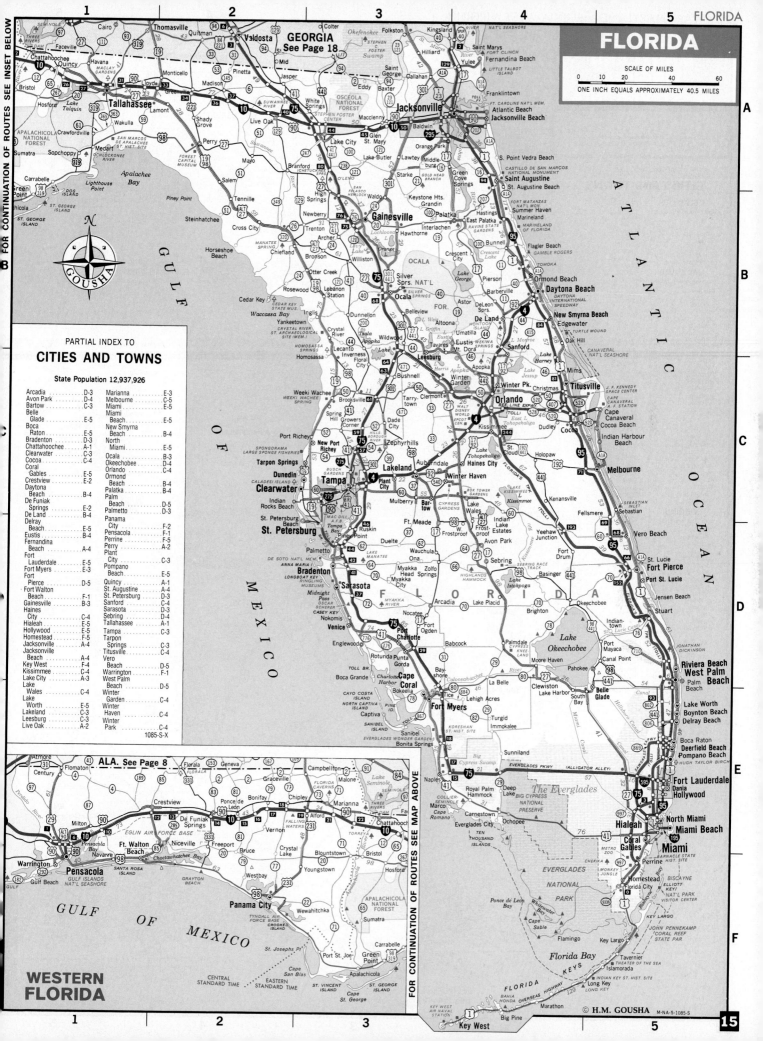

FLORIDA

SCALE OF MILES

ONE INCH EQUALS APPROXIMATELY 40.5 MILES

GEORGIA
See Page 18

PARTIAL INDEX TO
CITIES AND TOWNS

State Population 12,937,926

1085-S-X

ALA. See Page 8

WESTERN FLORIDA

CENTRAL STANDARD TIME · EASTERN STANDARD TIME

© H.M. GOUSHA   M-NA-5-1085-S

15

FOR CONTINUATION OF ROUTES SEE INSET BELOW

FOR CONTINUATION OF ROUTES SEE MAP ABOVE

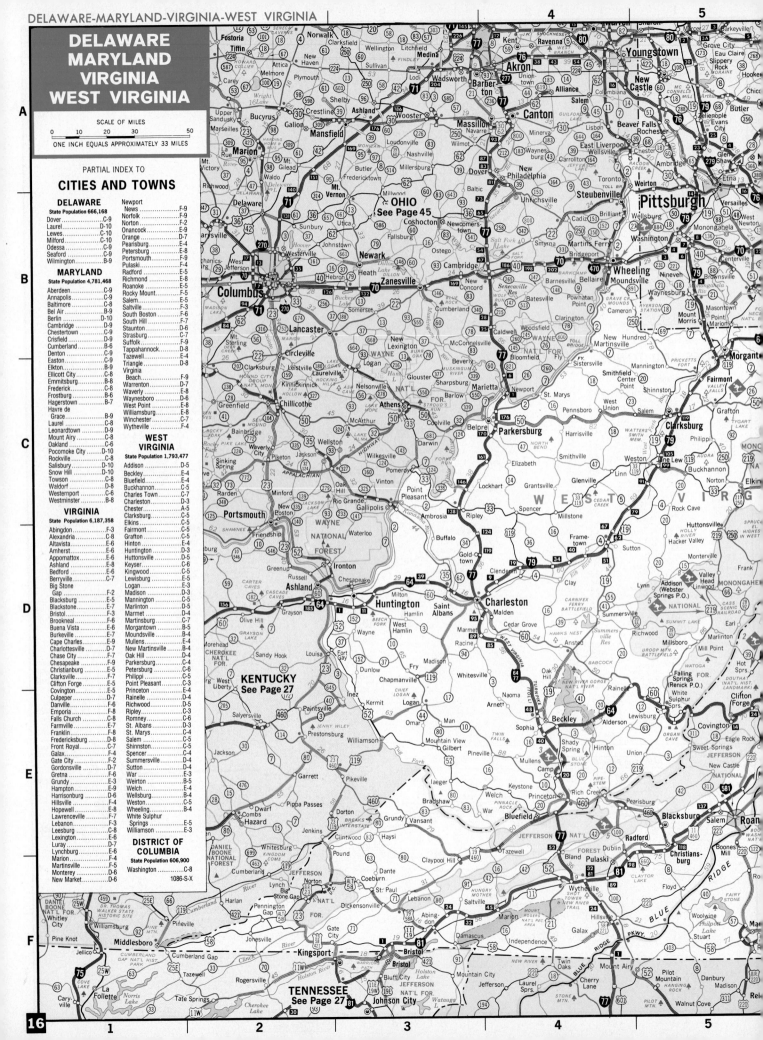

DELAWARE
MARYLAND
VIRGINIA
WEST VIRGINIA

SCALE OF MILES

0   10   20   30   50

ONE INCH EQUALS APPROXIMATELY 33 MILES

PARTIAL INDEX TO
CITIES AND TOWNS

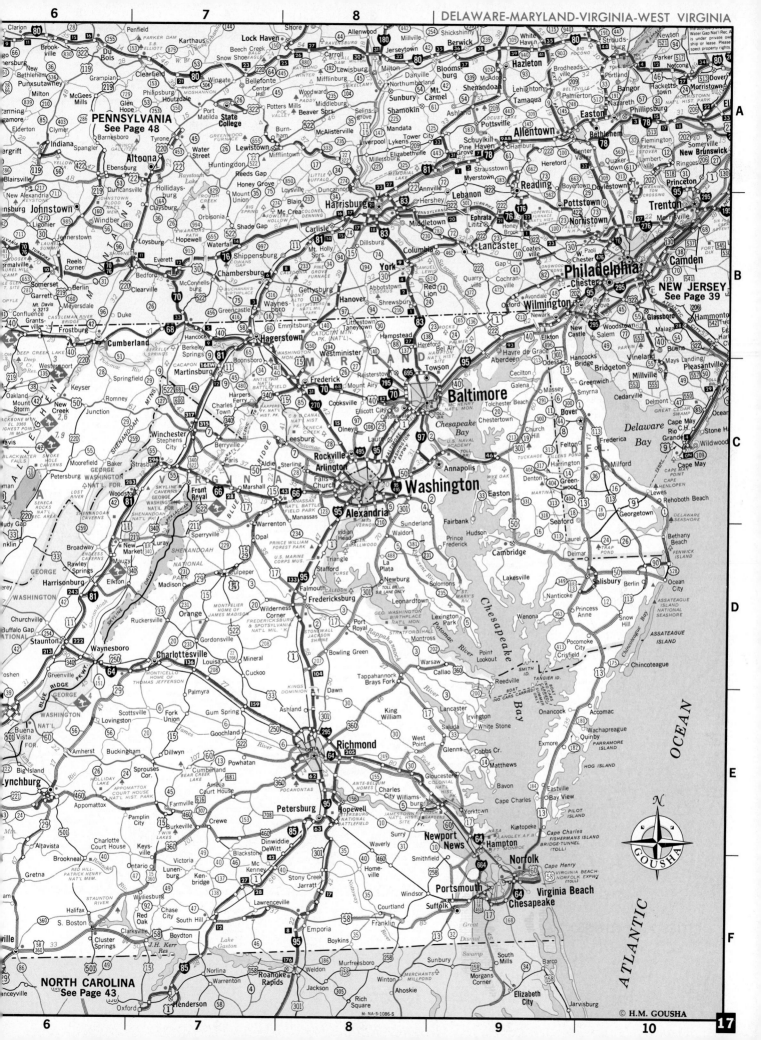

PENNSYLVANIA
See Page 48

MARYLAND

VIRGINIA

NEW JERSEY
See Page 39

NORTH CAROLINA
See Page 43

OCEAN

ATLANTIC

© H.M. GOUSHA

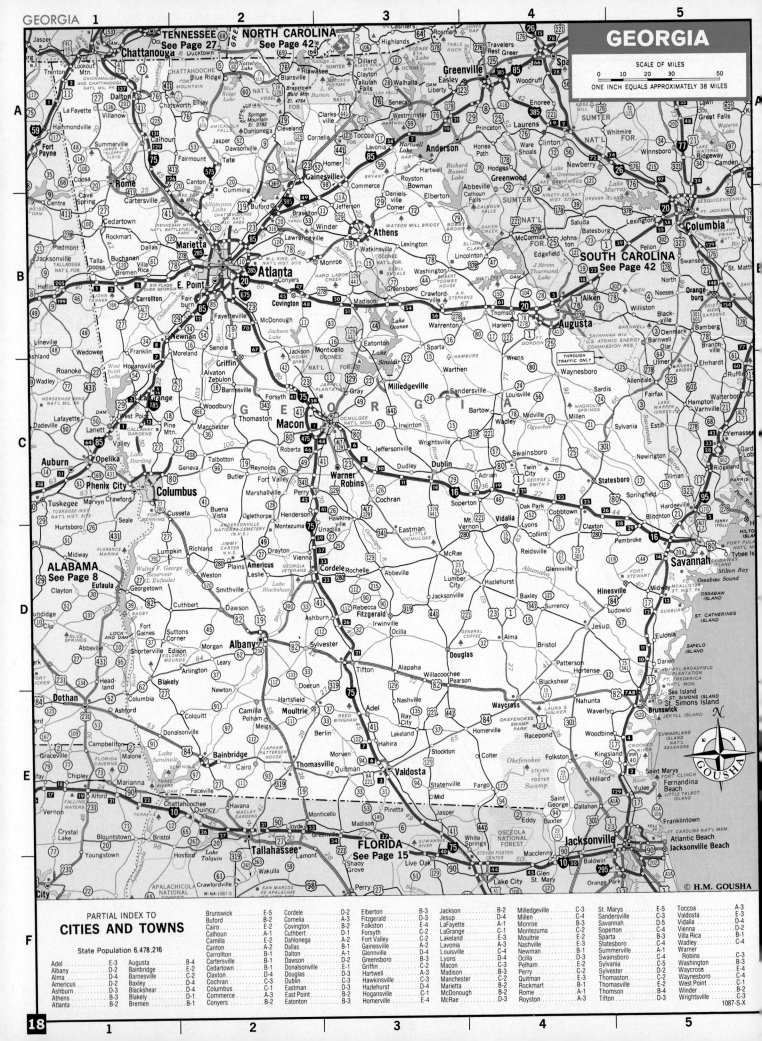

GEORGIA

GEORGIA

SCALE OF MILES

0 10 20 30 40 50

ONE INCH EQUALS APPROXIMATELY 38 MILES

© H.M. GOUSHA

1087-S-X

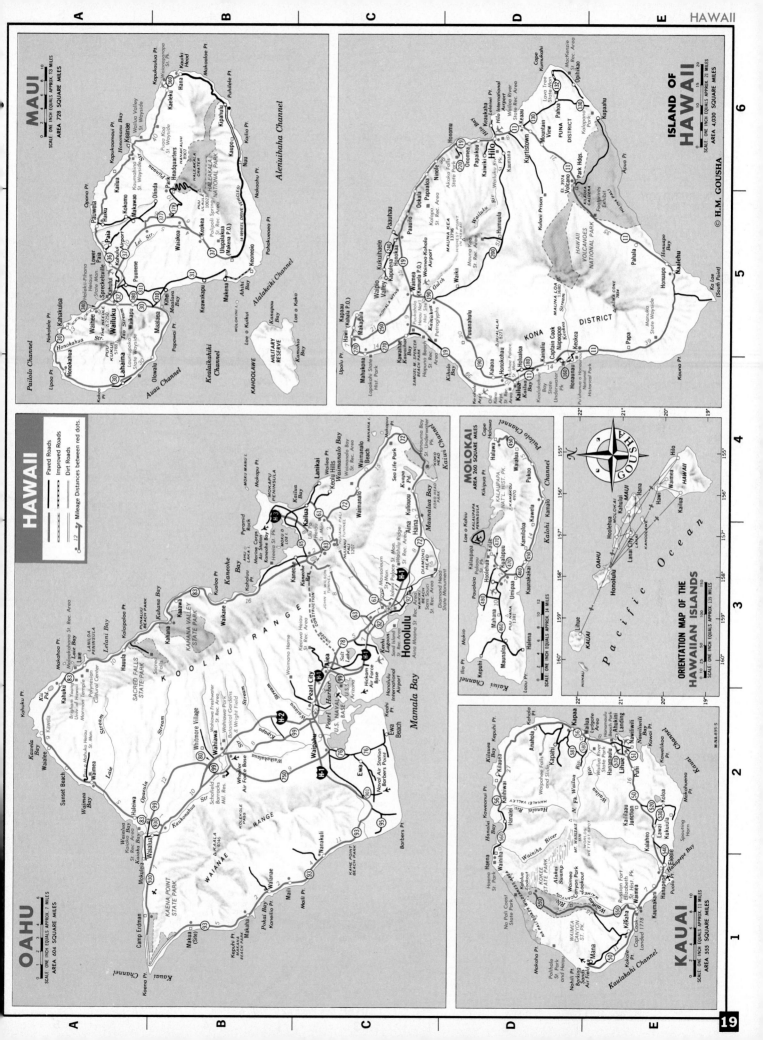

OAHU

SCALE ONE INCH EQUALS APPROX 7 MILES

AREA 604 SQUARE MILES

HAWAII

Paved Roads
Improved Roads
Dirt Roads
12 Mileage Distances between red dots.

MAUI

SCALE ONE INCH EQUALS APPROX 13 MILES

AREA 728 SQUARE MILES

ISLAND OF HAWAII

SCALE ONE INCH EQUALS APPROX 21 MILES

AREA 4,030 SQUARE MILES

© H.M. GOUSHA

MOLOKAI

AREA 260 SQUARE MILES

SCALE ONE INCH EQUALS APPROX 14 MILES

ORIENTATION MAP OF THE HAWAIIAN ISLANDS

SCALE ONE INCH EQUALS APPROX 139 MILES

Pacific Ocean

KAUAI

SCALE ONE INCH EQUALS APPROX 11 MILES

AREA 555 SQUARE MILES

M-NA-895-S

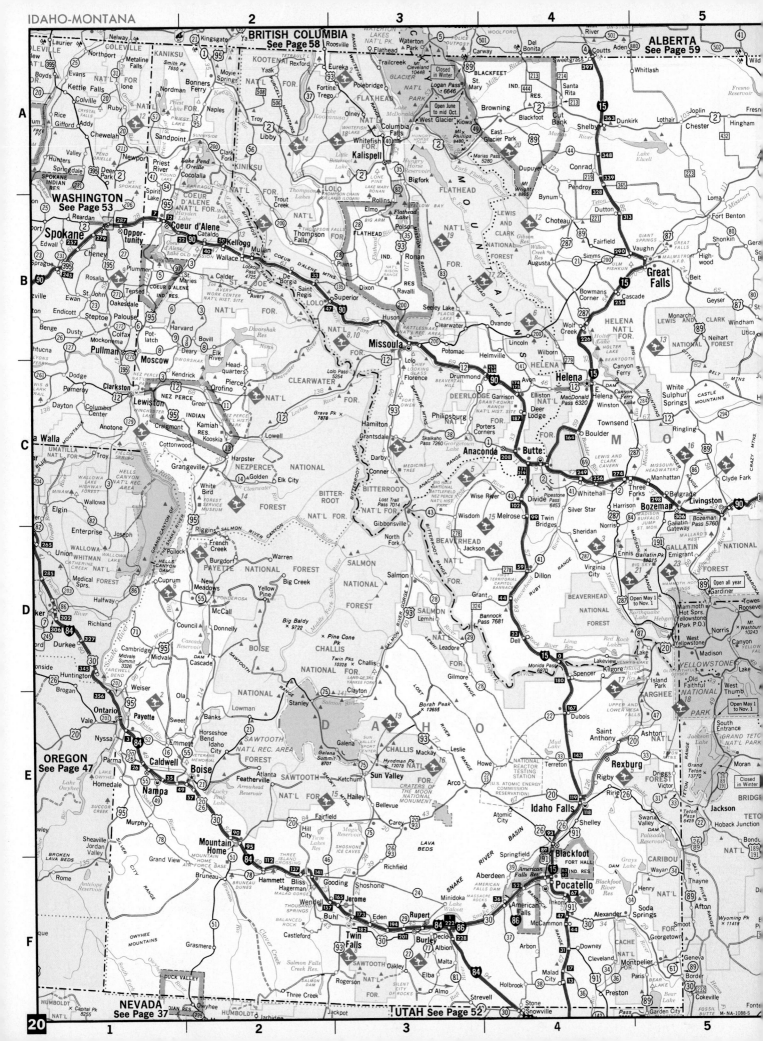

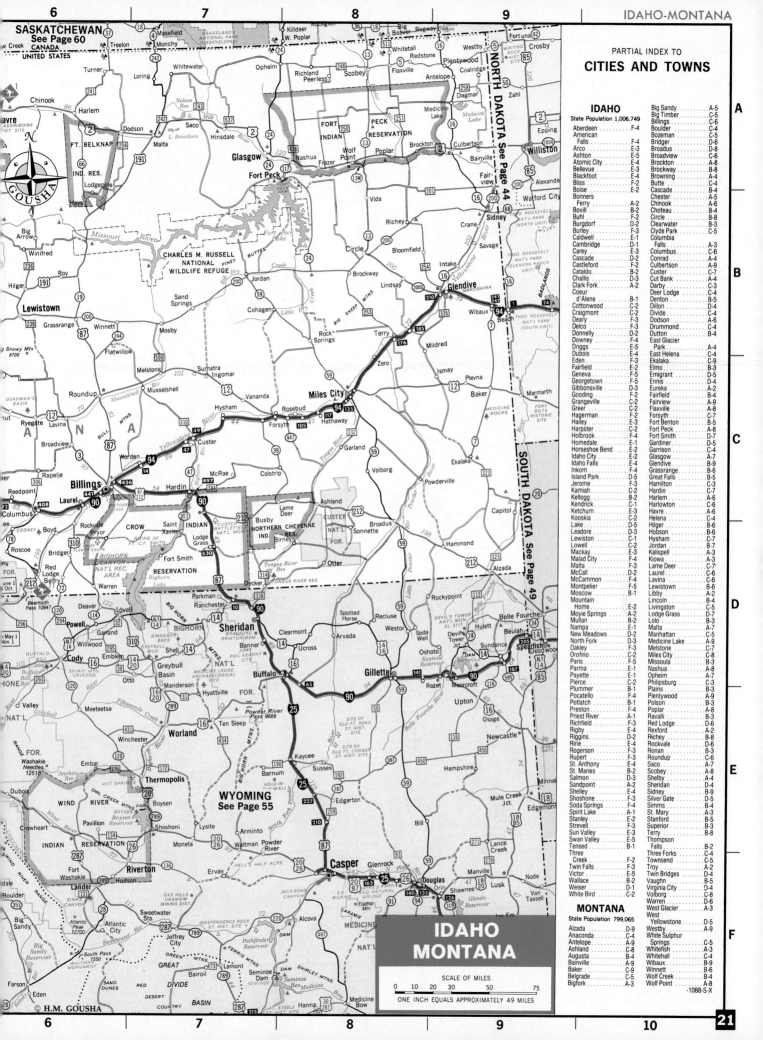

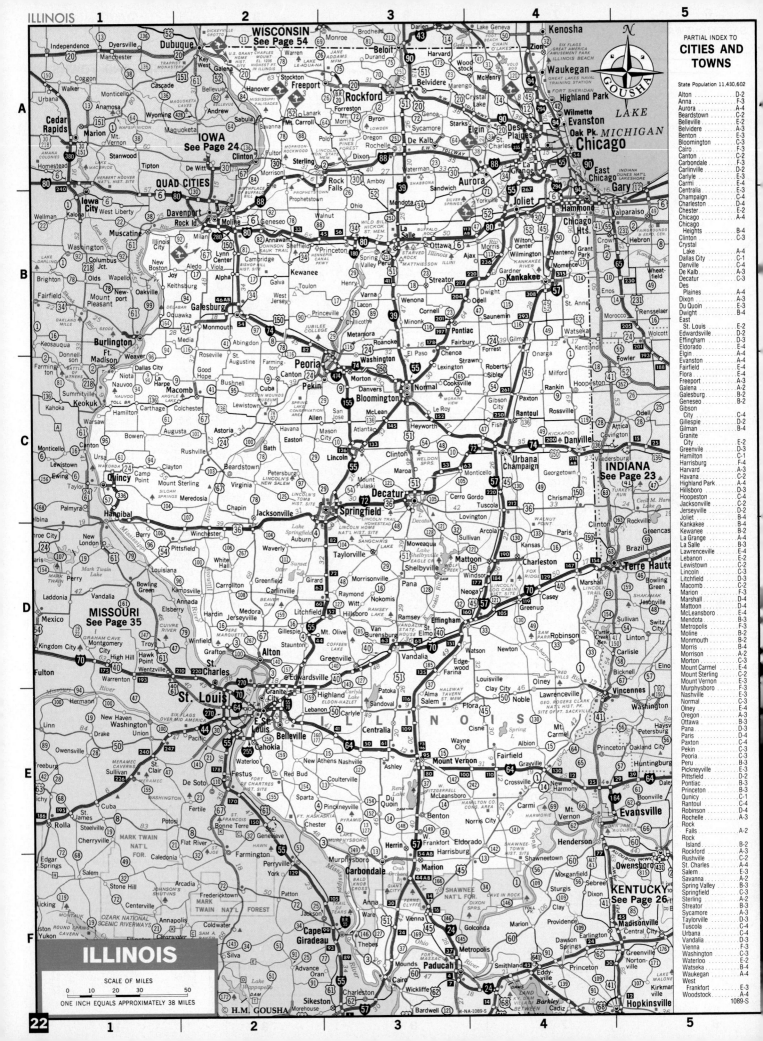

ILLINOIS

ILLINOIS

SCALE OF MILES

0 10 20 30   50

ONE INCH EQUALS APPROXIMATELY 38 MILES

© H.M. GOUSHA

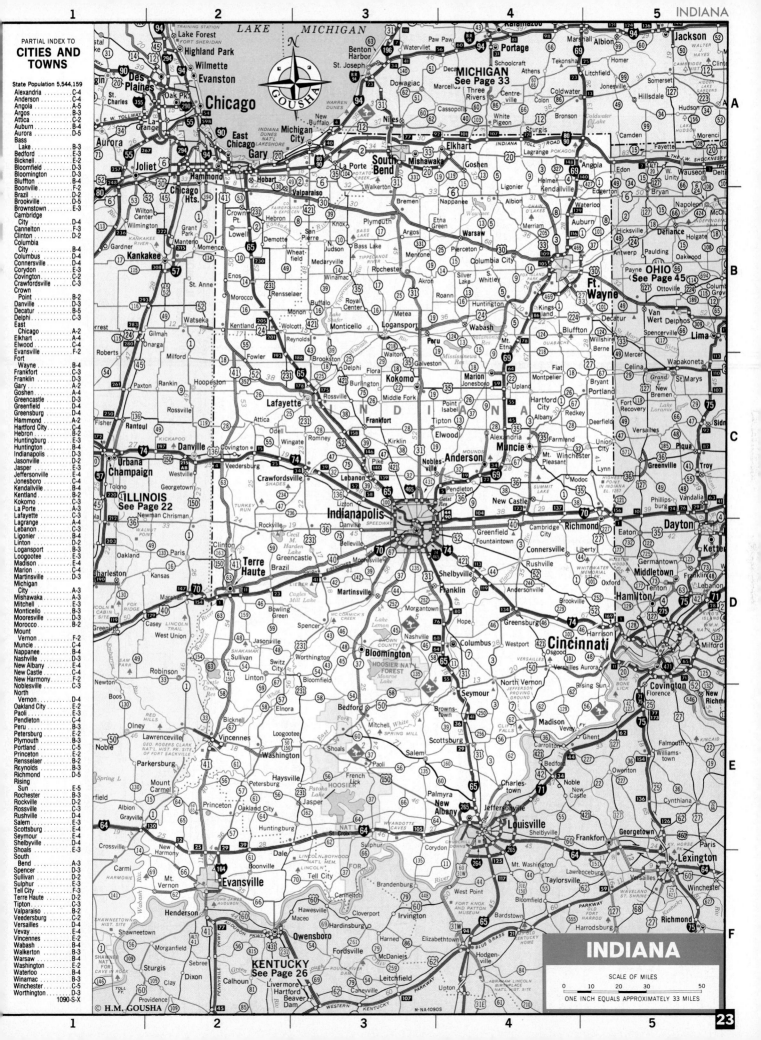

INDIANA

© H.M. GOUSHA

INDIANA

SCALE OF MILES

0   10   20   30   50

ONE INCH EQUALS APPROXIMATELY 33 MILES

23

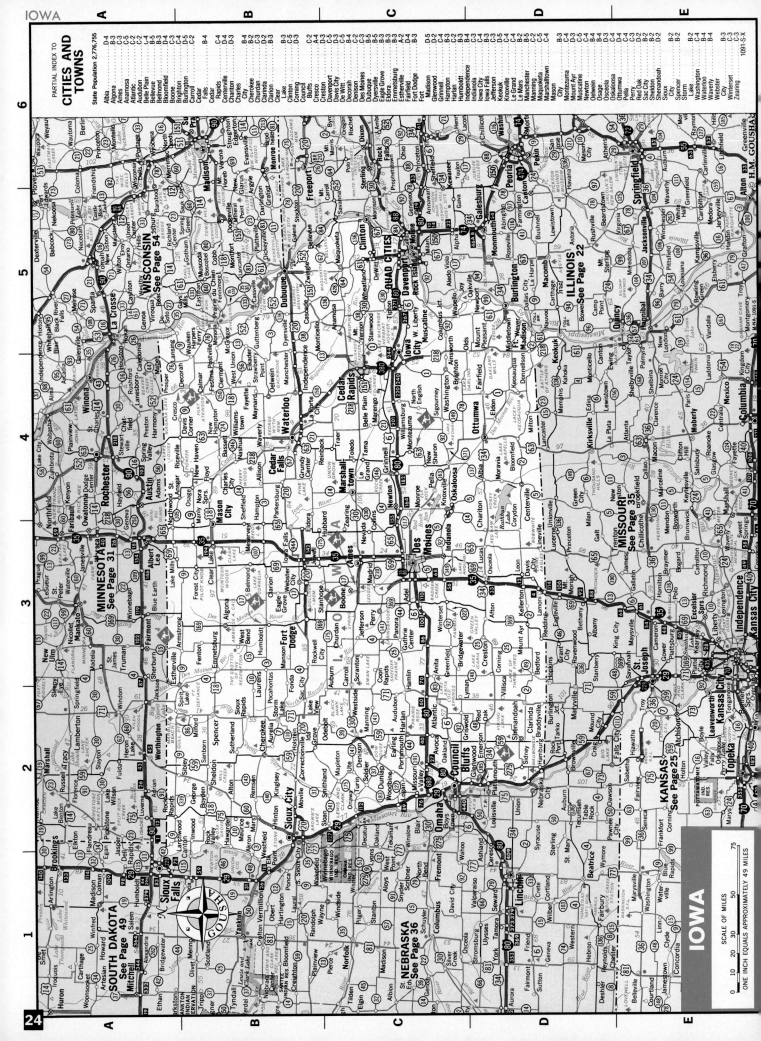

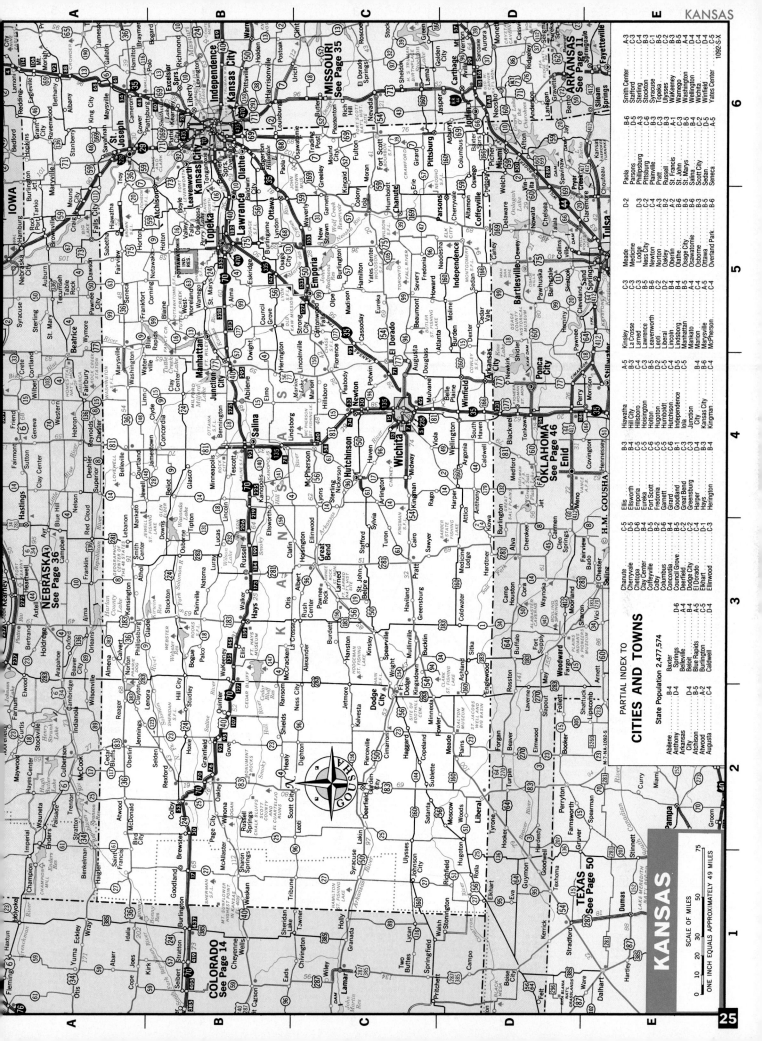

KANSAS

1092-S-X

M-7-NA-1092-S.

SCALE OF MILES

0 10 20 30 50 75

ONE INCH EQUALS APPROXIMATELY 49 MILES

NEBRASKA See Page 36

COLORADO See Page 14

TEXAS See Page 50

OKLAHOMA See Page 46

MISSOURI See Page 35

IOWA

ARKANSAS See Page 11

H.M. GOUSHA

25

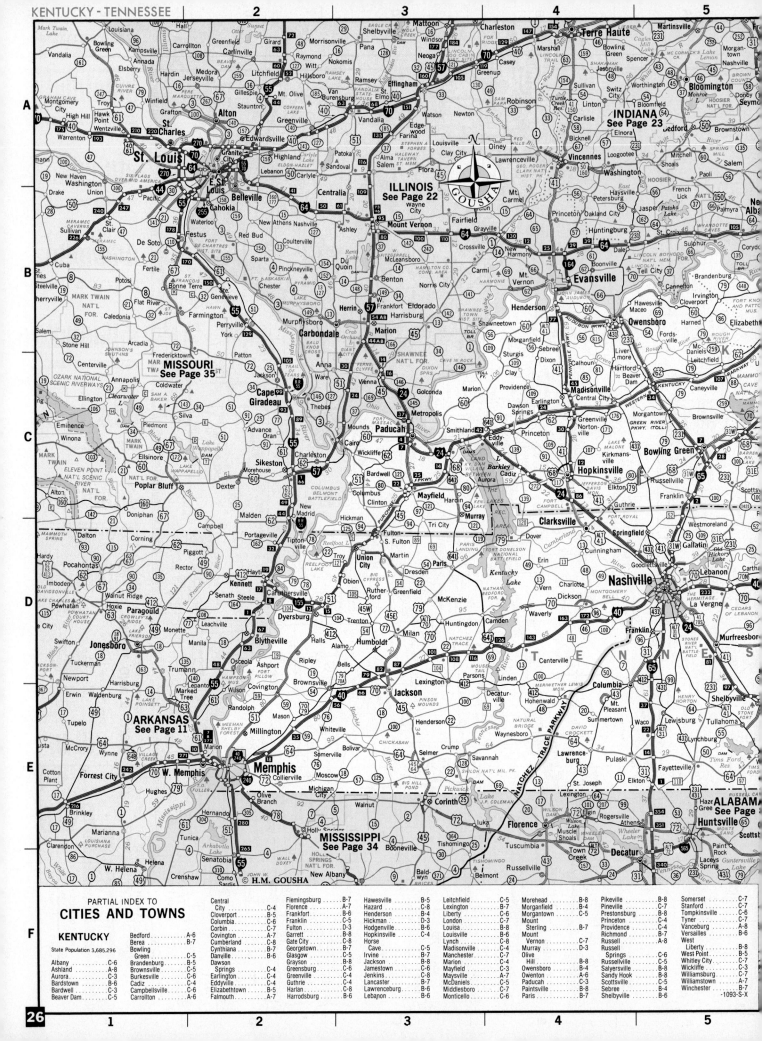

ILLINOIS See Page 22

INDIANA See Page 23

MISSOURI See Page 35

ARKANSAS See Page 11

MISSISSIPPI See Page 34

ALABAMA See Page

© H.M. Gousha

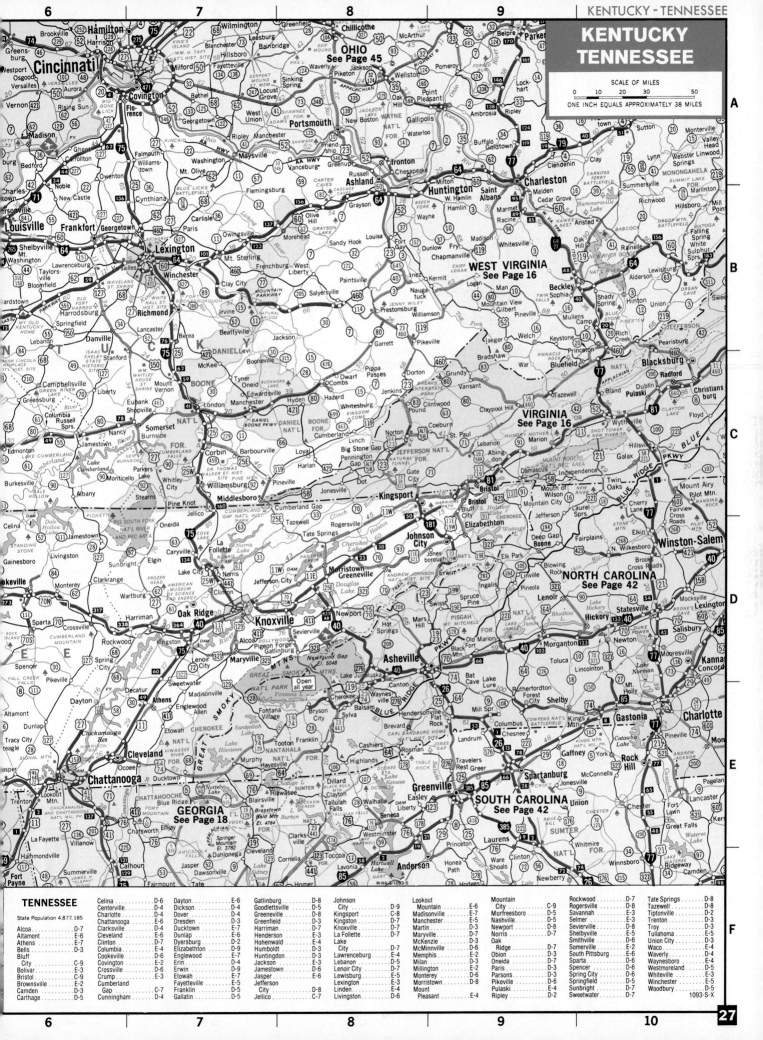

KENTUCKY TENNESSEE

SCALE OF MILES
0 10 20 30 50
ONE INCH EQUALS APPROXIMATELY 38 MILES

TENNESSEE
State Population 4,877,185

1093-S-X

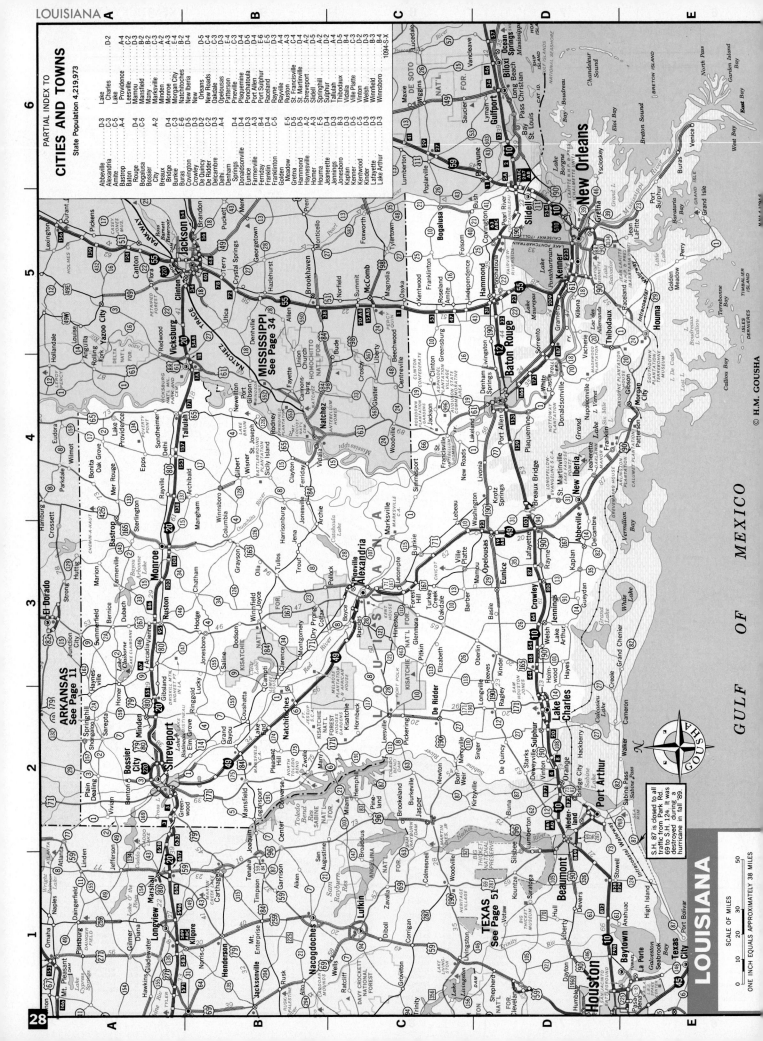

PARTIAL INDEX TO CITIES AND TOWNS

State Population 4,219,973

ARKANSAS See Page 11

MISSISSIPPI See Page 34

TEXAS See Page 51

LOUISIANA

GULF OF MEXICO

© H.M. Gousha

S.H. 87 is closed to all traffic from Park Rd. 69 to S.H. 124. It was destroyed during a hurricane in fall '89.

SCALE OF MILES
0   10   20   30   50
ONE INCH EQUALS APPROXIMATELY 38 MILES

28

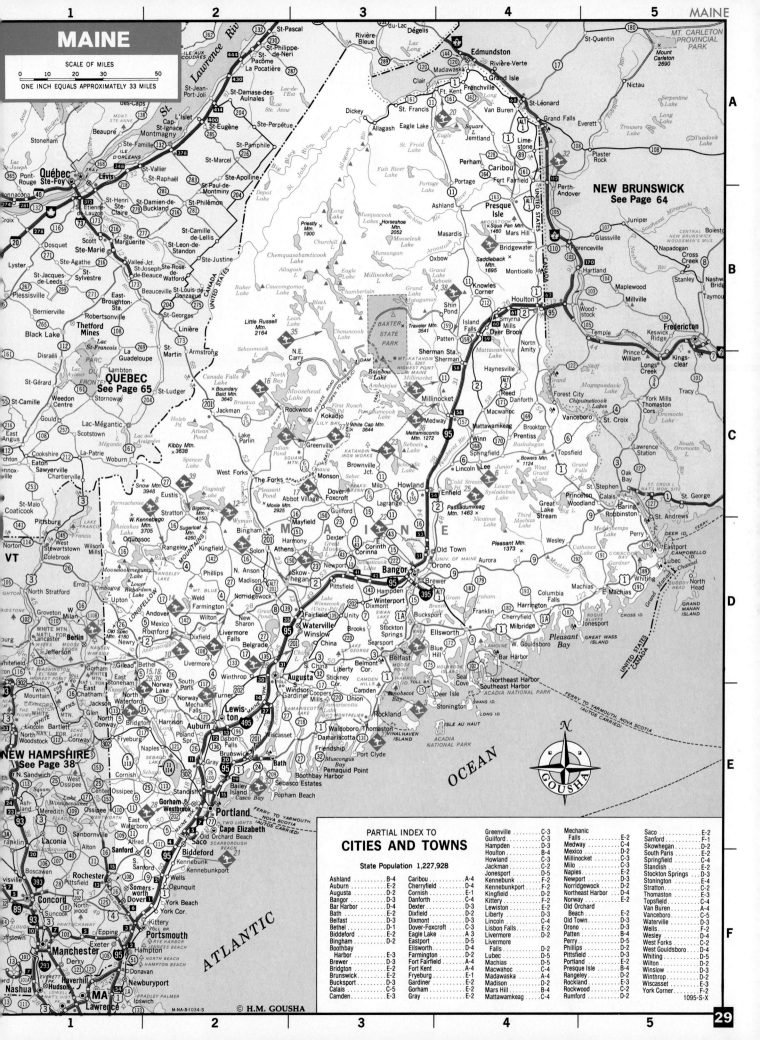

MAINE

SCALE OF MILES

0 10 20 30 40 50

ONE INCH EQUALS APPROXIMATELY 33 MILES

QUEBEC
See Page 65

NEW BRUNSWICK
See Page 64

NEW HAMPSHIRE
See Page 38

OCEAN

ATLANTIC

GOUSHA

FERRY TO YARMOUTH, NOVA SCOTIA (AUTOS CARRIED)

© H.M. GOUSHA

M-NA-5-1034-S

1095-S-X

29

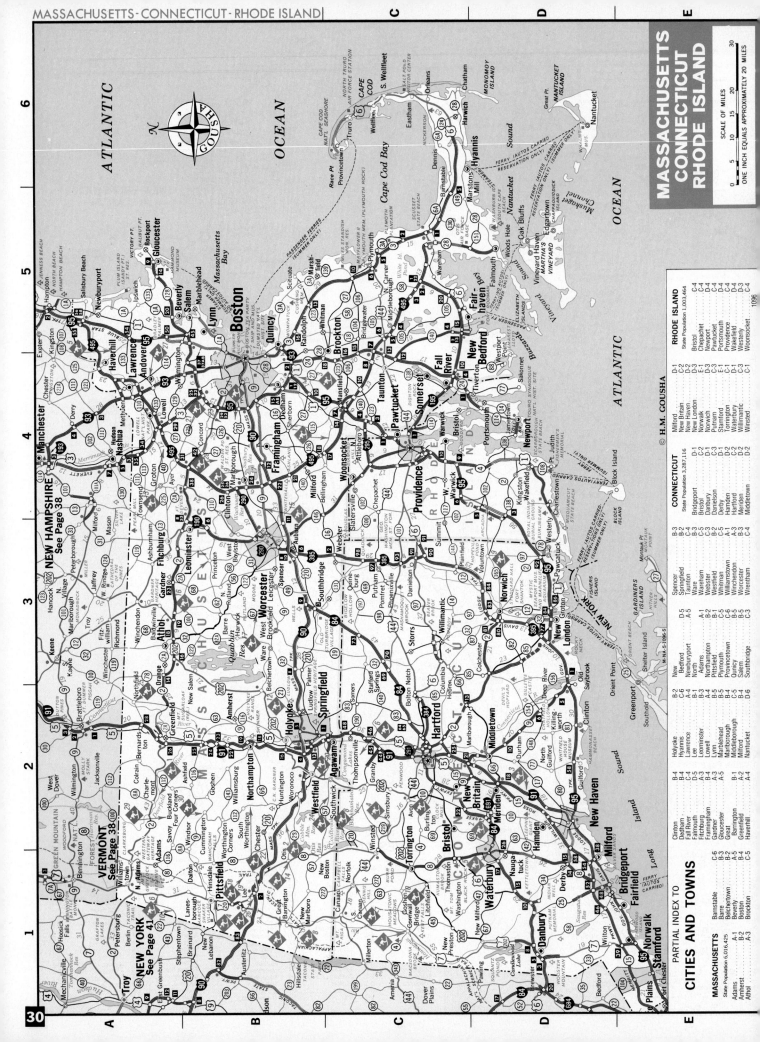

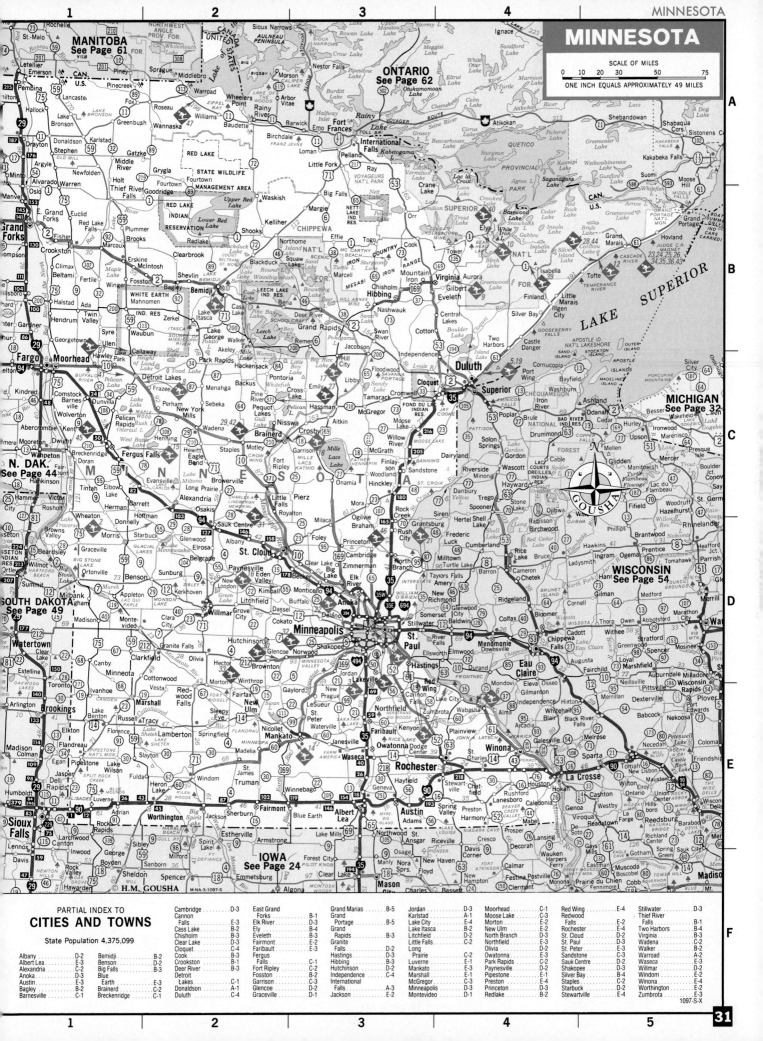

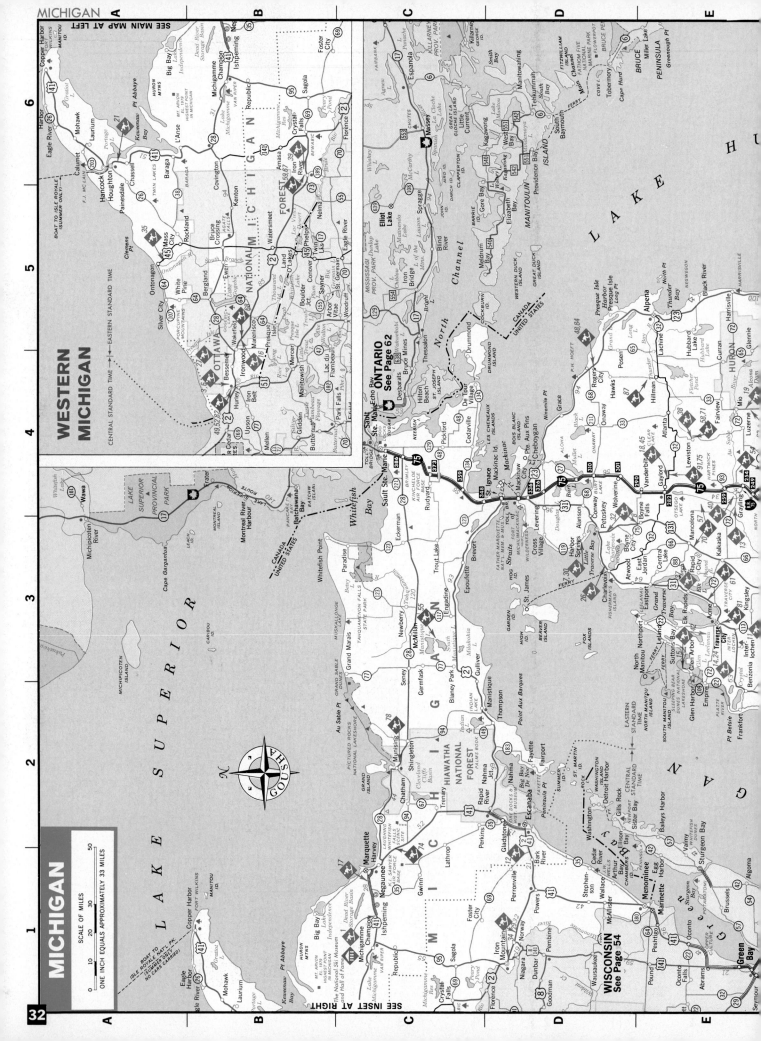

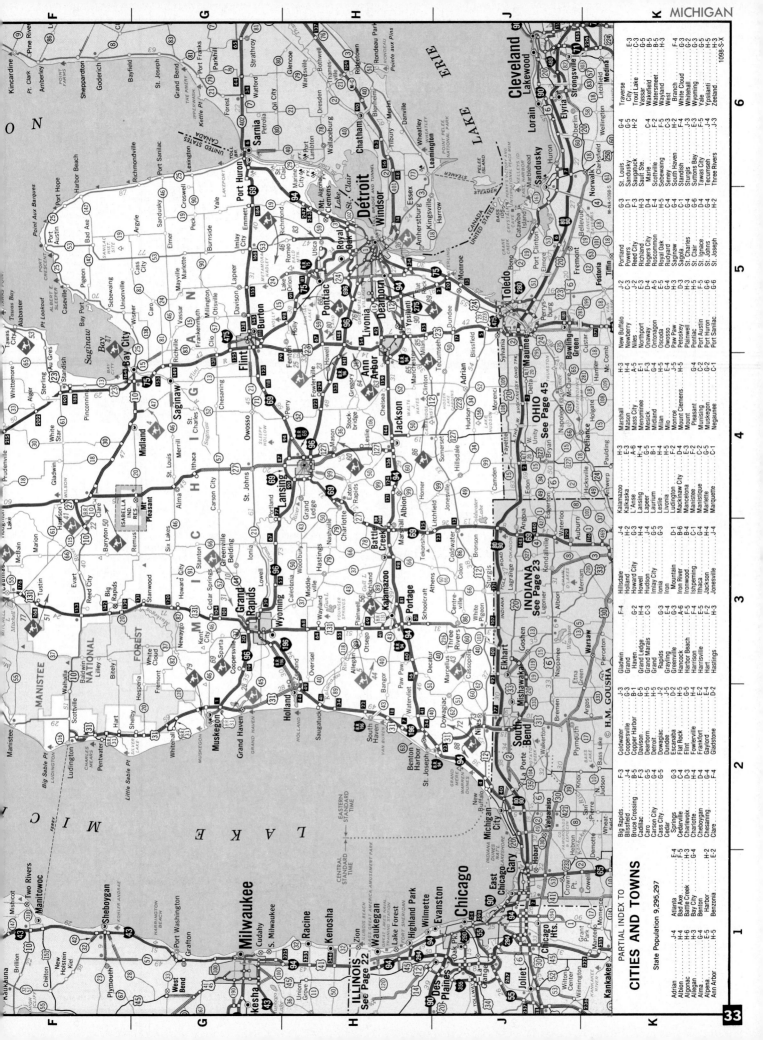

PARTIAL INDEX TO CITIES AND TOWNS

State Population 9,295,297

H.M. GOUSHA

Adrian ... E-4	Big Rapids ... F-4	Gladwin ... J-3	Hillsdale ... F-4
Albion ... F-5	Blissfield ... J-4	Grand Haven ... J-4	Holland ... G-2
Algonac ... H-3	Bruce Crossing ... B-5	Grand Ledge ... B-1	Howell ... C-3
Allegan ... E-5	Cadillac ... F-3	Grand Marais ... G-5	Hudson ... E-3
Alma ... E-2	Caro ... G-5	Grayling ... G-4	Imlay City ... D-4
Alpena ... H-5	Carson City ... E-4	Greenville ... E-4	Ionia ... A-6
Ann Arbor ... H-2	Cass City ... G-5	Hancock ... B-6	Iron Mountain ... A-6
Atlanta ... J-4	Cedar Springs ... E-5	Harbor Beach ... H-4	Ironwood ... F-5
Bad Axe ... H-6	Charlevoix ... E-3	Harrisville ... E-4	Ishpeming ... E-1
Battle Creek ... H-3	Charlotte ... H-4	Harrison ... G-2	Jackson ... H-4
Bay City ... H-3	Cheboygan ... G-4	Hart ... E-4	Jonesville ... D-2
Benzonia ... H-5	Chesaning ... H-2	Hastings ... H-3	
	Clare ... E-2		

Kalamazoo ... J-4	Marshall ... H-3	New Buffalo ... H-3	Portland ... J-2
Kalkaska ... H-2	Mason ... E-3	Niles ... A-5	Powers ... E-5
L'Anse ... A-6	Mass City ... A-6	Northport ... E-1	Reed City ... E-3
Lapeer ... G-5	Menominee ... H-4	Onaway ... F-3	Richland ... D-2
Laurium ... B-1	Mesick ... G-5	Ontonagon ... A-5	Rogers City ... A-5
Leslie ... H-4	Midland ... H-4	Oscoda ... G-4	Roscommon ... G-4
Livonia ... H-5	Mio ... H-5	Paw Paw ... H-5	Royal Oak ... H-3
Ludington ... D-2	Monroe ... F-2	Petoskey ... J-5	Rudyard ... D-3
Mackinaw City ... B-6	Mount Clemens ... D-4	Plainwell ... G-4	Saginaw ... H-3
Mackinac ... D-3	Mount Pleasant ... C-2	Pontiac ... G-2	Sagola ...
Manistee ... C-2	Munising ... G-5	Port Austin ... G-1	St. Charles ... H-3
Manistique ... G-4	Muskegon ... C-1	Port Huron ... G-6	St. Ignace ... G-2
Marlette ... G-5		Port Sanilac ... G-6	St. Johns ... G-2
Marquette ... C-1			St. Joseph ... G-6

St. Louis ... G-3	Traverse City ... G-4
Sandusky ... D-1	Trout Lake ... H-2
Saugatuck ... F-3	Vassar ... C-4
Sault Ste. Marie ... C-4	Wakefield ... F-5
Scottville ... D-4	Watersmeet ... F-2
Sebewaing ... H-5	Wayland ... F-5
Seney ... G-4	West Branch ... F-4
South Haven ... G-3	White Cloud ... G-2
Standish ... C-1	Whitehall ... G-2
Sturgis ... G-6	Wyoming ... G-5
Suttons Bay ... D-4	Yale ... G-5
Tawas City ... J-3	Ypsilanti ... H-2
Tecumseh ... J-4	Zeeland ... J-3
Three Rivers ... J-3	

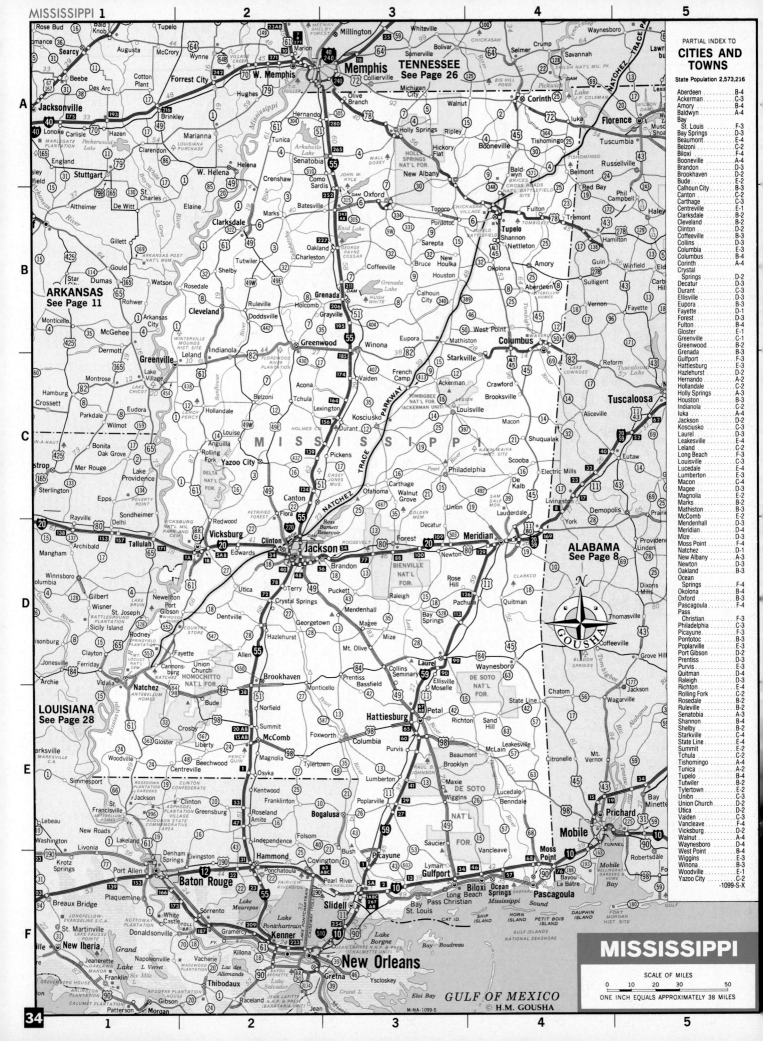

MISSISSIPPI

SCALE OF MILES

0 10 20 30 50

ONE INCH EQUALS APPROXIMATELY 38 MILES

M-NA-1099-S   © H.M. GOUSHA

34

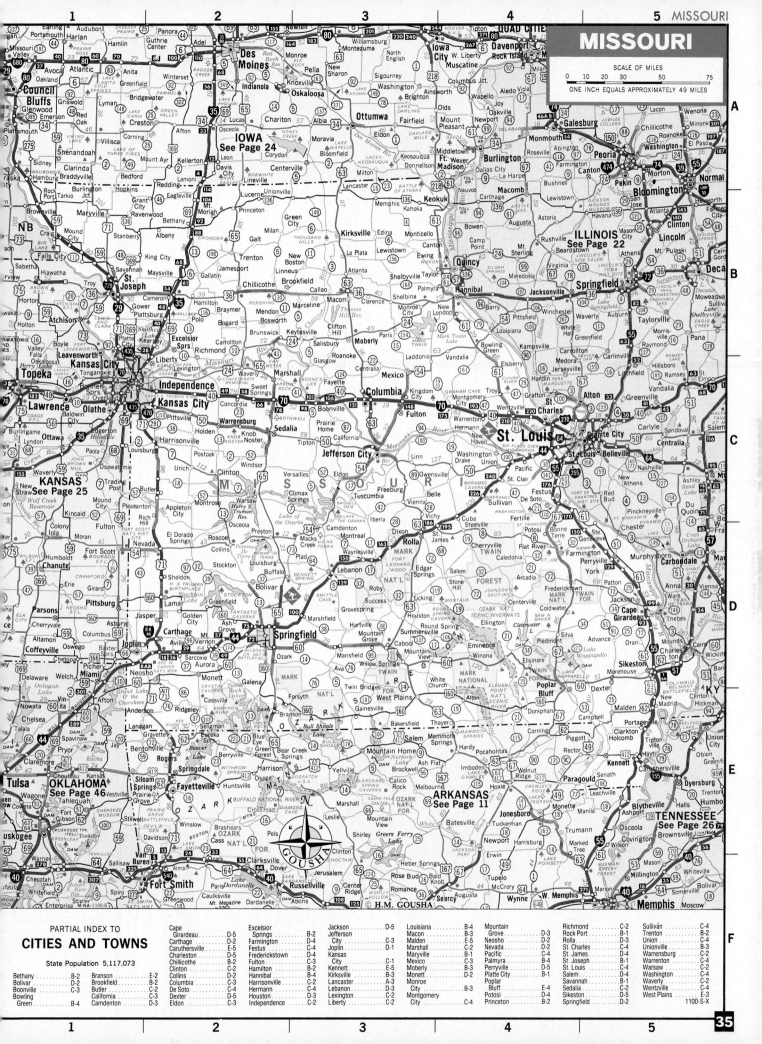

MISSOURI

SCALE OF MILES

0 10 20 30   50   75

ONE INCH EQUALS APPROXIMATELY 49 MILES

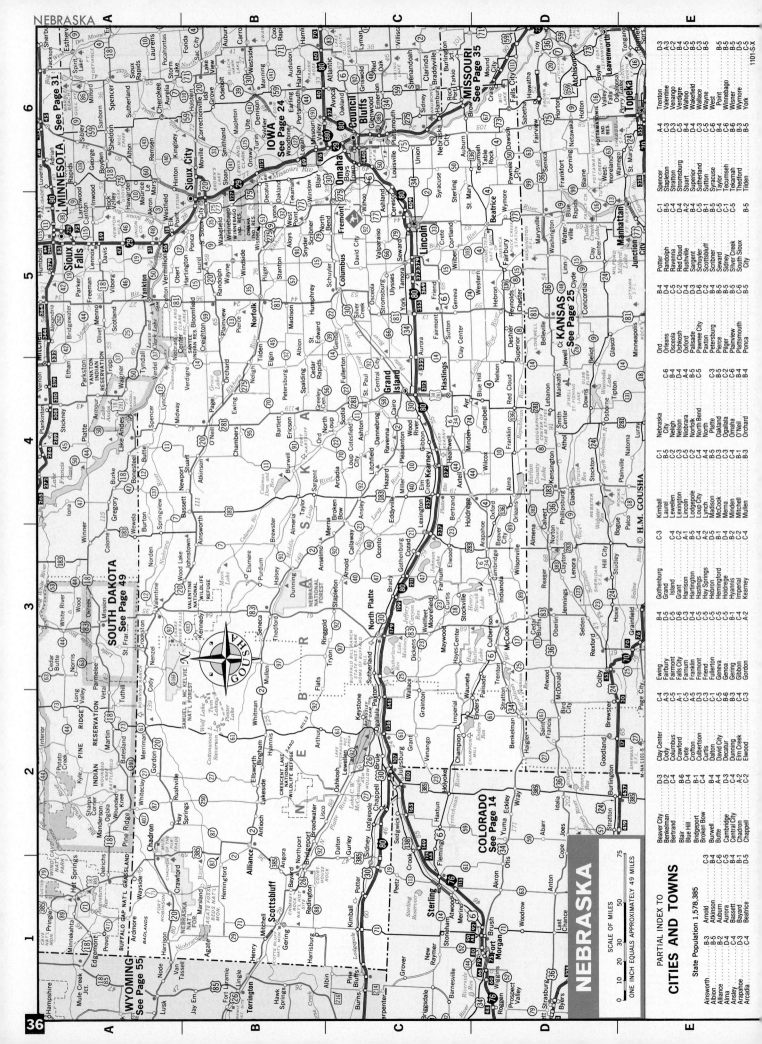

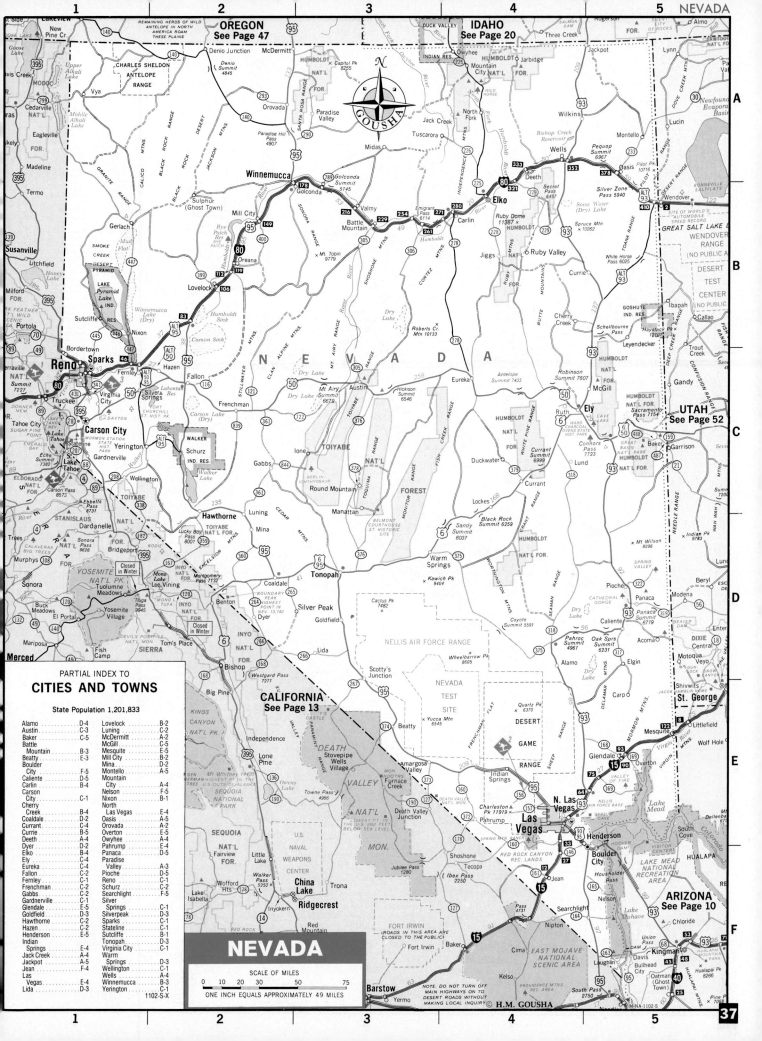

NEVADA

OREGON
See Page 47

IDAHO
See Page 20

CALIFORNIA
See Page 13

UTAH
See Page 52

ARIZONA
See Page 10

NEVADA

SCALE OF MILES

0 10 20 30 50 75

ONE INCH EQUALS APPROXIMATELY 49 MILES

NOTE: DO NOT TURN OFF
MAIN HIGHWAYS ON TO
DESERT ROADS WITHOUT
MAKING LOCAL INQUIRY

© H.M. GOUSHA

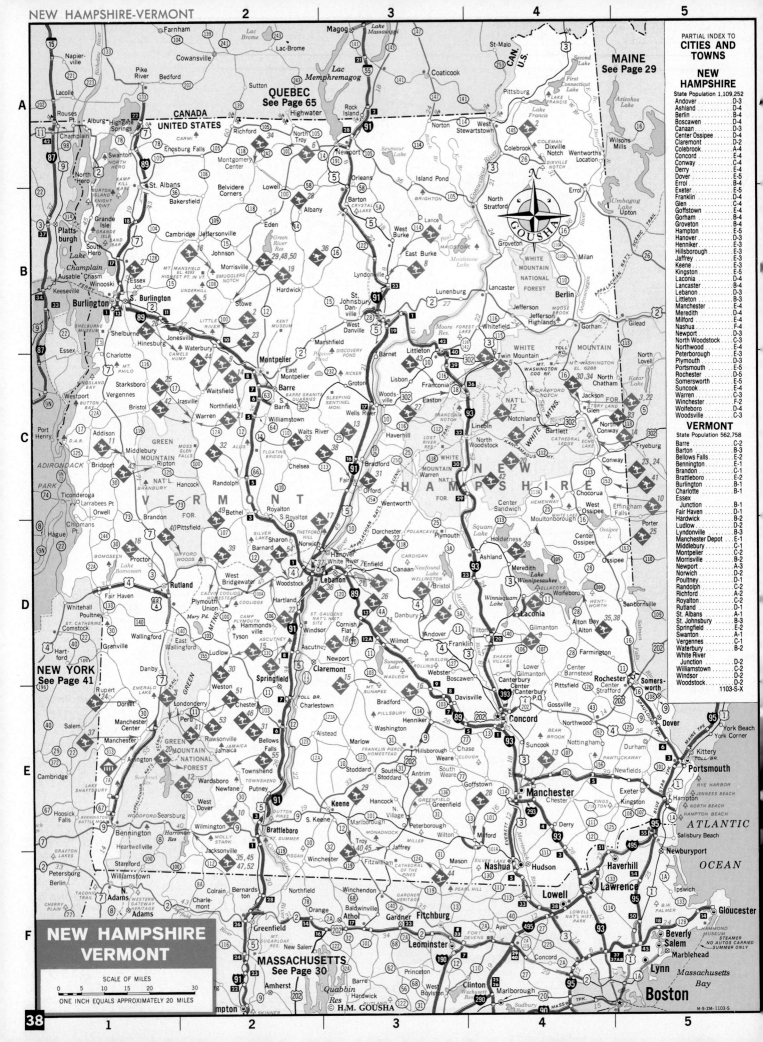

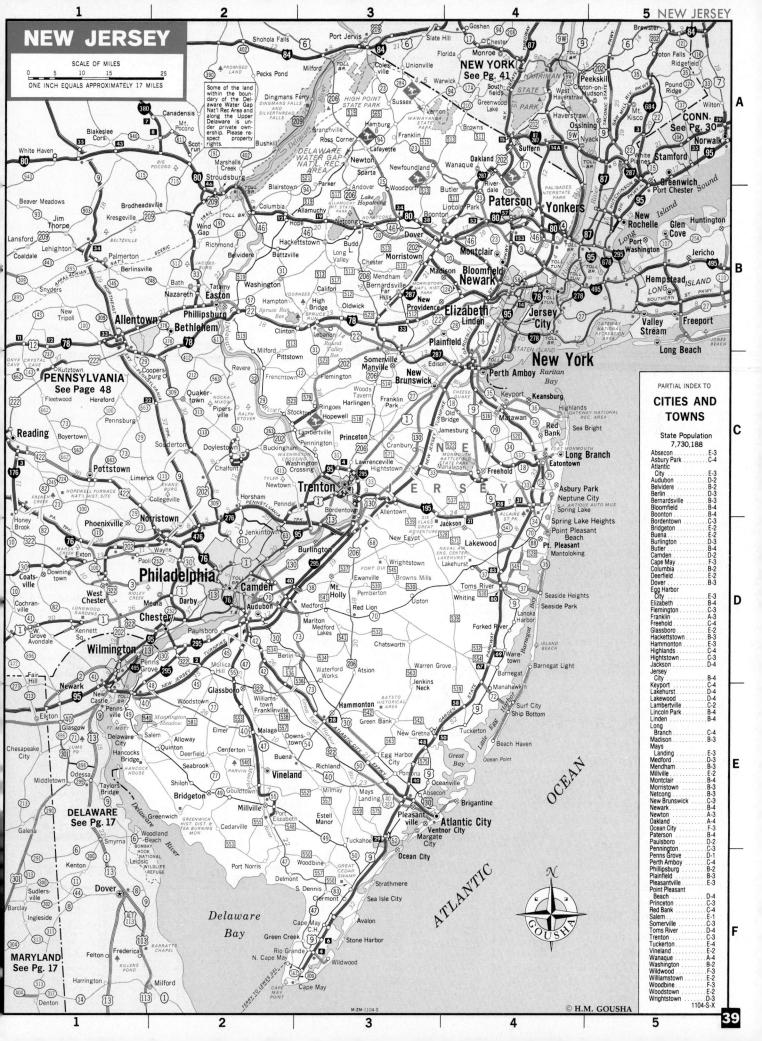

NEW JERSEY

SCALE OF MILES

0   5   10   15   25
ONE INCH EQUALS APPROXIMATELY 17 MILES

© H.M. GOUSHA

M-ZM-1104-S

1104-S-X

39

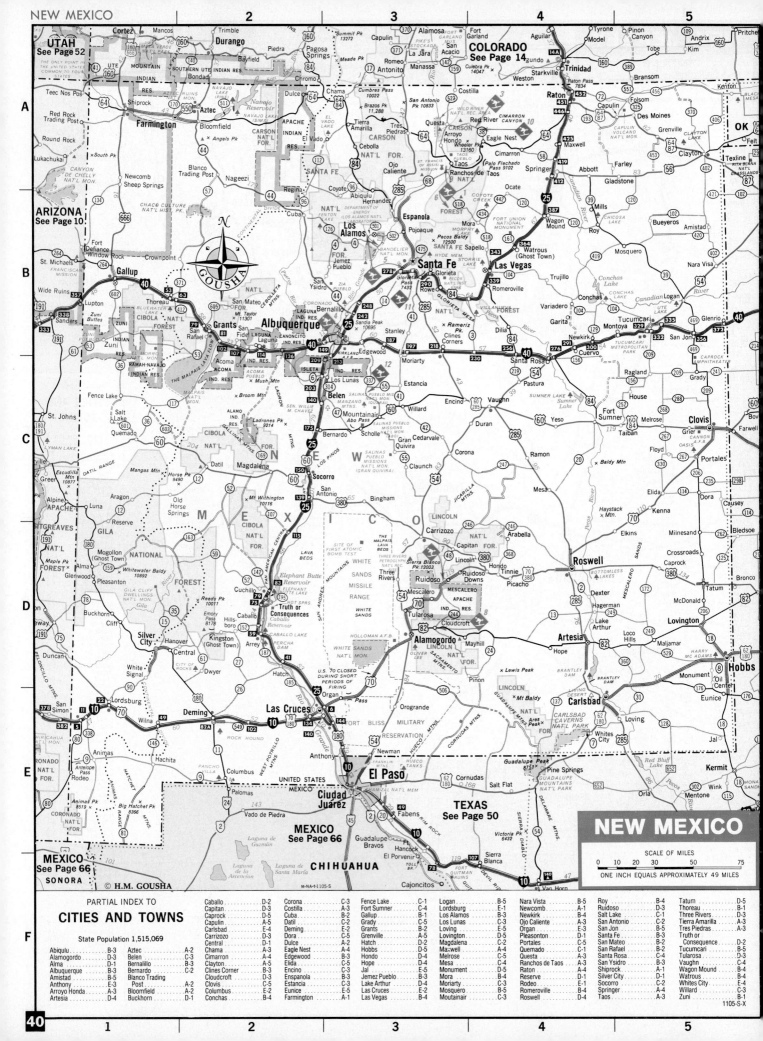

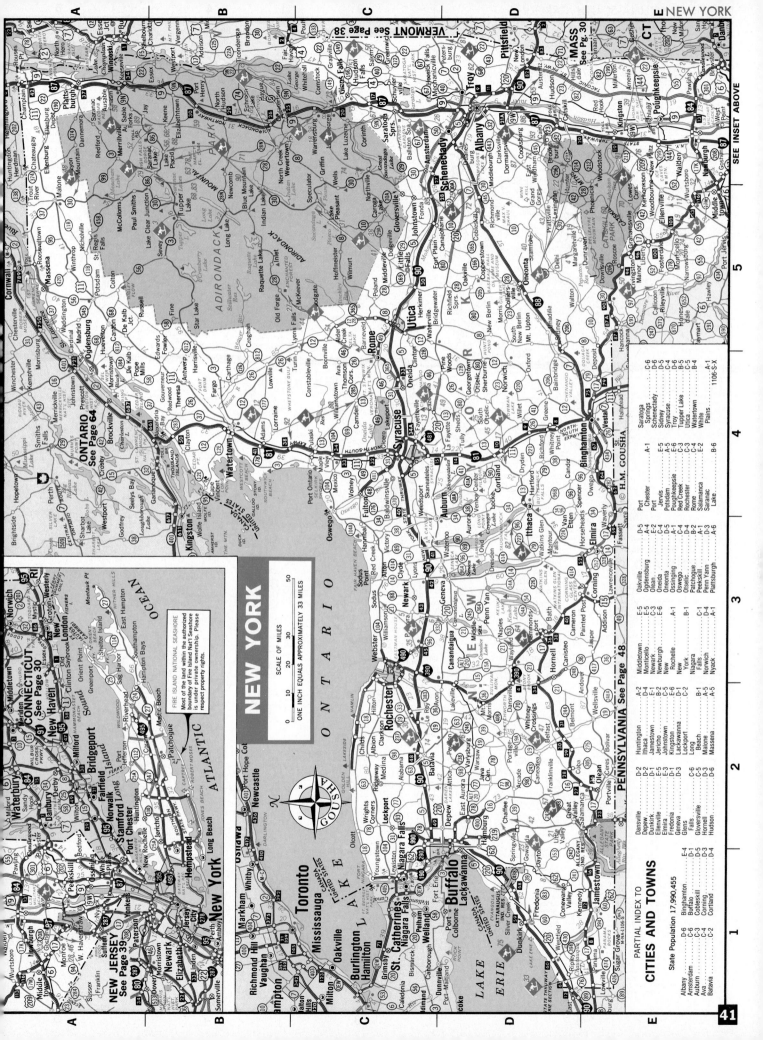

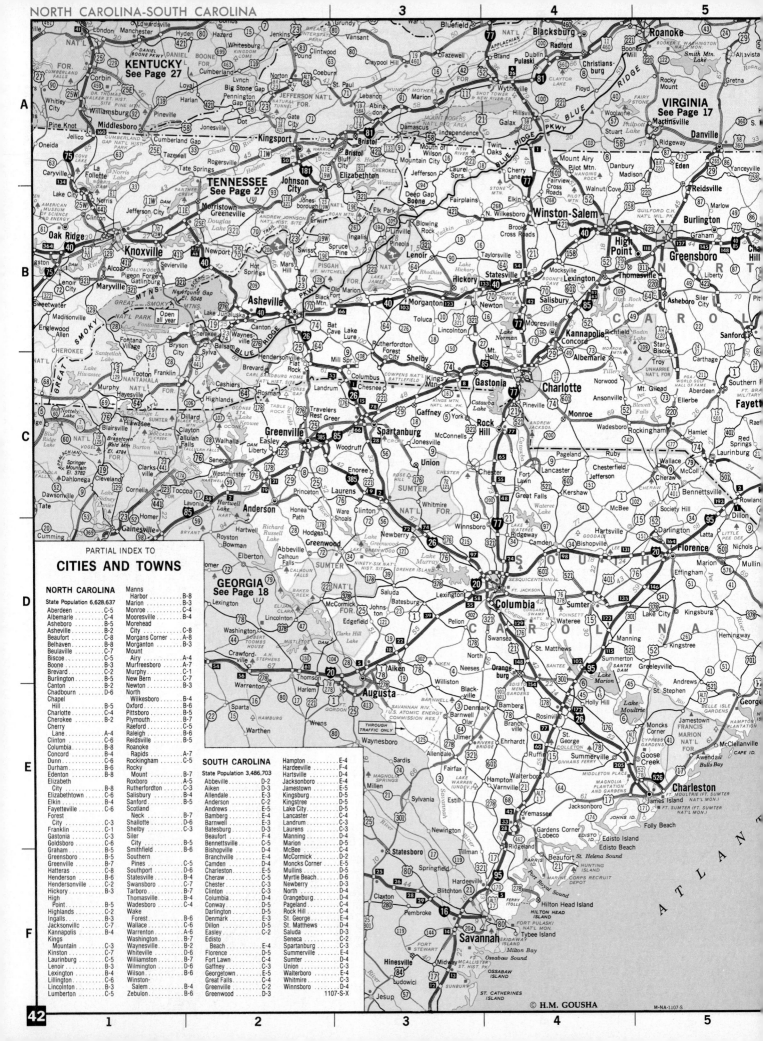

© H.M. GOUSHA

M-NA-1107-S

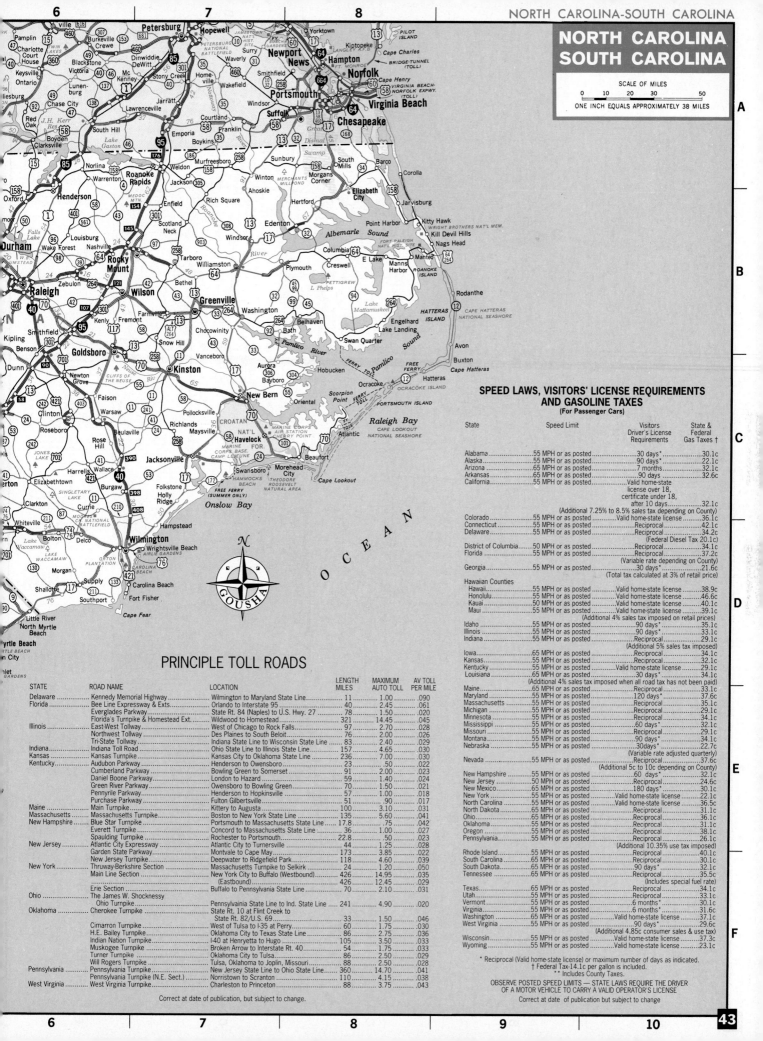

NORTH CAROLINA
SOUTH CAROLINA

SCALE OF MILES
0 10 20 30 50
ONE INCH EQUALS APPROXIMATELY 38 MILES

GOUSHA

PRINCIPLE TOLL ROADS

STATE	ROAD NAME	LOCATION	LENGTH MILES	MAXIMUM AUTO TOLL	AV TOLL PER MILE
Delaware	Kennedy Memorial Highway	Wilmington to Maryland State Line	11	1.00	.090
Florida	Bee Line Expressway & Exts.	Orlando to Interstate 95	40	2.45	.061
	Everglades Parkway	State Rt. 84 (Naples) to U.S. Hwy. 27	78	1.50	.020
	Florida's Turnpike & Homestead Ext.	Wildwood to Homestead	321	14.45	.045
Illinois	East-West Tollway	West of Chicago to Rock Falls	97	2.70	.028
	Northwest Tollway	Des Plaines to South Beloit	76	2.00	.026
	Tri-State Tollway	Indiana State Line to Wisconsin State Line	83	2.40	.029
Indiana	Indiana Toll Road	Ohio State Line to Illinois State Line	157	4.65	.030
Kansas	Kansas Turnpike	Kansas City to Oklahoma State Line	236	7.00	.030
Kentucky	Audubon Parkway	Henderson to Owensboro	23	.50	.022
	Cumberland Parkway	Bowling Green to Somerset	91	2.00	.023
	Daniel Boone Parkway	London to Hazard	59	1.40	.024
	Green River Parkway	Owensboro to Bowling Green	70	1.50	.021
	Pennyrile Parkway	Henderson to Hopkinsville	57	1.00	.018
	Purchase Parkway	Fulton Gilbertsville	51	.90	.017
Maine	Main Turnpike	Kittery to Augusta	100	3.10	.031
Massachusetts	Massachusetts Turnpike	Boston to New York State Line	135	5.60	.041
New Hampshire	Blue Star Turnpike	Portsmouth to Massachusetts State Line	17.8	.75	.042
	Everett Turnpike	Concord to Massachusetts State Line	36	1.00	.027
	Spaulding Turnpike	Rochester to Portsmouth	22.8	.50	.023
New Jersey	Atlantic City Expressway	Atlantic City to Turnersville	44	1.25	.028
	Garden State Parkway	Montvale to Cape May	173	3.85	.022
	New Jersey Turnpike	Deepwater to Ridgefield Park	118	4.60	.039
New York	Thruway-Berkshire Section	Massachusetts Turnpike to Selkirk	24	1.20	.050
	Main Line Section	New York City to Buffalo (Westbound)	426	14.95	.035
		(Eastbound)	426	12.45	.029
	Erie Section	Buffalo to Pennsylvania State Line	70	2.10	.031
Ohio	The James W. Shocknessy Ohio Turnpike	Pennsylvainia State Line to Ind. State Line	241	4.90	.020
Oklahoma	Cherokee Turnpike	State Rt. 10 at Flint Creek to State Rt. 82/U.S. 69	33	1.50	.046
	Cimarron Turnpike	West of Tulsa to I-35 at Perry	60	1.75	.030
	H.E. Bailey Turnpike	Oklahoma City to Texas State Line	86	2.75	.036
	Indian Nation Turnpike	I-40 at Henryetta to Hugo	105	3.50	.033
	Muskogee Turnpike	Broken Arrow to Interstate Rt. 40	54	1.75	.033
	Turner Turnpike	Oklahoma City to Tulsa	86	2.50	.029
	Will Rogers Turnpike	Tulsa, Oklahoma to Joplin, Missouri	88	2.50	.028
Pennsylvania	Pennsylvania Turnpike	New Jersey State Line to Ohio State Line	360	14.70	.041
	Pennsylvania Turnpike (N.E. Sect.)	Norristown to Scranton	110	4.15	.038
West Virginia	West Virginia Turnpike	Charleston to Princeton	88	3.75	.043

Correct at date of publication, but subject to change.

SPEED LAWS, VISITORS' LICENSE REQUIREMENTS AND GASOLINE TAXES
(For Passenger Cars)

State	Speed Limit	Visitors' Driver's License Requirements	State & Federal Gas Taxes †
Alabama	55 MPH or as posted	30 days*	30.1c
Alaska	55 MPH or as posted	90 days*	22.1c
Arizona	65 MPH or as posted	7 months	32.1c
Arkansas	65 MPH or as posted	90 days	32.6c
California	55 MPH or as posted	Valid home-state license over 18, certificate under 18, after 10 days	32.1c
		(Additional 7.25% to 8.5% sales tax depending on County)	
Colorado	55 MPH or as posted	Valid home-state license	36.1c
Connecticut	55 MPH or as posted	Reciprocal	42.1c
Delaware	55 MPH or as posted	Reciprocal	34.2c
		(Federal Diesel Tax 20.1c)	
District of Columbia	50 MPH or as posted	Reciprocal	34.1c
Florida	55 MPH or as posted	Reciprocal	37.2c
		(Variable rate depending on County)	
Georgia	55 MPH or as posted	30 days*	21.6c
		(Total tax calculated at 3% of retail price)	
Hawaiian Counties			
Hawaii	55 MPH or as posted	Valid home-state license	38.9c
Honolulu	55 MPH or as posted	Valid home-state license	46.6c
Kauai	50 MPH or as posted	Valid home-state license	40.1c
Maui	55 MPH or as posted	Valid home-state license	39.1c
		(Additional 4% sales tax imposed on retail sales)	
Idaho	55 MPH or as posted	90 days*	35.1c
Illinois	55 MPH or as posted	90 days*	33.1c
Indiana	55 MPH or as posted	Reciprocal	29.1c
		(Additional 5% sales tax imposed)	
Iowa	65 MPH or as posted	Reciprocal	34.1c
Kansas	55 MPH or as posted	Reciprocal	32.1c
Kentucky	55 MPH or as posted	Valid home-state license	29.1c
Louisiana	55 MPH or as posted	30 days*	34.1c
		(Additional 4% sales tax imposed when all road tax has not been paid)	
Maine	65 MPH or as posted	Reciprocal	33.1c
Maryland	55 MPH or as posted	120 days*	37.6c
Massachusetts	55 MPH or as posted	Reciprocal	35.1c
Michigan	55 MPH or as posted	Reciprocal	29.1c
Minnesota	55 MPH or as posted	Reciprocal	34.1c
Mississippi	55 MPH or as posted	60 days*	32.1c
Missouri	55 MPH or as posted	Reciprocal	29.1c
Montana	55 MPH or as posted	90 days*	34.1c
Nebraska	55 MPH or as posted	30days*	22.7c
		(Variable rate adjusted quarterly)	
Nevada	55 MPH or as posted	Reciprocal	37.6c
		(Additional 5c to 10c depending on County)	
New Hampshire	55 MPH or as posted	60 days*	32.1c
New Jersey	50 MPH or as posted	Reciprocal	24.6c
New Mexico	65 MPH or as posted	180 days*	30.1c
New York	55 MPH or as posted	Valid home-state license	22.1c
North Carolina	55 MPH or as posted	Valid home-state license	36.5c
North Dakota	65 MPH or as posted	Reciprocal	31.1c
Ohio	55 MPH or as posted	Reciprocal	36.1c
Oklahoma	55 MPH or as posted	Reciprocal	31.1c
Oregon	55 MPH or as posted	Reciprocal	38.1c
Pennsylvania	55 MPH or as posted	Reciprocal	26.1c
		(Additional 10.35% use tax imposed)	
Rhode Island	55 MPH or as posted	Reciprocal	40.1c
South Carolina	55 MPH or as posted	Reciprocal	30.1c
South Dakota	65 MPH or as posted	90 days*	32.1c
Tennessee	65 MPH or as posted	Reciprocal	35.5c
		(Includes special fuel rate)	
Texas	65 MPH or as posted	Reciprocal	34.1c
Utah	55 MPH or as posted	Reciprocal	33.1c
Vermont	55 MPH or as posted	6 months	30.1c
Virginia	55 MPH or as posted	6 months*	31.6c
Washington	65 MPH or as posted	Valid home-state license	37.1c
West Virginia	55 MPH or as posted	90 days*	29.6c
		(Additional 4.85c consumer sales & use tax)	
Wisconsin	55 MPH or as posted	Valid home-state license	37.3c
Wyoming	55 MPH or as posted	Valid home-state license	23.1c

* Reciprocal (Valid home-state license) or maximum number of days as indicated.
† Federal Tax-14.1c per gallon is included.
** Includes County Taxes.

OBSERVE POSTED SPEED LIMITS — STATE LAWS REQUIRE THE DRIVER OF A MOTOR VEHICLE TO CARRY A VALID OPERATOR'S LICENSE

Correct at date of publication but subject to change

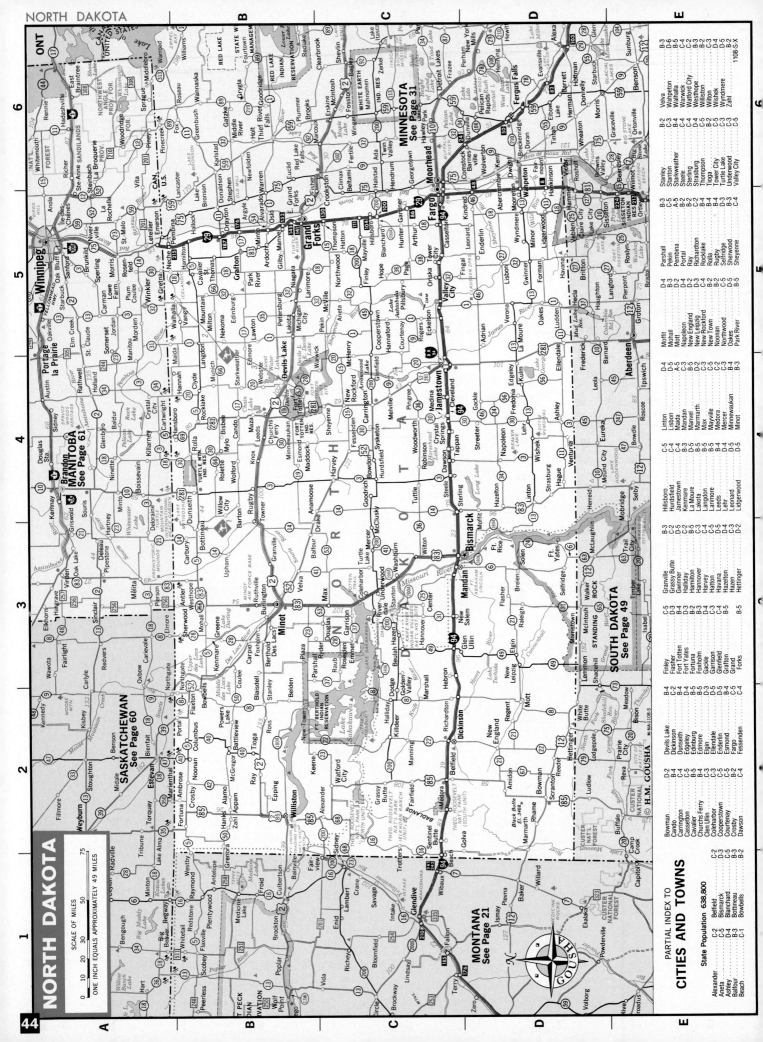

NORTH DAKOTA

NORTH DAKOTA

SCALE OF MILES

0 10 20 30 50 75

ONE INCH EQUALS APPROXIMATELY 49 MILES

44

© H.M. GOUSHA

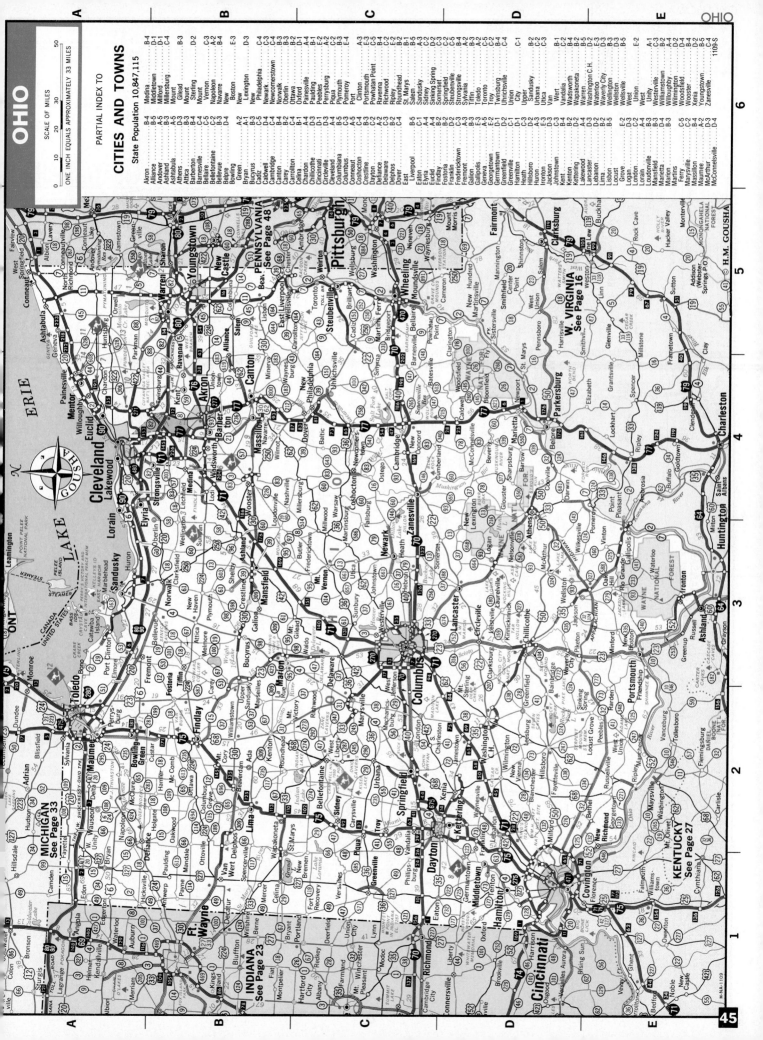

OHIO

SCALE OF MILES
0 10 20 30 50
ONE INCH EQUALS APPROXIMATELY 33 MILES

PARTIAL INDEX TO CITIES AND TOWNS

State Population 10,847,115

City	Grid
Akron	B-4
Alliance	B-5
Andover	A-5
Ashland	C-3
Ashtabula	A-5
Athens	D-3
Attica	C-3
Barberton	B-4
Barnesville	C-4
Bellaire	C-5
Bellefontaine	C-2
Bellevue	C-2
Belpre	D-4
Bowling Green	B-2
Bryan	B-1
Bucyrus	C-3
Cadiz	C-4
Caldwell	C-4
Cambridge	C-4
Canton	B-4
Carey	C-2
Carrollton	B-4
Celina	C-1
Chardon	A-4
Chillicothe	D-3
Cincinnati	E-1
Circleville	D-3
Cleveland	A-4
Columbiana	B-5
Columbus	C-3
Conneaut	A-5
Coshocton	C-3
Crestline	C-3
Dayton	D-1
Defiance	B-1
Delaware	C-3
Delphos	C-1
Dover	C-4
East Liverpool	B-5
Eaton	D-1
Elyria	A-3
Euclid	A-4
Findlay	C-2
Fostoria	C-2
Franklin	D-1
Fredericktown	C-3
Fremont	B-2
Galion	C-3
Gallipolis	D-3
Geneva	A-4
Georgetown	E-2
Germantown	D-1
Greenfield	D-2
Greenville	D-1
Hamilton	D-1
Heath	C-3
Hillsboro	D-2
Huron	B-3
Ironton	E-3
Jackson	D-3
Johnstown	C-3
Kent	B-4
Kenton	C-2
Kettering	D-1
Lakewood	A-4
Lancaster	C-3
Lebanon	D-1
Lima	C-1
Lisbon	B-5
Logan	D-3
London	C-2
Lorain	A-3
Loudonville	C-3
Mansfield	C-3
Marietta	D-4
Marion	C-2
Martins Ferry	C-5
Marysville	C-2
Massillon	B-4
McArthur	D-3
McConnelsville	D-4
Medina	B-4
Middletown	D-1
Milford	E-1
Millersburg	C-4
Mount Gilead	C-3
Mount Sterling	D-2
Mount Vernon	C-3
Napoleon	B-1
Navarre	B-4
New Boston	E-3
New Lexington	D-3
New Philadelphia	C-4
Newark	C-3
Newcomerstown	C-4
Norwalk	B-3
Oberlin	B-3
Ottawa	C-1
Oxford	D-1
Painesville	A-4
Paulding	B-1
Peebles	E-2
Perrysburg	B-2
Piqua	D-1
Plymouth	C-3
Pomeroy	D-4
Port Clinton	B-2
Portsmouth	E-3
Powhatan Point	C-5
Ravenna	B-4
Richwood	C-2
Ripley	E-2
Roundhead	C-2
St. Marys	C-1
Salem	B-5
Sandusky	B-3
Sidney	D-1
Sinking Spring	E-2
Somerset	D-3
Springfield	C-2
Steubenville	B-5
Strongsville	A-3
Sylvania	A-2
Tiffin	C-2
Toledo	B-2
Toronto	B-5
Troy	D-1
Twinsburg	A-4
Uhrichsville	C-4
Union City	D-1
Upper Sandusky	C-2
Urbana	C-2
Utica	C-3
Van Wert	C-1
Vandalia	D-1
Wadsworth	B-4
Wapakoneta	C-1
Warren	A-5
Washington C.H.	D-2
Waterloo	E-3
Waverly City	D-3
Wellington	B-3
Wellston	D-3
Wellsville	B-5
West Union	E-2
Westerville	C-3
Williamstown	D-4
Willoughby	A-4
Wilmington	D-2
Woodsfield	C-5
Wooster	B-4
Xenia	D-2
Youngstown	A-5
Zanesville	C-4

1109-S

M-NA-1109

45

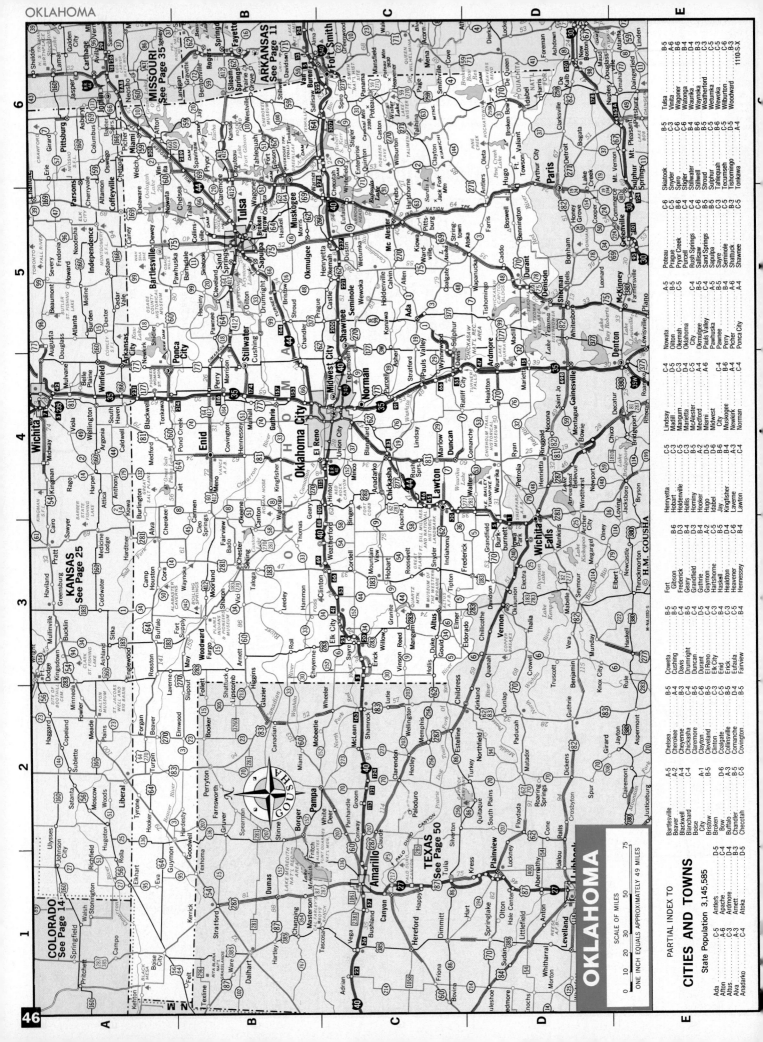

OKLAHOMA

SCALE OF MILES

0 10 20 30 50 75

ONE INCH EQUALS APPROXIMATELY 49 MILES

© H.M. GOUSHA

CITIES AND TOWNS

State Population 3,145,585

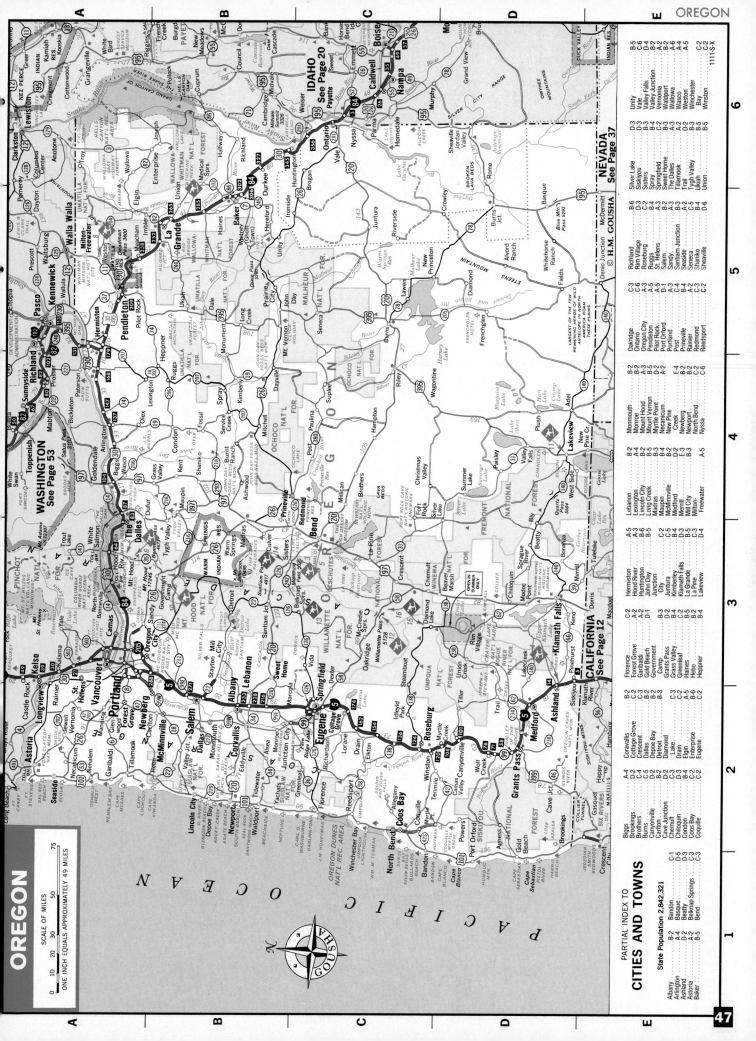

OREGON

SCALE OF MILES
0 10 20 30 50 75
ONE INCH EQUALS APPROXIMATELY 49 MILES

PACIFIC OCEAN

© H.M. GOUSHA

WASHINGTON
See Page 53

IDAHO
See Page 20

NEVADA
See Page 37

CALIFORNIA
See Page 12

1111-S-X

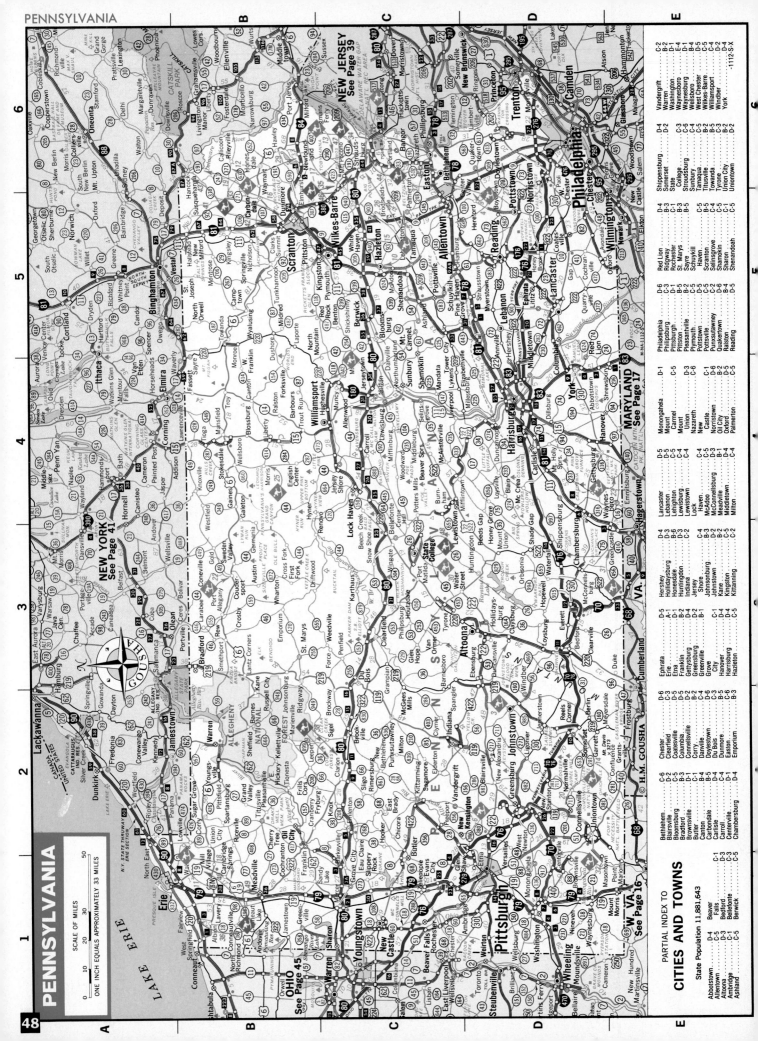

PENNSYLVANIA

SCALE OF MILES
0 10 20 30 50
ONE INCH EQUALS APPROXIMATELY 33 MILES

48

H.M. GOUSHA

NEW YORK See Page 41

NEW JERSEY See Page 39

OHIO See Page 45

MARYLAND See Page 17

W. VA. See Page 16

LAKE ERIE

M-NJ.1112-S-X

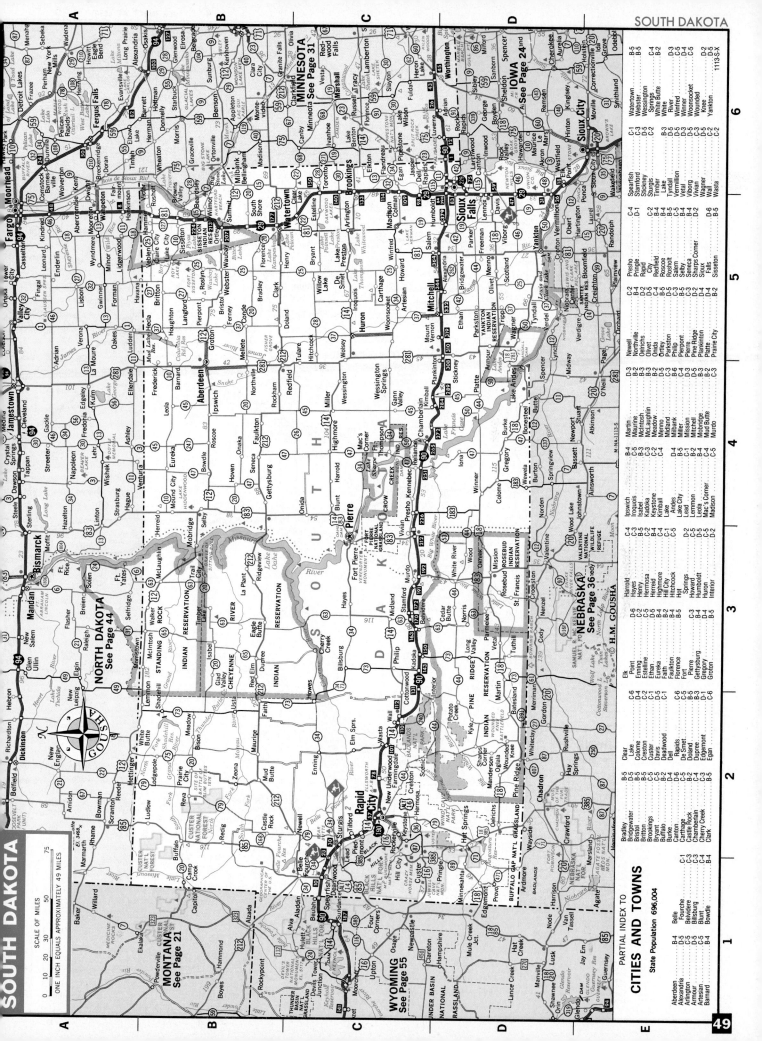

SOUTH DAKOTA

SCALE OF MILES
0 10 20 30 50 75
ONE INCH EQUALS APPROXIMATELY 49 MILES

MONTANA
See Page 21

NORTH DAKOTA
See Page 44

WYOMING
See Page 55

MINNESOTA
See Page 31

IOWA
See Page 24

NEBRASKA
See Page 36

PARTIAL INDEX TO
CITIES AND TOWNS
State Population 696,004

© H.M. GOUSHA

49

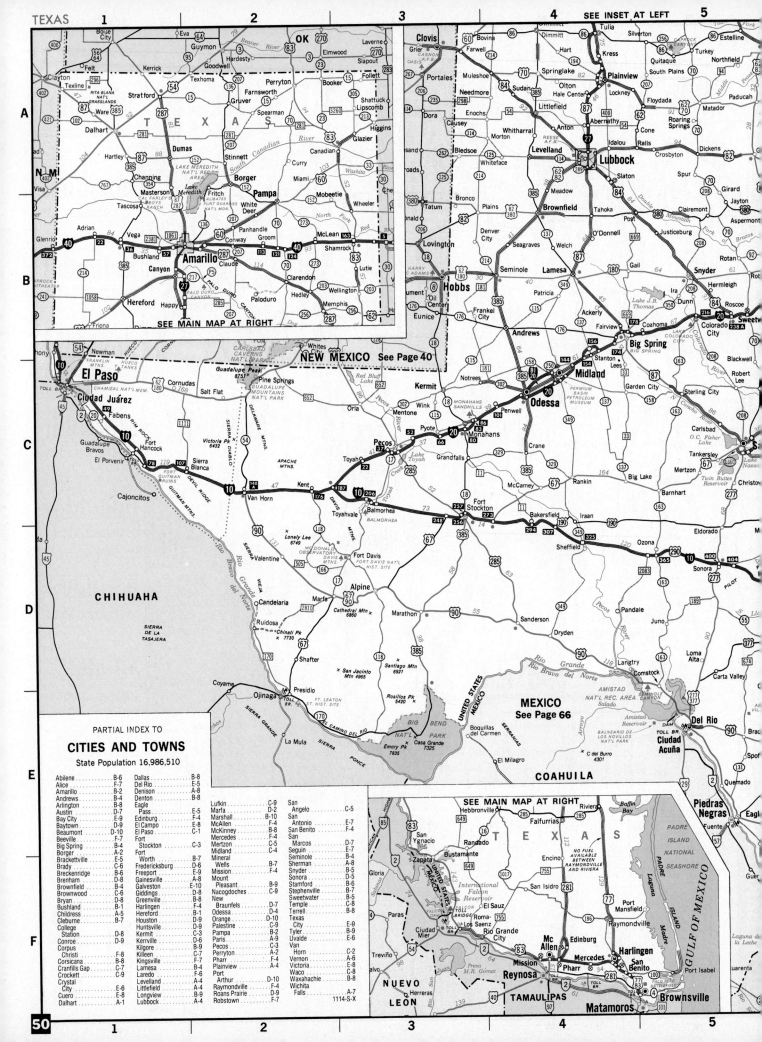

TEXAS

PARTIAL INDEX TO

CITIES AND TOWNS
State Population 16,986,510

50

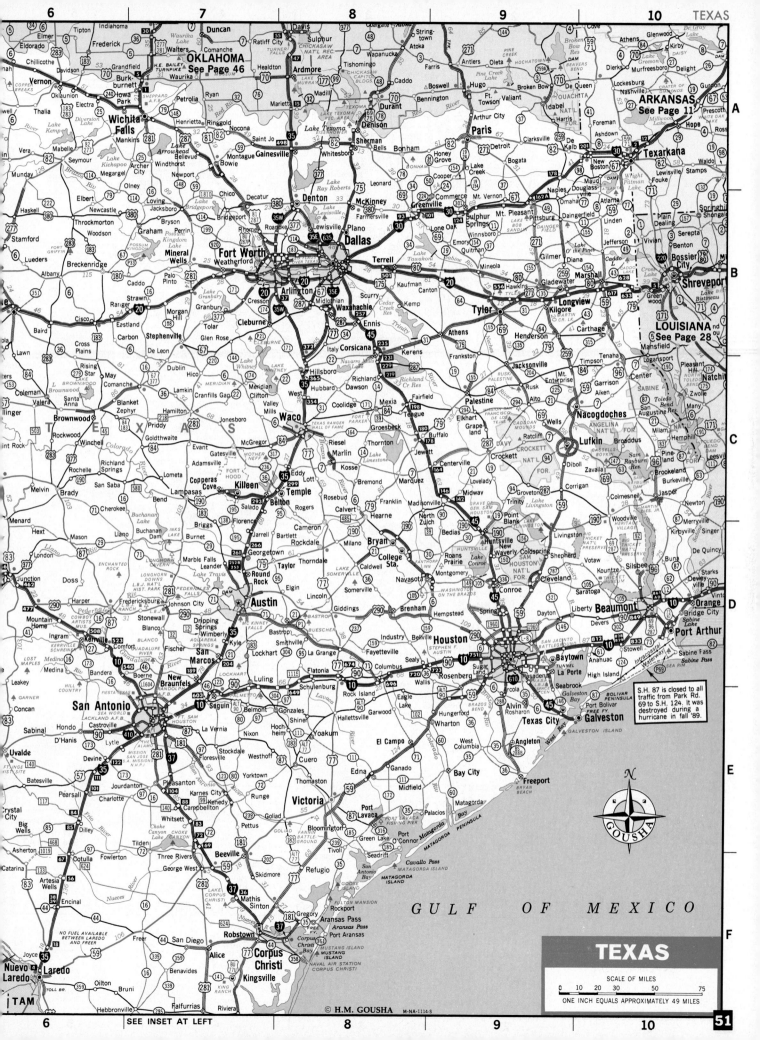

S.H. 87 is closed to all
traffic from Park Rd.
69 to S.H. 124. It was
destroyed during a
hurricane in fall '89.

ARKANSAS
See Page 11

LOUISIANA
See Page 28

OKLAHOMA
See Page 46

T E X A S

GULF OF MEXICO

NO FUEL AVAILABLE
BETWEEN LAREDO
AND FREER

© H.M. GOUSHA   M-NA-1114-S

TEXAS

SCALE OF MILES
0   10   20   30   50   75
ONE INCH EQUALS APPROXIMATELY 49 MILES

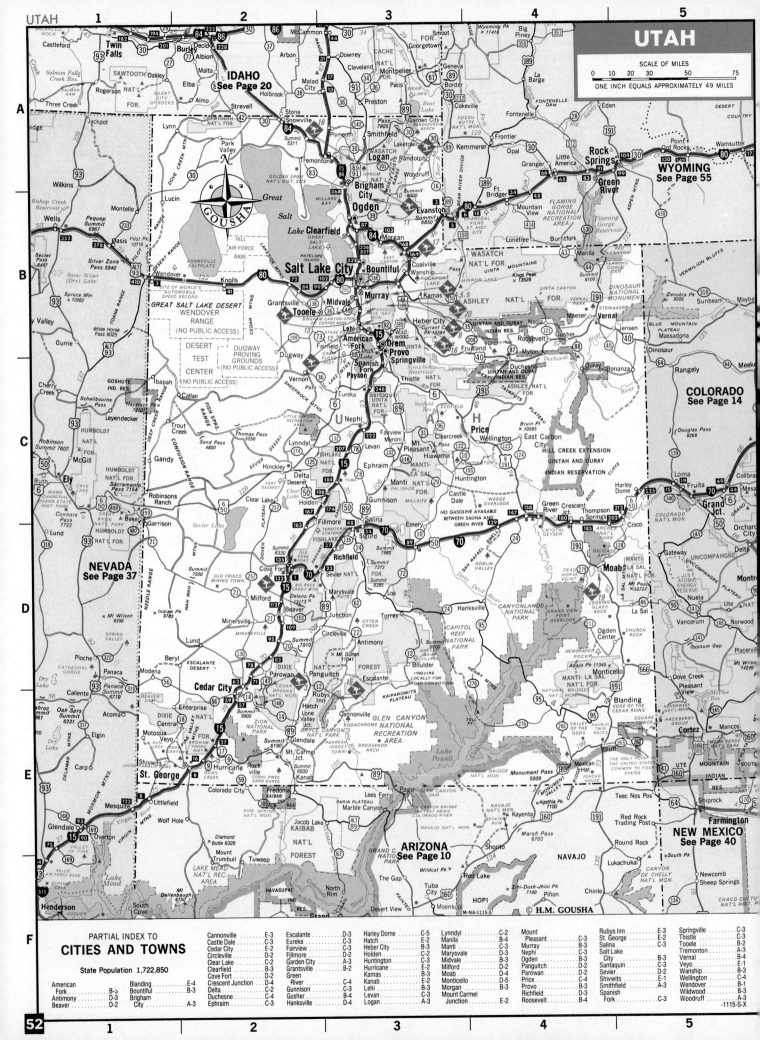

UTAH

SCALE OF MILES

0 10 20 30 50 75

ONE INCH EQUALS APPROXIMATELY 49 MILES

© H.M. GOUSHA

M-NA-1115-S

-1115-S-X

IDAHO See Page 20

WYOMING See Page 55

COLORADO See Page 14

NEVADA See Page 37

ARIZONA See Page 10

NEW MEXICO See Page 40

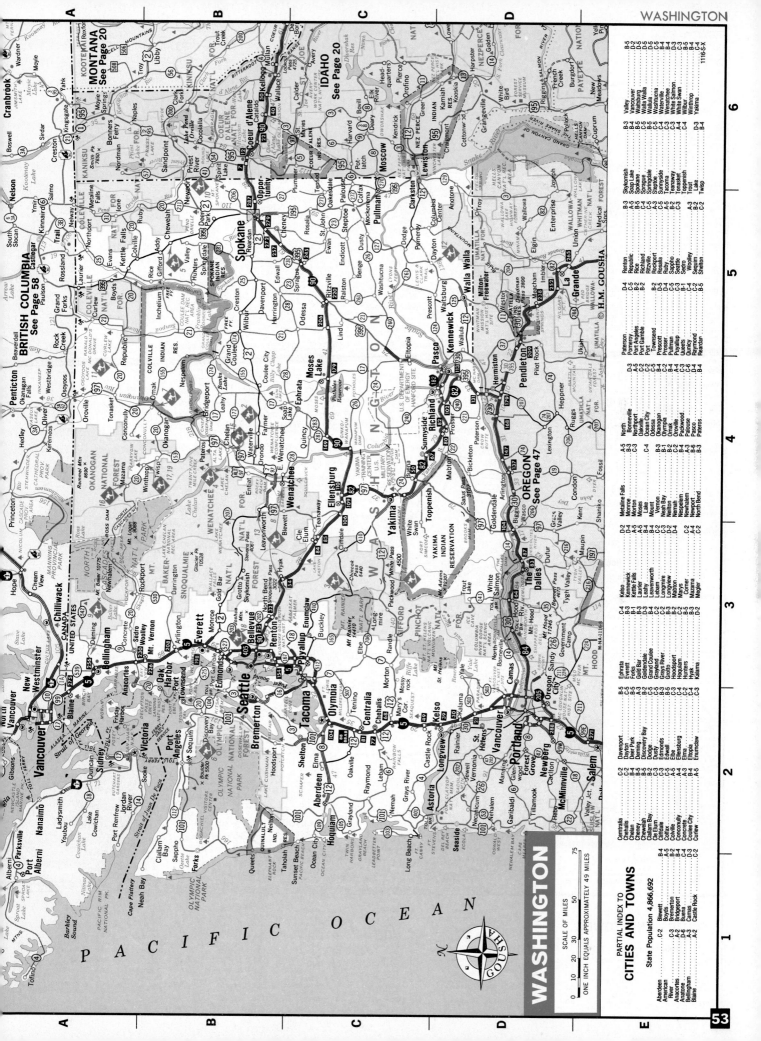

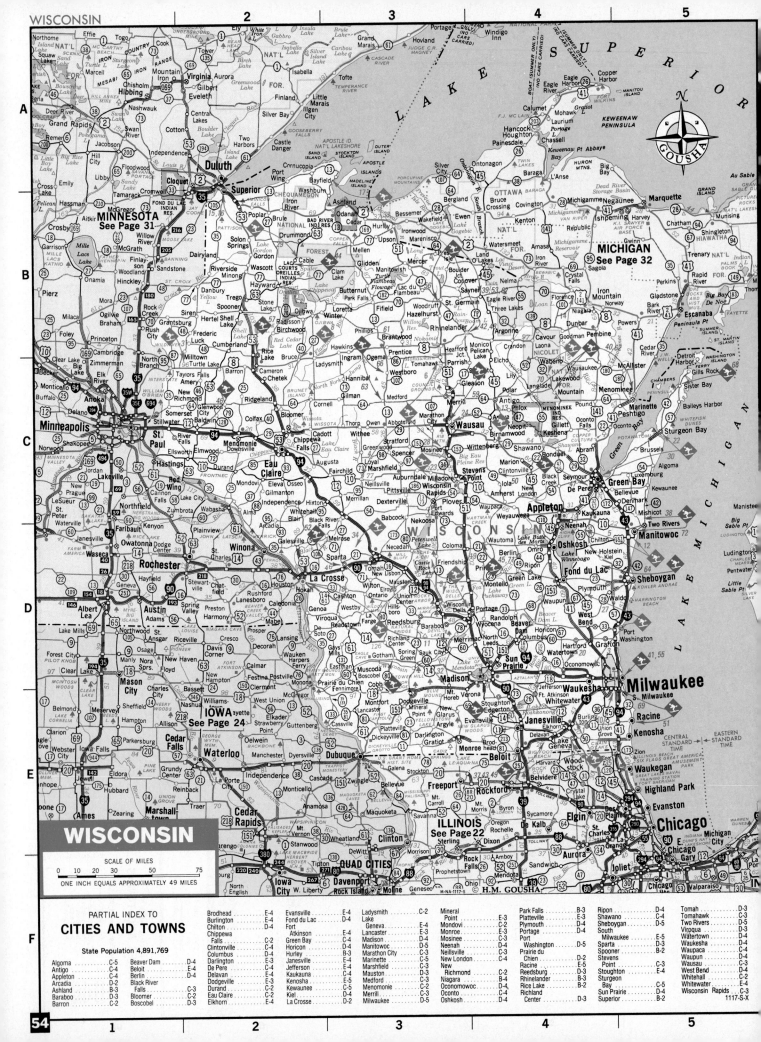

WISCONSIN

SCALE OF MILES

0 10 20 30   50   75

ONE INCH EQUALS APPROXIMATELY 49 MILES

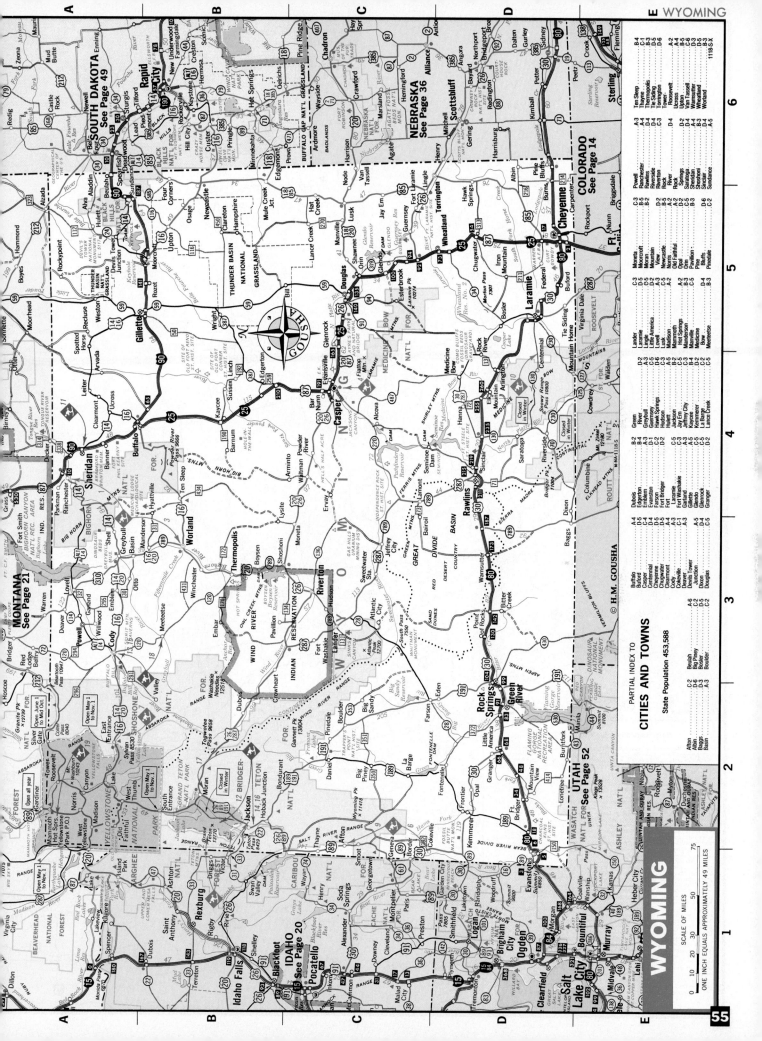

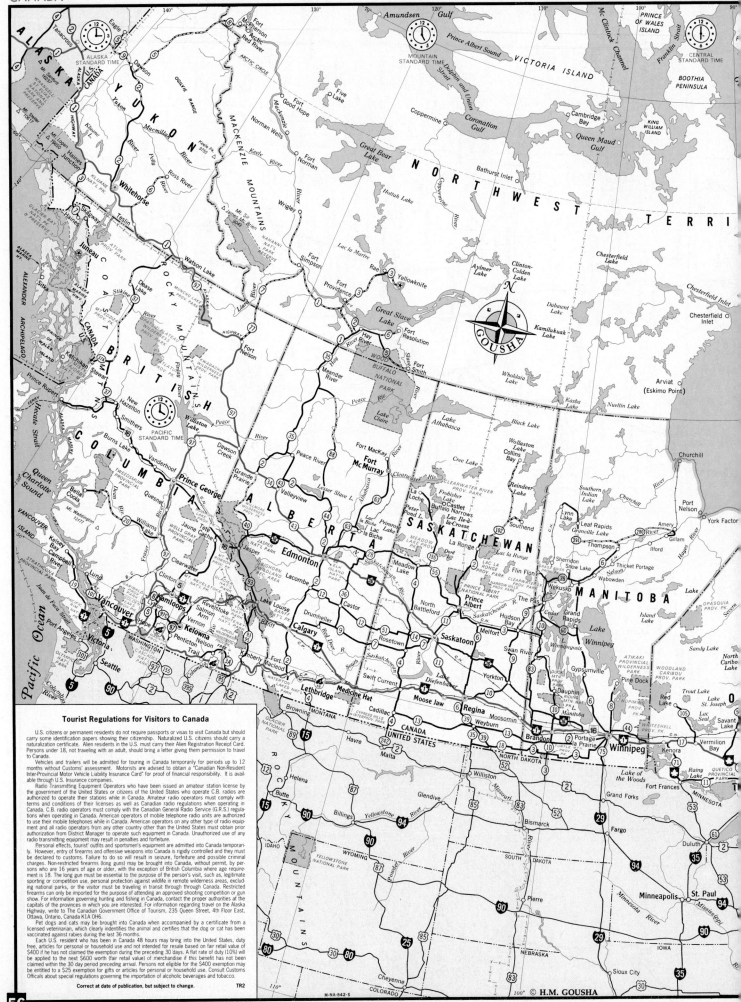

Tourist Regulations for Visitors to Canada

U.S. citizens or permanent residents do not require passports or visas to visit Canada but should carry some identification papers showing their citizenship. Naturalized U.S. citizens should carry a naturalization certificate. Alien residents in the U.S. must carry their Alien Registration Receipt Card. Persons under 18, not traveling with an adult, should bring a letter giving them permission to travel to Canada.

Vehicles and trailers will be admitted for touring in Canada temporarily for periods up to 12 months without Customs' assessment. Motorists are advised to obtain a "Canadian Non-Resident Inter-Provincial Motor Vehicle Liability Insurance Card" for proof of financial responsibility. It is available through U.S. insurance companies.

Radio Transmitting Equipment Operators who have been issued an amateur station license by the government of the United States or citizens of the United States who operate C.B. radios are authorized to operate their stations while in Canada. Amateur radio operators must comply with terms and conditions of their licenses as well as Canadian radio regulations when operating in Canada. C.B. radio operators must comply with the Canadian General Radio Service (G.R.S.) regulations when operating in Canada. American operators of mobile telephone radio units are authorized to use their mobile telephones while in Canada. American operators on any other type of radio equipment and all radio operators from any other country other than the United States must obtain prior authorization from District Manager to operate such equipment in Canada. Unauthorized use of any radio transmitting equipment may result in penalties and forfeiture.

Personal effects, tourist' outfits and sportsmen's equipment are admitted into Canada temporarily. However, entry of firearms and offensive weapons into Canada is rigidly controlled and they must be declared to customs. Failure to do so will result in seizure, forfeiture and possible criminal charges. Non-restricted firearms (long guns) may be brought into Canada, without permit, by persons who are 16 years of age or older, with the exception of British Columbia where age requirement is 18. The long gun must be essential to the purpose of the person's visit, such as, legitimate sporting or competition use, personal protection against wildlife in remote wilderness areas, excluding national parks, or the visitor must be traveling in transit through through Canada. Restricted firearms can only be imported for the purpose of attending an approved shooting competition or gun show. For information governing hunting and fishing in Canada, contact the proper authorities at the capitals of the provinces in which you are interested. For information regarding travel on the Alaska Highway, write to The Canadian Government Office of Tourism, 235 Queen Street, 4th Floor East, Ottawa, Ontario, Canada K1A 0H6.

Pet dogs and cats may be brought into Canada when accompanied by a certificate from a licensed veterinarian, which clearly indentifies the animal and certifies that the dog or cat has been vaccinated against rabies during the last 36 months.

Each U.S. resident who has been in Canada 48 hours may bring into the United States, duty free, articles for personal or household use and not intended for resale based on fair retail value of $400 if he has not claimed the exemption during the preceding 30 days. A flat rate of duty (10%) will be applied to the next $600 worth (fair retail value) of merchandise if this benefit has not been claimed within the 30 day period preceding arrival. Persons not eligible for the $400 exemption may be entitled to a $25 exemption for gifts or articles for personal or household use. Consult Customs Officials about special regulations governing the importation of alcoholic beverages and tobacco.

Correct at date of publication, but subject to change.   TR2

M-NA-842-S   © H.M. GOUSHA

Time Zones
- EASTERN STANDARD TIME
- ATLANTIC STANDARD TIME
- GREENLAND STANDARD TIME
- OSCAR STANDARD TIME
- NEWFOUNDLAND STANDARD TIME

CANADA

SCALE OF MILES
0 50 100 200 300
ONE INCH EQUALS APPROXIMATELY 209 MILES

LEGEND
- Paved Roads
- Improved Roads
- Graded Roads
- Trans-Canada Highway
- 90 U.S. Interstate System
- Capital Cities
- —x—x— Time Zone Boundaries
- Railroads
- 11 Provincial and State Hys.
- 19 U.S. Highway Numbers
- 20 Quebec Autoroutes

To find the approximate distance between two towns, over principal Canadian through routes, trace down the vertical column of one town to its intersection with the horizontal column of the other town.

Distance Chart

	CALGARY, ALTA.	CHARLOTTETOWN	EDMONTON, ALTA.
CHARLOTTETOWN	3075		
EDMONTON, ALTA.	3055	183	
FREDERICTON N.B.	2826	229	2846
HALIFAX N.S.	290	3116	147
MONTREAL, QUE.	843	554	2272
OTTAWA, ONT.	916	1033	1876
PRINCE RUPERT, B.C.	117	960	670
QUEBEC, QUE.	2156	3072	3189
REGINA, SASK.	3349	1192	277
SASKATOON, SASK.	1978	1371	785
THUNDER BAY, ONT.	157	2105	1243
TORONTO, ONT.	1785	1657	485
VANCOUVER, B.C.	2782	1007	1114
VICTORIA, B.C.	43	2825	1050
WHITEHORSE, YUKON	1556	1513	3372
WINDSOR, ONT.	3288	2742	2699
WINNIPEG, MAN.	1219	2070	1523

(Full triangular mileage chart — additional columns: FREDERICTON N.B., HALIFAX N.S., MONTREAL, QUE., OTTAWA, ONT., PRINCE RUPERT, B.C., QUEBEC, QUE., REGINA, SASK., SASKATOON, SASK., THUNDER BAY, ONT., TORONTO, ONT., VANCOUVER, B.C., VICTORIA, B.C., WHITEHORSE, YUKON, WINDSOR, ONT., WINNIPEG, MAN.)

Selected place names
GREENLAND (Denmark), Nuk (Godthaab), Julianehaab, Cape Farewell, Cape Desolation, BAFFIN ISLAND, Cape Dyer, Pangnirtung, Cumberland Sound, Cape Mercy, Davis Strait, Labrador Sea, PRINCE CHARLES ISLAND, Foxe Basin, AUYUITTUQ NAT'L PARK, Iqaluit, Frobisher Bay, Resolution Island, MELVILLE PENINSULA, SOUTHAMPTON ISLAND, Foxe Channel, Hudson Strait, Cape Chidley, COATS ISLAND, MANSEL ISLAND, Fisher Strait, Evans Strait, Rivière Kovic, Lac Nantais, Ungava Bay, Rivière Arnaud, Rivière aux Feuilles, Rivière aux Mélèzes, Rivière à la Baleine, Kuujjuaq, BELCHER ISLANDS, Inukjuak, Lac à l'Eau Claire, Lac Bienville, Grande Rivière de la Baleine, NEW FOUNDLAND, LABRADOR, Hopedale, Cartwright, Hamilton Inlet, Goose Bay, Michikamau Lake, Lake Melville, Churchill, Schefferville, Menihek Lakes, Lac Caniapiscau, Lac Opiscotéo, Lac Nichicun, Réservoir Pipmuacin, BELLE ISLE, St. Anthony, CAPE BAULD, Red Bay, Blanc-Sablon, FOGO ISLAND, GROS MORNE NAT'L PK, Gander, Goobies, St. John's, Deer Lake, Corner Brook, Stephenville, Channel-Port-aux-Basques, MIQUELON I. (FRANCE), CAPE RACE, Trading Post, Havre-St-Pierre, ÎLE D'ANTICOSTI, Sept-Îles, Gulf of St. Lawrence, Gaspé, GASPÉ PENINSULA, MAGDALEN ISLANDS, CAPE BRETON HIGHLANDS NAT'L PARK, North Sydney, Sydney, Cabot Strait, CAPE BRETON ISLAND, PRINCE EDWARD ISLAND, Charlottetown, NEW BRUNSWICK, Edmundston, Campbellton, Moncton, Fredericton, Saint John, NOVA SCOTIA, Halifax, Bridgewater, Digby, KEJIMKUJIK NAT'L PARK, Bangor, Calais, Woodstock, Augusta, Portland, Bar Harbor, Boston, Rivière-du-Loup, Baie-Comeau, Labrieville, Lac St-Jean, Chicoutimi, St-Siméon, Québec, Trois-Rivières, Sherbrooke, Montreal, Ottawa, La Tuque, Sanmaur, Senneterre, Amos, Rouyn-Noranda, Val-d'Or, Mont-Laurier, RÉS. FAUNIQUE LA VÉRENDRYE, Chibougamau, Matagami, Cochrane, Hearst, Kapuskasing, North Bay, Sudbury, Sault Ste. Marie, Peterborough, Kingston, Toronto, Hamilton, London, Sarnia, Windsor, Detroit, Cleveland, Buffalo, Scranton, New York, Albany, Moosonee, James Bay, POLAR BEAR PROV. PARK, Kesagami Lake, Lake Abitibi, Kirkland Lake, Parry Sound, Orillia, Owen Sound, Tobermory, Georgian Bay, ALGONQUIN PROVINCIAL PARK, PUKASKWA NAT'L PK, Nipigon, White River, Hemlo, Wawa, St. Ignace, LAKE SUPERIOR PROV. PK, ISLE ROYALE NAT'L PK

Atlantic Ocean

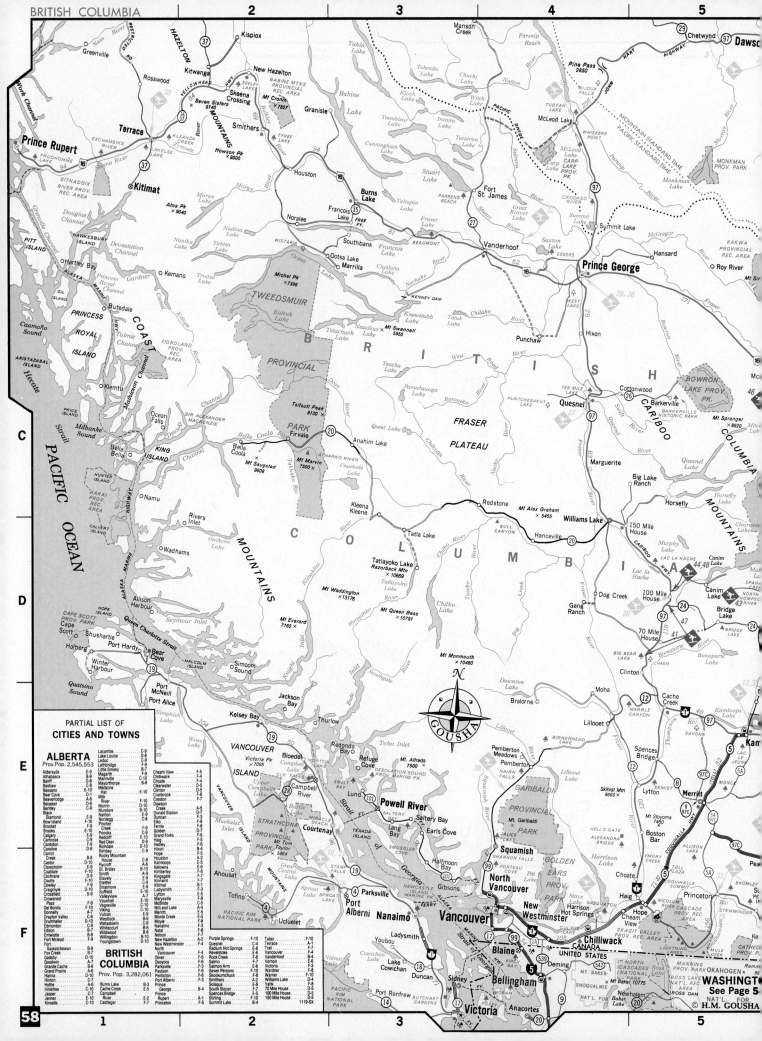

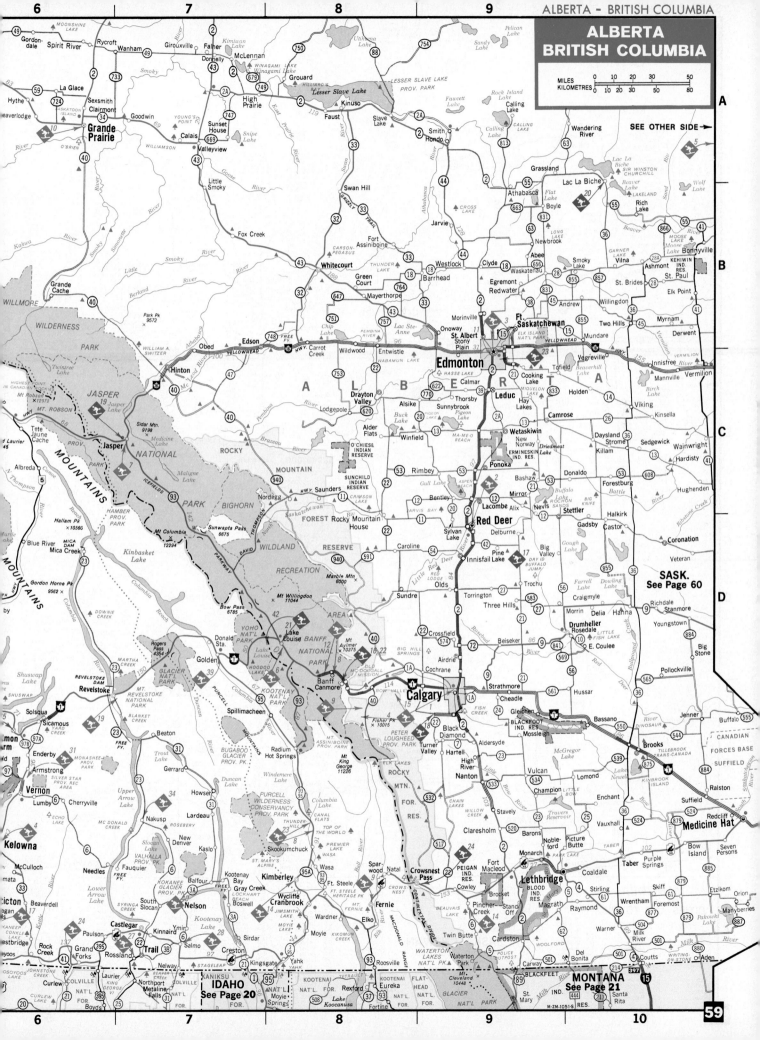

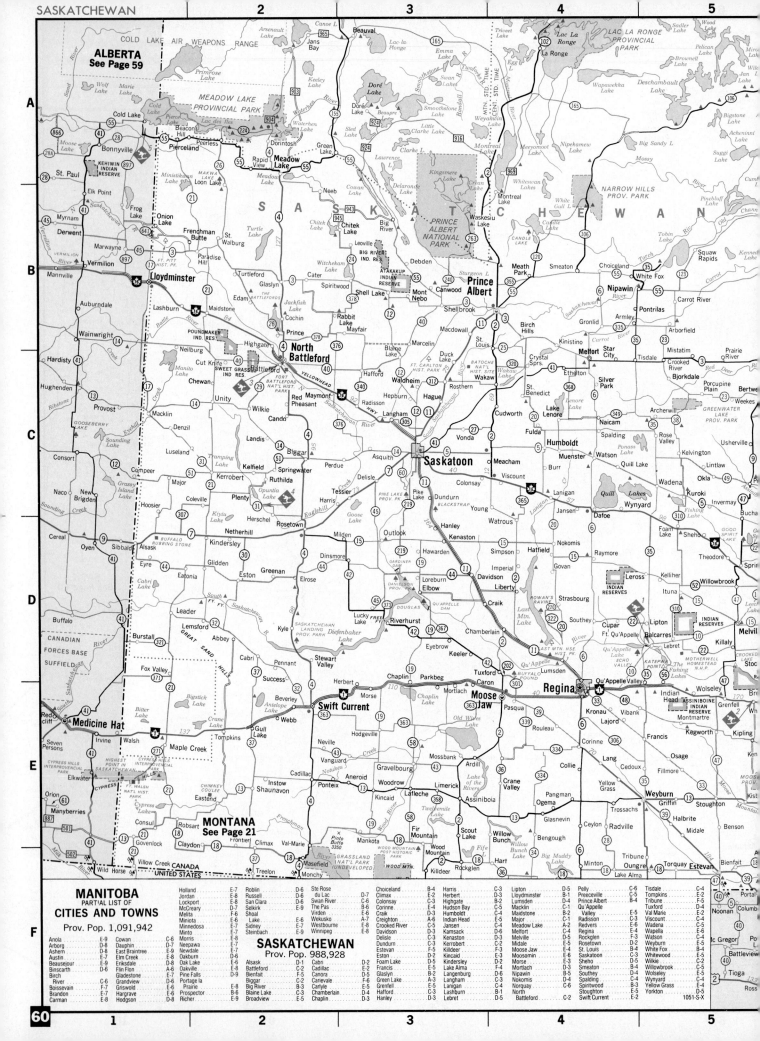

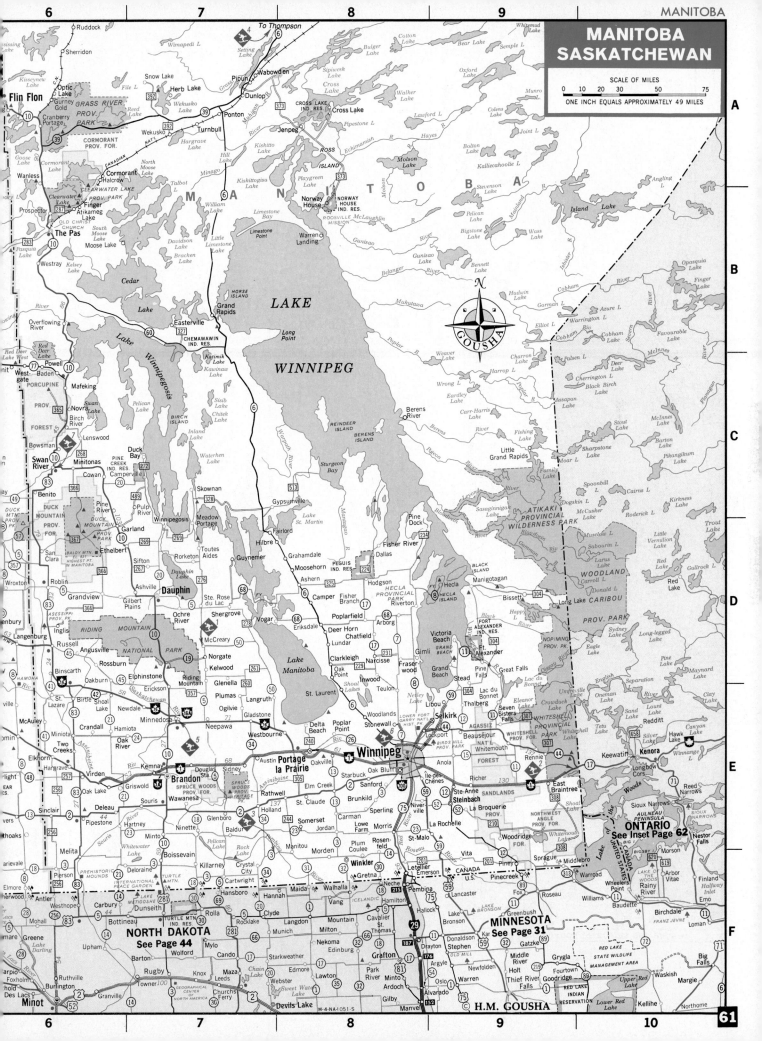

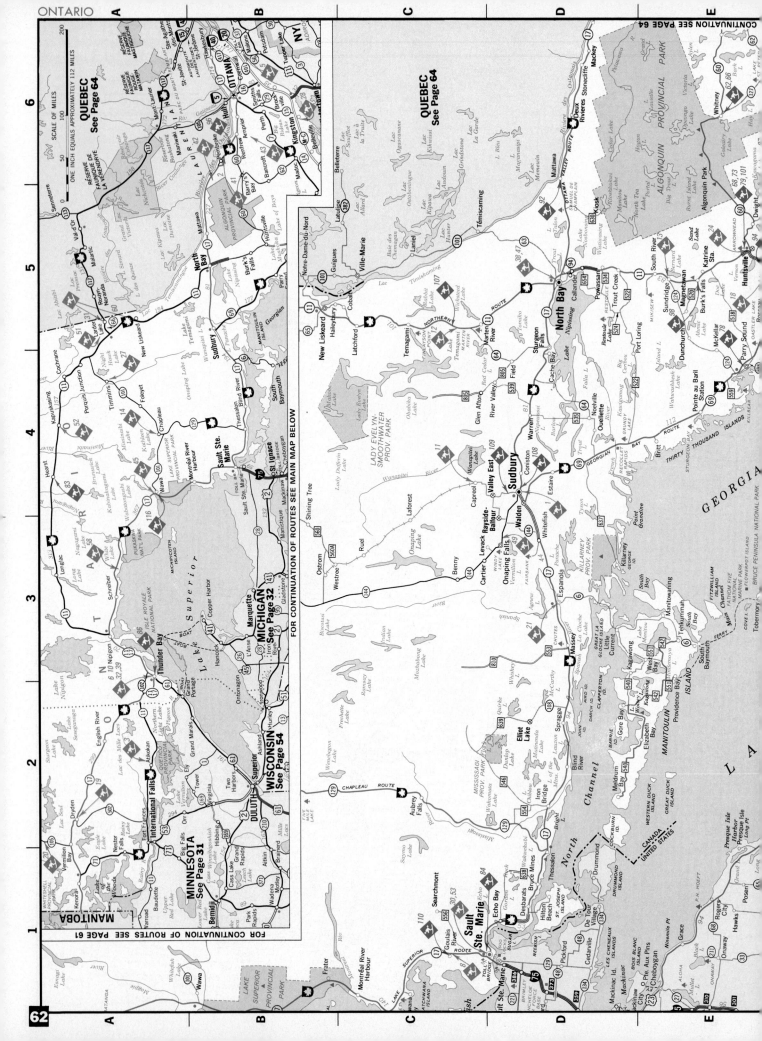

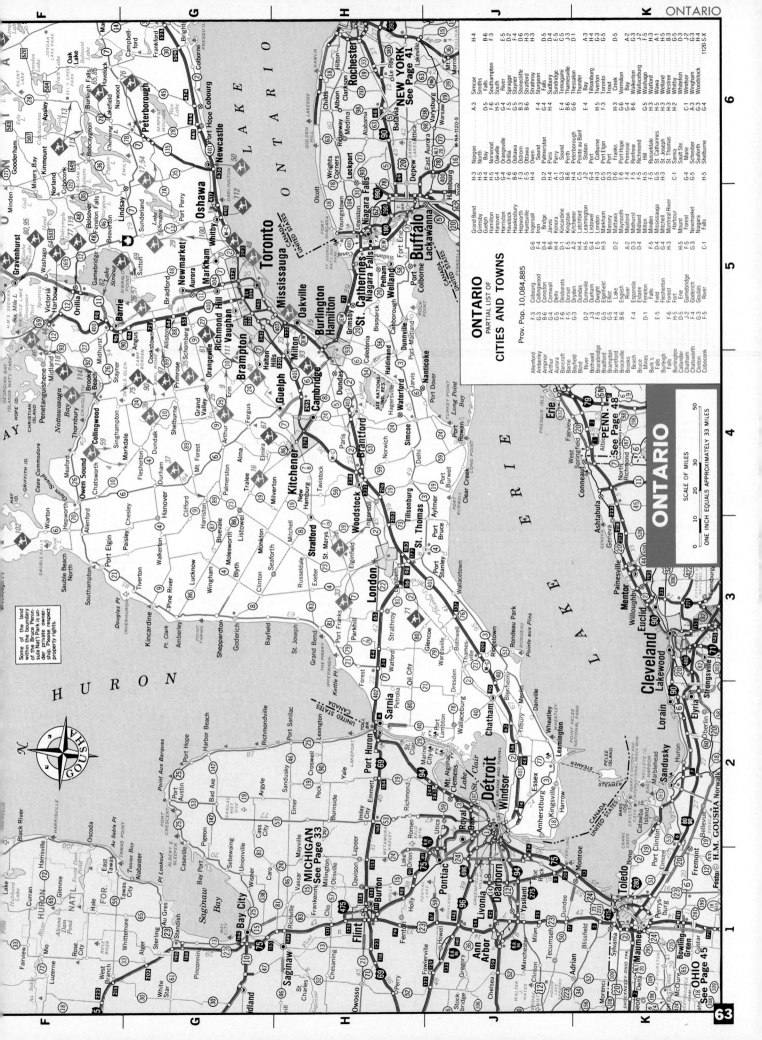

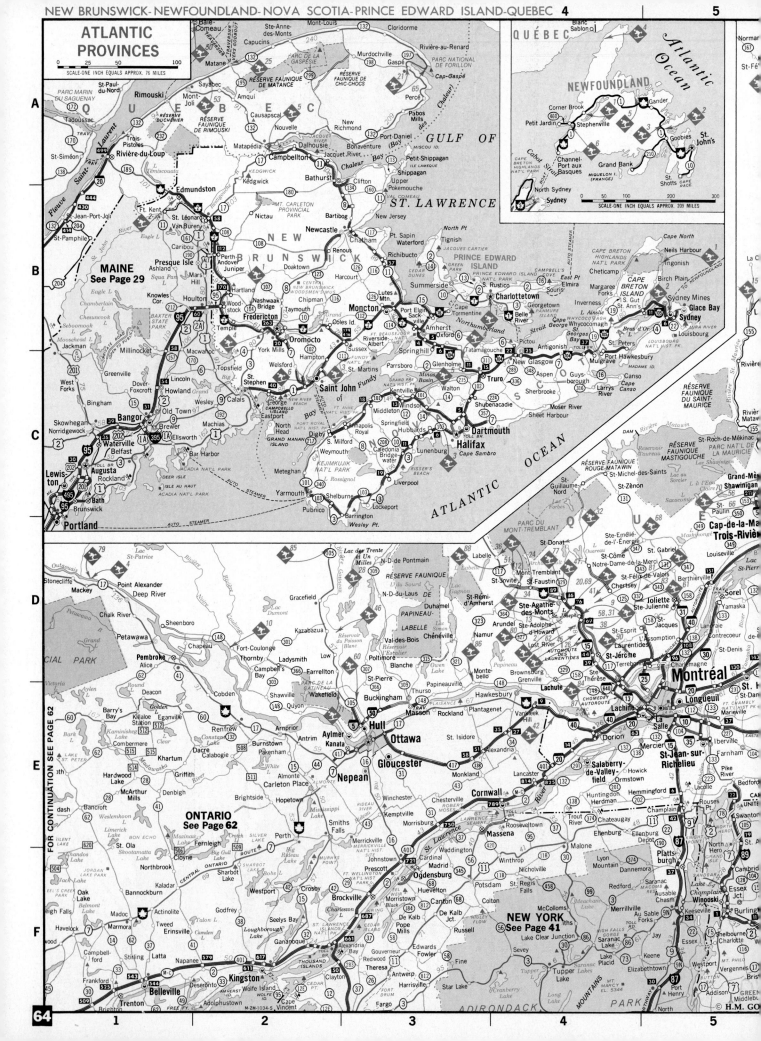

ATLANTIC PROVINCES

SCALE-ONE INCH EQUALS APPROX. 76 MILES
0   25   50   100

MAINE
See Page 29

ONTARIO
See Page 62

NEW YORK
See Page 41

FOR CONTINUATION SEE PAGE 62

© H.M. GO

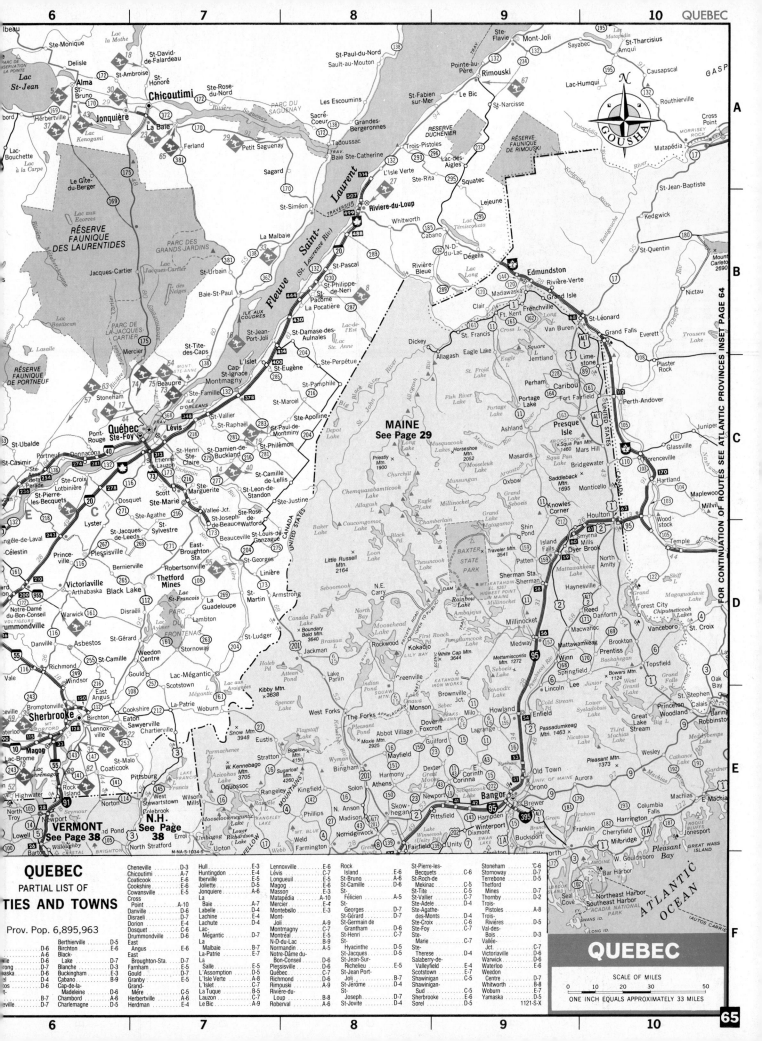

QUEBEC
PARTIAL LIST OF
TIES AND TOWNS

Prov. Pop. 6,895,963

QUEBEC

SCALE OF MILES
0 10 20 30 50
ONE INCH EQUALS APPROXIMATELY 33 MILES

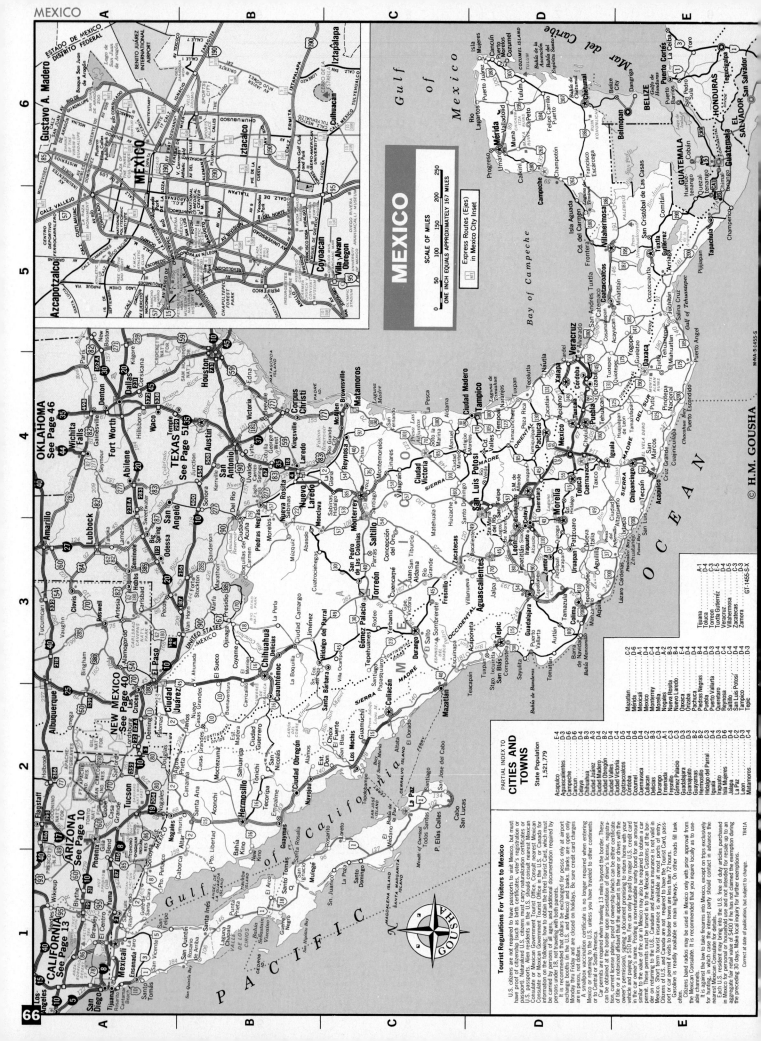

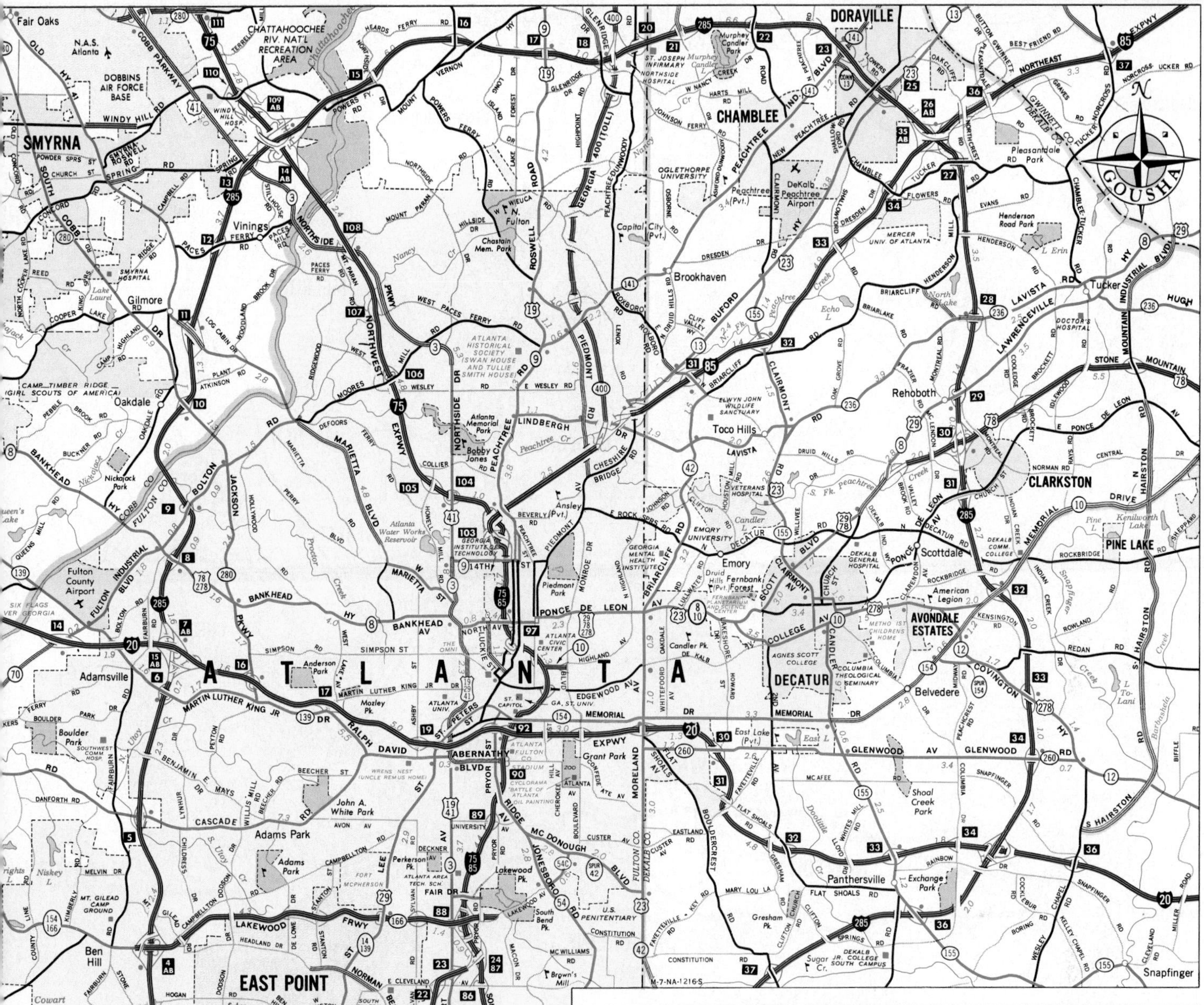

ATLANTA

SCALE OF MILES

0 1 2 3 4 5

SCALE: ONE INCH EQUALS APPROXIMATELY 2.7 MILES

© H.M. GOUSHA

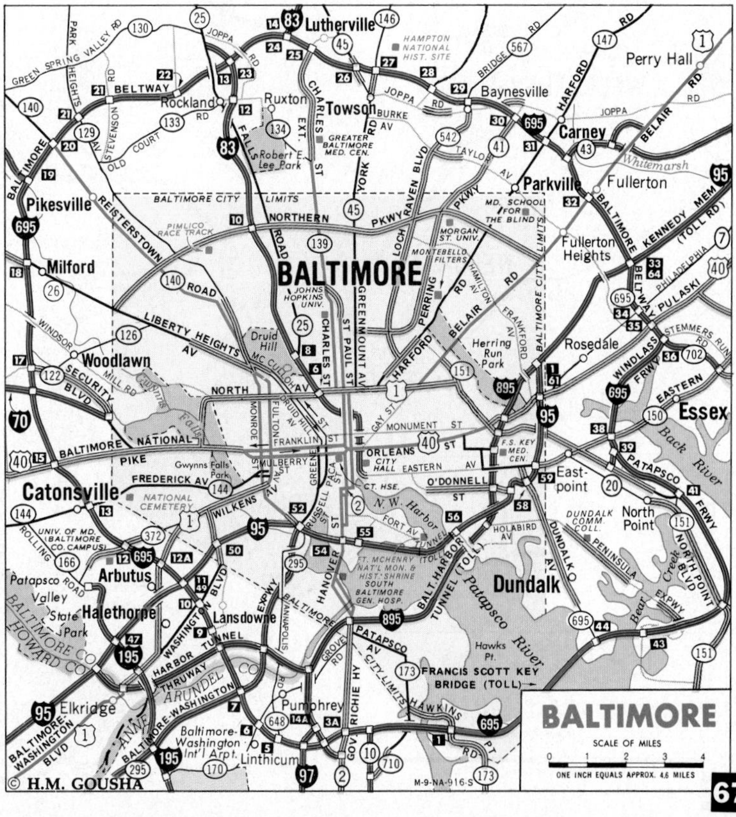

BALTIMORE

SCALE OF MILES

0 1 2 3 4

ONE INCH EQUALS APPROX. 4.6 MILES

© H.M. GOUSHA

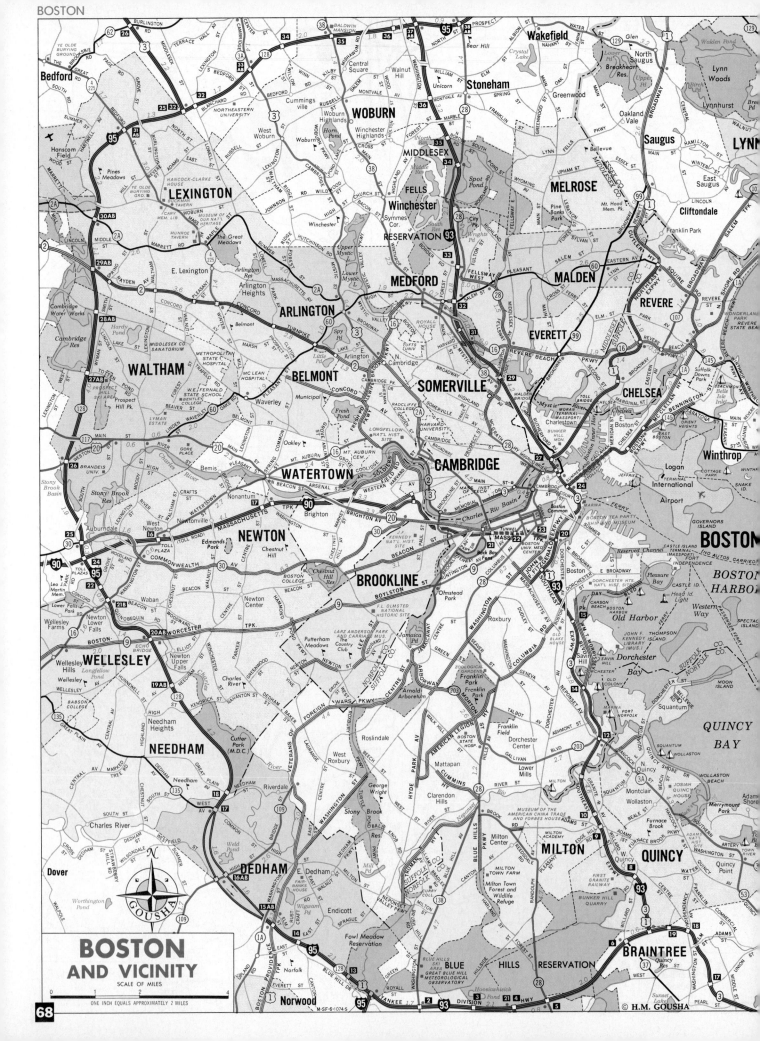

BOSTON
AND VICINITY

SCALE OF MILES

0   1   2   3   4

ONE INCH EQUALS APPROXIMATELY 2 MILES

68

© H.M. Gousha

M-SF-6-1074-S

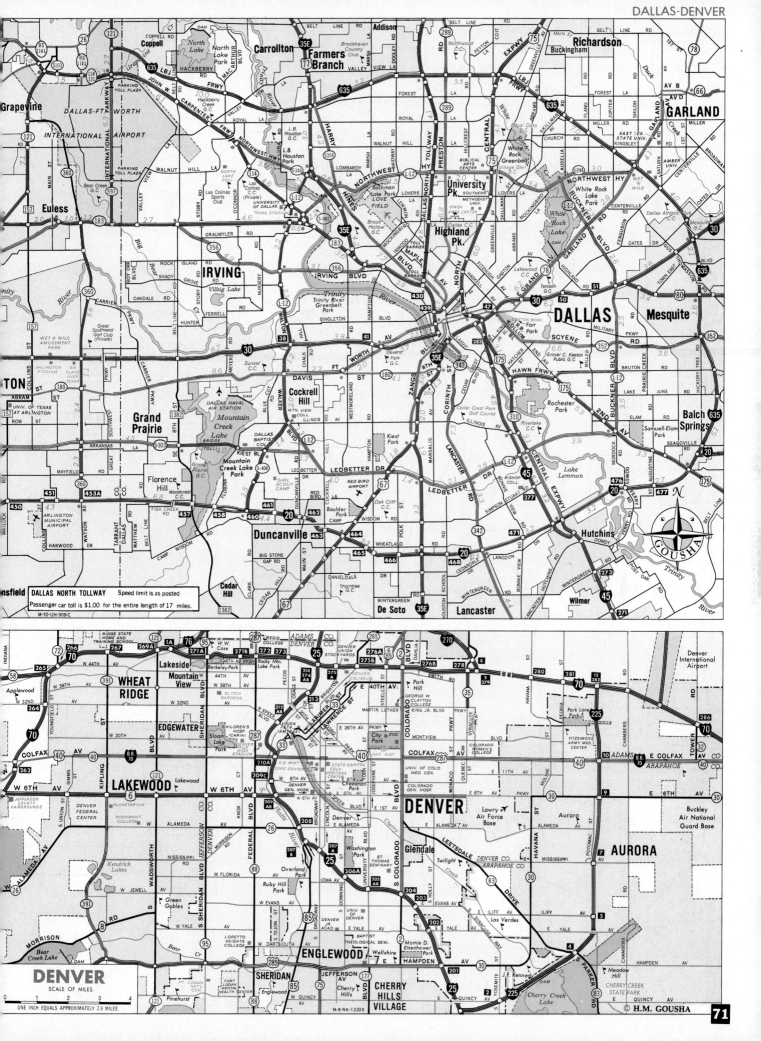

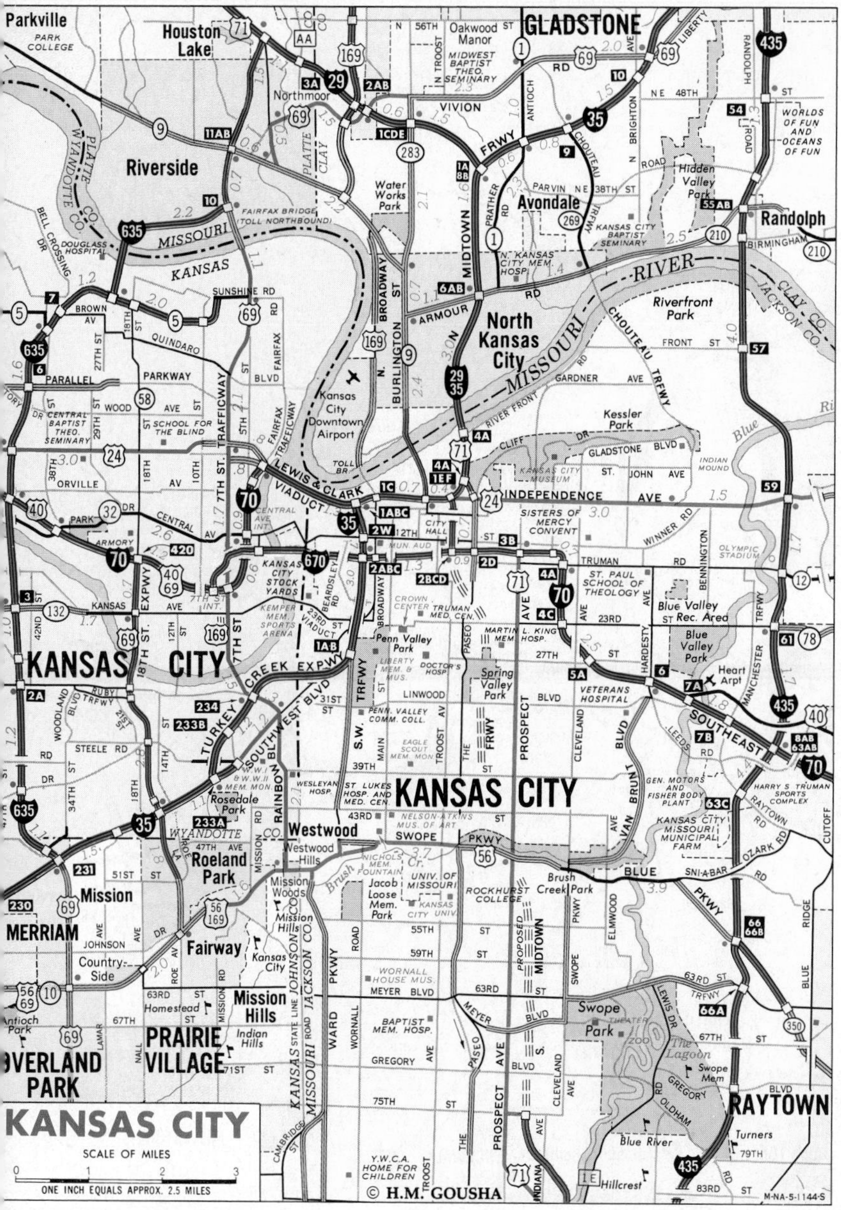
KANSAS CITY
SCALE OF MILES
ONE INCH EQUALS APPROX. 2.5 MILES
Parkville
PARK COLLEGE
Houston Lake
GLADSTONE
Oakwood Manor
MIDWEST BAPTIST THEO. SEMINARY
Northmoor
Riverside
WORLDS OF FUN AND OCEANS OF FUN
Hidden Valley Park
Randolph
Avondale
FAIRFAX BRIDGE (TOLL NORTHBOUND)
MISSOURI
KANSAS
RIVER
Riverfront Park
North Kansas City
Kansas City Downtown Airport
Kessler Park
INDEPENDENCE AVE
SISTERS OF MERCY CONVENT
ST. PAUL SCHOOL OF THEOLOGY
Blue Valley Rec. Area
Penn Valley Park
Spring Valley Park
VETERANS HOSPITAL
Heart Arpt
KANSAS CITY
CITY
Rosedale Park
Westwood
Westwood Hills
Roeland Park
Mission
MERRIAM
Mission Woods
Mission Hills
Jacob Loose Mem. Park
ROCKHURST COLLEGE
Brush Creek Park
KANSAS CITY MISSOURI MUNICIPAL FARM
Fairway
Country Side
Homestead
PRAIRIE VILLAGE
OVERLAND PARK
Swope Park
The Lagoon
Swope Mem
RAYTOWN
Blue River
Hillcrest
© H.M. GOUSHA
M-NA-5-1144-S

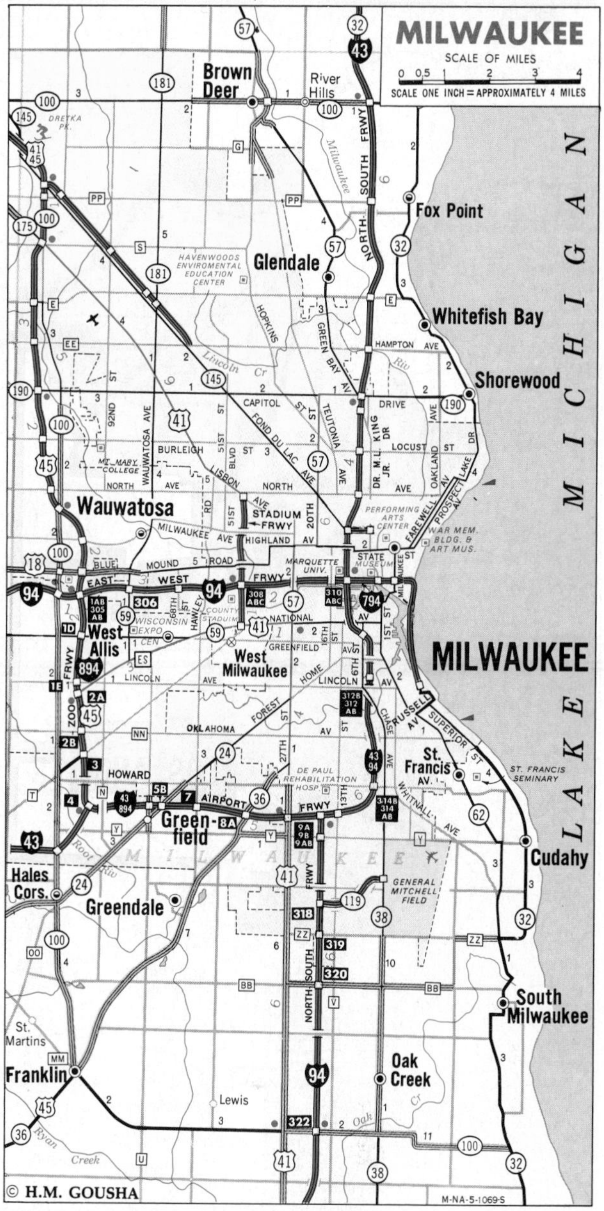
MILWAUKEE
SCALE OF MILES
SCALE ONE INCH = APPROXIMATELY 4 MILES
Brown Deer
River Hills
Fox Point
Glendale
HAVENWOODS ENVIRONMENTAL EDUCATION CENTER
Whitefish Bay
Shorewood
LAKE MICHIGAN
MT. MARY COLLEGE
Wauwatosa
PERFORMING ARTS CENTER
WAR MEM. BLDG. & ART MUS.
MARQUETTE UNIV.
STATE MUSEUM
MILWAUKEE
West Allis
WISCONSIN EXPO CEN
West Milwaukee
St. Francis
ST. FRANCIS SEMINARY
DE PAUL REHABILITATION HOSP
Green-field
Hales Cors.
Greendale
GENERAL MITCHELL FIELD
Cudahy
South Milwaukee
St. Martins
Franklin
Oak Creek
Lewis
© H.M. GOUSHA
M-NA-5-1069-S

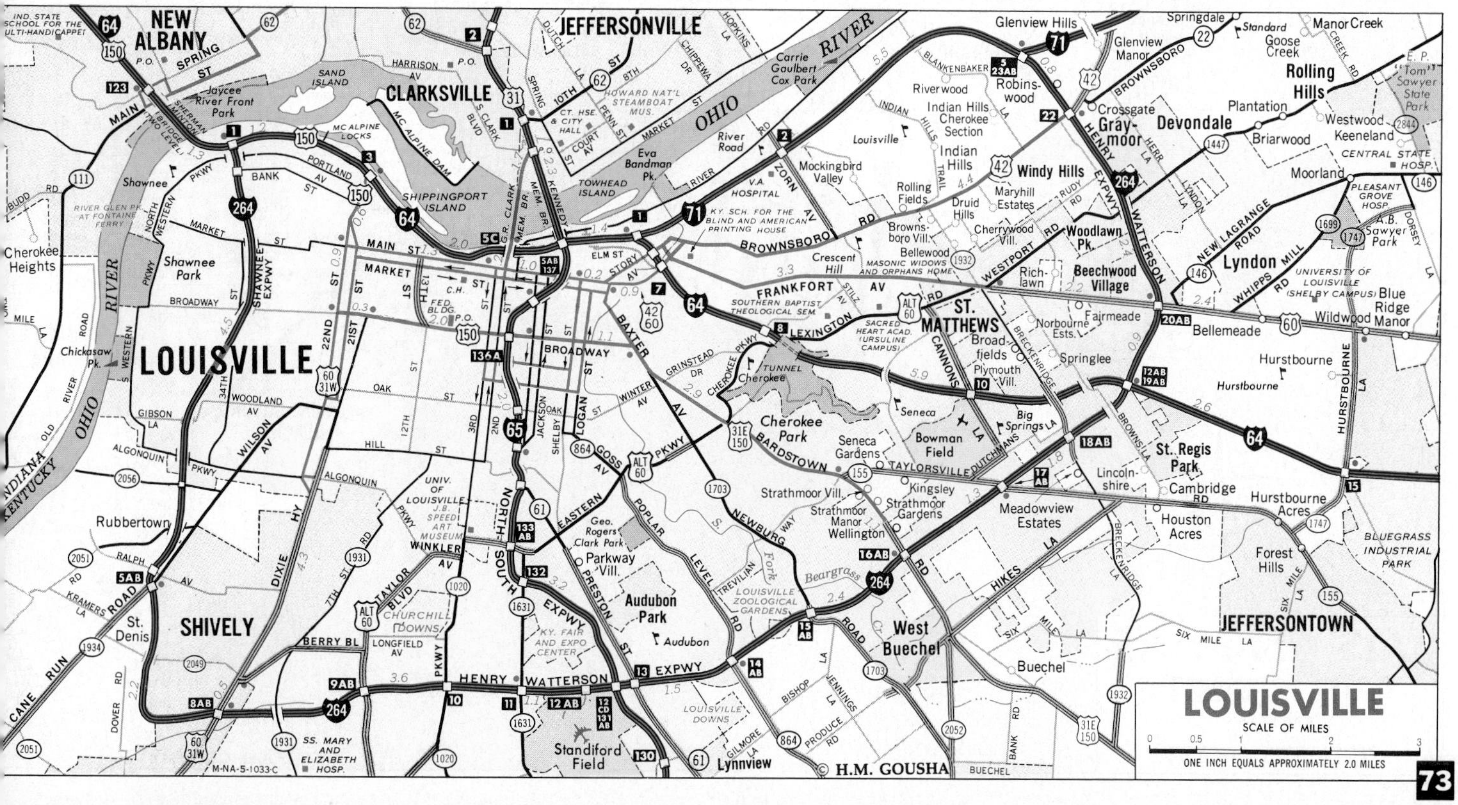
LOUISVILLE
SCALE OF MILES
ONE INCH EQUALS APPROXIMATELY 2.0 MILES
IND. STATE SCHOOL FOR THE MULTI-HANDICAPPED
NEW ALBANY
JEFFERSONVILLE
CLARKSVILLE
OHIO RIVER
Jaycee River Front Park
SAND ISLAND
MC ALPINE LOCKS
MC ALPINE DAM
SHIPPINGPORT ISLAND
HOWARD NAT'L STEAMBOAT MUS.
Carrie Gaulbert Cox Park
Glenview Hills
Glenview Manor
Robinswood
Riverwood
Indian Hills Cherokee Section
Gray-moor
Crossgate
Devondale
Rolling Hills
Plantation
Briarwood
Westwood
Keeneland
Moorland
Eva Bandman Pk.
Mockingbird Valley
Windy Hills
Maryhill Estates
KY. SCH. FOR THE BLIND AND AMERICAN PRINTING HOUSE
Cherokee Heights
Shawnee Park
Crescent Hill
Beechwood Village
Lyndon
UNIVERSITY OF LOUISVILLE (SHELBY CAMPUS)
Blue Ridge Manor
Wildwood
ST. MATTHEWS
Norbourne Ests.
Fairmeade
Bellemeade
SOUTHERN BAPTIST THEOLOGICAL SEM.
LOUISVILLE
Springlee
Hurstbourne
Chickasaw Pk.
Cherokee Park
Seneca Gardens
Bowman Field
Big Springs
St. Regis Park
Lincolnshire
Cambridge
Hurstbourne Acres
Strathmoor Vill.
Kingsley
Strathmoor Gardens
Strathmoor Manor
Wellington
Meadowview Estates
Houston Acres
BLUEGRASS INDUSTRIAL PARK
Forest Hills
Rubbertown
UNIV. OF LOUISVILLE
J.B. SPEED ART MUSEUM
Geo. Rogers Clark Park
Parkway Vill.
Audubon Park
LOUISVILLE ZOOLOGICAL GARDENS
SHIVELY
St. Denis
CHURCHILL DOWNS
KY. FAIR AND EXPO CENTER
West Buechel
Buechel
JEFFERSONTOWN
Standiford Field
Lynnview
SS. MARY AND ELIZABETH HOSP.
© H.M. GOUSHA
M-NA-5-1033-C

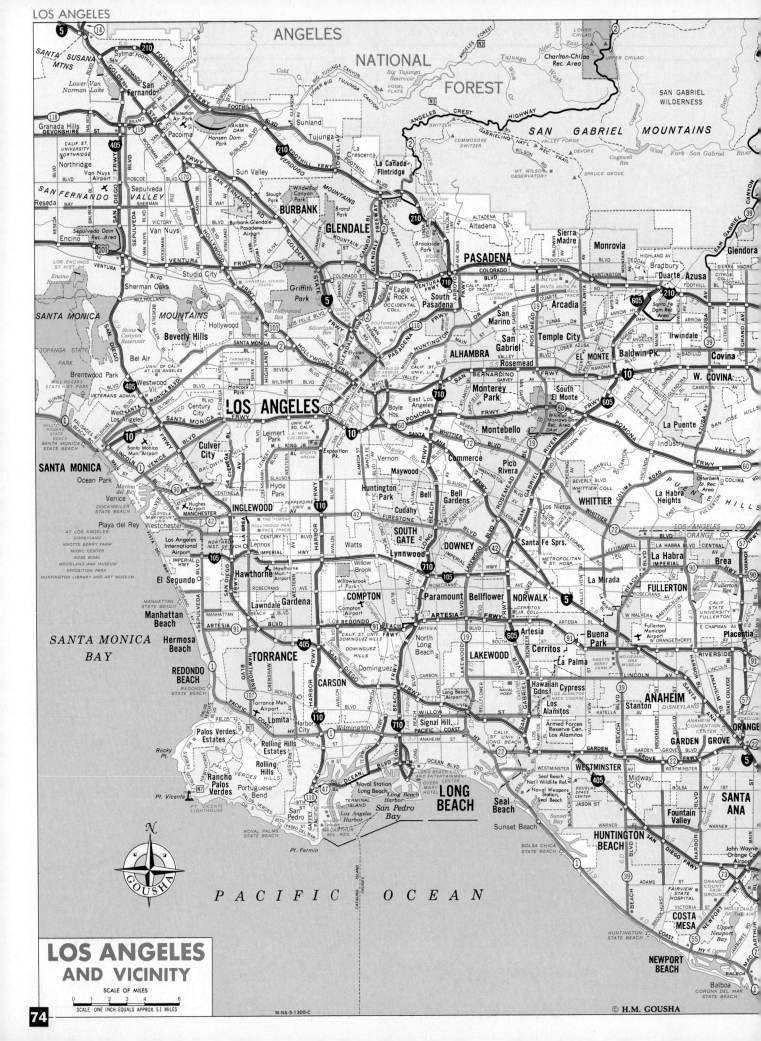

ANGELES

NATIONAL

FOREST

SAN GABRIEL WILDERNESS

SAN GABRIEL MOUNTAINS

SANTA SUSANA MTNS

San Fernando

BURBANK

GLENDALE

PASADENA

Sierra Madre

Monrovia

Glendora

SAN FERNANDO VALLEY

Northridge

Reseda

Encino

Sherman Oaks

Studio City

SANTA MONICA MOUNTAINS

Beverly Hills

Hollywood

Bel Air

Griffith Park

Eagle Rock

South Pasadena

Altadena

Duarte

Azusa

Arcadia

San Marino

Temple City

El Monte

Baldwin Pk.

Covina

W. Covina

Brentwood Park

Westwood Vil.

West Los Angeles

LOS ANGELES

Alhambra

Rosemead

San Gabriel

Monterey Park

South El Monte

La Puente

Industry

SANTA MONICA

Ocean Park

Culver City

Hyde Park

Vernon

Maywood

Huntington Park

Bell

Commerce

Pico Rivera

Montebello

WHITTIER

La Habra Heights

Venice

Inglewood

Bell Gardens

Cudahy

SOUTH GATE

Downey

Santa Fe Spgs.

La Habra

Brea

El Segundo

Hawthorne

Lennox

Watts

Willow Brook

Lynwood

Paramount

Bellflower

Norwalk

La Mirada

FULLERTON

Placentia

Manhattan Beach

Lawndale

Gardena

Compton

NORTH LONG BEACH

LAKEWOOD

Artesia

Cerritos

La Palma

Buena Park

Hermosa Beach

Redondo

SANTA MONICA BAY

TORRANCE

REDONDO BEACH

Dominguez Hills

Hawaiian Gdns.

Cypress

Los Alamitos

ANAHEIM

Stanton

ORANGE

CARSON

Lomita

Harbor City

Wilmington

Signal Hill

Long Beach Airport

GARDEN GROVE

Palos Verdes Estates

Rolling Hills Estates

Rolling Hills

Rancho Palos Verdes

Portuguese Bend

San Pedro

LONG BEACH

Seal Beach

WESTMINSTER

Midway City

SANTA ANA

Pt. Vicente

San Pedro Bay

Sunset Beach

FOUNTAIN VALLEY

P A C I F I C   O C E A N

Catalina Island

HUNTINGTON BEACH

COSTA MESA

NEWPORT BEACH

Balboa

N
GOUSHA

LOS ANGELES AND VICINITY

SCALE OF MILES

0 1 2 3 4 5 6

SCALE: ONE INCH EQUALS APPROX. 5.1 MILES

74

M-NA-5-1300-C

© H.M. GOUSHA

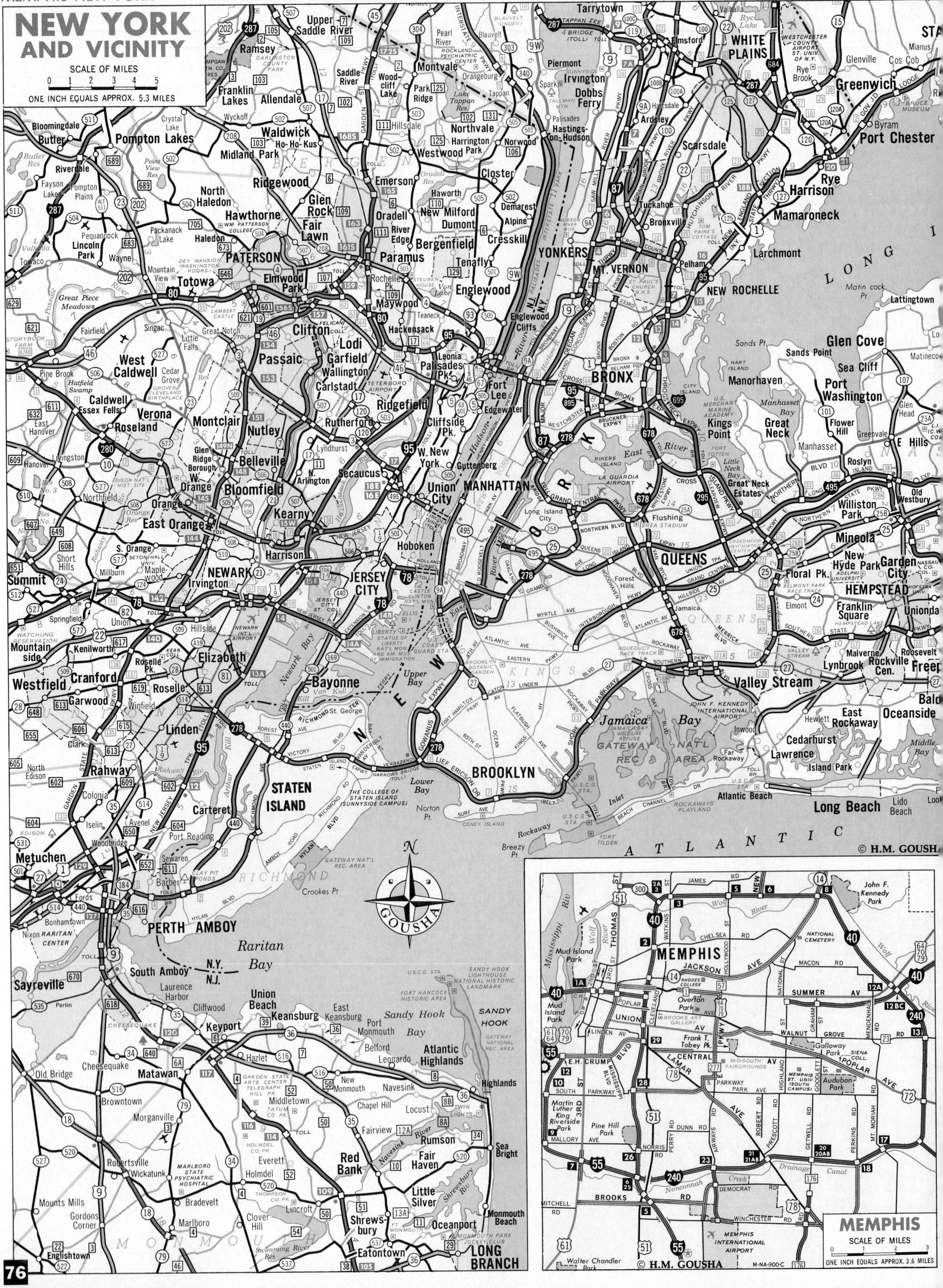
NEW YORK AND VICINITY
SCALE OF MILES
0 1 2 3 4 5
ONE INCH EQUALS APPROX. 5.3 MILES
Tarrytown
Upper Saddle River
Ramsey
White Plains
Elmsford
Greenwich
Port Chester
Rye
Harrison
Mamaroneck
Larchmont
New Rochelle
Scarsdale
Bronxville
Tuckahoe
Pelham
Mt. Vernon
Yonkers
Hastings-on-Hudson
Dobbs Ferry
Irvington
Piermont
Ardsley
Montvale
Pearl River
Park Ridge
Woodcliff Lake
Saddle River
Allendale
Franklin Lakes
Waldwick
Ho-Ho-Kus
Midland Park
Ridgewood
Northvale
Norwood
Harrington Park
Westwood
Hillsdale
Closter
Emerson
Haworth
Demarest
Alpine
Cresskill
Oradell
River Edge
New Milford
Dumont
Bergenfield
Tenafly
Englewood
Englewood Cliffs
Paramus
Glen Rock
Fair Lawn
Hawthorne
North Haledon
Haledon
Paterson
Elmwood Park
Rochelle Pk.
Maywood
Hackensack
Teaneck
Leonia
Palisades Pk.
Fort Lee
Edgewater
Cliffside Pk.
Ridgefield
Bloomingdale
Butler
Pompton Lakes
Riverdale
Pompton Plains
Fayson Lakes
Lincoln Park
Wayne
Towaco
Totowa
Great Piece Meadows
Fairfield
West Caldwell
Caldwell
Essex Fells
Verona
Montclair
Little Falls
Clifton
Passaic
Lodi
Garfield
Wallington
Carlstadt
Rutherford
Lyndhurst
Nutley
Belleville
Glen Ridge
Bloomfield
Orange
East Orange
West Orange
Roseland
Livingston
East Hanover
Hanover
Florham Park
Short Hills
Millburn
Maplewood
S. Orange
Summit
Springfield
Irvington
Union
Hillside
Newark
Harrison
Kearny
Secaucus
N. Arlington
Union City
W. New York
Guttenberg
Hoboken
Jersey City
Bayonne
Elizabeth
Roselle
Roselle Pk.
Kenilworth
Cranford
Westfield
Garwood
Mountainside
Linden
Clark
Rahway
Colonia
Iselin
Avenel
Woodbridge
Carteret
Port Reading
Sewaren
Metuchen
Edison
Fords
Perth Amboy
South Amboy
Sayreville
Laurence Harbor
Cliffwood
Keyport
Union Beach
Keansburg
East Keansburg
Port Monmouth
Belford
Leonardo
Atlantic Highlands
Highlands
Hazlet
Matawan
Cheesequake
Old Bridge
Browntown
Morganville
Middletown
New Monmouth
Navesink
Chapel Hill
Fairview
Locust
Rumson
Sea Bright
Red Bank
Fair Haven
Little Silver
Holmdel
Everett
Lincroft
Shrewsbury
Oceanport
Eatontown
Monmouth Beach
Long Branch
Robertsville
Wickatunk
Bradevelt
Marlboro
Mounts Mills
Gordons Corner
Englishtown
Clover Hill
Staten Island
St. George
Raritan Bay
Sandy Hook Bay
Sandy Hook
Lower Bay
Upper Bay
Newark Bay
Manhattan
Bronx
Queens
Brooklyn
Long Island City
Flushing
Jamaica
Forest Hills
Kings Point
Great Neck
Great Neck Estates
Manhasset
Manorhaven
Sands Point
Port Washington
Sea Cliff
Glen Cove
Roslyn
Williston Park
Mineola
New Hyde Park
Garden City
Floral Pk.
Hempstead
Franklin Square
Elmont
Valley Stream
Lynbrook
Rockville Cen.
Malverne
Uniondale
Roosevelt
Freeport
Baldwin
Oceanside
East Rockaway
Hewlett
Inwood
Cedarhurst
Lawrence
Island Park
Long Beach
Lido Beach
Atlantic Beach
Far Rockaway
Jamaica Bay
Gateway Nat'l Rec. Area
John F. Kennedy International Airport
La Guardia Airport
Newark Int'l Airport
Coney Island
Breezy Pt.
Rockaway Inlet
Long Island Sound
Atlantic
N.Y.
N.J.
GOUSHA
© H.M. GOUSHA
MEMPHIS
SCALE OF MILES
0 1 2 3
ONE INCH EQUALS APPROX. 3.6 MILES
Mississippi Riv
Wolf River
Mud Island Park
John F. Kennedy Park
National Cemetery
Rhodes College
Overton Park
Brooks Art Gallery
Frank T. Tobey Park
Mid-South Fairgrounds
Galloway Park
Siena Coll.
Audubon Park
Memphis St. Univ (South Campus)
Martin Luther King Riverside Park
Pine Hill Park
Memphis International Airport
Walter Chandler Park
Nonconnah Creek
Drainage Canal
© H.M. GOUSHA
M-NA-900-C

NEW ORLEANS

SCALE OF MILES

ONE INCH EQUALS APPROXIMATELY 3.6 MILES

© H.M. GOUSHA

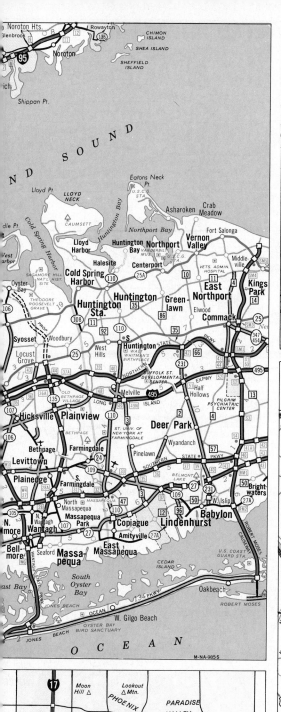

PHILADELPHIA

SCALE OF MILES

ONE INCH EQUALS APPROX. 2.7 MILES

© H.M. GOUSHA

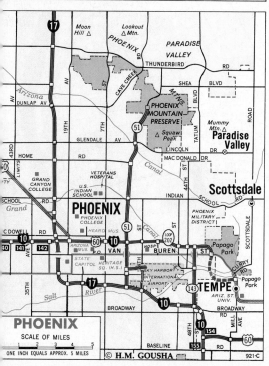

PHOENIX

SCALE OF MILES

ONE INCH EQUALS APPROX. 5 MILES

© H.M. GOUSHA

921-C

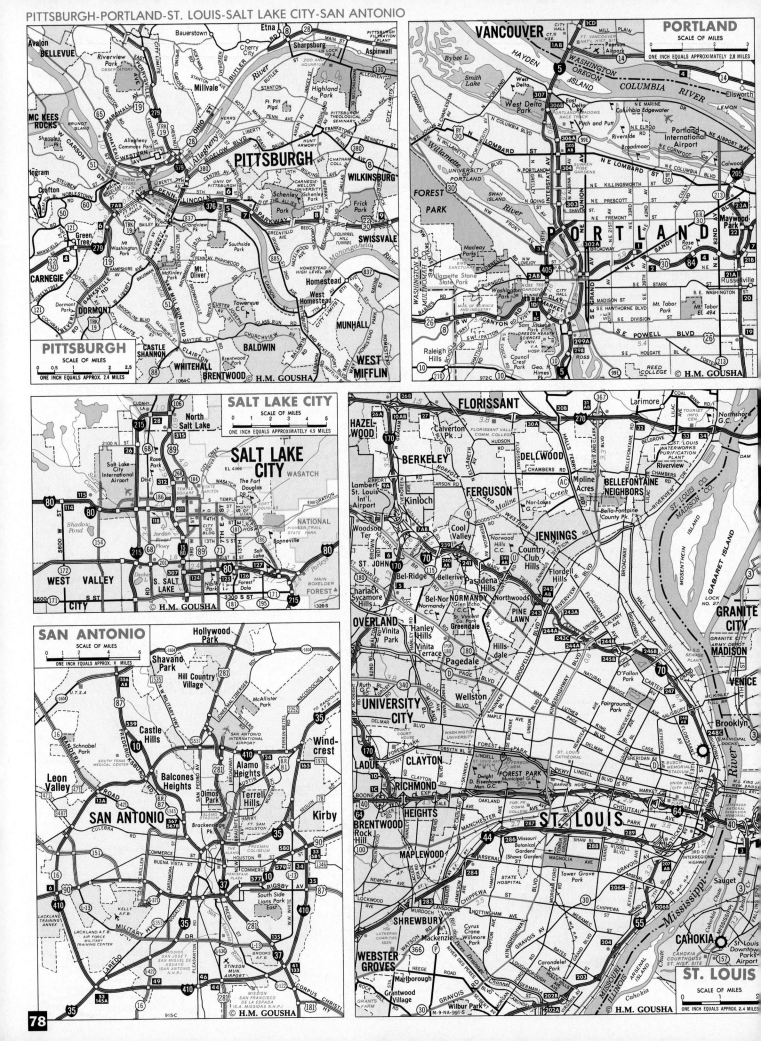

PITTSBURGH
SCALE OF MILES
0 .5 1 1.5 2 2.5
ONE INCH EQUALS APPROX. 2.4 MILES

© H.M. GOUSHA

PORTLAND
SCALE OF MILES
ONE INCH EQUALS APPROXIMATELY 2.8 MILES

© H.M. GOUSHA

SALT LAKE CITY
SCALE OF MILES
0 1 2 3 4 5
ONE INCH EQUALS APPROXIMATELY 4.9 MILES

© H.M. GOUSHA

SAN ANTONIO
SCALE OF MILES
0 1 2 4 6 MILES
ONE INCH EQUALS APPROX. 6 MILES

© H.M. GOUSHA

ST. LOUIS
SCALE OF MILES
ONE INCH EQUALS APPROX. 2.4 MILES

© H.M. GOUSHA

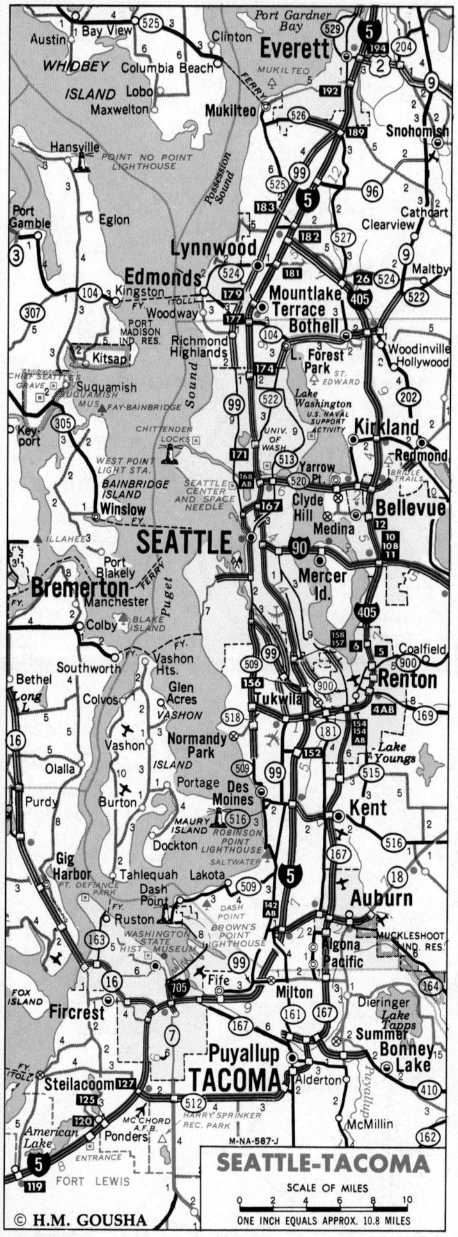

SEATTLE-TACOMA

SCALE OF MILES
ONE INCH EQUALS APPROX. 10.8 MILES

© H.M. GOUSHA

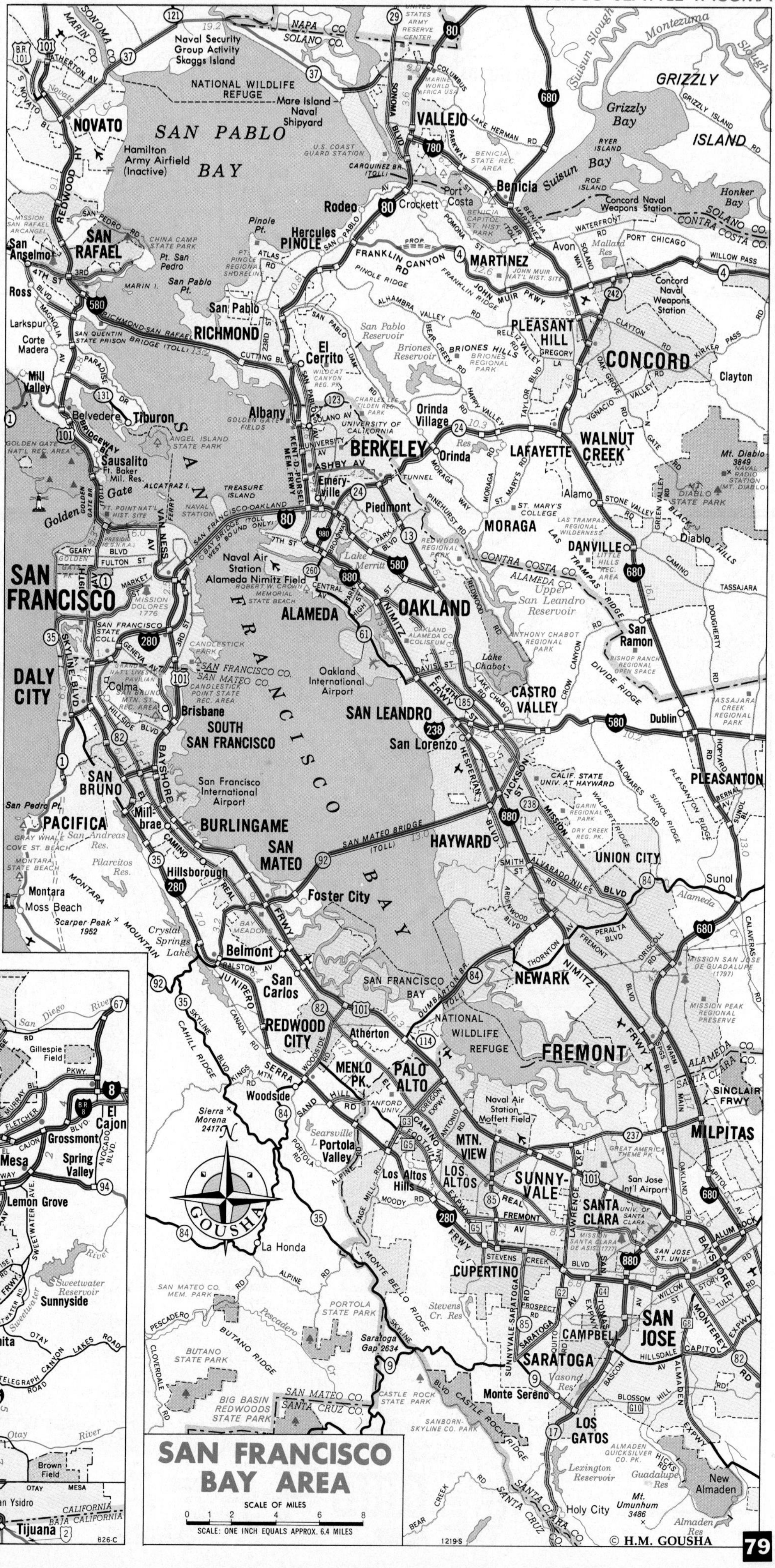

SAN FRANCISCO BAY AREA

SCALE OF MILES
SCALE: ONE INCH EQUALS APPROX. 6.4 MILES

GOUSHA

© H.M. GOUSHA

1219-S

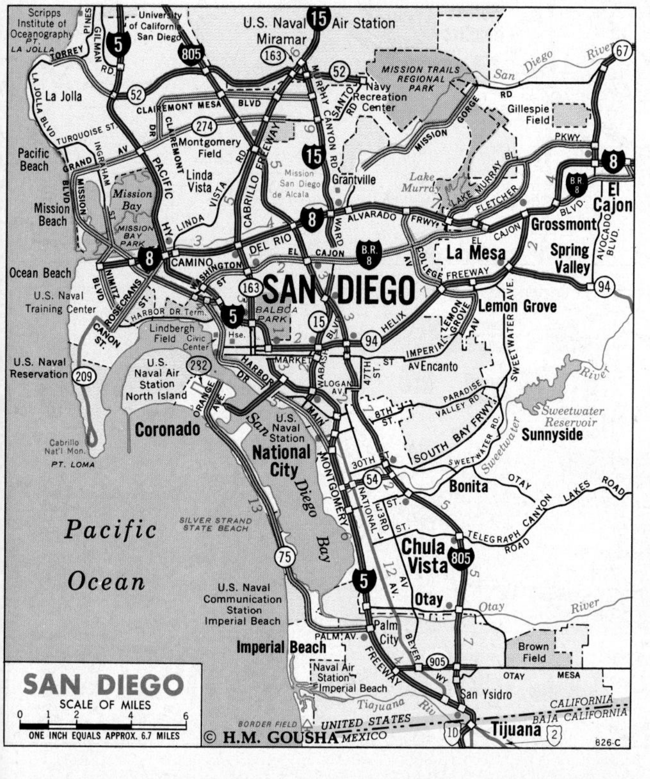

SAN DIEGO

SCALE OF MILES
ONE INCH EQUALS APPROX. 6.7 MILES

© H.M. GOUSHA

826-C

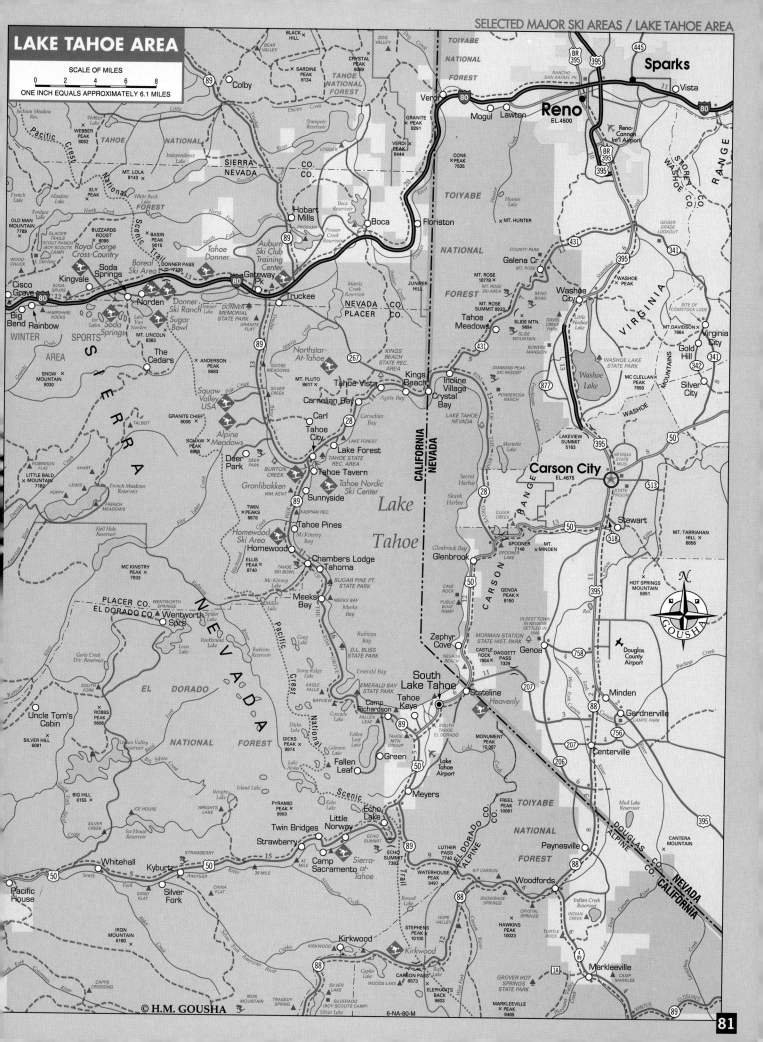

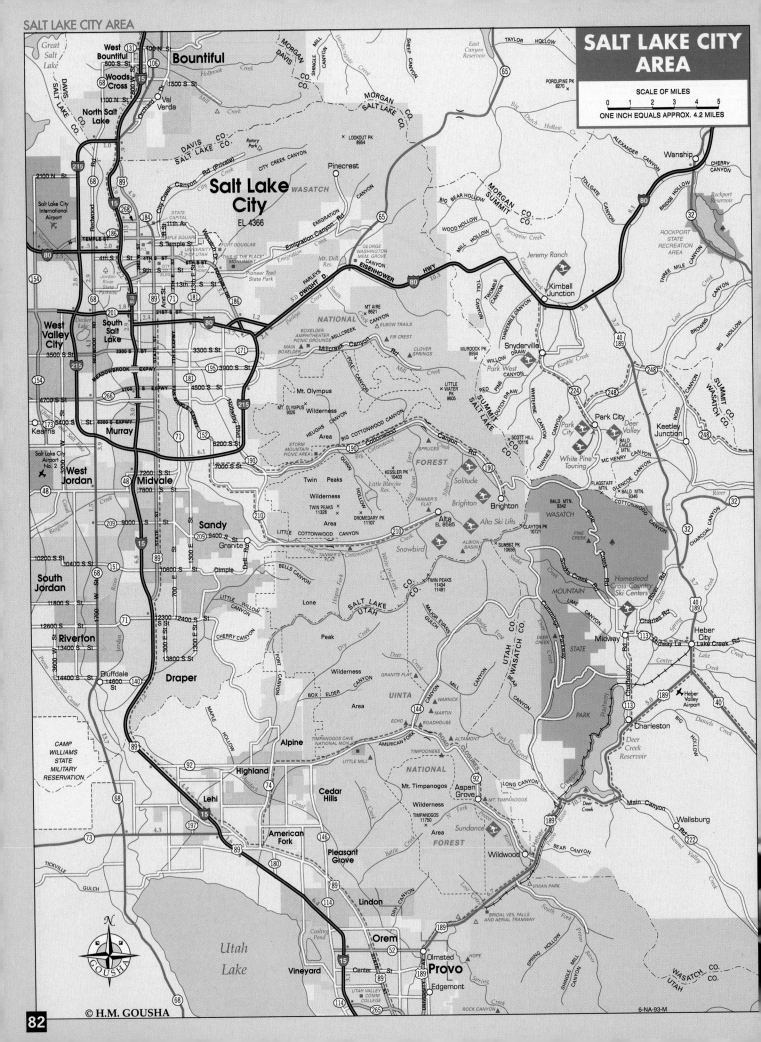

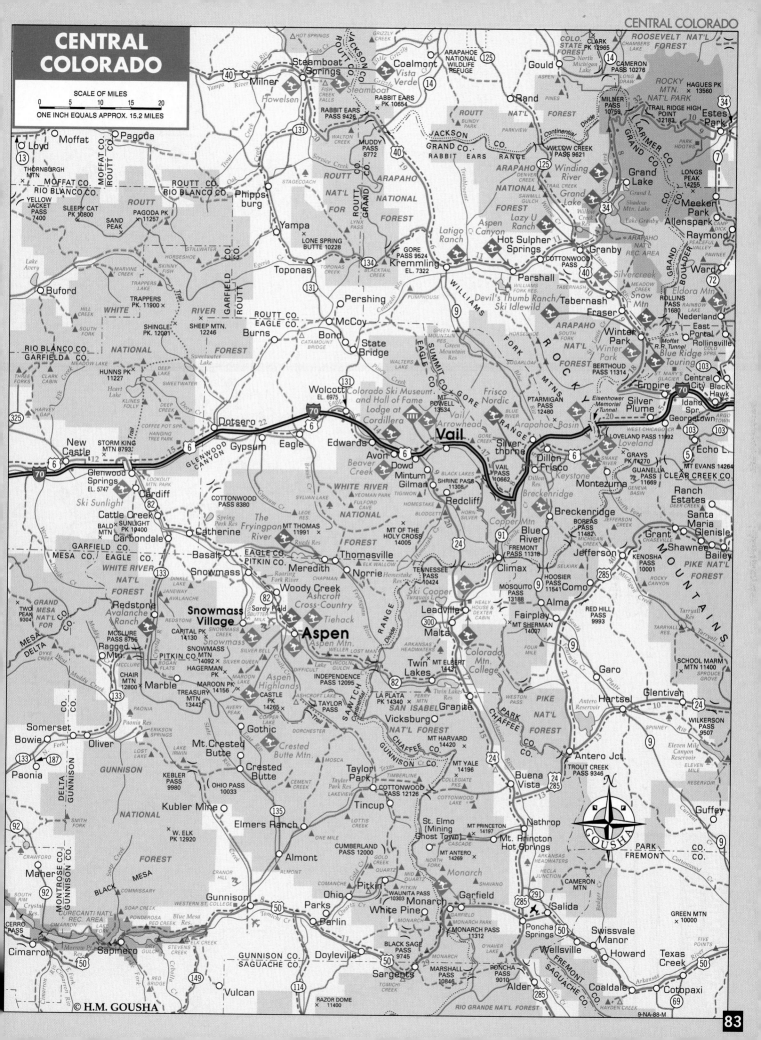

CENTRAL COLORADO

SCALE OF MILES
0 5 10 15 20
ONE INCH EQUALS APPROX. 15.2 MILES

© H.M. GOUSHA

9-NA-88-M

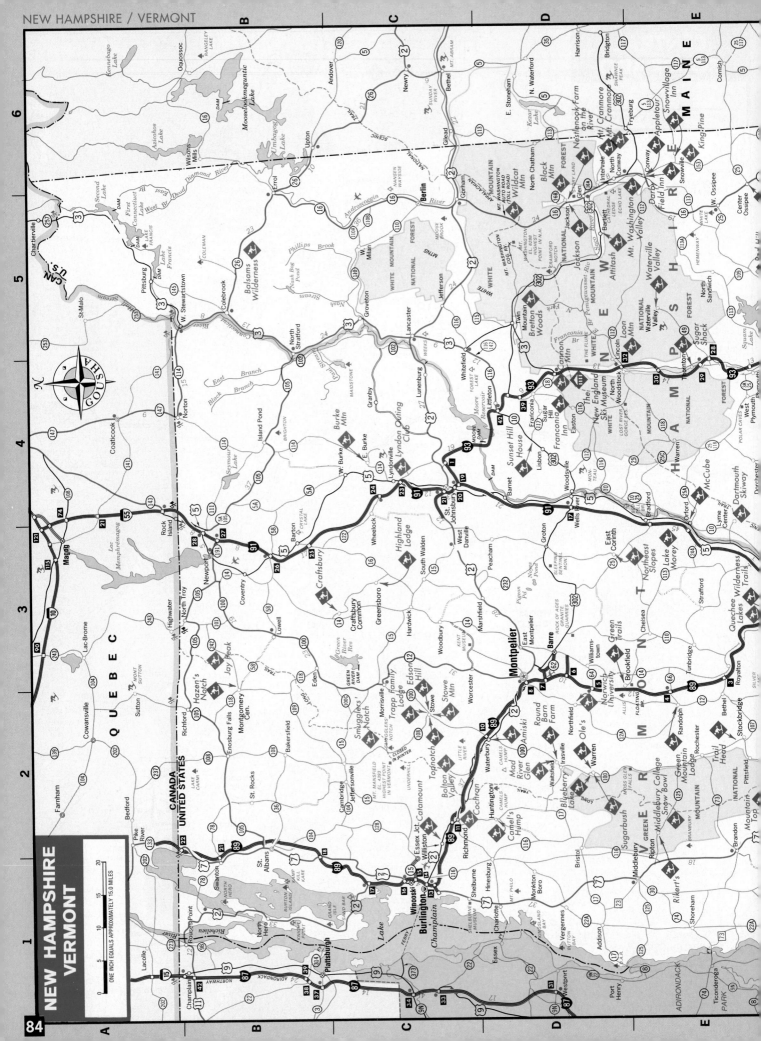

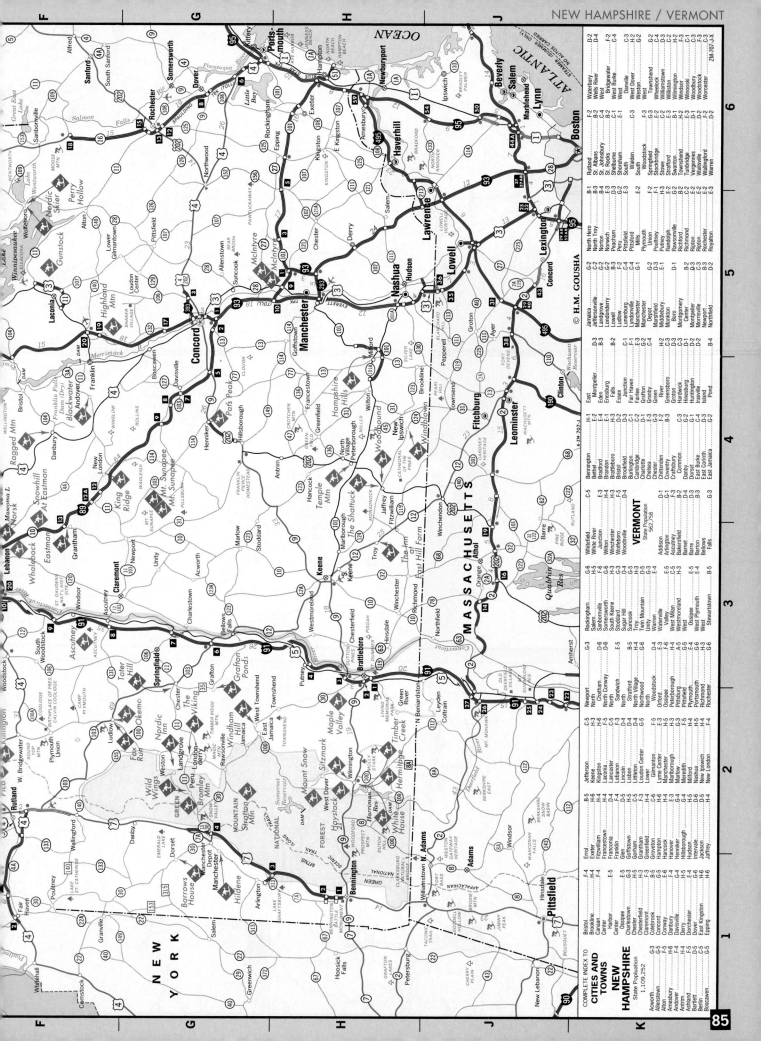

© H.M. GOUSHA

6-2M-707-J

ZM-707-J-X

CATSKILLS
NEW YORK

SCALE OF MILES
0   5   10   15
ONE INCH EQUALS APPROXIMATELY 12 MILES

POCONOS
PENNSYLVANIA

SCALE OF MILES
0   5   10   15
ONE INCH EQUALS APPROXIMATELY 12 MILES

SNOWFALL

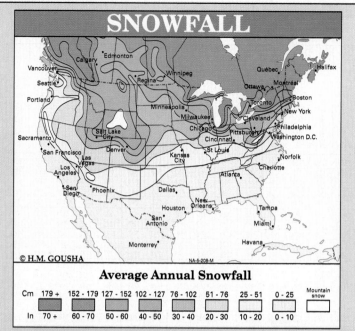

Average Annual Snowfall

Cm	179 +	152 - 179	127 - 152	102 - 127	76 - 102	51 - 76	25 - 51	0 - 25	Mountain snow
In	70 +	60 - 70	50 - 60	40 - 50	30 - 40	20 - 30	10 - 20	0 - 10	

© H.M. GOUSHA   NA-5-208-M

RAINFALL

Average Annual Rainfall

Centimeters	203 +	163 - 203	122 - 163	81 - 122	41 - 81	0 - 41
Inches	80 +	64 - 80	48 - 64	32 - 48	16 - 32	0 - 16

© H.M. GOUSHA   NA-5-206-M

SUNSHINE

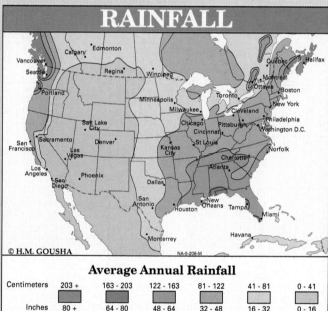

Annual Percentage of Sunshine

Over 85	75 - 85	65 - 75	55 - 65	45 - 55	35 - 45	Below 35

© H.M. GOUSHA   NA-5-207-M

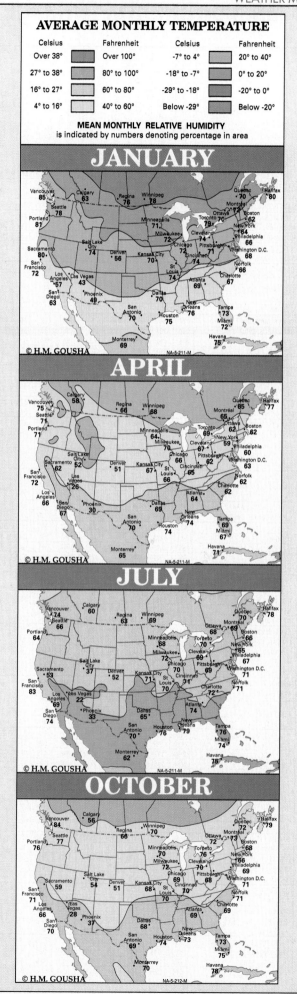

AVERAGE MONTHLY TEMPERATURE

Celsius	Fahrenheit	Celsius	Fahrenheit
Over 38°	Over 100°	-7° to 4°	20° to 40°
27° to 38°	80° to 100°	-18° to -7°	0° to 20°
16° to 27°	60° to 80°	-29° to -18°	-20° to 0°
4° to 16°	40° to 60°	Below -29°	Below -20°

MEAN MONTHLY RELATIVE HUMIDITY
is indicated by numbers denoting percentage in area

JANUARY

© H.M. GOUSHA   NA-5-211-M

APRIL

© H.M. GOUSHA   NA-5-211-M

JULY

© H.M. GOUSHA   NA-5-211-M

OCTOBER

© H.M. GOUSHA   NA-5-212-M

Transcontinental Mileage Chart

	ATLANTA, GA.	BOSTON, MASS.	CHICAGO, ILL.	CINCINNATI, OHIO	CLEVELAND, OHIO	DENVER, COLO.	DETROIT, MICH.	EL PASO, TEXAS	HOUSTON, TEXAS	KANSAS CITY, MO.	LOS ANGELES, CALIF.	MEMPHIS, TENN.	MIAMI, FLA.	MINNEAPOLIS-ST. PAUL, MINN.	MONTREAL, QUE., CAN.	NEW ORLEANS, LA.	NEW YORK, N.Y.	PHILADELPHIA, PA.	PITTSBURGH, PA.	PORTLAND, ORE.	ST. LOUIS, MO.	SALT LAKE CITY, UTAH	SAN FRANCISCO, CALIF.	SEATTLE, WASH.	WASHINGTON, D.C.
ALBANY, N.Y.	1059	172	800	717	471	1841	539	2261	1832	1275	2880	1239	1495	1209	227	1554	157	231	454	2995	1021	2252	3011	2935	358
ASHEVILLE, N.C.	205	965	656	368	603	1514	630	1662	1083	873	2409	533	771	1076	1067	744	746	652	586	2826	619	2009	2720	2840	463
ATLANTA, GA.	•	1084	715	481	727	1412	741	1450	875	882	2252	414	662	1136	1241	518	863	776	741	2873	582	1959	2464	2651	641
AUGUSTA, MAINE	1297	168	1113	1018	777	2142	840	2562	2129	1576	3264	1540	1733	1533	326	1793	387	481	755	3240	1322	2565	3332	3174	628
BALTIMORE, MD.	680	404	696	493	361	1624	524	2056	1555	1070	2724	955	1146	1106	586	1206	191	106	232	2892	800	2120	2899	2792	39
BIRMINGHAM, ALA.	148	1250	684	460	741	1364	755	1307	711	723	2091	230	783	1080	1335	344	990	893	812	2676	525	1855	2393	2707	759
BISMARCK, N.DAK.	1569	1850	847	1172	1220	683	1144	1355	1447	791	1723	1250	2231	441	1535	1600	1712	1630	1336	1260	1045	982	1589	1313	1567
BOISE, IDAHO	2340	2797	1789	2018	2137	891	2056	1266	1889	1492	908	1957	2974	1470	2637	2167	2616	2531	2238	433	1744	341	662	493	2480
BOSTON, MASS.	1084	•	976	853	643	2008	706	2428	1961	1442	3000	1389	1547	1399	327	1625	215	308	595	3229	1188	2431	3132	2977	443
BUFFALO, N.Y.	963	466	553	430	191	1554	263	1974	1545	988	2676	952	1479	945	407	1260	380	365	224	2775	734	1977	2744	2709	379
CHARLESTON, W.VA.	449	786	498	198	277	1381	357	1778	1269	797	2398	689	1115	918	834	1051	567	477	227	2649	543	1868	2626	2609	364
CHATTANOOGA, TENN.	119	1088	603	347	597	1343	612	1453	873	702	2200	321	783	1003	1175	537	869	775	637	2655	448	1838	2511	2686	628
CHEYENNE, WYO.	1479	1955	972	1198	1312	95	1241	789	1131	680	1196	1139	2141	826	1822	1385	1791	1709	1426	1253	951	432	1169	1323	1646
CHICAGO, ILL.	715	976	•	301	343	1017	279	1447	1073	505	2028	534	1386	416	854	938	818	767	468	2250	296	1411	2160	2030	696
CINCINNATI, OHIO	481	853	301	•	245	1245	273	1590	1115	604	2292	492	1143	721	819	846	623	578	292	2495	348	1682	2449	2485	519
CLEVELAND, OHIO	727	643	343	245	•	1373	163	1785	1356	799	2358	763	1251	769	578	1060	497	421	128	2599	545	1796	2490	2372	358
COLUMBUS, OHIO	560	769	316	103	142	1236	180	1654	1212	668	2356	619	1236	736	722	988	555	473	180	2559	408	1746	2526	2500	389
DALLAS, TEXAS	826	1753	936	988	1225	797	1194	639	241	505	1431	466	1305	940	1775	495	1540	1561	1282	2145	643	1240	1740	2093	1320
DENVER, COLO.	1412	2008	1017	1245	1373	•	1302	696	1038	604	1189	1053	2126	871	1883	1292	1852	1770	1420	1347	858	497	1267	1426	1707
DES MOINES, IOWA	933	1313	340	582	678	673	607	1243	943	193	1841	636	1595	238	1188	1006	1165	1083	789	1824	365	1071	1885	1962	1061
DETROIT, MICH.	741	706	279	273	163	1302	•	1754	1326	752	2285	751	1395	693	581	1075	632	588	294	2523	514	1725	2417	2299	525
DULUTH, MINN.	1199	1474	481	796	844	1065	768	1642	1361	637	2192	1004	1861	151	1056	1419	1336	1254	960	1840	695	1469	2155	1774	1191
EL PASO, TEXAS	1450	2428	1447	1590	1785	696	1754	•	752	942	784	1080	2068	1377	2335	1101	2209	2127	1842	1747	1193	883	1209	1822	2052
GLACIER NAT'L PARK, MONT.	2378	2618	1639	1940	1988	951	1912	1573	2071	1500	1373	2023	3040	1203	2145	2352	2480	2398	2104	673	1809	690	1217	580	2335
GRAND CANYON NAT'L PARK, ARIZ.	1884	2718	1807	1880	2075	798	2044	581	1352	1303	542	1463	2515	1774	2625	1577	2499	2417	2132	1230	1530	374	831	1310	2340
GRAND RAPIDS, MICH.	790	833	184	309	284	1216	156	1683	1277	668	2362	723	1452	594	715	1138	759	700	406	2433	460	1639	2406	2367	637
HELENA, MONT.	2111	2479	1500	1789	1849	796	1773	1386	1845	1294	1321	1762	2773	1080	2187	2082	2341	2259	1965	709	1542	498	1134	622	2196
HOUSTON, TEXAS	875	1961	1073	1115	1356	1038	1326	752	•	714	1564	580	1306	1181	1896	363	1742	1648	1396	2368	780	1502	1984	2445	1501
INDIANAPOLIS, IND.	549	948	182	114	305	1047	273	1431	1010	503	2182	438	1219	598	826	831	729	647	356	2385	242	1528	2353	2375	572
JACKSON, MISS.	411	1497	753	739	980	1197	968	1024	451	624	1877	199	979	1043	1549	176	1278	1184	1020	2638	505	1662	2206	2669	1037
JACKSONVILLE, FLA.	349	1204	1032	791	1028	1789	1058	1722	960	1148	2539	672	346	1449	1395	568	982	888	924	3101	904	2284	2892	3132	756
KANSAS CITY, MO.	882	1442	505	604	799	604	752	942	714	•	1631	459	1485	435	1333	809	1223	1141	856	1953	255	1105	1903	1984	1066
LAS VEGAS, NEV.	2004	2810	1866	1972	2167	765	2123	704	1484	1417	288	1637	2582	1688	2704	1740	2591	2509	2224	1027	1668	418	576	1204	2434
LITTLE ROCK, ARK.	560	1530	636	663	904	957	874	945	444	373	1701	132	1221	794	1455	430	1311	1217	944	2299	356	1478	2046	2334	1070
LOS ANGELES, CALIF.	2165	3000	2028	2292	2358	1021	2285	784	1564	1631	•	1877	2690	1893	3029	1875	2795	2829	2544	1016	1830	706	377	1134	2649
LOUISVILLE, KY.	432	989	309	100	352	1167	363	1512	1004	526	2214	373	1101	729	930	737	771	689	404	2479	266	1662	2433	2493	638
MEMPHIS, TENN.	414	1389	534	492	763	1053	751	1080	580	459	1877	•	1018	835	1332	393	1173	1076	803	2421	290	1536	2188	2452	944
MEXICO CITY, MEX.	1853	3099	2168	2198	2439	2001	2387	1261	978	1491	2070	1669	2216	2174	3231	1335	2848	2746	2491	3067	1847	2147	2494	3242	2609
MIAMI, FLA.	662	1547	1386	1143	1251	2054	1395	2068	1306	1485	2690	1018	•	1786	1732	881	1325	1231	1261	3438	1231	1222	3045	3299	1096
MILWAUKEE, WIS.	814	1069	95	391	439	1036	363	1526	1150	585	2149	625	1476	335	944	1018	931	849	555	2130	370	1434	2186	2043	786
MINNEAPOLIS-ST. PAUL, MINN.	1136	1399	416	721	769	871	693	1377	1181	435	1893	835	1786	•	1194	1228	1201	1179	885	1830	553	1251	1975	1615	1116
MONTREAL, QUE., CAN.	1241	327	854	819	578	1883	581	2335	1896	1333	3029	1332	1732	1194	•	1710	368	473	607	2914	1095	2306	3073	2848	618
NASHVILLE, TENN.	250	1168	439	291	542	1205	553	1351	814	564	2098	206	921	876	1120	549	949	855	582	2517	310	1700	2409	2548	659
NEW ORLEANS, LA.	518	1528	938	846	1060	1292	1075	1101	363	809	1875	393	881	1228	1710	•	1315	1312	1172	2654	690	1735	2247	2602	1165
NEW YORK, N.Y.	863	215	818	623	497	1783	632	2209	1742	1223	2745	1173	1325	1201	368	1315	•	103	376	3088	969	2180	2934	2816	236
OKLAHOMA CITY, OKLA.	911	1745	795	907	1102	628	1071	700	450	354	1350	464	1572	775	1652	724	1526	1444	1159	2076	502	1118	1695	2155	1369
OMAHA, NEB.	1027	1451	477	702	816	538	745	1054	931	180	1668	644	1686	371	1326	994	1295	1213	919	1749	439	938	1726	1824	1150
ORLANDO, FLA.	449	1331	1159	940	1143	1904	1173	1846	978	1278	2551	806	224	1585	1530	651	1117	1023	1059	3065	1017	2436	2917	3403	874
OTTAWA, ONT., CAN.	1231	464	784	754	513	1798	511	2232	1837	1263	2867	1262	1985	1068	117	1645	434	453	542	2770	1025	2224	2982	2683	702
PHILADELPHIA, PA.	776	308	767	578	421	1770	588	2127	1648	1141	2829	1076	1231	1179	473	1312	91	•	305	3006	887	2193	2960	2943	140
PHOENIX, ARIZ.	1894	2746	1837	1908	2103	904	2072	404	1206	1274	379	1493	2417	1669	2653	1553	2527	2445	2160	1383	1543	646	806	1597	2370
PITTSBURGH, PA.	741	595	468	292	128	1420	294	1842	1396	856	2544	803	1261	885	607	1172	376	305	•	2712	602	1933	2710	2649	231
PORTLAND, MAINE	1237	111	1053	958	717	2082	780	2502	2073	1516	3204	1480	1673	1473	266	1733	328	421	695	3180	1262	2505	3272	3114	568
PORTLAND, ORE.	2873	3229	2250	2495	2599	1347	2523	1747	2368	1953	1016	2421	3438	1830	2914	2654	3088	3006	2712	•	2207	768	638	173	2943
PUEBLO, COLO.	1415	2086	1148	1248	1431	112	1396	611	939	644	1264	1032	2076	965	1977	1198	1867	1785	1500	1330	898	582	1320	1515	1710
QUEBEC, QUE., CAN.	1468	392	1026	989	750	2055	717	2507	2079	1505	3201	1504	1904	1366	165	1882	547	652	777	3086	1267	2478	3245	3020	799
RALEIGH, N.C.	410	731	825	543	602	1773	689	1894	1347	1132	2668	792	834	1245	897	957	512	418	471	3038	878	2225	2979	3009	261
RAPID CITY, S.DAK.	1569	1922	899	1230	1292	386	1216	1087	1312	702	1409	1161	2231	572	1770	1522	1784	1702	1408	1275	956	663	1447	1188	1639
RENO, NEV.	2611	2953	1980	2196	2310	1038	2239	1213	1975	1654	501	2087	3217	1782	2820	2350	2789	2707	2413	666	1908	520	219	856	2644
RICHMOND, VA.	549	549	788	524	454	1762	617	1993	1489	1121	2740	863	995	1205	737	1099	351	257	323	3018	867	2205	2972	2972	105
ST. LOUIS, MO.	582	1188	296	348	545	858	514	1193	780	255	1830	290	1231	553	1095	690	969	887	602	2207	•	1359	2157	2238	840
SALT LAKE CITY, UTAH	1910	2388	1411	1682	1746	497	1673	883	1502	1105	706	1536	2252	1231	2306	1735	2190	2193	1933	768	1359	•	730	924	2081
SAN ANTONIO, TEXAS	1022	2108	1245	1247	1488	975	1458	559	193	788	1388	725	1435	1188	2039	574	1889	1795	1528	2224	949	1364	1793	2301	1648
SAN DIEGO, CALIF.	2230	3285	2277	2257	2625	1243	2544	747	1578	1651	126	1904	2881	2083	3125	1934	2851	2779	2505	1137	1931	812	525	1314	2705
SAN FRANCISCO, CALIF.	2646	3198	2160	2449	2490	1267	2417	1209	1984	1903	377	2188	3045	1975	3073	2247	2934	2960	2710	638	2103	730	•	786	2825
SANTA FE, N.MEX.	1461	2295	1372	1457	1652	386	1576	330	877	808	889	1042	2092	1150	2202	1154	2008	1936	1709	1464	1107	627	1200	1631	1919
SAVANNAH, GA.	246	1072	954	676	872	1741	952	1662	1062	1087	2479	676	502	1374	1239	672	853	759	768	3053	846	2236	2808	3084	580
SEATTLE, WASH.	2651	2977	2030	2485	2372	1311	2299	1822	2445	1984	1134	2452	3299	1615	2848	2602	2816	2943	2649	173	2094	837	786	•	2716
SHREVEPORT, LA.	643	1729	873	871	1112	973	1084	816	238	542	1614	330	1155	1020	1665	331	1171	1416	1152	2262	558	1417	1972	2340	1400
SIOUX CITY, IOWA	1129	1482	529	784	852	590	776	1163	1039	268	1736	774	1791	272	1357	1193	1344	1262	968	1804	560	1013	1780	1738	1199
SPOKANE, WASH.	2501	2857	1878	2179	2227	1143	2151	1642	2211	1678	1256	2146	3163	1405	2542	2471	2719	2637	2343	349	1932	732	929	284	2609
TAMPA, FLA.	458	1427	1215	972	1209	1933	1224	1807	1045	1292	2554	782	270	1615	1594	639	1208	1114	1123	3245	1060	2424	2977	3276	967
TOLEDO, OHIO	685	756	239	206	115	1267	59	1702	1274	708	2404	699	1342	661	634	1090	611	529	235	2487	462	1690	2457	2421	466
TORONTO, ONT., CAN.	963	582	503	482	304	1532	228	1984	1556	982	2678	981	1594	923	325	1373	495	480	333	2753	744	1955	2722	2687	494
TULSA, OKLA.	853	1627	720	773	984	736	953	813	486	244	1473	434	1514	730	1534	762	1408	1326	1041	2085	400	1225	1814	2162	1251
VANCOUVER, B.C., CAN.	3041	3215	2236	2525	2585	1537	2509	1940	2580	2209	1327	2776	3709	1816	2943	2783	3077	2995	2701	216	2465	1053	928	146	2932
WASHINGTON, D.C.	641	443	696	519	358	1707	525	2052	1501	1066	2649	944	1096	1116	618	1165	236	140	231	2943	840	2081	2897	2880	•
WICHITA, KANS.	980	1660	722	822	1017	519	970	748	632	196	1383	561	1603	685	1551	842	1441	1359	1074	1856	460	1016	1759	1899	1284
WINNIPEG, MAN., CAN.	1584	1859	880	1181	1229	1089	1153	1652	1608	867	2067	1324	2246	456	1463	1739	1721	1639	1345	1550	1015	1323	1959	1463	1575
YELLOWSTONE NAT'L PARK, WYO.	1946	2333	1354	1624	1703	514	1609	1301	1647	1085	1079	1570	2608	1015	2089	1854	2195	2113	1819	889	1377	320	971	809	2050

ZM-1-113

MILEAGES ARE APPROXIMATE AND ARE COMPUTED OVER COMMONLY TRAVELED THROUGH ROUTES

Glaciers, fjords, Eskimos, dog sleds, "Northern Exposure." So why don't more people think of skiing Alaska? No mountains? What about Mt. McKinley, the highest point in the United States? ❅ Alaska is one of the better kept secrets in skiing. Top racers like Olympic medalists Tommy Moe and Hilary Lindh honed their craft here. Not only is there some fearsome terrain awaiting hardcore skiers, but the weather isn't as harsh as you'd think, thanks to gentle Pacific currents and dry air—the same ingredients that contribute dumps of feathery powder. It's also a prime spot for sighting wildlife, especially while cross-countrying. The nordic facilities offer far fewer amenities than their "lower 48" counterparts (thus our guidelines for listings are not as strict). Some of the splendid sites include Chugach State Park, Hatcher Pass Recreation Area, Turnagain Pass outside Anchorage, and Chena Hot Springs near Fairbanks. ❅ So demanding is Alaska's forbidding wilderness terrain that the World Extreme Skiing Championships are held annually on the gullies, chutes, and couloirs of the Chugach Mountains outside Valdez. ❅ And of course, there's the famed Iditarod dog sled race, covering the 1,049 miles between Anchorage and Nome every March. ❅ Best of all may be the nightly spectacle of the kaleidoscopic Northern Lights—and the opportunity to night ski until 11 A.M.!

ALPINE

ALPENGLOW AT ARCTIC VALLEY
(P. 9, C-3, #1) 11000 Cange Rd., Anchorage
907-248-0367 (snow)
SEASON: Dec. 1-April 25 (open Fri.-Sun.)
ANNUAL SNOWFALL: 300"
TERRAIN: 20 trails over 200 acres; longest run 2,500'; ◆ 15%; ■ 65%; ● 20%.
LIFTS: 4 (2 doubles, 2 surface); capacity, 3,200 per hour.
SUMMIT: 3,900'
VERTICAL: 1,400'
ACTIVITIES: Snowboarding; telemarking.
FEATURES: Child care; ski school; restaurant; rentals.
►NORDIC: Mostly ungroomed terrain; rentals; lessons.
Operated by the Anchorage Ski Club and open only Fridays, weekends and holidays, friendly Alpenglow defines a locals' area: There are hardly any out-of-towners, and it almost feels as though it would open specially if a member's family came to visit. It features a good racing program, and mostly intermediate terrain.

ALYESKA RESORT
(P. 9, C-3, #2) 100 Olympic Circle, Girdwood
907-783-2222; 907-783-2121 (snow)
SEASON: Nov. 1-April 25
ANNUAL SNOWFALL: 550"
TERRAIN: No official trails, bowl and tree-skiing over 1,200 acres; longest run 2.5 mi.; ◆ 59%; ■ 36%; ● 5%.
LIFTS: 7 (1 high-speed quad, 1 quad, 3 doubles, 2 surface); capacity, 6,800 per hour.
SUMMIT: 3,160'
VERTICAL: 2,850'
ACTIVITIES: Snowboarding; NASTAR; night skiing; dogsledding; flightseeing (sightseeing by plane); ice climbing.
FEATURES: USAA racing; child care; ski school; restaurants; rentals.
►NORDIC: Unlimited, mostly ungroomed trails; lessons.
Funky, elemental Alyeska is rapidly becoming better known, thanks to recent, savvy upgrading, including the first high-speed quad, tram, and luxury hotel in Alaska—though these are unlikely to change its hard-core, easy-going ambiance. The base is only 280 feet above sea level, the lowest in North America, but you wouldn't know it from the dumps up top. When fog shrouds the gray sheet of water below, Alyeska feels like the top of the world. Nearly half the mountain is above timberline (in Alaska, 1,200 feet). The upper section offers mainly wide open porcelain bowls serrated with ridges, headwalls, and gullies; the lower, primarily tree skiing. Strong skiers will enjoy two treats: alternating between upper and lower slopes under Chairs 1 and 4, or skiing the entire vertical in one unbroken run. Glacier Bowl will have stomachs, hearts, and throats in a jumble, as will the ferocious runs plummeting like waterfalls from the black diamond cat track High Traverse. Beginners will find little suitable terrain and should stick to the area accessed by Chair 3. Nordic skiers can try the Winner Creek trail. While not very difficult, the rolling track is ungroomed and weaves through pristine woods and meadows.

CLEARY SUMMIT SKI AREA
(P. 9, B-3, #3) 3451 College Rd. (at Steese Highway), Fairbanks
907-456-5520; 907-456-SNOW (snow)
SEASON: Nov. 15-May 1
ANNUAL SNOWFALL: 100"
TERRAIN: 20 trails over 100 acres; longest run 6,000'; ◆ 15%; ■ 65%; ● 20%.
LIFTS: 3 (3 surface); capacity, 2,400 per hour.
SUMMIT: 3,100'
VERTICAL: 1,200'
ACTIVITIES: None.
FEATURES: Snowmaking 100%; ski school; restaurant; rentals.
With no chairs (although the antiquated lifts were overhauled in 1993-1994) and little challenging terrain, Cleary Summit is predominantly used as a learning mountain by locals. A drawback is its location on the "dark" side of the mountain, meaning little sunshine before March. It had financial problems in 1994, so call ahead.

EAGLECREST SKI AREA
(P. 9, C-4, #4) 115 S. Seward St., Juneau
907-790-2000; 907-586-5330 (snow)
SEASON: Dec. 1-April 15
ANNUAL SNOWFALL: 200"
TERRAIN: 31 trails over 640 acres; longest run 2 mi.; ◆ 40%; ■ 40%; ● 20%.
LIFTS: 3 (2 doubles, 1 surface); capacity, 2,600 per hour.
SUMMIT: 2,600'
VERTICAL: 1,400'
ACTIVITIES: Snowboarding; night skiing.
FEATURES: Snowmaking 7%; ski school; restaurant; rentals.
►NORDIC: 8 groomed km.; lessons; rentals.
Despite having only 20% beginner terrain, Eaglecrest is particularly suited to novices and families. The ski school specializes in teaching parents how to instruct their toddlers (and children how to be patient with their parents). The Outer Limits program takes already experienced young skiers and introduces them to techniques like mogul and powder skiing. The new Trickster run is a series of interconnnected meadows ideal for advanced beginners. Experts won't be bored by the East Bowl and Steep Chutes and the more expansive West Bowl. Eaglecrest has a nice blend of bowls, steeps, glades, and broad groomed boulevards.

HILLTOP SKI AREA
(P. 9, C-3, #5) 7015 Abbott Rd., Anchorage
907-346-1446 (snow)
TRAILS, 7; LIFTS, 2; VERTICAL, 294'.
►NORDIC: Ungroomed trails.

MOOSE MOUNTAIN
(P. 9, B-3, #6) 100 Moose Mountain Rd., 10 mi. W of Fairbanks
907-479-8362; 907-459-8132 (snow)
SEASON: Nov. 15-April 15 (open weekends and holidays)
ANNUAL SNOWFALL: 60"
TERRAIN: 10 trails over 100 acres; longest run 2 mi.; ◆ 25%; ■ 75%.
LIFTS: See below.
SUMMIT: 1,987'
VERTICAL: 1,300'
ACTIVITIES: None.
FEATURES: Restaurant.
After its first full season in 1993-1994, Moose Mountain planned to add rentals and instruction for 1995. A unique feature is its use of terrestrial trams: heated buses that climb the road winding around the

CONTINUED ON NEXT PAGE

ARIZONA

Arizona is more noted for the yawning Grand Canyon than for its towering peaks, but the Rockies extend as far south as Flagstaff, with several summits exceeding 11,000 feet. ❄ An added bonus for skiing Arizona areas can be breathtaking views of surrounding high desert plateaus. ❄ The Flagstaff Winterfest, held every February, is billed as an "Extravagan-ski," with everything from sled dog races to snow softball, and plenty of bargain ski activities. ❄ Combine a ski vacation with a golf holiday outside Phoenix, a side trip to New Age Sedona, or even hiking in Grand Canyon National Park (after a Nordic ski tour of the North Rim).

ALPINE

ARIZONA SNOWBOWL
(P. 10, B-3, #1) Highway 180 & Snowbowl Road, Flagstaff
602-779-1951; 602-779-4577 (snow)
SEASON: Dec. 10-April 10
ANNUAL SNOWFALL: 250"
TERRAIN: 32 trails over 120 acres; longest run 2 mi.; ◆ 30%; ■ 40%; ● 30%.
LIFTS: 4 (2 triples, 2 doubles); capacity, 4,260 per hour.
SUMMIT: 11,500'
VERTICAL: 2,300'
ACTIVITIES: Snowboarding.
FEATURES: Ski school; restaurants; rentals.
One of the nation's 10 oldest areas, the Snowbowl has been in business since 1939. It sits atop an extinct volcano, with stunning views of the Painted Desert and the Grand Canyon to the north. The terrain is reasonably well separated: Beginners should head to the Aspen and Hart Prairie chairs; intermediates to the Sunset chair; and advanced skiers to the Agassiz lift, which offers the most challenging skiing in Arizona. Real experts can go out-of-bounds for the 4,000-foot drop off the South Side. Snowboarders can trick in the new Snowboard Park, with a half-pipe and obstacle course. Children 7 and under ski free.

MT. LEMMON SKI VALLEY
(P. 10, E-4, #2) 1161 El Dorado Pl., Tucson
602-885-1181; 602-576-1400 (snow)
SEASON: Dec. 15-April 15
ANNUAL SNOWFALL: 125"
TERRAIN: 15 trails over 80 acres; longest run 1.5 mi.; ◆ 30%; ■ 45%; ● 25%.
LIFTS: 3 (1 double, 2 surface); capacity, 1,000 per hour.
SUMMIT: 9,150'
VERTICAL: 870'
ACTIVITIES: Snowboarding.
FEATURES: Snowmaking 100%; ski school; restaurant; rentals.
Less than an hour from balmy Tucson, Mt. Lemmon is the southernmost ski area in North America.

SUNRISE PARK RESORT
(P. 10, C-5, #3) Highway 260, 20 mi. E of McNary
602-735-7676; 800-882-SNOW (snow)
SEASON: Dec. 6-March 29
ANNUAL SNOWFALL: 250"
TERRAIN: 65 trails over 800 acres; longest run 2.75 mi.; ◆ 20%; ■ 40%; ● 40%.
LIFTS: 11 (2 quads, 4 triples, 2 doubles, 3 surface); capacity, 15,000 per hour.
SUMMIT: 11,000'
VERTICAL: 1,800'
ACTIVITIES: Snowboarding;

night skiing.
FEATURES: Snowmaking 55%; ski school; restaurants; rentals.
▶NORDIC: 10 groomed km; rentals; lessons.
Spread out over three mountains, Arizona's largest ski area is ideally suited to families. Most special ski school programs are tailored to children 6-12. Sunrise Peak is primarily beginner and low intermediate. Apache Peak features miles of ego-massaging cruisers. Cyclone Circle provides some hair-raising steeps like Suicide and Thunder. Set on Native American tribal land, Sunrise is operated by the White Mountain Apache.

WILLIAMS SKI AREA
(P. 10, B-3, #4) Fourth Street (off Highway 40), Williams
602-635-9330 (snow)
TRAILS, 5; LIFTS, 2; VERTICAL, 850'.

NORDIC

FLAGSTAFF NORDIC CENTER
(P. 10, B-3, #5) Route 4, Flagstaff
No phone.
FACILITIES: 40 groomed km; rentals; lessons; telemarking; restaurant.

Perched high above red rocks country, this is one of the more scenic areas in the West. It was recently sold but should be operational in 1995. Call information for new number.

FOREST LAKES TOURING CENTER
(P. 10, B-4, #6) Forest Lakes
602-535-4047
FACILITIES: 40 groomed km; rentals; lessons; grocery store.

MORMON LAKE SKI CENTER
(P. 10, C-3, #7) Mormon Lake
602-354-2240
FACILITIES: 28.8 groomed km; rentals; lessons; store.

NORTH RIM NORDIC CENTER AT KAIBAB LODGE
(P. 10, B-3, #8) North Rim Grand Canyon National Park (Off Route 67, which is closed in winter; only access by snow van)
602-526-0924
FACILITIES: 74 km (54 groomed, with skating lane); rentals; lessons; restaurant and lodging.
Views of the Grand Canyon here are awe-inspiring. The lodge itself is intimate and exclusive and offers guided overnight ski/hut or snow-van tours to the striking Saddle Mountain Wilderness Area.

STATBOX

Tourism: 800-842-8257
Time zone: Mountain
Population: 3,665,228
Square miles: 113,575

Average annual precipitation: 7.5"
Highest elevation: 12,670'
Lowest elevation: 70'

CONTINUED FROM LAST PAGE

perimeter of the mountain up to the top. The six buses make three trips an hour, ensuring that skiers remain toastily warm. While the snowfall seems meager, it's steady and accumulates all winter long, guaranteeing packed powder throughout. All the slopes are groomed. The terrain is mostly rolling amid glades of birch and aspen. Very similar to New England, but better snow quality.

SKILAND
(P. 9, B-3, #7) 1 mi. E of Steese

Highway at mi. 20.5, Fairbanks
907-389-2314; 907-459-ISKI (snow)
SEASON: Nov. 25-April 15
ANNUAL SNOWFALL: 100"
TERRAIN: 25 trails over 100 acres; longest run 2 mi.; ◆ 40%; ■ 40%; ● 20%.
LIFTS: 3 (1 double, 2 surface); capacity, 1,500 per hour.
SUMMIT: 2,000'
VERTICAL: 1,057'
ACTIVITIES: Snowboarding.
FEATURES: Ski school; restaurant; rentals.

Don't miss the folksy funny signs posted everywhere. One example: "We have rocks, stumps, frozen skiers, and giant blueberries. If you hit 'em, it's your fault, so be kind, courteous, and cheerful and have fun." But there is some challenging terrain for intermediates and experts, with both open bowls and glade skiing, like Mama Bear and Willie's Way. The lodge remains open at night for viewing the aurora borealis.

NORDIC

HATCHER PASS LODGE
(P. 9, C-3, #8) Hatcher Pass

Mine, Palmer Trunk Road, Palmer
907-745-5897
FACILITIES: 10 groomed km; lodging and restaurant.

KINCAID PARK
(P. 9, C-3, #9) Anchorage
907-248-4346
FACILITIES: 50 groomed km; lessons.
There is wonderful touring in this beautiful city park when snow cover is sufficient. Kincaid Park was the site of the 1983 Cross-Country World Cup competition.

So vast is the glittering sapphire of Tahoe, North America's largest and highest alpine lake, that the area's original residents, the Washoe, called it "Lake of the Sky." They thought it was one of their god's dwellings, for its intense blue mirrored the sky itself. Straddling the California-Nevada border, Tahoe is heaven on earth for skiers, with the highest concentration of ski areas in the country, nearly all of them world-class. It boasts an unrivalled range of terrain, gorgeous scenery, great snow, sunny days (spring skiing is usually in jams), top-tier lodging, dining, and around-the-clock excitement at Nevada's casinos. (The North Shore is for the quiet, up-on-the-first-lift crowd; the 24-hour South Shore for party-hearty types.) ❄ The Sierras also extend south to the Mammoth Lakes area, a magnet for Southern Californians. After a day at the beach, you'll even find some righteous snow in SoCal, where ski areas—notably free of Hollywood glitz—cater largely to families and college kids on the prowl. A haven for snowboarders, the region offers the sole shredding-only area (not listed): Big Air Green Valley near Running Springs.

ALPINE

ALPINE MEADOWS SKI AREA

(P. 12, E-3, #1) 2600 Alpine Meadows Rd., Tahoe City
800-441-4423, 916-583-4232 ; 916-581-8374 (snow)
SEASON: Nov. 15-May 31
ANNUAL SNOWFALL: 350"
TERRAIN: 105 trails over 2,000 acres; longest run 2.5 mi.; ◆ 35%; ■ 40%; ● 25%.
LIFTS: 12 (2 high-speed quads, 2 triples, 7 doubles, 1 surface); capacity, 16,025 per hour.
SUMMIT: 8,637'
VERTICAL: 1,557'
ACTIVITIES: NASTAR.
FEATURES: Snowmaking 12%; ski school; restaurant; rentals.
Resolutely unchic and no frills Alpine Meadows is a local favorite for its great powder days and varied terrain. There are phenomenal bowls for intermediates, where they can practice quick turns to their hearts' content, like the beautiful Alpine Bowl and Roundhouse runs. Experts have their own steeper bowls, led by Sherwood, Wolverine, Beaver, and Estelle. If you want heart-pounding dive-bomber runs, Our Father and the infamous Scott Chute fit the bill. Alpine often has the best spring conditions in Tahoe, and stays open late in the season. No attitude here—just stupendous skiing.

BADGER PASS SKI AREA

(P. 12, E-3, #2) Badger Pass, Yosemite National Park
209-372-1330 ; 209-372-1338 (snow)
SEASON: Nov. 15-April 15
ANNUAL SNOWFALL: 300"
TERRAIN: 9 trails over 88 acres; longest run 1 mi.; ◆ 15%; ■ 50%; ● 35%.
LIFTS: 5 (1 triple, 3 doubles, 1 surface); capacity, 5,300 per hour.
SUMMIT: 8,000'
VERTICAL: 800'
ACTIVITIES: NASTAR; snowcat rides.
FEATURES: ski school; restaurant; rentals.
▶NORDIC: Yosemite Cross-Country Ski School; 209-372-1244; 35 groomed km; rentals; lessons; telemarking.
Badger Pass and the affiliated Yosemite Cross-Country area offer spectacular views, deserted trails, and top ski schools. Seniors over 65 ski free. The downhill trails are relentlessly groomed, but Yosemite offers 350 additional miles of demanding backcountry touring. Its guide service offers full-day and overnight hut skiing in the enthralling national park. Despite the low percentage of beginner terrain, Yosemite is one of the best instructional locations in the West.

BEAR MOUNTAIN SKI RESORT

(P. 13, H-4, #3) 43101 Gold Mine Dr., Big Bear Lake
909-585-2517 ; 909-585-2519 (snow)
SEASON: Nov. 8-April 21
ANNUAL SNOWFALL: 200"
TERRAIN: 35 trails over 175 acres; longest run 2 mi.; ◆ 25%; ■ 50%; ● 25%.
LIFTS: 11 (1 high-speed quad, 1 quad, 3 triples, 4 doubles, 2 surface); capacity, 15,490 per hour.
SUMMIT: 8,805'
VERTICAL: 1,665'
ACTIVITIES: Snowboarding; tubing; sledding; tobogganing.
FEATURES: Snowmaking 100%; ski school; restaurants; rentals.
Bear Mountain is not as religiously groomed as its neighbor, Snow Summit (see below), so it offers some adequate bump skiing. Nor are its trails as well marked or its lake views as stunning. Still, it offers more of a test than its manicured neighbor. As proof, catch the Showdown chair; to the right is The Outlaw, a snowboarding-only run, and you can watch those renegades of the slopes catching big air. Experts will enjoy Geronimo and the off-trail tree-skiing (when conditions permit). Beginners learn under the Inspiration chair; intermediates play on the Goldmine, Silver, and Showdown peaks. With the highest summit in SoCal, Bear usually boasts the longest season. There is a frequent skier program that allows skiers to accumulate points toward free lift tickets.

BEAR VALLEY SKI AREA

(P. 12, D-3, #4) Mt. Reba Road, Bear Valley
209-753-2301; 209-753-2308 (snow)
SEASON: Nov. 30-April 15
ANNUAL SNOWFALL: 450"
TERRAIN: 60 trails over 1,280 acres; longest run 3 mi.; ◆ 30%; ■ 40%; ● 30%.
LIFTS: 11 (2 triples, 7 doubles, 2 surface); capacity, 12,000 per hour.
SUMMIT: 8,500'
VERTICAL: 1,900'
ACTIVITIES: Snowboarding; snowmobiling; ice skating.
FEATURES: Snowmaking 35%; ski school; restaurant; rentals.
▶NORDIC: 209-753-2834; 65 groomed km; rentals; lessons.
Only in northern California would an area this size be considered small. It does not contain any high-tech lifts, yet despite the occasional Bay Area crowds, you can ski a lot of vertical in one day here. There are few distractions in the area (virtually no après ski and nightlife), and the entire staff adroitly keeps things moving. Six chairs fan out from the base, efficiently separating skiers of varying ability. Experts should head for the cliffs of Grizzly, but intermediates can test their prowess on the satisying blend of bowls and glades. Children under 7 ski free. The state's first snowboard park opened here in 1990 and several areas have been designated for non-skiers; ever since, shredders have descended in droves. The Nordic center also has an impressive layout—larger than many better-known resorts, with a range of tracks through meadows and forests.

BOREAL SKI AREA

(P. 12, C-3, #5) I-80 Castle Peak Exit, Truckee
916-426-3666 (snow)
SEASON: Oct. 31-May 1
ANNUAL SNOWFALL: 300"
TERRAIN: 41 trails over 380 acres; longest run 1 mi.; ◆ 15%; ■ 55%; ● 30%.
LIFTS: 9 (1 high-speed quad, 1 quad, 2 triples, 5 doubles); capacity, 13,200 per hour.
SUMMIT: 7,800'
VERTICAL: 600'
ACTIVITIES: Snowboarding; night skiing.
FEATURES: Snowmaking 35%; ski school; restaurant; rentals.
The recently added high-speed detachable quad means there are almost never any lift lines at this already uncrowded area, despite its easy-to-reach location right off the highway. Boreal is a gem for beginners and intermediates, with a notable ski school. The snowboard park is California's largest.

BUCKHORN SKI AREA

(P. 13, H-4, #6) Highway 2, La Canada
714-775-7513 (for info only)
SLOPES, 2; LIFTS, 2; VERTICAL, 700'.
▶NORDIC: 40 ungroomed km.
A private area that you can check out for $5.

CEDAR PASS SKI HILL
(P. 12, B-3, #7) 501 Short St., Alturas
916-233-3323
TRAILS, 5; LIFTS, 2; VERTICAL, 400'.

DODGE RIDGE SKI AREA
(P. 12, D-3, #8) Dodge Ridge Road, Pinecrest
209-965-3474; 209-965-4444 (snow)
SEASON: Nov. 25-April 10
ANNUAL SNOWFALL: 400"
TERRAIN: 28 trails over 550 acres; longest run 2.25 mi.; ◆ 20%; ■ 60%; ● 20%.
LIFTS: 11 (2 triples, 5 doubles, 4 surface); capacity, 12,000 per hour.
SUMMIT: 8,200'
VERTICAL: 1,600'
ACTIVITIES: Snowboarding.
FEATURES: Ski school; restaurants; repair; and rentals.
A recent expansion doubled the vertical and skiable acres at this superb learning area, whose ski school has consistently been rated as good or better than larger resorts. Children under 9 and seniors over 62 ski free; there's a "Fun to Ski Money Back Guarantee" (just what it sounds like), as well as two-for-one lift tickets midweek. Intermediates will find plenty of cruising on empty slopes.

DONNER SKI RANCH
(P. 12, C-3, #9) Old Highway 40, Norden
916-426-3635 (snow)
SEASON: Oct. 31-May 31
ANNUAL SNOWFALL: 300"
TERRAIN: 40 trails over 400 acres; longest run 1 mi.; ◆ 25%; ■ 50%; ● 25%.
LIFTS: 6 (1 triple, 5 doubles); capacity, 7,800 per hour.
SUMMIT: 7751'
VERTICAL: 720'
ACTIVITIES: Snowboarding; night skiing.
FEATURES: Snowmaking 10%; ski school; restaurants; rentals.
Tiny by nearby Tahoe standards, Donner is nonetheless a good bet for intermediates when the lakeside crowds surge.

GRANLIBAKKEN SKI RESORT
(P. 12, D-3, #10) End of Granlibakken Road, Tahoe City
916-583-9896 (snow)
TRAILS, 2; LIFTS, 2; VERTICAL, 280'.
▶NORDIC: Unlimited ungroomed terrain.

HEAVENLY SKI RESORT
(P. 12, D-3, #11) Wildwood & Saddle Roads, South Lake Tahoe
916-541-1330 ; 916-541-7544 (snow)
SEASON: Nov. 15-April 30
ANNUAL SNOWFALL: 300"
TERRAIN: 79 trails over 4,800 acres; longest run 5.5 mi.; ◆ 35%; ■ 45%; ● 20%.
LIFTS: 25 (1 tram, 2 high-speed quads, 8 triples, 8 doubles, 6 surface); capacity, 33,000 per hour.
SUMMIT: 10,040'
VERTICAL: 3,500'
ACTIVITIES: Snowboarding; NASTAR.
FEATURES: Snowmaking 65%; ski school; restaurants; rentals.
Straddling the California-Nevada border, Heavenly is just that for skiers of all types. The California side gets all the press clippings. It has the much-photographed tram, the mind-boggling lake views, and the stomach-churning Gunbarrel bump run. It also has the traffic jams.
Consider the Nevada side: It's generally less crowded; the runs are even more varied; and its summit stands nearly 1,000 feet higher, making it less prone to wet snow (if it's raining on the California side, chances are it's powdery here). Lovely silky cruisers here include Big Dipper and Orion, with bumps forming on the Milky Way, Big and Little Dipper bowls. Nevada also has those extreme dreams Mott and Killebrew canyons, a series of steep bowls, steeper gullies, and elevator shafts through thick stands of pine. California has some more intermediate beauties like Betty's and Liz's Canyon. The only skiers left out of the equation at the gigantic Heavenly are rank beginners, who have a small play area: a sandbox amidst the Sahara.

JUNE MOUNTAIN
(P. 12, E-3, #12) 85 Boulder Rd., June Lake
619-648-7733; 619-934-6166 (snow)
SEASON: Nov. 1-April 31
ANNUAL SNOWFALL: 325"
TERRAIN: 32 trails over 500 acres; longest run 2.5 mi.; ◆ 20%; ■ 45%; ● 35%.
LIFTS: 8 (1 tram, 2 high-speed quads, 5 doubles); capacity, 12,000 per hour.
SUMMIT: 10,135'
VERTICAL: 2,590'
ACTIVITIES: Snowboarding; snowmobiling; dog sledding.
FEATURES: Ski school; restaurant; child care; and rentals.
June Mountain is affiliated with the central Sierras giant, Mammoth Mountain. June is ideal for advanced intermediate skiers who can attack ridges and chutes that rival Mammoth's for sheer precipitousness. There are no bowls; everything is below treeline, which translates into some superlative glade skiing and better snowpack than its famed neighbor. June is also the choice of snowboarders, who like the half pipe and chutes like Davos Drop. Come here weekends when Mammoth is packed; June's quaint European ambience (it's nicknamed "North America's Switzerland") will be a welcome change of pace.

KIRKWOOD SKI RESORT
(P. 12, D-3, #13) Kirkwood Meadows Drive, Kirkwood
209-258-6000; 209-258-3000 (snow)
SEASON: Nov. 15-April 30
ANNUAL SNOWFALL: 450"
TERRAIN: 65 trails over 2,000 acres; longest run 2.5 mi.; ◆ 35%; ■ 50%; ● 15%.
LIFTS: 11 (6 triples, 4 doubles, 1 surface): capacity, 15,000 per hour.
SUMMIT: 9,800'
VERTICAL: 2,000'
ACTIVITIES: Snowboarding; sleigh rides.
FEATURES: Ski school; child care; restaurants; rentals.
▶NORDIC: 80 groomed km; rentals; lessons.
Locals know Kirkwood gets the best snow in the area. And that's the problem: its high, open location means that the lifts and access roads close during savage storms. But once you're there, you'll find a wealth of terrain no matter what your ability. Beginners have their own areas off the Bunny and Snowkirk chairs on either side of the mountain. Intermediates enjoy groomed boulevards off the Sunrise chair or the lower section served by the Solitude and Hole 'n' Wall chairs. And experts know they have plenty of bruising runs off chutes and cornices. The West side off False Peak has the best tree skiing; the Cornice chair accesses hellacious bump runs. And the double diamond steeps off the Sisters Ridge like The Wall and All the Way are true stomach-churners, as are the powder-magnets off Thunder Saddle. Snowboarders love all the above—and, especially, the habit the mountain has of creating its own half-pipe trenches. The Nordic center offers double tracks, skating lanes, and three interconnected trails systems. Signs along the White Pine trail mark the region's flora and fauna.

KRATKA RIDGE
(P. 13, H-4, #14) Star Route, La Canada
818-578-1079; 818-449-1749 (snow)
SEASON: Dec. 15-April 15
ANNUAL SNOWFALL: 80"
TERRAIN: 13 trails over 56 acres; longest run 2,600'; ◆ 40%; ■ 30%; ● 30%.
LIFTS: 3 (1 double, 1 single chair, 1 surface); capacity, 2,500 per hour.
SUMMIT: 7,650'
VERTICAL: 750'
ACTIVITIES: Snowboarding.
FEATURES: Ski school; restaurants; and rentals.
With unpredictable snow and limited terrain, Kratka Ridge is best as a quick beginner getaway from Los Angeles, which sits a mere 35 miles southwest. Children under 13 ski free.

LASSEN PARK SKI AREA
(P. 12, C-2, #15) 2150 N. Main #7 at Highway 89, Red Bluff
916-595-3376; 916-595-4464 (snow)
SEASON: Nov. 25-April 15 (open Thurs. to Sun., holidays only)
ANNUAL SNOWFALL: 250"
TERRAIN: 10 trails over 100 acres; longest run 3,900'; ◆ 20%; ■ 40%; ● 40%.
LIFTS: 3 (1 triple, 2 surface); capacity, 2,800 per hour.
SUMMIT: 7,200'
VERTICAL: 600'
ACTIVITIES: Snowboarding.
FEATURES: Snowmaking; ski school; restaurant; rentals.
▶NORDIC: 80 km of marked ungroomed trails in park; rentals; lessons.
Located at the south entrance to Lassen Volcanic National Park, the area boasts some stunning panoramas of Lassen's tortured snow-covered lunarscape. Under 8 and over 69 ski free.

MAMMOTH MOUNTAIN SKI AREA
(P. 12, E-3, #16) 1 Minaret Rd., Mammoth Lakes
619-934-2571; 916-934-6166 (snow)
SEASON: Nov. 10-June 7
ANNUAL SNOWFALL: 335"
TERRAIN: 150 trails over 3,500 acres; longest run 2.5 mi.; ◆ 30%; ■ 40%; ● 30%.
LIFTS: 30 (2 gondolas, 2 high-speed quads, 4 quads, 7 triples, 13 doubles, 2 surface); capacity, 55,000 per hour.
SUMMIT: 11,053'
VERTICAL: 3,100'
ACTIVITIES: Snowboarding; bobsled; dog sled rides; tubing; tobogganing; ice skating.
FEATURES: Snowmaking 6%; ski school; child care; restaurants; rentals.
The name fits: Mammoth is a behemoth in every sense of the word. Imagine a volcano that blew its top, leaving a series of ridges, canyons, and endless bowls. That's Mammoth, and no place in California—perhaps even the USA—offers such a rich variety of terrain. Of course, every skier has heard the horror stories about weekends at Mammoth, when it becomes worse than the Santa Monica Freeway at rush hour. But with all that terrain, and a state-of-the-art lift network, it's not always as bad as legend has it. At Mammoth, runs don't have names,

they have chair numbers. Real experts should head for 22, whose ridges and chutes empty out into pristine bowls. No. 1 delivers bumps on The Wall; the gondola gets you the Cornice and Hangman's (as forbidding as they sound). Intermediates should chant "2, 4, 6, 8, who do we appreciate?" They'll also like 3, 10, 16, and 24. Seven and 11 are lucky for beginners. And for avoiding crowds? Nineteen, 22, and 25 are local favorites.

MT. BALDY SKI AREA
(P. 13, H-4, #17) End of Mt. Baldy Road, Mt. Baldy
909-982-0800; 909-981-3344 (snow)
SEASON: Nov. 15-April 15
ANNUAL SNOWFALL: 100"
TERRAIN: 27 trails over 400 acres; longest run 2,100'; ◆◆ 20%; ◆ 20%; ■ 40%; ● 20%.
LIFTS: 4 (4 doubles); capacity, 5,000 per hour.
SUMMIT: 8,600'
VERTICAL: 2,100'
ACTIVITIES: Snowboarding.
FEATURES: Snowmaking 20%; ski school; restaurants; rentals.
 With the greatest vertical drop in Southern California, Mt. Baldy offers some long runs and some steep slopes by SoCal standards. With the highest summit in the San Gabriels, it usually has more reliable snow and conditions. It's less popular than the Big Bear areas, though, because of its antiquated lift system (one double chair accesses most of the terrain) and limited snowmaking, especially on the black runs.

MT. SHASTA SKI PARK
(P. 12, B-2, #18) 104 Siskiyou Ave., Mt. Shasta
916-926-8610 ; 916-926-8686 (snow)
SEASON: Dec. 15-April 15
ANNUAL SNOWFALL: 250"
TERRAIN: 21 trails over 300 acres; longest run 1.25 mi.; ◆ 20%; ■ 60%; ● 20%.
LIFTS: 3 (2 triples, 1 surface); capacity, 3,900 per hour.
SUMMIT: 6,600'
VERTICAL: 1,100.
ACTIVITIES: Snowboarding; night skiing.
FEATURES: Snowmaking 70%; ski school; restaurant; rentals.
▶NORDIC: 25 groomed km; rentals; lessons.
 Another good learning area with riveting views of its eponymous peak. Skiing ranges from the green wanderer Wintun Way to the challenging steeps of the West Face. The Nordic center offers diagonal tracks, skating lanes, and guided backcountry tours.

MT. WATERMAN SKI AREA
(P. 13, H-4, #19) 87 Lynnhaven

Courtesy: Squaw Valley USA (see California, p. 94).

Lane, La Canada
818-440-1041; 818-440-2002 (snow)
SEASON: Nov. 15-May 1
ANNUAL SNOWFALL: 80"
TERRAIN: 23 trails over 135 acres; longest run 1 mi.; ◆ 40%; ■ 40%; ● 20%.
LIFTS: 3 (3 doubles); capacity, 3,600 per hour.
SUMMIT: 8,030'
VERTICAL: 1,000'
ACTIVITIES: Snowboarding.
FEATURES: Snowmaking 20%; ski school; restaurant; rentals.
 Less than a half hour from Pasadena, Mt. Waterman may be the most convenient Southern California area of all. Children under 12 ski free, a plus for families that come here to learn and practice.

MOUNTAIN HIGH WEST/EAST
(P. 13, H-4, #20) Highway 2, 3 mi. W of Wrightwood
714-972-9242 (snow)
SEASON: Nov. 15-April 15
ANNUAL SNOWFALL: 120"
TERRAIN: 30 trails over 205 acres; longest run 1.5 mi.; ◆ 25%; ■ 50%; ● 25%.
LIFTS: 11 (1 high-speed quad, 1 quad, 3 triples, 6 doubles); capacity, 16,000 per hour.
SUMMIT: 8,200'

VERTICAL: 1,600'
ACTIVITIES: Snowboarding; tubing; night skiing.
FEATURES: Snowmaking 93%; ski school; restaurants; rentals.
 Mountain High's high points are its fine, well-groomed cruisers, and accessibility, just 15 miles off I-15. West is ideal for intermediates; East has beginner runs at the base and summit, as well as Olympic Bowl for experts.

NORTHSTAR-AT-TAHOE
(P. 12, C-3, #21) Highway 267 & Northstar Drive, Truckee
916-562-1010 ; 916-562-1330 (snow)
SEASON: Nov. 25-April 30
ANNUAL SNOWFALL: 300"
TERRAIN: 57 trails over 500 acres; longest run 2.9 mi.; ◆ 25%; ■ 50%; ● 25%.
LIFTS: 11 (1 gondola, 3 high-speed quads, 2 triples, 3 doubles, 2 surface); capacity, 18,270 per hour.
SUMMIT: 8,600'
VERTICAL: 2,200'
ACTIVITIES: Snowboarding; sleigh rides; telemarking; snowshoeing.
FEATURES: Snowmaking 50%; ski school; restaurants; child care; rentals.
▶NORDIC: 65 groomed km; rentals; lessons.

True, the meticulous grooming may not appeal to the mogul-meisters who frequent Tahoe. There are no hellish bump runs or death-defying chutes. But there's no better place at Tahoe to work on your form. Northstar offers a series of long, steady, just-steep-enough runs—like the ones off the Lookout and Backside Express chairs. But watch out on powder days—or the day after when everywhere else is skied off. The expert eagles swoop down on Northstar seeking every pretty little glade run in sight. The Nordic trails, which include skating lanes, are among the most tranquil in the Tahoe area.

PLUMAS-EUREKA SKI BOWL
(P. 12, C-13, #22) 808 W. Old Valley Meadow Rd. (at Highway 70), Quincy
916-836-2317 (snow)
TRAILS, 6; LIFTS, 3; VERTICAL, 650'.

SHIRLEY MEADOWS SKI AREA
(P. 13, G-4, #23) 1600 Rancheria Rd., Green Horn
619-376-4186 (snow)
SEASON: Nov. 25-April 5 (open Fri. to Sun., holidays)
ANNUAL SNOWFALL: 80"
TERRAIN: 7 trails over 80 acres; longest run 1,500'; ◆ 25%; ■ 50%; ● 25%.
LIFTS: 2 (2 surface); capacity, 500 per hour.
SUMMIT: 7,500'
VERTICAL: 800'
ACTIVITIES: Snowboarding.
FEATURES: Ski school; restaurant; rentals.
 The minimal grooming at this small area can provide a few thrills in heavy snow seasons.

SIERRA AT TAHOE
(P. 12, D-3, #24) 9921 Sierra Ski Ranch Rd., Twin Bridges
916-659-7535 ; 916-659-7475 (snow)
SEASON: Nov. 15-April 15
ANNUAL SNOWFALL: 450"
TERRAIN: 40 trails over 2,000 acres; longest run 3.5 mi.; ◆ 25%; ■ 50%; ● 25%.
LIFTS: 9 (3 high-speed quads, 1 triple, 5 doubles); capacity, 14,920 per hour.
SUMMIT: 8,852'
VERTICAL: 2,212'
ACTIVITIES: Snowboarding; telemarking.
FEATURES: Snowmaking 5%; ski school; restaurants; rentals.
 Sierra At Tahoe recently added its third high-speed detachable quad and opened a snowboarding terrain garden. The mountain offers several wide-sweeping bowls and non-stop runs top-to-bottom. This is another lesser-known gem that skiers forget. Kids under 6 ski free,

and there are numerous promotions, like a complimentary lift ticket every third visit.

SIERRA SUMMIT SKI AREA

(P. 13, E-3, #25) 59265 Highway 168, Lakeshore
209-233-2500; 209-443-6111 (snow)
SEASON: Nov. 15-April 15
ANNUAL SNOWFALL: 130″
TERRAIN: 20 trails over 250 acres; longest run 2.25 mi.; ◆ 25%; ■ 65%; ● 10%.
LIFTS: 9 (2 triples, 3 doubles, 4 surface); capacity, 8,605 per hour.
SUMMIT: 8,709′
VERTICAL: 1,600′
ACTIVITIES: Snowboarding.
FEATURES: Snowmaking 100%; ski school; restaurants; rentals.
Sierra Summit has the most consistent snow in central California, thanks to top-to-bottom snowmaking coverage and some delightful cruising and steep runs.

SKI HOMEWOOD

(P. 12, D-3, #26) 5145 West Lake Blvd., Homewood
916-525-2992 (snow)
SEASON: Nov. 25-April 15
ANNUAL SNOWFALL: 200″
TERRAIN: 57 trails over 1,260 acres; longest run 2 mi.; ◆ 35%; ■ 50%; ● 15%.
LIFTS: 10 (1 quad, 2 triples, 2 doubles, 5 surface); capacity, 8,500 per hour.
SUMMIT: 7,880′
VERTICAL: 1,650′
ACTIVITIES: Snowboarding.
FEATURES: Snowmaking 10%; ski school; restaurant; rentals.
In-the-know locals head to friendly Homewood for three reasons: its low elevation virtually guarantees it will remain open when severe storms close other areas (or make access impossible); its slopes are often uncrowded, even on powder days; and its 180-degree lake views are unsurpassed. The skiing is mostly intermediate, with some sensational tree runs and gnarlier bumps on the Quail Face. Shredders enjoy the terrain park and half-pipe. Children under 9 ski free.

SKI SUNRISE

(P. 13, H-4, #27) 1 Table Mountain Rd., Wrightwood
619-249-6150 (snow)
SEASON: Dec. 1-March 31
ANNUAL SNOWFALL: 100″
TERRAIN: 22 trails over 100 acres; longest run 1 mi.; ◆ 30%; ■ 55%; ● 15%.
LIFTS: 4 (1 quad, 3 surface); capacity, 3,800 per hour.
SUMMIT: 7,600′
VERTICAL: 800′
ACTIVITIES: Snowboarding.
FEATURES: Snowmaking 25%;

ski school; restaurant; rentals.
A local learning area (beginners have a large separate section) with some tremendous views of the San Gabriel peaks.

SNOW SUMMIT SKI AREA

(P. 13, H-5, #28) 880 Summit Blvd., Big Bear Lake
909-866-5766 (snow)
SEASON: Nov. 15-April 15
ANNUAL SNOWFALL: 75″
TERRAIN: 27 trails over 230 acres; longest run 1.25 mi.; ◆ 25%; ■ 65%; ● 15%.
LIFTS: 11 (3 quads, 3 triples, 5 doubles); capacity, 17,450 per hour.
SUMMIT: 8,200′
VERTICAL: 1,200′
ACTIVITIES: Snowboarding; night skiing.
FEATURES: Snowmaking 100%; ski school; child care; restaurants; rentals.
Everything about Snow Summit—consistently rated the No. 1 day skiing area in California—is groomed to be user-friendly. They'll give you a voucher if for any reason you're dissatisfied with the skiing in the first 75 minutes. "Time our lifts," reads one sign, "they're not as long as you think." "Least skied run top to bottom," proclaims another. There are color-coded signs at the top of each chair indicating the crowd factor on different lifts. Many liftpoles offer a helpful hint—snippets of information about the area or ski trivia. And the views of Big Bear Lake rival those of the Tahoe areas up North. Snow Summit is also friendly to snowboarders, who carve up the slopes in droves (that's what the state-of-the-art grooming machinery is for). The more difficult runs are clustered to the left of the mountain as you face it; but Snow Summit has no fearsome runs, with the exception of Olympic, a steep narrow chute through trees. Otherwise, even on the double diamond, The Wall, the shaky skiers who hotdog down make it more perilous than its pitch.

SNOW VALLEY SKI AREA

(P. 13, H-4, #29) Highway 18, 5 mi. E of Running Springs
909-867-2751; 909-867-515 (snow)
SEASON: Nov. 25-April 15
ANNUAL SNOWFALL: 132″
TERRAIN: 35 trails over 230 acres; longest run 1.25 mi.; ◆ 30%; ■ 35%; ● 35%.
LIFTS: 13 (5 triples, 8 doubles); capacity, 18,550 per hour.
SUMMIT: 7,841′
VERTICAL: 1,141′
ACTIVITIES: Snowboarding; night skiing.
FEATURES: Snowmaking 75%; ski school; restaurants; rentals.
A couple of decent if short pitches (Slide Peak, which also builds moguls, stands out) and some smashing desert views. Good inter-

mediates can easily handle the black terrain. It tends to be less crowded than neighboring Big Bear on busy weekends.

SODA SPRINGS SKI AREA

(P. 12, D-3, #30) Highway 40 (Soda Springs Exit), Truckee
916-427-3666 (snow)
SEASON: Nov. 15-April 15 (open weekends, holidays)
ANNUAL SNOWFALL: 300″
TERRAIN: 16 trails over 200 acres; longest run 1 mi.; ◆ 20%; ■ 50%; ● 30%.
LIFTS: 2 (1 triple, 1 double); capacity, 4,800 per hour.
SUMMIT: 7,350′
VERTICAL: 650′
ACTIVITIES: Snowboarding.
FEATURES: Ski school; restaurant; rentals.
A small but friendly area with the cheapest prices in the Tahoe region: in other words, a great learning mountain. The entire area is available to rent for functions. The lift ticket can be used to ski Boreal at night.

SQUAW VALLEY USA

(P. 12, D-3, #31) End of Squaw Valley Road, Olympic Valley
916-583-6985, 800-545-4350 ; 916-583-6955 (snow)
SEASON: Nov. 15-May 31
ANNUAL SNOWFALL: 400″
TERRAIN: Open skiing over 4,500 acres; longest run 3.5 mi.; ◆ 30%; ■ 45%; ● 25%.
LIFTS: 33 (1 tram, 1 gondola, 3 high-speed quads, 8 triples, 15 doubles, 5 surface); capacity, 49,000 per hour.
SUMMIT: 9,050′
VERTICAL: 2,850′
ACTIVITIES: Snowboarding; ice skating; bungee jumping; night skiing.
FEATURES: Snowmaking 5%; ski school; child care; restaurants; rentals.
► NORDIC: 30 groomed km; rentals; lessons.
Not content to coast on its reputation, Squaw Valley (host of the 1960 Winter Olympics), has undergone a huge expansion the past few years, adding several high-speed quads and more luxury amenities and facilities, including the Resort at Squaw Creek. Squaw is one of those ultimate ski experiences: If you think you're good, you come here to find out just how good. Instead of cut trails, Squaw has more than 4,000 acres of open fields that range from expansive bowls to some of North America's tightest, most forbidding chutes, glades, and cliffs—a mecca for extreme skiers. If you like air, head for gladed Poulsen's Gully (off the new Big Red chair), Eagle's Nest, and the Palisades. Mere experts will find thrills aplenty on the KT22 side. Chute 75 is reputedly the steepest trail in Tahoeland (a 10- to

20-foot jump from a cornice gets you to its mega-bumps). Then there are the aptly named Funnel, Waterfall, and Elevator Shaft. Squaw's six separate peaks offer different exposures and snow conditions—no way will good skiers get bored here. For the rest? Actually, 70% of Squaw's terrain is rated blue and green. Intermediates will have a snowfield day on Chicken Bowl (unfairly named) and Sun Bowl (a black diamond challenge with perfect spring conditions), as well as the runs in the Shirley Lake, Newport, Gold Coast, and Mainline areas. Beginners have their own gorgeous bowl called Bailey's Beach. Boarders can enjoy all those nasty bumps and pitches, as well as their own half-pipe. And the Nordic system offers a similar challenge, with hills that vault over 500 feet as well as gentler terrain.

SUGAR BOWL SKI RESORT

(P. 12, D-3, #32) Old Highway 40, Norden (W of Donner Ski Ranch)
916-426-3651; 916-426-3847 (snow)
SEASON: Nov. 15-May 15
ANNUAL SNOWFALL: 475″
TERRAIN: 47 trails over 1,100 acres; longest run 3 mi.; ◆ 50%; ■ 30%; ● 20%.
LIFTS: 8 (1 gondola, 2 quads, 5 doubles); capacity, 8,500 per hour.
SUMMIT: 8,383′
VERTICAL: 1,500′
ACTIVITIES: Snowboarding.
FEATURES: Snowmaking 4%; ski school; child care; restaurants; rentals.
Sugar Bowl defines "sleeper." Nobody seems to know that it gets the most snow annually in California (except a few locals—and they're not telling). Powder hounds will find this area sweet indeed, despite its relatively short vertical. It's an advanced area, with rollercoaster rides galore on the gullies of Mt. Lincoln. Skiers love choosing a different line of descent every time: The intersecting runs zig and zag crazily across the slopes. Mt. Disney is the spot for wide-open cruising with a modicum of challenge for both intermediates and novices. Sugar Bowl is the closest major area to Sacramento and the Bay Area.

TAHOE DONNER SKI BOWL

(P. 12, D-3, #33) Northwoods Boulevard, 2 mi. W of Truckee
916-587-9400
SEASON: Nov. 25-April 6
ANNUAL SNOWFALL: 300″
TERRAIN: 11 trails over 120 acres; longest run 1 mi.; ■ 50%; ● 50%.
LIFTS: 3 (2 doubles, 1 surface); capacity, 2,000 per hour.
SUMMIT: 7,350′

VERTICAL: 600'
ACTIVITIES: Sledding.
FEATURES: Ski school; restaurants; rentals.
▶NORDIC: 916-587-9484; 15275 Alder Creek Rd., Truckee; 70 groomed km; rentals; lessons.
 A learning area. The fine Nordic center offers spectacular views of the Sierra Crest, with 33 trails over 4,800 acres and a vertical drop of 1,300 feet.

NORDIC

AUBURN SKI CLUB TRAINING CENTER
(P. 12, D-3, #34) Soda Springs
916-426-3313
FACILITIES: 7 groomed km; ski jump; biathlon range; lessons.
 A private club that charges only $15 annually for membership, Auburn doesn't meet our strict criteria for inclusion, but as a preeminent training center it's an excellent venue for potential racers or even amateur competitors. Clinics offered regularly.

COFFEE CREEK RANCH
(P. 12, B-2, #35) HC 2, Trinity Center
800-624-4480
FACILITIES: Several ungroomed km; rentals; lessons; telemarking; ice skating; goldpanning; restaurant and lodging.

EAGLE MOUNTAIN NORDIC CENTER
(P. 12, D-2, #36) 908 Taylorville Rd., Grass Valley
916-994-3613
FACILITIES: 20 groomed km; rentals; restaurant.

GREEN VALLEY LAKE CROSS-COUNTRY CENTER
(P. 13, H-3, #37) Green Valley Lake
909-867-7754
FACILITIES: 25 groomed km (with skating lane); rentals; lessons; restaurant.
 Near the Big Air Green Valley snowboarding area and convenient to the Big Bear downhill areas, Green Valley Lake is the largest Nordic center in Southern California. It offers miles of ungroomed trails in the San Bernardino National Forest with outstanding desert, mountain, lake, and even ocean views.

LELAND HIGH SIERRA SNOW PLAY
(P. 12, D-2, #38) Leland Meadows, 5 mi. E of Strawberry
209-965-4719
FACILITIES: 100 groomed km; rentals; lessons; restaurant; tobogganing; snowmobiling.
 Great for kids, with a sledding hill, Leland High Sierra is expanding its operations to include cross-country skiing (with both double tracks and skating lanes), snowmobiling, and backcountry tours for 1994-1995.

MARRIOTT-TENAYA LODGE
(P. 12, E-3, #39) 1122 Highway 41, Fish Camp
209-683-6555
FACILITIES: Unlimited backcountry; rentals; lessons; restaurant and lodging.

MONTECITO-SEQUOIA CROSS-COUNTRY
(P. 13, F-3, #40) Grants Grove, Kings Canyon National Park
800-227-9900
FACILITIES: 35 groomed km (with skating lane); rentals; lessons.

MT. PINOS/FRAZIER SKI AREA
(P. 13, H-3, #41) 3620 Mt. Pinos Way, Frazier Park
805-248-6014
FACILITIES: Unlimited backcountry skiing; rentals; lessons.

PALM SPRINGS NORDIC SKI AREA
(P. 13, J-5, #42) 1 Tramway Rd., Palm Springs
619-327-6002
FACILITIES: Unlimited ungroomed terrain; rentals; lessons; snowshoeing.
 Located 8,500 feet above the valley floor on Mt. San Jacinto, Palm Springs offers the almost eerie sensation of brisk Nordic skiing while overlooking the miles of emerald golf courses and azure pools for which the Palm Springs area is famous.

RIM NORDIC SKI AREA
(P. 13, H-4, #43) 1 Highway 18, Running Springs
909-867-2600
FACILITIES: 12 groomed km; rentals; lessons; restaurant.

ROYAL GORGE CROSS-COUNTRY
(P. 12, D-3, #44) Pahatsi Road, Soda Springs
916-426-3871
FACILITIES: 321 groomed km; rentals; lessons; lodging and restaurants; 3 lifts.
 Quite simply the emperor of Nordic resorts, Royal Gorge deserves every accolade heaped upon it. Its 81 meticulously groomed trails access more than 9,000 acres and are all double tracked with skating lanes. Striking scenery includes vistas of the craggy Devil's and Castle Peaks and the gaping Royal Gorge itself (a 4,400-foot deep canyon); the varied topography, traversing 1,600 feet vertically, includes frozen lakes, jagged ridges, and gentle meadows. To give you an idea of its sheer size, you could ski from San Francisco to Lake Tahoe if the system were laid end to end. It suits every level of skier.

SIERRA MEADOWS CROSS-COUNTRY
(P. 12, E-3, #45) Inyo National Forest, Mammoth Lakes
619-934-6161
FACILITIES: 55 groomed km; rentals; lessons; sleigh rides; restaurant.

TAHOE NORDIC SKI CENTER/ALLIED SPORTS
(P. 12, D-3, #46) 925 Country Club Dr., Tahoe City
916-583-0484
FACILITIES: 65 groomed km (with skating lane); rentals; lessons; restaurant.

TAMARACK LODGE RESORT
(P. 12, E-3, #47) Twin Lakes Road, Mammoth Lakes
619-934-2442
FACILITIES: 45 groomed km (with skating lane); rentals; lessons; lodging and restaurant.

Courtesy: Squaw Valley Ski Corp. (see California, p. 94).

For many people, Colorado means glitz, glamour, and glorious skiing. The state boasts 20% of the total annual skier visits in the USA, the most high-speed quads, and the greatest variety of dining, lodging, and cultural options. Not to mention over 22 feet of eiderdown-soft powder—and 300 days of sunshine—annually. ❄ The bonus of skiing Colorado is its rich frontier heritage: several areas are located in or near beautifully restored Victorian mining towns. ❄ Many resorts allow skiers to mix and match. The four areas of Summit County (A-Basin, Keystone, Breckenridge, and Copper Mountain), marketed together as "Ski the Summit," offer special multi-day lift tickets. The four ski areas owned by Aspen Skiing Company can be skied on one ticket. ❄ Don't overlook the so-called "Gems" of Colorado—smaller areas, many of which are larger and more varied than top resorts in other states, that offer microscopic lift lines and prices. You can also save money by staying in "satel-lite" towns like Frisco, Ouray, and Silverton, whose incentives include cheaper accommodations and lift tickets discounted by as much as 50%. ❄ Cross-country enthusiasts can enjoy the same pampering as downhillers, since many centers are either affiliated with the leading alpine areas or deluxe lodges and dude ranches. They can also make tracks amid the glorious scenery of Colorado's state parks and national forests and monuments. Few sensations match that of gliding past abandoned tail minings and ghost towns; the haunting ancient cliff dwellings of the Anasazi in the Four Corners region; the craggy moraines and glaciers of Rocky Mountain National Park; or the eerie, gnarled rock formations of the Garden of the Gods and Colorado National Monument. ❄ The best news for skiers may be the new Denver International Airport, where state-of-the-art facilities increased space mean fewer delays and cancellations due to weather.

ALPINE

ARAPAHOE BASIN
(P. 14, B-3, #1) U.S. 6, Keystone
800-222-0188; 303-468-4111 (snow)
SEASON: Nov. 15-June 1
ANNUAL SNOWFALL: 360"
TERRAIN: 61 trails over 490 acres; longest run 1.5 mi.; ◆◆ 25%; ◆ 25%; ▪ 40%; ● 10%
LIFTS: 5 (1 triple, 4 doubles); capacity, 6,066 per hour.
SUMMIT: 13,050'
VERTICAL: 2,270'
ACTIVITIES: Snowboarding; see Keystone below for rest.
FEATURES: USAA racing; child care; ski school; restaurant; rentals.
 Owned by Ralston Purina, America's highest ski area, with a base of 10,800', opened in 1945; some say it hasn't changed since (the lifts *are* ancient). A-Basin's devoted fans couldn't care less. They love the short lift lines, breathtaking views, above-timberline skiing, and wide-open bowls that seem on top of the world. This legendary, gnarly area is not for beginners. The howling winds and menacing clouds make for some heart-pounding adventures, as does the east wall with its plunging chutes and gullies. Intermediate and advanced skiers can push themselves on those lovely, stark, expansive bowls, which stay open well into June.

ARROWHEAD AT VAIL
(P. 14, B-3, #2) 0677 Sawatch Dr., Edwards
800-332-3029; 303-926-3029 (snow)
SEASON: Dec. 17-April 3
ANNUAL SNOWFALL: 140"
TERRAIN: 13 trails over 180 acres; longest run 2.5 mi.; ◆ 30%; ▪ 50%; ● 20%.
LIFTS: 2 (1 surface, 1 high-speed quad); capacity, NA per hour
SUMMIT: 9,100'
VERTICAL: 1,700'
ACTIVITIES: Snowmobiling; sleigh rides; ice skating.
FEATURES: Snowmaking 25%; child care; ski school; restaurants; rentals.
▶NORDIC: 8 mi. of groomed tracks; 303-926-3029; lessons; rentals.
 Built on private land, Arrowhead was designed to give a minimum number of people the maximum ski experience. Top-notch restaurants, uncrowded slopes, 1,700 uninterrupted vertical feet and state-of-the-art grooming make it seem much larger than it is. It's particularly good for families and beginners: for example, one child skies free when an adult purchases a multi-day lift ticket, and a complimentary group lesson is offered to anyone who buys a full-day ticket. With over 2,000 undeveloped acres owned by the mountain, and the Vail Valley nearby, Arrowhead may be a comer.

ASPEN HIGHLANDS
(P. 14, B-3, #3) 1600 Maroon Creek Rd., Aspen
800-356-8811; 303-925-5300 (snow)
SEASON: Nov. 25-April 10
ANNUAL SNOWFALL: 300"
TERRAIN: 78 trails over 555 acres; longest run 3.5 mi.; ◆◆ 15%; ◆ 14%; ▪ 48%; ● 23%.
LIFTS: 9 (7 doubles, 2 surfaces, 2 high-speed quads); capacity, 10,000 per hour.
SUMMIT: 11,800'
VERTICAL: 3,800'
ACTIVITIES: Snowboarding; snowmobiling; winter horseback riding; snowshoeing.
FEATURES: Snowmaking 20%; USAA racing; child care; ski school; restaurants; rentals.
▶NORDIC: see Aspen Mountain below.
 An era ended in 1993 when the Aspen Skiing Company purchased Highlands, the self-styled "maverick" ski area. Welcome changes include replacing two notoriously slow lifts with high-speed quads (this alone will attract greater crowds). The new owners promise Highlands' anti-establishment spirit will live on, in such enduring traditions as the freestyle competition held every Friday and the death-defying leap of the Ski Patrol over the Cloud Nine Picnic Hut deck (and startled skiers) daily at noon. Weather permitting, of course.

Highlands has a lot more to offer: the best views of the four Aspen ski areas, Colorado's longest vertical, great powder days, the hair-raising steeps of Steeplechase and Olympic Bowl, and equally fine intermediate terrain.

ASPEN MOUNTAIN
(P. 14, B-3, #4) 601 E. Dean St., Aspen
800-925-9000; 303-925-1221 (snow)
SEASON: Nov. 25-April 10
ANNUAL SNOWFALL: 300"
TERRAIN: 76 trails over 625 acres; longest run 3 mi.; ◆◆ 30%; ◆ 35%; ▪ 35%
LIFTS: 8 (1 high-speed quad, 1 gondola, 4 doubles, 2 quads); capacity, 10,775 per hour.
SUMMIT: 11,212'
VERTICAL: 3,267'
ACTIVITIES: Ice skating; snow-cat skiing; snowmobiling; winter horseback riding; sleigh rides; hot air ballooning.
FEATURES: Snowmaking 33%; USAA racing; child care; ski school; restaurants; rentals.
▶NORDIC: Aspen Touring Center; 303-925-2145; 81 groomed km., 265 total; lessons; rentals.
 Aspen. The name conjures up images of the rich and famous enjoying chic boutiques and champagne cocktails, of celebrities who need only be identified by first name: Kurt and Goldie, Jane and Ted, Don and Melanie. It's all true; even the streets, lined with impeccably maintained Victorians, are an eye-popping display of conspicuous consumption. But "real people" come to—and enjoy—Aspen,

STATBOX

Tourism: 800-265-6723
Time zone: Mountain
Population: 3,294,394
Square miles: 104,247

Average annual precipitation: 15"
Highest elevation: 14,431'
Lowest elevation: 3,350'

thanks to a surprising range of modest lodging and dining options. And Aspen has always been a mecca for countercultural types. Events like the Aspen Music Festival draw longhairs in droves, and veteran journalist Hunter S. Thompson is an Aspen institution (you can sometimes catch him at the Woody Creek Tavern).

As for the skiing, Ajax (the local name for the mountain, after the original silver mine) remains a definitive test of skiing ability, quickly separating the great from the merely good. There are no beginner runs. The narrow mountain is really a series of fearsomely precipitous ridges and gullies requiring the utmost concentration and pinpoint navigation. Intermediates should head for the knob circling the summit and the valleys between the ridges, where they can practice on Ruthie's Run, Buckhorn, International, or Copper Bowl. Bell Mountain, Kristi's, Hyrup's, Cone Dump, and the ironically named Trainer Hill provide enough thrilling—and chilling—descents for even the most jaded expert.

The Nordic trail network linking Aspen to Snowmass is dubbed by locals "Aerobic Avenue," and it does provide a high-impact workout to go along with the inspiring vistas. Free of charge, it's the best (perhaps only) bargain in town. The terrain and scenery vary; tracks meander through meadows and stands of evergreen, past babbling brooks and elk herds. There are both wide "corduroy-weal" lanes for skaters and double grooves for diagonalists. The flat Rio Grande trail and Aspen and Snowmass golf courses are perfect for beginners; more experienced gliders will adore the 20-km Owl Creek trail.

BEAVER CREEK RESORT

(P. 14, B-3, #5) Avon
303-949-5750; 303-476-4889 (snow)
SEASON: Nov. 20-April 17
ANNUAL SNOWFALL: 330"
TERRAIN: 61 trails over 1,125 acres; longest run 2.75 mi.; ◆ 43%; ■ 39%; ● 18%.
LIFTS: 10 (2 high-speed quads, 4 triples, 4 doubles); capacity, 19,075 per hour.
SUMMIT: 11,440'
VERTICAL: 3,440'
ACTIVITIES: Snowboarding; snowmobiling; ice skating; snowshoeing; skate skiing; heliskiing; hot air ballooning.
FEATURES: Snowmaking 30%; USAA racing; child care; ski school; restaurants; rentals.
▶NORDIC: Beaver Creek Cross-Country Ski Center; 303-845-5313; 30 groomed km; rentals; lessons.

Elegant Beaver Creek is finally emerging from big sister Vail's shadow as a premier ski area. The resort anticipates a guest's every need, with some of the USA's finest on-site dining and lodging. Guests enjoy the unhurried pace and quiet pampering. Lacking Vail's mystique, Beaver Creek's slopes are often wonderfully deserted even on the valley's busiest days. It also has tremendous family appeal, with such model developments as "Children's Adventure Zones," where kids slalom around Old West sets of ghost towns and Indian villages.

The area built its reputation on immaculate grooming and snowmaking, making skiing here the stuff of dreams. Seventy-five more acres of intermediate tree-skiing recently opened in the Harriet and Grouse Glade areas. Other classic cruisers are Latigo, Centennial, and Larkspur Bowl. But don't overlook the challenging ungroomed skiing on Grouse Mountain and the aptly-named Birds of Prey—mogul heaven on powder days.

The state-of-the-art Nordic facility at McCoy Park includes a skating track and biathlon course, with primarily intermediate difficulty.

BRECKENRIDGE SKI RESORT

(P. 14, B-3, #6) 1599 Summit County Rd. 3, Breckenridge
800-221-1091; 303-453-6118 (snow)
SEASON: Nov. 13-April 17
ANNUAL SNOWFALL: 255"
TERRAIN: 126 trails over 1,915 acres; longest run 3.5 mi.; ◆ 55%; ■ 27%; ● 18%.
LIFTS: 16 (4 high-speed quads, 1 triple, 8 doubles, 3 surface); capacity, 24,430 per hour.
SUMMIT: 12,998'
VERTICAL: 3,398'
ACTIVITIES: Snowboarding; ice skating; telemarking; snow skating; snowmobiling; sleigh rides.
FEATURES: Snowmaking 18%; USAA racing; Child care; ski school; restaurants; rentals.
▶NORDIC: Breckenridge Nordic Center; 303-453-6855; 23 groomed km; rentals; lessons.

Ralston Purina purchased Breckenridge in 1993. Plans to link it more closely with Keystone/A-Basin will create a mega-resort with eight mountains, 276 trails, and 4,142 acres of skiing. Breckenridge itself had already completed expansion to a fourth mountain, Peak 7, which offers steep bowls, twisting chutes, and bumptious bumps. This complements the expert terrain of the Back Bowls off Peak 8, the North Face of Peak 9 (with the infamous Devil's Crotch, Hades, and Inferno), and the bucking moguls of Mustang and Dark Rider on Peak 10. But Breckenridge isn't for experts only: Peak 10 also offers some great cruisers and Peak 8's varied terrain includes a sizable beginner's area. The biggest drawback is the poling required to get from one mountain to the other, crowned by the hike onto Peak 7. Be sure to leave plenty of time to meet your friends.

Settled during the gold rush of 1859, Breckenridge is the oldest continuously occupied town on the Western Slope (save for a brief stint on the offical ghost town itinerary in the 1950s). It comprises one of Colorado's largest National Historic Districts, though today it's hard to imagine that the pretty pastel Victorian false fronts and gingerbreads once housed gambling parlors and bordellos. But Breckenridge also prides itself on looking forward: It was the first major Colorado area to welcome snowboarders and hosts the World Snowboarding Championships annually. Known for its friendly, approachable bars, Breckenridge's après ski scene is considered top-notch.

The mostly gentle Nordic trails wind through spruce stands and open meadows, with amazing vistas of several fourteeners, a Rockies term for peaks over 14,000'.

COPPER MOUNTAIN RESORT

(P. 14, B-3, #7) I-70, exit 195, Copper Mountain
800-458-8386; 303-968-2100 (snow)
SEASON: Nov. 15-April 24
ANNUAL SNOWFALL: 256"
TERRAIN: 98 trails over 1,360 acres; longest run 2.8 mi.; ◆◆ 16%; ◆ 35%; ■ 27%; ● 22%.
LIFTS: 20 (2 high-speed quads, 6 triples, 8 doubles, 4 surface); capacity, 28,250 per hour.
SUMMIT: 12,313'
VERTICAL: 2,760'
ACTIVITIES: Snowboarding; telemarking; heliskiing; ice skating; sleigh rides.
FEATURES: Snowmaking 20%; USAA racing; child care; ski school; restaurants; rentals.
▶NORDIC: Copper Mountain / Trak Cross-Country Center; 303-968-2882, ext. 6342; 25 groomed km; rentals; lessons.

There's a saying in Summit County: Copper for skiing, Breckenridge for lodging, and Keystone for food. Everything at Copper is designed to keep skiers happy. The modern development may be an eyesore to some, but it's admirably compact and completely self-contained, with enough variety of lodging, dining, and activities to suit all ages and pocketbooks. The area's award-winning design is creatively contoured to the natural terrain; the layout separates the beginner, intermediate, and expert sections (right, center, and left respectively, as you face the mountain), meaning experts needn't slalom around beginners who can't get into trouble. Copper also offers 350 acres of guided adventure skiing for die-hards who can't get enough thrills and spills in Spaulding Bowl or the Enchanted Forest. Families will appreciate the superb day-care center and ski school. Nordic skiers have a choice between groomed tracks and skating lanes of varying difficulty. Not content to rest on its laurels, Copper is planning a 500-acre expansion on the back side of Union Peak.

CRESTED BUTTE MOUNTAIN RESORT

(P. 14, C-3, #8) 12 Snowmass Rd., Mt. Crested Butte
800-927-8883; 303-349-2323 (snow)
SEASON: Nov. 19-April 3
ANNUAL SNOWFALL: 260"
TERRAIN: 86 trails over 1,162 acres; longest run 2.6 mi.; ◆◆ 47%; ◆ 10%; ■ 30%; ● 13%; plus Extreme Limits, 550 expert-only acres.
LIFTS: 13 (1 high-speed quad, 3 triples, 5 doubles, 4 surface); capacity, 16,610 per hour.
SUMMIT: 12,162'
VERTICAL: 3,062' (2,775' via lift)

USA SNAPSHOTS®

A look at statistics that shape the sports world

Keeping slopes snowy

Percentage of U.S. ski areas with snow-making equipment:

83%

90%
80%
70%
60%
50%
40%
30%
20%
10%
0%

1980-81   1991-92

Source: Ski Industries America   By Sam Ward, USA TODAY

ACTIVITIES: Snowboarding; telemarking; dog sledding; snowmobiling; hot air ballooning; winter horseback riding.
FEATURES: Snowmaking 20%; USAA racing; child care; ski school; restaurants; rentals.
▶NORDIC: Crested Butte Nordic Ski Center; 512 2nd Street; 303-349-6201; 29 groomed km. over 3 track networks; rentals; lessons.

Crested Butte views itself as the downhome alternative to more upscale resorts. (The area once had the audacity to call itself "Aspen like it used to be and Vail like it never was.") Iconoclastic? You bet. Crested Butte is a countercultural haven. Part of its charm is the quirky contrast of a Victorian, Old West ambiance with a modern nonconformist attitude. Not many furs here; bellbottoms and tie dyes are more likely in this low-key, friendly resort. The town of Crested Butte is a National Historic Landmark District, with a surprising number of fine boutiques and galleries, plus some of Colorado's best restaurants. The mountain village, three miles away, is standard functional 60s architecture.

So are the lifts; thankfully they replaced the creaky old Silver Queen with a high-speed quad (another is on the way). And perhaps because Crested Butte is still off the beaten track, it initiated a daring, successful scheme in 1991—Ski Free the first month of the season. That—and the predominance and variety of cruiser runs—now attract a loyal following, with a high percentage of Texans. "The Butte" also hosts the U.S. Extreme Skiing Championships: The heart-stopping runs on The North Face and Extreme Limits are finally putting this superb area on the map. In the summer, Crested Butte reigns as Colorado's mountain biking capital.

The affiliated Nordic center offers mostly rolling terrain through aspen groves with enthralling alpine views. The only challenging section is the steeps on Gibson Ridge. Crested Butte also sparked the 70s telemarking renaissance; this is the best place to learn that demanding yet graceful discipline.

CUCHARA VALLEY SKI RESORT
(P. 14, D-4, #9) 946 Panadero Ave., Cuchara
800-227-4436; 719-742-3163 (snow)
SEASON: Dec. 16-April 2
ANNUAL SNOWFALL: 200"
TERRAIN: 24 trails over 230 acres; longest run 2.5 mi.; ◆ 20%; ▪ 40%; ● 40%.
LIFTS: 4 (1 triple, 3 doubles); capacity, 5,000 per hour.
SUMMIT: 10,810'
VERTICAL: 1,600'
ACTIVITIES: Snowboarding; telemarking; horse-drawn wagon

Courtesy: Ski The Summit (see Colorado, p. 96).

rides; snowmobiling.
FEATURES: Snowmaking 74%; USAA racing; child care; ski school; restaurants; rentals.
▶NORDIC: 10 groomed km; rentals; lessons.

This intimate people-oriented area, set in a tranquil get-away-from-it-all part of the state, is ideal for families and beginners. Advanced skiers will be pleasantly surprised by El Diablo and The Burn, a new ungroomed 40-acre double diamond bowl. The limited but scenic cross-country trails are accessed from the summit.

ELDORA MOUNTAIN RESORT
(P. 14, B-4, #10) State Route 119, Nederland
303-440-8700; 303-440-8800 (snow)
SEASON: Nov. 8-April 24
ANNUAL SNOWFALL: 185"
TERRAIN: 43 trails over 386 acres; longest run 2 mi.; ◆ 25%; ▪ 55%; ● 20%.
LIFTS: 8 (1 triple, 5 doubles, 2 surface); capacity, 6,150 per hour.
SUMMIT: 10,600'
VERTICAL: 1,400'
ACTIVITIES: Snowboarding; telemarking; night skiing.
FEATURES: Snowmaking 48%; USAA racing; child care; ski school; restaurants; rentals.
▶NORDIC: Eldora Nordic Center; 45 groomed and back-country km; rentals; lessons.

Convenient Eldora is a favorite day trip of Boulderites who enjoy the surprisingly varied terrain. The Front Side offers mellow cruising, the Corona Side tricky glades and steeps. The mountain recently upgraded lifts (including adding the new triple) and snowmaking capability. The Nordic trails wind through glorious Roosevelt National Forest.

HESPERUS SKI AREA
(P. 14, D-2, #11) U.S. 160, Durango
303-259-3711
SEASON: Dec. 3-April 3
ANNUAL SNOWFALL: 200"
TERRAIN: 18 trails over 80 acres; longest run 1 mile; ◆ 30%; ▪ 40%; ● 30%.
LIFTS: 2 (1 double, 1 surface); capacity, NA per hour.
SUMMIT: 8,880'
VERTICAL: 700'
ACTIVITIES: Snowboarding; telemarking; night skiing.
FEATURES: Ski school; restaurants; rentals.

Hesperus is known as the learning mountain for northern New Mexicans before they attack the big boys. It is largely ungroomed, so it can offer experts some hellacious skiing and boarding for an area its size. It also boasts the only night skiing in Southwest Colorado. The Navajos used the mountain as a directional landmark and regard it as a sacred peak.

HOWELSEN SKI AREA
(P. 14, A-3, #12) Lincoln Avenue, Steamboat Springs

303-879-8499
SEASON: Nov. 24-March 25
ANNUAL SNOWFALL: 250"
TERRAIN: 13 trails over 110 acres; longest run 1 mile; ◆ 50%; ▪ 25%; ● 25%.
LIFTS: 3 (1 double, 2 surface); capacity, 2,085 per hour.
SUMMIT: 7,136'
VERTICAL: 440'
ACTIVITIES: Ski jumping; bobsledding (call 303-879-2170); ice skating; night skiing.
FEATURES: Snowmaking 75%; FIS ski jumping; ski school; rentals.

Founded in 1914 by Norwegian Carl Howelsen, this is the oldest ski area in Colorado. While the skiing is basic, Howelsen is the preeminent ski jumping facility (and Olympic training ground) in the USA. It also offers the "Champagne of Thrills" bobsled course.

KEYSTONE RESORT
(P. 14, B-3, #13) 22010 Highway 6, Keystone
800-222-0188; 303-468-4111 (snow)
SEASON: Oct. 31-April 15
ANNUAL SNOWFALL: 230"
TERRAIN: 91 trails over 1,737 acres; longest run 3 mi.; ◆ 53%; ▪ 34%; ● 13%.
LIFTS: 19 (2 gondolas, 4 quads—3 high-speed, 3 triples, 6 doubles, 4 surface); capacity, 26,250 per hour.
SUMMIT: 11,980'
VERTICAL: 2,680'
ACTIVITIES: Snowboarding; ice skating; sleigh rides; snowmobiling; night skiing.
FEATURES: Snowmaking 49%; USAA racing; child care; ski school; restaurants; rentals.
▶NORDIC: Keystone Nordic Center at Ski Tip Lodge; 18 groomed km and 57 backcountry km; rentals; lessons.

Keystone Corporation (parent Ralston Purina) has become an industry giant now that it owns three Summit County areas, all of which can be skied on one ticket (hardcores can start at A-Basin and finish up with America's largest night skiing operation on Keystone Mountain). Keystone itself is a self-contained ultra-modern development, designed to blend harmoniously with its surroundings. The Keystone Resort has pursued an aggressive policy of environmentally sensitive expansion, opening up the North Peak and the Outback in recent years, and more than doubling the terrain and lift capacity. The ski school is among Colorado's best, including the high-performance Steve and Phil Mahre Training Center Intensive Workshop—the world champion Mahre twins taught their methods to the instructors.

Three mountains comprise the Keystone area, offering a superbly balanced blend of skiing for all levels. Keystone Peak was already the finest intermediate mountain in Colorado. Now, thanks to The Outback, advanced and expert skiers have nothing to complain about, while North Peak's sharp pitches are ideal for working on technique. Après ski, the restaurants are Summit County's finest.

LOVELAND SKI AREA

(P. 14, B-3, #14) I-70, exit 216, Georgetown
800-225-5683; 303-569-3203 (snow)
SEASON: Oct. 15-May 15
ANNUAL SNOWFALL: 375"
TERRAIN: 60 trails over 836 acres; longest run 1.5 mi.; ◆ 27%; ▪ 48%; ● 25%.
LIFTS: 10 (1 quad, 2 triples, 5 doubles, 2 surface); capacity, 12,550 per hour
SUMMIT: 12,280'
VERTICAL: 1,680'
ACTIVITIES: Snowboarding.
FEATURES: Snowmaking 18%; USAA racing; child care; ski school; restaurants; rentals.
 Loveland is Colorado's 11th-largest ski area—bigger than the legendary Aspen. It's also highly accessible (the closest major area to Denver, just over the Continental Divide), and stays open later seasonally than any other area save A-Basin. It even offers a money-back guarantee: If you're not pleased with the conditions, get a full refund by 10 A.M. So why isn't it better known? Aficionados rave about the short lift lines and great snow. Beginners and families head for the Loveland Valley section, which has its own facilities, including rental shop, restaurants, and a ski school. Stronger skiers play amid the chutes and above-timberline bowls of European-style Loveland Basin. The more adventuresome will enjoy the powder and protected bowls of 150-acre Zip Basin. And true ski-maniacs can always head to perilous Loveland Pass or St. Mary's Glacier (not part of the area), where intrepid shredders and extremists hike up and bomb down.

MONARCH SKI RESORT

(P. 14, C-4, #15) #1 Powder Place (22720 U.S. Highway 50), Monarch
800-332-3668; 719-539-3578 (snow)
SEASON: Nov. 20-April 10
ANNUAL SNOWFALL: 350"
TERRAIN: 54 trails over 637 acres; longest run 2 mi.; ◆ 28%; ▪ 46%; ● 26%.
LIFTS: 4 (4 doubles); capacity, 4,650 per hour.
SUMMIT: 11,950'
VERTICAL: 1,160'
ACTIVITIES: Snowboarding; telemarking; ice skating; snowmobiling.
FEATURES: USAA racing; child

BACKCOUNTRY COLORADO

Colorado's rugged terrain lends itself to a range of backcountry adventures, from ski touring to snowcat and heliskiing. The state offers four of the finest hut-to-hut systems in the country, with the Tenth Mountain Division Hut Association, which links Vail and Aspen (303-925-5775), leading the way. These occasionally grueling excursions are recommended for advanced skiers in good physical condition only. If you're not with a guided tour, be sure to carry sufficient food, water, and clothing and study the terrain beforehand.

During World War II, the Tenth Mountain Division trained for alpine combat in Europe in freezing temperatures and blinding conditions. Their endurance is commemorated by a system of 12 huts spaced three to eight miles apart. Surprisingly comfortable and fully outfitted, each sleeps up to 16. They include mattresses—and pillows!—a propane stove and utensils for cooking, and woodburning stoves and cut wood for heating. Summit County is developing a series of huts to link up with the network. Among the reliable outfitters running tours are Paragon Guides (Vail, 303-926-5299) and Aspen Alpine Guides (Aspen, 303-925-6680).

The other great Aspen backcountry network is the Alfred A. Braun Hut System (Aspen, 303-925-7345)—arguably even more strenuous than the Tenth Mountain Division System—connecting Aspen with Crested Butte. The six spartan huts sleep eight to 12. This route is prone to avalanche (always check with the Forest Service rangers for prevailing conditions on unguided tours), but many consider the views of the Maroon Bells worth the risk.

The Never Summer Nordic Yurt System (Fort Collins, 303-484-3903) winds through the pristine Colorado State Forest, offering splendid views of the Never Summer range and the Continental Divide. The terrain is of moderate difficulty.

The best learning network is the admirable San Juan Hut System (Telluride, 303-728-6935). Prior experience is not necessary (though preferable), and groups are limited to eight people. The terrain is less hazardous, the scenery is stirring, and the huts compare favorably to the "five-star" luxury of the Tenth Mountain Division System.

Heliskiing is rapidly increasing in popularity, though it remains exorbitantly priced. But the opportunity to ski fresh powder is unmatched. Full-day outings usually include four or five runs totaling 10,000 vertical feet. Two reputable companies run tours: Telluride Helitrax (303-728-4904) and Colorado Heli-Ski (Breckenridge, 303-668-5600); the latter is one of the few outfits in the world that can accommodate disabled skiers.

Another growing trend is snowcat skiing. In addition to the backcountry options listed above at Copper Mountain and Ski Cooper, Aspen Powder Tours (303-925-1227) and Steamboat Powder Cats (303-879-5188) explore virgin terrain on the back sides of their respective mountains.

But unquestionably, the best place to learn powder skiing in Colorado, if not the entire country, is Irwin Lodge (303-349-5140), a cozy aerie nestled 10 miles outside Crested Butte that receives an average of over 500 inches annually! The snowcats access more than 2,000 vertical feet, which can be negotiated by strong intermediates. Instructors have included gold medalists in the World Powder Championships. The lodge also offers fun snowmobiling tours.

care; ski school; restaurants; rentals.
▶NORDIC: 3 groomed km; rentals; lessons.
 Monarch has garnered several Colorado Tourism Hospitality Awards due to its friendly, efficient service. The Skiing Improvement Center is especially noted for its KidSki program, considered a model for the industry. Powder hounds will love the uncrowded, untracked runs, which provide a fair amount of variety though nothing really difficult.

POWDERHORN SKI CORPORATION

(P. 14, B-2, #16) Highway 65, Mesa
800-241-6997; 303-242-5637 (snow)
SEASON: Nov. 25-April 4
ANNUAL SNOWFALL: 250"
TERRAIN: 27 trails over 300 acres; longest run 2 mi.; ◆ 20%; ▪ 60%; ● 20%.
LIFTS: 4 (1 quad, 2 doubles, 1 surface); capacity, 4,370 per hour.
SUMMIT: 9,800'
VERTICAL: 1,600'
ACTIVITIES: Snowboarding; telemarking; snowmobiling; sleigh rides.
FEATURES: Snowmaking 16%; child care; ski school; restaurants; rentals.
▶NORDIC: Nordic Center at the Summit on Grand Mesa; 12 groomed km; rentals; lessons.
 Powderhorn is perched atop the Grand Mesa, the world's highest flattop mountain. The runs follow the fall line of the mesa, scooping natural bowls and glades that prove more challenging than they first appear. But the best reason to ski here is the sensational panorama of the multihued Bookcliffs and the fine vineyards of the Grand Valley below. The cross-country skiing, while not terribly strenuous, skirts hundreds of frozen lakes amid towering stands of aspen and spruce.

PURGATORY-DURANGO SKI RESORT

(P. 14, D-2, #17) #1 Skier Place, (Highway 550, 25 mi. N of Durango)
SEASON: Nov. 24 -April 4
ANNUAL SNOWFALL: 250"
TERRAIN: 70 trails over 692 acres; longest run 2 mi.; ◆ 26%; ▪ 50%; ● 24%.
LIFTS: 9 (4 triples, 5 doubles); capacity, 12,180 per hour.
SUMMIT: 10,822'
VERTICAL: 2,029'
ACTIVITIES: Snowboarding; telemarking; snowmobiling; sleigh rides.
FEATURES: Snowmaking 22%; USAA racing; child care; ski

school; restaurants; rentals.

►NORDIC: Purgatory Cross-Country Center; 3001 W. Third Avenue, Durango; 16 groomed km; rentals; lessons.
Purgatory-Durango narrowly averted bankruptcy in 1993 when a deal was worked out enabling the area to operate as usual—at least until 1995. (Too bad they won't have the money to overhaul the archaic lifts.) Hard-core skiers have dubbed Purgatory "Pleasant Ridge," since it offers surprisingly few challenges for an area its size. Actually, the rolling terrain is unusual and intriguing: lots of humps and dips, and pitches followed by flats, which makes it ideal learning terrain for both beginners and intermediates. There are also some terrific powder stashes off Lift 3 that provide a good workout. Purgatory is about as laid-back as it gets; popular with families, cowboys, and college kids on break, it lives up to its ad campaign, "You don't have to be a celebrity to be treated like a star." (Look for Uncelebrities Week: "No black tie galas, no wine tastings, no photo ops.") Kids under 12 ski free when an adult buys a ticket, and free first-timer lessons in skiing and snowboarding are included with the purchase of a lift ticket. Nearby Durango is a riproaring yet sophisticated old railroad town that serves as the gateway to the Four Corners region, including the beautiful ancient cliff dwellings of Mesa Verde National Park.
The Nordic trails weave through the thirteeners (peaks over 13,000 feet) of the Needles Range. There's also backcountry ski touring north of the resort along Molas Pass.

SILVERCREEK SKI AREA
(P. 14, B-3, #18) 1000 Village Rd., SilverCreek
800-448-9458; 303-887-3384 (snow)
SEASON: Dec. 7-April 3
ANNUAL SNOWFALL: 180"
TERRAIN: 25 trails over 208 acres; longest run 1 mile; ♦ 20%; ■ 50%; ● 30%.
LIFTS: 4 (2 triples, 1 double, 1 surface); capacity, 5,400 per hour.
SUMMIT: 9,202'
VERTICAL: 1,000'
ACTIVITIES: Snowboarding; telemarking; ice skating; snowmobiling; sleigh rides.
FEATURES: Snowmaking 40%; child care; ski school; restaurants; rentals.
►NORDIC: See Devil's Thumb Ranch, Grand Lake Touring Center, and Snow Mountain Ranch below.
SilverCreek is earning a reputation for its family-oriented approach. Its personalized service extends to free lollipop races, free ice cream parties, free pizza nights, and free skiing in January for kids. It also offers "Guaranteed Start to Ski Vacations or Your Money Back." If you're not

tackling the beginner runs with confidence within one day you get a refund—or additional lessons. More experienced skiers will enjoy the wide intermediate trails down the East Mountain and the bump runs off the West Mountain.

SKI COOPER
(P. 14, B-3, #19) Highway 24, 8 mi. N of Leadville
719-486-3684; 719-486-2277 (snow)
SEASON: Nov. 20-April 3
ANNUAL SNOWFALL: 250"
TERRAIN: 26 trails over 385 acres; longest run 1.5 mi.; ♦ 30%; ■ 40%; ● 30%.
LIFTS: 4 (1 triple, 1 double, 2 surface); capacity, 3,420 per hour.
SUMMIT: 11,700'
VERTICAL: 1,200'
ACTIVITIES: Snowcat skiing; telemarking.
FEATURES: USAA racing; child care; ski school; restaurant; rentals.
►NORDIC: Ski Cooper Nordic Center; 719-486-1750; 30 groomed km; rentals; lessons.
Affordable Cooper is an historic mountain, where the Tenth Mountain Division trained for alpine combat during World War II. Its lodging base is Leadville, a great old mining town 10 miles away, with over 300 buildings on the National Historic Register. Skiing is solidly beginner and intermediate, but advanced and expert skiers can snowcat ski on 1,800 ungroomed acres of powder on Chicago Ridge to an elevation of 12,850 feet.

SKI SUNLIGHT
(P. 14, B-2, #20) 10901 Road 117, Glenwood Springs
800-221-0098; 303-945-7491 (snow)
SEASON: Nov. 24-April 10
ANNUAL SNOWFALL: 200"
TERRAIN: 45 trails over 465 acres; longest run 2.5 mi.; ♦♦ 5%; ♦ 20%; ■ 55%; ● 20%
LIFTS: 4 (1 triple, 2 doubles, 1 surface); capacity, 4,600 per hour.
SUMMIT: 9,895'
VERTICAL: 2,010'
ACTIVITIES: Snowboarding; telemarking.
FEATURES: Snowmaking 2%; USAA racing; child care; ski school; restaurants; rentals.
►NORDIC: Ski Sunlight Cross-Country and Nordic Center; 29 groomed km (with skating lane); rentals; lessons.
This affordable area outside Glenwood Springs offers good value, virtually nonexistent lift lines, stunning views, and fairly varied terrain. Sunlight opened the East Ridge section in 1993, providing the only truly demanding skiing, with grades of up to 52%. Snowboarders love the mountain,

where they can catch "radical air." Sunlight hosts several snowboarding competitions and includes a snowboard terrain garden, made up of natural obstacles, a rail, half pipe, and air jump.
The Nordic center is popular for the inspiring vistas of William's Peak, Sunlight Peak, and Compass Mountain.

SNOWMASS SKI AREA
(P. 14, B-3, #21) 40 Carriage Way Rd. (at Owl Creek Road), Snowmass Village
800-598-2005; 303-923-2000 (snow)
SEASON: Nov. 25-April 10
ANNUAL SNOWFALL: 300"
TERRAIN: 72 trails over 2,500 acres; longest run 4 mi.; ♦♦ 21%; ♦ 18%; ■ 51%; ● 10%.
LIFTS: 16 (5 high-speed quads, 2 triples, 7 doubles, 2 surface); capacity, 23,000 per hour
SUMMIT: 11,835'
VERTICAL: 3,612'
ACTIVITIES: Snowboarding; telemarking; sleigh rides; dog sledding; hot air ballooning.
FEATURES: Snowmaking 2%; USAA racing; child care; ski school; restaurants; rentals.
►NORDIC: Snowmass Club Touring Center; 303-923-3148; rentals; lessons.
Snowmass is often called Aspen's "family" area. All ages do enjoy the self-contained modern development, whose amenities and facilities are beginning to rival those of her chic sister. With over 50% of its terrain rated intermediate, Snowmass is considered a premier cruising mountain; the silky runs off the Big Burn lift are justly famous. But people forget that this sprawling area is four times the size of Ajax at Aspen, with nearly triple its double diamond terrain. One look at the plunging chutes of Hanging Valley should settle (or unsettle) the matter once and for all. Recent improvements feature two more high-speed quads and a snowboarding transition park including a tortuous new half pipe, several quarter pipes, and a fun box, all complementing Colorado's longest half pipe. It's part of an ambitious five-year plan that will include a gondola and still more terrain (you can already get lost between its five mountains if you don't study the trail map carefully). Snowmass shares the country's finest Nordic system with Aspen.

STEAMBOAT SKI & RESORT CORPORATION
(P. 14, A-3, #22) 2305 Mt. Werner Circle, Steamboat Springs
800-922-2722; 303-879-6111 (snow)
SEASON: Nov. 25-April 10
ANNUAL SNOWFALL: 325"
TERRAIN: 106 trails over 2,500 acres; longest run 3 mi.; ♦ 31;

■ 54%; ● 15%.
LIFTS: 20 (1 gondola, 3 quads— 2 high-speed, 6 triples, 8 doubles, 2 surface); capacity, 30,000 per hour.
SUMMIT: 10,585'
VERTICAL: 3,685'
ACTIVITIES: Snowboarding; telemarking; ski touring; snow skating; snowmobiling; sleigh rides; dog sledding; hot air ballooning; ice skating.
FEATURES: Snowmaking 15%; USAA racing; child care; ski school; restaurants; rentals.
►NORDIC: Steamboat Touring Center; Steamboat Springs; 303-879-8180, also 303-879-0740 for individual properties offering skiing on their property; rentals; lessons.
Steamboat is becoming an increasingly hot destination; devotees appreciate the superlative skiing and down-home Western appeal. While the mountain village is a plastic collection of deluxe condos, trendy boutiques, and fern bars, the town itself, a 10-minute drive away, offers a refreshing change of pace from glitzier resorts. Despite attempts to gussy it up, Steamboat Springs remains a cowtown at heart, a ranching community where studs and chaps are sold for use and not as souvenirs. The rodeo circuit is still a big draw in summer and galleries showcase Western art and collectibles.
Steamboat is also known as "Ski Town USA" for the more than 30 athletes it has sent to the Winter Olympics. The most famous is undoubtedly Billy Kidd, silver medalist in the 1964 slalom, who conducts tours of the mountain when he's around. Following in his tracks (and that bobbing 10-gallon hat) is tremendous fun. His Kidd Center for Performance Skiing is one of the best places to learn disciplines like powder, mogul, and tree skiing, as well as racing techniques. The area also earns raves for its comprehensive children's programs, including Kids Ski Free.
The terrain is extremely varied, especially for beginners and intermediates, with Storm Peak and Sunshine Bowl being favorites. Experts won't find many true steeps, but connoisseurs of tree and glade skiing agree Steamboat's rank among the best in America, creating a natural slalom course on such runs as The Ridge and Crowtrack. Afterwards, you can soak your weary bones in one of the many revitaling hot springs that give the town its name.
The Nordic skiing is limited, though the scenery is sublime, winding around Fish Creek and over to the Strawberry Park Natural Hot Springs (a particularly romantic jaunt by moonlight). There is also fine backcountry skiing at Rabbit Ears Pass. The Nordic center is managed by Sven Wiik, a former coach of the U.S. Olympic team.

TELLURIDE SKI RESORT

(P. 14, C-2, #23) Telluride
800-525-3455; 303-728-3614 (snow)

SEASON: Nov. 24-April 10
ANNUAL SNOWFALL: 300″
TERRAIN: 65 trails over 1,120 acres; longest run 3 mi.; ◆◆ 32%; ◆ 0%; ■ 47; ● 21%.
LIFTS: 10 (1 high-speed quad, 2 triples, 6 doubles, 1 surface); capacity, 10,000 per hour.
SUMMIT: 12,247′
VERTICAL: 3,522′
ACTIVITIES: Snowboarding; tele-marking; ice skating; ice climbing; heliskiing; sleigh rides; snowmobiling; hot air ballooning; hut-to-hut ski touring.
FEATURES: Snowmaking 15%; USAA racing; child care; ski school; restaurants; rentals.
▶NORDIC: Telluride Nordic Center; 52 groomed km; rentals; lessons.

Victorian Telluride, tucked like a jewel into a narrow box canyon, was once so inaccessible, despera-does like Butch Cassidy (who robbed his first bank here) used it as a hideout. The rugged surround-ing terrain still attracts macho men—and women—seeking an adrenaline rush by skiing, snow-boarding, climbing, or mountain biking the steep chutes and inclines. Telluride has become the standard by which good skiers judge themselves, on legendary runs like The Plunge and The Spiral Staircase, and the 400 acres of "ulti-mate" skiing on Gold Hill. Beginners will be pleasantly sur-prised by its expansive learning section, but intermediates should steer clear since the high, adver-tised percentage of moderate runs is misleading; they'd be rated advanced almost anywhere else, and Black and blue will more likely refer to bruises than the trails. The cross-country network provides lit-tle challenge, although the high mesa views are certainly incompa-rable.

The town is often called Colorado's prettiest, with gorgeous lacy gin-gerbreads and picture-postcard views. But locals are divided about the steadily growing, sterile Mountain Village (the latest devel-opment is a gondola from town for the 1994-1995 season). Despite its lingering hippie trappings, Telluride is marketing itself as another upscale alternative to Aspen and Vail. Its fans appreciate not only the unparalleled skiing and atmosphere, but the wide variety of cultural opportunities throughout the year. It deserves inclusion in *Guinness* under the heading "Most Annual Festivals," ranging from the prestigious Telluride Film, Jazz and Bluegrass Festivals to hang gliding and wild mushroom festivals.

TIEHACK

(P. 14, B-3, #24) 37800 Highway 82, Aspen
800-925-9000; 303-925-1221 (snow)

SEASON: Dec. 11-April 3
ANNUAL SNOWFALL: 200″
TERRAIN: 45 trails over 410 acres; longest run 3 mi.; ◆ 26%; ■ 39%; ● 35%.
LIFTS: 7 (1 high-speed quad, 5 doubles, 1 surface); capacity, 7,500 per hour.
SUMMIT: 9,900′
VERTICAL: 2,030′
ACTIVITIES: Snowboarding; tele-marking; snow skating; ski touring.
FEATURES: Snowmaking 27%; child care; ski school; restau-rants; rentals.
▶NORDIC: see Aspen and Snowmass

In an effort to change Tiehack's "learning" mountain reputation, the Aspen Skico dropped Buttermilk from the title and installed a new high-speed quad and snowboard terrain garden, to go with the half-pipe at Spruce Run. West Buttermilk still sets the stan-dard by which beginners' areas measure themselves; thoughtful touches include the Max the Moose express, which picks kids up at Aspen area hotels, leaving their parents to fend for themselves. But the Tiehack side features some beautifully cut advanced intermedi-ate runs (as well as lingering pow-der dumps), enough to make that "sissy" reputation undeserved.

VAIL

(P. 14, B-3, #25) 600 Lionshead Mall, Vail
303-949-5750; 303-476-4888 (snow)

SEASON: Nov. 13-April 17
ANNUAL SNOWFALL: 335″
TERRAIN: 121 trails over 4,014 acres; longest run 4.5 mi.; ◆ 32%; ■ 36%; ● 32%; plus 2,614 acres of intermediate-expert skiing in the Back Bowls.
LIFTS: 25 (8 high-speed quads, 1 gondola, 2 quads, 3 triples, 6 doubles, 5 surface); capacity, 40,000 per hour.
SUMMIT: 11,450′
VERTICAL: 3,250′
ACTIVITIES: Snowboarding; tele-marking; ice skating; bobsled-ding; hut-to-hut ski touring; heliskiing; snowshoeing; hot air ballooning; sleigh rides.
FEATURES: Snowmaking 7%; USAA racing; child care; ski school; restaurants; rentals.
▶NORDIC: Cross-Country Ski Center at Golden Peak; 303-845-5313; 74 groomed km; rentals; lessons.

Vail is Nirvana for skiers, annually ranked the number one ski resort in America. The reasons are obvious: a thoroughly professional service, the sophisticated ambiance, and of course, the phenomenal skiing. It's a model resort and mountain

Courtesy: Ski The Summit (see Keystone Resort, Colorado, p. 98).

development. Although the pre-fab Bavarian-style buildings are begin-ning to show their age, the village remains quaint and charming. Vail has always attracted a large num-ber of Europeans, giving the resort a delightfully cosmopolitan air. Indeed, its most beloved citizen is probably Austrian Pepi Gramshammer, whose Wedel Weeks are one of the country's best intensive instructional programs.

Despite the mountain's mammoth size, it's easy to negotiate, thanks to the intelligently designed layout and connecting series of lifts. The variety of terrain is impressive, with the famed Back Bowls like China, Siberia, and Mongolia and the clas-sic bump runs off Prima Ridge the stuff of strong skiers' dreams. Beginners have their own areas at Golden Peak and Lionshead, while intermediates can romp almost at will over that astonishing expanse. Snowboarders enjoy the Boardertown Park, with its half pipe and 300-foot berm.

You can even visit the Colorado Ski Museum across Lionshead Drive, whose exhibits include historical equipment and the 10th Mountain Division.

Is there a downside to paradise? Well, despite the amazing range of terrain, there's no truly extreme section. The extensive cross-coun-try network is a bit like a snow-cov-ered golf course. And Vail is con-gested (don't tell someone to meet you at mid-Vail around lunchtime). It hosts 20,000 skiers on an average day, after all (Vail Associates tried to address the problem by recently adding its eighth high-speed quad). It's a small price to pay for the best.

WINTER PARK RESORT

(P. 14, B-3, #26) 677 Winter Park Dr. (off U.S. 40), Winter Park
800-453-2525; 303-726-5514 (snow)

SEASON: Nov. 17-April 17
ANNUAL SNOWFALL: 360″
TERRAIN: 113 trails over 1,311 acres; longest run 4.5 mi.; ◆ 20%; ■ 58%; ● 22%.
LIFTS: 20 (5 quads-4 high-speed, 4 triples, 11 doubles); capacity 30,000 per hours
SUMMIT: 12,060′
VERTICAL: 3,060′
ACTIVITIES: Snowboarding; sleigh rides; snowmobiling; hot air ballooning; snow tub-ing.
FEATURES: Snowmaking 20%; child care; ski school; restau-rants; rental.
▶NORDIC: See Devil's Thumb Ranch/Ski Idlewild and Snow Mountain Ranch below.

Denverites consider Winter Park their own personal area. It's owned by the City of Denver, and is a quick scenic ride by car—or for daytrip-pers by the delightful Ski Train. Moreover, it's the most affordable of Colorado's major areas and boasts expansive terrain spread out over three mountains. The area earmarked nearly $5 million for improvements for the 1993-1994 season, including the innovative Discovery/Learn-to-Ski Park, a 20-acre non-threatening environment that allows weaker skiers to sample varied conditions, including bump and tree skiing. This dovetails perfectly with its pioneering training center for the disabled and highly regarded children's program.

Skiers will find plenty of terrain to their liking, whatever their level of ability. Winter Park Base area accesses primarily beginner and lower intermediate trails, with the Alice in Wonderland section a standout. Vazquez Ridge and the recently opened Parsenn's Bowl are cruising heaven, while the steeper runs off Zephyr in the West Portal area hint at the fun to come on the Mary Jane peak, with some of Colorado's most awesome steeps and moguls (those on the backside are the most difficult).

WOLF CREEK SKI AREA
(P. 14, D-3, #27) U.S. 160 at top of Wolf Creek Pass, 23 miles NE of Pagosa Springs
303-264-5629
SEASON: Nov. 4-April 15
ANNUAL SNOWFALL: 450″
TERRAIN: 52 trails over 800 acres; longest run 2 mi.; ◆ 30%; ■ 50%: ● 20%.
LIFTS: 5 (2 triples, 2 doubles, 1 surface); capacity 4,500 per hour.
SUMMIT: 11,775′
VERTICAL: 1,425′
ACTIVITIES: Snowboarding; telemarking.
FEATURES: Child care; ski school; restaurant; rentals.
Wolf Creek is one of Colorado's best-kept secrets. Thanks to the whopping annual snowfall and a base height of 10,350′, skiers are virtually guaranteed fresh, deep champagne powder. The terrain is admirably balanced, with few real steeps and almost no tree skiing (save for a few plunging glades)—just wide-open, uncrowded bowls. But experts don't care: How often does the fluffy stuff stick around until last run? Unfortunately, there is no on-site lodging: The nearest rooms are located over 20 miles away in Pagosa Springs and South Fork.

NORDIC

ASHCROFT CROSS-COUNTRY
(P. 14, B-3, #28) 11399 Castle Creek Rd., Aspen
303-925-1971
FACILITIES: 35 groomed km; rentals; lessons; restaurant.
In addition to exquisite alpine scenery, trails weave past ghost towns and historic log cabins. Pine Creek Cookhouse, the gourmet restaurant, is alone worth the trip.

BEAVER MEADOWS
(P. 14, A-3, #29) Red Feather Lakes
800-462-5870; 303-881-2450
FACILITIES: 25 groomed km; rentals; lessons; restaurant and lodging; ice skating.

C LAZY U RANCH
(P. 14, A-3, #30) Granby
303-887-3344
FACILITIES: 20 groomed km; rentals; lessons; ice skating; sleigh rides; winter horseback riding; lodging and restaurant.
The C LAZY U is one of Colorado's more exclusive dude ranches, with sumptuous accommodations and meals. In addition to the machine-tracked trails, there is plenty of backcountry skiing on the ranch's 2,000 acres.

COLORADO MOUNTAIN COLLEGE
(P. 14, B-3, #31) Timberline Campus, Leadville
719-486-2015
FACILITIES: 10 groomed km; snowshoeing.
This is a state-accredited institution where students learn grooming, patrol, snowmaking, and trail design. The course is open to the public.

DEVIL'S THUMB RANCH/SKI IDLEWILD
(P. 14, B-3, #32) Winter Park
303-726-5564; 303-726-8231
FACILITIES: 90 groomed km; rentals; lessons; restaurant and lodging.
These two Nordic centers banded together to create one of the most attractive networks in the West, with superbly varied terrain ideal for both skating and skiing.

FRISCO NORDIC SKI CENTER
(P. 14, B-3, # 33) I-70 and Highway 9, Frisco
303-668-0866
FACILITIES: 35 groomed km; rentals; lessons; restaurant.

THE FRYINGPAN RIVER
(P. 14, B-3, #34) 32042 Fryingpan River Rd., Meredith
800-352-0980
FACILITIES: 35 groomed km; rentals; lessons; restaurant and lodging; snowshoeing; sleigh rides.

GRAND LAKE TOURING CENTER
(P. 14, A-3, #35) 1415 County Rd. 48, Grand Lake
303-627-8008
FACILITIES: 25 groomed km; rentals; lessons; restaurant.

HOME RANCH RESORT
(P. 14, A-3, #36) Clark
303-879-1780
FACILITIES: 30 groomed km; rentals; lessons; restaurant and lodging; winter horseback riding.
Another deluxe dude ranch and a member of Relais et Chateaux, the prestigious international lodging association whose members must meet rigorous standards. The Elk River Valley terrain ranges from open meadows for beginners to hilly stretches for intermediates.

LATIGO RANCH NORDIC SKIING
(P. 14, B-3, #37) Kremmling
800-227-9655
FACILITIES: 40 groomed km; rentals; lessons; lodging and restaurant.

LODGE AT CORDILLERA
(P. 14, B-3, #38) Edwards
303-926-2200
FACILITIES: 20 groomed km; rentals; lessons; restaurant and lodging; sleigh rides.
This secluded, romantic hideaway is one of Colorado's most luxurious spa/resorts. Thirty-one hundred surrounding acres have been declared a wildlife preserve. It's not uncommon to spot elk or rare bighorn sheep during treks.

MEDICINE MOUNTAIN CROSS COUNTRY CENTER
(P. 14, A-4, #39) Wellington
303-568-3339
FACILITIES: 20 groomed km; rentals; lessons.

PAGOSA PINES TOURING CENTER
(P. 14, D-3, #40) Pagosa Springs
303-731-4141
FACILITIES: 12 groomed km; rentals; lessons; restaurant and lodging.

PEACEFUL VALLEY LODGE AND SKI RANCH
(P. 14, A-4, #41) Star Route, Lyons
303-747-2881
FACILITIES: 15 groomed km; rentals.

REDSTONE TOURING INN
(P. 14, B-2, #42) 0082 Redstone Blvd., Redstone
303-963-9489
FACILITIES: 20 groomed km; rentals; repairs; restaurant and lodging.
Trails snake through aspen stands and skirt red sandstone cliffs and outcroppings. The Tyrolean-style inn is on the National Registry of Historic Places and the town itself is an artists' colony.

SNOW MOUNTAIN NORDIC CENTER
(P. 14, B-3, #43) Winter Park
303-887-2152
FACILITIES: 100 groomed km; 3 km lit; biathlon range; rentals; repairs; restaurant and lodging.
Most of the network overlooks a beautiful valley. There's plenty of variety, with tracks groomed for both skating and diagonal, a biathlon range, and such state-of-the-art additions as a 3K, lighted loop.

SPRUCE LODGE
(P. 14, C-2, #44) Cedaredge
303-856-3210
FACILITIES: Unlimited backcountry skiing; rentals; lodging and restaurant.
Spruce Lodge accesses the glorious Grand Mesa, the world's highest flattop mountain, filigreed with thousands of frozen lakes and ponds.

VISTA VERDE GUEST & SKI TOURING RANCH
(P. 14, A-3, #45) Steamboat Springs
303-879-3858; 800-526-7433
FACILITIES: 30 groomed km; rentals; lessons; restaurant and lodging; telemarking.

WINDING RIVER RESORT
(P. 14, A-3, #46) 491 County Rd., Grand Lake
303-627-3215
FACILITIES: Rentals; restaurant and lodging.
While the resort doesn't offer a groomed network of trails, it does feature access to Rocky Mountain National Park, with a staff that provides helpful advice and information.

CONNECTICUT

Skiers who associate Connecticut with nothing more than sailing on the Sound and the ivied halls of Yale are in for a big surprise. While there are few truly challenging slopes, Connecticut offers pleasant family-oriented areas and miles of groomed cross-country trails that wind through typically scenic forests and picturesque colonial villages. ❄ For a break, head to Hartford to watch the NHL Whalers, and to Storrs to applaud the perennial Big East basketball powerhouse, the Connecticut Huskies, or learn about New England's rich nautical tradition at Mystic Seaport and New London.

ALPINE

MOHAWK MOUNTAIN SKI AREA
(P. 30, C-1, #1) 46 Great Hollow Rd., Cornwall
203-672-6100 (snow)
SEASON: Nov. 25-April 1
ANNUAL SNOWFALL: 92"
TERRAIN: 23 trails over 107 acres; longest run 1.25 mi.; ◆ 20%; ■ 60%; ● 20%.
LIFTS: 5 (1 triple, 4 doubles); capacity, 7,400 per hour.
SUMMIT: 1,600'
VERTICAL: 640'
ACTIVITIES: Snowboarding; night skiing.
FEATURES: Snowmaking 95%; ski school; restaurant; rentals.
 Mohawk is generally credited for inventing snowmaking nearly 50 years ago, and has worked mightily to keep up with all the advances since. Connecticut's largest area, Mohawk appeals to families—it's even alcohol free—and features mainly gentle terrain with a few steep pitches like the bumped up Wildwood. The adjacent state park features 20 ungroomed km of trails.

MT. SOUTHINGTON SKI AREA
(P. 30, D-2, #2) 396 Mt. Vernon Rd., Southington
203-628-0954 (snow)
SEASON: Dec. 1-March 25
ANNUAL SNOWFALL: 85"
TERRAIN: 14 trails over 55 acres; longest run 1 mi.; ◆ 20%; ■ 50%; ● 30%.
LIFTS: 6 (1 triple, 1 double, 4 surface); capacity, 5,000 per hour.
SUMMIT: 525'
VERTICAL: 425'
ACTIVITIES: Snowboarding; night skiing.
FEATURES: Snowmaking 95%; ski school; restaurant; rentals.
 This converted country farm offers varied terrain best for intermediate skiers. Terrain garden and half pipe for snowboarders.

POWDER RIDGE SKI RESORT
(P. 30, D-2, #3) 99 Powder Hill Rd., Middlefield
203-349-3454 (snow)
SEASON: Nov. 15-April 1
ANNUAL SNOWFALL: 70"
TERRAIN: 14 trails over 75 acres; longest run 1 mi.; ◆ 20%; ■ 40%; ● 40%.
LIFTS: 5 (1 quad, 3 doubles, 1 surface); capacity, 5,500 per hour.
SUMMIT: 750'
VERTICAL: 500'
ACTIVITIES: Snowboarding; night skiing.
FEATURES: Snowmaking 100%; ski school; restaurant; rentals.
 Basically a learning area for locals, Powder Ridge offers a guarantee: If you're not pleased, ski free next time.

SKI SUNDOWN
(P. 30, C-2, #4) 126 Ratlum Rd., New Hartford
203-379-9851 ; 203-379-SNOW (snow)
SEASON: Dec. 1-April 1
ANNUAL SNOWFALL: 60"
TERRAIN: 16 trails over 65 acres; longest run 1 mi.; ◆ 20%; ■ 40%; ● 40%.
LIFTS: 4 (3 triples, 1 surface); capacity, 6,200 per hour.
SUMMIT: 1,075'
VERTICAL: 625'
ACTIVITIES: Snowboarding; night skiing.
FEATURES: Snowmaking 100%; ski school; restaurant; rentals.
 Sundown probably features the prettiest scenery and most advanced technology of the state's areas. Gunbarrel, a fairly steep, heavily mogulled run, ranks as one of Connecticut's toughest slopes.

WOODBURY SKI & RACQUET AREA
(P. 30, D-2, #5) Route 47, Woodbury
203-263-2203 (snow)
SEASON: Nov. 1-March 15
ANNUAL SNOWFALL: 65"
TERRAIN: 12 trails over 33 acres; longest run 2,600'; ◆ 33%; ■ 34%; ● 33%.
LIFTS: 4 (1 double, 3 surface); capacity, 2,544 per hour.
SUMMIT: 850'
VERTICAL: 300'
ACTIVITIES: Snowboarding; sledding; night skiing.
FEATURES: Snowmaking 100%; ski school; restaurant; rentals.
▶NORDIC: 40 groomed km; rentals; lessons; night skiing (2.5 km lit).
 While there's nothing really appropriate for advanced skiers, Woodbury offers cruising and some decent bump practice for intermediates just beginning to feel their oats. Features a mix of wide-open and tree-lined slopes. One trail with jumps and three half-pipes are set aside for snowboarders. The wooded Nordic trails are easy to moderate in difficulty.

NORDIC

CEDAR BROOK CROSS COUNTRY SKI AREA
(P. 30, C-2, #6) 1481 Ratley Rd. (off Route 168), West Suffield
203-668-5026
FACILITIES: 10 groomed km; rentals; lessons; restaurant.
 This novice to intermediate trail network is located on a working Morgan horse farm—a source of delight to kids.

MAPLEWOOD FARM CONSERVATION CENTER
(P. 30, C-2, #7) 129 Grantville Rd., Norfolk
203-542-5882
FACILITIES: 8 groomed km; rentals; lessons; restaurant.
 The complex includes a conservation center with interpretive trails and information on land preservation. The trails wind through both meadows and forestland, past several streams and ponds. Mostly rolling terrain with a few short steep hills.

PINE MOUNTAIN SKI TOURING CENTER
(P. 30, C-2, #8) Route 179, 2 mi. S of E. Hartland
203-653-4279
FACILITIES: 10 groomed km; rentals; lessons; restaurant.

QUINEBAUG VALLEY SKI
(P. 30, D-3, #9) 79 Roosevelt Ave., Preston
203-886-2284
FACILITIES: 10 groomed km; rentals; lessons; restaurant.

WHITE MEMORIAL FOUNDATION
(P. 30, C-1, #10) 71 Whitehall Rd. (Route 202, Route 8 exit 42), Litchfield
203-567-0857
FACILITIES: 35 mi.; restaurant.
 There are several activities of interest to non-skiers here at the Conservation Center, including changing exhibits and dioramas of local wildlife. Rentals and lessons can be obtained through The Wilderness Shop in Litchfield.

WINDING TRAILS CROSS COUNTRY SKI CENTER
(P. 30, B-4, #11) 50 Winding Trails Dr., Farmington
203-678-9582
FACILITIES: 20 groomed km (with skating lane); rentals; lessons; restaurant.

STATBOX

Tourism: 800-CT-BOUND	**Average annual precipitation:** 43"
Time zone: Eastern	
Population: 3,287,116	**Highest elevation:** 2,380'
Square miles: 5,009	**Lowest elevation:** Sea level

Papa Hemingway cultivated his sportsman's image in the laid-back wilderness of Idaho. The state's allure stems from ravishing scenery (including North America's deepest gorge, the striking Hell's Canyon, and sparkling alpine lakes like Couer d'Alene), superb fishing, idyllic retreats and country that spirals from majestic snow-capped mountains to the barren lunarscape of the Craters of the Moon National Monument (an unforgettable place for cross-country). And then there's the skiing, led by legendary Sun Valley, whose tradition is being challenged by upstarts like Schweitzer and Silver Mountain. ※ Idaho boasts the largest wilderness area outside Alaska; there are several state parks and national forests that groom trails for skiers. Call Sun Valley Trekking (208-788-9585) and Sawtooth Mountain Guides (208-774-3324) for backcountry hut-to-hut touring.

ALPINE

BALD MOUNTAIN
(P. 20, C-2, #1) Orofino
208-464-2311(snow)
SEASON: Nov. 25-April 10
ANNUAL SNOWFALL: 225"
TERRAIN: 15 trails over 195 acres; longest run 1.5 mi.; ◆ 34%; ■ 33%; ● 33%.
LIFTS: 2 (2 surface); capacity, 500 per hour.
SUMMIT: 7,770'
VERTICAL: 975'
ACTIVITIES: Snowboarding.
FEATURES: Ski school; restaurant; rentals.
A good uncrowded learning mountain that gets some nice powder dumps, used almost exclusively by locals.

BOGUS BASIN
SKI RESORT
(P. 20, E-2, #2) 2045 Bogus Basin Rd., 16 mi. N of Boise
208-332-5100; 208-342-2100 (snow)
SEASON: Nov. 25-April 5
ANNUAL SNOWFALL: 250"
TERRAIN: 46 trails over 2,600 acres; longest run 1.75 mi.; ◆ 36%; ■ 44%; ● 20%.
LIFTS: 10 (6 doubles, 4 surface); capacity, 6,700 per hour.
SUMMIT: 7,600'
VERTICAL: 1,800'
ACTIVITIES: Snowboarding; NASTAR; night skiing; sleigh rides.
FEATURES: Snowmaking 10%; ski school; restaurants; rentals.
▶NORDIC: 27 groomed km; rentals; lessons.
Bogus Basin (so-named because counterfeit gold was manufactured here in the 19th century) is anything but bogus if you like top-notch glade skiing. Nighthawk is a typical advanced steep run; Showcase offers leisurely cruising. The night skiing operation is one of the West's largest, with several black diamond runs lighted in addition to the usual easier stuff. Snowboarders also love the terrain garden and half pipe. The trails descend from a flat butte summit with incredible views of the capital.

And surprise, it's Idaho's biggest area, with over 500 skiable acres more than Sun Valley.

BRUNDAGE MOUNTAIN
SKI AREA
(P. 20, D-2, #3) 1410 Mill St., McCall
208-634-7462; 208-634-5650 (snow)
SEASON: Nov. 25-April 15
ANNUAL SNOWFALL: 240"
TERRAIN: 36 trails over 1,300 acres; longest run 1.5 mi.; ◆ 10%; ■ 70%; ● 20%.
LIFTS: 4 (1 triple, 2 doubles, 1 surface); capacity, 3,925 per hour.
SUMMIT: 7,600'
VERTICAL: 1,800'
ACTIVITIES: Snowboarding; telemarking.
FEATURES: Ski school; restaurant; child care; rentals.
The uncrowded runs of Brundage boast eye-popping views of gorgeous Payette Lake and the Seven Devils vaulting up from Hell's Canyon. Aside from some fun powder glades and some nasty cliffs and chutes, the skiing is solidly intermediate, with just enough sharp pitches to keep you on your toes (or rather, the balls of your feet in ski parlance). Standout runs include the 45th Parallel and Alpine. Conditions permitting, the area offers snowcat skiing on the backside. Children under 6 ski free.

COTTONWOOD BUTTE
(P. 20, C-1, #4) Country Road off U.S. 95, Cottonwood
208-962-3631
SEASON: Dec.-April 10 (open weekends and holidays)
ANNUAL SNOWFALL: 180"
TERRAIN: 4 trails over NA acres; ◆ 25%; ■ 50%; ● 25%.
LIFTS: 2 (2 surface); capacity, 450 per hour.
SUMMIT: 5,460'

VERTICAL: 845'
ACTIVITIES: Snowmobiling; sledding.
FEATURES: Ski school; restaurant; rentals.
▶NORDIC: 10 groomed km.
A tiny area, most often used as a learning mountain for locals.

KELLY CANYON
SKI AREA
(P. 20, E-4, #5) 706 S. Berlin, off Highway 26, Idaho Falls (3 mi. east of Heise)
208-538-6261 (snow)
SEASON: Dec. 10-April 10 (closed Mon.)
ANNUAL SNOWFALL: 200"
TERRAIN: 20 trails over 300 acres; longest run 6,800'; ◆ 30%; ■ 40%; ● 30%.
LIFTS: 5 (4 doubles, 1 surface); capacity, 2,100 per hour.
SUMMIT: 6,600'
VERTICAL: 938'
ACTIVITIES: Night skiing.
FEATURES: Ski school; restaurant; rentals.
Some great cruisers and a few steeps make this uncrowded area a good stopover if you're in the neighborhood.

LITTLE SKI HILL
(P. 20, D-2, #6) 3635 Highway 55, McCall
208-634-5691 (snow)
SEASON: Dec. 1-March 15 (closed Mon.)
ANNUAL SNOWFALL: 180"
TERRAIN: 5 trails over 40 acres; longest run 3,000'; ◆ 20%; ■ 40%; ● 40%.
LIFTS: 1 (1 surface); capacity, 1,000 per hour.
SUMMIT: 5,700'
VERTICAL: 405'
ACTIVITIES: Snowboarding; ski jumping; night skiing.
FEATURES: Ski school; restaurant.

An excellent training area, Little Ski Hill is popular with locals for its 25-meter ground jump, its varied cross country terrain (largely wooded, passing through pine and Aspen groves, with a marathon 25-km loop), and its top-notch restaurant (considered one of McCall's best). A snowboard park has been added for the 1994-1995 season.

LOOKOUT PASS
SKI AREA
(P. 20, B-2, #7) Lookout Pass, U.S. 90, Wallace
208-744-1301(snow)
SEASON: Nov. 15-April 1 (open Thurs. to Sun., holidays)
ANNUAL SNOWFALL: 220"
TERRAIN: 12 trails over 100 acres; longest run 1 mi.; ◆ 30%; ■ 40%; ● 30%
LIFTS: 2 (1 double, 1 surface); capacity, 1,200 per hour.
SUMMIT: 5,650'
VERTICAL: 850'
ACTIVITIES: Snowboarding; snowmobiling; dog sledding.
FEATURES: Ski school; restaurant; rentals.
▶NORDIC: 160 plus groomed km in St. Regis Basin; rentals; lessons.
There is an expert run along the ridge that can be harrowing. Some sheer drops off the three faces will challenge most advanced skiers. Novices can take Fitzgerald's from the top.

MAGIC MOUNTAIN
SKI RESORT
(P. 20, F-3, #8) 3367 N 3600 East, Kimberley
208-423-6221 (snow)
SEASON: Dec. 1-April 1 (closed Mon.)
ANNUAL SNOWFALL: 250"
TERRAIN: 20 trails over 210 acres; longest run 3,900'; ◆ 25%; ■ 45%; ● 30%.
LIFTS: 3 (1 double, 2 surface); capacity, 1,240 per hour.
SUMMIT: 7,200'
VERTICAL: 700'
ACTIVITIES: Snowboarding.
FEATURES: Ski school; restaurant; rentals.

STATBOX

Tourism: 800-635-7820
Time zone: Pacific and Mountain
Population: 1,006,000
Square miles: 83,557

Average annual precipitation: 12"
Highest elevation: 12,662'
Lowest elevation: 738'

►NORDIC: 32 groomed km.
A friendly family area with some good groomed steeps (like Tricky and Abracadabra) and cruisers.

NORTH SOUTH SKI BOWL
(P. 20, B-1, #9) St. Maries
208-245-4222 (snow)
SEASON: Dec. 1-March 31
ANNUAL SNOWFALL: 175″
TERRAIN: 15 trails over 80 acres; longest run 3,900′; ◆ 30%; ▪ 40%; ● 30%.
LIFTS: 2 (1 double, 2 surface); capacity, 1,000 per hour.
SUMMIT: 4,200′
VERTICAL: 600′
ACTIVITIES: Snowboarding.
FEATURES: Ski school; restaurant; rentals.
►NORDIC: 30 groomed km.
Mainly wide open bowls with some variation of pitch.

PEBBLE CREEK SKI AREA
(P. 20, F-4, #10) Off Highway 15 (Inkom exit), Pocatello
208-775-4451(snow)
SEASON: Dec. 15-April 1 (closed Mon.)
ANNUAL SNOWFALL: 250″
TERRAIN: 24 trails over 600 acres; longest run 1.25 mi.; ◆ 25%; ▪ 42%; ● 33%.
LIFTS: 3 (1 triple, 2 doubles); capacity, 3,300 per hour.
SUMMIT: 8,300′
VERTICAL: 2,000′
ACTIVITIES: Night skiing.
FEATURES: Snowmaking 50%; ski school; restaurant; rentals.
A good blend of wide open groomed runs and steeper tree skiing.

POMERELLE SKI RESORT
(P. 20, F-3, #11) Off state Route 77, Albion
208-638-5599; 208-638-5555 (snow)
SEASON: Nov. 15-April 10
ANNUAL SNOWFALL: 100″
TERRAIN: 17 trails over 200 acres; longest run 1.5 mi.; ◆ 20%; ▪ 50%; ● 30%.
LIFTS: 3 (1 triple, 1 double, 1 surface); capacity, 2,500 per hour.
SUMMIT: 9,000′
VERTICAL: 1,000′
ACTIVITIES: Night skiing.
FEATURES: Ski school; restaurant; rentals.
►NORDIC: Unlimited ungroomed trails; rentals; lessons.
The slopes are mostly wide open, with a few stands of aspen. Children under 7 ski free.

SCHWEITZER MOUNTAIN RESORT
(P. 20, A-2, #12) 10000 Schweitzer Mountain Rd., Sandpoint
800-831-8810; 208-263-9555,

208-263-9562 (snow)
SEASON: Nov. 24-April 9
ANNUAL SNOWFALL: 280″
TERRAIN: 50 trails and bowls over 2,350 acres; longest run 2.7 mi.; ◆◆ 5%; ◆ 35%; ▪ 40%; ● 20%.
LIFTS: 6 (1 high-speed quad, 5 doubles); capacity, 7,090 per hour.
SUMMIT: 6,400′
VERTICAL: 2,400′
ACTIVITIES: Snowboarding; NASTAR; sleigh rides; night-skiing; snowshowing; snow-mobiling.
FEATURES: Snowmaking 10%; ski school; restaurants; rentals.
►NORDIC: 8 groomed km; rentals; lessons.
Schweitzer is fast becoming a success story. Despite its remote location, more and more people are discovering this gem. They rave about the homey ambience, top-notch lodging, friendly people, awe-inspiring views of Lake Pend Oreille and, oh yes, the stupendous skiing on 2,350 uncrowded acres. This is an intermediate's and expert's dream area. Packed with gobs of fresh powder, breathtaking bowls and steeps, like the signature Stiles, cut through stately cedar forests. Recent expansion added a half-pipe, several beginner and low intermediate runs, and the kids-only Enchanted Forest Terrain Garden. With $100 million committed to additions and improvements into the next millennium, Schweitzer is poised to become one of the West's downhill meccas.

SILVER MOUNTAIN
(P. 20, A-2, #13) 610 Bunker Ave., Kellogg
208-783-1111
SEASON: Nov. 15-April 5
ANNUAL SNOWFALL: 260″
TERRAIN: 50 trails over 1,500 acres; longest run 2.5 mi.; ◆ 40%; ▪ 45%; ● 15%.
LIFTS: 7 (1 gondola, 1 quad, 2 triples, 2 doubles, 1 surface); capacity, 8,100 per hour.
SUMMIT: 6,300′
VERTICAL: 2,300′
ACTIVITIES: Snowboarding; NASTAR; snowshoeing; night skiing.
FEATURES: Snowmaking 20%; ski school; restaurants; rentals.
If Schweitzer has a rival, it's fast-growing Silver Mountain. When the silver lodes finally went bust in the early 1980s, locals saw their future in snow. The last few years Silver has expanded its trail system and added three lifts, including the world's longest (3.1 miles) single-stage gondola. There's plenty of mean double-diamond terrain with precipitous walls and glades, in addition to splendid forested bowls where intermediates can challenge themselves. Cruisers include Centennial and Silver Belt. Kellogg has a tiny bed base, so most people

stay in the delightful resort town of Couer d'Alene, 35 miles south.

SNOWHAVEN
(P. 20, B-2, #14) 225 W. North, Grangeville
208-983-2581
SEASON: Dec. 1-March 15
ANNUAL SNOWFALL: 130″
TERRAIN: 3 trails over 35 acres; longest run 3,000′; ◆ 34%; ▪ 33%; ● 33%.
LIFTS: 2 (2 surface); capacity, 500 per hour.
SUMMIT: 5,100′
VERTICAL: 400′
ACTIVITIES: Snowboarding.
FEATURES: Ski school; restaurant; rentals.
A small family-oriented local area, good for learning and practicing the basics.

SOLDIER MOUNTAIN
(P. 20, E-2, #15) 13 mi. N of Route 20, Fairfield
208-764-2300 (snow)
SEASON: Nov. 25-April 1 (closed Mon. to Wed.)
ANNUAL SNOWFALL: 210″
TERRAIN: 36 trails over 220 acres; longest run 1 mi.; ◆ 25%; ▪ 50%; ● 25%.
LIFTS: 3 (2 doubles, 1 surface); capacity, 2,200 per hour.
SUMMIT: 7,200′
VERTICAL: 1,400′
ACTIVITIES: Snowboarding.
FEATURES: Ski school; restaurant; rentals.
►NORDIC: 10 groomed km.
A very affordable mountain, well worth the trip if you're nearby and want some good undisturbed powder runs.

SUN VALLEY RESORT
(P. 20, E-3, #16) State Route 75, Sun Valley
208-622-4111; 800-635-2140 (snow)
SEASON: Nov. 25-May 1
ANNUAL SNOWFALL: 220″
TERRAIN: 73 trails over 2,000 acres; longest run 3 mi.; ◆ 17%; ▪ 45%; ● 38%.
LIFTS: 16 (6 high-speed quads, 5 triples, 5 doubles); capacity, 26,380 per hour.
SUMMIT: 9,150′
VERTICAL: 3,400′
ACTIVITIES: Snowboarding; NASTAR; ski jump; sleigh rides; ice skating.
FEATURES: Snowmaking 73%; ski school; restaurants; rentals.
►NORDIC: 40 groomed km; rentals; lessons; telemarking.
Created by statesman and railroad baron Averill Harriman, frequented by the likes of Gary Cooper and Ernest Hemingway (who penned *For Whom the Bell Tolls* in the venerable lodge), Sun Valley has long been a haunt of the rich and famous. Aficionados have always come not just for the skiing, but for

the incomparable ambiance, an almost perfect blend of European sophistication and Western warmth. But like all grande dames, Sun Valley needed a face lift—and got one from reclusive owner Earl Holding, who has pumped nearly $40 million into the resort since 1987. Everything shines, especially at the new Warm Springs and Seattle Ridge lodges (the bathrooms are all gleaming marble and brass). Two new high-speed quads, Seattle Ridge and Lookout Express, transport thousands more skiers per hour to a mountain that is already surprisingly empty, given its reputation.
The skiing, too, is incomparable. Dollar Mountain is the enclave of beginners and its neighbor Elkhorn features some steeper bowls for lower intermediates—neither of whom dare approach the famed Bald Mountain (Baldy to fans), a series of ridges sitting daintily atop flowing bowls. Baldy's long steep cruisers are just the ticket for working on form. Try the Bowls, Seattle Ridge, Warm Springs, College—each a perfect groomed boulevard, not so wide that you get cocky, just wide enough to get the turns right. Exhibition is a classic knock-your-knees bump run, and Fire Trail appeals to tree-skiing fanatics. Believe it or not, you're likely to find some runs virtually all to yourself. Sun Valley isn't easy to get to, and, of course, that has always been the point.

NORDIC

LUCKY DOG RETREAT
(P. 20, D-5, #17) Route 20, Island Park
208-558-7455
FACILITIES: 20 groomed km; rentals; restaurant and lodging.

TETON RIDGE RANCH
(P. 20, E-5, #18) 200 Valley View Rd., Tetonia
208-456-2650
FACILITIES: 20 groomed km; rentals; lessons; telemarking; sleigh rides; restaurant and lodging.

WARM SPRINGS RANCH
(P. 20, E-3, #19) Warm Springs Road, Ketchum
208-726-3322
FACILITIES: 5 groomed km; rentals; lessons.

ILLINOIS

Even though snow blankets most of northern Illinois in winter, Chicagoans prefer to stay warm in their favorite cubby holes watching Da Bulls and Da Bears. Chicago's a sporting town, all right, and the athleticism can extend to the slopes, most of which are perched above the mighty Mississippi, within a few hours' drive to the southwest. (Fortunately, the nickname Windy City doesn't usually apply at these sheltered areas.)

ALPINE

CHESTNUT MOUNTAIN SKI RESORT
(P. 22, A-2, #1) 8700 West Chestnut Rd., Galena
815-777-1320 (snow)
SEASON: Nov. 25-March 15
ANNUAL SNOWFALL: 42″
TERRAIN: 17 trails over 100 acres; longest run 3,600'; ◆ 30%, ■ 40%, ● 30%.
LIFTS: 8 (1 quad, 2 triples, 5 surface); capacity, 9,000 per hour.
SUMMIT: NA
VERTICAL: 475'
ACTIVITIES: NASTAR; night skiing.
FEATURES: Snowmaking 100%; ski school; restaurants; rentals. Chestnut offers wide open skiing, with the occasional steep section. Ninety percent of the slopes overlook—and seem poised to empty into—the Mississippi. Under 6 and over 70 ski free.

FOUR LAKES VILLAGE
(P. 22, A-4, #2) U.S. 53, Lisle
708-964-2551; 708-964-2550 (snow)
TRAILS, 6; LIFTS, 6; VERTICAL, 100'. Boarders have their own run with jump and half pipe.

PLUMTREE SKI AREA
(P. 22, A-2, #3) 200 Plumtree Dr., Lake Carroll
815-493-2881 (snow)
TRAILS, 10; LIFTS, 2; VERTICAL, 210'.
▶NORDIC: 10 groomed km.

SNOWSTAR SKI AREA
(P. 22, B-2, #4) 9500 126th St. West, Taylor Ridge
309-798-2666
TRAILS, 9; LIFTS, 4; VERTICAL, 228'.

VILLA OLIVIA SKI AREA
(P. 22, A-4, #5) Route 20 & Naperville Road, Bartlett
708-289-5200
TRAILS, 8; LIFTS, 7; VERTICAL, 180'.
▶NORDIC: 2 groomed km.; rentals; lessons.

NORDIC

EAGLE RIDGE INN & RESORT
(P. 22, A-2, #6) Galena
815-777-2500
FACILITIES: 60 groomed km; rentals; lessons; lodging and restaurant; ice skating; sledding; winter golf center.

NORDIC HILLS RESORT
(P. 22, A-4, #7) Nordic Road, Itasca
708-773-2750
FACILITIES: 5 ungroomed km; rentals; lessons (weekends only); lodging and restaurant.

TWIN LAKES X-C TOURING CENTER
(P. 22, A-4, #8) 1200 E. Lake Dr., Palatine
708-934-6050
FACILITIES: 6 ungroomed km.; rentals; restaurant.

STATBOX

Tourism: 800-223-0121
Time zone: Central
Population: 11,430,602
Square miles: 56,400
Average annual precipitation: 32-48″ (north); 48-64 (south)
Highest elevation: 1,241'
Lowest elevation: 269'

INDIANA

Hoosiers may be wild about basketball (this is Larry Bird and Bobby Knight territory), the Indianapolis 500 and Notre Dame football, but skiers will be surprised by the amount of terrain in this basically flat state, most of it concentrated in the south, near the Ohio River, and the northeast, near Lake Michigan.

ALPINE

PERFECT NORTH SLOPES
(P. 23, D-5, #1) 1074 Perfect Lane, Lawrenceburg
812-537-3754 (snow)
SEASON: Dec. 1-March 15
ANNUAL SNOWFALL: 12″
TERRAIN: 14 trails over 50 acres; longest run 3,900'; ◆ 18%, ■ 32%, ● 50%.
LIFTS: 9 (3 triples, 6 surface); capacity, 6,700 per hour.
SUMMIT: 800'
VERTICAL: 400'
ACTIVITIES: Snowboarding; NASTAR; night-skiing.
FEATURES: Snowmaking 100%; ski school; restaurant; rentals. Alternating between open slopes and tighter tree-lined trails, Perfect offers some challenge by lower Midwest standards—particularly in the varied pitch on bumpy runs like Center Stage and Deception.

There's skiing until 4 A.M. weekends, making it popular with the college crowd.

SKI PAOLI PEAKS
(P. 23, E-3, #2) Route 3, Paoli
812-723-4696 (snow)
SEASON: Dec. 1-March 15
ANNUAL SNOWFALL: 19″
TERRAIN: 14 trails over 60 acres; longest run 3,300'; ◆ 7%, ■ 71%, ● 22%.
LIFTS: 8 (1 quad, 3 triples, 4 surface); capacity, 10,200 per hour.
SUMMIT: 900'
VERTICAL: 300'
ACTIVITIES: Snowboarding; NASTAR; night-skiing.
FEATURES: Snowmaking 100%; ski school; restaurant; rentals. The largest operation in Indiana, Paoli Peaks offers some pleasant tree skiing, ideal for low intermediates graduating to true paralleling. New half pipe. Skiing until 6 A.M. weekends.

SKI VALLEY
(P. 23, E-3, #3) Forrester Road, 1 mi. N of Highway 2, La Porte
219-326-0123 (snow)
TRAILS, 5; LIFTS, 6; VERTICAL, 120'.

SKI WORLD RECREATION AREA
(P. 23, D-3, #4) Off Highway 46, Nashville
812-988-6638 (snow)
SEASON: Dec. 1-March 10
ANNUAL SNOWFALL: 30″
TERRAIN: 12 runs over 100 acres; longest run 2,500'; ◆ 25%, ■ 50%, ● 25%.
LIFTS: 5 (1 quad, 1 triple, 3 surface); capacity, 4,800 per hour.
SUMMIT: 1,100'
VERTICAL: 310'
ACTIVITIES: Snowboarding; NASTAR; night skiing.
FEATURES: Snowmaking 100%; ski school; restaurant; rentals. Ski World frequently offers fun promotions and side activities. A new, short advanced run will dive 300 vertical feet in just 400 feet—a dizzying 45-degree descent.

NORDIC

GNAW BONE CAMP
(P. 23, D-3, #5) Rural Route 2, Nashville
812-988-4852
FACILITIES: 5 groomed km; rentals.

STATBOX

Tourism: 800-289-6646
Time zone: Central
Population: 5,544,159
Square miles: 36,291
Average annual precipitation: 39″
Highest elevation: 1,257'
Lowest elevation: 320'

IOWA

Thinking of plains and corn-fields? Think again. Iowa offers surprisingly satisfying—and inexpensive—skiing on the bluffs overlooking the Mississippi River. These are premier places to learn, especially popular with families and college kids—who enjoy the many fun, nighttime events. ❄ Combine your ski vacation with trips to the Iowa (Hawkeye) and Iowa State (Cyclones) campuses or with legalized riverboat gambling out of the Quad Cities.

ALPINE

FUN VALLEY SKI AREA
(P. 24, C-4, #1) Rural Route 1, Montezuma
515-623-3456 (snow)
TRAILS, 10; LIFTS, 5; VERTICAL, 240'.

MT. CRESCENT SKI AREA
(P. 24, C-2, #2) Off I-29, 2 mi. N of Crescent
712-545-3850 (snow)
SEASON: Dec. 15-March 15
ANNUAL SNOWFALL: 20''
TERRAIN: 10 trails over 40 acres; longest run 2,000'; ◆ 30%; ■ 30%; ● 40%.
LIFTS: 3 (1 double, 2 surface); capacity, 3,200 per hour.
SUMMIT: 1,330'
VERTICAL: 300'
ACTIVITIES: Snowboarding; night-skiing.
FEATURES: Snowmaking 100%; ski school; restaurant; rentals. Mostly open slopes, straight up and down. Good for practicing turns.

NOR-SKI RUNS
(P. 24, B-4, #3) 602 E. Broadway, Decorah
319-382-8373 or 4158 (snow)
TRAIL, 5; LIFTS, 3; VERTICAL, 250'.

RIVERSIDE HILLS SKI AREA
(P. 24, A-4, #4) rural Route 3, Estherville
712-362-5376 (snow)
TRAILS, 6; LIFTS, 3; VERTICAL, 190'.

SILVER CREEK RECREATION
(P. 24, B-3, #5) Rural Route 2, Humboldt
515-332-3329 (snow)
SEASON: Dec. 1-March 15 (weekends only)
ANNUAL SNOWFALL: 28''
TERRAIN: 11 runs over 20 acres; longest run 1,000'; ◆ 20%; ■ 40%; ● 40%.
LIFTS: 6 (6 surface); capacity, 3,500 per hour.
SUMMIT: N. A.
VERTICAL: 130'
ACTIVITIES: Snowboarding; tubing; night-skiing.
FEATURES: Snowmaking 100%; ski school; restaurant; rentals. A fine place to learn with gentle wide open slopes, Silver Creek offers free lessons to beginners. The entire area is lit at night.

SKI VALLEY
(P. 24, C-3, #6) RFD 4, Boone
515-432-2423 (snow)
TRAIN, 10; LIFTS, 4; VERTICAL, 180'.

SUNDOWN MOUNTAIN SKI AREA
(P. 24, B-5, #7) 17017 Asbury Rd., Dubuque
319-556-6676 ; 800-634-5911 (snow)
SEASON: Nov. 25-March 17
ANNUAL SNOWFALL: 40''
TERRAIN: 26 trails over 49 acres; longest run 4,000'; ◆◆ 5%; ◆ 15%; ■ 40%; ● 40%.
LIFTS: 6 (1 quad, 2 triples, 2 doubles, 1 surface); capacity, 9,000 per hour.
SUMMIT: 1,059'
VERTICAL: 475'
ACTIVITIES: Snowboarding; NASTAR; night-skiing.
FEATURES: Snowmaking 100%; ski school; restaurant; rentals.
▶NORDIC: 1 groomed km. Easily the finest area in Iowa, with solidly beginner and low intermediate terrain and a few intriguing pitches. The 250-foot wide Andy's Run is 35 degrees at top, and Gunbarrel exceeds 40 degrees.

NORDIC

CAMP HANISHA
(P. 24, C-3, #8) Rural Route 1, Boone
515-432-1417
FACILITIES: 5 groomed km; rentals.

STATBOX

Tourism: 800-345-4692
Time zone: Central
Population: 2,776,755
Square miles: 56,290

Average annual precipitation: 32''
Highest elevation: 1,600'
Lowest elevation: 500'

CONDITIONING

Conditioning is vital for skiers. You don't have to be buffed, but regular exercise is the best way to prevent injury on the slopes. Aerobics is excellent training for high altitude exertion, since it gets the heart pumping and processing oxygen. A low-impact workout every other day for a few weeks prior to your ski trip will vastly improve your stamina on the mountain. Always stretch before you attack the slopes. Skis have a habit of skidding this way and that; the more limber you are, the less likely you are to strain something. Pay special attention to your hamstrings and inner thigh muscles, but don't ignore your upper body, if only to prepare yourself for poling on a cat track or hiking up a ridge.

Even the best physical specimens are prone to skier's ailments. Hey, say you live at sea level and suddenly you're two miles in the air. There's less oxygen up there. Suddenly your head is pounding, you're nauseous, and you can't sleep. No, it's not a hangover or a mild flu. You just caught yourself a case of altitude sickness. If you're prone, consider spending a day at an interim altitude, say Denver or Salt Lake City, to acclimate yourself. Always drink lots of water, cut down on your intake of caffeine and alcohol (which dehydrate you, further impeding your blood's oxygen intake), and take it easy the first day or so.

Wear goggles or sunglasses that filter out UV rays when you ski. Radiation is more intense at high altitudes and even sunlight reflected off the snow damages the retina; snow blindness can result if you don't wear protective eye gear. If you burn easily, use a sunscreen with an SPF of at least 8 on your face and lips.

We've all had bad hair days on the slopes. Unfortunately, they're unavoidable: hats are not just a fashion statement, they're a necessity. You lose 50% of your body heat through your head. In less extreme weather you can make do with a headband. Ski gloves or mittens (usually warmer) are specially reinforced with thinsulate or other insulators; white evening gloves or your woolens won't cut it. A face mask and / or neck gaiter provides excellent protection against the wind. Dress in layers, starting with long underwear and wool or acrylic socks. Silk is very effective at trapping body heat. Don't overdress: Clothes soaked with perspiration are extremely good conductors of cold. Hypothermia or frostbite can easily result on chilly, blustery days if you expose yourself to the elements.

✦ 107 ✦

IA

Craggy peaks cast a bullying shadow over valleys and meadows silvered with streams, while 3,500 miles of rocky inlets scissor the Atlantic coast. Fully 75% forestland, Maine's rugged scenery has attracted the rich and famous for years, from John D. Rockefeller to George Bush, yet it's as famous for its down home, Down East hospitality as for its lobsters and potatoes. Ski areas feature stunning views and varied terrain, with Sugarloaf USA and Sunday River ranked among the best in the East, if not the entire country. But don't forget such top-notch areas as Saddleback and Shawnee Peak, long the choice of many locals. The cross-country terrain is predictably isolated and pristine, especially in the numerous wilderness camps (see sidebar p. 110).

ALPINE

BIG ROCK SKI AREA
(P. 29, B-4, #1) Off Route 1, Mars Hill
207-425-6711
SEASON: Dec. 1-March 15
ANNUAL SNOWFALL: 105"
TERRAIN: 9 trails over 50 acres; longest run 1.25 mi.; ◆ 30%; ■ 50%; ● 20%.
LIFTS: 4 (1 double, 3 surface); capacity, 3,400 per hour.
SUMMIT: 1,750'
VERTICAL: 980'
ACTIVITIES: Snowboarding; night skiing.
FEATURES: Snowmaking 25%; ski school; restaurant; rentals.
A strong intermediate area with spectacular views, Big Rock recently installed its first chair, with another to follow in 1995.

BLACK MOUNTAIN OF MAINE
(P. 29, D-2, #2) 50 Congress St., Rumford
207-364-8977
TRAILS, 9; LIFTS, 2; VERTICAL, 470'.
▶NORDIC: 10 groomed km.

CAMDEN SNOW BOWL
(P. 29, E-3, #3) John St., Camden
207-236-3438; 207-236-4418 (snow)
SEASON: Dec. 15-March 15
ANNUAL SNOWFALL: 95"
TERRAIN: 11 trails over 40 acres; longest run 1.25 mi.; ◆ 10%; ■ 80%; ● 10%.
LIFTS: 3 (1 double, 2 surface); capacity, 2,000 per hour.
SUMMIT: 1,100'
VERTICAL: 950'
ACTIVITIES: Snowboarding; tobogganing; ice skating; night skiing.
FEATURES: Snowmaking 40%; ski school; restaurant; rentals.
Camden offers limited skiing, but its location overlooking Penobscot Bay is breathtaking. You can get so distracted by the view, especially on Lookout, that the few steep sections may seem poised to pitch you into the whitecaps.

EATON MOUNTAIN
(P. 29, D-2, #4) HCR 71, Skowhegan
207-474-2666
SEASON: Dec. 15-March 15
ANNUAL SNOWFALL: 70"
TERRAIN: 14 trails over 117 acres; longest run 1 mi.; ◆◆ 7%; ◆ 28%; ■ 36%; ● 29%.
LIFTS: 2 (1 double; 1 surface); capacity, 1,000 per hour.
SUMMIT: 2,200'
VERTICAL: 600'
ACTIVITIES: Snowboarding; night skiing.
FEATURES: Snowmaking 100%; ski school; restaurant; rentals.
Another agreeable locals' area, with some surprising if short steeps like the ungroomed double black diamond Fox. A new snowboard fun park was added in 1994.

LOST VALLEY SKI AREA
(P. 29, E-2, #5) Lost Valley Road, Auburn
207-784-1561
TRAILS, 15; LIFTS, 3; VERTICAL, 240'.
FEATURES: Snowboard park. Nordic trails will probably be added for 1995.

MT. JEFFERSON SKI AREA
(P. 29, C-4, #6) Off Route 6, Lee
207-738-2377
TRAILS, 10; LIFTS, 2; VERTICAL, 432'.

NEW HERMON MOUNTAIN
(P. 29, D-3, #7) RFD 1, Searsport
207-848-5192
SEASON: Dec. 1-March 31
ANNUAL SNOWFALL: 90"
TERRAIN: 18 trails over 60 acres; longest run 4,000'; ◆ 20%; ■ 40%; ● 40%.
LIFTS: 2 (2 surface); capacity, 1,200 per hour.

SUMMIT: 1,410'
VERTICAL: 350'
ACTIVITIES: Snowboarding; night skiing.
FEATURES: Snowmaking 100%; ski school; restaurant; rentals.
Largely of interest to locals, though boarders enjoy the half pipe and lack of crowds.

SADDLEBACK SKI AREA
(P. 29, D-2, #8) Saddleback Ski Road, Rangeley
207-864-5671; 207-864-3380 (snow)
SEASON: Nov. 15-April 10
ANNUAL SNOWFALL: 105"
TERRAIN: 40 trails over 120 acres; longest run 2.5 mi.; ◆ 35%; ■ 35%; ● 30%.
LIFTS: 5 (2 doubles, 3 surface); capacity, 4,400 per hour.
SUMMIT: 4,120'
VERTICAL: 1,830'
ACTIVITIES: Snowboarding; ice skating.
FEATURES: Snowmaking 55%; ski school; child care; restaurant; rentals.
▶NORDIC: 40 groomed km; rentals; lessons.
With all the hoopla over Sugarloaf and Sunday River, Saddleback tends to get overlooked. Its ardent fans aren't complaining. They love discovering secret powder stashes days after the last storm, the glittering panoramas of the Rangeley Lakes, and the beautifully contoured serpentine runs that go on and on. Intermediates can challenge themselves with the constantly changing pitch and terrain of Haymaker and White Stallion. Beginners can drink in the sublime views from the 2.5-mile, ego-inflating Lazy River. And experts can enjoy the ferocious rides on Broncobuster and two gladed steeps: Nightmare, which slaloms around islands of fir and spruce, and Muleskinner, which, after a deceptive traverse, kamikazes into an unrelenting series of moguls and pitches.

SHAWNEE PEAK SKI AREA
(P. 29, E-2, #9) Rural Route 1, Bridgton
207-647-8444
SEASON: Dec. 1-April 10
ANNUAL SNOWFALL: 120"
TERRAIN: 30 trails over 210 acres; longest run 1.5 mi.; ◆ 25%; ■ 50%; ● 25%.
LIFTS: 5 (1 triple, 3 doubles, 1 surface); capacity, 3,200 per hour.
SUMMIT: 1,949'
VERTICAL: 1,300'
ACTIVITIES: Snowboarding; night skiing.
FEATURES: Snowmaking 98%; ski school; restaurant; rentals.
Shawnee Peak is best experienced at night. Fully 80% of the mountain is open and the high spirits of the skiers are contagious. It's a wonderful family area, with warm people and lots of great, groomed cruising. Moreover, the beginners' areas tend to be separated, allowing new skiers to develop at their own pace without fear of comparison. The views are spectacular: Haggett's, an intermediate run (with one side allowed to bump up for mogul practice) looks out onto Mt. Washington, while the black Appalachian surveys the lake district. One of the first areas in the USA to permit snowboarding, Shawnee remains popular with shredders and its snowboarding instruction programs are highly recommended by experts.

SKI MT. ABRAM
(P. 29, D-2, #10) Howe Hill Road, Locke Mills
207-875-5003
SEASON: Dec. 10-April 1
ANNUAL SNOWFALL: 115"
TERRAIN: 25 trails over 130 acres; longest run 2.5 mi.; ◆ 20%; ■ 60%; ● 20%.
LIFTS: 5 (2 doubles, 3 surface); capacity, 4,400 per hour.
SUMMIT: 2,000'
VERTICAL: 1,030'
ACTIVITIES: Snowboarding.
FEATURES: Snowmaking 70%; ski school; restaurant; rentals.
▶NORDIC: 10 ungroomed km.
Mt. Abram is particularly noted for its impeccable grooming, which makes it a prime learning mountain

STATBOX

Tourism: 800-533-9595	**Average annual precipitation:**
Time zone: Eastern	40" (north); 42" (coastal)
Population: 1,227,928	**Highest elevation:** 5,268'
Square miles: 33,040	**Lowest elevation:** sea level

for novices and intermediates seeking improvement or ego massage. But experts can enjoy the headwalls of Boris Badonov, the bumps of Fearless Leader, and the constantly changing pitch and terrain on Rocky's Run. Children under 6 ski free.

SKI SQUAW MOUNTAIN

(P. 29, C-3, #11) Route 6/15, Greenville
207-695-2272
SEASON: Dec. 1-April 1
ANNUAL SNOWFALL: 95″
TERRAIN: 18 trails over NA acres; longest run 2.5 mi.; ♦ 34%; ▪ 33%; ● 33%.
LIFTS: 4 (1 triple, 1 double, 2 surface); capacity, 3,500 per hour.
SUMMIT: 2,700′
VERTICAL: 1,750′
ACTIVITIES: Snowboarding.
FEATURES: Snowmaking 60%; ski school; restaurant; rentals.
This relatively unknown area is set amid the moodily beautiful scenery of Baxter State Park, with enthralling views of Moosehead Lake. Its vertical ranks fourth in the state, translating into long runs, like the gloriously scenic Penobscot. They are ideal for strong intermediates who want uncrowded slopes on which to practice and grow. The area plans to reopen its Nordic center in 1995.

SUGARLOAF/USA

(P. 29, D-2, #12) Route 27, Carrabassett Valley
207-237-2000
SEASON: Nov. 5-May 1
ANNUAL SNOWFALL: 168″
TERRAIN: 94 trails over 430 acres; longest run 3 mi.; ♦ 33%; ▪ 34%; ● 33%.
LIFTS: 14 (1 gondola, 2 high-speed quads, 1 triple, 8 doubles, 2 surface); capacity, 17,500 per hour.
SUMMIT: 4,237′
VERTICAL: 2,820′
ACTIVITIES: Snowboarding; NASTAR; ice skating.
FEATURES: Snowmaking 90%; ski school; restaurants; rentals.
▶NORDIC: 207-237-6830; 85 groomed km; rentals; lessons.
Sugarloaf USA stands out. Literally. The imposing mountain towers over the Carrabassett Valley, thrusting up with a vengeance, the runs resembling streamers zigging and zagging through a jade forest. Experts won't be disappointed, for the 'Loaf offers a dizzying range of adrenaline-pumping steeps (try those off the King Pine quad). There are wide plunges like Narrow Gauge (the only World Cup downhill course in New England), as well as some great bump runs like Choker and Skidder. And there are four, narrow twisty beauts called Wedge, Winter's Way, Bubblecuffer, and Boomauger that swan dive down

the mountain. Intermediates may be intimidated at first glance, but plenty of long lazy cruisers like the 3.5-mile Tote Road and all the runs serviced by the Wiffletree Quad await them. Beginners adore the lovely Stub's Glade and West Mountain lifts. Snowboarders can shred at will all over the mountain, or on a half pipe.

The mountain's astonishing vertical (signs three-quarters of the way up tweak the area's main rival, "If you were skiing Sunday River, you'd be at the top now"); comparatively uncrowded slopes; top-ranked ski school; superb dining, lodging, and nightlife; and wild scenic beauty are reason enough to ski here. But what really makes Sugarloaf unique among Eastern resorts is its above-timberline skiing on the Snowfields, now open year-round, thanks to recently installed snowmaking. If there's one complaint, it's the chill resulting from the combination of high altitude and sunless north-facing slopes. But that's precisely why the snow falls earlier and lingers later than at other areas.

The nearby semi-affiliated ski touring center is likewise among the East's best, winding through bogs, spruce flats, ponds, and alongside the roaring, foaming Carrabassett River. Experts enjoy the challenge of climbing through the hardwood

stands on Burnt Mountain, then screaming down the other side. As a reward, they can strike out on one of the ski trails sitting atop the old rail beds once used to haul lumber, like the 9-km Narrow Gauge.

SUNDAY RIVER SKI RESORT

(P. 29, D-1, #13) Sunday River Road, Bethel
800-824-3000; 207-824-6400 (snow)
SEASON: Nov. 10-May 15
ANNUAL SNOWFALL: 150″
TERRAIN: 90 trails over 505 acres; longest run 3 mi.; ♦ 35%; ▪ 41%; ● 24%.
LIFTS: 12 (2 high-speed quads, 4 quads, 5 triples, 1 double); capacity, 24,000 per hour.
SUMMIT: 2,793′
VERTICAL: 2,011′
ACTIVITIES: Snowboarding; sleigh rides; ice skating.
FEATURES: Snowmaking 95%; ski school; restaurants; child care; rentals.
Sunday River has become the darling of ski writers, who rave about everything from the lessons to the lifts and lodging. In terms of crafting the complete ski experience, it has few rivals: The Vail of the East might well describe it. Although the

area sits on a wide mountain range, a brilliantly linked lift network enables skiers to explore the six peaks with a minimum of cat tracks and poling. A state-of-the-art snowmaking system guarantees lighter, fluffier powder. Beginners have their own trail network—South Ridge. Intermediates can romp on broad, long, perfectly groomed boulevards off Spruce Peak or a new gladed section on Barker Mountain. Experts will delight in the hair-raising descents and big bumps on the Barker, White Cap, and Aurora Peaks, with Obsession, Vortex, Shock Wave, Agony, and White Heat among the most challenging. You'll find scintillating views of the quaint town of Bethel and the surrounding valley nearly everywhere you ski. The ski school is justly praised as one of the USA's finest. Instead of lessons and instructors, you get clinics and ski pros. Never skied? Sunday River's "Guaranteed Learn-to-Ski in One Day" program is an industry model. And the "Perfect Turn" development course (offered throughout the day, all over the mountain) will make better skiers rethink their approach and see immediate improvement. Even boarders love Sunday River, which recently converted Upper Starlight into a snowboarder-only park, including a half pipe. A new area with its own base lodge, Jordan Bowl, will add five trails and two lifts.

TITCOMB MOUNTAIN

(P. 29, D-2, #14) Morrison Hill Road, Farmington
207-778-9031
TRAILS, 10; LIFTS, 2; VERTICAL, 500′.

BETHEL INN SKI CENTER

(P. 29, D-1, #15) Village Common, Bethel
207-824-2175
FACILITIES: 36 groomed km; rentals; lessons; restaurant and lodging; sleigh rides; ice skating.
Heavily angled toward beginners, the wooded terrain offers some challenge. Aside from typically gorgeous scenery, other pluses are free use of the inn's fitness center until 2 P.M. for non-guests.

THE BIRCHES CROSS-COUNTRY

(P. 29, C-2, #16) On Moosehead Lake, Rockwood
207-534-7305
FACILITIES: 43 groomed km; rentals; restaurant.

BOREALIS NORDIC

(P. 29, C-3, #17) Dover-Foxcroft
207-564-2159
FACILITIES: 25 groomed mi.; yurts.

Courtesy: Keystone Resort (see Colorado, p. 98).

Borealis is in the process of becoming a year-round conservation education center. It formerly offered superb skiing on its 10,000 acres, as well as overnight yurts. Borealis expects to reopen for skiing by 1995. Call for details.

CARTER'S CROSS-COUNTRY SKI CENTERS
(P. 29, D-1, #18) Route 26, Oxford and Middle Intervale Roads, Bethel
207-539-4848
FACILITIES: 80 groomed km; rentals; lessons; restaurant; child care; night skiing (20 km).

CHRISTMAS TREE FARM TOURING CENTER
(P. 29, D-2, #19) West Ridge Road, Skowhegan
207-474-2859
FACILITIES: 15 groomed km; rentals; lessons.

FORT KENT CROSS-COUNTRY
(P. 29, A-4, #20) Lonesome Pines Trail, Fort Kent
207-834-5202
FACILITIES: 18 groomed km; lessons; restaurant.

HARRIS FARM CROSS-COUNTRY SKI CENTER
(P. 29, E-2, #21) 252 Buzzell Rd., Biddeford
207-499-2678
FACILITIES: 40 groomed km (with skating lane); rentals; lessons; restaurant; ice skating.

HERMON MEADOW SKI TOURING CENTER
(P. 29, D-3, #22) RFD 2, Billings Rd., Bangor
207-848-3741
FACILITIES: 5 groomed mi.; rentals; restaurant.

HILLTOP HOMESTEAD CROSS-COUNTRY SKI AREA
(P. 29, C-3, #23) HCR 66, Route 2, Seboeis
207-732-3561
FACILITIES: 10 groomed km; rentals; restaurant.

MT. CHASE LODGE
(P. 29, B-4, #24) Upper Chase Pond, Patten
207-528-2183
FACILITIES: 10 groomed mi.; rentals; snowmobiling; restaurant and lodging.
 Baxter State Park offers some of the most scintillating—and demanding—wilderness terrain in the East. This lodge caters primarily to snowmobilers but grooms several level tracks by the lake, and the backcountry opportunities are

MAINE'S WILDERNESS CAMPS

Maine is noted for its many wilderness camps that offer the ultimate in isolation and getting away from it all. Usually four-season retreats, they are popular with both Nordic skiers and ice fishermen in the winter. All offer unbeatable overnight deals including a private cabin with the basics and meals. The cabins range in comfort and amenities from simple affairs with a wood-burning stove and a clean modern outhouse to rustic lodges. Some offer bedding; you must bring your sleeping bag to others. Depending on the package, meals are included in a communal dining room, or you cook your own food on propane stoves. Showers are usually solar-heated 5-gallon plastic bags. These are generally recommended for experienced skiers and hardy souls only. Access is often limited to four-wheel drive and then skiing or snowcatting in. Listed below are some of the most reputable; consult Nordic icons on the state map for locations.

Bowlin Camps
(P. 29, C-3, #34) On E branch Penobscot River, between Oxbow and Millinocket
207-528-2022
FACILITIES: 10 groomed km; unlimited backcountry skiing; rentals; lodging and dining room.

Chesuncook Lake Ski Touring
(P. 29, B-3, #35) Route 76, Chesuncook
207-745-5330 (radio phone)
FACILITIES: Unlimited ungroomed backcountry; cabins; dining room.

Katahdin Lake Wilderness Camps
(P. 29, C-3, #36) T3R8 E of Baxter State Park, Millinocket
207-723-4050 (radio phone)
FACILITIES: Unlimited backcountry skiing; lodging; dining room.

Little Lyford Pond Camps
(P. 29, C-3, #37) Route 6/15, Greenville
207-695-2821 (radio phone)
FACILITIES: Cabins; dining room.

Macannamac Camps
(P. 29, C-4, #38) T8R11, Patten
207-528-2855
FACILITIES: Unlimited backcountry skiing; cabins; lodge; dining room.

Tea Pond Camps
(P. 29, C-2, #39) Stratton
207-243-2943
FACILITIES: Unlimited backcountry skiing; century-old log camps; dining room; sauna.

unmatched.

MOUNTAIN RECREATION
(P. 29, D-4, #25) Smarts Hill Farm, Lowell
603-447-1786
FACILITIES: 32 groomed km; rentals; restaurant.

NATANIS CROSS-COUNTRY SKI TRAILS
(P. 29, D-3, #26) Route 201, Vassalboro
207-622-6533
FACILITIES: 24 groomed km.; rentals; restaurant.

SAMOSET RESORT CROSS-COUNTRY
(P. 29, E-3, #27) 220 Warrenton St., Rockport
207-594-2511

FACILITIES: 5 groomed km; rentals; restaurant and lodging.

SKI-A-BIT
(P. 29, E-2, #28) Route 112, West Buxton
207-929-4824
FACILITIES: 25 groomed km; rentals; snacks.

SUNDAY RIVER INN SKI TOURING CENTER
(P. 29, D-1, #29) Sunday River Road, Bethel
207-824-2410
FACILITIES: 40 groomed km (with skating lane); rentals; lessons; lodging and restaurant; telemarking; night skiing (3 km).
 Though just a mile down the road, this cozy inn is not affiliated with the downhill area. It's noted for its mellow ambience and fine system for both experienced skaters and gliders.

TELEMARK INN
(P. 29, D-1, #30) Kings Highway, Bethel
207-836-2703
FACILITIES: 20 groomed km; rentals; lessons; restaurant and lodging; horse-drawn sleigh rides; ice skating.
 Only 10 non-guests are allowed to use the trails here daily, making this area in the White Mountain National Forest feel like a secluded wilderness. Owner Steve Crone cuts at least one new trail each year, but there's plenty of rugged backcountry terrain skirting frozen ponds and waterfalls. From May to October, the inn offers llama treks.

TROLL VALLEY CROSS-COUNTRY AND FITNESS CENTER
(P. 29, D-2, #31) Red School House Road, Farmington
207-778-3656
FACILITIES: 35 groomed km; rentals; lessons; restaurant.

UP COUNTRY WINTER SPORTS CROSS-COUNTRY
(P. 29, A-4, #32) Forest Ave., Fort Fairfield
207-473-7265
FACILITIES: 20 groomed km; rentals; lessons.

VAL HALLA SKI TOURING CENTER
(P. 29, E-2, #33) 1 Val Halla Rd., Cumberland
207-829-2225
FACILITIES: 20 groomed km; rentals; lessons; restaurant.

MASSACHUSETTS

It's true that Massachusetts' mountains are molehills compared to the Rockies—or even New England's steeper and deeper White and Green Mountains in Vermont, Maine, and New Hampshire. And that's precisely what accounts for the popularity here: Massachusetts makes an excellent training ground for families who might then strike out in search of whiter pastures. Indeed, most of the ski areas offer a special, all-inclusive (rentals, lift ticket, lesson) "Learn to Ski" package mid-week for roughly $15. ❄ Rolling terrain also makes the Bay State a cross-country mecca. Everything is fair game: a frozen pond, a golf course, a state park—even the footpaths along Boston's Charles River!. ❄ Night-skiing is big here, too, and many areas have skating rinks: It's not uncommon to join in a pick-up hockey game before dinner. All of which goes to show Massachusetts people take their winters seriously. ❄ Most of the downhill areas are set in the delightful Berkshires, chock-a-block with quaint hamlets, artists colonies, antique shops, and cozy B&Bs. ❄ Check out the National Basketball Hall of Fame in Springfield or the annual Bean Pot collegiate hockey tournament in the venerable Boston Garden for more non-skiing thrills.

ALPINE

BERKSHIRE EAST SKI AREA

(P. 30, A-2, #1) South River Road, off Route 2, 2 mi. S of Charlemont
413-339-6617
SEASON: Dec. 1-March 31
ANNUAL SNOWFALL: 65"
TERRAIN: 31 trails over NA acres; longest run 2 mi.; ◆ 30%; ▪ 40%; ● 30%.
LIFTS: 4 (3 doubles, 1 surface); capacity, 4,200 per hour.
SUMMIT: 1,720'
VERTICAL: 1,180'
ACTIVITIES: Snowboarding; night skiing.
FEATURES: Snowmaking 100%; ski school; child care; restaurant; rentals.
▶NORDIC: 19 groomed km.; rentals; lessons.
Along with its respectable vertical, Berkshire East offers fine cruising, a few tough pitches, some fairly long wraparound runs, and glorious views. Beginners love the lengthy Mohawk run; racers hone their skills on Competition.

BLANDFORD SKI AREA

(P. 30, B-2, #2) Nye Brook Road, Blandford
413-848-2860
SEASON: Dec. 15-March 10 (open Fri. to Sun., holidays)
ANNUAL SNOWFALL: 60"
TERRAIN: 24 trails over 132 acres; longest run 4,000'; ◆ 20%; ▪ 40%; ● 40%.
LIFTS: 4 (3 doubles, 1 surface); capacity, 4,000 per hour.
SUMMIT: 1,500'
VERTICAL: 465'
ACTIVITIES: Snowboarding.
FEATURES: Snowmaking 90%; ski school; restaurant; rentals.
Essentially a learning mountain for Springfield locals, Blandford can get fairly crowded; but it boasts sufficiently diverse, open terrain for intermediates seeking practice, as well as two short steep pitches from mini-cliffs, Put's Peril and the Ledge.

BLUE HILLS SKI AREA

(P. 30, B-4, #4) 4001 Washington St., Canton
617-828-5090
SEASON: Dec. 1-March 30
TRAILS, 7; LIFTS, 4; VERTICAL, 350'.
▶NORDIC: Friends of Blue Hills Nordic Center (617-326-0079); 750 ungroomed km.

BOUSQUET SKI AREA

(P. 30, B-1, #4) Tamarack Road, Pittsfield
413-442-8316
SEASON: Dec. 1-April 1 (weekends and holidays only)
ANNUAL SNOWFALL: 83"
TERRAIN: 21 trails over 200 acres; longest run 1.5 mi.; ◆ 33%; ▪ 33%; ● 34%.
LIFTS: 5 (2 doubles, 3 surface); capacity, 3,000 per hour.
SUMMIT: 1,875'
VERTICAL: 750'
ACTIVITIES: Snowboarding; tubing; night skiing.
FEATURES: Snowmaking 98%; ski school; restaurants; rentals.
Bousquet offers some exceptionally pretty views of the Berkshires and decent beginner and lower intermediate terrain, as well as a half pipe for snowboarders. Experts can tackle the bumps and steeps of Louisa's Folly when it's open. Under 6 and over 70 ski free.

BRADFORD SKI AREA

(P. 30, A-4, #5) South Cross Road, Haverhill
508-373-0071
TRAILS, 10; LIFTS, 6; VERTICAL, 250'.

BRODIE MOUNTAIN SKI RESORT

(P. 30, A-1, #6) U.S. 7, New Ashford
413-443-4752
SEASON: Nov. 25-April 10
ANNUAL SNOWFALL: 85"
TERRAIN: 28 trails over 325 acres; longest run 2.5 mi.; ◆ 20%; ▪ 50%; ● 30%.
LIFTS: 6 (4 doubles, 2 surface); capacity, 6,000 per hour.
SUMMIT: 2,700'
VERTICAL: 1,250'
ACTIVITIES: Snowboarding; night skiing.
FEATURES: Snowmaking 100%; ski school; child care; restaurants; rentals.
▶NORDIC: 25 groomed km; rentals; lessons.
Brodie is enormously popular with young singles for the variety of lodging, dining, and nightlife—both at the resort and nearby. It's nicknamed "Kelly's Irish Alps," after the patriotic owner, and there's usually rollicking Irish folk music in the lodge of the same name. The skiing is fairly basic, though there are a few steep humps and dips, as well as Massachusetts' longest run, Tipperary. Stronger skiers should enjoy Shamrock.

BUTTERNUT BASIN

(P. 30, B-1, #7) Route 23 East, Great Barrington
413-528-2000
SEASON: Dec. 1-April 7
ANNUAL SNOWFALL: 70"
TERRAIN: 20 trails over 120 acres; longest run 9,500'; ◆ 25%; ▪ 60%; ● 15%.
LIFTS: 8 (1 quad, 1 triple, 4 doubles, 2 surface); capacity, 9,200 per hour.
SUMMIT: 1,800'
VERTICAL: 1,000'
ACTIVITIES: Snowboarding.
FEATURES: Snowmaking 100%; ski school; child care; restaurants; rentals.
▶NORDIC: 10 groomed km; rentals; lessons.
If you think this is a novices' delight, you're right. Families adore this area, located in one of the region's most charming towns, for its friendly feel, first-class ski school, and beautiful scenery, featuring the tight, gently graded slashes through spruce forests that define skiing in the East. Applejack surprises intermediates with its constantly changing terrain. The varied trails and tranquil woods of the Nordic center draw appreciative gliders.

CATAMOUNT SKI AREA

(P. 30, B-1, #8) Route 23 W, South Egremont
413-528-1262
SEASON: Dec. 1-March 30
ANNUAL SNOWFALL: 70"
TERRAIN: 23 trails over 100 acres; longest run 2 mi.; ◆ 30%; ▪ 40%; ● 30%.
LIFTS: 6 (4 doubles, 2 surface); capacity, 5,000 per hour.
SUMMIT: 1, 950'
VERTICAL: 1,000'
ACTIVITIES: Snowboarding; night skiing.
FEATURES: Snowmaking 95%; ski school; child care; restaurant; rentals.
In many respects, Catamount, which straddles the border with New York, is an anomaly. The slopes appear comparatively barren, as if forest fires have decimated the area. Still, it's a charming throwback to the 1950s, and several generations have learned to ski here. The straight up and down runs, such as the misleadingly titled The Glade, have an eerily western feel. Boarders enjoy the half pipe; expert skiers should salivate over a new 35-degree trail being cut for 1995.

STATBOX

Tourism: 800-447-MASS
Time zone: Eastern
Population: 6,016,425
Square miles: 8,257

Average annual precipitation: 44"
Highest elevation: 3,563'
Lowest elevation: Sea level

JERICHO SKI AREA
(P. 30, B-4, #9) 500 Brigham St., Marlborough
508-460-3718
TRAILS, 5; LIFTS, 2; VERTICAL, 180'.

JIMINY PEAK SKI AREA
(P. 30, A-1, #10) Corey Road, Hancock
413-738-5500; 413-738-PEAK (snow)
SEASON: Nov. 15-April 7
ANNUAL SNOWFALL: 90"
TERRAIN: 28 trails over 105 acres; longest run 2 mi.; ◆ 40%; ■ 30%; ● 30%.
LIFTS: 6 (1 quad, 1 triple, 2 doubles, 2 surface); capacity, 6,000 per hour.
SUMMIT: 2,500'
VERTICAL: 1,200'
ACTIVITIES: Snowboarding; ice skating; night skiing.
FEATURES: Snowmaking 95%; ski school; child care; restaurant; rentals.
Jiminy Peak is yet another fine Berkshire area that kindles fond memories of learning to ski in the East, with its gentle tree-lined slopes and picture-postcard views. The undulating pitch and occasionally radical bumps of Whitetail (right under the quad) and Jericho attract the hotdoggers. The new surface lift and Chipmunk trail add to an already fine teaching section. Snowboarders have a half pipe and terrain park.

KLEIN INNSBRUCK SKI AREA
(P. 30, C-4, #11) Off Route 126, S of Franklin
617-528-5660
TRAILS, 5; LIFTS, 3; VERTICAL, 200'.

MOUNT TOM SKI AREA
(P. 30, B-2, #12) Route 5, Holyoke
413-536-0516
SEASON: Dec. 15-March 31
ANNUAL SNOWFALL: 50"
TERRAIN: 17 trails over NA acres; longest run 3,600'; ◆ 10%; ■ 60%; ● 30%.
LIFTS: 6 (4 doubles, 2 surface); capacity, 7,770 per hour.
SUMMIT: 1,380'
VERTICAL: 680'
ACTIVITIES: Snowboarding; night skiing.
FEATURES: Snowmaking 100%; ski school; restaurant; rentals.
Mount Tom sees a large number of students from nearby Amherst and Mt. Holyoke Colleges, giving it a youthful flair in contrast to the state's predominantly family-oriented areas.

NASHOBA VALLEY SKI AREA
(P. 30, A-4, #13) Power Road, Westford
508-692-3033; 508-692-8577 (snow)

TRAILS, 10; LIFTS, 8; VERTICAL, 240'.
Half pipe.

OTIS RIDGE SKI AREA
(P. 30, B-1, #14) Route 23, Otis
413-269-4444
TRAILS, 11; LIFTS, 6; VERTICAL: 400'.

SKI WARD HILL
(P. 30, B-4, #15) 1000 Main St., Shrewsbury
508-845-2814; 508-842-6346 (snow)
TRAILS, 7; LIFTS, 7; VERTICAL, 210'.

WACHUSETT MOUNTAIN
(P. 30, B-3, #16) 499 Mountain Rd., Princeton
508-464-2300; 508-464-5101 (snow)
SEASON: Nov. 25-April 1
ANNUAL SNOWFALL: 90"
TERRAIN: 18 trails over 104 acres; longest run 2 mi.; ◆ 30%; ■ 40%; ● 3-%.
LIFTS: 5 (1 quad, 1 triple, 1 double, 2 surface); capacity, 5,100 per hour.
SUMMIT: 2,006'
VERTICAL: 1,000'
ACTIVITIES: Snowboarding; NASTAR; night skiing.
FEATURES: Snowmaking 100%; USAA racing; ski school; restaurants; rentals.
▶NORDIC: 18 groomed mi.; rentals; lessons.
For an area its size, Wachusett boasts a hefty number of skiers per day: more than 300,000 annually, despite a cap on the number of ticket sales. Part of the secret is its first-class night skiing. Wachusett defines user-friendly. Beginners are particularly coddled, with their own isolated section that was blasted to create a 10-degree pitch (considered ideal for learning). Otherwise, the skiing is solidly low intermediate cruising. Conifer Connection stands out among the blue runs, and Tenth Mountain Trail should satisfy mogul meisters. Equipment is constantly upgraded, and the snowmaking and grooming systems are more sophisticated than many larger mountains. The mountain—a true monadnock, not part of a ridge but standing alone—offers stunning views that inspired Thoreau.

NORDIC

BROOKFIELD ORCHARDS TOURING CENTER
(P. 30, B-3, #17) 12 Lincoln Rd., North Brookfield
508-867-6858
FACILITIES: 12 groomed km; restaurant.

BUCKSTEEP CROSS-COUNTRY SKI CENTER
(P. 30, B-1, #18) Washington

Mountain Road, Washington
413-623-5535
FACILITIES: 40 groomed km; rentals; lessons; restaurant and lodging.
There is a nice blend of wooded terrain here that will appeal to all levels. Take advantage of the moonlight tours if you're staying.

CANTERBURY FARM
(P. 30, B-1, #19) Snow Road, Becket
413-623-8765
FACILITIES: 11 groomed km, 50 ungroomed; rentals; lessons (call ahead); restaurant; child care.
This working farm offers a good mix of terrain.

EAST MOUNTAIN SKI TOURING CENTER
(P. 30, C-2, #20) 1458 East Mountain Rd., Westfield
413-568-1539
FACILITIES: 3 groomed km; rentals; restaurant.

GREAT BROOK FARM SKI TOURING CENTER
(P. 30, B-4, #21) 1018 Lowell St., Carlisle
508-369-7486
FACILITIES: 15 groomed km; rentals; lessons; restaurant; night skiing (1.5 km).

HICKORY HILL SKI TOURING CENTER
(P. 30, B-2, #22) Buffington Hill Road, Worthington
413-238-5813
FACILITIES: 20 groomed km; rentals; lessons; restaurant.

LINCOLN GUIDE SERVICE CENTER
(P. 30, B-4, #23) 152 Lincoln Rd., Lincoln
617-259-1111
FACILITIES: 57 groomed mi.; snowshoeing; rentals; lessons; restaurant.

MAPLE CORNER FARM CROSS-COUNTRY SKI CENTER
(P. 30, C-2, #24) Beech Hill Road, Granville
413-357-8829
FACILITIES: 20 groomed km; rentals; lessons; telemarking; restaurant.

NORTHFIELD MOUNTAIN CROSS-COUNTRY SKI AREA
(P. 30, A-2, #25) Route 63, Northfield
413-659-3715
FACILITIES: 40 groomed km; rentals; lessons; restaurant (weekends only).
This picturesque wooded area

is especially noted for its fine seniors and womens programs.

OAK 'N' SPRUCE
(P. 30, B-1, #26) Meadow Street, South Lee
413-243-3500
FACILITIES: 2 groomed km; rentals (for guests only); restaurant and lodging.

ROLLING GREEN SKI CENTER
(P. 30, A-4, #27) Route 133, Andover
508-475-4066
FACILITIES: 5 groomed km; rentals; restaurant and lodging.

STOW ACRES COUNTRY CLUB
(P. 30, B-4, #28) 58 Randall Rd., Stow
508-568-1100
FACILITIES: 10 groomed km (with skating lane); rentals; restaurant.

STUMP SPROUTS SKI TOURING
(P. 30, B-2, #29) West Hill Road, West Hawley
413-339-4265
FACILITIES: 18 groomed km; rentals; lessons; restaurant and lodging.

SWIFT RIVER INN
(P. 30, B-2, #30) 151 South St., Cummington
413-634-5751
FACILITIES: 23 groomed km; rentals; lessons; restaurant and lodging; night skiing (3 km); tubing; sleigh rides; ice skating.
This is a full-service resort, added on to a turn-of-the-century "gentleman's farm," popular both with families and small business groups. Abundant beginner terrain meanders through fields, with some expert gliding in the woods.

WESTON SKI TRACK
(P. 30, B-4, #31) Park Road, Weston
617-891-6575
FACILITIES: 15 groomed km (with skating lane); rentals; lessons; night skiing (3 km); restaurant.

Skiing in the Midwest doesn't get any better than this, with the consistently longest vertical drops, breathtaking Great Lakes views, miles of pristine cross-country terrain, and by far the most abundant snowfall—averaging upwards of 200 inches annually in the Upper Peninsula. In addition, tobogganing is wildly popular, with courses permitting speeds up to 70 mph. Local bungee-types also indulge in ski flying at Copper Peak in the U.P.'s Iron Mountain! ❄. Prices are low by industry standards, making Michigan a good bet for families. Save and ski a cluster of three areas in the U.P. (Big Powderhorn, Blackjack, and Indianhead) and one (Whitecap) in Wisconsin known collectively as "Big Snow Country." ❄ Youpers (the local term for U.P. residents, as in "We're youpers, not yuppies") are noted for their wry humor and rugged outdoorsy lifestyle, with night-time entertainment running toward beer bashes and sumo wrestling bowling. Maybe that's why many of the USA's leading ski jumpers (a notoriously zany lot) hail from Michigan. ❄ Visit the National Ski Museum and Hall of Fame in Ishpeming or Bronner's, the world's largest Christmas store, in Frankenmuth, a kitschy but entertaining hamlet nicknamed "Michigan's Little Bavaria." ❄ Several events compete for your attention, including the Michigan 200 Dog Sled race, a worthy rival to the famed Iditarod in Alaska, and the North American Vasa Cross Country Ski race.

ALPINE

AL QUAAL RECREATION
(P. 32, C-1, #1) 100 E. Division St., Ishpeming
906-486-6181
TRAILS, 3; LIFTS, 3; VERTICAL, 100'.
▶NORDIC: 5 groomed km.
Boasts a 1,500-foot toboggan run. Municipally operated Al Quaal is convenient for visits to the National Ski Museum and Hall of Fame. A ski jump and Nordic trails are located a few blocks away in Suicide Bowl.

ALPINE VALLEY SKI AREA
(P. 33, H-5, #2) 6775 E. Highland Rd., White Lake
313-887-2180; 313-887-4183 (snow)
SEASON: Nov. 25-March 15
ANNUAL SNOWFALL: 60"
TERRAIN: 23 trails over 103 acres; longest run 2,000'; NA.
LIFTS: 22 (NA quads, NA triples, NA doubles, 12 surface); capacity, 21,330 per hour.
SUMMIT: 1,210'
VERTICAL: 910'
ACTIVITIES: Snowboarding; night skiing.
FEATURES: Snowmaking 100%; ski school; restaurants; rentals.
Alpine Valley's lift capacity is astonishing—and necessary, given the hordes of novices and low intermediates from nearby Detroit.

BIG POWDERHORN MOUNTAIN
(P. 32, B-4, #3) Powderhorn Road, Bessemer
906-932-4838; 800-272-7000 (snow)
SEASON: Nov. 25-April 10
ANNUAL SNOWFALL: 214"
TERRAIN: 24 trails over 215 acres; longest run 1 mi.; ◆ 30%; ▪ 35%; ● 30%.
LIFTS: 9 (9 doubles); capacity, 10,800 per hour.
SUMMIT: 1,840'
VERTICAL: 622'
ACTIVITIES: Snowboarding; NASTAR; night skiing.
FEATURES: Snowmaking 90%; ski school; restaurants; rentals. One of the four "Big Snow Country" resorts with interchangeable lift tickets and joint packages, Powderhorn boasts the greatest variety of dining, lodging, and nightlife, as well as surprisingly varied terrain. Choose from steep chutes, narrow glades, wide open bowls, and meandering cruisers at this excellent intermediate mountain. Cannonball is the top mogul run; Ricochet, Bovidae, and Buckshot the smooth-as-silk cruisers. A new chair will increase uphill capacity, already the highest in the U.P.

BINTZ APPLE MOUNTAIN RESORT
(P. 33, G-4, #4) North River Road, Freeland
517-781-2550
TRAILS, 7; LIFTS, 5; VERTICAL, 200'.
▶NORDIC: 4 groomed km.

BITTERSWEET SKI RESORT
(P. 33, H-3, #5) 600 River Rd., Otsego
616-694-2820; 616-694-2032 (snow)
SEASON: Dec. 1-March 15
ANNUAL SNOWFALL: 100"
TERRAIN: 16 trails over 100 acres; longest run 2,800'; ◆ 30%; ▪ 40%; ● 30%.
LIFTS: 13 (4 triples, 2 doubles, 7 surface); capacity, 10,000 per hour.
SUMMIT: 700'
VERTICAL: 300'
ACTIVITIES: Snowboarding; night skiing.
FEATURES: Snowmaking 100%; ski school; restaurant; rentals. The skiing is strictly for advanced beginners at this pleasant area, except for the fairly sustained pitch of Hawthorne.

BLACKJACK
(P. 32, B-4, #6) Just off U.S. 2, Bessemer
906-229-5115
SEASON: Nov. 25-April 10
ANNUAL SNOWFALL: 180"
TERRAIN: 17 trails over 80 acres; longest run 1 mi.; ◆ 40%; ▪ 40%; ● 20%.
LIFTS: 6 (1 triple, 3 doubles, 2 surface); capacity, 5,000 per hour.
SUMMIT: 1,650'
VERTICAL: 456'
ACTIVITIES: Snowboarding; snowshoeing; tobogganing.
FEATURES: Snowmaking 40%; ski school; restaurants; rentals. Another "Big Snow Country" area, Blackjack is a mecca for snowboarders who thrill to its state-of-the-art terrain park with half pipe, obstacles, and jumps. The solid advanced terrain (mostly clustered in the center) features some potentially bruising, wide bump runs like Spillaway and Cameron. Narrow chutes dart from their flanks, both perfect for practicing or showing off. Children enjoy the Rainbow Run terrain garden. The area's main drawback, a less extensive and sophisticated snowmaking system than its neighbors', will be corrected gradually over the next few years.

BOYNE HIGHLANDS
(P. 32, D-3, #7) Hedrick Road, Harbor Springs
800-GO-BOYNE; 616-549-2441 (snow)
SEASON: Nov. 25-April 10
ANNUAL SNOWFALL: 150"
TERRAIN: 32 trails over 200 acres; longest run 1 mi.; ◆ 35%; ▪ 35%: ● 30%.
LIFTS: 9 (4 quads, 4 triples, 1 surface); capacity, 17,500 per hour.
SUMMIT: 1,290'
VERTICAL: 545'
ACTIVITIES: Snowboarding; NASTAR; snowshoeing; tobogganing; night skiing.
FEATURES: Snowmaking 95%; ski school; restaurants; rentals.
▶NORDIC: 26 groomed km; rentals; lessons.
Boyne Highlands is under the same ownership as Boyne Mountain (less than a half hour drive away) and can be skied on the same ticket, one of the Midwest's great bargains. Highlands is in the midst of an expansion that will add 10 runs and two chairlifts on North Peak by 1996. Like its sister resort, the uphill capacity is among the highest in North America, and the snowmaking is similarly state-of-the-art. The terrain is admirably balanced for all skiers, with a pleasing blend of narrow winding trails reminiscent of New England and wide open bowls. The gentler runs are concentrated on the extreme west and east sides. Boyne's signature steeps—Challenger and Olympic—have consistent pitch, plummeting straight down the fall line. The pointed summit means that skiers

can access any area of the mountain from the top with a minimum of poling. Both the ski school and Nordic center are highly regarded.

BOYNE MOUNTAIN

(P. 32, E-3, #8) Off U.S. 131, Boyne Falls
616-549-2441, 800-GO-BOYNE
SEASON: Nov. 25-April 10
ANNUAL SNOWFALL: 145"
TERRAIN: 17 trails over 115 acres; longest run 1 mi.; ◆ 35%, ■ 40%, ● 25%.
LIFTS: 10 (1 high speed six-seater, 4 quads, 1 triple, 3 doubles, 1 surface); capacity, 18,600 per hour.
SUMMIT: 1,120'
VERTICAL: 500'
ACTIVITIES: Snowboarding; ice skating; night skiing.
FEATURES: Snowmaking 100%; ski school; child care; restaurants; rentals.
▶NORDIC: 35 groomed km; rentals; lessons; 5 km lit.
 The big news is the first six-seat high-speed chair in the USA, which alone transports 3,600 skiers per hour—yet another reason Boyne is among the class of Midwest resorts. Its top-rated snowmaking equipment already sets the standard for the region. Boyne skis bigger than its vertical drop and size would suggest. This is an advanced skier's haven, with bumps and chutes galore, including the infamous Hemlock. Super Bowl offers a choice of three fall lines, with lots of dips and jumps to keep things lively. The middle of the mountain is basically one wide slope with varying pitches, ideal for intermediates. Aurora and Victor are the top cruisers. Beginners have their own small isolated area. The architecture sports a pleasing Tyrolean look; and the lodging and dining in the area is legendary for comfort and elegance. The Nordic center ranks among the best in North America, with a 4-mile lift-serviced trail snaking from the summit. Despite the distance, the Boyne resorts draw droves of weekenders from Detroit who bypass their local areas when they want more demanding runs. The sole downside is Boyne's flattop summit, which necessitates a fair bit of traversing to get where you want.

CABERFAE PEAKS SKI RESORT

(P. 33, F-3, #9) Caberfae Road, Cadillac
616-862-3300; 800-YOU-SKII (snow)
SEASON: Nov. 25-April 10
ANNUAL SNOWFALL: 125"
TERRAIN: 20 trails over 65 acres; longest run 3,960'; ◆ 30%, ■ 40%, ● 30%.
LIFTS: 9 (1 quad, 1 triple, 3 doubles, 4 surface); capacity, 9,000 per hour.

SUMMIT: 1,597'
VERTICAL: 485'
ACTIVITIES: Snowboarding; night skiing.
FEATURES: Snowmaking 77%; ski school; restaurant; rentals.
▶NORDIC: 15 groomed km; rentals; lessons; night skiing (2 km).
 Caberfae, the Midwest's oldest ski area, recently added runs on its North Peak, creating more variety for intermediate skiers who will appreciate the reasonably sharp drops and interesting dips on both mountains. South Peak is the choice for more advanced skiers. The Nordic system, run by the Forest Service, offers trails for all levels.

CANNONSBURG SKI AREA

(P. 33, G-3, #10) 6800 Cannonsburg Rd., Cannonsburg
616-874-6711; 616-874-6728 (snow)
SEASON: Nov. 25-March 15
ANNUAL SNOWFALL: 110"
TERRAIN: 18 trails over 100 acres; longest run 1,800'; ◆ 20%, ■ 40%, ● 40%.
LIFTS: 12 (1 quad, 1 triple, 1 double, 9 surface); capacity, 12,000 per hour.
SUMMIT: 1,100'
VERTICAL: 250'
ACTIVITIES: Snowboarding; night skiing.
FEATURES: Snowmaking 100%; ski school; restaurants; rentals.
 Grand Rapids' premier local area sees considerable skier traffic weekends, but there's rarely a lift line.

CRYSTAL MOUNTAIN RESORT

(P. 32, E-3, #11) M-115 at Lindy Road
800-968-7686; 616-378-2000; 800-748-0114

SEASON: Nov. 25-April 6
ANNUAL SNOWFALL: 135"
TERRAIN: 23 trails over 90 acres; longest run 2,640'; ◆ 30%, ■ 45%, ● 25%.
LIFTS: 7 (1 quad, 2 triples, 2 doubles, 2 surface); capacity, 10,000 per hour.
SUMMIT: 1,132'
VERTICAL: 375'
ACTIVITIES: Snowboarding; NASTAR; sleigh rides; night skiing.
FEATURES: Snowmaking 95%; ski school; restaurants; rentals.
▶NORDIC: 26 groomed km; rentals; lessons; night skiing.
 Another top-notch resort, Crystal is a superlative family area, with primarily beginner and low intermediate skiing. It boasts a remarkably friendly staff (the hands-on owner George Petritz still interviews every staff member personally), as well as a fine ski school and incentives like mid-week packages where children ski and stay free. It is one of the pioneers of time-increment skiing, with lift tickets sold in four-hour lots. Despite the meager vertical, Crystal is spread out and offers wonderfully varied terrain on wide, magic-carpet slopes. Buck is a blue beauty (rated black here). Advanced skiers can tackle the bumps on Wipeout or drop down The Gorge, which while short is savagely steep and mogulled. As good as the downhill area is, the Nordic facility surpasses it. Crystal recently added four more kilometers, and recontoured two advanced trails for intermediate skiers, but still boasts the only genuine double diamond Nordic trail in the Midwest, Screaming Eagle. The 26 km of lighted trails qualify as one of the USA's longest cross country night-skiing networks.

GLADSTONE SPORTS PARK

(P. 32, D-2, #12) Gladstone
906-428-9130; 906-428-2311 (snow)

TRAILS, 4; LIFTS, 5; VERTICAL, 110'.
▶NORDIC: 5 groomed km.

HANSON HILLS RECREATION AREA

(P. 32, E-4, #13) Off state Routes 73 & 93, 3 mi. west of Grayling
517-348-9266
TRAILS, 9; LIFTS, 5; VERTICAL, 200'.
▶NORDIC: 35 groomed km (with skating lane).
 Half pipe.

HICKORY HILLS SKI AREA

(P. 32, E-3, #14) Traverse City
616-947-8566
TRAILS, 7; LIFTS, 5; VERTICAL, 250'.
 A small municipally-run area, Hickory Hills boasts enough good pitch that local high schoolers train here for races.

THE HOMESTEAD

(P. 32, E-3, #15) Wood Ridge Road, Glen Arbor
616-334-5000
SEASON: Dec. 1-March 31
ANNUAL SNOWFALL: 115"
TERRAIN: 14 trails over 25 acres; longest run 1,320'; ◆ 14%, ■ 50%, ● 36%.
LIFTS: 4 (2 triples, 1 double, 1 surface); capacity, 3,300 per hour.
SUMMIT: 905'
VERTICAL: 375'
ACTIVITIES: Snowboarding; snowshoeing; ice skating; night skiing.
FEATURES: Snowmaking 100%; ski school; restaurants; rentals.
▶NORDIC: 36 groomed km; rentals; lessons; night skiing (2 km).
 The Homestead runs a respected ski school, with several programs for youngsters (those under 6 ski free). While the skiing is limited, so are ticket sales, and the sweeping panoramic views of Lake Michigan and the Manitou Islands are extraordinary. The Homestead offers "Ski-x-press," which entitles skiers to a 10% discount (and no wait on line) when they purchase packages at least three days in advance. But the real allure is the nine Nordic trails, many of which wind through the adjacent Sleeping Bear Dunes National Lakeshore, whose stunning terrain embraces thick pine forests and tawny windswept dunes embroidered with scrub. The resort itself is one of Michigan's finest, and includes a charming slopeside village—a rarity in the state.

INDIANHEAD MOUNTAIN RESORT

(P. 32, B-5, #16) 500 Indianhead Rd., Wakefield
906-229-5181, 800-3-INDIAN;

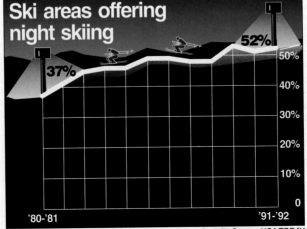

USA SNAPSHOTS®

A look at statistics that shape the sports world

Ski areas offering night skiing

37%

52%

50%
40%
30%
20%
10%
0

'80-'81   '91-'92

Source: Ski Industries America   By Julie Stacey, USA TODAY

800-272-7000 (snow)
SEASON: Nov. 9-April 5
ANNUAL SNOWFALL: 211″
TERRAIN: 19 trails over 160 acres; longest run 5,000′; ♦ 42%; ▪37%; ● 21%.
LIFTS: 9 (1 quad, 1 triple, 3 doubles, 4 surface); capacity, 8,550 per hour.
SUMMIT: 1,935′
VERTICAL: 638′
ACTIVITIES: Snowboarding; NASTAR; snowshoeing; tobogganing; night skiing.
FEATURES: Snowmaking 90%; ski school; restaurants; rentals.
 The third "Big Snow Country" area in Michigan, Indianhead differs from its neighbors in that it's geared to the family and intermediates. The snow tends to be the best in the area, and the runs are all wide, flowing, and impeccably groomed. Visitors love the lodge, which is perched atop the area. The slopes tumble down to thick stands of evergreen below, especially in the Bear Creek area, accentuating the wilderness ambience. The runs in the middle section average a mile in length; the isolated east and west sections are uncrowded and pleasant, but much shorter. Runs tend to feature steeper pitches followed by flats; perfect for racing practice. The toughest challenges are the bumpy Tomahawk, and the steep Winnebago West and East headwalls. Indianhead has also beefed up its snowboarding facilities with a new park, following Powderhorn's lead.

MARQUETTE MOUNTAIN SKI AREA

(P. 32, C-1, #17) County Route 550, Marquette
906-225-1155
SEASON: Dec. 1-April 1
ANNUAL SNOWFALL: 200″
TERRAIN: 17 trails over 95 acres; longest run 1.25 mi.; ♦ 25%; ▪ 50%; ● 25%.
LIFTS: 4 (2 doubles, 2 surface); capacity, 3,500 per hour.
SUMMIT: 1,800′
VERTICAL: 600′
ACTIVITIES: Snowboarding; NASTAR; night skiing.
FEATURES: Snowmaking 80%; ski school; restaurant; rentals.
 Marquette is a fairly steep little mountain popular with snowboarders (it also has a half pipe). The area recently added a new lift and cut more intermediate trails. Cliffs Ridge builds up some awesome bumps by Midwest standards and is one of the rare mogul runs lit at night. To the right off Chair Two are gentler, follow-the-fall-line cruisers like Snowfield and Chute. The U.S. Luge Association practices on the area's track (not open to the public).

MICHAWAYE-AUSABLE

(P. 32, E-4, #18) Opal Lake Road, Gaylord
517-939-8919

TRAILS, 9; LIFTS, 5; VERTICAL, 215′.
▶NORDIC: 20 groomed km.
 Most popular for its fine Nordic trails.

MIO MOUNTAIN SKI AREA

(P. 32, E-4, #19) Routes 72 & 33, Mio
517-826-5569
SEASON: Dec. 15-April 1 (open Fri. to Sun.; holidays; Thur. to Sat. eve.)
ANNUAL SNOWFALL: 120″
TERRAIN: 18 trails over 60 acres; longest run 1,500′; NA.
LIFTS: 5 (5 surface); capacity, 1,500 per hour.
SUMMIT: NA
VERTICAL: 250′
ACTIVITIES: Snowboarding; night skiing.
FEATURES: Snowmaking 25%; ski school; restaurant; rentals.
 The skiing is predominantly low intermediate, with some beautiful forest views.

MISSAUKEE MOUNTAIN

(P. 33, F-3, #20) State Route 66, 2 mi. N of Lake City
616-839-7575
TRAILS, 4; LIFTS, 2; VERTICAL, 470′.
▶NORDIC: 9 groomed km.
 The cross-country trails are more demanding than the Alpine runs; lack of snowmaking makes conditions spotty—when it's open.

MONT RIPLEY

(P. 32, A-6, #21) Off U.S. 40, Houghton
906-487-2340
SEASON: Dec. 10-March 31
ANNUAL SNOWFALL: 200″
TERRAIN: 8 trails over 23 acres; longest run 1,500′; ♦ 25%; ▪ 50%; ● 25%.
LIFTS: 2 (1 double, 1 surface); capacity, 2,400 per hour.
SUMMIT: 1,120′
VERTICAL: 423′
ACTIVITIES: Snowboarding; snowshoeing; tobgganing; night skiing.
FEATURES: Ski school; restaurant; rentals.
 Operated by Michigan Tech University, Mont Ripley is a mini-bowl shaped like a barcalounger; the top half is super-steep, the bottom virtually flat. Best either for advanced skiers or first-timers. The university may install snowmaking over the next few years; for now call ahead since the area closes with insufficient snow cover.

MOTT MOUNTAIN

(P. 33, F-3, #22) Off U.S. 10, 1 mi. S of Farwell
517-588-2945
TRAILS, 7; LIFTS, 5; VERTICAL, 200′.

MT. BRIGHTON SKI AREA

(P. 33, H-4, #23) 4141 Bauer Rd., Brighton
810-229-9581; 810-227-1451 (snow)
SEASON: Nov. 20-March 10
ANNUAL SNOWFALL: 60″
TERRAIN: 25 runs over 130 acres; longest run 1,500′; ♦ 30%; ▪ 40%; ● 30%.
LIFTS: 7 (4 triples, 3 doubles); capacity, 17,200 per hour.
SUMMIT: NA
VERTICAL: 250′
ACTIVITIES: Snowboarding; NASTAR; night skiing.
FEATURES: Snowmaking 100%; ski school; restaurants; rentals.
 This sparsely wooded pyramidical mountain essentially offers two broad, multi-faceted humps scored by lifts. The front side facing the lodge is gentle, as is the groove formed by the humps on the back side. The smaller hump (to the left as you face the mountain) offers a much sharper drop, accessed by the yellow chair. Snowboarders have a half pipe.

MT. HOLIDAY

(P. 32, E-3, #24) 1861 U.S. 31 N, Traverse City
616-938-2500
TRAILS, 12; LIFTS, 8; VERTICAL, 200′.
▶NORDIC: 4 groomed km.
 Half pipe.

MT. HOLLY SKI AREA

(P. 33, H-5, #25) 3536 S. Dixie Highway, Holly
313-634-8260
SEASON: Nov. 15-March 15
ANNUAL SNOWFALL: 60″
TERRAIN: 17 trails over 102 acres; longest run 2,100′; ♦ 35%; ▪ 45%; ● 20%.
LIFTS: 11 (2 quads, 3 triples, 2 doubles, 4 surface); capacity, 12,000 per hour.
SUMMIT: NA
VERTICAL: 350′
ACTIVITIES: Snowboarding; NASTAR; night skiing.
FEATURES: Snowmaking 100%; ski school; restaurants; rentals.
 An excellent mountain for locals that can get crowded on weekends, though a new quad has eased congestion. Hotdoggers and boarders enjoy the bumpy Thunderbolt and Mogulmania; intermediates enjoy several recently lengthened blue runs.

MT. MCSAUBA

(P. 32, D-3, #26) McSauba Road & Pleasant Street, Charlevoix
616-547-3267
TRAILS, 5; LIFTS, 3; VERTICAL, 160′.
▶NORDIC: 3 groomed km (2 km lit).

MT. ZION SKI AREA

(P. 32, B-4, #27) E 4946 Jackson Rd., Ironwood
906-932-3718
TRAILS, 9; LIFTS, 3; VERTICAL, 302′.
▶NORDIC: 3 groomed km.
 Mt. Zion has expanded its advanced terrain recently and has a few steep pitches, but it's still most appropriate as a learning mountain.

MULLIGAN'S HOLLOW SKI BOWL

(P. 33, G-2, #28) Harbor Avenue, Grand Haven
616-842-0634
TRAILS, 8 trails; LIFTS, 3; VERTICAL, 130′.

NORWAY MOUNTAIN

(P. 32, D-1, #29) Norway
800-272-5445
SEASON: Dec. 1-April 1
ANNUAL SNOWFALL: 180″
TERRAIN: 12 trails over 70 acres; longest run 1 mi.; ♦ 25%; ▪ 50%; ● 25%.
LIFTS: 3 (2 doubles, 1 surface); capacity 2,800 per hour.
SUMMIT: NA
VERTICAL: 500′
ACTIVITIES: Snowboarding.
FEATURES: Snowmaking 75%; ski school; restaurant; rentals.
▶NORDIC: 1 groomed km.
 This deserted mountain is ideal for practicing, with some fairly long runs, good snow, and slight variation in pitch.

NUB'S NOB SKI AREA

(P. 32, D-3, #30) 4021 Nubs Nob Rd., Harbor Springs
616-526-2131; 616-878-NUBS (snow)
SEASON: Nov. 25-April 10
ANNUAL SNOWFALL: 140″
TERRAIN: 23 trails over 160 acres; longest run 5,000′; ♦ 30%; ▪ 40%; ● 30%.
LIFTS: 8 (1 quad, 3 triples, 2 doubles, 2 surface); capacity, 12,000 per hour.
SUMMIT: 1,338′
VERTICAL: 427′
ACTIVITIES: Snowboarding; NASTAR; night skiing.
FEATURES: Snowmaking 100%; ski school; child care; restaurants; rentals.
 A truly skier-friendly resort, Nub's Nob executives listened when families complained there wasn't enough intermediate terrain and have cut two new trails, Dories Bowl and Revelry, as well as a 10-acre terrain garden for children. Splendid beginner and intermediate terrain runs through stands of maple, oak, beech, and basswoods. But Nub's Nob still has the reputation as an advanced mountain, with a troika of gnarly runs called Twilight Zone, Scarface, and Chute (with an oscillating fall line). The

snowmaking is considered some of the best anywhere (the crew was invited to take their guns to the Sarajevo Winter Olympics in 1984). And two new chairs have been added to ease weekend traffic from Detroit. Best of all, the bulk of the mountain is protected from the fierce winds that plague many Midwest resorts on the water.

PANDO
(P. 33, G-3, #31) State Route 44 East, Rockford
616-874-8343
TRAILS, 6; LIFTS, 6; VERTICAL, 125'.
▶NORDIC: 8 groomed km (3 km lit).

PETOSKEY WINTER SPORTS PARK
(P. 32, D-3, #32) Petoskey
616-347-2500
TRAILS, 1; LIFTS, 1; VERTICAL, 100'.

PINE KNOB SKI RESORT
(P. 33, H-5, #33) 7777 Pine Knob Rd., Clarkston
810-625-0801
SEASON: Nov. 25-March 15
ANNUAL SNOWFALL: 50"
TERRAIN: 17 trails over 85 acres; longest run 1,350'; ◆◆ 5%; ◆ 30%; ■ 35%; ● 30%.
LIFTS: 9 (4 triples, 1 double, 4 surface); capacity, 9,600 per hour.
SUMMIT: 1,300'
VERTICAL: 300'
ACTIVITIES: Snowboarding; night skiing.
FEATURES: Snowmaking 100%; ski school; restaurant; rentals.
Pine Knob's main distinction is its metro Detroit location. The fiercely steep and ungroomed Wall is the only true expert run in southern Michigan, and Bumper is top-notch mogul run.

PINE MOUNTAIN
(P. 32, D-1, #34) N 3332 Pine Mountain Rd., Iron Mountain
906-774-2747
SEASON: Nov. 25-April 5
ANNUAL SNOWFALL: 120"
TERRAIN: 15 trails over 100 acres; longest run 1 mi.; ◆ 30%; ■ 40%; ● 30%.
LIFTS: 4 (3 doubles, 1 surface); capacity, 3,900 per hour.
SUMMIT: 1,600'
VERTICAL: 450'
ACTIVITIES: Snowboarding; snowmobiling; NASTAR.
FEATURES: Snowmaking 100%; ski school; restaurants; child care; rentals.
▶NORDIC: 8 groomed km.
The original Pine Mountain was created by the Pabst family, but burnt down. It was rebuilt after World War II; the new owners were ski jumpers, and their 90-meter ski jumping complex still stands. The

bulk of the skiing is green and blue, with a couple of steep headwalls. The area recently added a half pipe and new chair, with increased snowmaking and refurbished lodging planned.

PORCUPINE MOUNTAINS
(P. 32, A-5, #35) Route 107, Ontonagon
906-885-5275; 800-272-7000 (snow)
SEASON: Dec. 20-April 1
ANNUAL SNOWFALL: 110"
TERRAIN: 14 trails over 80 acres; longest run 6,000'; ◆ 36%; ■ 36%; ● 28%.
LIFTS: 4 (1 triple, 1 double, 2 surface); capacity, 3,500 per hour.
SUMMIT: 1,550'
VERTICAL: 600'
ACTIVITIES: Snowboarding; snowmobiling.
FEATURES: Ski school; restaurant; rentals.
▶NORDIC: 42 groomed km; rentals; lessons.
Porcupine offers some nicely pitched runs that snake through virgin stands of birch, pine, and hemlock. But the main reasons to ski here are the low prices (it's state-owned) and extraordinary panoramas of Lake Superior—so close it feels as if you could ski off a lip and do a split right into the water. The expert runs are essentially short feed-ins to the low intermediate expanse. The long green runs off either flank of the mountain are endless by Midwestern standards.

RIVERVIEW HIGHLANDS SKI AREA
(P. 33, H-5, #36) 15015 Sibley Rd., Riverview
313-281-4257; 479-2266 (snow)
TRAILS, 10; LIFTS, 5; VERTICAL, 195';
Half pipe.

SHANTY CREEK/SCHUSS MOUNTAIN RESORT
(P. 32, E-3, #37) Route 3, Bellaire
616-533-8621; 800-678-4111 (snow)
SEASON: Nov. 25-April 10
ANNUAL SNOWFALL: 200"
TERRAIN: 29 trails over 170 acres; longest run 1 mi.; ◆ 25%; ■ 50%; ● 25%.
LIFTS: 9 (1 triple, 5 doubles, 3 surface); capacity, 7,800 per hour.
SUMMIT: 1,115'
VERTICAL: 400'
ACTIVITIES: Snowboarding; ice skating; night skiing.
FEATURES: Snowmaking 100%; ski school; restaurants; rentals.
▶NORDIC: 31 groomed km; rentals; lesson; night skiing (2.5 km).
These two resorts—best known for their world-class golf courses,

including an Arnold Palmer-designed beaut—are under the same ownership, sit four miles apart, and can be skied on the same ticket. Guests have access to all amenities and facilities at both; a shuttle runs regularly between the two. Children under 18 ski and stay free (in parents' room) midweek. Shanty is a more modern, comfortable development, popular with families and honeymooners, while Schuss resembles Disney World in its riot of cotton candy colors. Schuss also provides more challenging skiing, with sharp inclines like Kingdom Come and Goose Bumps. Good Knight and Sapporo are the cruise-control blues; while green runs cling to the periphery of the mountain. With its lodge at the mountain top, Shanty offers plenty of wide open, meticulously groomed cruisers. Recent additions include a snowboard terrain garden with half pipe. Special events nearly every weekend.

SHERIDAN VALLEY SKI AREA
(P. 32, E-4, #38) Lewiston
517-786-4231
TRAILS, 7; LIFTS, 2; VERTICAL, 150'.
▶NORDIC: 7 groomed km.
Another good learning area for locals. The Nordic system here is more challenging than the downhill runs.

SKI BRULE/HOMESTEAD
(P. 32, B-6, #39) 397 Brule Mountain Rd., Iron River
906-265-4957; 800-362-7853 (snow)
SEASON: Nov. 15-April 7
ANNUAL SNOWFALL: 130"
TERRAIN: 14 trails over 95 acres; longest run 1 mi.; ◆ 30%; ■ 40%; ● 30%.
LIFTS: 9 (3 doubles, 6 surface); capacity, 4,700 per hour.
SUMMIT: 1,861'
VERTICAL: 420'
ACTIVITIES: Snowboarding; snowmobiling; NASTAR; night skiing.
FEATURES: Snowmaking 100%; ski school; restaurants; rentals.
▶NORDIC: 23 groomed km; rentals; lessons.
This fine little area has a steady family and business clientele and is slowly expanding, most recently with a new chair and intermediate trail.

SKYLINE SKI AREA
(P. 32, E-4, #40) 4 mi. Rd. exit 251, Grayling
517-275-5445
SEASON: Dec. 15-March 31
ANNUAL SNOWFALL: 110"
TERRAIN: 11 trails over 60 acres; longest run 1,800'; ◆ 15%; ■ 75%; ● 15%
LIFTS: 10 (1 double, 9 surface); capacity, 9,500 per hour.

SUMMIT: 1,515'
VERTICAL: 210'
ACTIVITIES: Snowboarding; night skiing.
FEATURES: Ski school; restaurant; rentals.
Skyline's lodge is perched atop the mountain and offers superb views, but beginners have only a small trail off to the side. Truly challenging skiing can be found on The Bowl.

SNOW SNAKE SKI AREA
(P. 33, F-4, #41) 3407 Mann Siding Rd., Harrison
517-539-7793
SEASON: Dec. 15-March 15
ANNUAL SNOWFALL: 85"
TERRAIN: 12 trails over 40 acres; longest run 2,650'; ◆ 10%; ■ 70%; ● 20%.
LIFTS: 6 (1 triple, 5 surface); capacity, 3,600 per hour.
SUMMIT: NA
VERTICAL: 210'
ACTIVITIES: Snowboarding; night skiing.
FEATURES: Snowmaking 90%; ski school; restaurant; rentals.
▶NORDIC: 7 groomed km; rentals.
The owner has cleared several stands of trees, reducing the number of trails, but widening runs for effortless intermediate skiing.

SUGAR LOAF RESORT
(P. 32, E-3, #42) Off Route 651 North, Cedar
616-228-5461; 800-748-0117; 616-228-5461 (snow)
SEASON: Nov. 25-March 15
ANNUAL SNOWFALL: 180"
TERRAIN: 23 trails over 80 acres; longest run 1 mi.; ◆ 30%; ■ 40%; ● 30%.
LIFTS: 7 (1 triple, 5 doubles, 1 surface); capacity, 8,365 per hour.
SUMMIT: 1,150'
VERTICAL: 500'
ACTIVITIES: Snowboarding; NASTAR; night skiing.
FEATURES: Snowmaking 85%; ski school; restaurants; child care; rentals.
▶NORDIC: 26 groomed km; rentals; lessons.
Talk about something for everyone! Wonderful, broad-gladed boulevards on the backside offer dramatic views of Lake Michigan and the Manitou Islands. Short but menacing drops on the front face include Awful-Awful, arguably the steepest in the Midwest. Sugarloaf also boasts mean bump runs like Waffle and AAA (aka Awful-Awful-Awful), and impeccable grooming. For boarders, there is a half pipe and renowned school. A new beginner's section with its own chair features ski-through tepees and fort. High-quality midweek learn-to-ski packages cater to all levels, including racing. Don't overlook the first-class Nordic facility,

with extensive night skiing. A free shuttle runs to the nearby Leelanau Sands Casino (operated by the Chippewa and Ottawa tribes). A skier could get spoiled at the "Tahoe of the Midwest."

SWISS VALLEY SKI AREA

(P. 33, J-3, #43) Patterson Hill Road, Jones
616-244-5635; 616-244-8016 (snow)
SEASON: Dec. 15-March 15
ANNUAL SNOWFALL: 80″
TERRAIN: 11 trails over 55 acres; longest run 2,200′; ◆ 20%; ■ 60^; ● 20%.
LIFTS: 7 (2 quads, 1 triple, 4 surface); capacity, 9,800 per hour.
SUMMIT: NA
VERTICAL: 225′
ACTIVITIES: Snowboarding; night skiing.
FEATURES: Snowmaking 80%; ski school; restaurants; rentals.
 This family area boasts the highest summit in southwest Michigan, but the terrain is limited. The expert slope is occasionally allowed to develop bumps.

TIMBER RIDGE SKI AREA

(P. 33, H-3, #44) 07500 23 1/2 St., Gobles
800-253-2928; 616-694-9158 (snow)
SEASON: Dec. 1-March 10
ANNUAL SNOWFALL: 75″
TERRAIN: 15 trails over 50 acres; longest run 2,000′; ◆ 20%; ■ 40%; ● 40%.
LIFTS: 8 (1 quad, 1 triple, 2 doubles, 4 surface); capacity, 6,000 per hour.
SUMMIT: NA
VERTICAL: 250′
ACTIVITIES: night skiing.
FEATURES: Snowmaking 100%; ski school; restaurant; rentals.
 The name doesn't deceive: The skiing is mostly among mini-glades on runs carved into the hill. Timber Ridge's layout offers a few interesting steeps, curves, and dips, but nothing appropriate for strong skiers except Hemlock, which develops bumps and unusual whales from the snowmaking. The area has been increasing its snowmaking quality and capabilities, as well as expanding the beginner terrain.

TREETOPS SYLVAN RESORT

(P. 32, E-4, #45) 3962 Wilkinson Rd., Gaylord
517-732-6711
SEASON: Nov. 25-March 31
ANNUAL SNOWFALL: 150″
TERRAIN: 18 trails over 80 acres; longest run 2,200′; ◆ 20%; ■ 60%; ● 20%.
LIFTS: 7 (2 triples, 1 double, 4 surface); capacity, 4,800 per hour.
SUMMIT: 1,360′

VERTICAL: 225′
ACTIVITIES: Snowboarding; NASTAR; tubing; night skiing.
FEATURES: Snowmaking 100%; ski school; child care; restaurants; rentals.
▶NORDIC: 20 groomed km; rentals; lessons; night skiing (7 km).
 This four-season, full-service resort offers fairly varied, mostly tree-lined skiing and a popular Nordic system. The lodge sits atop the mountain

NORDIC

ADDISON OAKS COUNTY PARK SKI CENTER

(P. 33, G-5, #46) 1480 West Romeo Rd., Leonard
313-693-2432
FACILITIES: 18 groomed km; rentals; lessons; restaurant; ice skating; night skiing.

BAY VALLEY HOTEL AND RESORT

(P. 33, G-4, #47) Bay City
800-292-5028
FACILITIES: 6 groomed km; rentals; lodging and restaurant.

BLACK MOUNTAIN FOREST PATHWAY

(P. 32, D-4, #48) Rogers City
800-622-4148
FACILITIES: 50 groomed km; rentals; lodging and restaurant.

BLACK RIVER HARBOR CROSS-COUNTRY TRAILS

(P. 32, B-4, #49) Ironwood
906-932-2144
FACILITIES: 15 groomed km; lessons; lodging and restaurant.

CHALET CROSS-COUNTRY

(P. 33, F-4, #50) Clare
517-386-9697
FACILITIES: 10 groomed km; rentals; lessons; night skiing.

COOL SKI AREA

(P. 32, F-3, #51) 5557 N. 210th Ave., LeRoy
616-768-4624
FACILITIES: 40 groomed km; rentals; lessons; lodging and restaurant; snowshoeing; mountain biking.
 Tracked for diagonal and skating, the system winds through a range of terrain from rolling hills to frozen swampland, open meadows to hardwood, and evergreen forests. This friendly, family-run operation includes the Old Bottle Museum and a working tree farm, both of which appeal to kids.

COPPER PEAK NORDIC CENTER

(P. 32, B-4, #52) Ironwood
906-932-3857
FACILITIES: 30 groomed km; rentals; lessons; lodging and restaurant; snowshoeing; dog sledding; sleigh rides; snowcat rides.
 An excellent center for both instruction and solitary gliding.

CORSAIR SKI TRAILS

(P. 32, F-5, #53) I-75 Business Loop, Tawas City
800-55-TAWAS
FACILITIES: 56 groomed km; rentals; lessons.
 In addition to the varied groomed terrain, Corsair accesses over 120,000 backcountry acres in Huron National Forest. Trails follow high bluffs and descend into valleys, crossing forests and meadows.

CROSS-COUNTRY SKI CENTER OF ROSCOMMON

(P. 32, E-4, #54) 9435 County Route 100, Higgins Lake,

Roscommon
517-821-6661
FACILITIES: 24.5 groomed km; rentals; lessons; restaurant; night skiing (4.5 km).

CURTIS AREA TRAILS

(P. 32, C-3, #55) Curtis
906-586-9700
FACILITIES: NA groomed km; rentals; instructions; lodging and restaurant; night skiing; snowshoeing; tobogganing.

ECHO VALLEY

(P. 33, H-3, #56) Kalamazoo
616-349-3291
FACILITIES: 0.25 groomed km; rentals; instructions; restaurant; night skiing.

FORBUSH CORNER

(P. 32, E-4, #57) 4971 County Route 612, Frederic
517-348-5989
FACILITIES: 36 groomed km; rentals; lessons; night skiing; restaurant and lodging.

GARLAND

(P. 32, E-4, #58) Route 1, County Route 489, Lewsiton
800-968-0042
FACILITIES: 40 groomed km; rentals; lessons; restaurant and lodging; ice skating; night skiing (1.5 km).
 One of the Rolls-Royces of Nordic skiing, posh Garland even has a private jet to whisk guests around. The luxurious accommodations are in individual cabins, condos, or the largest log lodge east of the Mississippi. Don't miss the "Gourmet Glide," held weekends in February and March (skiing from hut to hut, sampling a different course at each stop) or the bacchanalian Zhivago nights (taking a horse-drawn sleigh to a romantic cabin for a sumptuous dinner).

Courtesy: Michigan Travel Bureau (see p. 113).

GEORGE YOUNG RECREATIONAL CENTER
(P. 32, B-6, #59) Iron River
906-265-3401
FACILITIES: 25 groomed km; rentals; instructions; restaurant; snowshoeing.

GRAND RIVER WINTER SPORTS AREA
(P. 33, H-4, #60) Mason
517-676-6109
FACILITIES: 11 groomed km; rentals; restaurant and lodging; tobogganing.

GRAND TRAVERSE RESORT
(P. 32, E-3, #61) 6300 U.S. 31 N, Acme
800-748-0303, ext. 3675
FACILITIES: 75 groomed km; rentals; lessons; restaurants and lodging; sleigh rides; snowmobiling; ice skating; night skiing (2 km).
This top-notch four-star spa resort offers every conceivable amenity. The superb Nordic center serves as headquarters for the annual Vasa Race. Non-skiers can tour the several fine wineries in the region (try the dry Johannisberg rieslings). Skiing is wonderfully varied, with some arduous forest trails in addition to milder tracks on the resort grounds, including The Bear golf course (designed by Jack Nicklaus).

HINCHMAN ACRES RESORT
(P. 32, E-4, #62) Mio
517-826-3267
FACILITIES: 24 groomed km; rentals; lessons; restaurant and lodging.

HUDSON MILLS METROPARK/INDIAN SPRINGS
(P. 33, H-5, #63) Dexter
800-477-2757
FACILITIES: 13 groomed km; rentals; restaurant.

HURON-CLINTON METROPARKS
(P. 33, H-5, #64) Brighton
800-47-PARKS
FACILITIES: 115 groomed km; rentals; lessons; restaurant and lodging; night skiing; tobogganing.

HURON HILLS SKI CENTER
(P. 33, H-5, #65) Ann Arbor
313-971-6840
FACILITIES: 11 groomed km; rentals; lessons.

INDEPENDENCE OAKS COUNTY PARK SKI CENTER
(P. 33, H-5, #66) 9501 Sashabaw Rd., Clarkston

313-625-0877
FACILITIES: 18 groomed km; rentals; lessons; restaurant; ice skating.

IRON RIVER NORDIC
(P. 32, B-6, #67) Highway 424 & Young Lane, Iron River
906-265-3401
FACILITIES: 25 groomed km; rentals; lessons; restaurant and lodging.

JOHNSON'S NORDIC TRAILS
(P. 32, B-5, #68) 160 Old U.S. 2, Wakefield
906-224-4711
FACILITIES: 30 groomed km; rentals; lessons; restaurant and lodging.
Fine skiing for both experts and beginners at this Midwest training site of the U.S. Ski Team.

KENT COUNTY PARKS
(P. 33, G-3, #69) Grand Rapids
616-774-3697
FACILITIES: 37 groomed km; rentals; restaurant.

LAKES OF THE NORTH
(P. 32, E-3, #70) Pineview Drive, Mancelona
616-585-6000
FACILITIES: 20 groomed km; rentals; restaurant; tobogganing.

LAKEVIEW HILLS COUNTRY INN RESORT
(P. 32, E-4, #71) Fleming Drive, Lewiston
517-786-2000
FACILITIES: 20 groomed km; rentals; lessons; restaurant and lodging.

LOVE CREEK NATURE CENTER
(P. 33, J-2, #72) Berrien Center
616-471-2617
FACILITIES: 10 groomed km; rentals; lessons; night skiing; snowshoeing.

MADELINE BERTRAND COUNTY PARK
(P. 33, J-2, #73) Niles
616-683-8280
FACILITIES: 8 groomed km; rentals; lessons; restaurant; night skiing; snowshoeing.

MAPLE LANE
(P. 32, C-2, #74) 124 Krieger Dr., Skandia
906-942-7662
FACILITIES: 14 groomed km; rentals; lessons; restaurant; snowshoeing.

MARSH RIDGE
(P. 32, E-4, #75) 4815 Historic Old 27 South, Gaylord
800-743-7529
FACILITIES: 26 groomed km; rentals; lessons; restaurant and lodging; ice skating.
This new resort offers spa facilities for the end of a strenuous workout on the varied terrain.

MAYBURY STATE PARK
(P. 33, H-5, #76) Northville
313-348-1190
FACILITIES: 15 groomed km; rentals; restaurant.

MCGUIRE'S RESORT
(P. 33, F-3, #77) Mackinaw Trail, Cadillac
800-632-7302
FACILITIES: 7 groomed km; rentals; lessons; restaurant and lodging; night skiing (3 km).

MUNISING TRAIL NETWORKS
(P. 32, C-2, #78) Munising
906-387-3700
FACILITIES: 44 groomed km; rentals; restaurant and lodging; night skiing.
The local parks department operates several interconnected trail systems, including Valley Spur, McKeever Hills, and the Christmas Lighted Ski Trail (whose name derives from the majestic stands of spruce lining the trails).

MUSKEGON STATE PARK
(P. 33, G-2, #79) North Muskegon
616-744-9629
FACILITIES: 8 groomed km; rentals; night skiing; luge run.

PROUD LAKE RECREATION AREA
(P. 33, H-5, #80) Milford
313-685-2379
FACILITIES: 10 groomed km; rentals; instructions; night skiing.

RANCH RUDOLF
(P. 32, E-3, #81) Traverse City
5616-947-9529
FACILITIES: 25 groomed km; rentals; restaurant and lodging; snowshoeing.

RIVER FALLS TRAILS
(P. 32, B-4, #82) Ironwood
906-932-5638
FACILITIES: 10 groomed km; rentals; lessons; lodging and restaurant; snowshoeing; tobogganing.

ROCHESTER-UTICA RECREATION AREA
(P. 33, H-5, #83) Utica
313-652-1321

FACILITIES: 15 groomed km; rentals; lessons; tobogganing.

ROGERS CITY TRAIL NETWORKS
(P. 32, D-4, #84) Rogers City
800-622-4148
FACILITIES: 133 groomed km; rentals; restaurant and lodging. Several networks, including those of Hoeft State Park, Presque Isle Trails, Ocquoc Falls Pathway, Thompson's Harbor State Park, and the Herman Vogler Conservation Area interconnect, with a breathtaking range of scenery and terrain.

ROLLING HILLS COUNTY PARK
(P. 33, H-5, #85) Ypsilanti
313-484-7669
FACILITIES: 5 groomed km; rentals; lessons; night skiing; tobogganing.

SAUK VALLEY FARMS
(P. 33, H-4, #86) 10750 Prospect Hill, Brooklyn
517-467-2061
FACILITIES: 10 groomed km; rentals; restaurant and lodging; tobogganing.

THUNDER BAY RESORT
(P. 32, D-4, #87) 1 Village Corner, State Route 32 E, Hillman
517-742-4732
FACILITIES: 15 groomed km; rentals; lessons; restaurant and lodging; snowmobiling; sleigh rides; ice skating.

WARREN DUNES STATE PARK
(P. 33, J-2, #88) Sawyer
616-426-4013
FACILITIES: 10 ungroomed km; rentals; restaurant; snowshoeing.

WARREN VALLEY TRAILS
(P. 33, H-5, #89) Dearborn Heights
313-561-1040
FACILITIES: 6 groomed km; rentals; lessons; restaurant.

WAYNE COUNTY DEPT. OF PARKS AND RECREATION
(P. 33, H-5, #90) Westland
313-261-1990
FACILITIES: 6 groomed km; rentals; lessons.

WILDERNESS VALLEY CROSS-COUNTRY
(P. 32, E-4, #91) 7519 Mancelona Rd., Gaylord
616-585-7141
FACILITIES: 56 groomed km (with skating lane); rentals; lessons; restaurant and lodging; night skiing (1.5 km).

MINNESOTA

It's cold, true, but the snow conditions are uniformly excellent in the scenic northern half of the state where most downhill areas are located. The peaks here are the region's highest, with verticals up to 800 feet. ❅ "The Land of 10,000 Lakes" is cross-country heaven wherever you chose to stride and glide, with the Grand Marais Gunflint, Iron Range, North Shore Mountains, and Grand Rapids-Voyageurs Trail Systems rated among the nation's best. The scenery is wonderfully varied, including rolling, lake-studded farmland and magnificent oak, maple, and evergreen forests; Mississippi bluffs and the shores of Lake Superior. Most cross-country trails require you to show a Great Minnesota Season Pass (only $5 for the winter, available at most trailheads). The fees are used to groom, maintain, and expand the state's many trail systems. ❅ Minnesota has developed several top racers, including Olympic medalist Cindy Nelson.

ALPINE

AFTON ALPS SKI AREA
(P. 31, D-3, #1) 6600 Peller Ave. South, Hastings
800-328-1328; 612-436-5245 (snow)
SEASON: Nov. 15-April 15
ANNUAL SNOWFALL: 55"
TERRAIN: 36 runs over 105 acres; longest run 3,000'; ◆ 20%; ▪ 60%; ● 20%.
LIFTS: 20 (3 triples, 15 doubles, 2 surface); capacity, 20,000 per hour.
SUMMIT: 1,000'
VERTICAL: 350'
ACTIVITIES: Snowboarding; night skiing.
FEATURES: Snowmaking 100%; ski school; restaurant; rentals.
Convenient to the Twin Cities, Afton Alps draws huge weekend crowds, but the amazing number of lifts guarantees virtually no lift lines (though once you're on the mountain itself, traffic can be bumper-to-bumper). Boarders have a half pipe.

ANDES TOWER HILLS SKI AREA
(P. 31, D-2, #2) 4505 Andes Rd. SW, Kensington
612-965-2455
SEASON: Nov. 10-March 25
ANNUAL SNOWFALL: 50"
TERRAIN: 14 trails over 110 acres; longest run 2,000'; ◆ 35%; ▪ 35%; ● 30%.
LIFTS: 5 (1 quad, 2 triples, 2 surface); capacity, 4,000 per hour.
SUMMIT: NA
VERTICAL: 280'
ACTIVITIES: Snowboarding; night skiing.
FEATURES: Snowmaking 100%; ski school; restaurant; rentals.
▶NORDIC: 18 groomed km (with skating lane); rentals; lessons; night skiing (2 km).
Located amid beautiful lake country in the western part of the state, Andes Tower Hill is most popular for its cross country center, some of whose tracks follow the old pioneer Red River oxcart trail, rumbling through basswood and maple forests. The downhill terrain is balanced but undemanding, with a few steeps. Children under 6 ski free.

BUCK HILL SKI AREA
(P. 31, D-3, #3) 15400 Buck Hill Rd., Burnsville
612-435-7174
TRAILS, 10; LIFTS, 7; VERTICAL: 306'.

BUENA VISTA
(P. 31, B-2, #4) County Route 15, Bemidji
218-243-2231
SEASON: Nov. 25-March 25 (open Thur. to Sun.)
ANNUAL SNOWFALL: 50"
TERRAIN: 15 trails over 70 acres; longest run 2,000'; ◆ 20%; ▪ 55%; ● 25%.
LIFTS: 5 (2 triples, 2 doubles, 1 surface); capacity, 7,000 per hour.
SUMMIT: NA
VERTICAL: 230'
ACTIVITIES: Snowboarding; NASTAR; horse-drawn sleigh rides; night skiing.
FEATURES: Snowmaking 100%; ski school; restaurant; rentals.
▶NORDIC: 25 groomed km. (with skating lane)
Buena Vista is best known for its Nordic facilities (it's the site of the important annual Minnesota Finlandia race). The headwaters of the Mississippi create a landscape of open bogland and rolling hardwood forest. Popular with groups and families who enjoy the rustic setting; the downhill slopes are on the mild side.

CHESTER MUNICIPAL PARK
(P. 31, C-4, #5) Off Skyline Drive, Duluth
218-724-9832
TRAILS, 3; LIFTS, 1; VERTICAL, 175'.
▶NORDIC: 3 groomed km.

COFFEE MILL SKI AREA
(P. 31, E-4, #6) Route 2, Highway 60, Wabasha
612-565-2777
SEASON: Dec. 1-March 31
ANNUAL SNOWFALL: 44"
TERRAIN: 10 trails over 50 acres; longest run 3,100'; ◆ 20%; ▪ 50%; ● 30%.
LIFTS: 3 (2 doubles, 1 surface); capacity, 3,800 per hour.
SUMMIT: 1,155'
VERTICAL: 425'
ACTIVITIES: Snowboarding; NASTAR; night skiing.
FEATURES: Snowmaking 100%; ski school; restaurant; rentals.
Located in the southern part of the state, Coffee Mill is another locals' learning area; it has one nasty, bumpy steep called O'Chute. Boarders have a lengthy half pipe. The views of the Mississippi Valley are a bonus.

COMO SKI CENTER
(P. 31, D-3, #7) W. 4th Street, St. Paul
612-488-9673
TRAILS, 2; LIFTS, 5; VERTICAL, 175'.
▶NORDIC: 7.5 groomed km (2.5 km lit).

DETROIT MOUNTAIN SKI AREA
(P. 31, C-1, #8) Rural Route 4, Detroit Lakes
218-847-1661
SEASON: Nov. 15-March 15
ANNUAL SNOWFALL: 45"
TERRAIN: 14 trails over 55 acres; longest run 2,500'; ◆ 40%; ▪ 30%; ● 30%.
LIFTS: 5 (1 triple, 1 double, 3 surface); capacity 4,800 per hour.

SUMMIT: 1,600'
VERTICAL: 250'
ACTIVITIES: Snowboarding; night skiing.
FEATURES: Snowmaking 100%; ski school; restaurant; rentals.
▶NORDIC: 15 groomed km.
Another area best for cross-country; the diagonal tracks that wind through meadowlands and maple stands are of primarily moderate difficulty. The newly installed triple has eased congestion on busy days (another will be added for 1995). Boarders have a 500-foot half pipe.

GIANTS RIDGE SKI AREA
(P. 31, B-4, #9) County Route 138, Biwabik
800-688-7669; 218-865-4143 (snow)
SEASON: Nov. 15-April 10
ANNUAL SNOWFALL: 90"
TERRAIN: 24 trails over 124 acres; longest run 3,800'; ◆ 20%; ▪ 20%; ● 60%.
LIFTS: 5 (1 triple, 3 doubles, 1 surface); capacity, 6,000 per hour.
SUMMIT: 1,850'
VERTICAL: 500'
ACTIVITIES: Snowboarding; night skiing.
FEATURES: Snowmaking 100%; ski school; restaurant; rentals.
▶NORDIC: 55 groomed km (29 skating); rentals; lessons; biathlon range; night skiing (4 km lit).
Giants Ridge is more varied than the other Duluth-area resorts, despite its smaller vertical. The slope pitch constantly shifts, meaning more challenge, and the terrain also features bowls and headwalls carved from rocky outcroppings. But the area's glory is its cross-country network, the official training center for the U.S. Ski and Biathlon associations. Difficulty ranges from first-time to super-expert; many trails meander along pine- and birch-covered ridges with eye-popping lake views. Wildlife sightings are the rule.

HIDDEN VALLEY RECREATION AREA
(P. 31, B-4, #10) Hidden Valley

STATBOX

Tourism: 800-657-3700
Time zone: Central
Population: 4,375,099
Square miles: 84,068

Average annual precipitation: 26"
Highest elevation: 2,301'
Lowest elevation: 602'

Road, Ely
218-365-3097
TRAILS, 4; LIFTS, 3; VERTICAL, 165'.
▶NORDIC: 15 groomed km.

HYLAND HILLS SKI AREA
(P. 31, D-3, #11) 8800 Chalet Rd., Bloomington
612-835-4250
SEASON: Nov. 25-March 15
ANNUAL SNOWFALL: 50"
TERRAIN: 14 runs over 35 acres; longest run 1,300'; ◆ 30%; ■ 30%; ● 40%.
LIFTS: 6 (3 triple, 3 surface); capacity, 3,800 per hour.
SUMMIT: NA
VERTICAL: 175'
ACTIVITIES: Snowboarding; night skiing.
FEATURES: Snowmaking 100%; ski school; restaurant; rentals.
▶NORDIC:25 groomed km (with skating lane); rentals; lessons.
 Again, primarily a Nordic facility (actually located in the adjoining Hyland-Bush-Anderson Park Reserve). The almost cliched classic terrain includes flat meadows, forested hills, and a lake. Hyland Hills has been courting shredders by beefing up rentals and opening the half pipe at night.

LUTSEN MOUNTAINS
(P. 31, B-5, #12) Highway 61, Lutsen
218-663-7281
SEASON: Nov. 25-April 10
ANNUAL SNOWFALL: 105"
TERRAIN: 30 trails over 200 acres; longest run 6,000'; ◆ 30%; ■ 40%; ● 30%.
LIFTS: 7 (1 gondola, 5 doubles, 1 surface); capacity, 8,000 per hour.
SUMMIT: 1,277'
VERTICAL: 1,008'
ACTIVITIES: Snowboarding; NASTAR.
FEATURES: Snowmaking 95%; ski school; restaurant; rentals.
 Lutsen is the Big Kahuna of Minnesota resorts, with a whopping (for the Midwest) 1,008-foot vertical, highest in the region. The slopes are tight and tree-lined, like New England, with unusual rocky outcroppings and imposing headwalls. Moose Mountain features wide boulevards with breathtaking vistas of Lake Superior. While Lutsen lacks an official Nordic center, there is easy access to the splendid 196K North Shore Network.

MT. FRONTENAC
(P. 31, E-4, #13) Red Wing
612-345-3504
SEASON: Dec. 1-March 15 (closed Mon.)
ANNUAL SNOWFALL: 53"
TERRAIN: 10 trails over 44 acres; longest run 5,000'; ◆

30%; ■ 40%; ● 30%.
LIFTS: 5 (2 doubles, 3 surface); capacity, 3,000 per hour.
SUMMIT: 1,120'
VERTICAL: 400'
ACTIVITIES: night skiing.
FEATURES: Snowmaking 100%; ski school; restaurant; rentals.
 Another Twin Cities area with ideal learning terrain.

MT. KATO
(P. 31, E-3, #14) Route 1, Mankato
507-625-3363
ANNUAL SNOWFALL: 75"
TERRAIN: 17 trails over 55 acres; longest run 2,800'; ◆◆ 20%; ◆ 25%; ■ 35%; ● 20%.
LIFTS: 8 (5 quads, 3 doubles); capacity, 14,550 per hour.
SUMMIT: NA
VERTICAL: 240'
ACTIVITIES: Snowboarding; night skiing.
FEATURES: Snowmaking 100%; ski school; restaurant; rentals.
 Despite its lack of vertical, Kato has a nice blend of terrain, with lots of rolls, though nothing either sustained or demanding.

OLD SMOKEY SKI HILL
(P. 31, C-1, #15) Adolphus Avenue, Fergus Falls
218-739-3205
TRAILS, 4; LIFTS, 2; VERTICAL; 90'.

POWDER RIDGE SKI AREA
(P. 31, D-2, #16) 15015 93rd

Ave., Kimball
612-398-5295
SEASON: Nov. 15-March 15
ANNUAL SNOWFALL: 45"
TERRAIN: 15 trails over 60 acres; longest run 2,650'; ◆ 20%; ■ 40%; ● 40%.
LIFTS: 6 (1 quad, 2 doubles, 3 surface); capacity, 7,400 per hour.
SUMMIT: NA
VERTICAL: 310'
ACTIVITIES: Snowboarding; night skiing.
FEATURES: Snowmaking 100%; ski school; restaurant; rentals.
 Powder Ridge has made a concerted effort of late to appeal to hardcore skiers, adding a quad, refurbishing a double, improving snowmaking, and increasing the vertical by 40 feet—all of which is making it a player in central Minnesota. The ski school is considered first-rate.

QUADNA MOUNTAIN RESORT
(P. 31, C-3, #17) 100 Quadna Rd., Hill City
218-697-8444
SEASON: Dec. 1-March 31
ANNUAL SNOWFALL: 55"
TERRAIN: 15 trails over 72 acres; longest run 2,600'; ◆ 33%; ■ 34%; ● 33%.
LIFTS: 4 (1 quad, 3 surface); capacity, 2,400 per hour.
SUMMIT: 1,110'
VERTICAL: 350'
ACTIVITIES: snowmobiling; night skiing.
FEATURES: Snowmaking 100%; ski school; restaurant; rentals.

Courtesy: Michigan Travel Bureau (see p. 113).

▶NORDIC: 30 groomed km; rentals.
 This area offers solid intermediate terrain in both Alpine and Nordic.

SKI GULL SKI AREA
(P. 31, C-2, #18) Off Highway 77, Brainerd
218-963-4353
TRAILS, 14; LIFTS, 3; VERTICAL, 230'.
▶NORDIC: 5 groomed km.

SPIRIT MOUNTAIN
(P. 31, C-4, #19) 9500 Spirit Mountain Pl., Duluth
218-628-2891
SEASON: Nov. 25-April 8
ANNUAL SNOWFALL: 85"
TERRAIN: 20 trails over 180 acres; longest run 1 mi.; ◆ 25%; ■ 50%; ● 25%.
LIFTS: 8 (1 high-speed quad, 1 quad, 2 triples, 1 double, 3 surface); capacity, 11,000 per hour.
SUMMIT: 1,320'
VERTICAL: 700'
ACTIVITIES: Snowboarding; NASTAR; tobogganing; ski jump; night skiing.
FEATURES: Snowmaking 86%; ski school; restaurant; rentals.
▶NORDIC: 10 groomed km; rentals; lessons.
 After Lutsen, Spirit Mountain is the cream of Minnesota ski areas. It features classically gorgeous lake views (and some great panoramas of Duluth and its harbor), narrow gladed trails, and long lazy runs by Midwest standards. Unfortunately for experts, those runs are practically straight up and down and groomed within an inch of their bumpy lives. But intermediates and novices will have a ball stroking their egos. Shredders like the state-of-the-art snowboard park.

WELCH VILLAGE SKI AREA
(P. 31, E-3, #20) County Route 7, Welch
612-258-4567; 612-222-7079 (snow)
SEASON: Nov. 25-April 1
ANNUAL SNOWFALL: 50"
TERRAIN: 36 trails over 120 acres; longest run 4,000'; ◆ 19%; ■ 50%; ● 31%.
LIFTS: 9 (2 quads, 1 triple, 5 doubles, 1 surface); capacity, 12,300 per hour.
SUMMIT: 1,050'
VERTICAL: 360'
ACTIVITIES: Snowboarding; NASTAR; night skiing.
FEATURES: Snowmaking 100%; ski school; restaurant; rentals.
 Despite the limited vertical, the trail layout is intriguing: lots of tight glade skiing with some decent pitch variation. Still, the mountain is solidly for beginners and intermediates, especially now that the moguls are groomed regularly.

Snowboarders have a new terrain park to play in.

WILD MOUNTAIN SKI AREA
(P. 31, D-3, #21) 37350 Wild Mountain Rd., Taylors Falls
621-465-6315
SEASON: Oct 31-April 4
ANNUAL SNOWFALL: 50"
TERRAIN: 21 trails over 82 acres; longest run 4,500'; ◆ 30%; ■ 40%; ● 30%.
LIFTS: 6 (4 quads, 2 surface); capacity, 11,000 per hour.
SUMMIT: 1,113'
VERTICAL: 300'
ACTIVITIES: Snowboarding; night skiing.
FEATURES: Snowmaking 100%; ski school; restaurant; rentals.
  Superior snowmaking and consistently cold nights allow Wild Mountain to open early. The slopes feature some good tree skiing, though few hairy pitches or twisty runs. The Wall, Wild, and Competition are popular for their steepness. Shredders have a half pipe and snowboard park.

WIRTH WINTER RECREATION AREA
(P. 31, D-3, #22) Theodore Wirth Regional Park, Minneapolis
612-522-4584
TRAILS, 2; LIFTS, 2; VERTICAL, 150'.

NORDIC

BEAR TRACK OUTFITTING
(P. 31, B-5, #23) Grand Marais
800-795-8068
FACILITIES: 25 groomed km (with 8-km skating lane); rentals; ice skating.
  A scenic blend of deep forest, gentle hills, and frozen ponds. Accesses several other trail networks.

BEARSKIN LODGE RESORT
(P. 31, B-5, #24) 275 Gunflint Trail, Grand Marais
800-338-4170
FACILITIES: 55 groomed km; rentals; lessons; lodging and restaurant; ice skating; night skiing (1.5 km).

BORDERLAND LODGE
(P. 31, B-5, #25) 855 Gunflint Trail, Grand Marais
800-451-1667
FACILITIES: 100 groomed km; rentals; lessons; lodging and restaurant; ice skating; dog sled rides.

BOUNDARY COUNTRY TREKKING
(P. 31, B-5, #26) 590 Gunflint Trail, Grand Marais

800-322-8327
FACILITIES: 37 groomed km; rentals; lessons; yurts.
  These backcountry guides offer yurt-to-yurt packages along the USA's longest tracked wilderness trail, the Banadad.

BREEZY POINT RESORT
(P. 31, C-2, #27) HCR 2, Breezy Point
800-432-3777
FACILITIES: 16 groomed km; rentals; lodging and restaurant.

CASCADE LODGE
(P. 31, B-5, #28) HC 3, Lutsen
218-387-1112
FACILITIES: 56 groomed km; rentals; lessons; lodging and restaurant.
  This rustic lodge lies in beautiful Cascade River State Park and forms part of the ravishing 196-km North Shore Trail. The lonely runs boast astounding views of Lake Superior amid ghostly white stands of aspen and jade evergreens. The highest point along the system in the Sawtooth Mountains is 1,800 feet, translating into a 1,200-foot vertical from the lodge.

CRAGUN'S LODGE
(P. 31, C-2, #29) 2001 Pine Beach Rd., Brainerd
800-272-4867
FACILITIES: 45 groomed km; rentals; lessons; lodging and restaurant; sleigh rides; ice skating; dog sled rides.
  Another of Minnesota's superlative winter resorts, with spa facilities for soaking after a grueling day out on the challenging trails serpentining through hardwood and pine forests, often flanking the Mississippi.

CROW NORDIC CENTER
(P. 31, D-2, #30) 13494 Lace Ave., Glencoe
612-864-5503
FACILITIES: 10 groomed km; rentals; restaurant.

EAGLE MOUNTAIN RESORT
(P. 31, D-2, #31) Grey Eagle
612-573-2222
FACILITIES: 10 groomed km; rentals; lodging and restaurant; tubing.

ELM CREEK PARK RESERVE
(P. 31, D-3, #32) 13080 Territorial Rd., Osseo
612-424-5511
FACILITIES: 14.7 groomed km; rentals.
  Possibly the most rewarding of several trails in the Twin Cities metro area, thanks to the fine nature center exhibits. The intermediate terrain (12.8 km for skaters) runs through both woodlands and wetlands. The trail links up with the

other Hennepin State Park trails (call 612-559-9000 for more information). Snacks available at warming hut.

FLANDRAU STATE PARK
(P. 31, E-2, #33) 1300 Summit Ave., New Ulm
507-354-3519
FACILITIES: 11 groomed km; rentals.

GOLDEN EAGLE LODGE
(P. 31, B-5, #34) 325 Gunflint Trail, Grand Marais
800-346-2203
FACILITIES: 55 groomed km; rentals; lessons; lodging and restaurant; ice skating; night skiing (1.5 km).
  Golden Eagle is one of many lodges accessing the Gunflint Trail, with tracks for both diagonal and skating. Trails weave past menacing cliffs, spruce bogs, and frozen lakes.

GUNFLINT LODGE
(P. 31, B-5, #35) 750 Gunflint Trail, Grand Marais
218-388-2294
FACILITIES: 100 groomed km; rentals; lessons; lodging and restaurant; night skiing (2 km).

GUNFLINT PINES RESORT
(P. 31, B-5, #36) 755 Gunflint Trail, Grand Marais
800-533-5814
FACILITIES: 100 groomed km; rentals; lessons; lodging and restaurant; sleigh rides; ice skating; snowshoeing.

MAPLELAG
(P. 31, C-1, #37) Route 1, Callaway
218-375-4466; 800-654-7711
FACILITIES: 53 groomed km; rentals; lessons; lodging and restaurant; ice skating.
  Another highly touted resort with all amenities, very popular with families and honeymooners. Trails snake around lakes through majestic maple and basswood forests.

MINNESOTA ZOOLOGICAL GARDEN
(P. 31, D-3, #38) 13000 Zoo Blvd., Apple Valley
612-432-9000
FACILITIES: 10 groomed km; rentals.
  Despite the comparative lack of facilities, this is one of the more intriguing trails (mostly intermediate, with 2 km for skaters), winding past outdoor exhibits of exotic animals.

NATIONAL FOREST LODGE
(P. 31, B-4, #39) 3226 Highway 1, Isabella
218-323-7676
FACILITIES: 40 groomed km;

rentals; lodging and restaurant.

NORTHWIND LODGE
(P. 31, B-4, #40) Ely
218-365-5489
FACILITIES: 35 groomed km; rentals; lessons; lodging and restaurant.

OAK RIDGE RESORT TRAILS
(P. 31, C-1, #41) Highway 10, 3 mi. W of Detroit Lakes
218-439-6192
FACILITIES: 10 groomed km; rentals; lodge and restaurant.

PAUL BUNYAN ARBORETUM
(P. 31, C-3, #42) Brainerd
218-829-8770
FACILITIES: 19 groomed km; lessons; night skiing (2 km).

PINCUSHION B&B
(P. 31, B-5, #43) 220 Gunflint Trail, Grand Marais
218-387-1276; 800-542-1226
FACILITIES: 25 groomed km; rentals; lessons; lodging and restaurant; night skiing (2 km).

SOLBAKKEN RESORT
(P. 31, B-5, #44) HCR 3, Lutsen
218-663-7566
FACILITIES: 30 groomed km; rentals; lessons; lodging and restaurant.
  A get-away-from-it-all resort (no phones), Solbakken offers the ultimate in solitude, accessing the 200-km North Shore Mountain Ski Trail.

SPIDAHL SKI GARD
(P. 31, C-1, #45) Route 1, Erhard
218-736-5097
FACILITIES: 32 groomed km (10 skating); rentals; lessons.

ST. CROIX WILD RIVER STATE PARK
(P. 31, D-3, #46) 39755 Park Trail, Center City
612-583-2125
FACILITIES: 56 groomed km; rentals; restaurant.

TAMARACK OUTFITTERS
(P. 31, A-2, #47) Warroad
218-386-3928; 800-626-1478
FACILITIES: 48 groomed km; rentals; lessons; lodging and restaurant; snowmobiling.

MN

Nickname is Big Sky Country.
The scenery is so rugged and unspoiled, the local joke goes, "If God doesn't live here, he must own a vacation home." (And so do Harrison Ford and Michael Keaton, among others.) This is the Wild West at its woolliest, a magnificent landscape of shimmering blue-tinged glaciers and craggy moraines, where elk, moose, and bighorn sheep sightings are frequent during cross-country jaunts. The most riveting vistas can be found in astounding Glacier National Park. ❄ Montana is known for its dude ranches, many of which offer groomed trails (though unfortunately no rentals or lessons, one criterion for listing). In addition, there are several guide services that offer ski touring in Yellowstone and Glacier. (For more information on both dude ranches and wilderness outfitters, contact the state tourist board). ❄ The downhill areas are among the nation's least crowded and most expansive, with bowls—and views—that seem to go on forever. No wonder they call it Big Sky Country. Big Ski would be equally appropriate.

ALPINE

BEAR PAW SKI BOWL
(P. 21, A-6, #1) Havre
406-265 8404
SEASON: Dec. 10-March 31
ANNUAL SNOWFALL: 200"
TERRAIN: 9 trails over NA acres; longest run NA; ◆ 50; ■ 25%; ● 25%.
LIFTS: 2 (1 double, 1 surface); capacity, 720 per hour.
SUMMIT: 5,280'
VERTICAL: 900'
ACTIVITIES: Snowboarding.
FEATURES: Ski school; restaurant; rentals.
Bear Paw is remote, just outside the charming old mining town of Havre in the middle of magnificent wilderness, with some decent steeps.

THE BIG MOUNTAIN
(P. 20, A-3, #2) Big Mountain Road, 8 mi. N of Whitefish on MT 93
800-858-5439; 406-862-3511 (snow)
SEASON: Nov. 25-April 15
ANNUAL SNOWFALL: 300"
TERRAIN: 61 trails (and unlimited unmarked tree skiing) over 3,000 acres; longest run 2.5 mi.; ◆ 20%; ■ 55%; ● 25%.
LIFTS: 9 (1 high speed quad, 1 quad, 4 triples, 1 double, 2 surface); capacity, 11,684 per hour.
SUMMIT: 7,000'
VERTICAL: 2,300'
ACTIVITIES: Snowboarding; telemarking; sleigh rides; dog sledding; night skiing.
FEATURES: Snowmaking 2%; ski school; DREAM adaptive ski program; child care; restaurants; rentals.
▶NORDIC: 10 groomed km; rentals; lessons.
Big is an understatement. The mountain seems to go on forever, as do the glorious views of Whitefish Lake. Some skiers carp that it's hard to get to and there's no nightlife. But gee, once you're here, all you have to do is ski. (You can always head down to Whitefish for fancy grub, dosy-doeing and low-stakes gambling.) And it's a transcendant experience: The views, the feathery powder, even the "snow ghosts" (the local term for trees blanketed with hoarfrost like delicate ice sculptures) are hard to match. So are the warm reception (free mountain host tours daily), low prices, and constant improvements (new base lodge, two recently added lifts including the high-speed Glacier Chaser, and even more snowmaking). Plenty of cruisers are accessible from the Chaser, including the Toni Mott, Inspiration, and Big Ravine (all traversing a whopping 2,000 feet of vertical). Total novices enjoy an isolated area under Chair 6. Strong beginners and low intermediates have a large playground off Chairs 2 and 3 (most of which is lighted at night). Beginning bumpsters will have a field day practing on North Bowl. Although there is little heart-stopping terrain on this vast expanse, there are some gorgeous tree steeps alternating with extensive powder fields, where advanced and expert skiers can choose their preferred line, from tight slalom to sweeping Giant Slalom to figure eights. The only real drawback is that because Big Mountain faces north, it gets little sun and lots of Cascade-like fog (but plenty of powder dumps). In addition to the fine Nordic center, tours of Glacier National Park (a must day off for any visitor) can be arranged.

BIG SKY RESORT
(P. 20, D-5, #3) 1 Lone Mountain Trail, Big Sky
800-548-4486; 406-995-4211 (snow)
SEASON: Nov. 25-April 10
ANNUAL SNOWFALL: 400"
TERRAIN: 55 trails over 2,100 acres; longest run 3 mi.; ◆ 40%; ■ 44%; ● 16%.
LIFTS: 11 (2 gondolas, 2 high-speed quads, 2 triples, 2 doubles, 3 surface); capacity, 12,030 per hour.
SUMMIT: 10,000'
VERTICAL: 3,030'
ACTIVITIES: Snowboarding; snowshoeing; sleigh rides; snowmobiling.
FEATURES: Snowmaking 20%; ski school; restaurants; rentals.
▶NORDIC: 75 groomed km; rentals; lessons.
Chet Huntley (yes, of the famed news team) created Big Sky and started the Montana skiing boom, giving many grateful schussers cause for jubilation ever since. In the hands of the Kircher family (owners of the Boyne USA resorts in Michigan) since 1976, Big Sky has retained its low-key ambiance despite increasing popularity (doubling its skier visits in less than a decade). Fortunately, increased lift capacity, with the high-speed Ram Charger and Thunder Wolf gondolas, has dispersed any potential crowds, and skiers always rave about the "empty" slopes. They also praise the rich variety of terrain on Lone and Andesite Mountains. Elevator shaft couloirs perch atop wide bowls. Gentle walls slope into open meadows. Experts should head for the Challenger lift, which accesses 450 acres of bumps and steeps. Little Rock Tongue here also boasts some superb tree skiing. The patrol can also let you know if any "out-of-bound" in-bounds chutes and cornices off the Country Club tows are open, like the aptly named Parachute and The Pinnacles. But Big Sky (and sunshine) also smile on beginners and intermediates. The Southern Comfort triple leads to miles of groomed boulevards that remain sunstruck all day. In fact, skiers can follow the sun all day long, starting with the two gondolas. Children under 10 ski free with a paying adult. Nordic skiers should head for nearby Lone Mountain, one of the USA's great cross-country hideaways, or arrange tours of Yellowstone.

BRIDGER BOWL
(P. 20, D-5, #4) 15795 Bridger Canyon Rd., 15 mi. N of Bozeman on State Route 86
800-223-9609; 406-586-2389 (snow)
SEASON: Dec. 10-April 5
ANNUAL SNOWFALL: 400"
TERRAIN: 51 trails over 1,200 acres; longest run 2.5 mi.; ◆◆ 10%; ◆ 30%; ■ 35%; ● 25%.
LIFTS: 6 (5 doubles, 1 surface); capacity, 5,100 per hour.
SUMMIT: 8,100'
VERTICAL: 2,000'
ACTIVITIES: Snowboarding; telemarking.
FEATURES: Snowmaking 5%; ski school; Eagle Adaptive ski program; child care; restaurants; rentals.
This is a lesser-known beauty, whose devotees enjoy its savage tree-lined steeps. Only about a third of the mountain is groomed, and many so-called slopes are actually controlled avalanche paths. Experts also can hike the ridge for another 400 acres and 500' vertical. But a "mogul-cutter" winch-cat smooths out some of those steeps for mere mortals. A powderhound's dry dream.

DISCOVERY BASIN
(P. 20, C-4, #5) 505 Hickory, Anaconda
406-563-2184
SEASON: Nov. 24-April 10
ANNUAL SNOWFALL: 200"
TERRAIN: 30 trails over 360 acres; longest run 2 mi.; ◆ 33%; ■ 34%; ● 33%.
LIFTS: 5 (3 doubles, 2 surface); capacity, 3,400 per hour.
SUMMIT: 8,150'
VERTICAL: 1,300'
ACTIVITIES: Snowboarding; hot

STATBOX

Tourism: 800-541-1447	Average annual precipitation: 11"
Time zone: Mountain	
Population: 799,065	Highest elevation: 12,799'
Square miles: 147,138	Lowest elevation: 1,800'

springs; water slide.

FEATURES: Ski school; restaurant; rentals.

▶NORDIC: 5 groomed km, unlimited ungroomed; rentals; lessons.

A very pleasant, strongly intermediate mountain, with an excellent children's program. The real attraction is the associated Fairmont Hot Springs Resort, with its two Olympic-sized thermal pools and 350' water slide.

GREAT DIVIDE
(P. 20, C-4, #6) Marysville
406-449-3746

SEASON: Dec. 10-April 5 (closed Tues.)
ANNUAL SNOWFALL: 150"
TERRAIN: 50 trails, 2 bowls, and a snowfield over 720 acres; longest run 3 mi.; ♦♦ 15%; ♦ 40%; ▪ 30%; ● 15%.
LIFTS: 4 (3 doubles, 1 surface); capacity, 2,400 per hour.
SUMMIT: 7,230'
VERTICAL: 1,520'
ACTIVITIES: Snowboarding; night skiing.
FEATURES: Ski school; restaurants; rentals.

The Great Divide is popular among Helena locals for its wide open bowls and Summit Snowfields, an endless white expanse. One mile away, Marysville is a restored ghost town, a delight for kids—who are also catered to with a number of special deals. The mountain itself is primarily advanced, with the new Rawhide Gulch expansion offering 90 acres of near-extreme skiing.

LOST TRAIL/POWDER MOUNTAIN
(P. 20, C-3, #7) Top of Lost Trail Pass on U.S. 93, Darby
800-351-3508; 406-821-3211 (snow)

SEASON: Dec. 10-April 10 (Thurs. to Sun. and holidays only)
ANNUAL SNOWFALL: 300"
TERRAIN: 18 trails over 600 acres; longest run 1.5 mi.; ♦ 20%; ▪ 60%; ● 20%.
LIFTS: 4 (2 doubles, 2 surface); capacity, 1,925 per hour.
SUMMIT: 7,800'
VERTICAL: 1,200'
ACTIVITIES: Snowboarding.
FEATURES: Ski school; restaurant; rentals.

This is a superb learning area, for both first-timers and intermediates honing their skills. Offers a series of expansive bowls and a few narrow chutes. The 30 km of trails of the Chief Joseph Nordic System (no rentals or lessons available) are located at Lost Trail Pass.

MARSHALL SKI AREA
(P. 20, B-3, #8) Highway 200, 4 mi. E of Missoula
406-258-6000

SEASON: Dec. 1-March 31
ANNUAL SNOWFALL: 250"
TERRAIN: 17 trails over 200 acres; longest run 2 mi.; ♦ 30%; ▪ 40%; ● 30%.
LIFTS: 3 (1 triple, 2 surface); capacity, 2,900 per hour.
SUMMIT: 5,400'
VERTICAL: 1,500'
ACTIVITIES: Snowboarding; night skiing.
FEATURES: Ski school; restaurant; rentals.

The area is popular with families and students from nearby Missoula who enjoy its predominantly gladed runs.

MAVERICK MOUNTAIN
(P. 20, D-3, #9) Maverick Mountain Road, Polaris
406-834-3454

SEASON: Nov. 25-April 1 (open Thurs. to Sun. and holidays only)
ANNUAL SNOWFALL: 180"
TERRAIN: 17 trails over 500 acres; longest run 2.25 mi.; ♦ 40%; ▪ 40%; ● 20%.
LIFTS: 2 (1 double, 1 surface); capacity, 700 per hour.
SUMMIT: 9,220'
VERTICAL: 2,120'
ACTIVITIES: Snowboarding.
FEATURES: Ski school; restaurant; child care; rentals.

Although the lift capacity is low, Maverick is usually uncrowded—a surprise since it's a great mountain for learning and practicing. Long, broad groomed slopes, gladed meadows, and deep powder bowls abound. But there's plenty of hairy terrain as well. Rock 'n' Roll is a popular double-diamond run; Showtime is a great gladed trail. The surrounding area provides attractions like ghost towns and hot springs (nearby Elkhorn Ranch, though not affiliated, is a wonderful place to soak your bones, and offers 40 miles of Nordic trails—no rentals or lessons). Maverick hosts a unique event each January: the Cowboy Downhill Western Winter games, where locals compete in rodeo one day, team ski races the next.

MONTANA SNOW BOWL
(P. 20, B-3, #10) 1700 Snowbowl Rd., Missoula
406-549-9777

SEASON: Nov. 25-April 1 (closed Tues.)
ANNUAL SNOWFALL: 300"
TERRAIN: 32 trails over 1,200 acres (plus 700 acres of "extreme" skiing); longest run 3 mi.; ♦♦ 15; ♦ 25%; ▪ 40%; ● 20%.
LIFTS: 4 (2 doubles, 2 surface); capacity, 4,400 per hour.
SUMMIT: 7,600'
VERTICAL: 2,600'
ACTIVITIES: Snowboarding; ski jump; night skiing.

FEATURES: Snowmaking 20%; ski school; restaurants; rentals. Although its summit is lower than the base of many Colorado ski areas, the Snow Bowl offers supreme powder conditions. Runs range from wide cruisers, like Paradise, and narrow lengthy tree runs to the bowls that gave the area its name. The extreme section offers the ultimate challenge in reading terrain. Angel Face is a memorable bump run, Grizzly Chute a savage slash. Nearby Missoula is a rip-roaring, rowdy university town.

RED LODGE MOUNTAIN
(P. 21, D-6, #11) 101 Ski Run, 1 mi. W of Red Lodge
406-446-2610

SEASON: Nov. 25-April 10
ANNUAL SNOWFALL: 250"
TERRAIN: 36 trails over 500 acres; longest run 2.5 mi.; ♦ 25%; ▪ 60%; ● 15%.
LIFTS: 6 (4 doubles, 1 triple, 1 surface); capacity, 6,690 per hour.
SUMMIT: 9,416'
VERTICAL: 2,016'
ACTIVITIES: Snowboarding.
FEATURES: Snowmaking 40%; ski school; Eagle Adaptive Ski Program; restaurants; rentals.
▶NORDIC: 406-425-1070; unlimited backcountry skiing; rentals; lessons; telemarking.

Red Lodge is a quintessential intermediate mountain, with superb grooming virtually throughout the area. Lazy M is a confidence-building, rolling, intermediate run. Wilder and woollier stretches include the chutes of the Main and Cole Creek drainages. The town is a classic, too: a lively Western town with a rich history and architectural heritage. The Nordic area is exceptionally scenic.

ROCKY MOUNTAIN HI SKI AREA
(P. 20, B-4, #12) Teton Pass, Choteau
406-278-5308

SEASON: Nov. 25-April 15 (Fri. to Sun. and holidays only)
ANNUAL SNOWFALL: 300"
TERRAIN: 25 trails over 150 acres; longest run 1.5 mi.; ♦ 30%; ▪ 50%; ● 20%.
LIFTS: 3 (1 double, 2 surface); capacity, 1,300 per hour.
SUMMIT: 7,400'
VERTICAL: 1,000'
ACTIVITIES: Snowboarding; snowmobiling.
FEATURES: Ski school; restaurant; rentals.

A relatively inaccessible area, its name applies to the exceptionally scenic surroundings. When it comes to the skiing, the acreage and vertical are small by Western standards.

SHOWDOWN SKI AREA
(P. 20, C-5, #13) Neihart
800-433-0022; 406-771-1300 (snow)

SEASON: Nov. 25-April 10 (closed Mon. and Tues.)
ANNUAL SNOWFALL: 240"
TERRAIN: 34 trails over 640 acres; longest run 2 mi.; ♦ 30%; ▪ 40%; ● 30%.
LIFTS: 4 (1 triple, 1 double, 2 surface); capacity, 3,020 per hour.
SUMMIT: 8,200'
VERTICAL: 6,800'
ACTIVITIES: Snowboarding; snowmobiling.
FEATURES: Ski school; Eagle Adaptive Ski Program; restaurant; rentals.
▶NORDIC: 12 groomed km.

Somewhat remote, Showdown offers balanced terrain with a predominance of gladed runs. The beginning terrain is clustered toward the right side, with a new beginners' lift planned for 1995. The left side offers several steep chutes from the summit like Geronimo, Glory Hole, and Gun Barrel.

TURNER MOUNTAIN
(P. 20, B-2, #14) 22 mi. NW of Libby
406-293-4317

SEASON: Dec. 20-March 15 (weekends and holidays only)
ANNUAL SNOWFALL: 200"
TERRAIN: 14 trails over 300 acres; longest run 2.5 mi.; ♦ 60%; ▪ 30%; ● 10%.
LIFTS: 2 (2 surface); capacity, 1,000 per hour.
SUMMIT: 6,000'
VERTICAL: 2,165'
ACTIVITIES: Snowboarding; snowmobiling.
FEATURES: Ski school; restaurant.

Tucked in Montana's northeastern corner, Turner is a local area with two antiquated lifts that serve some ferocious steeps, bowls, and tightly gladed runs. Truly the ultimate getaway; the nearest lodging is in Libby.

NORDIC

BIG HOLE LODGE
(P. 20, D-4, #15) Wise River
406-832-3252

FACILITIES: 30 groomed km; rentals; lessons; lodging and restaurant.

BOHART RANCH
(P. 20, C-5, #16) 16621 Bridger Canyon Rd., Bozeman
406-586-9070

FACILITIES: 30 groomed km; rentals; lessons; lodging and restaurant; biathlon range.

DOUBLE ARROW LODGE
(P. 20, B-3, #17) Seeley Lake

406-677-2777
FACILITIES: 8 groomed km; rentals; lessons; lodging and restaurant.

GLACIER NORDIC TOURING CENTER

(P. 20, A-3, #18) 1205 Highway 93 West, Whitefish
406-862-3000
FACILITIES: 15 groomed km (with skating lane); rentals; lessons; lodging and restaurant; night skiing (3 km).
The center is affiliated with the deluxe Grouse Mountain Lodge.

HOLLAND LAKE LODGE

(P. 20, B-3, #19) Highway 83, Condon

800-648-8859
FACILITIES: Backcountry skiing (with some groomed trails); rentals; lessons (weekends); lodging and restaurant.

IZAAK WALTON INN

(P. 20, A-3, #20) Essex
406-888-5700
FACILITIES: 33 groomed km; rentals; lessons; lodging and restaurant; telemarking.
Izaak Walton is the choice of skiers looking to explore the wondrous adjacent Glacier National Park (guided tours of its backcountry are available) and the equally splendid Great Bear Wilderness.

LONE MOUNTAIN RANCH

(P. 20, D-5, #21) Meadow Village, Big Sky
406-995-4644
FACILITIES: 75 groomed km; rentals; lessons; lodging and restaurant; sleigh rides; winter fly fishing.
Lone Mountain is considered one of the great Nordic centers in the country, thanks to rustic elegant accommodations, gourmet dining, magnificent terrain, and superb guided tours into Yellowstone. Lone Mountain also offers snowcat skiing and naturalist guided tours into the 25,000-acre Moonlight Basin (overnight yurts available).

TAMARACKS RESORT/SEELEY CREEK NORDIC

(P.20, B-3, #22) Seeley Lake
800-477-7216
Facilities: 18 groomed km; rentals; lodging and restaurant.

YELLOWSTONE EXPEDITIONS

(P. 20, D-5, #23) West Yellowstone
800-728-9333
FACILITIES: Unlimited backcountry skiing; rentals; lessons; lodging and restaurant; telemarking.
One of the preeminent guide services into Yellowstone, they offer yurt dining and overnight huts.

Courtesy: Ski The Summit (see Colorado, p. 96).

Talk about a classic. White-steepled churches, covered bridges, frosted colonial farmhouses, red-brick Federalist homes: New Hampshire is a Currier and Ives print come to life. ❄ Ski studs of both sexes test themselves on notorious Tuckerman's Ravine, scaling the narrow screaming 3,400-foot slash down Mt. Washington (the East's highest peak) in spring, once the avalanche danger is past. ❄ For additional savings, head for the five areas of the glorious Mt. Washington Valley (Attitash, Black Mountain, Cranmore, King Pine, and Wildcat), which offer special multi-day mix-and-match packages. The valley also offers quaint hamlets, cozy inns, gourmet restaurants, and factory outlet shopping in Conway and North Conway for non-skiers. ❄ Four top-flight areas—Bretton Woods, Cannon, Loon, and Waterville Valley—can be skied on a multi-day interchangeable ticket.

ALPINE

ATTITASH SKI RESORT
(P. 38, C-4, #1) Route 302, Bartlett
603-374-2368
SEASON: Nov. 19-April 15
ANNUAL SNOWFALL: 90″
TERRAIN: 28 trails over 220 acres; longest run, 2 mi.; ◆ 25%; ■ 50%; ● 25%.
LIFTS: 6 (2 triples, 4 doubles); capacity, 5,500 per hour.
SUMMIT: 2,300′
VERTICAL: 1,750′
ACTIVITIES: Snowboarding; NASTAR.
FEATURES: Snowmaking 98%; ski school; child care; restaurant; rentals.

One of the East's best family areas, Attitash offers a variety of packages and programs geared toward enhancing kids' ski experiences, including the Attitots on-slope clubhouse and fun-packed Adventure Kids Terrain Garden. Another steal is the transferable, computerized point Smart Ticket, which enables skiers to pay by the vertical foot. The skiing is ideally suited to beginners and intermediates, with impeccable grooming, although Ptarmigan, Tim's Trauma, and Idiot's Option (the latter achieving a 42% pitch) provide a few expert thrills. A new snowboard park includes such obstacles as a log slide, barrels, and benches.

BALSAMS WILDERNESS
(P. 38, A-4, #2) Route 26, Dixville Notch
800-255-0600; 603-255-3951 (snow)
SEASON: Dec. 1-April 1
ANNUAL SNOWFALL: 90″
TERRAIN: 13 trails over 95 acres; longest run, 2 mi.; ◆ 15%; ■ 65%; ● 20%.
LIFTS: 4 (1 double, 3 surface); capacity, 2,250 per hour.
SUMMIT: 2,700′
VERTICAL: 1,000′
ACTIVITIES: Snowboarding; NASTAR; telemarking.
FEATURES: Snowmaking 88%; ski school; child care; restaurant; rentals.
▶NORDIC: 100 km (73 km groomed); rentals; lessons.

Tucked in the northern part of the state, just 13 miles from the Canadian border, Balsams has long been a major summer resort as well. The skiing isn't very challenging, but the relaxed après-skiing at the grand old resort hotel is nonpareil.

In addition to the scenic touring, ranging from novice to expert—with a 1,000-foot vertical to traverse, there are occasional natural history tours of the region, as well as telemark tours on Alpine and Nordic trails. Trails wrap around high ridges and Lake Gloriette.

BLACK MOUNTAIN SKI AREA
(P. 38, C-4, #3) Route 16B, Jackson
603-383-4490
SEASON: Dec. 15-March 25
ANNUAL SNOWFALL: 80″
TERRAIN: 22 trails over 85 acres; longest run, 1.25 mi.; ◆ 30%; ■ 40%; ● 30%.
LIFTS: 3 (1 triple, 1 double, 1 surface); capacity, 3,700 per hour.
SUMMIT: 2,350′
VERTICAL: 1,110′
ACTIVITIES: Snowboarding; NASTAR.
FEATURES: Snowmaking 98%; ski school; child care; restaurant; rentals.

Another family beauty, Black Mountain offers several enticing packages for parents and coddling for toddlers to teens. Only one run is desginated expert, so this is nirvana for cruisers. Best of all, the area faces south, ensuring sunny skiing and warmer temperatures throughout the day. While snowboarding is banned in much of the area, a 350-foot half pipe helps compensate. Black Mountain adjoins the Jackson Ski Touring Foundation network, and Nordic types can ski the mountain for free, which explains the high percentage of telemarkers on the slopes.

BLACKWATER SKI AREA
(P. 38, D-3, #4) Main Street, Andover
603-735-5128
TRAILS, 3; LIFTS, 1; VERTICAL, 407′.
▶NORDIC: 10 groomed km.
Ski jump.

A private area for students, faculty, and townspeople, Blackwater is open on a limited basis to the public. The trails are fairly steep.

BRETTON WOODS SKI RESORT
(P. 38, C-4, #5) Route 302, Twin Mountain
603-278-5000; 603-278-5051 (snow)
SEASON: Nov. 25-April 10
ANNUAL SNOWFALL: 180″
TERRAIN: 30 trails over 180 acres; longest run, 2 mi.; ◆ 23%; ■ 46%; ● 31%.
LIFTS: 5 (1 quad, 1 triple, 2 doubles, 1 surface); capacity, 6,000 per hour.
SUMMIT: 3,100′
VERTICAL: 1,500′
ACTIVITIES: Snowboarding; NASTAR; night skiing.
FEATURES: Snowmaking 98%; ski school; child care; restaurant; rentals.
▶NORDIC: 100 km (88 km groomed); rentals; lessons; biathlon range.

Bretton Woods may just be the prototypical New England ski area. The trails are old-fashioned beauties winding through thick stands of evergreen. The heavy-timbered base lodge strikes an immediate note of elegance. It receives the most snow of any area in New Hampshire. The views of Mt. Washington (especially at dusk when alpenglow paints a quilt of mauve and rose) are enthralling. The colonial-style inns ooze Yankee warmth and tradition, there's even one of the country's grand old resort hotels nearby. The Mt. Washington (whose management periodically announces its intention to winterize it), has been a playground for wealthy city-folk since the turn-of-the-century. Aside from a few steep pitches, there is little to distract strong skiers from those heavenly views.

The three interconnected trail systems that comprise the Nordic area are set for both classic and skating amid the Mt. Washington Valley. Its base occupies a handsome Victorian stable.

CANNON MOUNTAIN
(P. 38, C-3, #6) Franconia Notch, Franconia
603-823-5563; 603-823-7771 (snow)
SEASON: Nov. 6-May 1
ANNUAL SNOWFALL: 150″
TERRAIN: 35 trails over 150 acres; longest run, 2.3 mi.; ◆ 29%; ■ 52%; ● 19%.
LIFTS: 6 (1 tram, 1 quad, 1 triple, 2 doubles, 1 surface); capacity, 6,000 per hour.
SUMMIT: 4,146′
VERTICAL: 2,146′
ACTIVITIES: Snowboarding; NASTAR.
FEATURES: Snowmaking 95%; ski school; child care; restaurants; rentals.
▶NORDIC: 60 groomed km; rentals; lessons.

State-operated Cannon is a classic in more ways than one. The USA's first ski lift and ski school were established here in 1929 on what was then called Peckett's Hill. The first aerial tram in North America opened at Cannon in 1938. In 1967, Cannon hosted the first World Cup races to be held in North America. (Its rich history is celebrated in the New England Ski Museum at the base.) The famed, craggy granite outcropping, the "Old Man of the Mountain," adorns Cannon's south face. Tight, tree-lined trails literally snake down the mountain in a series of sinuous curves. They take full advantage of New Hampshire's highest vertical. Eighty percent of the runs are blue and black, contributing to Cannon's reputation as a preeminent skier's mountain. Any expert would derive satisfaction from the Peabody Slopes on the lower half and the fabled Front Five: Rocket, Gary's, Avalanche,

Paulie's Folly, and the bumptious beauty Zoomer (the latter three are true black diamonds). But intermediates needn't despair, since increased snowmaking and grooming have tamed much of the mountain. Notable but steep stand-outs include Vista Way (which offers the best views of the Notch), Profile, Tramway, and Upper Cannon.

DARTMOUTH SKIWAY
(P. 38, D-3, #7) Canaan Turnpike, Hanover
603-795-2143
TRAILS, 16; LIFTS, 3; VERTICAL, 968'.
▶NORDIC: 10 groomed km.

GUNSTOCK SKI AREA
(P. 38, D-4, #8) Off I-93, Gilford
800-GUNSTOCK
SEASON: Nov. 15-April 1
ANNUAL SNOWFALL: 100"
TERRAIN: 41 trails over 215 acres; longest run, 2.5 mi.; ◆ 24%; ▪ 60%; ● 16%.
LIFTS: 7 (1 quad, 2 triples, 2 doubles, 2 surface); capacity, 8,445 per hour.
SUMMIT: 2,300'
VERTICAL: 1,400'
ACTIVITIES: Snowboarding; winter camping; ski jump; night skiing.
FEATURES: Snowmaking 98%; ski school; child care; restaurants; rentals.
▶NORDIC: 42 groomed km (with skating lane); rentals; lessons; telemarking.
The quintessential family resort, Gunstock has an excellent ski school, friendly ambiance, gorgeous lake views, and a nice mix of trails for all levels, primarily intermediate cruisers. It recently added a half pipe to keep the teen members of the family occupied.

HIGHLAND MOUNTAIN SKI AREA
(P. 38, D-4, #9) Bean Hill Road, Northfield
800-353-2414; 603-286-1414 (snow)
TRAILS, 21; LIFTS, 5; VERTICAL, 800'.
▶NORDIC: Unlimited backcountry skiing.

KING PINE SKI AREA
(P. 38, C-4, #10) Route 153, East Madison
603-367-8896
TRAILS, 16; LIFTS, 4; VERTICAL, 350'.

KING RIDGE SKI AREA
(P. 38, D-3, #11) King Ridge Road, New London
603-526-6966; 800-343-1312 (snow)
SEASON: Nov. 25-March 31
ANNUAL SNOWFALL: 90"

TERRAIN: 24 trails over 100 acres; longest run, 5,000'; ◆ 12%; ▪ 33%; ● 55%.
LIFTS: 7 (2 triples, 1 double, 4 surface); capacity, 7,250 per hour.
SUMMIT: 1,800'
VERTICAL: 850'
ACTIVITIES: Snowboarding; NASTAR.
FEATURES: Snowmaking 90%; ski school; child care; restaurant; rentals.
Truly a beginner's paradise with lots of gentle runs, predictably popular with families.

LOON MOUNTAIN
(P. 38, C-4, #12) RFD 1, Kancamagus Highway, Lincoln
603-745-8111; 603-745-8100 (snow)
SEASON: Nov. 15-April 15
ANNUAL SNOWFALL: 125"
TERRAIN: 41 trails over 234 acres; longest run, 3 mi.; ◆ 20%; ▪ 55%; ● 25%.
LIFTS: 9 (1 gondola, 2 triples, 5 doubles, 1 surface); capacity, 10,200 per hour.
SUMMIT: 3,050'
VERTICAL: 2,100'
ACTIVITIES: Snowboarding; NASTAR.
FEATURES: Snowmaking 85%; ski school; child care; restaurants; rentals.
▶NORDIC: 35 groomed km; rentals; lessons.
Loon addressed its one major liability when it recently upgraded its snowmaking system. It helped pioneer limiting ticket sales and advance purchase of tickets. And the Unconditional Conditions Guarantee promises you'll ski free your next day if you're not happy with the conditions. Loon perennially records the highest skier days in New Hampshire, largely due to easy freeway access and the greatest number and variety of accommodations. Skiing gets high marks, too, especially among intermediates who appreciate the religious grooming and the challenge of negotiating close trails at the top that fan out into wide cruisers. They can wander at will over the mountain, since even the advanced runs on North Peak, while steep, are rarely allowed to get bumped up (save perhaps Angel Street). Beginners have their own area off the Kissin' Cousins lift. Lower intermediates can practice on the gentle powder blue runs off the Seven Brothers chair. The Nordic trail network follows the tumbling Pemigewasset River, with 30 km set for skating. Under 6 and over 70 ski free.

MCINTYRE SKI AREA
(P. 38, E-4, #13) 625 Mammoth Rd., Manchester
603-624-6571

TRAILS, 3; LIFTS, 3; VERTICAL, 169'.

MT. CRANMORE SKI AREA
(P. 38, C-4, #14) Off Route 16, North Conway
603-356-5543
SEASON: Dec. 1-March 31
ANNUAL SNOWFALL: 100"
TERRAIN: 30 trails over 185 acres; longest run, 1.75 mi.; ◆ 20%; ▪ 40%; ● 40%.
LIFTS: 5 (1 triple, 4 doubles); capacity, 3,500 per hour.
SUMMIT: 1,697'
VERTICAL: 1,200'
ACTIVITIES: Snowboarding; NASTAR; night skiing.
FEATURES: Snowmaking 100%; ski school; restaurants; rentals.
▶NORDIC: 20 groomed km; rentals; lessons.
Founded in 1938, Cranmore is one of North America's oldest ski areas and boasts a vital piece of history: Famed instructor Hannes Schneider, inventor of the Arlberg Technique that modernized skiing, set up shop here after he escaped Nazi Germany. His son Herbert is still active at the school. Cranmore has invested several million dollars in improvements and expansions (including a base fitness center and a half pipe for boarders) this decade. The terrain is pleasingly varied, although nothing will strike fear in the hearts of strong skiers.

MT. SUNAPEE SKI AREA
(P. 38, E-3, #15) Route 103, Mt. Sunapee State Park
603-763-2356; 603-763-4020 (snow)
SEASON: Dec. 1-April 4
ANNUAL SNOWFALL: 100"
TERRAIN: 36 trails over 210 acres; longest run, 1.75 mi.; ◆ 5%; ▪ 75%; ● 20%.
LIFTS: 7 (3 triples, 3 doubles, 1 surface); capacity, 8,550 per hour.
SUMMIT: 2,743'
VERTICAL: 1,510'
ACTIVITIES: Snowboarding; NASTAR.
FEATURES: Snowmaking 80%; ski school; child care; restaurants; rentals.
The other state-owned area, Sunapee, would suffer from an inferiority complex if it were a person, since it's often ignored when people list the top areas in New Hampshire. Still, its acreage exceeds that at Cannon and its lower elevation guarantees less extreme conditions. The skiing is primarily intermediate, though advanced skiers will enjoy the runs of the Sunbowl and several narrow squiggles from the summit.

PAT'S PEAK SKI AREA
(P. 38, E-3, #16) Off Route 114, Henniker
603-428-3245; 800-258-3218

(snow)
TRAILS, 19; LIFTS, 7; VERTICAL, 710'.

RAGGED MOUNTAIN SKI AREA
(P. 38, D-3, #17) Ragged Mountain Road, Danbury
603-768-3475; 603-768-3971 (snow)
SEASON: Dec. 1-April 1
ANNUAL SNOWFALL: 95"
TERRAIN: 23 trails over 80 acres; longest run, 1.75 mi.; ◆ 30%; ▪ 50%; ● 20%.
LIFTS: 4 (3 doubles, 1 surface); capacity, 3,000 per hour.
SUMMIT: 2,250'
VERTICAL: 1,250'
ACTIVITIES: Snowboarding.
FEATURES: Snowmaking 90%; ski school; child care; restaurants; rentals.
▶NORDIC: 15 groomed km; rentals; lessons.
Ragged Mountain recently added a mid-mountain lodge and another double chair, and increased snowmaking capacity, in an effort to smooth its rough edges and solidify its family base. The skiing will occupy all levels for a few hours. Exhibition is the superb cruiser; the steep mogulled Cemetery Gates beckons experts. Children under 6 ski free. The Nordic center boasts sterling views.

SNOWHILL AT EASTMAN
(P. 38, D-3, #18) Old Route 10, Grantham
603-863-4241
TRAILS, 3; LIFTS, 1; VERTICAL, 243'.
▶NORDIC: 30 groomed km. Sleigh rides.

TEMPLE MOUNTAIN SKI AREA
(P. 38, E-3, #19) Route 101, Peterborough
603-924-6949
TRAILS, 15; LIFTS, 6; VERTICAL, 568'.
▶NORDIC: 40 km (20 km groomed, 5 km skating).

WATERVILLE VALLEY SKI RESORT
(P. 38, C-4, #20) Town Square, Waterville Valley
800-468-2553; 603-236-4144 (snow)
SEASON: Nov. 14-April 18
ANNUAL SNOWFALL: 140"
TERRAIN: 53 trails over 255 acres; longest run, 3 mi.; ◆ 20%; ▪ 60%; ● 20%.
LIFTS: 13 (1 quad, 3 triples, 5 doubles, 4 surface); capacity, 15,660 per hour.
SUMMIT: 4,004'
VERTICAL: 2,020'
ACTIVITIES: Snowboarding; NASTAR; sleigh rides; ice skating.

FEATURES: Snowmaking 96%; ski school; child care; restaurants; rentals.
▶NORDIC: 105 km (70 km groomed); rentals; lessons.
Waterville Valley appeals to nearly everyone. Families appreciate the midweek free skiing and lodging for kids under 12, highly rated ski school, nursery, Ski Wee program, and supervised teen center. Singles and young couples revel in the thriving nightlife. Snowboarders love their own lift-served area with half pipe (the area's second) on Snow Mountain. Best of all, the five-day family pass permits skiing at 16 state areas.
The mountain, designed in the 1960s when wider trails were fashionable, is particularly friendly to intermediates. Low blue skiers can frolic on Valley Run and Periphery. Advanced intermediates have Snow Mountain, White Caps, Old Tecumseh, and Tippecanoe. Mogul mashers can test their knee strength off the Sunny Side chair.
The superb grooming and instruction, challenging terrain, 70 km of skating track, and extensive facilities at the modern village make the Nordic center one of the USA's most popular. Eight dollars buys a trip up Snow Mountain and some brilliant all-day skiing back onto the network.

WHALEBACK SKI AREA
(P. 38, D-3, #21) Lebanon
603-448-1489
TRAILS, 16; LIFTS, 2; VERTICAL, 700'.
Half pipe.

WILDCAT MOUNTAIN
(P. 38, C-4, #22) Off Route 16, Jackson
800-255-6439; 603-466-3326 (snow)
SEASON: Nov. 15-May 5
ANNUAL SNOWFALL: 150"
TERRAIN: 29 trails over 120 acres; longest run, 2.75 mi.; ◆ 45%; ■ 35%; ● 20%.
LIFTS: 6 (1 gondola, 4 triples, 1 double); capacity, 8,500 per hour.
SUMMIT: 4,050'
VERTICAL: 2,100'
ACTIVITIES: Snowboarding; NASTAR.
FEATURES: Snowmaking 90%; ski school; child care; restaurant; rentals.
▶NORDIC: 10 groomed mi.; rentals; lessons.
The name suits. Wildcat was always the choice for hellacious skiing. Regrettably for experts, several slopes were recently widened and all but two are groomed to a satiny finish. But the steeps are still there for intermediates and advanced skiers seeking challenge and improvement. Wildcat is also famous for installing the USA's first two-person gondola, unmatched views of Mt. Washington, and

Tuckerman's Ravine—and bitter chill winds. A 10-mile cross-country trail descends from the summit to Jackson.

NORDIC

APPLETOUR
(P. 38, C-4, #23) Route 88, Conway
603-926-3721
FACILITIES: 10 groomed km; rentals; lessons; restaurant.

DARBY FIELD INN
(P. 38, C-4, #24) Bald Hill, Conway
800-426-4147
FACILITIES: 18 groomed km; lodging and restaurant.
This charming inn offers private touring for guests only; rentals are expected for 1994-1995.

DEER CAP SKI TOURING CENTER
(P. 38, D-4, #25) Center Ossipee
603-539-6030
FACILITIES: 15 groomed km (with skating lane); rentals; lodging and restaurant.

EASTMAN TOURING CENTER
(P. 38, D-3, #26) Club House Lane, Gratham
603-863-4500
FACILITIES: 30 groomed km; rentals; lessons; restaurant.
Twenty kilometers are on the golf course, another 10 in the woods. Call in advance for lessons. The restaurant is only open Thurs. to Sun. The center itself is closed Mon. and Tues.

FRANCONIA INN CROSS-COUNTRY
(P. 38, C-3, #27) Route 116, Easton Road
603-823-5542
FACILITIES: 65 km (35 km groomed, 30 km tracked); rentals; lessons; lodging and restaurant.

HAMPSHIRE HILLS
(P. 38, E-4, #28) 50 Emerson Rd., Milford
603-673-7123
FACILITIES: 4 groomed km (with skating lane); rentals; lessons; night skiing; lodging and restaurant.

Courtesy: Woodstock Inn & Resort (see Suicide Six Ski Area, Vermont, p. 150).

THE INN AT EAST HILL FARM
(P. 38, E-3, #29) Mountain Road, Troy
603-242-6495
FACILITIES: 16 km (14 km groomed); rentals; lessons; lodging and restaurant.
This comfortable country inn opens onto wonderfully varied, picturesque terrain.

JACKSON SKI TOURING FOUNDATION
(P. 38, C-4, #30) Jackson
503-383-9355
FACILITIES: 160 km (91 km groomed); rentals; lessons; lodging and restaurants.
One of the finest cross-country systems in the country, with Mt. Washington towering from every perspective, Jackson also provides 40 km for skaters. The cross-country ticket can be used to ski Black Mountain. Twenty-two delightfully quaint member inns along the way provide lodging and dining. Among the top properties are the Christmas Farm Inn, Ellis River House, Inn at Thorn Hill, New England Inn, The Village House, and the Wildcat Inn.

MCCUBE CROSS-COUNTRY
(P. 38, C-3, #31) Route 25A, Orford
603-353-4709
FACILITIES: 20 groomed km; rentals; restaurant.

MOOSE MOUNTAIN LODGE
(P. 38, D-3, #32) Etna
603-643-3529
FACILITIES: 50 km; rentals; lessons; restaurant and lodging.
The terrain surrounding this homey lodge is ungroomed backcountry open only to guests. The guides are particularly fine telemark instructors.

MT. WASHINGTON VALLEY SKI TOURING ASSOCIATION
(P. 38, C-4, #33) Route 15, Intervale
603-356-9920
FACILITIES: 60 groomed km; rentals; lessons; lodging and restaurants.
Another highly rated system, with evenly distributed terrain and 8 km for skaters. There are several inns and restaurants along the network.

NESTLENOOK FARM ON THE RIVER
(P. 38, C-4, #34) Dinsmore Road, Jackson
603-383-0845

CONTINUED ON NEXT PAGE

NH

NEW JERSEY

With the sole exception of Vernon Valley/Great Gorge, New Jersey ski areas are little more than extended bunny slopes, but they provide lots of family fun, especially in the evening. ❄ Otherwise, there's more action in the Meadowlands (with the Giants, Jets, Nets, and Devils), any Asbury Park bar (especially when the "Boss" is in town), or the casinos of Atlantic City.

ALPINE

BELLE MOUNTAIN SKI AREA
(P. 39, C-2, #1) Valley Road (Route 29), Lambertville
TRAILS, 7; LIFTS, 4; VERTICAL, 235'.

CAMPGAW MOUNTAIN SKI CENTER
(P. 39, A-4, #2) Campgaw Road, Mahwah
201-327-7800
TRAILS, 8; LIFTS, 4; VERTICAL, 275'.
▶NORDIC: 2 groomed km.
Another good learning hill, convenient to New York City (with dazzling views of Manhattan by night), Campgaw boasts one of the Northeast's largest SkiWee enrollments (the children's program developed by Ski Magazine) and a state-of-the-art snowboard terrain garden, including a 625-foot half pipe, the first installed on the East Coast.

CRAIGMEUR SKI AREA
(P. 39, B-3, #3) 1175 Green Pond Rd., Newfoundland
TRAILS, 4; LIFTS, 4; VERTICAL, 250'.

HIDDEN VALLEY SKI AREA
(P. 39, A-3, #4) Breakneck Road, Vernon
201-764-6161; 201-764-4200 (snow)
SEASON: Dec. 1-March 31
ANNUAL SNOWFALL: 80"
TERRAIN: 12 trails over 55 acres; longest run, 4,000'; ◆ 50%; ■ 40%; ● 10%.
LIFTS: 3 (1 triple, 2 doubles); capacity, 3,600 per hour.
SUMMIT: 1,460'
VERTICAL: 640'
ACTIVITIES: Snowboarding; night skiing.
FEATURES: Snowmaking 100%; ski school; child care; restaurants; rentals.
While its vertical is nothing to sneeze at, Hidden Valley cannot match the breadth of nearby Vernon Valley/Great Gorge; still you'll hardly ever wait on lift lines, and more advanced skiers enjoy the steady pitch and sharp rolls of trails like Helenback.

VERNON VALLEY/GREAT GORGE
(P. 39, A-3, #5) Route 94, Vernon
201-827-2000; 201-827-3900 (snow)
SEASON: Nov. 25-April 15
ANNUAL SNOWFALL: 89"
TERRAIN: 52 trails over 150 acres; longest run, 4,680'; ◆ 30%; ■ 45%; ● 25%.
LIFTS: 17 (1 triple, 13 doubles, 3 surface); capacity, 17,500 per hour.
SUMMIT: 1,480'
VERTICAL: 1,040'
ACTIVITIES: Snowboarding; night skiing.
FEATURES: Snowmaking 100%; ski school; restaurants; rentals.
▶NORDIC: 15 groomed km; rentals; lessons.
Great Gorge is notable in several respects: it has an amazing vertical for New Jersey, a surprising range of terrain for all levels (though nothing really steep or ferociously bumpy), an extensive lift network, excellent night skiing, full spa facilities—and it once had a Playboy Club (whence may have come the term "ski bunny"). It's still extremely popular with singles from "the city," as well as suburban families, who take advantage of numerous special rates and package deals.

NORDIC

FAIRVIEW LAKE SKI TOURING CENTER
(P. 39, A-3, #6) 1035 Fairview Lake Rd., Newton
201-383-9282
FACILITIES: 16 groomed km.; rentals; lessons; restaurant.

STATBOX	
Tourism: 800-JERSEY7	**Average annual precipitation:** 40"-51"
Time zone: Eastern	
Population: 7,730,188	**Highest elevation:** 1,803'
Square miles: 7,836	**Lowest elevation:** Sea level

CONTINUED FROM LAST PAGE

FACILITIES: 20 groomed km (with an 8-km skating lane); rentals; lessons; sleigh rides; lodging and restaurant.

NORDIC SKIER
(P. 38, D-4, #35) 19 North Main St., Wolfeboro
603-569-3151
FACILITIES: 20 groomed km (with 10-km skating lane); rentals; lessons; restaurant.

NORSK CROSS-COUNTRY SKI CENTER
(P. 38, D-3, #36) Route 11, Lebanon
604-526-4685
FACILITIES: 95 km (85 km groomed, with 20-km skating lane); rentals; lessons; lodging and restaurant.

OCCOM CROSS-COUNTRY CENTER
(P. 38, D-3, #37) Occom Road, Hanover
603-646-2440
FACILITIES: 15 groomed km; rentals; lessons; restaurant.

PERRY HOLLOW CROSS-COUNTRY
(P. 38, D-4, #38) Wolfeboro
603-569-3055
FACILITIES: 25 groomed km (with 5-km skating lane); rentals; lessons; restaurant.

RED HILL INN AND SKI TOURING CENTER
(P. 38, D-4, #39) Centre Harbor
603-279-7001
FACILITIES: 5 km; rentals; lodging and restaurant.

THE SHATTUCK NORDIC CENTER
(P. 38, E-3, #40) 28 Dublin Rd., Jaffrey
603-532-4300
FACILITIES: 10 groomed km; rentals; lessons; restaurant.
Trails romp through the highly rated golf course and wooded sugarbush, with stunning views of Mt. Monadnock. The sugar house is open during maple tapping season, for an entertaining break.

SNOWVILLAGE INN
(P. 38, C-4, #41) Foss Mountain Road, Snowville
603-447-2818
FACILITIES: 13 groomed km; rentals; lessons; lodging and restaurant.

SUGAR SHACK NORDIC VILLAGE
(P. 38, C-3, #42) Route 175, Thornton
603-726-3867
FACILITIES: 30 groomed km (with 8-km skating lane); rentals; night skiing; restaurant.

SUNSET HILL HOUSE TOURING CENTER
(P. 38, C-3, #43) Sunset Road, Sugar Hill
603-823-5522
FACILITIES: 60 km (20 km groomed); rentals; sleigh rides; lodging and restaurant.

WINDBLOWN CROSS-COUNTRY
(P. 38, F-3, #44) RFD 2, New Ipswich
603-878-2869
FACILITIES: 40 groomed km; rentals; lessons; lodging and restaurant.
This tree farm (two basic cabins are for rent) offers admirably balanced terrain, with 15 km set for skaters. The grooming is exquisite, as are the vistas of the Monadnock region.

WOODBOUND INN
(P. 38, E-3, #45) Woodbound Road, Jaffery
603-532-8341
FACILITIES: 15 groomed km; rentals; lessons; lodging and restaurant; 1.5 km lighted.

NEW MEXICO

Desert and pueblos usually come to mind when people think of New Mexico, not skiing. Yet the mountainous spine of the Rockies extends almost as far south as the Tex/Mex border. High desert sunshine caresses these mountains, ensuring pleasant fair-weather skiing most winter days. Indeed, come spring you can often ski and golf in the same day.❄ Purchase a Ski Three Pass and get a discount on tickets at Taos, Red River, and Angel Fire, part of the so-called Enchanted Circle. ❄ Take an afternoon off and visit the superlative galleries in Santa Fe and Taos, the ingenious cliff dwellings of the Anasazi in Chama Canyon or the hauntingly beautiful Taos, Santa Clara, and San Ildefonso pueblos. ❄ Contrary to a popular misconception among vistors, yes, you can drink the water in New Mexico.

ALPINE

ANGEL FIRE SKI RESORT
(P. 40, A-4, #1) North Angel Fire Road, off Route 234, Angel Fire
800-633-7463; 505-377-4219 (snow)
SEASON: Dec. 9-April 3
ANNUAL SNOWFALL: 220"
TERRAIN: 67 trails over 320 acres; longest run, 3.5 mi.; ◆ 18%; ▪ 48%; ● 34%.
LIFTS: 6 (3 triples, 4 doubles); capacity, 7,900 per hour.
SUMMIT: 10,680'
VERTICAL: 2,180'
ACTIVITIES: Snowboarding; NASTAR.
FEATURES: Snowmaking 60%; ski school; restaurants; rentals.
 Your first clue that Angel Fire is a supreme family area is the passel of lovely wide cruisers nestled amid stands of fir and spruce as you approach, including the 3.5-mile Headin' Home. Then you notice the separate learning area for pre-schoolers. The innovative ski school inculcates its instructors (trained to work with all ages) with the dynamics of a child's stance and style as opposed to an adult's, teaches kids greater body awareness, indoctrinates parents how to ski with their children, and encourages families to take special instructional packages together. At the other end of the spectrum, seniors ski free.
 Angel Fire boasts a pleasing blend of terrain: wide open runs, narrower trails with rollercoaster pitches reminiscent of New England, a couple of long steeps from the top of the triple. The tougher terrain isn't visible from the base. The area has operated under a mountain of debt in recent years (it's currently in Chapter 11), which makes the new ownership's ambitious plans to overhaul the 1960s vintage lifts (a 29-minute triple is a prime candidate for New Mexico's first high-speed detachable quad) moot. But steadily rising skier visits (mainly from Texas) bode well for this appealing, friendly place.

PAJARITO MOUNTAIN
(P. 40, B-3, #2) Off Route 4, Los Alamos
505-662-7669
SEASON: (open only Wed., weekends, holidays)
ANNUAL SNOWFALL: 220"
TERRAIN: 41 trails over 220 acres; longest run, 1.5 mi.; ◆ 45%; ▪ 45%; ● 10%.
LIFTS: 5 (1 triple, 3 doubles, 1 surface); capacity, 5,150 per hour.
SUMMIT: 10,441'
VERTICAL: 1,600'
ACTIVITIES: Snowboarding.
FEATURES: Professional ski patrol; ski school; restaurant; rentals.
▶NORDIC: 10 groomed km.
 Run by the Los Alamos Ski Club, Pajarito was laid out by local nuclear scientists with cabin fever in the 1950s. To this day, the access road is lined with signs warning, "DANGER! EXPLOSIVE TRUCKS!" As the local joke goes, "If they ever started night skiing, they wouldn't have to install lights." The skiing is atomic, to say the least. The runs plummet from a long ridge, all steep, hairy, and ungroomed. The one blessing for intermediates is that the majority are fairly wide. Privately owned and non-profit, Pajarito isn't allowed to promote itself. And the turn-off is so poorly marked, you'd think they don't welcome strangers. Well, they'd prefer not to let the secret out, but once you're there, an ultra-casual, friendly atmosphere prevails: The lodge's walls and racks are lined with coats, even purses. It really is the 1950s revisited.

RED RIVER SKI AREA
(P. 40, A-4, #3) Pioneer Road, Red River
800-331-7669; 505-754-2382 (snow)
SEASON: Nov. 25-April 3
ANNUAL SNOWFALL: 188"
TERRAIN: 53 trails over 135 acres; longest run, 2.5 mi.; ◆ 30%; ▪ 38%; ● 32%.
LIFTS: 7 (2 triples, 4 doubles, 1 surface); capacity, 7,920 per hour.
SUMMIT: 10,350'
VERTICAL: 1,600'
ACTIVITIES: Snowboarding; NASTAR.
FEATURES: Snowmaking 75%; ski school; restaurants; rentals.
 Don't be intimidated by The Face—most of the hardest terrain is right above the base chalet. Several green runs are on the backside. Beginners can go all the way to the top, where they glide through aspen groves (treeline is above 10,000 feet) and the terrain garden at Pricklepines, with tepees, cutout farm animals, and a mining camp. Advanced skiers will enjoy the windy West Bowl's narrow, winding, slightly bumped up trails.
 And experts can tackle the short steeps of Liftline, Mine Shaft, and Catskinner. You can't get into major trouble, as most nasty pitches are followed by flats, and families can ski together since the layout often creates two or three short trails that reconnect for skiers of different abilities.
 Texans love this area and the old-fashioned Western town of the same name (the slopes descend practically down to Main Street). The saloons are classics, the folks are warm (most everyone wears several hats—all of them Stetsons—so your ski instructor might be your bartender that night), even the liftpoles are down-home, with hay bales used for cushioning.

SANDIA PEAK
(P. 40, B-3, #4) 10 Tramway Loop NE, Albuquerque
505-242-9133; 296-9585; 505-242-9052 (snow)
SEASON: Dec. 11-March 20
ANNUAL SNOWFALL: 183"
TERRAIN: 26 trails over 100 acres; longest run, 2.5 mi.; ◆ 10%; ▪ 55%; ● 35%.
LIFTS: 6 (4 doubles, 2 surface); capacity, 4,500 per hour.
SUMMIT: 10,378'
VERTICAL: 1,700'
ACTIVITIES: Snowboarding.
FEATURES: Snowmaking 25%; ski school; restaurants; rentals.
 Access to Sandia Peak is either via a leisurely scenic drive or a 15-minute ride on the world's longest tram. The tram takes you straight to the top of the area, where there is no ski shop (bring your own equipment or rent elsewhere). Sandia Peak is an excellent learning area, with a fine ski school and miles of gentle green and blue runs. Children under 46 inches ski free. Experts will find little to do, although there are some gladed runs with decent pitch.

SANTA FE SKI AREA
(P. 40, B-3, #5) End of Route 475, Santa Fe
800-776-SNOW; 505-982-4429; 505-983-9155 (snow)
SEASON: Nov. 25-April 10
ANNUAL SNOWFALL: 225"
TERRAIN: 38 trails over 600 acres; longest run, 3 mi.; ◆ 40%; ▪ 40%; ● 20%.
LIFTS: 7 (1 quad, 1 triple, 2 double, 3 surface); capacity, 7,300 per hour.
SUMMIT: 12,000'
VERTICAL: 1,650'
ACTIVITIES: Snowboarding; NASTAR.
FEATURES: Snowmaking 30%; ski school; child care; restaurants; rentals.
 A picturesque road spirals its way up several switchbacks from "The City Different" to one of the highest—and oldest—areas in North America. You can see the desert from its lofty summit. The skiing offers far more variety than at first glance. While true beginner's terrain is limited to a small secluded area, there are plenty of cruisers like Gayway, Midland, Open Slope, Sunset, and Easy Street. Expert runs lie mainly to the left of the Tesuque chair. Whatever kind of skiing you're looking for, you'll find it here. Tequila Sunrise, Wizard, Easter Bowl, and Molly Hogan offer excellent tree skiing. Avalanche Bowl and Double Eagle II offer good steep bumps. Big Rock and Camp Robber, both accessible by a

hike from the Super Chief quad, provide the intrepid expert with tight nearly vertical glades that hold snow beautifully. Plans are afoot (pending environmental impact studies) to install a lift in the Big Tesuque Bowl, currently reached by a hike from Cornice. On powder days, this is magnificent advanced intermediate skiing: wide open at the top, closely gladed at the bottom. Skiers new to the area should go with someone familiar with the bowl: It's huge and people have gotten lost. Once at the bottom, you'll have to hitchhike back—it's part of the experience.

SIPAPU SKI AREA

(P. 40, B-3, #6) Highway 518, Vadito
505-587-2240
TRAILS, 19; LIFTS, 3; VERTICAL, 865'.

Owned by the same family since its opening in 1952, Sipapu is a delightful throwback. Most employees have worked here for at least a decade, and the president helps with the snowmaking. Its all-purpose lodge includes a liquor store and trading post. Three minutes is the longest wait on lift lines at peak periods; and children under 6 and seniors over 69 ski free. The narrow, tree-lined runs fan out from the center lift and are contoured to the natural terrain, similar to many Northeastern runs. The trails wind fairly steeply through aspen and pine. While there is no official cross-country network, forest service trails weave through nearby canyons and President Bruce Bolander, a true mountain man, leads wilderness backpacking and telemarking expeditions. Though the Bolanders have filed for a permit to expand to nearly 1,000 acres (and double the vertical with a new lift), the atmosphere is unlikely to change. No wonder families adore Sipapu and come back year after year.

SKI APACHE

(P. 40, D-3, #7) Route 532, Ruidoso
505-336-4356; 505-257-9001 (snow)
SEASON: Nov. 25-April 10
ANNUAL SNOWFALL: 183''
TERRAIN: 52 trails over 300 acres; longest run, 2.7 mi.; ◆ 45%; ■ 30%; ● 25%.
LIFTS: 10 (1 gondola, 1 quad, 5 triples, 2 doubles, 1 surface); capacity, 15,360 per hour.
SUMMIT: 11,500'
VERTICAL: 1,900'
ACTIVITIES: Snowboarding.
FEATURES: Snowmaking 40%; ski school; restaurants; rentals.

The Mescalero Apache own this resort, which lies partly on their reservation, and skiers schuss over traces of their historic trails. The slopes sit below the sacred Sierra Blanca peak; they offer panoramic vistas of Texas, Arizona, the unforgettable White Sands National Monument, and the site of the Trinity Project. Ski Apache boasts the state's only gondola and its highest lift capacity, and the slopes never feel crowded. Though closer to El Paso than to Albuquerque (the bilingual ski school is a reminder of Mexico's proximity), the mountain is situated in one of those odd metereological mini-zones, and its face is usually gleaming white while the landscape for miles around is parched and brown. Ski Apache is noted for its groomed steeps, one with a pitch of 38 degrees. There are chutes, glades, and open bowls galore. A concerted effort has been made to improve service here. The nearest lodging is at the deluxe tribe-owned Inn of the Mountain Gods or in the charming Western town of Ruidoso.

SNOW CANYON AT CLOUDCROFT

(P. 40, D-3, #8) Off Route 82, Cloudcroft
505-682-2333; 800-333-7542 (snow)
TRAILS, 21; LIFTS, 3; VERTICAL, 700'.

The runs at Snow Canyon are mild and sunny, ideal for beginners. Children under 41 inches and seniors over 62 ski free. The elegant Lodge at Cloudcroft offers ski touring through the majestic Lincoln National Forest. The town of Cloudcroft is an entrancing artists' colony, with general stores displaying handmade crafts and fruit preserves from nearby orchards.

TAOS SKI VALLEY

(P. 40, A-3, #9) End of Highway 150, Taos Ski Valley
800-776-1111; 505-776-2291; 505-776-2916 (snow)
SEASON: Nov. 25-April 10
ANNUAL SNOWFALL: 320''
TERRAIN: 72 trails over 1,000 acres; longest run, 5.25 mi.; ◆ 51%; ■ 25%; ● 24%.
LIFTS: 11 (3 quads, 1 triple, 6 doubles, 1 surface); capacity, 13,500 per hour.

Courtesy: Ski The Summit (see Copper Mountain Resort, Colorado, p. 97).

SUMMIT: 11,819'
VERTICAL: 2,612'
ACTIVITIES: Snowboarding.
FEATURES: Snowmaking 45%; ski school; child care; restaurants; rentals.

Al's Run, the legendary, intimidating slope, greets you with nearly a mile of tightly packed moguls as tall (according to local lore) as you are. Legend has it that founder Ernie Blake used to dangle airline bottles of vodka from the trees to buck up terrified skiers. But then there's the sign at the base of Al's: "Only 1/30th of our mountain looks like this. We have easy runs, too." One of the great secrets in skidom is that this bully has a gentle side. Helpful ski patrollers are stationed everywhere to ease anxiety. They'll point less experienced skiers to the west side of the mountain, where Honeysuckle, Shalako, and Totemoff await. The only green run down the east side is Bambi—though the greens (aside from cat tracks) might qualify as low blues elswhere. And true intermediates have little more selection, though there are lovely bowls (with some surprises) off Kachina Quad. Another huge drawback is the layout: Many "green" and black-and-blue runs criss cross, then converge in congested cat tracks at the bottom. But if you want to improve, there's no better place: Taos boasts the top-rated ski school in North America, and its intensive Learn to Ski Better Weeks make good skiers brilliant. Seniors over 70 ski free.

Let's face it, though, Taos is not for weak-kneed skiers. There are magical hidden chutes and glades at nearly every turn. Tree skiers will find blood-curdling slalom courses in Castor and Pollux, with trees spaced as narrowly as two feet apart. An integral part of the Taos mystique is Kachina Ridge, accessible only after a 75-minute hike—the area will never install a lift as a point of pride. Actually, several ridges (Highline is the other favorite) plummet from the summit, offering the ultimate in thrill-seeking for experts. You used to have to sign in with the patrol; now they simply give you and your partner—that's mandatory—a quick test. Study the ridge procedure signs: They're serious and should be.

The town and ski valley offer a winning combination of European and Southwestern ambiance. Yet despite its cosmopolitan air and chic image, the Valley remains relatively down-home; the elegant new Inn at Snakedance is the first lodging at the area that offers the combination of such luxuries as TV, fireplace, and private bath. It's the kind of place where celebrities come to wind down, and everyone babbles about the quality of the light.

NORDIC

ENCHANTED FOREST

(P. 40, A-4, #10) 3 mi. E of Red River
505-745-2374
FACILITIES: 34 groomed km; rentals; lessons; restaurant.

The trails (set for both gliding and skating) off Bobcat Pass wind through ancient forests, snow-covered red rocks, aspen groves, and rolling meadows with sweeping panoramic views of the Sangre de Cristos.

JEMEZ NORDIC

(P. 40, B-3, #11) 2 Del Gado St., Santa Fe
505-989-7056
FACILITIES: 20 groomed km (with skating lane); rentals; lessons; restaurant.

Trails weave through a spectacular combination of meadow and rolling forest adjacent to the volcanic caldera of Valle Grande in the Jemez Range.

MANZANO MOUNTAIN

(P. 40, C-3, #12) Torreon
505-384-2209
FACILITIES: 25 groomed km (with skating lane); rentals; lessons; restaurant.

New York could be considered the Big Apple of Mid-Atlantic ski states, with a wide variety of both Alpine and Nordic terrain. As proof, Lake Placid has hosted the winter Olympics twice—only Innsbruck, Austria, has enjoyed the same honor—and many of Lake Placid's Olympic venues are open to the public. ❄ There are three major ranges: the Catskills, Adirondacks, and Alleghenys. Each has its own unique side attractions. In addition to their proximity to New York City, the Catskills region offers several charming artistic communities like Woodstock, as well as the grand old "Borscht Belt" hotels, where you'll still find top music and comedy entertainment weekends and holidays. The Adirondacks chime in with the spa and horse racing retreat Saratoga Springs and gorgeous Lake Champlain. And the scattered Allegheny chain takes in the beautiful Finger Lakes, whose attractions include several wineries and Cornell University, with Rochester, Buffalo and Niagara Falls also within easy reach. ❄ Two areas not listed below are open only to club members, guests, and prospective members but may allow skiers access if they say they're interested in joining: Hunt Hollow and Ski Valley Club, both in Naples.

ALPINE

BELLEAYRE MOUNTAIN SKI CENTER

(P. 41, D-5, #1) Off Route 28, Belleayre Mountain Road, Highmount
914-254-5600; 800-942-6904 (snow)
SEASON: Nov. 25-April 10
ANNUAL SNOWFALL: 110'
TERRAIN: 33 trails over 220 acres; longest run, 6,378'; ◆ 17%; ■ 59%; ● 24%.
LIFTS: 8 (1 triple, 3 doubles, 4 surface); capacity, 9,210 per hour.
SUMMIT: 3,429'
VERTICAL: 1,404'
ACTIVITIES: Snowboarding; NASTAR; night skiing.
FEATURES: Snowmaking 88%; ski school; child care; restaurants; rentals.
▶NORDIC: 10 groomed km; rentals; lessons.
Belleayre is family-oriented and reasonably priced (it's owned by the state, which keeps prices low, but also guarantees slow modernization since the resort is a chronic money loser). Still, it sees far fewer skiers than its neighbors Hunter and Windham. Novices play on the bottom half of the mountain, two virtual plateaux whose trail names bear witness to the area's rich Native American heritage (Iroquois is a particular favorite with beginners). Several advanced intermediate runs fan out from the top ridge. Unfortunately, because of the unusual layout (there are lodges and parking areas at the base, mid-mountain and summit) there are no true uninterrupted runs to take advantage of that respectable vertical. Seniors over 70 ski free; beginners can get free lessons.

BIG BIRCH SKI AREA

(P. 41, A-2, E-6, #2) off Route 22, Paterson
914-878-3181
TRAILS, 15; LIFTS, 4; VERTICAL, 500'.

BIG TUPPER SKI AREA

(P. 41, B-5, #3) Country Club Road, Tupper Lake
518-359-3651
SEASON: Nov. 18-April 15 (weekends only before Christmas)
ANNUAL SNOWFALL: 128"
TERRAIN: 23 trails over 105 acres; longest run, 1.25 mi.; ◆ 10%; ■ 30%; ● 60%.
LIFTS: 5 (3 doubles, 2 surface); capacity, 5,240 per hour.
SUMMIT: 3,050'
VERTICAL: 1,152'
ACTIVITIES: Snowboarding; night skiing; luge run.
FEATURES: Snowmaking 25%; ski school; child care; restaurants; rentals.
▶NORDIC: 25 groomed km; rentals; lessons.
One of the supreme Adirondack learning areas, with low prices, an acclaimed ski school, relatively deserted slopes—even a few steeps for stronger skiers in the family. The problem is the usual northern New York bugaboo—ice and wind.

BOBCAT SKI CENTER

(P. 41, D-5, #4) Gladstone Hollow Road, Andes
914-676-3143
SEASON: Dec. 1-March 31 (open weekends and holidays)
ANNUAL SNOWFALL: 88"
TERRAIN: 18 trails over 73 acres; longest run, 1.5 mi.; ◆ 50%; ■ 39%; ● 11%.
LIFTS: 2 (2 surface); capacity, 500 per hour.
SUMMIT: 2,560'
VERTICAL: 1,050'
ACTIVITIES: None.
FEATURES: Snowmaking 20%;
ski school; child care; restaurant; rentals.
Even its aficionados think Bobcat is an odd area. You get the feeling that it could be better, much better, if someone lavished money and attention here. It has no chairs, yet a decent vertical and some nasty steeps and bumps. It's only open weekends (of course, it's in a slightly less touristy part of the Catskills). Maybe it's just living up to its name: a little untamed.

BRANTLING SKI SLOPES

(P. 41, C-3, #5) 4015 Fish Farm Rd., Sodus
315-331-2365
TRAILS, 6; LIFTS, 6; VERTICAL, 240'.
`

BRISTOL MOUNTAIN

(P. 41, D-3, #6) 5658 Route 64, Canandaigua
716-374-6000; 716-271-5000 (snow)
SEASON: Nov. 15-April 10
ANNUAL SNOWFALL: 110"
TERRAIN: 22 trails over 130 acres; longest run, 2 mi.; ◆ 20%; ■ 60%; ● 20%.
LIFTS: 5 (2 triples, 2 doubles, 1 surface); capacity, 6,600 per hour.
SUMMIT: 2,200'
VERTICAL: 1,200'
ACTIVITIES: Snowboarding; night skiing.
FEATURES: Snowmaking 100%; ski school; child care; restaurant; rentals.
A great family area, Bristol is intermediate heaven with lots of lovely long cruisers like Northstar and Southern Cross. But advanced skiers can streak down Comet, Upper Rocket, and a new double diamond slope being cut for 1995. Kids under 8 ski free, and a new beginner area has been expanded and removed from the heavier skier traffic. If you're dissatisfied with conditions within the first hour of purchasing your lift ticket, you can get a voucher for another day.

CATAMOUNT SKI AREA

(P. 41, D-6, #7) Route 23, Hillsdale
518-325-3200
SEE LISTING IN MASSACHUSETTS.

COCKAIGNE

(P. 41, D-1, #8) County Route 66 N, Cherry Creek
716-287-3223
TRAILS, 15; LIFTS, 4; VERTICAL, 430'.
Cockaigne offers a "sweet" learning experience for locals: Its runs are named after desserts. Beginners adore Kandy Kaigne, Baked Apple, and Sugar Plum. Intermediates eat up Marzipan and Crackerjack. Experts have to settle for the crumbs of Macaroon and Honey Bun.

CONCORD HOTEL

(P. 41, E-5, #9) 1 mi. N of Quickway, Kiamesha Lake
914-794-4000
TRAILS, 4; LIFTS, 4; VERTICAL, 200'.
✕NORDIC: 15 groomed km.
Once upon a time the Catskills were known as the Borscht Belt, and hosted the nation's leading comics as the solidly upper-middle class scarfed down matza balls, kasha, cole slaw, and stuffed cabbage. You can still catch top acts (well, mainly those skidding downhill), join up for a singles weekend and make your mother happy, and if you've never skied and maybe want to flirt a little, you can hit the bunny slopes. All kidding aside, the Nordic skiing is pleasant, if not strenuous, and the Concord remains a class act for lodging and entertainment.

CORTINA VALLEY SKI AREA

(P. 41, D-6, #10) Off Route

STATBOX	
Tourism: 212-827-6255	Average annual precipitation: 40"
Time zone: Eastern	
Population: 17,990,455	Highest elevation: 5,344'
Square miles: 49,576	Lowest elevation: Sea level

23A, Haines Falls
518-589-6500
TRAILS, 11; LIFTS, 4; VERTICAL, 625'.

▶NORDIC: 20 groomed km.

DAVOS
(P. 41, E-5, #11) Davos Road, Route 17 (Exit 109), Woodridge
914-434-1000
TRAILS, 12; LIFTS, 2; VERTICAL, 500'.

▶NORDIC: 10 groomed km.
Davos has had periodic financial problems over the last two decades. A pity, because many New Yorkers learned to ski here—or at least learned the joys of wilderness beyond Central Park. Its gentle, gladed slopes are perfect for novices. Over 65 and under 6 ski free.

DRY HILL SKI AREA
(P. 41, B-4, #12) Brookside Drive, Watertown
315-782-8584
TRAILS, 6; LIFTS, 3; VERTICAL, 300'.

FOUR SEASONS SKI CENTER
(P. 41, C-4, #13) State Route 5, 1 mi. E of Fayetteville
315-637-9023
TRAILS, 4; LIFTS, 2; VERTICAL, 100'.

▶NORDIC: 5 groomed km.

FROST RIDGE SKI AREA
(P. 41, D-2, #14) Conlon Road, LeRoy
716-768-9730; 716-594-2304 (snow)
TRAILS, 9; LIFTS, 3; VERTICAL, 140'.

▶NORDIC: 10 groomed km.

GORE MOUNTAIN SKI AREA
(P. 41, B-6, #15) Peaceful Valley Road, off Routes 8 & 28, North Creek
518-251-2411
SEASON: Nov. 15-April 15
ANNUAL SNOWFALL: 85''
TERRAIN: 43 trails over 270 acres; longest run, 3 mi.; ◆ 20%; ■ 70%; ● 10%.
LIFTS: 8 (1 triple, 5 doubles, 2 surface); capacity 8,600 per hour.
SUMMIT: 3,600'
VERTICAL: 2,100'
ACTIVITIES: Snowboarding.
FEATURES: Snowmaking 90%; ski school; child care; restaurants; rentals.
▶NORDIC: 25 groomed km; rentals; lessons.
Quiet and family-oriented, Gore sits in the shadow of more glamorous Lake Placid, even though its history and tradition are equally venerable. The sizable vertical

means long cruisers, and this is one of the best eastern mountains for intermediates, with a whopping three-quarters of the terrain rated blue. Best of all, every one of those slopes exceeds a mile in length, with the winding scenic Cloud Trail the standout.

GRANIT HOTEL SKI CENTER
(P. 41, E-6, #16) Kerhonkson
914-626-3141
TRAILS, 3; LIFTS, 1; VERTICAL, 60'.

▶NORDIC: 15 groomed km.

GREEK PEAK SKI RESORT
(P. 41, D-4, #17) 2000 State Route 392, 6 mi. S of Cortland
607-835-6111; 800-365-SNOW (snow)
SEASON: Nov. 25-April 10
ANNUAL SNOWFALL: 75''
TERRAIN: 24 trails over 95 acres; longest run, 1.5 mi.; ◆ 33%; ■ 43%; ● 24%.
LIFTS: 7 (1 triple, 4 doubles, 2 surface); capacity, 8,500 per hour.
SUMMIT: 2,100'
VERTICAL: 900'
ACTIVITIES: Snowboarding; night skiing.
FEATURES: Snowmaking 85%; ski school; child care; restaurants; rentals.
▶NORDIC: 40 groomed km; rentals; lessons.
This user-friendly resort offers numerous special packages. The skiing is admirably balanced, with wide cruisers and narrow gladed slopes. The beautiful Finger Lakes region is less than an hour's drive away.

HICKORY SKI CENTER
(P. 41, C-6, #18) Route 418, Warrensburg
518-623-2825
SEASON: Dec. 25-April 1 (open weekends and holidays)
ANNUAL SNOWFALL: 80''
TERRAIN: 12 trails over 38 acres; longest run, 1.5 mi.; ◆ 50%; ■ 33%; ● 17%.
LIFTS: 3 (3 surface); capacity, 1,800 per hour
SUMMIT: 1,900'
VERTICAL: 1,230'
ACTIVITIES: None.
FEATURES: Professional ski patrol; ski school; restaurant; rentals.
▶NORDIC: 20 groomed km.
A tough little area known for its steeps and difficult conditions.

HIGHMOUNT SKI CENTER
(P. 41, D-5, #19) Drybrook Road, Highmount
914-254-5265
TRAILS, 15; LIFTS, 5; VERTICAL, 1,050'.
Call ahead; will probably close.

HOLIDAY MOUNTAIN SKI AREA
(P. 41, E-5, #20) Bridgeville Road (Route 17, Exit 107), Monticello
914-796-3161
TRAILS, 14; LIFTS, 9; VERTICAL, 400'.

HOLIDAY VALLEY
(P. 41, D-5, #21) Route 219, Ellicottville
716-699-2345; 716-699-2644 (snow)
SEASON: Nov. 27-April 8
ANNUAL SNOWFALL: 180''
TERRAIN: 52 trails over 230 acres; longest run, 4,300'; ◆ 32%; ■ 38%; ● 30%.
LIFTS: 11 (4 quads, 2 triples, 3 doubles, 2 surface); capacity, 20,000 per hour.
SUMMIT: 2,250'
VERTICAL: 750'
ACTIVITIES: Snowboarding; night skiing.
FEATURES: Snowmaking 95%; ski school; restaurants; rentals.
▶NORDIC: 20 groomed km; rentals.
Want a surprise? Holiday Valley is numero uno in skier visits in New York. Yes, it outstrips Hunter, Gore, and Whiteface/Lake Placid. There are several reasons: glorious views, classic evergreen forests lining the slopes, varied terrain, ample snowfall, easy access from Buffalo, Cleveland, and Toronto, and new improvements every year. Recent additions include the classy Tannenbaum Lodge in the Upper Area and a new high-speed quad accessing the Chute runs. Bumpbashers head toward Falcon, Ego Alley, Chute, and the tricky now-we're-groomed-now-we're-not Champagne. Low intermediates have a field day in the Morning Star area. Snowboarders have their own section on steep Foxfire, including half pipe. And everyone gets a chance to experience glade skiing at its finest.

HUNTER MOUNTAIN SKI BOWL
(P. 41, D-6, #22) Route 23A, Hunter
518-263-4223; 800-FOR-SNOW (snow)
SEASON: Nov. 15-May 1
ANNUAL SNOWFALL: 125''
TERRAIN: 47 trails over 210 acres; longest run, 2 mi.; ◆ 30%; ■ 40%; ● 30%.
LIFTS: 16 (1 quad, 2 triples, 8 doubles, 5 surface); capacity, 18,000 per hour.
SUMMIT: 3,200'
VERTICAL: 1,600'
ACTIVITIES: Snowboarding; NASTAR.
FEATURES: Snowmaking 100%; ski school; restaurants; rentals.
▶NORDIC: 5 groomed km; lessons.

Here's an Eastern skiing legend, as renowned for its weekend crowds as for mean steeps like Annapurna, Westway, and K-27. The traffic reports are no exaggeration, as huge groups descend (or ascend) on Hunter from New York City every weekend and Wednesday (when several metro area ski shops run day trips). Hunter is social. You might be riding the lifts with members of a firefighting company, a Columbia University frat house, or Friends of the Frick. You just never know. Hunter West is an advanced skier's dream; the original Bowl caters to intermediates (watch out for the hordes on Broadway and Park Avenue), and Hunter One's laid-back runs are perfect for novices. Aside from slaloming your fellow skiers, the slopes remain satiny smooth thanks to some of the finest snowmaking and grooming anywhere. But do yourself a favor and go weekdays.

KISSING BRIDGE
(P. 41, D-2, #23) Route 240, Glenwood
716-592-4963; 716-592-4961 (snow)
SEASON: Dec. 1-April 1
ANNUAL SNOWFALL: 185''
TERRAIN: 37 trails over 700 acres; longest run, 3,000'; ◆ 20%; ■ 50%; ● 30%.
LIFTS: 10 (2 quads, 4 doubles, 4 surface); capacity, 12,400 per hour.
SUMMIT: 1,750'
VERTICAL: 550'
ACTIVITIES: Snowboarding; night skiing.
FEATURES: Snowmaking 75%; ski school; child care; restaurants; rentals.
Kissing Bridge does a lot with limited terrain. Despite the short vertical, there's sufficient variety, though the runs are short so there's no sustained challenge. It's a very good learning and practicing area, as the snow is usually excellent.

KUTSHER'S COUNTRY CLUB
(P. 41, E-5, #24) Kutsher Road, Monticello
914-794-6000
TRAILS, 2; LIFTS, 2; VERTICAL, 150'.

LABRADOR MOUNTAIN
(P. 41, D-4, #25) Off Route 91, just N of Truxton
607-842-6204; 800-446-9559 (snow)
SEASON: Dec. 1-April 1
ANNUAL SNOWFALL: 80''
TERRAIN: 22 trails over 90 acres; longest run, 4,500'; ◆ 30%; ■ 40%; ● 30%.
LIFTS: 5 (1 triple, 2 doubles, 2 surface); capacity, 6,675 per hour.
SUMMIT: 1,825'
VERTICAL: 700'

ACTIVITIES: NASTAR; night skiing.
FEATURES: Snowmaking 90%; ski school; restaurants; child care; rentals.
Another good learning area convenient to Syracuse locals; its Northern Peak is given over to first-timers and novices. Intermediates can romp over Central Peak, while experts enjoy runs, like Ptarmigan, Jacopie, and Cut Throat, that straddle the Southern and Central Peaks.

MAPLE SKI RIDGE
(P .41, D-6, #26) Route 159, W of Schenectady
518-381-4700
TRAILS, 6; LIFTS, 5; VERTICAL, 225'.

MCCAULEY MOUNTAIN
(P. 41, B-5, #27) Route 28, 2 mi. E of Old Forge
315-369-3225
TRAILS, 14; LIFTS, 5; VERTICAL, 663'.
▶NORDIC: 30 groomed km.

MT. PETER SKI AREA
(P. 41, A-1, #28) Route 17 & Old Mt. Peter Road, Greenwood Lake
914-986-4992
TRAILS, 8; LIFTS, 2; VERTICAL, 600'.

MT. PISGAH
(P. 41, B-6, #29) Mt. Pisgah Road, off Route 86, Saranac Lake
518-891-0970
TRAILS, 4; LIFTS, 1; VERTICAL, 300'.

NORTHHAMPTON PARK
(P. 41, C-2, #30) Route 31, Brockport
716-352-9995
TRAILS, 1; LIFTS, 1; VERTICAL, 100'.

OAK MOUNTAIN SKI CENTER
(P. 41, C-5, #31) Route 30, Speculator
518-548-7311
TRAILS, 13; LIFTS, 3; VERTICAL, 600'.

ORANGE COUNTY SKI AREA
(P. 41, A-1, E-6, #32) Montgomery
914-457-3000
TRAILS, 1; LIFTS, 1; VERTICAL, 131'.
▶NORDIC: 10 groomed km. Ice skating; sledding.

PEEK'N PEAK RESORT
(P. 41, E-1, #33) Ye Olde Road, Route 430, Clymer
716-355-4141
TRAILS, 24; LIFTS, 9; VERTICAL, 400'.

PINES SKI AREA
(P. 41, E-5, #34) Route 17 (Exit 106/107), South Fallsburg
914-434-6000
TRAILS, 6; LIFTS, 3; VERTICAL, 260'.

POWDER MILLS SKI SLOPE
(P. 41, C-3, #35) Route 96, Perinton
716-586-9209
TRAILS, 1; LIFTS, 1; VERTICAL, 75'.

RIDIN-HY
(P. 41, C-6, #36) 3 mi. off Exit 24 of I-87, Warrensburg
518-494-2742
TRAILS, 1; LIFTS, 1; VERTICAL, 150'.
▶NORDIC: 15 groomed km.

ROCKING HORSE
(P. 41, E-6, #37) 600 Route 44-55, Highland
914-691-2927
TRAILS, 3; LIFTS, 2; VERTICAL, 150'.

ROYAL MOUNTAIN SKI AREA
(P. 41, C-5, #38) Route 10, Caroga Lake
518-835-6445
TRAILS, 13; LIFTS, 3; VERTICAL, 550'.

SAWKILL FAMILY SKI CENTER
(P. 41, E-6, #39) Hill Road, Kingston
914-336-6977
TRAILS, 3; LIFTS, 1; VERTICAL, 70'.
▶NORDIC: 10 groomed km.

SCOTCH VALLEY
(P. 41, D-5, #40) Route 10, 3 mi. N of Stamford
607-652-3132; 800-558-SNOW (snow)
SEASON: Nov. 25-April 10
ANNUAL SNOWFALL: 86"
TERRAIN: 15 trails over 68 acres; longest run, 1.5 mi.; ◆ 10%; ▪ 75%; ● 15%.
LIFTS: 3 (1 triple, 2 doubles); capacity, 4,100 per hour.
SUMMIT: 2,950'
VERTICAL: 750'
ACTIVITIES: Snowboarding; sledding; night skiing.
FEATURES: Snowmaking 85%; ski school; restaurant; rentals.
▶NORDIC: 55 groomed km; rentals; lessons.
Another top-notch mountain for low intermediates. The touring center is similarly ideal for those wanting to work on their form. Under 5 ski free.

SHUMAKER MOUNTAIN
(P. 41, E-5, #41) Off Route 167, Little Falls
315-823-4470; 315-823-1110 (snow)
SEASON: Dec. 1-March 15
Annual snowfall: 85"
TERRAIN: 17 trails over 180 acres; longest run, 4,500'; ◆ 13%; ▪ 69%; ● 18%.
LIFTS: 4 (2 doubles, 2 surface); capacity, 3,200 per hour.
SUMMIT: 1,900'
VERTICAL: 750'
ACTIVITIES: Snowboarding; night skiing.
FEATURES: Snowmaking 90%; ski school; restaurant; rentals.
An expansive mountain with both wide slopes and tree-lined trails that remains relatively uncrowded.

SKI TAMARACK
(P. 41, D-2, #42) Route 240 South, Colden
716-941-6821; 716-941-5654 (snow)
TRAILS, 13; LIFTS, 4; VERTICAL, 500'.
▶NORDIC: 8 groomed km.
The mountain's fairly steep face makes it a good choice for intermediates who need to practice carving their turns.

SKI WINDHAM
(P. 41, D-6, #43) Route 23W to Clarence D. Lane Road, Windham
518-734-4300; 800-719-SKIW (snow)
SEASON: Nov. 15-April 11
ANNUAL SNOWFALL: 110"
TERRAIN: 33 trails over 220 acres; longest run, 2.25 mi.; ◆ 25%; #% 45%; ● 30%.
LIFTS: 8 (1 high-speed quad, 4 triples, 2 doubles, 1 surface); capacity, 9,800 per hour.
SUMMIT: 3,100'
VERTICAL: 1,500'
ACTIVITIES: Snowboarding.
FEATURES: Snowmaking 97%; ski school; restaurants; rentals.
Windham has been seeing more and more run-off traffic from Hunter, and has thoughtfully replaced the Whistler double chair with the Whirlwind high-speed quad, giving advanced skiers direct access from the base area to Wedel, The Wall, Upper Wolverine, and Upper Wheelchair. Beginners can toodle along Wraparound, the longest run, in the Catskills, while snowboarders enjoy Windham's half pipe and long, mellow intermediate runs. Everyone appreciates the fine grooming, attention to detail (with brightly garbed Courtesy Patrol volunteers to answer questions), and the classic fall-line skiing.

SNOW RIDGE
(P. 41, C-4, #44) 4501 West Rd., Turin
315-348-8456
TRAILS, 12; LIFTS, 7; VERTICAL, 500'.
▶NORDIC: 10 groomed km.
One of skiing's holdouts relented when owner Peter Harris installed snowmaking equipment in 1993. Because of its fortunate location, winds blowing off Lake Ontario usually dump several feet at a time on the aptly-named mountain; since 1970, it has seen less than 150 inches annually only once. As a result of the new acquisition, this relatively unknown beauty will start opening earlier. It features fine if short intermediate terrain.

SONG MOUNTAIN
(P. 41, D-4, #45) Tully
315-696-5711
TRAILS, 12; LIFTS, 5; VERTICAL, 700'.

STERLING FOREST SKI CENTER
(P. 41, A-1, #46) Route 17A W, Tuxedo
914-351-2163; 914-351-4788 (snow)
TRAILS, 10; LIFTS, 4; VERTICAL, 450'.
Set in lovely Bear Mountain State Park with some great views of the Hudson, Sterling has some decent steeps like Double Rainbow and the Bowl, as well as a racing slope.

SWAIN SKI CENTER
(P. 41, D-2, #47) Swain
607-545-6511
SEASON: Nov. 25-April 8
ANNUAL SNOWFALL: 150"
TERRAIN: 20 trails over 110 acres; longest run, 1 mi.; ◆ 15%; ▪ 45%; ● 40%.
LIFTS: 4 (3 quads, 1 double); capacity, 8,400 per hour.
SUMMIT: 1,950'
VERTICAL: 650'
ACTIVITIES: Snowboarding; NASTAR; night skiing.
FEATURES: Snowmaking 95%; ski school; restaurants; rentals.
Another gem unknown to many skiers, Swain provides ample snow cover, excellent grooming, and a mix of open slopes and narrower glades best suited to intermediate and novice skiers.

TITUS MOUNTAIN
(P. 41, A-5, #48) Johnson Road, 6 mi. S of Malone on Route 30
518-483-3740
SEASON: Dec. 15-April 15
ANNUAL SNOWFALL: 100"
TERRAIN: 25 trails over 125 acres; ◆ 10%; ▪ 80%; ● 10%.
LIFTS: 8 (2 triples, 5 doubles, 1 surface); capacity, 6,400 per hour.
SUMMIT: 2,350'
VERTICAL: 1,200'
ACTIVITIES: Snowboarding; night skiing.
FEATURES: Snowmaking 80%; ski school; restaurant; rentals.
Another locals' secret, Titus has a

loyal following for its good mix of trails that consistently challenge low intermediates.

TOGGENBURG SKI CENTER
(P. 41, C-4, #49) 1/4 mi. S of Route 80, Fabius
315-683-5842; 315-446-6666 (snow)
TRAILS, 18; LIFTS, 6; VERTICAL, 600'.
▶NORDIC: 40 groomed km.
Toggenburg offers a fine blend of slopes and glades, but it is most notable for its extensive night skiing operation. Virtually the entire mountain is lit.

VILLA ROMA
(P. 41, E-5, #50) Polster Road, Exit 104 of Route 17B, Callicoon
914-887-4880
TRAILS, 5; LIFTS, 2; VERTICAL, 500'.
▶NORDIC: 10 groomed km.

WEST MOUNTAIN SKI AREA
(P. 41, C-6, #51) West Mountain Road, 3 mi. W of Exit 18 I-87, Glens Falls
518-793-6606
SEASON: Dec. 1-April 1
ANNUAL SNOWFALL: 85''
TERRAIN: 21 trails over 95 acres; longest run, 1.5 mi.; ◆ 15%; ■ 60%; ● 25%.
LIFTS: 6 (1 triple, 2 doubles, 3 surface); capacity, 4,300 per hour.
SUMMIT: 1,470'
VERTICAL: 1,010'
ACTIVITIES: Snowboarding; bungee jumping; night skiing.
FEATURES: Snowmaking 65%; ski school; restaurant; rentals.
A nice intermediates' mountain, with such fine cruisers as Midway and Mach 2; extreme skiers in the family can always try the bungee jump if the narrow Cure and A.O.A. won't suffice.

WHITEFACE MOUNTAIN SKI CENTER
(P. 41, A-6, #52) Route 86, Wilmington
518-523-1655
SEASON: Nov. 15-April 15
ANNUAL SNOWFALL: 110''
TERRAIN: 65 trails over 285 acres; longest run, 3.5 mi.; ◆ 36%; ■ 37%; ● 27%.
LIFTS: 9 (2 triples, 7 doubles); capacity, 10,115 per hour.
SUMMIT: 4,436'
VERTICAL: 3,216'
ACTIVITIES: Snowboarding.
FEATURES: Snowmaking 95%; ski school; restaurant; rentals.
▶NORDIC: 100 groomed km; rentals; lessons.
Let the games begin. Two Olympics, in 1932 and 1980, tell the

Courtesy: Michigan Travel Bureau (see p. 113).

story. Athletes of all winter sports disciplines make the pilgrimage to Lake Placid, headquarters of the Winter Olympics Authority. Nowhere else can you fling yourself down not only a bobsled but a Ricochet Rabbit luge run. Nowhere else can you take a glass elevator 26 stories to the top of the 90-meter ski jump—just to watch the Evel Knievels of the ski world. Not to mention gliding at the Olympic Oval skating center, site of the Miracle on Ice and Eric Heiden's unrivaled five-gold-medal-winning exploits. The charming town of Lake Placid gazes at its own perfect reflection in Lake Mirror—frozen endpoint of some hairy toboggan runs best attempted with some Dutch courage.
Then there's the skiing. Whiteface boasts the East's largest vertical, and that translates into some world-class steeps and bumps. Experts should tackle the men's and women's Olympic downhill runs, Cloudspin and Skyward, then check out the drops off Little Whiteface. Advanced skiers will enjoy the challenge of Empire and MacKenzie off the same face. The lake and valley views from the summit here are incomparable. Beginners have their own isolated area (don't be misled by the Cliff's tag), and once they feel their oats, have nearly the entire bottom half of the mountain to roam at will. Intermediates had better resign themselves to cruising the lower runs, or investing in enough lessons to attack the top half with confidence. Although it's plagued with more than the usual amount of ice and wind, Whiteface is a true goliath.

WILLARD MOUNTAIN
(P. 41, C-6, #53) Off Route 40, Greenwich

518-692-7337
TRAILS, 14; LIFTS, 3; VERTICAL, 505'.

WOODS VALLEY SKI AREA
(P. 41, C-5, #54) Route 46, Dopp Hill Road, Westernville
315-827-4721; 315-827-4206 (snow)
TRAILS, 12; LIFTS, 3; VERTICAL, 500'.

NORDIC

ADIRONDACK HUT-TO-HUT SYSTEM
(P. 41, D-6, #55) RD1, Ghent
518-828-7007
FACILITIES: Backcountry skiing; overnight huts; meals.
This guide service offers the only true wilderness experience in New York. Trips range from two to five days; bring your own equipment and sleeping bag. The skiing is not too challenging—mainly flats alternating with hills, frozen lakes, old carriage roads—but you should have command of the basics. The guides can give pointers along the way to help you improve technique.

ADIRONDAK LOJ
(P. 41, B-6, #56) Off Route 73, Lake Placid
518-523-3441
FACILITIES: Backcountry skiing; rentals; lessons; lodging.

ALLEGANY STATE PARK SKI CENTER
(P. 41, E-2, #57) RD 1, Salamanca
716-354-9121
FACILITIES: 21 groomed mi.; rentals; restaurant.

AUSABLE CHASM CROSS-COUNTRY SKI CENTER
(P. 41, A-6, #58) U.S. 9 & Route 373, Ausable Chasm
518-834-9990
FACILITIES: 26 groomed km; rentals; lessons; store.

BARK EATER INN
(P. 41, B-6, #59) Alstead Hill Road, Keene
518-576-2221
FACILITIES: 10 groomed km; rentals; lodging and restaurant; ice skating; sleigh rides.

BEAVERKILL VALLEY INN
(P. 41, E-5, #60) Lew Beach
914-439-4844
FACILITIES: 20 groomed mi.; rentals; lodging and restaurant. The trails are open only to inn guests (rentals free).

BRYNCLIFF RESORT
(P. 41, D-2, #61) Route 20A, Varysburg
716-535-7300
FACILITIES: 20 groomed km; rentals; lessons (weekends only); lodging and restaurant; night skiing (5 km lit).

BURDEN LAKE COUNTRY CLUB
(P. 41, D-6, #62) Totem Lodge Road, RD3, Averill Park
518-674-8917
FACILITIES: 3 groomed mi.; rentals; restaurant.
Mainly open meadows and hills are available on the golf course. It's open Thurs. to Sun. only.

CASCADE SKI TOURING CENTER
(P. 41, B-6, #63) Route 73, 5 mi. S of Lake Placid
518-523-1111
FACILITIES: 20 groomed km; rentals; lessons; lodging and restaurant; night skiing (1 km).
The varied trails also connect with the Mt. Van Hoeverberg system, including the Olympic and Jackrabbit trails.

CUMMING NATURE CENTER
(P. 41, D-3, #64) 6472 Gulick Rd., Naples
716-374-6160
FACILITIES: 12 groomed mi.; rentals; lessons (weekends only); restaurant.
Typically hilly wooded trails are offered here; a display on regional endangered species will intrigue kids.

CONTINUED ON NEXT PAGE

CUNNINGHAM'S SKI BARN
(P. 41, B-6, #65) 1 Main St., North Creek
518-251-3215
FACILITIES: 25 groomed km; rentals; lessons; restaurant.

CUNNINGHAM'S SKI BARN
(P. 41, B-6, #66) Lake Placid Club, Lake Placid
518-523-4460
FACILITIES: 25 groomed km; rentals; lessons; restaurant.

CUNNINGHAM'S SKI BARN
(P. 41, C-6, #67) Saratoga Spa State Park, Saratoga Springs
518-584-3116
FACILITIES: 20 groomed km; rentals; lessons; restaurant.

DEWEY MOUNTAIN
(P. 41, B-6, #68) 30 Main St., Saranac Lake
518-891-2697
FACILITIES: 15 groomed km; rentals; lessons (by appointment); restaurant (across street).

FRIENDS LAKE INN
(P. 41, B-6, #69) Friends Lake Road, Chestertown
518-494-4751
FACILITIES: 20 groomed km; backcountry skiing; rentals; lessons; sleigh rides; ice skating; lodging and restaurant.
A good mix of terrain lies outside this exquisite inn known for its gourmet restaurant.

FROST VALLEY TOURING CENTER
(P. 41, E-5, #70) 2000 Frost Valley Rd., Claryville
914-985-2291
FACILITIES: 20 groomed km; rentals; lessons (weekends only); lodging and restaurant; sleigh rides.

GARNET HILL LODGE
(P. 41, B-6, #71) 13th Lake Road, North River
518-251-2444
FACILITIES: 54 groomed km; rentals; lessons; lodging and restaurants; night skiing (5 km lit).
The lodge is a supreme example of the log lodge built as retreats for the wealthy in the 1930s. The highly rated trail network is a perfect blend of rolling hills, forestland, and open meadows. There is also 50,000 acres of backcountry skiing in the sublime Siamese Ponds Wilderness Area. The high elevation guarantees good snow cover.

HOWE CAVERNS
(P. 41, D-5, #72) Howes Cave
518-296-8990
FACILITIES: 20 groomed km; rentals; restaurant.
These trails are the usual blend of woods and meadows for all abilities. The real attraction is the cave tour (with a 20-minute boat ride on the underground lake).

INSIDE EDGE
(P. 41, C-6, #73) 630 Glen St., Route 9, Queensbury
518-793-5676
FACILITIES: 5 groomed km. (lit at night); rentals; lessons (by appointment).
This top outdoors store also runs the oldest night skiing operation in the USA.

LAPLAND LAKE
(P. 41, C-6, #74) 277 Storer Rd., Northville
518-863-4974
FACILITIES: 45 km (35 km groomed); rentals; lessons; lodging and restaurant; night skiing (3.5 km lit); sleigh rides; ice skating; sledding; child care; sauna.
This exceptional facility is run by former Finnish Olympian Olavi Hirvonen. The groomed, varied terrain includes skating lanes.

MERRITT WINERY GLEN
(P. 41, D-1, #75) 2264 King Rd., Forestville
716-965-4800
FACILITIES: 3 groomed km; tasting room.
The novelty here is not the wooded terrain but the opportunity to taste wines after skiing (or before).

MOHONK MOUNTAIN HOUSE
(P. 41, E-6, #76) Springtown Road, Lake Mohonk, New Paltz
914-255-1000
FACILITIES: 35 groomed km; rentals; lessons; lodging and restaurant; sleigh rides; ice skating.
The peaceful woods offer a rigorous workout for experts; there are gentler trails for novices as well. There is also access to the lovely groomed trails at Minnewaska State Park.

MT. TRAIL
HYER MEADOWS
(P. 41, D-6, #77) Route 23A, Tannersville
518-589-5361
FACILITIES: 35 groomed km; rentals; lessons; restaurant.

MT. VAN HOEVERBERG
(P. 41, B-6, #78) Off Route 73, 7 mi. S of Lake Placid
518-523-2811
FACILITIES: 50 groomed km; rentals; lessons; restaurant.
Site of the Nordic events at the 1980 Olympics, Mt. Van Hoeverberg offers the opportunity to test your abilities on Olympic race courses (all labeled), or tune up on the practice course. The tracks are wide and range in difficulty, though are predominantly intermediate. Bridges cross the roads; and there's even limited snowmaking at this first-class facility.

OAK HILL FARMS
(P. 41, D-5, #79) Oak Hill Road, RD 1, Esperance
518-875-6700
FACILITIES: 15 groomed km; rentals; lessons; restaurant,

OSCEOLA/TUG HILL
(P. 41, C-4, #80) RD3, Camden
315-599-7377
FACILITIES: 25 groomed km; rentals; restaurant.

PINERIDGE CROSS COUNTRY SKI AREA
(P. 41, D-6, #81) RD1, E. Poestenkill, Petersburg
518-283-5509
FACILITIES: 30 groomed km; rentals; lessons; restaurant.

PODUNK SKI TOURING
(P. 41, D-4, #82) 6383 Podunk Rd., Trumansburg
607-387-6716
FACILITIES: 6 groomed mi.; rentals; lessons (weekends only); restaurant.

THE POINT
(P. 41, B-6, #83) Star Route, Saranac Lake
518-891-5674
FACILITIES: 10 groomed km; rentals; lessons; lodging and restaurant.
This elegant resort, formerly part of the Rockefeller estate, candidly admits that the best trails are off-property (the system is open only to guests—rentals free), but there are pleasant wooded hills and the managers often go off with guests to give, well, pointers. There is superb backcountry skiing in adjacent Adirondack Park.

SAGAMORE RESORT
(P. 41, B-6, #84) Sagamore Road, Bolton Landing
518-644-9400
FACILITIES: Open skiing; rentals; lodging and restaurant.

TREE HAVEN TRAILS
(P. 41, C-5, #85) County Route 45, 1227 W. Galway Rd., Hagaman
518-882-9455
FACILITIES: 45 groomed km; rentals; lessons (weekends); restaurant.

VILLAGGIO RESORT
(P. 41, D-6, #86) Route 23A, Haines Falls
518-589-5000
FACILITIES: 10 groomed km; rentals; lodging and restaurant.

WHITE BIRCHES
(P. 41, D-6, #87) Nauvoo Road, off Route 23W, Windham
518-734-3266
FACILITIES: 30 groomed km; rentals; lessons; restaurant.

WHITEFACE INN
(P. 41, B-6, #88) Whiteface Inn Road, Lake Placid
518-523-2551
FACILITIES: 40 groomed km; rentals; lessons; lodging and restaurant; night skiing (3 km lit); sleigh rides; ice skating.
Whiteface Inn offers superb skiing on both its golf course and in the surrounding woods. The rental shop is run by High Cyclery Peaks, with a respected staff of instructors.

WHITEFACE TERRACE CROSS-COUNTRY SKI AREA
(P. 41, A-6, #89) Wilmington
518-946-2576
FACILITIES: 15 groomed km; rentals; lessons (weekends); restaurant.

WILDERNESS LODGE
(P. 41, B-5, #90) End of Starbuck Road, Indian Lake
518-648-5995
FACILITIES: Unlimited backcountry terrain; rentals; lessons; restaurant and lodging.
The lodge accesses pristine terrain in the Siamese Ponds Wilderness area and offers guided inn-to-inn tours Sun. to Thurs.

WILLIAMS LAKE HOTEL
(P. 41, E-6, #91) Binnewater Road, Rosendale
800-382-3818
FACILITIES: 15 groomed km; rentals; lessons; lodging and restaurant; night skiing (2 km lit); ice skating.

WINONA LODGE
(P. 41, B-4, #92) Lacona
315-387-3886
FACILITIES: 40 groomed km; rentals; restaurant and lodging.

WINTER CLOVE INN
(P. 41, D-6, #93) Winter Clove Drive, Round Top
518-622-3267
FACILITIES: 15 groomed km; rentals; lessons; lodging and restaurant; child care; ice skating.

NORTH CAROLINA

The South may be noted for its hospitality, but many of North Carolina's Blue Ridge runs are anything but genteel. No longer do skiers scoff at Southern areas, branding them the "banana belt." North Carolina's high country, tucked in the northwest corner of the state, boasts the densest concentration of ski areas south of the Mason-Dixon line. Add to that historic mountain towns, exceptionally picturesque scenery, unusual granite outcroppings, and formations like Blowing Rock, and you have the makings of a cozy ski vacation.

ALPINE

APPALACHIAN SKI MOUNTAIN
(P. 42, B-3, #1) Ski Mountain Road, off U.S. 321, Blowing Rock
704-295-7828
TRAILS, 8; LIFTS, 6; VERTICAL, 365'.
A serious little mountain, renowned for its fine ski school, the French-Swiss Ski College. Twisty, bumpy Orchard Run and narrow Hard Core provide some challenges, while the friendly ski patrol patrols the Big and Candied Apple trails, offering helpful tips to newcomers. Plans are to open a new intermediate run and to upgrade a double chair to a quad.

BEECH MOUNTAIN SKI RESORT
(P. 42, B-3, #2) Beech Mountain Parkway, Route 184N, Banner Elk
704-387-2011
SEASON: Nov. 15-March 31
ANNUAL SNOWFALL: 85"
TERRAIN: 13 trails over 75 acres; longest run, 1 mi.; ◆ 20%; ■ 30%; ● 50%.
LIFTS: 9 (1 high-speed quad, 6 doubles, 2 surface); capacity, 9,000 per hour.
SUMMIT: 5,505'
VERTICAL: 830'
ACTIVITIES: Snowboarding, NASTAR; night skiing.
FEATURES: Snowmaking 100%; ski school; child care; restaurants; rentals.
One of two class acts in North Carolina, Beech is one of the best beginners' mountains in the South, with an excellent ski school. Novices can even practice true bowl skiing on Powder. It also has a couple of intermediate and advanced runs that can build up decent bumps like Shawneehaw, Tri-South, White Lightning (the steepest), and Southern Star. The highest ski area in the East, Beech offers splendid vistas of the surrounding peaks. Its major drawback is that all trails funnel into a narrow bottleneck at the bottom.

CATALOOCHEE SKI AREA
(P. 42, B-2, #3) Fie Top Road, Route 1, Maggie Valley
704-926-0285
SEASON: Dec. 3-March 12
ANNUAL SNOWFALL: 55"
TERRAIN: 8 trails over 17 acres; longest run, 4,000'; ◆ 25%; ■ 50%; ● 25%.
LIFTS: 3 (1 double, 2 surface); capacity, 3,000 per hour.
SUMMIT: 5,400'
VERTICAL: 740'
ACTIVITIES: Snowboarding; NASTAR; night skiing.
FEATURES: Snowmaking 100%; ski school; restaurant; rentals.
Don't be deceived by Cataloochee's apparently minuscule size. The tree-lined slopes like Omigosh and Snowbird are narrow and have some nice pitch; and there's also open, high country skiing off the ridge in High Meadow, adding another 80 acres when conditions permit. Seniors over 65 and children under 7 ski free.

FAIRFIELD/SAPPHIRE VALLEY
(P. 42, C-2, #4) 4000 Highway 64 West, Sapphire
704-743-3441
TRAILS, 4; LIFTS, 3; VERTICAL, 425'.
The attached resort usually attracts families looking to get away for the weekend and perhaps learn to ski.

HOUND EARS LODGE & CLUB
(P. 42, B-3, #5) Route 3, State Route 105, Blowing Rock
704-963-4321
TRAILS, 2; LIFTS, 2; VERTICAL, 107'.
Really a lodge (consistently earning four-star ratings) that offers a ski slope for its guests' amusement, Hound Ears' flat terrain actually attracts more Nordic and telemark skiers. They didn't offer skiing in 1993-1994, but may reopen for 1995, so call ahead.

SCALY MOUNTAIN
(P. 42, C-2, #6) Off Highway 106, Scaly Mountain
704-526-3737
TRAILS, 3; LIFTS, 2; VERTICAL, 225'.

SKI HAWKSNEST
(P. 42, B-3, #7) 1800 Skyland Dr., Seven Devils
704-963-6561
SEASON: Dec. 3-March 12
ANNUAL SNOWFALL: 65"
TERRAIN: 10 trails over 37 acres; longest run, 2,400'; ◆ 30%; ■ 50%; ● 20%.
LIFTS: 4 (2 doubles, 2 surface); capacity, 3,200 per hour.
SUMMIT: 4819'
VERTICAL: 619'
ACTIVITIES: Snowboarding; night skiing.
FEATURES: Snowmaking; ski school; restaurant; rentals.
A fine beginners' mountain (with limited ticket sales), Hawksnest has been expanding its advanced terrain of late. It's popular for snowboarding (a new park was added for 1994-1995) and one diabolic run, Sock-Em-Dog: a series of sharp pitches and tightly packed moguls (an even steeper if shorter slope will be added in 1995). The Right Stuff is a cruiser with just enough sudden drops; Narrow Gauge is a natural snow glade.

SKI MILL RIDGE
(P. 42, B-3, #8) Route 1, Banner Elk (8 mi. W of Boone)
704-963-4500
TRAILS, 5; LIFTS, 2; VERTICAL, 275'.
This teacup-bowl is basically a family outing kind of area, save for the short but savage Go-For-It run. But given its size, its offers at least one run for everyone. It may close; call ahead.

SUGAR MOUNTAIN RESORT
(P. 42, B-3, #9) Highway 184, Banner Elk
704-898-4521
SEASON: Nov. 15-March 15
ANNUAL SNOWFALL: 78"
TERRAIN: 18 trails over 100 acres; longest run, 1.5 mi.; ◆ 20%; ■ 40%; ● 40%.
LIFTS: 8 (1 triple, 4 doubles, 3 surface); capacity, 8,000 per hour.
SUMMIT: 5,300'
VERTICAL: 1,200'
ACTIVITIES: NASTAR; night skiing.
FEATURES: Snowmaking 100%; ski school; restaurants; rentals.
North Carolina's other class act. Sugar Mountain's 1,200-foot vertical ranks second in the South. It offers a few long, meandering runs like Easy Street, Big Birch, and New Slope for beginners and intermediates looking to stretch themselves and gain confidence. More advanced skiers in the family won't be bored. Try Tom Terrific, reputedly the steepest sustained slope south of New England (beware the ruts created by those who have no business being there), or its tighter, only slightly less vertiginous neighbor, Boulder Dash. A very attractive area, Sugar boasts endless vistas of Grandfather Mountain and three neighboring states; and its beech glades are truly magnificent. Volkl USA ski company, owned by the resort general manager Gunther Jochl, is headquartered at the base. Children under 5 and adults over 70 ski free.

WOLF LAUREL
(P. 42, B-2, #10) Route 3, Mars Hill
704-689-4111
SEASON: Nov. 25-March 15
ANNUAL SNOWFALL: 60"
TERRAIN: 12 trails over 40 acres; longest run, 1 mi.; ◆ 30%; ■ 40%; ● 30%.
LIFTS: 3 (1 quad, 1 double, 1 surface); capacity, 2,200 per hour.
SUMMIT: 4,600'
VERTICAL: 650'
ACTIVITIES: Night skiing.
FEATURES: Snowmaking 100%; ski school; rentals.
Yet another excellent learning mountain, noted for its patient ski school. The toughest runs, like The Howling and Flame Out, fan off the ridgetop. Intermediates can cruise on Eagle, Broadway, and Sideslip. Wolf Laurel sits right off the Appalachian Trail, for those wanting to do a little winter hiking, and near the historic town of Asheville, a literary legend that evokes Wolfe and Fitzgerald.

STATBOX

Tourism: 800-VISIT-NC	**Average annual precipitation:** 44"
Time zone: Eastern	
Population: 6,628,637	**Highest elevation:** 6,684'
Square miles: 52,712	**Lowest elevation:** Sea level

OHIO

Ohio might seem to confirm skiers' suspicions that the world really is flat in the Midwest, with no vertical exceeding 300 feet. But what the ski areas lack in height, they make up for in enthusiasm, offering numerous packages and promotions to tempt folks out onto the slopes. Cross-country is zooming in popularity, and several golf courses groom trails during the winter. Nordic Sports offers an informal snow hotline (216-238-2181) for up-to-date info.

❄ Ohioans are rabid sports fans, attested to by major pro franchises in Cleveland (baseball's Indians, football's Browns, basketball's Cavaliers) and Cincinnati (baseball's Reds and football's Bengals). And don't forget Ohio State, in Columbus, a hallowed institution in college sports. Football is probably number one in local fans' hearts: Ohio is proud home to both the College (just outside Cincinnati) and Pro Football (in Canton) Halls of Fame.

ALPINE

ALPINE VALLEY
(P. 45, A-5, #1) Off Route 322, Chesterland
216-285-2211
TRAILS, 7; LIFTS 6; VERTICAL, 240'.

BOSTON MILLS/BRANDY-WINE SKI RESORTS
(P. 45, B-5, #2) Off Routes 8 & 21, Peninsula
216-467-2242 (snow)
SEASON: Dec. 15-March 15
ANNUAL SNOWFALL: 54"
TERRAIN: 17 trails over 170 acres; longest run, 2,700'; ◆ 40%, ■ 40%, ● 20%.
LIFTS: 16 (4 quads, 5 triples, 2 doubles, 5 surface); capacity, 8,000 per hour.
SUMMIT: NA
VERTICAL: 240'
ACTIVITIES: Snowboarding; snow tubing; night skiing.
FEATURES: Snowmaking 100%; ski school; restaurants; rentals. Wide open runs are featured at both areas, which sit 2.5 miles apart and are linked by continuous complimentary shuttle service. North Bowl, Tiger, Race Hill, Grizzly, Champagne, and Regulator Johnston are the top expert runs, all steep and occasionally bumped up. Snowboarding is only permitted at Brandywine, which boasts a 650-foot long half pipe. Seniors over 70 ski free.

CLEAR FORK SKI AREA
(P. 45, B-4, #3) Resort Drive, Butler
419-883-2000; 800-237-5673 (snow)
SEASON: Dec. 1-March 15
ANNUAL SNOWFALL: 45"
TERRAIN: 9 trails over 60 acres; longest run, 3,960'; ◆ 30%; ■ 40%; ● 30%.
LIFTS: 6 (1 quad, 1 triple, 1 double, 3 surface); capacity, 6,900 per hour.
SUMMIT: 1475'
VERTICAL: 300'
ACTIVITIES: Snowboarding; night skiing.
FEATURES: Snowmaking 90%; ski school; restaurant; rentals.

▶NORDIC: 1.5 groomed km. The beginner area is separate from the rest of the mountain, a big plus in the Midwest. The slopes are wide open and carefully groomed (The Bowl is a particular favorite), save for the aptly-named Mogul Run.

MAD RIVER MOUNTAIN
(P. 45, C-2, #4) Off U.S. 33, Bellefontane
513-599-1015 (snow)
TRAILS, 8; LIFTS, 4; VERTICAL, 300'.
Half pipe.

SNOW TRAILS SKI AREA
(P. 45, C-2, #5) Possum Run Road off Route 13, Exit 169, Mansfield
419-522-7393; 800-332-7669 (snow)
SEASON: Nov. 25-March 15
ANNUAL SNOWFALL: 43"
TERRAIN: 12 trails over 45 acres; longest run, 2,000'; ◆ 20%, ■ 60%, ● 20%.
LIFTS: 6 (4 triples, 2 doubles); capacity, 8,650 per hour.
SUMMIT: 1,475'
VERTICAL: 300'
ACTIVITIES: Snowboarding; night skiing.
FEATURES: Snowmaking 100%; ski school; restaurant; rentals. Ohio's first ski area, Snow Trails prides itself on continually upgrading its facilities. Skiers enjoy improved grooming on cruisers like West Woods and the new Rustler. The expert runs to the left of the mountain, Outer Limits and Silver Bullet, are allowed to develop bumps; and boarders delight in the new half pipe.

NORDIC

BUNKER HILL GOLF & SKI CENTER
(P. 45, B-4, #6) 3060 Pearl Rd., Medina
216-722-4174
FACILITIES: 6 groomed km; rentals; sledding; restaurant.

CHAPIN FOREST
(P. 45, A-4, #7) Routes 6 & 306, Kirtland
216-256-3810; 256-2255 (snow)
FACILITIES: 10 groomed km (with skating lane); rentals; lessons; restaurant.

CROSS-COUNTRY SKI CENTER
(P. 45, D-2, #8) Triangle Park, Kettering
513-263-8400
FACILITIES: 8 groomed km; rentals; lessons; sledding; restaurant.

EDGEWOOD CROSS-COUNTRY
(P. 45, B-4, #9) 6900 Market, N. Canton
216-499-2353
FACILITIES: 4 groomed km; rentals; restaurant.

HIGHLAND PARK CROSS-COUNTRY
(P. 45, A-4, #10) 21400 Chagrin Blvd., Cleveland
216-348-7225
FACILITIES: 10 groomed km; rentals; lessons; restaurant. This golf course hasn't offered skiing in four years, but plans to reopen in 1995.

LAKE COUNTY YMCA
(P. 45, A-4, #11) 4540 River Rd., Perry
216-259-2724
FACILITIES: 7 groomed km; rentals; lessons (weekends); sledding; restaurant.

NORTHWEST OHIO NORDIC SKI CENTER
(P. 45, A-2, #12) 1 Walden Pond, Toledo
419-836-7317
FACILITIES: Unlimited ungroomed acres; rentals; lessons; restaurant. A concession operates this center on the 7,600-yard Ottawa Park Golf Course. Terrain is mostly flat, with a few hilly stretches for intermediate gliders. The park also offers ice skating and sledding.

PUNDERSON STATE PARK
(P. 45, A-4, #13) Routes 87 & 44, Newbury
216-564-2279; 216-564-5246 (rentals)
FACILITIES: 15 groomed km (with skating lane); rentals; lodging and restaurant.

QUAIL HOLLOW RESORT
(P. 45, A-4, #14) 11080 Concord Hambden Rd., Painesville
216-352-6201
FACILITIES: 13 groomed km; rentals; restaurant.

STATBOX

Tourism: 800-BUCKEYE	**Average annual precipitation:** 37"
Time zone: Eastern	
Population: 10,847,115	**Highest elevation:** 1,549'
Square miles: 41,222	**Lowest elevation:** 455'

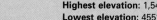

OREGON

Few places in North America can match Oregon for sheer beauty. The topography spirals from a wild tangle of surf and rock to high alpine to semi-arid desert, much of it on dazzling display for skiers from the craggy Cascade peaks. The Mt. Hood National Forest is one of the USA's premier recreational areas. Water thunders through the striking basalt cliffs of the Columbia River Gorge, plummeting 620 feet down the Multnomah Falls before creating a wind tunnel at Hood River, a mecca for windsurfers. Indeed, many hard-core types will ski the Mt. Hood glaciers in the morning, then don their wetsuits that afternoon. The enchanting modern city of Portland is only an hour away, as are the superlative vineyards of the Willamette Valley, making this one of the most varied vacation spots in the USA. ❄ Scenic beauty is also the lure of Oregon's Nordic centers; the more adventurous can glide amid the serene majesty of Crater Lake National Park, skirting the rim of that extinct volcano as mist shrouds the lake and its many jagged islands. ❄ Downhill thrills galore are on tap with Mt. Bailey Snowcats (503-793-3311). You can cram in 10 to 20 runs a day on the 8,400-foot peak, enjoying a vertical of up to 3,000 feet; and, tilting at 45-degree angles, there are 1,000-foot couloirs for the truly intrepid.

ALPINE

ANTHONY LAKES MOUNTAIN RESORT

(P. 47, B-5, #1) 61995 Quail Rd., Island City
503-963-4599
SEASON: Nov. 25-April 10
ANNUAL SNOWFALL: 200"
TERRAIN: 23 trails over 360 acres; longest run, 1 mi.; ◆33%; ■ 34%; ● 33%.
LIFTS: 2 (1 double, 1 surface); capacity, 1,500 per hour.
SUMMIT: 8,000'
VERTICAL: 900'
ACTIVITIES: Snowboarding.
FEATURES: Ski school; restaurant; rentals.
▶NORDIC: 13 groomed km; rentals; lessons.
 Anthony Lakes is developing a reputation for its tree skiing, with lots of steep glades for experts and stronger intermediates. Mogul mashers will find plenty of beauties like Rock Garden.

COOPER SPUR SKI AREA

(P. 47, A-3, #2) 11000 Cloud Cap Rd., Mt. Hood
503-352-7803
SEASON: Dec. 20-March 31
ANNUAL SNOWFALL: 120"
TERRAIN: 10 trails over 90 acres; longest run, 1,500'; ◆ 10%; ■ 40%; ● 50%.
LIFTS: 2 (2 surface); capacity, 1,000 per hour.
SUMMIT: 5,000'
VERTICAL: 500'
ACTIVITIES: Snowboarding; night skiing.
FEATURES: Ski school; restaurant; rentals.
▶NORDIC: 10 groomed km; rentals; lessons.
 Families constitute the bulk of Cooper Spur's clientele; they appreciate its small, human scale and friendly service. A great place to learn, Cooper Spur differs from the other Mt. Hood areas in that its wide-groomed slopes face northeast (meaning drier snow) and it sits completely below tree line. Boarders have a half pipe. The area is now offering snowcat skiing up to the Cloud Cap/Tilly Jane National Historic District, where a 2,500-foot vertical drop awaits true powder hounds.

HOODOO SKI BOWL

(P. 47, B-3, #3) Highway 20, Sisters
503-822-3799; 800-949-5438 (snow)
SEASON: Nov. 15-April 15
ANNUAL SNOWFALL: 180"
TERRAIN: 22 trails over 600 acres; longest run, 1 mi.; ◆ 30%; ■ 40%; ● 30%.
LIFTS: 4 (1 triple, 2 doubles, 1 surface); capacity, 4,100 per hour.
SUMMIT: 5,703'
VERTICAL: 1,035'
ACTIVITIES: Snowboarding; night skiing.
FEATURES: Ski school; restaurants; rentals.
▶NORDIC: 15.5 groomed km; rentals; lessons.
 All Hoodoo's runs funnel down to the base lodge, enabling parents to let their kids roam at will, knowing they won't get lost. The runs tend toward the steep, like the usually bumpy Grandstand. There are also secret powder stashes off the backside. Hoodoo also offers good, solid intermediate cruising, especially in the Red Valley. You can check out conditions for free between 9 A.M. and 10 A.M. The Nordic trails are typically scenic; you can also access more difficult terrain in the adjacent National Forest. The area has embarked on a 10-year master plan and will see major expansion through the 1990s.

MT. ASHLAND SKI AREA

(P. 47, D-2, #4) I-5, Exit 6, 7 mi. S of Ashland
503-482-2897; 503-482-2754 (snow)
SEASON: Nov. 25-April 15
ANNUAL SNOWFALL: 325"
TERRAIN: 23 trails over 110 acres; longest run, 1 mi.; ◆ 50%; ■ 35%; ● 15%.
LIFTS: 4 (2 triples, 2 doubles); capacity, 5,350 per hour.
SUMMIT: 7,500'
VERTICAL: 1,150'
ACTIVITIES: Snowboarding; night skiing.
FEATURES: Ski school; restaurant; rentals.
 The town of Ashland is nationally renowned for the Tony Award-winning Oregon Shakespeare Festival (its winter season starts in February). Befitting a community with an arty reputation, Ashland offers superb eateries, chic boutiques, top galleries, and a hip yet mellow ambiance. The mountain includes a glaciated bowl rimmed with a series of menacing steeps and chutes, but intermediates can enjoy top-to-bottom runs like the Tempest, Dream, and Romeo (many names are inspired by The Bard of Avon). Boarders have a half pipe.

MT. BACHELOR SKI RESORT

(P. 47, C-3, #5) Cascade Lakes Highway, 22 mi. S of Bend
503-382-2607
SEASON: Nov. 1-June 30
ANNUAL SNOWFALL: 325"
TERRAIN: 54 trails and bowls over 3,228 acres; longest run, 2 mi.; ◆◆ 25%; ◆ 25%; ■ 35%; ● 15%.
LIFTS: 12 (5 high-speed quads, 1 high-speed triple, 3 triples, 1 double, 2 surface); capacity, 19,720 per hour.
SUMMIT: 9,065'
VERTICAL: 3,100'
ACTIVITIES: Snowboarding; NASTAR.
FEATURES: Ski school; restaurant; child care; rentals.
▶NORDIC: 56 groomed km (with skating lane); rentals; lessons.
 Mt. Bachelor is king of Northwest skiing; a 10-year $100 million improvement and expansion plan is consolidating its position at the top of the high-tech heap. The Flextime lift ticket system allows skiers to pay only for what they ski. Six new high-speed lifts whisk skiers up to the summit, where they can happily disperse over the expansive terrain. Despite its mammoth size, it's a warm, friendly place where families feel right at home, with "Slow Family Skiing" signs posted over much of the area.
 Bachelor is intermediate heaven: Lots of wide, seemingly endless cruisers, gently scooped out bowls, and some of the lightest powder the Cascades have to offer. Lower intermediates should head for the Skyliner superchair. You'll discover more challenge, including bump practice, off the Pine Marten Express. Don't be misled by the 50% black terrain; strong intermediates can handle most of the barren above-tree line runs. These bowls are accorded diamond status more for their ungroomed surface than anything else. Real experts can find distraction on the Pinnacles (accessed via a short hike), the tight glades in the Outback area (especially between Boomerang and the pogo stick bumps of Down Under), and the lone Cinder Cone jutting up between the Red and Outback chairs. Beginners can play around the Orange and Yellow chairs, then graduate to the Sunrise Express runs. The top-tier ski school utilizes the innovative perfect turn method

STATBOX

Tourism: 800-547-7842
Time zone: Pacific
Population: 2,812,321
Square miles: 96,981

Average annual precipitation: 37"
Highest elevation: 11,237'
Lowest elevation: Sea level

of instruction. You can also work on your form at racing camps in both the winter and summer (when you ski mornings and raft, golf, or play tennis afternoons). The dozen Nordic loops range from the beginners' 1-km First Time Around to the hilly, 12-km Oli's Alley. All trails enjoy dramatic views of the wild, woolly, Cascades and Deschutes National Forest, with unusual formations like the Three Sisters and Broken Top. For a change of pace, try mushing at the Oregon Iditarod Training Camp, based at the mountain. Then head into lively Bend for everything from espresso bars to factory outlets.

MT. HOOD MEADOWS SKI RESORT

(P. 47, A-3, #6) Highway 35, Mt. Hood
503-337-2222
SEASON: Nov. 15-May 15
ANNUAL SNOWFALL: 360″
TERRAIN: 70 trails over 2,150 acres; longest run, 3 mi.; ◆ 35%; ■ 50%; ● 15%.
LIFTS: 11 (2 high-speed quads, 1 quad, 6 doubles, 2 surface); capacity, 14,400 per hour.
SUMMIT: 7,300′
VERTICAL: 2,777′
ACTIVITIES: Snowboarding; NASTAR; night skiing.
FEATURES: Ski school; restaurants; rentals.
▶NORDIC: 15 groomed km; rentals; lessons.
The pastoral name is deceiving: Mt. Hood Meadows implies a kinder, gentler ski area, when it really features tough, tough terrain. The runs cascade down the eastern flank of Mt. Hood, offering something for all abilities. Beginners have a segregated section to the left, served by three lifts. Intermediates frolic along wide lengthy cruisers like North Canyon or the wide-open, above-tree-line Texas area off the Cascade Express. Most skiers make the pilgrimage to the Meadows' signature run: the three-mile long, powdery Heather Canyon, which thunders down the mountain, attaining a 40-degree pitch in places. Shredders have a half pipe and plenty of chutes and ravines to test their skills. In addition to the Nordic center, the area accesses nearly 200 km of trails in the breathtaking Mt. Hood National Forest. The Meadows has been expanding and improving of late, replacing two chairs with high-speed quads (including the only one serving night skiing in the Pacific Northwest) and opening more intermediate terrain. One exciting development is a new snowcat skiing operation that will climb 700 feet up the mountain, adding five runs and 1,000 more vertical feet.

MT. HOOD SKI BOWL

(P. 47, B-3, #7) Highway 26, Ski Bowl

503-272-3206
SEASON: Nov. 15-April 15
ANNUAL SNOWFALL: 300″
TERRAIN: 61 trails over 910 acres; longest run, 3.5 mi.; ◆ 40%; ■ 40%; ● 20%.
LIFTS: 9 (4 doubles, 5 surface); capacity, 4,600 per hour.
SUMMIT: 5,056′
VERTICAL: 1,456′
ACTIVITIES: Snowboarding; night skiing.
FEATURES: Snowmaking 25%; ski school; restaurants; rentals.
The Ski Bowl is the USA's largest night ski area, with 33 lighted runs accessing 210 acres of terrain. As the name suggests, most of the runs are wide open. Although beginners can take the 3.5-mile Skyline trail from the top and have a sizable section off the Red Chair, most of the terrain is suited to stronger skiers, especially the recently added Outback section (a fave with boarders, who also have a half pipe). Starting at the Upper Bowl, skiers can drop the 1,500-foot vertical uninterrupted. The Multipor chair accesses a tremendous variety of terrain for all levels.

SPOUT SPRINGS

(P. 47, A-5, #8) Route 1, Weston
503-566-2164
TRAILS, 11; LIFTS, 4; VERTICAL, 550′.
▶NORDIC: 21 groomed km.

SUMMIT SKI AREA

(P. 47, B-3, #9) U.S. 26, Government Camp
503-272-0256
Trails, 3; Lifts, 2; Vertical, 400′.
▶NORDIC:14 groomed km.
A pleasant novice day area, Summit is slowly expanding its Nordic facilities, with 50 km of trails to be added over the next few years. Co-owner and Olympic silver medalist Bill Koch (an originator of the skating technique) designed the system, which is wooded and predominantly intermediate.

TIMBERLINE LODGE SKI AREA

(P. 47, B-3, #10) Off Highway 26, Timberline Lodge
503-272-3311
SEASON: Nov. 15-Sept. 1
ANNUAL SNOWFALL: 300″
TERRAIN: 31 trails over 1,000 acres; longest run, 1 mi.; ◆ 10%; ■ 60%; ● 30%.
LIFTS: 7 (1 quad, 1 triple, 5 doubles); capacity, 8,000 per hour.
SUMMIT: 8,500′
VERTICAL: 2,000′ (1,500′ in summer)
ACTIVITIES: Snowboarding; telemarking; mountaineering.
FEATURES: Ski school; restaurants; rentals.
Timberline's 1930s lodge is a National Historic Landmark, a veritable shrine to Americana from the WPA era. You'll find glorious handcrafted furniture and wainscoting, including intricate wrought iron chairs upholstered in rawhide, crocheted rugs, and hand-hewn wood beams. The ski area is open all summer, offering a variety of renowned camps for ski racers and snowboarders, creating a wonderfully cosmopolitan mix on the mountain. (It's a great opportunity to meet tomorrow's ski stars from around the world.) This section of the area, the Palmer Snowfield, is only open in summer due to severe avalanche danger the rest of the year. For wintry types, the skiing is solidly intermediate and the ideal family experience (Magic Mile is the classic cruiser), although advanced skiers will find deserted glades galore. Boarders have not only the Bone Zone terrain park, but will discover natural half pipes all over the mountain.

WARNER CANYON

(P. 47, D-4, #11) Lakeview
503-947-5001 or 6040
Other information NA

WILLAMETTE PASS

(P. 47, C-3, #12) Willamette Pass, Cascade Summit

503-484-5030; 503-345-SNOW (snow)
SEASON: Nov. 15-April 15
ANNUAL SNOWFALL: 250″
TERRAIN: 29 trails over 210 acres; longest run, 2.1 mi.; ◆ 35%; ■ 45%; ● 20%.
LIFTS: 5 (4 triples, 1 double; capacity, 8,400 per hour.
SUMMIT: 6,683′
VERTICAL: 1,563′
ACTIVITIES: Snowboarding; speed skiing; night skiing.
FEATURES: Snowmaking 30%; ski school; restaurant; child care; rentals.
Willamette Pass is best known as the U.S. Speed Skiing training center, and neophytes can try out the track during special events. The runs offer both intermediate boulevards and more treacherous steeps for those who like getting their hearts pumping and knees knocking. Seven runs plunge 35 degrees or more, including RTS (which doubles as the speed-skiing track). A new triple chair beefed up the vertical and affords a 360-degree view from Eagle Peak. Boarders have a half pipe and terrain park. You can ski by the hour, or join The Vertical Club, which provides bargain rates (ski free after your 18th day).

NORDIC

BLACK BUTTE RANCH

(P. 47, B-3, #13) Black Butte Ranch
503-595-1282
FACILITIES: 35 groomed km; rentals; sledding; lodging and restaurant.

BLUE LAKE NORDIC CENTER

(P. 47, B-3, #14) 13900 Blue Lake Dr., Sisters
503-595-6671
FACILITIES: 27 groomed km; rentals; lessons; ice skating; sledding; lodging and restaurant.

DIAMOND LAKE RESORT

(P. 47, C-3, #15) Diamond Lake Ranch
503-793-3333
FACILITIES: 10 groomed km, 80 ungroomed; rentals; lessons; snowmobiling; sliding hill; lodging and restaurant.

ODELL LAKE LODGE

(P. 47, C-3, #16) Crescent Lake
503-433-2540
FACILITIES: 8 groomed km; rentals; lessons; lodging and restaurant.

Courtesy: Keystone Resort (see Colorado, p. 98).

OR

PENNSYLVANIA

There are two major ski regions in Pennsylvania—the Poconos in the northeast and Laurel Highlands at the opposite end of the state. With a few notable exceptions, the Poconos areas are beginners' hills, most of them attached to full-service, fulfill-your-every-heart's-desire resorts (the "Honeymoon Capital of America" is famed for heart-shaped tubs and champagne-glass jacuzzis). There are also several private ski clubs in eastern Pennsylvania, like Wissahickon, Saw Creek, and Poconos Ranch whose ski areas operate on a private basis, open only to home-owners and their guests. Those in the southwest, part of the Allegheny range, offer generally better snow and more challenging terrain. ❄ Both major cities, Pittsburgh and Philadelphia, proudly follow their major pro franchises. Take in a Penguins or Flyers hockey game; gridiron action with the Steelers and Eagles; hoops hoopla with the 76ers; or diamond doings courtesy of the Phillies and Pirates. ❄ Philly's Independence National Historic Park offers the "most historic square mile in America." Other must-sees include the Victorian mansions of quaint Jim Thorpe, near the Poconos; the Dutch Country where old-fashioned Amish customs live on; and Pittsburgh's gleaming downtown.

ALPINE

ALPINE MOUNTAIN SKI AREA
(P. 48, C-6, #1) Route 447, Analomink
717-595-2150
SEASON: Dec. 9-April 9
ANNUAL SNOWFALL: 55"
TERRAIN: 18 trails over 60 acres; longest run, 2,640';◆ 25%, ▪ 50%, ● 25%.
LIFTS: 3 (2 quads, 1 double); capacity, 5,800 per hour.
SUMMIT: 1,150'
VERTICAL: 500'
ACTIVITIES: Snowboarding; snowmobiling.
FEATURES: Snowmaking 100%; ski school; restaurants; child care; rentals.
 A popular family area, Alpine is virtually 100% cruisers (including the longer expert slopes, although Power Line sometimes develops moguls). Rockaway and Outer Edge are the favorite ego runs. For beginners, Alpine Way is a wide avenue straight from the summit (otherwise they have only a small learning area).

BIG BOULDER SKI AREA
(P. 48, C-5, #2) Route 903, Lake Harmony
717-722-0100
SEASON: Dec. 1-March 30
ANNUAL SNOWFALL: 60"
TERRAIN: 14 trails over 65 acres; longest run, 2,900'; ◆ 20%, ▪ 40%, ● 40%.
LIFTS: 7 (2 triples, 5 doubles); capacity, 9,200 per hour.
SUMMIT: 2,175'
VERTICAL: 475'
ACTIVITIES: Snowboarding; night skiing.
FEATURES: Snowmaking 100%; ski school; restaurants; child care; rentals.
▶ NORDIC: 5 groomed km; rentals; lessons.
 Big Boulder is a prime example of what makes skiing the Poconos so popular. The snowmaking and grooming are impeccable. The ski school is first rate. Granted, despite the addition of more advanced terrain and a 400-foot half pipe, it's hardly a fearsome mountain. But that's the point: Everyone from families to honeymooners feels at home—and no one feels ashamed being a first-timer or novice. And if you get bored, Big Boulder and Jack Frost have a reciprocal lift ticket policy.

BLUE KNOB RECREATION
(P. 48, D-3, #3) Top of Mountain, Claysburg
814-239-5111; 800-458-3403 (snow)
SEASON: Dec. 1-March 31
ANNUAL SNOWFALL: 100"
TERRAIN: 21 trails over 80 acres; longest run, 9,200'; ◆ 37%, ▪ 34%, ● 29%.
LIFTS: 7 (2 triples, 2 doubles, 3 surface); capacity, 5,200 per hour.
SUMMIT: 3,152'
VERTICAL: 1,072'
ACTIVITIES: Snowboarding; NASTAR; night skiing.
FEATURES: Snowmaking 90%; ski school; restaurants; child care; rentals.
 The lodge and easier terrain are up top at Blue Knob, which boasts Pennsylvania's highest vertical. Mambo Alley is an advanced beginner's dream, with nearly two miles of cruising, while Expressway and Bunny Hop satisfy intermediates. Most stronger skiers will find the lower half—or right side as you look down—to their liking (Extrovert is one of the steepest slopes in the mid-Atlantic.) Snowboarders have a half pipe.

BLUE MARSH SKI AREA
(P. 48, C-5, #4) Route 183, Bernville
215-488-6399
TRAILS, 1; LIFTS, 5; VERTICAL, 300'.
Half pipe, snowboard terrain park.

BLUE MOUNTAIN
(P. 48, C-5, #5) 5 mi. E of Palmerton
215-826-7700
SEASON: Dec. 10-March 31
ANNUAL SNOWFALL: 42"
TERRAIN: 20 trails over 220 acres; longest run, 6,600'; ◆ 30%, ▪% 40%, ● 30%.
LIFTS: 7 (1 high-speed quad, 4 doubles, 2 surface); capacity, 7,600 per hour.
SUMMIT: 1,665'
VERTICAL: 1,075'
ACTIVITIES: Snowboarding; night skiing.
FEATURES: Snowmaking 100%; ski school; restaurants; child care; rentals.
 Blue Mountain has expanded its terrain, adding four slopes (including Paradise, a delightful cruiser), installing a high-speed quad, and lengthening the intermediate Sidewinder and advanced Challenge trails.

BOYCE PARK SKI AREA
(P. 48, D-2, #6) 675 Old Frankstown Rd., Boyce Park, Pittsburgh
412-733-4656; 412-733-4665 (snow)
TRAILS, 9; LIFTS, 4; VERTICAL, 172'.
Half pipe.

BLUE MARSH SKI AREA
CAMELBACK SKI AREA
(P. 48, C-6, #7) Off I-80 (Exit 45), Tannersville
717-629-1661
SEASON: Nov. 25-April 8
ANNUAL SNOWFALL: 40"
TERRAIN: 30 trails over 142 acres; longest run, 1 mi.; ◆ 40%, ▪ 40%, ● 20%.
LIFTS: 12 (2 quads, 2 triples, 8 doubles); capacity, 17,300 per hour.
SUMMIT: 2,050'
VERTICAL: 800'
ACTIVITIES: Snowboarding; night skiing.
FEATURES: Snowmaking 100%; ski school; restaurants; child care; rentals.
 Another Poconos ski factory, with the most extensive and varied terrain in the area, Camelback has taught thousands to ski, but also offers more challenging terrain on the upper third of the mountain—like the Rocket. A quad and three new trails were added for 1995.

CRYSTAL LAKE SKI CENTER
(P. 48, C-4, #8) Off Route 220 N, Hughesville
717-584-2698; 717-584-4209 (snow)
TRAILS, 5; LIFTS, 3; VERTICAL, 250'.
▶ NORDIC: 40 groomed km

DOE MOUNTAIN SKI AREA
(P. 48, D-6, #9) RD 1, Macungie
215-682-7108
SEASON: Dec. 15-March 31
ANNUAL SNOWFALL: 40"
TERRAIN: 12 trails over 90 acres; longest run, 4,700'; ◆ 30%, ▪ 40%, ● 30%.
LIFTS: 7 (1 triple, 3 doubles, 3 surface); capacity, 6,500 per hour.
SUMMIT: 1,100'
VERTICAL: 500'
ACTIVITIES: Snowboarding;

NASTAR; night skiing.
FEATURES: Snowmaking 100%; ski school; restaurant; child care; rentals.
Doe Mountain's major distinction used to be as the closest area to Philadelphia, but it recently added an advanced slope and half pipe to help change its image.

EAGLE ROCK SKI CENTER
(P. 48, C-5, #10) Hazleton
717-384-3223; 800-525-1210 (snow)
SEASON: Dec. 7-March 15
ANNUAL SNOWFALL: 40"
TERRAIN: 12 trails over 43 acres; longest run, 1 mi.; ◆ 30%; ■ 10%; ● 60%.
LIFTS: 4 (3 doubles, 1 surface); capacity, 3,900 per hour.
SUMMIT: 1,825'
VERTICAL: 550'
ACTIVITIES: Snowboarding; night skiing.
FEATURES: Snowmaking 100%; ski school; restaurant; rentals.
Eagle Rock is oddly configured, with a large beginners section, some steeper terrain (rated black but not terribly challenging), and not much in between, making it best for first-timers, novices, and stronger intermediates. Currently in Chapter 11, it may not reopen; call ahead.

EDINBORO SKI AREA
(P. 48, B-1, #11) Edinboro
814-734-1641
TRAILS, 11; LIFTS, 4; Vertical, 350'.

ELK MOUNTAIN SKI CENTER
(P. 48, B-9, #12) Route 374 E, Union Dale
717-679-2611; 800-233-4131 (snow)
SEASON: Dec. 5-Mar. 31
ANNUAL SNOWFALL: 45"
TERRAIN: 23 trails over 235 acres; longest run, 1.75 mi.; ◆ 40%; ■ 30%; ● 30%.
LIFTS: 6 (1 quad, 5 doubles); capacity, 7,800 per hour.
SUMMIT: 2,693'
VERTICAL: 1000'
ACTIVITIES: Snowboarding; night skiing.
FEATURES: Snowmaking 98%; ski school; restaurants; child care; rentals.
By Pennsylvania standards, Elk Mountain is a challenge, with a series of steeps and bumps up top on runs like Upper Tonkhannock and Seneca. Lackawanna is good practice for mogul-meister wannabes. The Delaware and the recently added Wissahickon are the great groomed cruisers. Even the bottom half of the mountain has some tricky sections for novices.

FERNWOOD SKI AREA
(P.48, C-6, #13) Route 209,

Bushkill
717-588-9500
TRAILS, 2; LIFTS, 1; VERTICAL, 250'.

HIDDEN VALLEY SKI AREA
(P. 48, D-2, #14) 4 Craighead Dr., Hidden Valley
814-443-2600
SEASON: Dec. 1-March 31
ANNUAL SNOWFALL: 150"
TERRAIN: 17 trails over 85 acres; longest run, 1 mi.; ◆ 30%; ■ 35%; ● 35%.
LIFTS: 8 (1 quad, 2 triples, 3 doubles, 2 tows); capacity, 12,000 per hour.
SUMMIT: 3,000'
VERTICAL: 610'
ACTIVITIES: Snowboarding; NASTAR; sleigh rides; night skiing.
FEATURES: Snowmaking 98%; ski school; restaurants; rentals.
►NORDIC: 50 groomed km, 30 ungroomed; rentals; lessons.
One of the top places to learn in Pennsylvania, Hidden Valley is renowned for its grooming and ski school. Thunderbird and Chabe are fairly exciting bump runs; Rambler is a gentle cruiser typical of most of the terrain. Under 6 and over 69 ski free.

JACK FROST MOUNTAIN
(P. 48, C-5, #15) Off I-80, Blakeslee
717-443-8425
SEASON: Dec. 3-March 31
ANNUAL SNOWFALL: 50"
TERRAIN: 21 trails over 75 acres; longest run, 3,200'; ◆ 40%; ■ 40%; ● 20%.
LIFTS: 7 (1 quad, 2 triples, 4 doubles); capacity, 8,800 per hour.
SUMMIT: 2,000'
VERTICAL: 600'
ACTIVITIES: Snowboarding; snowmobiling.
FEATURES: Snowmaking 100%; ski school; restaurants; rentals.
►NORDIC: 15 groomed km; rentals; lessons.
Another perennial Poconos favorite for its smooth operation and slopes, Jack Frost differs from its neighbors in that it offers slightly more challenging terrain on its east side; advanced skiers enjoy the bumpy ride on Thunderbolt and the dive down Rivershot. Jack Frost recently replaced a double with a quad to increase uphill capacity; more expansion may be in the works through 1996. It offers a reciprocal lift ticket with Big Boulder (they're marketed together as "The Big Two"). Over 69 and under 6 ski free.

MONTAGE SKI AREA
(P. 48, B-5, #16) 1000 Montage Mountain Rd., Scranton
717-969-7669; 800-GOT-

SNOW (snow)
SEASON: Nov. 10-April 1
ANNUAL SNOWFALL: 45"
TERRAIN: 21 trails over 150 acres; longest run, 6,300'; ◆ 33%; ■ 45%; ● 22%.
LIFTS: 5 (1 quad, 3 triples, 1 double); capacity, 8,300 per hour.
SUMMIT: 2,000'
VERTICAL: 1,000'
ACTIVITIES: Snowboarding; NASTAR; night skiing.
FEATURES: Snowmaking 100%; ski school; restaurant; rentals.
Montage has three faces, creating the impression that the area is larger than it is. The North Face contains the most advanced skiing. Cannonball has several different pitches and constantly shifting terrain through spruce stands. Smoke and Boomer are the double diamond bump runs, with another one being added for 1995. Montage's relatively empty, wide-open slopes, respectable vertical, and sizable acreage (by Pennsylvania standards) add up to hours of ego-massage for intermediates. The area has an advantage over most of its neighbors in its slope design. Very few trails intersect, allowing skiers of varying ability to stay with their own kind. Montage is not as well-known as the other major Poconos areas—maybe because it's not as meticulously manicured and attracts fewer novices—but skiers who've discovered it aren't complaining. Boarders have both a half pipe and park.

MT. AIRY LODGE
(P. 48, C-6, #17) Mt. Pocono
717-839-8811
TRAILS, 7; LIFTS, 2; VERTICAL, 280'.
►NORDIC: 5 groomed km.

MT. PLEASANT SKI AREA
(P. 48, B-1, #18) Off Route 86, Cambridge Springs
814-734-1641
TRAILS, 11; LIFTS, 3; VERTICAL, 350'.

MT. TONE SKI RESORT
(P. 48, B-6, #19) Wallerville Road, off Route 247, Lake Como
717-798-2707
TRAILS, 11; LIFTS, 5; VERTICAL, 450'.
►NORDIC: 11 groomed km.

SEVEN SPRINGS MOUNTAIN RESORT
(P. 48, D-2, #20) RD 1, Champion
814-352-7777; 800-523-7777 (snow)
SEASON: Dec. 1-April 1
ANNUAL SNOWFALL: 90"
TERRAIN: 31 trails over 540 acres; longest run, 1.25 mi.; ◆ 15%; ■ 45%; ● 40%.

LIFTS: 18 (2 quads, 7 triples, 2 doubles, 7 surface); capacity, 24,600 per hour.
SUMMIT: 2,990'
VERTICAL: 750'
ACTIVITIES: Snowboarding; NASTAR; sleigh rides; night skiing.
FEATURES: Snowmaking 95%; ski school; restaurants; child care; rentals.
Thanks to the foward-looking Dupres, owners since its inception in the 1930s, Seven Springs has worked hard to craft the total resort experience and is one of the pre-eminent family areas in the East. What lures so many families (it now records a half million skier visits annually) to this rather modest hill? The resort's strong suit is actually its wealth of indoor activities. Bad weather keep you indoors? Millions were lavished on the entertainment center in the base lodge, which is more suburban mall than ski chalet. Trade in your lift ticket for an activity pass to the bowling alley, indoor mini golf, racquetball courts, health club, and roller-rink. Without once stepping foot outside, the adjoining complex offers a mega-hotel, 12 restaurants, six bars, a shopping arcade, and game rooms. It's all housed in buildings made of chiseled flagstone and heavy timber.
Just as much care was lavished on the skiing. Though the two faces barely qualify as mountains, intermediates will have a field day on runs like Lost Boy. Beginners can romp at will over the Sun Bowl, than graduate to Fawn Lane and Wagner from the top. And even advanced skiers will get Goosebumps on a short but unrelenting mogul run of the same name. Gunner offers a steep drop. The ski school is top-notch, not surprisingly. And boarders love shuttling between the half pipe and video arcade. Besides, where else will you find ski-in, ski-out mini golf?

SHAWNEE MOUNTAIN
(P. 48, C-6, #21) Hollow Road, Shawnee-on-Delaware
717-421-7231; 800-233-4218 (snow)
SEASON: Nov. 25-March 30
ANNUAL SNOWFALL: 60"
TERRAIN: 23 trails over 115 acres; longest run, 1 mi.; ◆ 25%; ■ 50%; ● 25%.
LIFTS: 9 (1 triple, 8 doubles); capacity, 11,400 per hour.
SUMMIT: 1,350'
VERTICAL: 700'
ACTIVITIES: Snowboarding; night skiing.
FEATURES: Snowmaking 100%; ski school; restaurants; rentals.
Shawnee is geared to first-timers (who have their own area), novices, and intermediates. The runs, many sporting Native American names like Pocohontas, Little Brave, and Chief Thundercloud, are predominantly broad, groomed slopes with

little variety in pitch. Snowboarders prefer the half pipe. Those who don't ski can tour the Delaware Water Gap, explore the charming turn-of-the-century village, take in a jazz concert, or simply enjoy the après ski experience at the area's many resort hotels.

SKI DENTON

(P. 48, B-3, #22) U.S. 6, Coudersport
814-435-2115
SEASON: Dec. 1-March 31
ANNUAL SNOWFALL: 100"
TERRAIN: 20 trails over NA acres; longest run, 1 mi.; ◆ 33%; ■ 33%; ● 34%.
LIFTS: 4 (1 triple, 1 double, 2 surface); capacity, 3,850 per hour.
SUMMIT: 2,885'
VERTICAL: 650'
ACTIVITIES: Snowboarding; night skiing.
FEATURES: Snowmaking 95%; ski school; restaurant; rentals.
▶NORDIC: Unlimited ungroomed km; rentals.
Denton recently added two new advanced slopes, Extreme and The Wall, to complement the roller-coaster-steep Avalanche (with a 66-degree incline). Occasional bronco buster bumps lurk on The Link. But Denton still caters to novices and low intermediates who cruise happily on the mountain's wide gentle slopes. Standouts include two secluded green trails more than a mile long and Katy-O. Shredders have natural half pipe and snowboard park. Denton is situated in a state park that offers miles of backcountry trails for gliders.

SKI LIBERTY

(P. 48, E-4, #23) Route 116 & Sanders Road, Fairfield
717-642-8282; 800-829-4766 (snow)
SEASON: Nov. 25-March 15
ANNUAL SNOWFALL: 24"
TERRAIN: 14 trails over 94 acres; longest run, 1 mi.; ◆ 30%; ■ 40%; ● 30%.
LIFTS: 8 (3 quads, 3 doubles, 2 surface); capacity, 11,000 per hour.
SUMMIT: 1,186'
VERTICAL: 600'
ACTIVITIES: Snowboarding; night skiing.
FEATURES: Snowmaking 100%; ski school; restaurants; rentals.
Viewed from the base lodge, the mountain appears to be one long bunny hill—and beginners love Alpine Run, which slithers straight down its flank. But much steeper terrain (by mid-Atlantic standards) drops off the back side, including Ultra, Eastwind (the signature bump run), and the recently added Strata—all of which feature sharp double-diamond pitches at the top before turning into single black diamond runs. White Lightning, a beauty, is a seldom-skied steep on

WHITE SALES

When planning your ski vacation, contact the ski areas you plan to visit directly for information on savings. Many offer discounts for weekly lift tickets, or stay-and-ski packages. Beginners may be eligible for free lessons or equipment rentals. Children ski free, or at least receive a discount, at many areas when an adult purchases a ticket; seniors usually also realize savings. (We have noted this ski free policy whenever space allows in venue notes). Often, satellite communities provide free or discounted lift tickets with lodging packages. Indeed, the further from the area, generally the cheaper the accommodations. USAir, American, Continental, United, Delta, and Southwest all offer fly/stay package deals for the resort towns they service. And remember that ski resorts have high and low seasons, with concomitant price levels. Christmas break is always the most expensive time to travel, followed by February. You can find great bargains—and snow—in January and late March.

It's also a good idea to find out about activities and events planned during your stay. Many areas host winter festivals and World Cup, pro or celebrity charity races. Not only are these entertaining in themselves, but there are often side attractions, like equipment companies demoing their latest lines or offering sales.

Ski shows are another good source of information on ski travel. These are held in most major markets and advertised through local media. Check also the "Coming Events" columns in specialty publications like *Snow Country*, *Ski*, *Skiing*, *Ski Impact*, *Ski Canada* and *Powder*. Most of the main destination resorts, as well as product manufacturers are represented. It's a great way to get a feel for an area from the people who live and work there.

If you ski regularly, consider joining a ski club. Very often members receive discounts and travel deals. Consult your local yellow pages or ski shop for the club nearest you or best suited to your needs. You can also send a SASE to the National Ski Club Newsletter, P.O. Box 17385, Denver, CO 80217.

the front side. Heavenly and Blue Streak are great groomed cruisers. A new quad services Pennsylvania's largest beginner area. The area limits the number of lift ticket sales.

SKI ROUNDTOP

(P. 48, C-4, #24) 925 Roundtop Rd., Lewisberry
717-432-9631
SEASON: Nov. 25-March 31
ANNUAL SNOWFALL: 20"
TERRAIN: 14 trails over 100 acres; longest run, 4,100'; ◆ 35%; ■ 30%; ● 35%.
LIFTS: 10 (1 quad, 1 triple, 4 doubles, 4 surface); capacity, 8,000 per hour.
Summit: 1,355'
VERTICAL: 600'
ACTIVITIES: Snowboarding; NASTAR; night skiing.
FEATURES: Snowmaking 100%; ski school; restaurants; rentals.
Other than three fairly steep runs to the left of the mountain (as you face it), like Ramrod and the gnarly Gunbarrel, Ski Roundtop's terrain is

perfect for its bread-and-butter clientele—families. Young kids love the terrain garden; teens head for the lift-serviced half pipe. Cruisers like Lafayette's Leap and Minuteman comprise the bulk of the mountain. Children under 5 ski free. Lift tickets are sold in four- and eight-hour increments. Like its neighbor under the same ownership, Ski Liberty, Roundtop attracts skiers from Baltimore (just over an hour away) and Washington (just under two hours' drive).

SKI SAWMILL

(P. 48, B-4, #25) RD 1, Morris
717-353-7521
TRAILS, 8; LIFTS, 4; VERTICAL, 515'.

SPLIT ROCK SKI AREA

(P. 48, C-5, #26) Lake Harmony
717-722-9111
TRAILS, 7; LIFTS, 2; VERTICAL, 250'.
Half pipe.

SPRING MOUNTAIN SKI AREA

(P. 48, D-6, #27) Spring Mount
215-287-7900
SEASON: Dec. 15-March 15
ANNUAL SNOWFALL: 35"
TERRAIN: 7 trails over NA acres; longest run, 2,220'; ◆ 20%; ■ 40%; ● 40%.
LIFTS: 6 (1 triple, 3 doubles, 2 surface); capacity, 5,500 per hour.
SUMMIT: 528'
VERTICAL: 420'
ACTIVITIES: Snowboarding; night skiing.
FEATURES: Snowmaking 100%; ski school; restaurant; rentals.
Spring Mountain serves as a Philadelphia day area, and is trying to upgrade its image as an easy mountain with a new advanced trail; snowboarders have a half pipe.

TAMIMENT SKI AREA

(P. 48, C-6, #28) Tamiment
717-588-6652
TRAILS, 1; LIFTS, 1; VERTICAL, 200'.
▶NORDIC: 3 ungroomed km.

TANGLEWOOD SKI AREA

(P. 48, B-6, #29) Tafton
717-226-9500
TRAILS, 10; LIFTS, 5; VERTICAL, 415'.

TUSSEY MOUNTAIN SKI AREA

(P. 48, C-3, #30) Route 322, Boalsburg, 5 mi. E of State College
814-466-6810
TRAILS, 8; LIFTS, 4; VERTICAL, 500'.

WHITETAIL RESORT

(P. 48, E-3, #31) 13805 Blairs Valley Rd., Mercersburg
717-328-9400; 717-328-5300 (snow)
SEASON: Dec. 4-April 4
ANNUAL SNOWFALL: 60"
TERRAIN: 16 trails over 104 acres; longest run, 4,900'; ◆ 26%; ■ 54%; ● 20%.
LIFTS: 5 (1 high-speed quad, 2 quads, 1 double, 1 surface); capacity, 9,400 per hour.
SUMMIT: 1,800'
VERTICAL: 935'
ACTIVITIES: Snowboarding; night skiing.
FEATURES: Snowmaking 100%; ski school; restaurant; child care; rentals.
Whitetail, the most recent major ski area to open, is a sleek, high maintenance resort—for this neck of the woods. With the region's only high-speed quad, you get more skiing per hour, and the area constantly seeks to improve itself. Boarders have a half pipe and new park. Proposed expansion for 1995

will significantly enlarge the beginners' area. The skiing is tremendously varied. Exhibition and Bold Decision are usually allowed to bump up for mogul-mashers. Angel Drop and Home Run are long, flowing intermediate runs. And everyone enjoys the summit views, which seem to go on for miles.

WILLOWBROOK SKI AREA
(P. 48, D-1, #32) RD 2, Belle Vernon
412-872-7272
TRAILS, 1; LIFTS, 2; VERTICAL, 100'.

NORDIC

CALLENDER'S WINDY ACRES FARM
(P. 48, B-5, #33) Wrighter Lake Road, Thompson
717-727-2982
FACILITIES: 6 groomed km, 4 ungroomed; rentals; snowshoeing.

CAMP SPEARS ELJABAR
(P. 48, C-6, #34) RD 1, Dingmans Ferry
717-828-2329
FACILITIES: 16 groomed km;

Courtesy: Sunrise Park Resort (see Arizona, p. 90).

rentals; lessons; lodging and restaurant.

CHERRY RIDGE FARM
(P. 48, C-5, #35) Gallagher Road, Tobyhanna
717-676-4904
FACILITIES: 3 groomed km, 25 ungroomed; rentals; lessons; restaurant.

ELK VALLEY CROSS COUNTRY
(P. 48, B-1, #36) 7085 Van Camp Rd., Girard
814-474-2356
FACILITIES: 30 groomed km; rentals; lessons; restaurant.

EVERGREEN PARK CROSS-COUNTRY AREA
(P. 48, C-6, #37) Cherry Lane Road, Analomink
717-421-7721
FACILITIES: 3 groomed km; rentals; lessons (by appointment); restaurant.

GATEWAY LODGE
(P. 48, C-2, #38) Route 36, Cooksburg
814-744-8017
FACILITIES: Miles of ungroomed terrain; rentals; lodging and restaurant.

HANLEY'S HAPPY HILL
(P. 48, C-2, #39) Route 42, Eagles Mere
717-525-3461
FACILITIES: 40 groomed km, 10 ungroomed; rentals; lessons; restaurant.
  Hanley's offers an excellent mix of terrain on its 6,300 acres, with several changes in elevation and 10 km of wilderness to suit more advanced gliders.

INDIAN HEAD NORDIC CENTER
(P. 48, B-1, #40) RD 5, Waterford
814-796-2818
FACILITIES: NA groomed km; rentals; lessons; restaurant.

INDIAN MOUNTAIN INN
(P. 48, B-5, #41) Tripp Lake Road, Brackney
717-663-2645
FACILITIES: 8 groomed km; lodging and restaurant.

THE INN AT STARLIGHT LAKE
(P. 48, B-5, #42) Starlight
717-798-2519
FACILITIES: 20 groomed km; rentals; lessons; ice skating; lodging and restaurant.
  The system has a good variety of terrain for all abilities, with trails following abandoned logging roads through stone quarries and past numerous lakes.

MAPLE HILL FARM
(P. 48, B-6, #43) Starrucca
717-224-4191
FACILITIES: 42 groomed km; rentals; lessons; lodging and restaurant.

PACK SHACK ADVENTURES
(P. 48, C-6, #44) 88 Broad St., Delaware Water Gap
717-424-8533
FACILITIES: 65 manually groomed km; rentals; lessons; tubing; tobogganing.
  Pack Shack operates two areas with the cooperation of the National Park Service. Slateford Farms offers mostly beginner terrain with three trails (totalling 5.5 miles) that skirt farmers' fields and gently rolling woods. Blue Mountain Lakes has five 2-mile, a 3-mile, 4-mile, and a 5-mile loop that cover more rugged terrain. Luncheon, full moon, and three-day expedition tours are also available.

PENN HILLS LODGE
(P. 48, C-6, #45) Analomink
717-421-6464
FACILITIES: 8 groomed km;

rentals; lessons; lodging and restaurant.

POCONO HERSHEY NORDIC CENTER
(P. 48, C-6, #46) Pocono Manor
717-443-8411
FACILITIES: 3 groomed km; rentals; lessons; lodging and restaurant.

STERLING INN
(P.48, C-5, #47) South Sterling
717-676-3311
FACILITIES: 8 groomed km; rental; lessons; sleigh rides; ice skating; tobogganing; lodging and restaurant.

STONE VALLEY RECREATION CENTER
(P. 48, C-3, #48) Off Route 26 S, 17 mi. S of State College
814-863-1164
FACILITIES: 44 groomed km; rentals; lessons; ice skating.
  A pleasant university-run haven near the Penn State campus, Stone Valley has mainly hilly, wooded terrain perfect for intermediates. It also operates a rehabilitation center for injured birds of prey and has an environmental display area. Cabins for rent.

WILDERNESS LODGE
(P. 48, B-1, #49) Weeks Valley Road, Wattsburg
814-739-2946
FACILITIES: 25 groomed km, 25 ungroomed; rentals; lessons; lodging and restaurant.

UTAH

Utah license plates read "The Greatest Snow on Earth," and it's no idle boast. Some of the fluffiest white stuff anywhere—true champagne powder—falls on the slopes of the majestic Wasatch Range. No less than nine major resorts (several of them world-class) lie within an hour's drive of Salt Lake City. No city on earth rivals Utah's capital for accessibility and variety of both terrain and ambiance, a fact locals hope to showcase in the 2002 Winter Olympics, for which Salt Lake is a leading contender. And many of them represent astounding value. ❄ After hitting the slopes, take in a Jazz basketball game or performance of the Mormon Tabernacle Choir. Or just enjoy the first-class dining at resorts like Deer Valley and Snowbird. (It used to be that Utah's liquor laws were so complex they'd drive anyone to drink. But recent reforms allow diners to partake when they order food, or to belly up to the bar by purchasing a $5 temporary "private club" membership, good for two weeks.) ❄ Don't overlook the southern part of the state. Not only are there two fine downhill areas literally in the middle of nowhere (Brian Head and Elk Meadows), but groomed cross-country trails wind through the fantastic, wildly colorful rock formations of

Bryce Canyon National Park; the vaulting natural bridges in Arches National Monument; and the red rock country of Canyonlands National Park. ❄ Seeking adventure? Wasatch Powderbird Guides (801-742-2800) offers heliskiing well into the summer; Park Snowcats (801-649-6583) accesses pristine terrain in the Park City area. True ski-aholics will enjoy the Ski Utah Interconnect (801-534-1907), starting in Park City and continuing on foot and skis via select Alpine and backcountry trails to Brighton, Solitude, Alta, and Snowbird. (An abbreviated tour visits the latter four areas only.) Strong intermediates can negotiate the downhill skiing sections; the hiking and poling are mostly moderate in difficulty. ❄ For other winter sports, head to the Utah Winter Sports Park at Bear Hollow near Park City (801-649-5447). The complex features four ski jumps ranging from 18 to 90 meters, a snowboard half pipe, a bobsled, and a luge run. ❄ And the Wasatch Cache National Forest (801-943-1794) offers free "Ski with a Naturalist" tours on gentle terrain at Alta, Brighton, Snowbird, and Solitude, where trained volunteers point out sites of natural or historical significance.

ALPINE

ALTA SKI LIFTS
(P. 52, B-3, #1) Highway 210, Little Cottonwood Canyon, Alta
801-742-3333; 801-572-3939 (snow)
SEASON: Nov. 15-April 15
ANNUAL SNOWFALL: 500"
TERRAIN: 39 trails over 2,200 acres; longest run, 3.5 mi.; ◆ 35%; ■ 40%; ● 25%.
LIFTS: 8 (2 triples, 6 doubles); capacity, 8,750 per hour.
SUMMIT: 10,550'
VERTICAL: 2,000'
ACTIVITIES: None.
FEATURES: Ski school; restaurants; child care; rentals.
The area's slogan reads, "Alta is for Skiers." Alta is about loving the snow, the mountains, even your fellow skiers. To come here you must be passionate about the sport. Everyone else is. Altans don't like change or glitz. Some locals and regulars grumbled when Alta had the audacity to upgrade a couple of lifts to triples and widen a few trails. The philosophy behind those long lift lines and agonizingly slow rides is this: It puts fewer people on the slopes. And makes the powder last longer. So old-fashioned. So rustic. No frills, just thrills. More than half Alta's terrain is unmarked on the map. This is the place for secret powder stashes "that only the locals know." If you can see it,

you can ski it. Unfortunately, most powder caches are accessible only by hikes ranging from 10 to 60 minutes. And even the traverses can prove daunting. Diehards like it that way, too. Some of the classic stashes are Catherine's off the Supreme lift, Devil's Castle off Sugarloaf, and the Greeley Bowls off Germania. Experts will also enjoy the steeps off the Wildcat lift (where you can also hike up to the Baldy Chutes). If Alta has a signature named run, it's Alf's High Rustler, a steep steady drop that makes a great powder run in the morning and a sensational bump run after lunch. But beginners and intermediates won't feel left out. Novices have a huge area in the Albion Basin all to themselves. Intermediates can take groomed cruisers off Supreme, like Rock 'n Roll and Big Dipper; or they can waltz with the mountain on Ballroom and Mambo off the Germania lift. A few tips: Don't volunteer that your ski suit is by Bogner and don't say you skied Deer Valley earlier that week. The natives are very friendly, but Alta's skier's mountain reputation can breed a little insiders' snootiness. Alta shares Little Cottonwood Canyon with Snowbird. Both areas provide supreme powder skiing; but whereas Snowbird is a sleek

Jaguar, Alta's the old family Chevy. Would Alta converts ask for a trade-in? Nah. They can take a test drive at Snowbird whenever they want.

BEAVER MOUNTAIN
(P.52, A-3, #2) 1045 1/2 N. Main, off Highway 89 E, Logan
801-753-0921; 801-753-4822 (snow)
SEASON: Dec. 1-April 15
ANNUAL SNOWFALL: 450"
TERRAIN: 16 trails over 364 acres; longest run, 2.25 mi.; ◆25%; ■ 40%; ● 35%.
LIFTS: 3 (3 doubles); capacity, 3,000 per hour.
SUMMIT: 8,832'
VERTICAL: 1,632'
ACTIVITIES: Snowboarding.
FEATURES: Ski school; restaurant; rentals.
The northernmost area in Utah, Beaver Mountain caters to novices and intermediates just mastering powder. More advanced skiers will find plenty of virgin powder off the flanks and through the trees.

BRIAN HEAD SKI RESORT
(P. 52, D-2, #3) 329 S. Highway 143, Brian Head
801-677-2035; 800-272-7426

(snow)
SEASON: Nov. 15-April 15
ANNUAL SNOWFALL: 400"
TERRAIN: 55 trails over 825 acres; longest run, 1.5 mi.; ◆ 30%; ■ 40%; ● 30%.
LIFTS: 6 (5 triples, 1 doubles); capacity, 11,200 per hour.
SUMMIT: 10,920'
VERTICAL: 1,320'
ACTIVITIES: Snowboarding; night skiing.
FEATURES: Snowmaking 35%; ski school; restaurants; child care; rentals.
► NORDIC: 801-677-2029; 42 groomed km (with skating lane), 300 ungroomed km; rentals; lessons.
Stuck in the middle of nowhere, halfway between Los Angeles and Las Vegas, Brian Head is a funny sort of resort. You'd expect it to be solidly local—it's in a sparsely populated neck of the woods. Surprisingly, many of the latest neon Bogner and Obermeyer ski outfits are on display on the slopes; the resort seems to attract many skiers on their way to the almost-as-bright lights of Vegas. That makes the après-ski scene livelier than expected in southern Utah. The skiing can be sensational. Navajo Peak has fine novice trails. Other runs straight down the chair side are pure green; those to the left a nice powder blue. Stronger skiers head for Brian Head Peak, where runs like Giant Steps and Engens build up major-league bumps.

STATBOX

Tourism: 801-538-1030
Time zone: Mountain
Population: 1,722,850
Square miles: 84,916

Average annual precipitation: 13"
Highest elevation: 13,528'
Lowest elevation: 2,200'

Intermediates will find plenty of heavenly cruising off the Roulette chair. The Nordic trails weave through some of the most striking scenery in the Southwest, near the Cedar Breaks National Monument.

BRIGHTON SKI RESORT

(P. 52, B-3, #4) Top of Big Cottonwood Canyon, Brighton
801-532-4731; 801-943-8309 (snow)
SEASON: Nov. 15-April 25
ANNUAL SNOWFALL: 430″
TERRAIN: 61 trails over 850 acres; longest run, 3 mi.; ◆ 38%; ■ 38%; ● 24%.
LIFTS: 7 (2 high-speed quads, 2 triples, 3 doubles, 1 surface); capacity, 10,500 per hour.
SUMMIT: 10,500′
VERTICAL: 1,745′
ACTIVITIES: Snowboarding; night skiing.
FEATURES: Snowmaking 25%; ski school; restaurants; rentals.
Brighton touts itself as the area where Salt Lake City learns to ski and they've been coming since 1936. The layout turns potential liabilities into advantages. Much of the central area consists of a series of short interlinked runs. These give you a chance to test your skills on new terrain every few hundred feet and sample numerous little powder pockets. And trails usually merge into flatter cat tracks, making it difficult to get into trouble. Brighton is one of the few major Utah areas to allow boarders, and does an excellent job teaching board etiquette. Usually shredders dive off trails into out-of-bounds glades; but Brighton has curbed their penchant for using snow walls as a half pipe, posting signs reading "OFF THE WALL—NOT!" Lest you think Brighton is a pussycat, the Great Western Express accesses a vast bowl punctuated by islands of pine where you can pick any one of a hundred lines. And the isolated Millicent chair area reaches some nice steeps like Lone Pine and Scree Slope. Nestled snugly in the exquisite Big Cottonwood Canyon (one of the West's most scenic ski access roads, a wonderland of babbling brooks, rock formations, and snow sculptures), Brighton's no longer a secret. It only has itself to blame, having recently added two high-speed quads, an isolated beginners section, and 250 acres of patrolled skiable terrain.

DEER VALLEY RESORT

(P. 52, B-3, #5) 2250 Deer Valley Dr., S off Highway 224, Park City
801-649-1000; 801-649-2000 (snow)
SEASON: Dec. 5-April 4
ANNUAL SNOWFALL: 300″
TERRAIN: 66 trails over 1,000 acres; longest run, 1.4 mi.; ◆ 35%; ■ 50%; ● 15%.
LIFTS: 12 (2 high-speed quads, 9 triples, 1 double); capacity, 19,200 per hour.
SUMMIT: 9,400′
VERTICAL: 2,200′
ACTIVITIES: Ice skating; sleigh rides.
FEATURES: Snowmaking 25%; ski school; restaurants; child care; rentals.
Valets to unload your skis from the car. Cellular phones for rent on the slopes. Gourmet salad bars and sinful desserts at on-mountain restaurants. . . . Deer Valley is as posh and pampering as skiing gets. The slopeside development is remarkably tasteful; the day lodges define rustic chic in cedar and sandstone. And it boasts the finest assortment of five-star restaurants in the USA. (It's all true, but you get what you pay for). Some complain that the slopes are as immaculately groomed as the soigne clientele. Au contraire. True, nearly everything on Bald Eagle and Flagstaff Mountains (with its new and longer blue runs), as well as off the Sterling lift on Bald Mountain, is smooth as silk (the ski patrol actually stops to remove rocks). Cruisers like Stein's Way, Sidewinder, and Big Stick (the designated Olympic slalom run) are justly famous for their perfect fall lines. But Deer Valley has a less polished side, highlighted in its unique Experts Only trail map. It only grooms nine or 10 runs a night (check the Inside Edge newsletter for the day's on-slope dope). The ferocious bumps of Know You Don't and Rattler will rattle anyone's teeth. The steeps off the Mayflower and Sultan chairs like Ruins of Pompeii and the straight shot Mayflower Chutes will set knees aflame. And the tree skiing in Ontario Bowl, as well as the unmarked Triangle, is unsurpassed. If you fall, don't worry. Someone's almost always there at Deer Valley to pick you up—or, at least, offer a pick-me-up.

ELK MEADOWS SKI RESORT

(P. 52, D-2, #6) 1419 S. Main, Highway 153, 17 mi. E of Beaver
801-438-5433; 800-248-SNOW (snow)
SEASON: Nov. 25-April 1
ANNUAL SNOWFALL: 350″
TERRAIN: 30 trails over 345 acres; longest run, 2 mi.; ◆ 24%; ■ 62%; ● 14%.
LIFTS: 5 (1 triple, 2 doubles, 2 surface); capacity, 5,000 per hour.
SUMMIT: 10,400′
VERTICAL: 1,200′
ACTIVITIES: Snowboarding.
FEATURES: Snowmaking; ski school; restaurants; child care; rentals.
Elk Meadows is a family resort with miles of cruising terrain, and steeper stuff in the series of bowls crowning the ridge. Experts can hike to the top of Mt. Holly and ski down the Tushar backside.

NORDIC VALLEY

(P. 52, B-3, #7) 3567 Nordic Valley Rd., off Highway 39, Eden
801-745-3511
SEASON: Dec. 1-April 15
ANNUAL SNOWFALL: 300″
TERRAIN: 12 trails over 85 acres; longest run, 1 mi.; ◆ 20%; ■ 50%; ● 30%.
LIFTS: 2 (2 doubles); capacity, 1,800 per hour.
SUMMIT: 6,460′
VERTICAL: 960″
ACTIVITIES: Snowboarding; night skiing.
FEATURES: Ski school; restaurant; rentals.
Despite its name, Nordic Valley has no groomed cross-country trails but does offer strongly intermediate skiing and even fewer crowds than its highly touted neighbors. Unfortunately, the area's lower elevation means it's more subject to the vagaries of the weather. In other words, in good snow years it's very good value, but in bad . . . . The runs are wide and well-groomed, perfect for entry- and lower-level skiers seeking a floating-on-air sensation.

PARK CITY SKI AREA

(P. 52, B-3, #8) 1345 Lowell Ave., Highway 224, Park City
801-649-8111; 801-649-9571 (snow)
SEASON: Nov. 20-April 11
ANNUAL SNOWFALL: 350″
TERRAIN: 86 trails over 2,200 acres, plus an additional 650 acres of bowl skiing; longest run, 3.5 mi.; ◆ 38%; ■ 45%; ● 17%.
LIFTS: 14 (1 gondola, 2 high-speed quads, 1 quad, 5 triples, 5 doubles); capacity, 22,200 per hour.
SUMMIT: 10,000′
VERTICAL: 3,100′
ACTIVITIES: NASTAR; ice skating; sleigh rides; night skiing.
FEATURES: Snowmaking 16%; ski school; restaurants; rentals.
Park City offers the widest variety of terrain in Utah, as well as the state's only true ski town (which retains charming vestiges of its 19th century mining town origins). This is an intermediate paradise. Skiers love runs off the gondola like Pay Day and NASTAR, as well as trails that swoop off the new King Con high-speed quad and the equally fast Prospector lift. Short dives like Widowmaker and Dynamite provide fine bump practice. Even beginners can join in the fun, taking the lazy circuitous Claimjumper/Bonanza route from the top, or slipping down the windfree and sunny Pioneer lift trails. Experts will find more than enough diversion. There are steep mogulled beauties in Thaynes Canyon and still more precipitous drops off the Ski Team lift. But Park City's crowning glory is the series of bowls serenely perched up top. If you're not sure you're ready, check out the equally steep but much shorter Blueslip Bowl. Jupiter boasts the widest variety of terrain, from chutes to glades. If you're suddenly having second thoughts on the way down, head for its West Face (though, if it's been heavily skied, the cattrack leading there can be treacherous, winnowing tightly through trees, with huge trenches). Jupiter whet your appetite? Head further right of the lift to the elevator shafts called Portuguese Gap and Scott's. Not enough, you say? Take a hike to McConkey's and Puma Bowls. Yup, there's something for everybody at Park City. The only complaint is that it's virtually impossible to ski that 3,100-foot vertical uninterrupted (that's the price you pay for diversity). Also, the Prospector and King Con Quads can have long (15 minute!) waits. If so, take the Town or Ski Team lift and ski those runs for a while.

PARK WEST SKI AREA

(P. 52, B-3, #9) 4000 Park West Dr., Park City
801-649-5400
SEASON: Dec. 1-April 4
ANNUAL SNOWFALL: 350″
TERRAIN: 58 trails over 850 acres; longest run, 2.5 mi.; ◆ 48%; ■ 30%; ● 22%.
LIFTS: 7 (7 double); capacity, 6,700 per hour.
SUMMIT: 9,000′
VERTICAL: 2,200′
ACTIVITIES: Snowboarding.
FEATURES: Snowmaking; ski school; restaurant; child care; rentals.
Another of Utah's great buys, Park West offers an amazing $19 lift ticket. Don't expect frills here. You will find four mountains with wide open bowls (Bushwhacker is a great warm-up), ultra-gnarly bump runs like Geronimo Ridge and Maverick, and hellacious descents from the ridge on Iron Horse Peak, like Lone Pine, Bull Chute, and Rock 'n Roll. This is the place to shoot the chutes. Park West attracts a younger crowd, too, because it's the only Park City ski area that allows snowboarders, offering five half pipes and a gigantic terrain park.

POWDER MOUNTAIN RESORT

(P. 52, B-3, #10) State Route 158, Eden
801-745-3772
SEASON: Nov. 15-May 1
ANNUAL SNOWFALL: 500″
TERRAIN: 33 trails over 1,600 acres; longest run, 3 mi.; ◆ 30%; ■ 60%; ● 10%.
LIFTS: 6 (1 triple, 2 doubles, 3 surface); capacity, 4,800 per hour.
SUMMIT: 8,900′
VERTICAL: 1,300′

ACTIVITIES: Snowboarding; snowcat skiing; night skiing.
FEATURES: Ski school; restaurants; rentals.

A jealously guarded locals' secret, Powder Mountain stands out for its gorgeous bowls and of course, for the fluffy white stuff swaddling the mountain like a benediction. Watch your fellow skiers: You can see them sniffing the air when the clouds roll in. After a day, you'll swear you can smell it, too: talcum-soft powder. Everywhere you look you'll find untracked bliss in one direction or another. Even beginners can get a taste—early in the morning—on runs like Burntwood and Mushroom Valley, where drifts off to either side occasionally lay ungroomed. If the in-bounds skiing proves too tame, you can go cat skiing in the Meadows Express area, or hit the entire backside of the mountain—known as Powder Country—which is easily accessed off the Hidden Lake lift. A shuttle conveniently awaits at the bottom to take you back to the base. Beginning powder skiers can take the intermediate Boundary run and drop off into unnamed, gentler glade runs. The out-of-bounds skiing increases Powder's skiable acreage by 2,000.

SNOWBASIN

(P. 52, B-3, #11) End State Route 226, 17 mi. E of Ogden, Huntsville
801-399-1135; 801-399-0198
SEASON: Nov. 25-April 4
ANNUAL SNOWFALL: 400''
TERRAIN: 39 trails over 1,800 acres; longest run, 3 mi.; ◆ 30%; ▪ 50%; ● 20%.
LIFTS: 5 (4 triples, 1 double); capacity, 7,500 per hour.
SUMMIT: 8,800'
VERTICAL: 2,400'
ACTIVITIES: Snowboarding.
FEATURES: Ski school; restaurants; rentals.

Here's another cherished locals' favorite, with generous dumps of powder, empty slopes, and unmarked, open-faced knolls that remain untracked all morning! That may change if Salt Lake is awarded the 2002 Olympics. Snowbasin is scheduled to host the men's and women's downhill and Super G (a cross of downhill and slalom) races. Snowbasin is another area that casts a blind eye if you sneak off out of bounds to expansive powder magnets like Strawberry Bowl and John Paul. The trail cutters thoughtfully provided runs that link these sections with the base area. Beginners can pick their way down from the summit or stick to the runs to the left of the Becker chair. Intermediates seeking groomed runs can float down Chicken Springs, Wildcat Bowl, and Porcupine Face. Snowbasin has impeccable credentials. It was developed by Pete Seibert (the visionary behind Vail) and is now

owned by Earl Holding (the mogul behind Sun Valley).

SNOWBIRD SKI RESORT

(P. 52, B-3, #12) Little Cottonwood Canyon, Snowbird
801-742-2222
SEASON: Nov. 23-May 10
ANNUAL SNOWFALL: 500''
TERRAIN: 50 trails over 2,000 acres; longest run, 3.5 mi.; ◆ 50%; ▪ 30%; ● 20%.
LIFTS: 8 (1 125-passenger tram, 7 doubles); capacity, 8,810 per hour.
SUMMIT: 11,000'
VERTICAL: 3,100'
ACTIVITIES: Snowboarding; NASTAR.
FEATURES: Snowmaking 5%; ski school; restaurants; child care; rentals.

One of skiing's ultimate highs has to be making first tracks on powder days, then gazing up at that vast virgin expanse scored only by a single sinuous "S." Along with Alta, Snowbird excels at providing skiers with that Rocky Mountain High. But unlike Alta, Snowbird is utterly high-tech and contemporary. The development's concrete-and-glass buildings have been cannily designed to blend with the mountain, calling attention to the pristine surroundings. The ski experience is just as carefully crafted. Snowmass is the vision of billionaire Dick Bass, a renaissance entrepreneur who holds the distinction of scaling the highest peak on all seven continents. He dedicates Snowbird to the "enhancement of mind, body, and spirit," and you can often see him at the top of the gondola surveying his kingdom, telling anyone who'll listen about his dream. It is a powderhound's and shredder's fantasy world. Pilgrims crowd the mountain early on powder days; when the single tram unloads atop Hidden Peak, it resembles a stampede. But who can blame them? Skiers dart off madly in all directions, bombing down the renowned double diamond expanse of Silver Fox, Great Scott, and Upper Cirque. They swoop like eagles down into powder pockets of the Peruvian Gulch. When it's all skied off, they head for the bumps of Regulator Johnson; or the steeps of the Gad Chutes, Wilbere Bowl, and Mach Schnell; or high-speed cruising on Primrose Path. Or they try the Gad 2 lift (the only one off-limits to boarders) in search of narrower beauties like S.T.H. ("Steeper than Hell" in local parlance). And of course, like Alta, there's plenty of terrain not on the map. Ask locals about in-bounds gems like Restaurant Row, the "Get Serious" chutes, Egad, and Gaddamnit. Out-of-bounds, thousands of acres await in the leviathan drainages of Boundary Bowl and White Pine Valley. Yes, 50% of Snowbird is rated black and jet black. Looking up from the base, its fiercest terrain

looms above; but largely hidden from sight remains 1,000 acres reserved for beginners and intermediates. First-timers learn on Chickadee before graduating to the mid-Gad lift and the blue-tinged Big Emma. Intermediates have a whole play area off the tram on Chip's Run, as well as off Gad 2 on preeminent cruisers like Bassackwards, Election, and Banana. And a new section called Baby Thunder, expected to be ready by the 1995-1996 season at the latest, will create 500 more acres of intermediate terrain. Still, Snowbird is a tough mountain—but a rewarding one. If you're trying to master powder, this is one of the meccas.

SOLITUDE SKI RESORT

(P. 52, B-3, #13) Big Cottonwood Canyon Road, Salt Lake City
801-534-1400
SEASON: Nov. 15-April 20
ANNUAL SNOWFALL: 410''
TERRAIN: 63 trails over 1,100 acres; longest run, 2.5 mi.; ◆ 25%; ▪ 55%; ● 20%.
LIFTS: 7 (1 quad, 2 triples, 4 doubles); capacity, 10,350 per hour.
SUMMIT: 10,030'
VERTICAL: 2,030'
ACTIVITIES: None.
FEATURES: Ski school; restaurants; rentals.
▶NORDIC: 20 groomed km. (with skating lane); rentals; lessons.

Solitude has been expanding exponentially the last several years and ultimately will include an entire slopeside village. That won't make locals happy—because this is a jewel. Solitude is an incredibly user-friendly mountain with a growing and justly deserved reputation for quality skiing. The mountain has been entirely redesigned, minimizing the need to hike or traverse. The grooming is exceptional: The industry leader LMC uses Solitude as its testing ground for new equipment; even super-steep slopes can now receive coddling care. And there's something for everyone. Beginners have a large playground off the Moonbeam chair. Intermediates dive greedily down the cruisers off the Eagle Express and Sunrise chair. Bumpbashers gallop down the runs off Eagle Ridge, like Vertigo, Paradise Lost, and Rhapsody before attacking Courageous. The Headwall Forest offers superb courses through the trees. Cathedral and Milk Run surprise extreme wannabes with sudden cliffs. And if you just want a steep sustained pitch, check out Honeycomb Canyon—which offers lift-served "out-of-bounds" skiing. The Nordic center weaves through impressive high-alpine forests and meadows, living up to the resort's name, and is superb practice before striking out into the backcountry. Solitude also offers two unparalleled dining

experiences: a cross-country ski-in and ski-out gourmet, yurt dinner; and a sleigh ride to the Roundhouse restaurant for dinner.

SUNDANCE RESORT

(P. 52, B-3, #14) North Fork, Provo Canyon, Provo
801-225-4107
SEASON: Nov. 15-April 1
ANNUAL SNOWFALL: 320''
TERRAIN: 41 trails over 450 acres; longest run, 2.5 mi.; ◆ 40%; ▪ 40%; ● 20%.
LIFTS: 4 (2 triples, 2 doubles)
SUMMIT: 8,250'
VERTICAL: 2,150'
ACTIVITIES: Snowboarding.
FEATURES: Ski school; restaurant; child care; rentals.
▶NORDIC: 15 groomed km; rentals; lessons.

In 1969, Robert Redford purchased a tract of land on Mount Timpanogos, one of the highest peaks in the Wasatch range. The resort he developed, Sundance, represents his vision of a planned community that blends artistic, recreational, and environmentally minded pursuits. To that end, the prestigious Sundance Institute runs several programs for young filmmakers as well as the U.S. Film Festival, held annually in late January, perhaps the leading showcase for independent films. And the resort hosts several ecological conferences throughout the year. Sundance has a special aura. It's partly the other-worldly vistas, partly the near-flawless design of the public spaces, partly the infectious communal spirit. The skiing experience is special, too. There's something about enjoying a fresh-baked muffin and homemade soup up at Bearclaw's Cabin while the entire panorama of northern Utah unfolds before you. Unfortunately, novices are limited to the lower half of the mountain, and intermediates really have only one option from the top—Bearclaw. But advanced skiers will love riding the bumps on Tombstone, Jamie's, and Redfinger, or challenging Bishop's and Grizzly Bowls. And, after communing with nature, everyone can enjoy the refined ambiance in the Tree Room restaurant, which displays some of Redford's Native American art collection and is built around a tree.

NORDIC

BEST WESTERN RUBY'S INN

(P. 52, E-3, #15) Highway 63, Bryce Canyon
801-834-5341
FACILITIES: 30 groomed km (with skating lane),

CONTINUED ON NEXT PAGE

VERMONT

Two words characterize Vermont skiing best: accessible and affordable. Most areas are a four-to-six-hour drive from New York and Boston. Several airlines service the area, and Amtrak has revived its "ski train" to Burlington. The nearby resorts of Stowe, Smugglers' Notch, Sugarbush, and Jay Peak—marketed as "Ski Vermont's Classics"—offer special packages. And good old Yankee thrift is alive and well, with Vermont areas offering numerous bargains throughout the season, like free lessons, free lift tickets with lodging, or mid-week and early or late season discounts. ❄ Don't expect glamour: Rustic chic is the rule. While most mountain villages are distressingly functional and nondescript, a short drive takes you to the New England skiers expect: White steeples, covered bridges, 18th century farmhouses frosted with snow— a Christmas paperweight come to life. ❄ The combination of heavy snowfall (augmented by some of the most sophisticated snowmaking anywhere) and steep narrow slopes has created a tradition of top racers, many of whom trained at the renowned Burke Mountain Academy, Stratton Mountain School, or Sugarbush Green Mountain Valley School. Vermont has contributed more skiers to the U.S. Olympic ski team than any other state, including 1952 double-gold winner Andrea Mead Lawrence, Billy Kidd, Suzy Chaffee and 1992 moguls gold-medalist Donna Weinbrecht. ❄ Cross-country fanatics will find over 50 centers in Vermont. They can also follow the 280-mile Catamount Trail that extends from the Canadian to the Massachusetts border, connecting a series of rustic inns. In addition, many lodges participate in inn-to-inn tours. ❄ For a break, pay a visit to Brandon's Vermont Ski Museum in the central western part of the state, which exhibits over 700 items of ski memorabilia, including early lift and grooming equipment.

ALPINE

ASCUTNEY MOUNTAIN RESORT

(P. 38, D-2, #1) Route 44, Brownsville
802-484-7711
SEASON: Nov. 25-April 10
ANNUAL SNOWFALL: 220"
TERRAIN: 31 trails over 100 acres; longest run, 2 mi.; ◆ 35%; ▪ 39%; ● 26%.
LIFTS: 4 (3 triples, 1 double); capacity, 4,500 per hour.
SUMMIT: 2,250'
VERTICAL: 1,530'
ACTIVITIES: Snowboarding; ice skating.
FEATURES: Snowmaking 70%; ski school; restaurants; child care; rentals.
▶NORDIC: 32 groomed km; rentals; lessons.
 What a bargain! The skiing's good and affordable, sure, but new owners Steven and Susan Plausteiner stole Ascutney for $1.1 million at a bankruptcy auction—lock, stock, and barrel, including a deluxe hotel and health spa. They immediately pinpointed the previous owners' problem—insufficient grooming and snowmaking—and are improving both dramatically (though they can do little about the fierce winds that occasionally pummel the slopes). It's nice to have Ascutney back. The trail names have been changed but not the friendly attitude. And the skiing is wonderfully varied for a mid-sized resort. Intermediates will love the clean fall lines, the stepped terrain, and the mix of wide open Western-style slopes and typically narrow New England twisters. Cloudspin is a meandering cruiser, Exhibition a big bump run. And when the snow's good, Ascutney offers the best glade skiing in the southern half of the state.

STATBOX

Tourism: 800-VERMONT
Time zone: Eastern
Population: 562,758
Square miles: 9,609

Average annual precipitation: 34"
Highest elevation: 4,393'
Lowest elevation: 95'

BOLTON VALLEY RESORT

(P. 38, B-2, #2) Bolton Valley Access Road, Bolton
802-434-2131
SEASON: Nov. 25-April 15
ANNUAL SNOWFALL: 250"
TERRAIN: 48 trails over 150 acres; longest run, 2.5 mi.; ◆ 23%; ▪ 49%; ● 28%.
LIFTS: 6 (1 quad, 4 doubles, 1 surface); capacity, 6,100 per hour.
SUMMIT: 3,150'
VERTICAL: 1,625'
ACTIVITIES: Snowboarding; night skiing.
FEATURES: Snowmaking 66%; sleigh rides; ski school; restaurants; child care; rentals.
▶NORDIC: 43 groomed km, 47 ungroomed; rentals; lessons.
 Bolton is owned by the Des Lauriers family, three of whose kids (Rob, Adam, and Eric) are leading extreme skiers. The younger Des Lauriers run extreme clinics at several North American areas, including Bolton every December. Despite that, the area is essentially an intermediate's dream. Cobrass stands out among its groomed cruisers, while Stillway, Lost Boys, and Devil's Playground are among the more challenging runs. Many other trail names pay tribute to the area's rich history, including the sharp-shooting Green Mountain Boys of the Revolutionary era, like Beech Seal, the Bolton Outlaw, and Peggy Dow's Hymn Book. The atmosphere is mellow throughout, the owners still making the rounds from time to time in the dining room. The compact mountain village development is one of Vermont's best, and the attractions of Burlington are just minutes away. Nordic trails run the gamut, with a whopping 1,800-foot vertical for a strenuous, advanced workout. Less experienced gliders have a wealth of trails too.

CONTINUED FROM LAST PAGE

30 ungroomed; rentals; lessons; lodging and restaurant.
 Ruby's Inn lies at the base of Bryce Canyon and maintains a series of trails, from easy to strenuous, that connect with the rim and snake through towering stands of evergreen.

HOMESTEAD CROSS-COUNTRY SKI CENTER

(P. 52, B-3, #16) 700 N. Homestead Dr. or 975 West Golf Course Dr., Midway
801-654-1102; 800-327-7220
FACILITIES: 31 groomed km; rentals; lessons; sleigh rides; lodging and restaurant.
 Touring along a golf course which follows the Snake Creek. Hot springs.

JEREMY RANCH

(P. 52, B-3, #17) I-80, exit 143, Kimball Junction
801-649-2700
FACILITIES: 65 groomed km; rentals; restaurant.
 Jeremy Ranch had ceased operations but is expected to reopen on a limited scale.

SHERWOOD HILLS NORDIC CENTER

(P. 52, A-3, #18) Wellsville
801-245-5054
FACILITIES: 20 groomed km (5 skating); rentals; lessons; restaurant.

TAG-A-LONG EXPEDITIONS

(P. 52, D-4, #19) 452 N. Main St., Moab
801-259-8546 800-453-3292
FACILITIES: Unlimited ungroomed km; rentals; lessons; lodging.
 Tag-a-Long offers hut-to-hut ski touring in the red rock country of the La Sal mountains.

WHITE PINE TOURING

(P. 52, B-3, #20) Park City
801-649-8701
FACILITIES: 20 groomed km; rentals; lessons; restaurant.
 Touring is predominantly on the local golf course, a serpentine loop that skirts ponds and climbs a series of gentle swales.

BROMLEY MOUNTAIN

(P.38, E-1, #3) Route 11, Manchester Center
802-824-5522
SEASON: Nov. 15-April 10
ANNUAL SNOWFALL: 150″
TERRAIN: 35 trails over 160 acres; longest run, 2.5 mi.; ◆ 31%; ▪ 34%; ● 35%.
LIFTS: 9 (1 quad, 5 doubles, 3 surface); capacity, 9,045 per hour.
SUMMIT: 3,284′
VERTICAL: 1,334′
OTHER ACTIVITIES: Snowboarding; NASTAR.
FEATURES: Snowmaking 84%; ski school; restaurant; child care; rentals.

Bromley is beloved by fair weather souls. It's the only resort in Vermont that faces south, meaning temperatures are as much as 10 degrees higher than at neighboring areas (and skiers tan better). It's also big with families, who love ego-stroking cruisers like Thruway and West Meadow, and the innovative Ski Learning Center that specializes in getting tots started. Teen boarders rave about the Jib terrain park; snowboarding guru Jake Burton began testing here and at neighboring Stratton. But Bromley has a mean side, too—the ferocious East Side, that is, with menacing steeps like the bronco busting Pabst Peril, Havoc, and Stargazer.

BURKE MOUNTAIN

(P. 38, B-3, #4) Mountain Road, East Burke
802-626-3305
SEASON: Nov. 25-April 7
ANNUAL SNOWFALL: 170″
TERRAIN: 30 trails over 145 acres; longest run, 3.5 mi.; ◆ 30%; ▪ 40%; ● 30%.
LIFTS: 5 (1 quad, 1 double, 3 surface); capacity, 4,400 per hour.
SUMMIT: 3,200′
VERTICAL: 2,000′
ACTIVITIES: Snowboarding.
FEATURES: Snowmaking 35%; ski school; restaurants; child care; rentals.
▶NORDIC: 60 groomed km; rentals; lessons.

Burke is best known for its Burke Mountain Academy, perhaps the USA's foremost racing school, which has turned out Olympic medalists like Diane Roffe-Steinrotter. But you don't have to be Tommy Moe to appreciate the skiing, which is primarily upper intermediate. A series of slender squiggles run down the mountain. The Nordic trails are often deserted, and their snow tends to last longer. A new policy slashed lift ticket prices for everyone across the board.

COCHRAN SKI AREA

(P. 38, B-1, #5) RD 2, Richmond
802-434-2479
TRAILS, 6; LIFTS, 4; VERTICAL, 500′.

JAY PEAK RESORT

(P. 38, A-2, #6) Route 242, Jay
802-988-2611; 800-451-4449 (snow)
SEASON: Nov. 1-May 1
ANNUAL SNOWFALL: 309″
TERRAIN: 50 trails over 325 acres; longest run, 3 mi.; ◆ 25%; ▪ 55%; ● 20%.
LIFTS: 6 (1 tram, 1 quad, 1 triple, 1 double, 2 surface); capacity, 7,500 per hour.
SUMMIT: 3,968′
VERTICAL: 2,153′
ACTIVITIES: Snowboarding; ice skating; snowshoeing.
FEATURES: Snowmaking 80%; ski school; restaurants; child care; rentals.
▶NORDIC: 20 groomed km; rentals; lessons.

Just stateside of the Canadian border, Quebecois-owned Jay Peak boasts a cosmopolitan ambiance. Indeed, French is prevalently spoken in the public areas of the slopeside Hotel Jay. The cognoscenti come here for the gobs of snow and some of the best tree skiing in the East. The area has been trying to keep pace with the demand, cutting two to five new glade runs annually the past few years. (If you want fresh powder, better catch that first tram at 8:30!) Timbuktu and Beaver Pond are two of the most popular, with Ullr's Dream ideal for entry-level tree skiing. Looking for cruisers? Head for the Vermonter off the tram or the occasionally bumpy Can-Am off the Bonaventure chair. Mogulmeisters love the narrow, steep U.N. and Haynes. Boarders also cavort on a half pipe; gliders will enjoy the stunning views.

KILLINGTON SKI RESORT

(P. 38, D-2, #7) Killington Road, Killington
802-773-1330; 802-422-3261 (snow)
SEASON: Oct. 31-June 1
ANNUAL SNOWFALL: 244″
TERRAIN: 158 trails over 854 acres; longest run, 10.2 mi.; ◆ 32%; ▪ 18%; ● 50%.
LIFTS: 19 (1 high-speed gondola, 7 quads, 4 triples, 5 doubles, 2 surface); capacity, 36,627 per hour.
SUMMIT: 4,200′
VERTICAL: 3,175′
ACTIVITIES: Snowboarding.
FEATURES: Snowmaking 63%; ski school; restaurants; child care; rentals.

Killington is the Big Kahuna of the East, logging the most "mosts" in nearly every category dear to skiers. But it refuses to rest on its laurels; the $10 million in improvements for 1995 include replacing the original four-passenger gondola with an eight-passenger model, touted as the world's fastest, and cutting three new trails in the Needle's Eye sector. The previous year owners invested $5 million in cosmetic changes, expanding the base areas and increasing snowmaking by 38%. Killington really has it all, from tremendous variety of terrain to an equally varied nightlife. If you've never been to Killington, take the free mountain tour offered every morning at 9:45 A.M. The guides will give you a rundown on the six mountains and five base areas. Beginners have a vast playground here: 66 trails to choose from, including a 10-mile wanderer. Some of the best terrain is accessed via the Rams Head chair. Intermediates will love the smooth runs in the Snowdon and Needle's Eye areas; stronger skiers can try recently added terrain on Skye Peak (where if you're a Superstar, you'll get an Ovation). Experts will find few real tests but will enjoy the consistent pitch on the Killington Peak runs (Cascade, Down Draft, Big Dipper) before heading for one of ultimate thrills in skiing: the man-sized bumps on Outer Limits. These sit directly under the Bear Mountain quad. If in need of a warm-up beforehand, experts should try billowing down the other flanks of Bear Mountain on Wildfire or Devil's Fiddle. Drawbacks? Despite Killington's size, lift lines and bottlenecks are common on weekends. The sprawling six-mountain configuration can mean a lot of poling, especially if you don't study the trail map. The town is hardly upscale—but wait, that's an advantage. As one of skidom's most creative packagers, Killington can offer significant savings. Where else in the East can you ski from October to June?

LYNDON OUTING CLUB

(P. 38, B-3, #8) Lyndonville
802-626-8465
TRAILS, 7; LIFTS, 3; VERTICAL, 400′.

MAD RIVER GLEN

(P. 38, C-2, #9) Route 17, Waitsfield
802-496-3551; 802-496-2001 (snow)
SEASON: Dec. 15-April 15
ANNUAL SNOWFALL: 200″
TERRAIN: 33 trails over 87 acres; longest run, 3.5 mi.; ◆ 35%; ▪ 40%; ● 25%.
LIFTS: 4 (3 doubles, 1 single); capacity, 3,000 per hour.
SUMMIT: 3,600′
VERTICAL: 2,000′
ACTIVITIES: None.
FEATURES: Snowmaking 15%; ski school; restaurants; child care; rentals.

This is it: The East's ultimate test. Mad River Glen may not be the largest ski area, but it's certainly among the scariest. It doesn't challenge experts, it dares them—with a motto, "Ski it if you can." Even the green trails here would rank blue elsewhere. Mad River is a throwback (it won't make snow and has a single chair!); aficionados fervently believe this is skiing the way it was meant to be—no frills, just you and the mountain, mano a mano. Don't take the solo chair to the top if you have to think twice (only real experts can stand the lines anyway). Strong intermediates can ski anywhere off the Sunnyside chair; not even Birdland, supposedly the beginners' area, will bore them. And Mad River may seem to have invented tree skiing, with slinky runs like Lynx and The Glades. From the top? The truly suicidal can ask for directions to the out-of-bounds Paradise (watch out for the entrance, an eight-foot frozen waterfall) and the Octopus' Garden. The merely pathological can attack the man-sized bumps of Chute or the elevator shaft called Fall Line. If you have second thoughts, you can always bail out on Antelope or Catamount—they're just plain steep.

MAPLE VALLEY SKI AREA

(P.38, E-2, #10) Route 30, West Dummerston
802-254-6083
SEASON: Dec. 15-March 31
ANNUAL SNOWFALL: 150″
TERRAIN: 15 trails over 53 acres; longest run, 1.5 mi.; ◆ 20%; ▪ 60%; ● 20%.
LIFTS: 3 (2 doubles, 1 surface); capacity, 2,500 per hour.
SUMMIT: NA
VERTICAL: 1,000′
ACTIVITIES: Snowboarding; NASTAR; night skiing.
FEATURES: Snowmaking 95%; ski school; restaurant; child care; rentals.

This pleasant family area plans to upgrade its facilities and expand the terrain. Locals prize its solid cruisers; boarders appreciate the half pipe.

MIDDLEBURY COLLEGE SNOW BOWL

(P. 38, C-1, #11) Middlebury
802-388-4356
SEASON: Dec. 1-April 1
ANNUAL SNOWFALL: 200″
TERRAIN: 14 trails over 100 acres; longest run, 2.5 mi.; ◆ 33%; ▪ 34%; ● 33%.
LIFTS: 3 (1 triple, 2 doubles); capacity, 3,400 per hour.
SUMMIT: 2,520′
VERTICAL: 1,020′
ACTIVITIES: Snowboarding.
FEATURES: Snowmaking 35%; ski school; restaurant; rentals.

Yup, Middlebury's race team is so good the college built a ski area for it. But everyone can enjoy the varied runs, named after trustees, with Ross and Youngman earning high marks as bruising steeps.

MT. SNOW/HAYSTACK RESORT

(P. 38, E-2, #12) Mountain Road, Route 100, Mount Snow
802-464-3333; 802-464-2151 (snow)
SEASON: Nov. 1-May 1
ANNUAL SNOWFALL: 150″
TERRAIN: 127 trails over 603 acres; longest run, 2.5 mi.; ♦ 18%; ■ 61%; ● 21%.
LIFTS: 24 (1 high-speed quad, 1 quad, 9 triples, 10 doubles, 3 surface); capacity, 35,690 per hour.
SUMMIT: 3,600′
VERTICAL: 1,700′
ACTIVITIES: Snowboarding; sleigh rides.
FEATURES: Snowmaking 82%; ski school; restaurants; child care; rentals.

A monster resort got bigger when Mt. Snow leased neighboring Haystack in 1991. A shuttle bus now runs continuously between the two. Owners have an option to buy or extend the lease in 1994; and Haystack is not expected to revert to independent status. Mt. Snow probably comes closest to the skier's ideal image of Vermont. Nearby Dover and Wilmington are classic Yankee villages with white-steepled churches, village greens, lovingly restored farmhouses, and antiques and crafts shops made for browsing. This is a solidly intermediate mountain, noted for its perfectly groomed cruisers, wide by New England standards. The trails get progressively more difficult as you look right. Lower intermediates will waltz down the runs in the Sunbrook and Carinthia sections. Slightly steeper cruisers include Ego Alley, Sundance, and Snowdance. Skiers seeking more challenge should head for the seat belt moguls of Beartrap, or the North Face, whose runs aren't as fearsome as their names: Ripcord, Jaws of Death, Freefall, and Plummet. Mt. Snow is also a haven for shredders, who jib and bonk to their hearts' content all over the Un Blanco Gulch snowboard park, a 2,500-foot obstacle course including a half pipe, banks, barrel jumps, and wedges galore. Families will adore the 43 trails and 188 acres at less-crowded Haystack. The separated lower mountain appeals to novices, while its upper mountain features laid-back cruisers and the recently added Witches black runs. With accessibility, great grooming, quaint surroundings, and no glitz or attitude, Mt. Snow/Haystack keeps recreational skiers coming back for more.

NORTHEAST SKI SLOPES

(P. 38, C-3, #13) RD 1, East Corinth
802-439-5789
TRAILS, 1; LIFTS, 1; VERTICAL, 250′.

NORWICH UNIVERSITY SKI AREA

(P. 38, C-2, #14) Northfield
802-485-2145
SEASON: Dec. 15-March 15 (open weekends only or by appointment)
ANNUAL SNOWFALL: 50″
TERRAIN: NA trails over NA acres; longest run, NA; ♦ 10%; ■ 60%; ● 30%.
LIFTS: 2 (1 double, 1 surface); capacity, 1,200 per hour.
SUMMIT: 1,700′
VERTICAL: 902′
ACTIVITIES: Snowboarding.
FEATURES: Ski school; restaurant; rentals.
▶NORDIC: 8 groomed km; rentals.

This university training area is open to the public; the slopes are empty and enjoyable for practice. Since it relies on natural snow, the hours are spotty.

OKEMO RESORT

(P. 38, D-2, #15) Off Route 103, Ludlow
802-228-4041; 802-228-5222 (snow)
SEASON: Nov. 7-April 20
ANNUAL SNOWFALL: 200″
TERRAIN: 72 trails over 400 acres; longest run, 4.5 mi.; ♦ 20%; ■ 50%; ● 30%.
LIFTS: 10 (1 high-speed quad, 5 quads, 2 triples, 2 surface); capacity, 19,000 per hour.
SUMMIT: 3,300′
VERTICAL: 2,150′
ACTIVITIES: Snowboarding; NASTAR.
FEATURES: Snowmaking 95%; ski school; restaurants; child care; rentals.

No area in the East works harder to improve itself and please its loyal clientele. Okemo installed a new lift each year between 1983-1992. In 1993, it concentrated on refurbishing base facilities and increasing snowmaking. For 1994 and 1995, plans included adding three new lifts, five trails, and a snowboard park. The service is among the friendliest and most efficient in the Northeast. The snow is as soft as a baby's bottom, aiding and abetting a fine ski school in improving skiers' skills. Beginners will feel like intermediates here, intermediates like experts and experts, well, they may feel like moving on after a day. Even the black runs here are more a midnight blue. The toughest skiing is off the Glades Summit quad, on Double Black Diamond and Outrage. Intermediates can tackle anything else, including the bumps of Rimrock and Ledges, both wide enough to traverse if need be. Lower intermediates will have a field day off the Solitude Peak quad and Green Ridge triple, while boarders can run riot over the mountain and a half-pipe. Nearly everyone sports a goofy grin. And why not? Okemo knows the value of the old adage, "The customer's always right."

PICO SKI AREA

(P. 38, D-2, #16) HCR 34, off Route 4, Rutland
802-775-4346
SEASON: Nov. 7-May 1
ANNUAL SNOWFALL: 200″
TERRAIN: 40 trails over 200 acres; longest run, 2.5 mi.; ♦ 30%; ■ 50%; ● 20%.
LIFTS: 9 (2 high-speed quads, 2 triples, 3 doubles, 2 surface); capacity, 12,158 per hour.
SUMMIT: 4,000′
VERTICAL: 2,000′
ACTIVITIES: Snowboarding; NASTAR.
FEATURES: Snowmaking 82%; ski school; restaurants; child care; rentals.

Like rooting for underdogs? Low-key Pico's for you. Just a hop, skip, and ski jump away from Killington, the two areas have entered into sometimes fractious negotiations over the past several years. At the last minute, something always happens to the proposed merger and Pico asserts its feisty independence. It has plenty to offer in Killington's shadow. The area boasts spectacular vistas from the summit; long, winding uncrowded slopes; and a good mix of terrain from the primo cruiser, 49er, to the supreme bump run, Summit Glade.

QUECHEE LAKES

(P. 38, D-2, #17) River Road, Quechee
802-295-9356
TRAILS, 8; LIFTS, 2; VERTICAL, 650′.
▶NORDIC: 8 groomed km

A semi-private club, Quechee sells lift tickets on a limited basis. The runs are wide, groomed, and very lonely indeed. The Nordic trail meanders around the golf course, though there is also an ungroomed "wilderness" track.

SMUGGLERS' NOTCH SKI AREA

(P. 38, B-2, #18) Route 108, Smugglers' Notch
802-644-8851; 800-451-8752 (snow)
SEASON: Nov. 27-April 12
ANNUAL SNOWFALL: 260″
TERRAIN: 56 trails over 236 acres; longest run, 3.5 mi.; ♦ 34%; ■ 46%; ● 20%.
LIFTS: 6 (4 doubles, 2 surface); capacity, 4,200 per hour.
SUMMIT: 3,640′
VERTICAL: 2,610′
ACTIVITIES: Snowboarding; NASTAR; sleigh rides.
FEATURES: Snowmaking 57%; ski school; restaurants; child care; rentals.
▶NORDIC: Sugar Shack Nordic Center; 23 groomed km; rentals; lessons.

Smugglers' Notch is consistently rated one of the USA's top family resorts. Its Alice in Wonderland child care facility is second to none in the East. The creative ski camps appeal to all ages; and Smuggler's Notch even has an acclaimed Teen

Courtesy: Michigan Travel Bureau (see p. 113).

Central, which offers a disco and special programs from snow volleyball to chariot tubing. The raves begin with the model self-contained village—which, all within a short walk, offers everything from spa, indoor tennis courts, and pool to ice rinks, restaurants, and lodging. The three mountains have something for the whole family, too, as well as northern Vermont's biggest vertical. Morse is for those mighty mites and novices of all sizes. Sterling is the choice of savvy intermediates, including one mogul mine in Exhibition and an adult terrain garden that approximates variable snow conditions and terrain. And Madonna offers world-class steeps like F.I.S. and Freefall. It has a surprising, hidden glade that runs off the backside toward Stowe, along with posted tree gardens like Doc Dempsey's. Day-trippers and stronger skiers should bypass the main village entirely and head up the hill to the top parking lot, a quick stroll from the Sterling Mountain lift.

STOWE MOUNTAIN RESORT

(P. 38, B-2, #19) Mountain Road, Stowe
802-253-7311
SEASON: Nov. 15-April 20
ANNUAL SNOWFALL: 250″
TERRAIN: 45 trails over 480 acres; longest run, 3.7 mi.; ◆ 25%; ■ 59%; ● 16%.
LIFTS: 11 (1 high-speed quad, 1 gondola, 1 triple, 6 doubles, 2 surface); capacity, 12,326 per hour.
SUMMIT: 3,750′
VERTICAL: 2,360′
ACTIVITIES: Snowboarding; night skiing.
FEATURES: Snowmaking 73%; ski school; restaurants; child care; rentals.
▶NORDIC: Mt. Mansfield Nordic Center; 40 groomed km (with skating lane), 40 ungroomed; rentals; lessons.
An ambitious five-year plan has revitalized this grande dame among eastern resorts, with a high-speed eight-passenger gondola, recontoured trails to disperse traffic, increased snowmaking, and more efficient grooming among the most notable additions. The trails are sinuous New England classics dancing in and out of thick stands of spruce to reveal ravishing valley views. Most of Spruce Peak is ideal for intermediates, especially off the Forerunner quad; Lord, in particular, makes any skiing commoner feel like an aristocrat. Toll Road, a scenic, meandering run, has probably converted thousands to the sport. Novices also have sizable acreage at the bottom of Spruce Peak. But Stowe's reputation among ski fanatics is for the mogulled steeps on Mt. Mansfield. The fabled Front Four (Goat, Starr, Liftline, and National) are one of the litmus tests of skiing, especially

when they're icy. If you're not sure you're ready, try Nose Dive, then the usually groomed National. Boarders can show off on a 600-foot half pipe and a terrain park. The new night skiing operation is already among the most extensive in the East. The cross-country system is highly rated; and several other excellent Nordic centers in the vicinity make Stowe a mecca for gliders and skaters.

STRATTON MOUNTAIN RESORT

(P. 38, E-2, #20) Stratton Mtn. Access Road, off Route 30, Stratton Mtn.
802-297-2200; 802-297-4211 (snow)
SEASON: Nov. 15-April 22
ANNUAL SNOWFALL: 170″
TERRAIN: 92 trails over 476 acres; longest run, 3 mi.; ◆◆ 20%; ◆ 30%; ■ 27%; ● 23%.
LIFTS: 14 (1 gondola, 4 quads, 1 triple, 6 doubles, 2 surface); capacity, 20,020 per hour.
SUMMIT: 3,936′
VERTICAL: 2,003′
ACTIVITIES: Snowboarding; NASTAR; ice skating; sleigh rides.
FEATURES: Snowmaking 58%; ski school; restaurants; child care; rentals.
▶NORDIC: Sun Bowl Touring Center; 802-297-1880; 20 groomed km, 2 km skating lane, 50 km backcountry; rentals; lessons.
Stratton has a reputation as a "Yuppie Hill," in part because of its slick modern facilities and ultra-manicured slopes. As if to combat its softy image, Stratton has opened more demanding terrain like Bear Down and Freefall, which feature mammoth moguls. Otherwise most of the trails are so impeccably groomed, you'd swear it was by hand, and the black diamonds are graded on a curve that ensures skiers will pass with flying colors. The upper half provides more advanced cruisers like Lift Line, and narrower traditional runs off the Grizzly Chair. The flowing Sun Bowl is another favorite, especially on bitter days since it's on the leeward side with a southern exposure. Novices have their own huge Ski Learning Park. . . . Shredders see Stratton as hallowed ground; this is where Jake Burton tested the first board. The park features a lengthy half pipe and lots of banks, spines, and dips. The heavily wooded Nordic trails are suitable for all levels; the center also offers ski touring into the National Forest. The mountain village sports an appealing faux-Tyrolean design. And nearby Manchester is a shopaholic's dream, with everything from factory outlets to craft shops.

SUGARBUSH RESORT

(P. 38, C-2, #21) Off Route 100, Warren

802-583-2381; 802-583-7669 (snow)
SEASON: Nov. 1-May 1
ANNUAL SNOWFALL: 252″
TERRAIN: 110 trails over 400 acres; longest run, 2.5 mi.; ◆ 28%; ■ 49%; ● 23%.
LIFTS: 16 (1 high-speed quad, 2 quads, 3 triples, 6 doubles, 4 surface); capacity, 15,018 per hour.
SUMMIT: 4,135′
VERTICAL: 2,600′
ACTIVITIES: Snowboarding; NASTAR; sledding.
FEATURES: Snowmaking 50%; ski school; restaurants; child care; rentals.
▶NORDIC: Sugarbush Inn; Sugarbush Access Road; 802-583-2301; 20 groomed km, 5 ungroomed; rentals; lessons.
Once dubbed Mascara Mountain, Sugarbush was the East's first ski playground for the rich and famous—as still evidenced by its clutch of deluxe condos and gourmet restaurants. But management neglected it for many years while other resorts eclipsed Sugarbush not only in fashion but skier services. That has changed with a vengeance the past few years, as several million dollars have been invested in much-needed refurbishment and improvement. Chronic problems addressed were the plodding lifts (three new quads, including a high-speed, were installed on Sugarbush North) and inadequate snowmaking, which has nearly doubled. As a result, Sugarbush has made a comeback, with skiers rediscovering its superlative views and superior blend of terrain. There are two mountains (three if you include the independent Mad River Glen right down the valley). Intermediates can romp at will over Sugarbush North, the former Glen Ellen; its Rim Run ranks among the East's top cruisers, with stunning vistas of Lake Champlain on one side and the Green Mountains on the other. Exterminator and Bravo, the black runs, make a good challenge. Sugarbush South is an enormous bowl, with the terrain generally becoming harder as you look left. The major exception is the narrow steep off the Castlerock lift, which requires strong legs and a stronger stomach. Other classic thigh-burners include the double diamond bump run Stein's Way. Beginners have an expansive section to the extreme right off the Gate House lift, which also accesses low intermediate runs. Intermediates can explore the entire center of the mountain (avoiding only the short steeps dropping off under the Heaven's Gate chair), with a series of groomed boulevards like Jester, Snowball, and Domino. The Nordic trails skirt beaver ponds and wind through apple orchards, old logging roads, and spruce stands.

SUICIDE SIX SKI AREA

(P. 38, D-2, #22) Stage Road, 4 mi. N of Woodstock
802-457-6661
SEASON: Dec. 15-March 31
ANNUAL SNOWFALL: 180″
TERRAIN: 19 trails over 100 acres; longest run, 1 mi.; ◆ 30%; ■ 40%; ● 30%.
LIFTS: 3 (2 doubles, 1 surface); capacity, 3,000 per hour.
SUMMIT: 1,200′
VERTICAL: 650′
ACTIVITIES: Snowboarding.
FEATURES: Snowmaking 50%; ski school; restaurant; rentals.
▶NORDIC: Woodstock Ski Touring Center; 802-457-6674; 60 groomed km (25 skating); rentals; lessons.
Suicide Six is operated by the venerable Woodstock Inn, in the Norman Rockwell town of the same name, a picture postcard vision of white steepled churches and Georgian houses. The mountain claims a unique piece of ski history itself, as home of the USA's oldest continuously operating rope tow, installed in 1937. Though small, it features a fine blend of terrain, typified by the scenic Easy Mile for beginners and the super-steep The Face. Vermont's first tree farm is the locale of one of its top-rated Nordic centers, with varied trails for all abilities, many along 19th century carriage roads. While the area has been designated as a national historic park, the center will continue to operate.

NORDIC

AMISKI SKI AREA

(P. 38, B-2, #23) 97 S. Main St., Waterbury
802-244-5677
FACILITIES: 15 groomed km, with skating lane; rentals; lessons; ice skating; lodging and restaurant; night skiing (1.5 km lit).

BLUEBERRY HILL

(P. 38, C-1, #24) RD 3, Goshen
802-247-6735
FACILITIES: 72 groomed km; rentals; lessons; lodging and restaurant.
Nestled amid the glorious Green Mountain National Forest, the secluded, heavily wooded trails offer something for all levels.

BLUEBERRY LAKE CROSS-COUNTRY

(P. 38, C-2, #25) Plunkton Road, Warren
802-496-6687
FACILITIES: 23 groomed km (with skating lane); rentals; lessons; night skiing (1.5 km lit).
With 100% snowmaking, Blueberry Lake can guarantee good skiing no matter what the weather.

CAMEL'S HUMP
(P. 38, B-2, #26) Handy Road, Huntington
802-434-2704
FACILITIES: 35 groomed km (with 30 skating), 35 ungroomed; rentals; lessons; snowshoeing; restaurant.
Stunning mountain and valley views are one reason to come here. Norwegian Olympic gold medalist Babben Enger, who has taught there part-time, is another. Trails vary from gentle ridge runs to heavily wooded hills.

CATAMOUNT FAMILY CENTER
(P. 38, B-1, #27) 421 Governor Chittenden Rd., Williston
802-879-6001
FACILITIES: 30 groomed km (with skating lane), 10 ungroomed; rentals; lessons; ice skating; restaurant; night skiing (3 km lit).

CRAFTSBURY NORDIC CENTER
(P. 38, B-2, #28) Craftsbury Common
800-729-7751
FACILITIES: 120 groomed km (with skating lane), 50 ungroomed; rentals; lessons; ice skating; lodging and restaurant; night skiing (5 km lit).
One of the most complete Nordic centers in the state, with a mix of woods, meadow and lake trails. Twenty percent are beginner, with 40% each for intermediates and experts. The charming 1850 country inn of the same name also offers guided inn-to-inn touring.

EDSON HILL
(P. 38, B-2, #29) Rural Route 1, Stowe
802-253-8954
FACILITIES: 42 groomed km (20 skating); rentals; lessons; winter horseback riding; sleigh rides; snowshoeing; lodging and restaurant.

FOX RUN CROSS-COUNTRY
(P. 38, D-2, #30) Fox Lane, Routes 100 & 103, Ludlow
802-228-8871
FACILITIES: 18 groomed km (15 skating); rentals; lessons; restaurant.

GRAFTON PONDS
(P. 38, E-2, #31) Route 121, Main Street, Grafton
802-843-2231
FACILITIES: 30 groomed km; rentals; lessons; ice skating; sleigh rides; lodging and restaurant.

GREEN MOUNTAIN TOURING CENTER
(P. 38, C-2, #32) Randolph
802-728-5575
FACILITIES: 50 groomed km; rentals; lessons; lodging and restaurant.

GREEN TRAILS
(P. 38, C-2, #33) Brookfield
802-276-3412
FACILITIES: 35 groomed km; rentals; lessons; lodging and restaurant.

HAZEN'S NOTCH CROSS-COUNTRY
(P. 38, A-2, #34) Route 58, Montgomery Center
802-326-4708
FACILITIES: 30 groomed km (5 skating), 15 ungroomed; rentals; lessons; lodging and restaurant.

HERMITAGE TOURING CENTER
(P. 38, E-2, #35) Coldbrook Road, Wilmington
802-464-3511
FACILITIES: 40 groomed km (with skating lane), 10 ungroomed; rentals; lessons; lodging and restaurant.
The varied terrain is ideal for all levels, winding past streams, beaver ponds and pine forests all the way to the Mount Snow ski area.

HIGHLAND LODGE
(P. 38, B-3, #36) Craftsbury Road, Greensboro
802-533-2647
FACILITIES: 60 groomed km (30 skating); rentals; lessons; lodging and restaurant.

HILDENE
(P. 38, E-1, #37) Route 7A S, Manchester
802-362-1788
FACILITIES: 15 groomed km; rentals; lessons; restaurant.
The 21 mostly wooded trails are notable for traversing the former estate of Robert Todd Lincoln.

LAKE MOREY INN RESORT
(P. 38, C-3, #38) Lake Morey Road, Fairlee
802-333-4311
FACILITIES: 26 groomed km; rentals; lessons; ice skating; sleigh rides; snowmobiling; spa; lodging and restaurant.

MOUNTAIN MEADOWS
(P. 38, D-2, #39) Thundering Brook Road, Killington
802-775-7077; 800-221-0598
FACILITIES: 40 groomed km (with skating lane), 20 ungroomed; rentals; lessons; lodging and restaurant; night skiing (1.5 km lit).

MOUNTAIN TOP CROSS-COUNTRY
(P. 38, D-1, #40) Mountain Top Road, Chittenden
802-483-6089 800-445-2100
FACILITIES: 70 groomed km (with skating lane), 40 ungroomed; rentals; lessons; ice skating; sleigh rides; lodging and restaurant.
Mountain Top's 1,300-acre resort retreat has wonderful food and accommodations, and a sugar house where it bottles its own maple syrup. The excellent, balanced trail system winds through dense spruce and open meadows, like the expansive playground Interfield, while snowmaking allows Mountain Top to stay open nearly as long as neighboring Killington. The resort actually offered its first prepared track in 1964, five years before Trapp Family Lodge (which is usually credited as the first in the USA), but who's counting?

NORDIC INN CROSS-COUNTRY
(P. 38, E-1, #41) Route 11, Landgrove
802-824-6444
FACILITIES: 26 groomed km; rentals; lessons; lodging and restaurant.

OLE'S CROSS-COUNTRY CENTER
(P. 38, C-2, #42) Airport Road, Warren
802-496-3430
FACILITIES: 35 groomed km; rentals; lessons; restaurant.

RIKERT'S
(P. 38, C-2, #43) Ripton
802-388-2759
FACILITIES: 42 groomed km (15 skating); rentals; lessons; restaurant; night skiing (3.5 km lit).

ROUND BARN FARM
(P. 39, C-2, #44) East Warren Road, Waitsfield
802-496-6661
FACILITIES: 25 groomed km (12 skating); rentals; lessons; snowshoeing; lodging and restaurant.
The farm has been converted into a delightful and posh bed and breakfast; the trails boast equally resplendent views.

SITZMARK
(P. 38, E-2, #45) East Dover Road, Wilmington
802-464-5498
FACILITIES: 20 groomed km (8 skating), 20 ungroomed; rentals; lessons; lodging and restaurant.

TATER HILL CROSS-COUNTRY CENTER
(P. 38, E-2, #46) RFD 1, Chester
802-875-2517
FACILITIES: 25 groomed km, 10 ungroomed; rentals; lessons; restaurant.

TIMBER CREEK CROSS-COUNTRY
(P. 38, E-2, #47) Route 100, Wilmington
802-464-0999
FACILITIES: 16 groomed km; rentals; lessons; spa; lodging and restaurant.

TOPNOTCH
(P. 38, B-2, #48) Stowe
802-253-8585
FACILITIES: 40 groomed km; rentals; lessons; snowshoeing; spa; indoor tennis; lodging and restaurant.

TRAIL HEAD CROSS-COUNTRY SKI AREA
(P. 38, D-2, #49) Route 100, Stockbridge
802-746-8038
FACILITIES: 35 groomed km (with skating lane), 25 ungroomed; rentals; lessons; restaurant.

TRAPP FAMILY LODGE-CROSS-COUNTRY
(P. 38, B-2, #50) 42 Trapp Hill Rd., Stowe
802-253-8511
FACILITIES: 60 groomed km (48 with skating lanes), 40 ungroomed; rentals; lessons; sleigh rides; lodging and restaurant.
Ever wondered what happened to the von Trapps after *The Sound of Music*? They settled in Vermont and are credited with opening the USA's first Nordic center. It still ranks among the best after over a quarter century in operation. Trails range from gently sloping meadows to hilly forest, with up to a 1,600-foot vertical. The lodge is Tyrolean in look, naturally, and the ambiance cosmopolitan.

THE VIKING SKI TOURING CENTER
(P. 38, E-2, #51) Little Pond Road, Londonderry
802-824-3933
FACILITIES: 30 groomed km, 15 ungroomed; rentals; lessons; ice skating; lodging and restaurant; night skiing (3 km lit).
One of the oldest ski touring centers in the USA, Viking has trails for every level.

CONTINUED ON NEXT PAGE

VIRGINIA

Virginia's ski resorts lie nestled in the rugged Allegheny Blue Ridge Mountains, whose bewitching scenery is on display in Shenandoah National Park. The surprising amount of snow blanketing those towering peaks is complemented by state-of-the-art snowmaking. The areas double as world-class resorts, attracting an intriguing blend of families, foreigners, and Old World money. When snow cover permits, there is incomparable gliding through Shenandoah and along the Appalachian Trail. ❄ Historic Charlottesville is close by, where you can tour the 18th century mansions and Thomas Jefferson's University of Virginia, then watch the Virginia Cavaliers on the basketball court.

ALPINE

BRYCE RESORT
(P. 17, C-7, #1) Route 263, Basye
703-856-2121
SEASON: Dec. 1-March 15
ANNUAL SNOWFALL: 30"
TERRAIN: 6 trails over 25 acres; longest run, 3,500'; ◆ 10%; ■ 60%; ● 30%.
LIFTS: 4 (2 doubles, 2 surface); capacity, 2,500 per hour.
SUMMIT: 1,750'
VERTICAL: 500'
ACTIVITIES: Snowboarding; NASTAR; night skiing.
FEATURES: Snowmaking 100%; ski school; restaurants; rentals. The four main slopes at Bryce are roughly equal in length, allowing better skiers to enjoy a continuous vertical run, with White Lightning and Bootlegger the most popular cruisers. There is one short steep pitch dubbed Hangover, and the beginners' area is separate. The Horst Locher Ski School is highly rated; several learning packages are offered to entice families to this top-calibre destination resort nestled in the picturesque Shenandoah Valley.

THE HOMESTEAD SKI AREA
(P. 16, D-5, #2) State Route 220, Hot Springs
703-839-7721
SEASON: Dec. 15-March 15
ANNUAL SNOWFALL: 50"
TERRAIN: 10 trails over 45 acres; longest run, 4,200'; ◆ 30%; ■ 40%; ● 30%.
LIFTS: 5 (1 double, 4 surface); capacity, 3,000 per hour.
SUMMIT: 2,500'
VERTICAL: 700'
ACTIVITIES: Snowboarding; NASTAR; ice skating; sleigh rides; night skiing.
FEATURES: Snowmaking 100%; ski school; restaurants; rentals. One of the premier resorts in the South, noted for pampering service, deluxe accommodations and full spa facilities (including famed hot springs), the Homestead also ranks in the top echelon of ski areas. One reason is the acclaimed Sepp Kober Ski School, whose Austrian instructors contribute to the cosmopolitan ambiance. Another is the extensive beginners' area served by three lifts. The skiing is solidly intermediate, with Main Slope the standout cruiser, although there are some steeper pitches such as The Glades run.

MASSANUTTEN RESORT
(P. 17, D-6, #3) Route 644, Harrisonburg
703-289-9441
SEASON: Dec. 1-March 31
ANNUAL SNOWFALL: 30"
TERRAIN: 14 trails over 68 acres; longest run, 4,100'; ◆ 24%; ■ 38%; ● 38%.
LIFTS: 5 (1 quad, 3 doubles, 1 surface); capacity, 6,350 per hour.
SUMMIT: 2,880'
VERTICAL: 1,110'
ACTIVITIES: Snowboarding; NASTAR; night skiing.
FEATURES: Snowmaking 100%; ski school; restaurants; rentals. Another highly regarded four-season resort, Massanutten recently opened new advanced terrain served by Virginia's first quad, adding more than 300 feet of vertical. The two runs, Diamond Jim and Paradise, offer an uninterrupted 1,100-foot drop over three-quarters of a mile. The narrow Dixie Dare and wide but fairly steep Rebel Yell also will have strong skiers screaming for more, while lower intermediates can cruise down Mass Transit and Pace Setter. Beginners have the Southern Comfort learning area, then graduate to the isolated novice section composed of Turkey Trot, Geronimo and Tail Feather.

WINTERGREEN
(P. 17, E-6, #4) Route 664, Wintergreen
804-325-2200; 804-325-2100 (snow)
SEASON: Dec. 11-March 21
ANNUAL SNOWFALL: 40"
TERRAIN: 17 trails over 83 acres; longest run, 4,450'; ◆ 38%; ■ 42%; ● 20%.
LIFTS: 5 (4 triples, 1 double); capacity, 8,200 per hour.
SUMMIT: 3,515'
VERTICAL: 1,003'
ACTIVITIES: Snowboarding; night skiing.
FEATURES: Snowmaking 100%; ski school; restaurants; rentals. Yet another luxurious vacation retreat, Wintergreen still claims the largest total area in Virginia despite being eclipsed by Massanutten's increased vertical. It's a summit ski area, meaning you ski down from the lodge and lifts take you back home. Massanutten may claim the most beautiful setting in the state; The Appalachian Trail winds through its acreage. As for the skiing, it's ideal learning terrain. The Big Acorn area features both wide groomed boulevards and tighter mogul runs. And the Highlands section is tough enough that a ski patroller checks you out before you can stay. In good snow years, gliders can strike out for the nearby Blue Ridge Parkway.

NORDIC

MOUNTAIN LAKE RESORT
(P. 17, E-4, #5) Route 700, Mountain Lake
703-626-7121
FACILITIES: 25 groomed km; rentals; lessons; lodging and restaurant. This 19th century lodge commands a breathtaking wilderness area. The trails amble through beech and evergreen forests; a nature preserve; the rolling hills of a golf course, and beside Mountain Lake itself.

CONTINUED FROM LAST PAGE

WHITE HOUSE
(P. 38, E-2, #52) Route 9, Wilmington
800-541-2135
FACILITIES: 43 groomed km; rentals; lessons; snowshoeing; lodging and restaurant. The White House is a grand 1915 Edwardian mansion converted into a traditional country inn. The system traverses high alpine meadows and forested valleys, with trails equally distributed in difficulty.

WILD WINGS SKI TOURING CENTER
(P. 38, E-2, #53) North Road, Peru
802-824-6793
FACILITIES: 20 groomed km, 2 ungroomed; rentals; lessons; restaurant.

WILDERNESS TRAILS
(P. 38, D-2, #54) Clubhouse Road, Quechee
802-295-7620
FACILITIES: 12 groomed km, 6 ungroomed; rentals; lessons; sleigh rides; lodging and restaurant. The associated Bed & Breakfast (Quechee Inn at Marshland Farm) is a restored 1793 house.

WINDHAM HILL INN
(P. 38, E-2, #55) West Townsend
802-874-4080
FACILITIES: 10 groomed km, unlimited backcountry; rentals; lessons; lodging and restaurant. Windham Hill is considered a first-rate learning center, though facilities are available to guests only.

A land of fragrant forests and craggy snowcapped mountains, the "Evergreen State" is defined by water. The mighty Columbia and Snake rivers mold its southern and eastern borders. The vast Pacific batters the West Coast, while Puget Sound forms a mosaic of sheltered coves and pine-blanketed islands. All that water transforms Washington's towering Cascades into a moisture magnet, coaxing frequent feathery dumps of snow. There are several top ski areas within an hour's drive of Seattle. Or you can glide along hundreds of miles of trails in the glorious Olympic and Mt. Rainier national parks, traversing moraines and glaciers that seem poised to initiate another Ice Age. One of the best networks, the Mt. Tahoma Scenic Trails Association (206-832-4000), offers a 128-km trail system with sterling views of the highest peak in the lower 48. Have a taste for adventure? North Cascade Heli-Skiing (509-996-3272) accesses over 300,000 acres of backcountry skiing in unspoiled Okanogan National Forest. And Rendezvous Outfitters (509-996-2873) runs guided backcountry hut-to-hut tours in the North Cascades. ❄ Washington even offers indoor skiing year-round at Bellevue's Mini Mountain (206-746-7547), where beginners can learn and experts condition themselves on two conveyor-belt treadmill "mountains."

ALPINE

ALPENTAL/ SNOQUALMIE/ SKI ACRES/ HYAK

(P. 53, B-3, #1) Off I-90, Snoqualmie Pass
206-232-8182; 206-434-6364 (Alpental); 434-6363 (Snoqualmie); 434-6400 (Ski Acres); 434-7600 (Hyak); 206-236-1600 (snow)
SEASON: Nov. 15-April 15
ANNUAL SNOWFALL: 170"
TERRAIN: NA trails over 1,916 acres; longest run, 1.5 mi.; ◆ 37%; ■ 43%; ● 20%.
LIFTS: 33 (1 quad, 4 triples, 18 doubles, 10 surface); capacity, 30,140 per hour.
SUMMIT: 5,400'
VERTICAL: 2,200'
ACTIVITIES: Snowboarding; tubing; night skiing.
FEATURES: Ski school; restaurants; rentals.
▶NORDIC: 206-434-6646; 55 groomed km; rentals; lessons; night skiing (5 km lit).
These four interlinked areas hugging spectacular Snoqualmie Pass (just 50 miles from Seattle) are under the same ownership; the price of one lift ticket gets you one of the most varied day areas in the USA. You'll find every kind of skiing at ASSAH (a k a "The Pass" to locals). Alpental boasts twice the vertical of any of the other three, most of it steep and religiously ungroomed. Among its famed—and feared—runs are Widow Maker, Adrenaline, and Internationale. The latter offers your choice of moguls, glade skiing, and chutes during a hairy 2,200-foot ride. True experts will have a (snow) field day at the out-of-bounds unpatrolled Great Scott area, a wonderland of bowls, chutes, ridges and couloirs. . . . Ski Acres provides the best blend, with steep expert runs up top and gentle bunny slopes at the base, punctuated by several joy-riding cruisers. Trails like Easy Rider and Over Easy explain Snoqualmie's reputation as the best place to learn. . . . Hyak is bliss for snowboarders. In addition to a natural half-pipe and an uninterrupted 1,000-foot vertical, the mountain has a habit of creating natural pipes, trenches, and jumps, which groomers studiously avoid. The only drawback to skiing these areas is the low elevation, which promises that skiers will contend with a heavy share of Cascade Crud and slick ice.

BADGER MOUNTAIN

(P. 53, B-4, #2) Off Highway 2, Waterville
509-745-8409
SEASON: Dec. 20-March 1 (weekends only)
ANNUAL SNOWFALL: 100"
TERRAIN: 6 trails over NA acres; longest run, 1,800'; ◆ 40%; ■ 40%; ● 20%.
LIFTS: 3 (3 surface); capacity, 1,800 per hour.
SUMMIT: 3,700'
VERTICAL: 1,000'
ACTIVITIES: Snowboarding.
FEATURES: Ski school; restaurant.
Run by the Badger Mountain Ski Club, this small area represents superb value (tickets are only $5). There are three separate hills, all essentially wide open snowfields: the Bunny Hill, the B-Hill (for intermediates), and the surprisingly steep A-Hill (for experts, who can also drop off into the back trails for tree skiing when snow conditions permit). There are numerous Nordic opportunities in the immediate vicinity, mostly ungroomed.

CRYSTAL MOUNTAIN

(P. 53, C-3, #3) 1 Crystal Mountain Blvd., Crystal Mountain
206-663-2265
SEASON: Nov. 15-April 15
ANNUAL SNOWFALL: 204"
TERRAIN: 29 trails over 2,300 acres; longest run, 3.5 mi.; ◆ 43%; ■ 37%; ● 20%.
LIFTS: 10 (1 high-speed quad, 1 quad, 3 triples, 5 doubles); capacity, 15,600 per hour.
SUMMIT: 7,002'
VERTICAL: 3,100'
ACTIVITIES: Snowboarding; NASTAR; night skiing.
FEATURES: Snowmaking 1.3%; ski school; restaurants; child care; rentals.
Few resorts appeal equally to families and hard-core skiers. Crystal has the terrain and the ambiance to satisfy both. The layout is almost ideal, with green runs concentrated to the left of the mountain (as you face it), blue runs dead center, and black runs occupying the right half (including 1,000 acres of out-of-bounds tree, chute and bowl skiing not included in the trail count). Kids adore the new childrens' ski center and caring attention they get all over the area. Experts thrill to the steeps (names like Snorting Elk Bowl and Right Angle hint at what they can expect). Boarders love that same advanced terrain, as well as the new snowboard park. Intermediates will find few uninterrupted cruisers, but can dart between blue and black runs testing their mettle and bailing out when necessary.

ECHO VALLEY

(P. 53, B-4, #4) Lake Chelan
800-424-3526
TRAILS, 8; LIFTS, 4; VERTICAL, 1,400'.
▶NORDIC: 16 groomed km
A nice family area, Echo Canyon has a tiny bunny hill, two steeps (Face and Ptarmigan) and some scenic cruisers like Ridge.

49 DEGREES NORTH SKI RESORT

(P. 53, B-5, #5) Flowery Trail Road, 10 miles outside Chewelah
509-935-6649
SEASON: Dec. 15-April 15
ANNUAL SNOWFALL: 120"
TERRAIN: 23 trails over 800 acres, plus a 120-acre bowl; longest run, 3.25 mi.; ◆ 30%; ■ 40%; ● 30%.
LIFTS: 4 (4 doubles); capacity, 4,800 per hour.
SUMMIT: 5,773'
VERTICAL: 1,845'
ACTIVITIES: Snowboarding.
FEATURES: Ski school; restaurant; child care; rentals.
▶NORDIC: 10 groomed km.
Tucked in the northeast corner of Washington, 49 Degrees North enjoys lighter snow than areas in the state's western half, and a policy reserving 120 acres for powder skiing on weekends takes full advantage. Boarders have a half-pipe, and also like the steep and deep on Tombstone and Concentrator. No crowds.

HURRICANE RIDGE SKI AREA

(P. 53, B-2, #6) 17 mi. from Port Angeles
206-452-0330; 206-452-0329 (snow)
TRAILS, 4; LIFTS, 3; VERTICAL, 500'.
▶NORDIC: 30 groomed km.
Located in splendid Olympic National Park, the panoramic views are awe-inspiring.

LOUP LOUP SKI BOWL

(P. 53, B-4, #7) Highway 20, Omak
509-826-2720
TRAILS, 4; LIFTS, 3; VERTICAL, 1,240'.
▶NORDIC: 20 groomed km.
Loup Loup is a fine little local learning area, with wide open trails, though advanced skiers can dart off into the trees in search of powder.

MISSION RIDGE SKI AREA

(P. 53, B-4, #8) 212 South Mission St. off Highway 2, Wenatchee
509-663-7631; 800-374-1693 (snow)
SEASON: Nov. 15-April 15
ANNUAL SNOWFALL: 100"
TERRAIN: 33 trails over 300 acres; longest run, 5 mi.; ◆ 30%; ■ 60%; ● 10%.
LIFTS: 6 (4 doubles, 2 surface); capacity, 4,300 per hour.
SUMMIT: 6,770'
VERTICAL: 2,200'
ACTIVITIES: Snowboarding; night skiing.
FEATURES: Snowmaking 15%; ski school; restaurant; rentals.
▶NORDIC: 3 ungroomed km.
Mission Ridge is one of the best ski values in the Northwest—in good ski years. Its position on the east slope of the Cascades ensures drier—but less bountiful—snow. On the other hand, how many areas offer runs that average 2 miles in length? This is paradise for intermediates, with a great mix of cruisers and tougher terrain, like the upper sections of Snookum and Toketie. Advanced skiers won't be disappointed by Lip Lip, Robinson's, or such vicious little drops as the Bomber Chutes, which fan out into a lovely wide bowl of the same name. Pipeline is a scenic trail for Nordic devotees; boarders have a half pipe.

MT. BAKER

(P. 53, A-3, #9) Route 542, 56 mi. E of Bellingham
206-734-6771
SEASON: Nov. 1-May 12 (open daily through Jan. 7; Wed. to Sun. Jan. 8 to March 31; weekends afterward)
ANNUAL SNOWFALL: 750"
TERRAIN: NA trails over 1,000 acres; longest run, 6,500 feet; ◆◆ 7%; ◆ 21%; ■ 42%; ● 30%.
LIFTS: 9 (2 quads, 6 doubles, 1 surface); capacity, 6,000 per hour.
SUMMIT: 5,250'
VERTICAL: 1,500'
ACTIVITIES: Snowboarding.
FEATURES: Ski school; restaurants; child care; rentals.
▶NORDIC: 2 groomed km.
It's not a misprint: Mt. Baker receives an average of 750 inches of snow a year, making it a Mecca for hard-core skiers, telemarkers and shredders (local snowboarders perennially win the World Extreme Championships). The gleaming new White Salmon Base Area opens late 1994. There are two mountains: Pan Dome and Shuksan. Pan Dome is a series of unforgiving and daunting trails, with one chute and mogul field after another, like Pan Face, Rattrap, and Gunbarrel (which has two novice runs for the suddenly faint of heart). Shuksan offers gentle green boulevards and blue beauties off the 7 and 8 quads. It also has a natural half pipe alongside a creek bed and hellaciously steep powder stashes under the double chairs, like Nose Dive. Baker's pristine setting may be unrivalled for sheer beauty, and Nature asserts her awesome power with periodic avalanches that thunder thousands of feet (the area itself is safe—but the most spectacular slides are visible from nearly every lift).

MT. SPOKANE SKI AREA

(P. 53, B-5, #10) N. 7322 Division, Mead
509-238-6281
SEASON: Dec. 15-April 4
ANNUAL SNOWFALL: 200"
TERRAIN: 27 trails over 350 acres; longest run, 1.5 mi.; ◆ 40%; ■ 40%; ● 20%.
LIFTS: 5 (5 doubles); capacity, 5,000 per hour.
SUMMIT: 5,883'
VERTICAL: 2,065'
ACTIVITIES: Snowboarding; night skiing.
FEATURES: Ski school; restaurant; rentals.
Another top bargain, Mt. Spokane offers the lowest lift ticket prices of any major area in the Northwest, as well as excellent intermediate skiing, and some tight glades that hold powder beautifully for experts.

SITZMARK

(P. 53, A-4, #11) Havillah Road, 20 mi. NE of Tonasket
509-485-3323
TRAILS, 10; LIFTS, 2; VERTICAL, 650'.
▶NORDIC: 12 groomed km.
A pleasant local area with a decent vertical in a rural part of the state. It may close for 1995; call ahead.

SKI BLUEWOOD

(P. 53, C-5, #12) 116 N. Third St., Dayton
509-382-4725; 509-382-2877 (snow)
SEASON: Nov. 20-April 15
ANNUAL SNOWFALL: 180"
TERRAIN: 21 trails over 430 acres; longest run, 2.25 mi.; ◆ 28%; 3 24
LIFTS: 3 (2 triples, 1 surface); capacity, 4,200 per hour.
SUMMIT: 5,650'
VERTICAL: 1,125'
ACTIVITIES: Snowboarding.
FEATURES: Ski school; restaurant; rentals.
▶NORDIC: 509-581-4151; 5 groomed km.
Another lesser-known area off the beaten track (Walla Walla is the nearest city of any size), Bluewood offers an agreeable blend of wide open and gladed slopes, as well as a half pipe and park for boarders. The Nordic trails may be eliminated, or left ungroomed.

STEVENS PASS SKI AREA

(P. 53, C-5, #13) U.S. 2, 37 mi. W of Leavenworth
206-973-2441
SEASON: Nov. 15-April 15
ANNUAL SNOWFALL: 120"
TERRAIN: 36 trails over 1,125 acres; longest run, 1.5 mi.; ◆ 35%; ■ 54%; ● 11%.
LIFTS: 13 (1 quad, 3 triples, 6 doubles, 3 surface); capacity, 14,350 per hour.
SUMMIT: 5,800'
VERTICAL: 1,774'
ACTIVITIES: Snowboarding; night skiing.
FEATURES: Ski school; restaurants; child care; rentals.
▶NORDIC: 26.5 groomed km (with skating lane); rentals; lessons.
Once upon a time, Stevens Pass was ignored by serious skiers: the bulk of its terrain was beginner and easy intermediate. (Though how bad could it have been, since it's where local boys—and Olympic medalists—the Mahre twins learned to ski?) In 1988, the Southern Cross and 7th Heaven chairs opened, and 400 acres of advanced terrain in Mill Valley became available. Such runs as Pegasus Gulch, Corona Bowl, Andromeda Face, and Polaris Bowl offer a galaxy of out-of-this-world skiing. On powder days, skiers can dart off into the surrounding trees. Even novices and intermediates can play in Mill Valley—thanks to a new quad—by taking the Way Back and Skid Road to the base area and its miles of gentle groomed cruisers. Lodging is 37 miles east in the charming Bavarian-style town of Leavenworth.

WHITE PASS VILLAGE SKI AREA

(P. 53, C-3, #14) U.S. 12, 52 mi. W of Yakima
509-453-8731; 509-672-3100 (snow)
SEASON: Nov. 15-May 10
ANNUAL SNOWFALL: 250"
TERRAIN: 14 trails over 635 acres; longest run, 2 mi.; ◆ 20%; ■ 60%; ● 20%.
LIFTS: 6 (4 doubles, 2 surface); capacity, 5,525 per hour.
SUMMIT: 6,000'
VERTICAL: 1,500'
ACTIVITIES: Snowboarding; night skiing.
FEATURES: Ski school; restaurants; child care; rentals.
▶NORDIC: 15 groomed km (with skating lane); rentals; lessons.
A notable local area, with varied terrain (mostly long, wide intermediate cruisers), picturesque Nordic trails and uncrowded slopes.

NORDIC

BEAR MOUNTAIN RANCH

(P. 53, B-4, #15) Highway 97, 5 mi. S of Chelan
509-682-5444
FACILITIES: 55 groomed km (with skating lane); rentals; lessons; restaurant.

MAZAMA COUNTRY INN

(P. 53, A-4, #16) Mazama
800-843-7951
FACILITIES: 35 groomed km; rentals; lessons; lodging and restaurant.
The Mazama trails (part of the Methow Valley network) are mostly flat but boast incredible views of the mountains and Goat Wall formations. The gourmet restaurant is highly regarded.

METHOW VALLEY SPORT TRAILS ASSOCIATION

(P. 53, A-4, #17) Winthrop
509-996-3287
FACILITIES: 175 groomed km (with skating lane); rentals; lessons; lodging and restaurants.
This wonderfully varied system features several fine restaurants and cozy accommodations. The snow is light and plentiful.

NORDIC WAY X-C SKI SCHOOL & NORTHWEST TELEMARK INSTITUTE

(P. 53, B-3, #18) 70 E. Sunset Way, Issaquah
206-391-2782
FACILITIES: Unlimited groomed km; rentals; lessons.
One of the West's premier learning centers, utilizing several nearby National Forest service systems.

SUN MOUNTAIN LODGE

(P. 53, B-4, #19) Winthrop
800-572-0493
FACILITIES: 60 groomed km (with skating lane); rentals; lessons; child care; sleigh rides; lodging and restaurant.
Built on a mountain top commanding marvelous panoramas, Sun Mountain Lodge is one of the Northwest's leading resorts, with deluxe accommodations and service. The ski school is highly rated, as are the trails (part of the Methow Valley system).

WEST VIRGINIA

West Virginia is already renowned for its world-class mountain biking and whitewater rafting, but the dramatic Allegheny and Cumberland ranges form a rugged backbone of rocky outcroppings and bald knobs ideal for skiing, too. Locals say the combination of scenery and weather patterns makes it "a little bit of Canada gone astray." Many of the resorts are isolated, accessible only via twisting, vertiginous roads that would make a Grand Prix racer blanch. Seemingly hacked from the beech and evergreen forests, these hideaways maintain an exciting wilderness feel. And the prevailing weather patterns blanket the state with the most plentiful and consistent snow in the Southeast.

That same terrain makes West Virginia a Nordic paradise, and several state parks are noted for their tranquil trails, as well as cozy lodges.

ALPINE

ALPINE LAKE RESORT
(P. 16, C-6, #1) Route 2, Terra Alta
304-789-2481
TRAILS, NA; LIFTS, 3; VERTICAL, 400'.
▶NORDIC: Terra Alta Touring Center.
This small area mainly attracts locals with its upscale yet easygoing ambiance and lack of crowds. The resort blends harmoniously with the surroundings, earning it several ecological design awards.

CANAAN VALLEY RESORT
(P. 17, C-6, #2) Route 1, Canaan Valley State Park, Davis
304-866-4121
SEASON: Dec. 10-April 1
ANNUAL SNOWFALL: 160"
TERRAIN: 15 trails over 70-80 acres; longest run, 1 mile; ♦ 30%; ■ 40%; ● 30%.
LIFTS: 4 (1 quad, 2 triple, 1 surface); capacity, 6,100 per hour.
SUMMIT: 4,280'
VERTICAL: 850'
ACTIVITIES: Snowboarding; ice skating; night skiing.
FEATURES: Snowmaking 80%; ski school; restaurants; rentals.
The highest alpine valley in the East at 3,200 feet, Canaan Valley State Park is the site of West Virginia's first commercial ski area. Although isolated, skiers can plan a productive holiday, since Timberline is right next door, as is the fine White Grass Touring Center. Canaan Valley (pronounced ki-NANE) is a perfect cruising mountain, featuring beautiful, wide-open, well-groomed runs.

NEW WINTERPLACE
(P. 17, E-4, #3) I-77 (exit 28), Flat Top
304-787-3221; 800-874-SNOW (snow)
SEASON: Nov. 25-March 31
ANNUAL SNOWFALL: 120"
TERRAIN: 24 trails over 80 acres; longest run, 1.25 mi.; ♦24%; ■ 52%; ● 24%.

LIFTS: 5 (2 triples, 2 doubles, 1 surface); capacity, 7,600 per hour.
SUMMIT: 3,600'
VERTICAL: 603'
ACTIVITIES: Snowboarding; NASTAR; night skiing.
FEATURES: Snowmaking 100%; ski school; restaurants; rentals.
Winterplace's trump card is its accessibility; it sits right off the Interstate. Primarily a daytrippers' ski area, it also does a high percentage of night business, since 90% of the area is lit. Beginners can easily negotiate the longest trail, Ridgerunner, from the top. Unfortunately, the sprawling design necessitates taking two chairs to reach the summit. The steepest runs—Nightmare, Nosedive, Turkey Chute, and Plunge—plummet from the bald knob up top.

OGLEBAY PARK
(P. 16, B-4, #4) Oglebay Park, Wheeling
304-243-4000
TRAILS, 2; LIFTS, 3; VERTICAL, 330'.
▶NORDIC: NA groomed km.

SNOWSHOE MOUNTAIN RESORT/SILVER CREEK
(P. 16, D-5, #5) Snowshoe Drive, Snowshoe
304-572-1000; 304-572-4636
SEASON: Nov. 15-April 15
ANNUAL SNOWFALL: 180"
TERRAIN: 50 trails over 180 acres; longest run, 1.5 mi.; ♦ 27%; ■ 40%; ● 33%.
LIFTS: 11 (2 quads, 8 triples, 1 double); capacity, 18,100 per hour.
SUMMIT: 4,848'
VERTICAL: 1,500'
ACTIVITIES: Snowboarding; NASTAR; night skiing.
FEATURES: Snowmaking 98%; ski school; restaurants; rentals.
Snowshoe became a monster when it absorbed Silver Creek, which shares the same 4,800-foot ridge. Silver Creek now becomes the choice of novices and lower-intermediates who enjoy its wide-open, less crowded runs. As for Snowshoe, it's the Atlantic Coast's most substantial area south of New York—and has the subway-like congestion to prove it. Hordes come for some of the lightest snow east of the Mississippi. Beginners have longer runs to choose from than at Silver Creek, though many are glorified cat-tracks. Most of Cheat Mountain is paradise for middle-of-the-road skiers. Even the black runs are within a strong intermediate's grasp. There's Widow Maker (a bit of hyperbole—once you negotiate that first nasty headwall that strongly resembles a cliff). And there's Cupp's Run, endorsed by Jean-Claude Killy as one of the USA's top ten downhill runs. Its contouring is intriguing, with constantly changing terrain, humps and dips galore, and width varying from boulevard to trench. Snowshoe is the most bustling ski town in the South.

TIMBERLINE FOUR SEASONS RESORT
(P. 17, C-6, #6) Route 32, Canaan Valley, Davis
304-866-4801; 304-866-4828
SEASON: Dec. 1-April 1
ANNUAL SNOWFALL: 150"
TERRAIN: 25 trails over 75 acres; longest run, 2 mi.; ♦ 50%; ■ 20%; ● 30%.
LIFTS: 5 (1 triple, 1 double, 3 surface); capacity, 3,000 per hour.
SUMMIT: 4,268'
VERTICAL: 1,084'
ACTIVITIES: Snowboarding; NASTAR; night skiing.
FEATURES: Snowmaking 95%; ski school; restaurant; rentals.
Timberline offers the South's longest run, Salamander. A treasure for beginners, it has great valley views. Timberline's double diamond, The Drop, may not stack up to Western standards, but moguls and ice can present a challenge.

The area is bordered by acres of splendid wilderness terrain for Nordic skiers. Snowboarders have a 200-foot half pipe.

NORDIC

BLACKWATER NORDIC CENTER
(P. 17, C-6, #7) Blackwater State Park, Davis
304-259-5216
FACILITIES: 10 groomed km, 15 ungroomed; rentals; lessons; lodging and restaurant.
The tracks in this scenic state park follow old railroad tracks, skirting a canyon, with stirring views of the Blackwater River and Waterfalls.

ELK RIVER TOURING CENTER
(P. 16, D-5, #8) Highway 219, Slatyfork
304-572-3771
FACILITIES: 25 groomed km; rentals; lessons; restaurant.
The terrain is a perfect blend of fields and woods, following old logging roads and railroad grades.

WHITE GRASS SKI TOURING CENTER
(P. 17, C-6, #9) Canaan Valley, Davis
304-866-4114
FACILITIES: 50 groomed km; rentals; lessons; restaurant; night skiing (2 km lit).
White Grass is the top Nordic center in the South, offering backcountry tours and telemark glades in addition to its balanced trails. In many ways, it seems a throwback to the '60s, with a funky natural foods cafe and live acoustic music weekends. The area leads tours of the surrounding region, including Blackwater, Weiss Knob (the abandoned site of the South's first ski area), and the lunarscape of the Dolly Sods Wilderness. Moonlight headlamp tours are also available.

WISCONSIN

Even flatter than Michigan, its neighbor across the Great Lakes, Wisconsin nevertheless offers some of the best skiing in the Midwest. It makes up for lack of vertical with low prices, first-rate ski schools, top-notch grooming and snowmaking, and its rugged scenery. ❄ Gently rolling hills make Wisconsin a natural for gliding, and thousands of miles of trails crisscross the state, skirting frozen lakes and brooks, looping along limestone bluffs and ridges. The USA's most famous—and grueling—Nordic race, the Birkebeiner (affectionately known as "The Birkie") draws hundreds of eager competitors and thousands of rabid fans from around the globe each winter. ❄ Spectator sports are well represented: Take in a Green Bay Packers or Milwaukee Bucks game, or watch the Wisconsin Badgers hockey and basketball teams.

ALPINE

ALPINE VALLEY RESORT
(P. 54, E-4, #1) East Troy
414-642-7374
SEASON: Dec. 1-March 15
ANNUAL SNOWFALL: 60"
TERRAIN: 12 trails over 95 acres; longest run, 3,000'; ◆ 20%; ▪ 60%; ● 20%.
LIFTS: 16 (6 triples, 5 doubles, 5 surface); capacity, 14,800 per hour.
SUMMIT: NA
VERTICAL: 388'
ACTIVITIES: Snowboarding; night skiing.
FEATURES: Snowmaking 100%; ski school; restaurants; rentals.
The major player in the Milwaukee area, Alpine Valley attracts novices and intermediates from as far afield as Chicago. The lift capacity is more than adequate; but, unfortunately, the slopes themselves are packed many weekends. Broadway is the featured bump run; Sheltered Valley the signature cruiser.

AMERICANA SKI AREA
(P. 54, E-4, #2) Highway 50, Lake Geneva
414-248-8811
TRAILS, 13; LIFTS, 5; VERTICAL, 211'.
▶NORDIC: 8 groomed km; 1,000 backcountry acres.

AUSBLICK SKI AREA
(P. 54, D-4, #3) Mary Hill Road 1 mi. S of Highway 74, 2 mi. W of Sussex
414-246-3090
TRAILS, 6; LIFTS, 2; VERTICAL, 182'.
A private area with limited terrain (evenly distributed between narrow glades and open slopes). Members' guests and prospective members can stop by.

BRUCE MOUND WINTER SPORTS AREA
(P. 54, C-3, #4) 517 Court St., Neillsville
715-743-5140
TRAILS, 7; LIFTS, 4; VERTICAL, 325'.
▶NORDIC: 20 groomed km.

CALUMET SKI AREA
(P. 54, D-4, #5) N6150 Highway EE, Hilbert
414-439-1008
TRAILS, 6; LIFTS, 5; VERTICAL, 180'.
▶NORDIC: 5 groomed km.

CAMP TEN SKI AREA
(P. 54, C-3, #6) Camp Ten Road, County Highway A, Tomahawk
715-564-2265
TRAILS, 8; LIFTS, 3; VERTICAL, 240'.
▶NORDIC: 30 groomed km.

CASCADE MOUNTAIN
(P. 54, D-3, #7) W10441 Cascade Mountain Rd., Portage
608-742-5588; 800-992-2SKI (snow)
SEASON: Nov. 27-March 25
ANNUAL SNOWFALL: 42"
TERRAIN: 21 trails over 122 acres; longest run, 1 mile; ◆ 40%; ▪ 30%; ● 30%.
LIFTS: 9 (3 quads, 3 triples, 1 double, 2 surface); capacity, 14,300 per hour.
SUMMIT: 1,277'
VERTICAL: 460'
ACTIVITIES: NASTAR; night skiing.
FEATURES: Snowmaking 100%; ski school; restaurants; rentals.
Cascade attracts skiers from Chicago and Milwaukee in droves. Much appreciated are its mix of wide, groomed cruisers (like School Marm and Adele Valley); bump runs (Mogul Monster and North Wall earn raves); and steep headwalls (Cindy Pop is a sudden drop). Ironically, its beginner area was subpar until the recent addition of isolated terrain (served by its own triple chair). Cascade Mountain's vista, overlooking the Wisconsin River Valley from the Baraboo Bluffs, is one of the loveliest in the state.

CHRISTIE MOUNTAIN
(P. 54, B-2, #8) W13755 County Rd. O, Bruce
715-868-7275 (res); 715-868-7800 (snow)
TRAILS, 10; LIFTS, 4; VERTICAL, 350'.
This fine family area boasts a good variety of tree-lined trails, with Wildcat and Bobcat luring stronger skiers.

CHRISTMAS MOUNTAIN
(P. 54, D-3, #9) S944 Christmas Mountain Rd., Wisconsin Dells
608-254-3971
TRAILS, 8; LIFTS, 4; VERTICAL, 250'.
▶NORDIC: 10 groomed km.
This full-service resort makes an ideal base for touring the lovely Wisconsin Dells region. The skiing is family-oriented, with a top-rated ski school, but fairly basic.

CRYSTAL RIDGE
(P. 54, E-4, #10) 7900 W. Crystal Ridge, Franklin
414-529-7676; 414-529-SNOW (snow)
TRAILS, 8; LIFTS, 5; VERTICAL, 200'.
2 half pipes.

DEVIL'S HEAD LODGE
(P. 54, D-3, #11) S6330 Bluff Rd., Merrimac
608-493-2251
SEASON: Nov. 25-April 1
ANNUAL SNOWFALL: 42"
TERRAIN: 22 trails over 200 acres; longest run, 8,500'; ◆ 20%; ▪ 50%; ● 30%..
LIFTS: 15 (3 quads, 1 triple, 6 doubles, 5 surface); capacity, 15,800 per hour.
SUMMIT: 995'
VERTICAL: 500'
ACTIVITIES: Snowboarding; NASTAR; night skiing.
FEATURES: Snowmaking 100%; ski school; restaurants; child care; rentals.
▶NORDIC: 5 ungroomed km; rentals; lessons.
An upscale, full-service resort, Devil's Head is another favorite with city dwellers, who enjoy the ravishing scenery and the superlative, beginner-through-intermediate terrain. Skiers seeking greater variety and challenge should head for nearby Cascade, although Outer Limits offers some mean bumps.

HIDDEN VALLEY SKI AREA
(P. 54, D-5, #12) 1815 Maple St., Manitowoc
414-682-5475
TRAILS, 4; LIFTS, 4; VERTICAL, 200'.

KETTLEBOWL HILL
(P. 54, C-4, #13) State Route 52, 15 mi. NE of Antigo
715-623-3560
TRAILS, 5; LIFTS, 5; VERTICAL, 200'.
▶NORDIC: 3 groomed km.

KEYES PEAK SKI HILL
(P. 54, B-4, #14) Route 1, Florence
715-528-3228
TRAILS, 4; LIFTS, 3; VERTICAL, 250'.
▶NORDIC: 10 groomed km; ice skating.
Another learning area for locals.

LITTLE SWITZERLAND
(P. 54, B-2, #15) 105 Highway AA, Superior
414-644-5020
SEASON: Dec. 1-March 15
ANNUAL SNOWFALL: 35"
TERRAIN: 16 trails over NA acres; longest run, 1,800'; ◆ 30%; ▪ 40%; ● 30%.
LIFTS: 8 (1 quad, 4 doubles, 3 surface); capacity, 7,500 per hour.
SUMMIT: NA
VERTICAL: 200'
ACTIVITIES: Snowboarding; night skiing.
FEATURES: Snowmaking 100%; ski school; restaurant; rentals.
Another area that does a lot with a little, and offers enough variety to keep most families occupied for a day.

STATBOX

Tourism: 800-432-Trip
Time zone: Central
Population: 4,891,769
Square miles: 56,154

Average annual precipitation: 31"
Highest elevation: 1,952'
Lowest elevation: sea level

MONT DU LAC SKI AREA
(P. 54, B-2, #16) Highway 23, Superior
715-636-2642
TRAILS, 9; LIFTS, 3; VERTICAL, 300'.
Thrilling views of Lake Superior and the attractions of nearby Duluth are the big draws at this agreeable area.

MT. ASHWABAY
(P. 54, A-3, #17) State Route 13, 3 mi. outside Bayfield
715-779-3227
SEASON: Dec. 1-April 1 (open Wed., weekends)
ANNUAL SNOWFALL: 100"
TERRAIN: 13 trails over 65 acres; longest run, 3,000'; ◆ 40%; ▪ 30%; ● 30%.
LIFTS: 5 (5 surface); capacity, 5,500 per hour.
SUMMIT: 1,280'
VERTICAL: 317'
ACTIVITIES: Snowboarding; night skiing.
FEATURES: Ski school; restaurant; rentals.
▶NORDIC: 40 groomed km; rentals; lessons.
A terrific bargain for the price, Mt. Ashwabay offers relatively varied terrain and long runs for Wisconsin, D-4 being the top cruiser. Don't overlook the picturesque, wooded, cross-country trails and stunning Lake Superior views.

MT. LA CROSSE
(P. 54, D-2, #18) Route 3, Old Town Road, La Crosse
608-788-0044
SEASON: Nov. 25-March 15
ANNUAL SNOWFALL: 50"
TERRAIN: 17 trails over NA acres; longest run, 1 mile; ◆ 30%; ▪ 50%; ● 20%.
LIFTS: 4 (3 doubles, 1 surface); capacity, 3,500 per hour.
SUMMIT: 1,110'
VERTICAL: 516'
ACTIVITIES: Snowboarding; NASTAR; night skiing.
FEATURES: Snowmaking 100%; ski school; restaurant; rentals.
▶NORDIC: 10 groomed km; rentals; lessons.
The prototypical Wisconsin resort, Mt. La Crosse's runs are cut from rocky outcroppings, resulting in a series of tough headwalls and chutes that will challenge even expert skiers. Try the double diamond Damnation, or softer cruisers like Mileaway. Views of the Mississippi can be distracting.

NORDIC MOUNTAIN
(P. 54, D-3, #19) Route 1, Hancock
414-787-3324
SEASON: Dec. 1-March 15
ANNUAL SNOWFALL: 80"
TERRAIN: 13 trails over 80 acres; longest run, 1 mile; ◆

DRIVING SAFETY

When driving to an area, always check the weather forecasts, and consult the Highway Patrol for any potential road closings or hazardous conditions. Make sure you have your chains (which provide the surest traction on slick surfaces) and highway-tread tires on all four wheels (always carry a spare, as well). In heavy snow, try to stay in the tracks of cars ahead of you. A shovel will come in handy should you get stuck in drifts. Yellow sunglasses or goggles will improve your vision in whiteouts or fog, just as they do on the slopes.

Never start or stop suddenly or turn abruptly in slippery conditions. Traction is poor if your wheels start spinning. Always be on the lookout for patches of ice, especially on bridges, at intersections, or on steep winding roads. Stay even further back than you normally would of the car in front of you. If you skid, turn your wheels in the direction the car is skidding and take your foot off the accelerator immediately. Pump your breaks for the best control in sudden stops.

If you anticipate driving long distances, carry a sleeping bag and blankets. You can even take the precaution of packing some canned food. Should the worst happen and you stall in a blizzard or ice storm, huddle together and cover up with the blankets for warmth. Conserve your gas by running the engine just long enough to heat the interior. Never leave the protection of the car to go for help.

35%; ▪ 50%; ● 15%.
LIFTS: 5 (1 triple, 1 double, 3 surface); capacity, 6,000 per hour.
SUMMIT: 1,137'
VERTICAL: 265'
ACTIVITIES: Snowmobiling; night skiing.
FEATURES: Snowmaking 100%; ski school; restaurants; rentals.
▶NORDIC: 20 groomed km; rentals.
Nordic has a creative layout that skis bigger than the vertical suggests. The trails weave in and out of glades, forcing skiers to work on carving their turns. Several runs feature good pitch and changing terrain.

OLYMPIA VILLAGE
(P. 54, D-4, #20) 1350 Royale Mile Rd., Oconomowoc
414-567-2577
TRAILS, 5; LIFTS, 3; VERTICAL, 164'.
▶NORDIC: 11 groomed km. Half pipe.

PAUL BUNYAN SKI HILL
(P. 54, C-4, #21) 14502 Resort Lane, Lakewood
715-276-7610
TRAILS, 7; LIFTS, 5; VERTICAL, 160'.

POTAWATOMI PARK
(P. 54, C-5, #22) Park Drive, Sturgeon Bay
414-743-7033
TRAILS, 3; LIFTS, 3; VERTICAL, 120'.

▶NORDIC: 10 groomed km.

POWERS BLUFF WINTER RECREATION AREA
(P. 54, C-3, #23) 17 mi. outside Wisconsin Rapids
715-421-8422
TRAILS, 3; LIFTS, 1; VERTICAL, 250'.
▶NORDIC: 2.5 groomed km.

RIB MOUNTAIN SKI AREA
(P. 54, C-3, #24) 3506 North Mountain Rd., 3 mi. outside Wausau
715-845-2846
SEASON: Dec. 1-March 31
ANNUAL SNOWFALL: 60"
TERRAIN: 13 trails over NA acres; longest run, 1 mile; ◆ 20%; ▪ 60%; ● 20%.
LIFTS: 4 (1 triple, 2 doubles, 1 surface); capacity, 6,000 per hour.
SUMMIT: 1,942'
VERTICAL: 624'
ACTIVITIES: Night skiing.
FEATURES: snowmaking 100%; ski school; restaurant; rentals.
Rib Mountain boasts the biggest vertical in Wisconsin. Wide groomed boulevards alternate with tighter, tree-lined slopes here, though there are a couple of steeper faces.

SKY LINE SKI AREA
(P. 54, D-3, #25) 1900 13th Court, Friendship
608-339-3364
TRAILS, 7; LIFTS, 3; VERTICAL, 335'.

▶NORDIC: 10 groomed km.

STANDING ROCKS
(P. 54, C-3, #26) 1516 Church St., Stevens Point
715-824-3949
TRAILS, 5; LIFTS, 3; VERTICAL, 125'.
▶NORDIC: 715-346-1433; 16 groomed km.

SUNBURST
(P. 54, D-4, #27) 8355 Prospect Dr., Kewaskum
414-626-8404
SEASON: Dec. 1-March 15
ANNUAL SNOWFALL: 45"
TERRAIN: 10 trails over 35 acres; longest run, 2,600'; ◆◆ 10%; ◆ 30%; ▪ 30%; ● 30%.
LIFTS: 7 (3 doubles, 4 surface); capacity, 3,500 per hour.
SUMMIT: 1,100'
VERTICAL: 214'
ACTIVITIES: Snowboarding; NASTAR; night skiing.
FEATURES: Snowmaking 100%; ski school; restaurant; rentals.
Sunburst's wide-open slopes and bowls make it a favorite of Milwaukee families, especially after recent improvements in grooming and snowmaking. Along with a half pipe, a new chair has been added to service the novice and intermediate terrain. Over 65 and under 7 ski free.

SYLVAN SKI HILL
(P. 54, C-3, #28) Mosinee
715-847-5235
TRAILS, 4; LIFTS, 3; VERTICAL, 90'.
▶NORDIC: 54 groomed km.

TELEMARK SKI AREA
(P. 54, B-2, #29) Off Route 63, 2 mi. W of Cable
715-798-3811
SEASON: Nov. 25-April 4
ANNUAL SNOWFALL: 70"
TERRAIN: 10 trails over 120 acres; longest run, 2,600'; ◆ 20%; ▪ 40%; ● 40%.
LIFTS: 5 (2 doubles, 3 surface); capacity, 5,000 per hour.
SUMMIT: 1,770'
VERTICAL: 370'
ACTIVITIES: Snowboarding; NASTAR; ice skating.
FEATURES: Snowmaking 100%; ski school; restaurants; child care; rentals.
▶NORDIC: 100 groomed km; rentals; lessons.
This fine resort is highly popular with families and couples, who enjoy the extensive open bowls, wide slopes, and pristine Nordic trails that figure prominently in the "Birkie." The World Cup section offers the most thrilling 30 km, with a series of pitches and constantly changing terrain and scenery.

TRIANGLE SPORTS AREA
(P. 54, C-4, #30) 500 Beverly

Rd., Green Bay
414-448-3365
TRAILS, 1; LIFTS, 1; VERTICAL, 80'.
▶NORDIC: 10 groomed km.

TROLLHAUGEN SKI AREA
(P. 54, C-2, #31) County Road F, Dresser
715-755-2955
SEASON: Nov. 8-April 1
ANNUAL SNOWFALL: 50"
TERRAIN: 22 trails over 80 acres; longest run, 2,500'; ◆ 30%; ▪ 50%; ● 20%.
LIFTS: 10 (2 quads, 1 double, 7 surface); capacity, 8,000 per hour.
SUMMIT: 1,140'
VERTICAL: 260'
ACTIVITIES: Snowboarding; NASTAR; night skiing.
FEATURES: Snowmaking 100%; ski school; restaurants; rentals.
 A well-regarded family resort near the Twin Cities of Minnesota, whose clientele enjoys the religiously groomed trails, like Missibakken and Julebakken. One or two of these are usually allowed to bump up.

TYROL BASIN
(P. 54, D-3, #32) 3487 Bohn Rd., Mt. Horeb
608-437-4135
SEASON: Dec. 1-March 30
ANNUAL SNOWFALL: 40"
TERRAIN: 12 trails over 24 acres; longest run, 2,600'; ◆ 40%; ▪ 28%; ● 32%.
LIFTS: 5 (2 triples, 3 surface); capacity, 5,000 per hour.
SUMMIT: 1,150'
VERTICAL: 300'
ACTIVITIES: Snowboarding; night skiing.
FEATURES: Snowmaking 100%; ski school; restaurant; rentals.
 Tyrol Basin has labored to expand its client base, adding both a longer novice run named Nisse Sti and Sutter's Ridge, a virtual theme park of quarter pipes, rails, and bumps. Both skiers and boarders (who still have their half pipe) enjoy Sutter's so much they nicknamed it the Fun Run.

WHITECAP MOUNTAINS
(P. 54, B-3, #33) County Trunk Road E, Montreal
715-561-2227
SEASON: Nov. 25-April 1
ANNUAL SNOWFALL: 200"
TERRAIN: 33 trails over 390 acres; longest run, 5,000'; ◆ 33%; ▪ 34%; ● 33%.
LIFTS: 8 (1 quad, 1 triple, 4 doubles, 2 surface); capacity, 9,400 per hour.
SUMMIT: 1,834'
VERTICAL: 400'
ACTIVITIES: Snowboarding.
FEATURES: Snowmaking 80%; ski school; restaurants; rentals.

▶NORDIC: 3 groomed km.
 Whitecap and its sister resorts, Michigan's Blackjack, Big Powderhorn, and Indianhead comprise "Big Snow Country," offering interchangeable lift tickets and, taken as a whole, highly varied skiing for the Midwest. Like its neighbors, Whitecap offers rugged scenery and a mix of wide open cruisers, tighter tree runs, and steep headwalls. Sud Bowl, 150 acres of rolling, changeable terrain, allows skiers of any ability to pick the line right for them. Bump runs are clustered at the far southern end, with St. George, Southern Cross, and the more regularly groomed Val D'Isere the standouts. The snow, benefiting from "lake effect" dumps, is the lightest and most abundant by far in Wisconsin. The region itself is well worth exploring for its strongly ethnic heritage, thanks to the Finns, Italians, and Slavs who came a century earlier to work iron and copper mines.

WHITE TAIL RIDGE
(P. 54, D-3, #34) Highway 21, Fort McCoy
608-388-4498
TRAILS, 2; LIFTS, 2; VERTICAL, 185'.
▶NORDIC: 8 groomed km.

WILMOT MOUNTAIN
(P. 54, E-5, #35) Highway W, Wilmot
414-862-2301
SEASON: Dec. 1-March 31
ANNUAL SNOWFALL: 60"
TERRAIN: 30 trails over NA acres; longest run, 2,500'; ◆ 40%; ▪ 30%; ● 30%.
LIFTS: 14 (1 quad, 3 triples, 4 doubles, 6 surface); capacity, 12,500 per hour.
SUMMIT: NA
VERTICAL: 230'
ACTIVITIES: Snowboarding;

night skiing.
FEATURES: Snowmaking 100%; ski school; restaurants; rentals.
 Another area that does wonders with its limited vertical, Wilmot offers a surprising range of terrain, with some broad groomed avenues, steep faces, and mogul runs spread out over a wide ridge.

WOODSIDE RANCH RESORT
(P. 54, D-3, #36) Highway 82, Mauston
608-847-4275
TRAILS, 2; LIFTS, 1; VERTICAL, 100'.
▶NORDIC: 20 groomed km, 10 ungroomed.
 Ice skating; horseback riding; sleigh rides.
 The bunny hill is a free amusement for guests of this relaxing retreat, which offers a range of winter sports and services; lessons are also complimentary. The Nordic trails are far more extensive and challenging.

NORDIC

ABBEY SPRINGS
(P. 54, E-4, #37) South Shore Drive, Fontana
414-275-6113
FACILITIES: 8 groomed km; rentals; restaurant.

CAMP TAPAWINGO
(P. 54, C-5, #38) 915 TaPaWingo Rd., Mishicot
414-755-2785
FACILITIES: 5 groomed km; rentals; restaurant.

"THE CLUB" AT EAGLE RIVER NORDIC
(P. 54, B-4, #39) Eagle River
715-479-7285
FACILITIES: 4.5 groomed km

(with skating lane); rentals; lessons; restaurant.

CRIVITZ CROSS-COUNTRY SKI CENTER
(P. 54, C-4, #40) Route 4, Crivitz
715-854-7863
FACILITIES: 5 groomed km; rentals; lessons; restaurant.

CURRIE PARK
(P. 54, D-5, #41) 3535 N. Mayfair Rd., Milwaukee
414-257-5100
FACILITIES: 4 groomed km; rentals; restaurant.

FORT WILDERNESS CHRISTIAN CAMP
(P. 54, B-3, #42) 6180 Wilderness Trail, Rhinelander
715-277-2587
FACILITIES: 32 groomed km; rentals; lessons; snowshoeing; lodging and restaurant.

GEORGE WILLIAMS SKI TOURING CENTER
(P. 54, E-4, #43) 350 N. Lakeshore Drive, Williams Bay
414-245-5531
FACILITIES: 1.5 groomed km; rentals; lessons.

GLACIER PINES OUTFITTERS
(P. 54, B-2, #44) County Highway M, Cable
715-794-2055
FACILITIES: 40 groomed km; rentals; lessons; snowshoeing; restaurant.
 This top store offers guided ski touring, as well as lessons on the adjacent, narrow and hilly Rock Lake trail. Skiers snake through thick pine and hardwood forests and around several jewel-like lakes.

Courtesy: Wisconsin Division of Tourism.

GOAT FARM TRAILS
(P. 54, D-4, #45) Route 3, Wautoma
414-787-2425
FACILITIES: 30 groomed km (with skating lane); rentals; lessons.
 Located on a moraine, the challenging system at Goat Farm provides lots of steeps and rolling pitches. Even the easy loops can daunt novices: they're narrow, and trees have been left intact on the trails, adding to the rugged appeal.

HAMMOND GOLF CLUB
(P. 54, C-2, #46) 450 Davis St., Hammond
715-796-2266
FACILITIES: 4 groomed km; rentals; restaurant.

HILLY HAVENS SKI & GOLF
(P. 54, C-4, #47) 5911 Highway PP, DePere
414-336-6204
FACILITIES: 10 groomed km; rentals; restaurant.

HOLIDAY ACRES' HOLIDAY TRAILS
(P. 54, B-4, #48) Rhinelander
715-369-1500
FACILITIES: 18 groomed km (with skating lane); rentals; restaurant.

INTERLAKEN RESORT & COUNTRY SPA
(P. 54, E-4, #49) Highway 50 West, Lake Geneva
414-248-9121
FACILITIES: 90 ungroomed acres; rentals; spa; lodging and restaurant.

IOLA WINTER SPORTS COMPLEX
(P. 54, C-4, #50) E398 County Rd. MM, Iola
715-445-3411
FACILITIES: 20 groomed km (with skating lane); rentals; lessons; ice skating; restaurant.

JOHNSON PARK WINTER WONDERLAND
(P. 54, E-5, #51) 6200 Northwestern Ave., Racine
414-637-2840
FACILITIES: 5 groomed km; rentals; lessons; restaurant.

JUST-N-TRAILS
(P. 54, D-3, #52) Route 1, Sparta
608-269-4522 800-488-4521
FACILITIES: 20 groomed km; lessons; snowshoeing; lodging and restaurant.

LAKE FOREST RECREATION AREA
(P. 54, B-4, #53) 3801 Eagle Waters Rd., Eagle River
715-479-3251
FACILITIES: 8 groomed km; rentals; snowshoeing; restaurant.

LAKE LAWN LODGE
(P. 54, E-4, #54) Highway 50, Delavan
414-728-5511
FACILITIES: 15 groomed km; rentals; lodging and restaurant.

MILWAUKEE COUNTY ZOO
(P. 54, D-5, #55) 10001 W. Blue Mound Rd., Milwaukee
414-771-3040
FACILITIES: 4 groomed km; rentals; restaurant.
 No, the trail doesn't wind past cages, but rather follows the old train track on the zoo property.

MINOCQUA WINTER PARK
(P. 56, B-3, #56) 12375 Scotchman Lake Rd., Minocqua
715-356-3309
FACILITIES: 58 groomed km (with skating lane); rentals; lessons; child care; restaurant; night skiing (2.5 km lit).
 A fine family area, with lessons given by a member of the Professional Ski Instructors of America demo team, located amid hardwood forests and hilly glacial terrain.

MT. HARDSCRABBLE
(P. 54, B-2, #57) Route 4, Rice Lake
715-234-3412
FACILITIES: 16 groomed km; rentals; lessons; restaurant.

MOUNTAIN-NICOLET
(P. 54, C-4, #58) Mountain
715-276-7200
FACILITIES: 20 groomed km; rentals; restaurant.
 The local ski club grooms this balanced network; rentals are available through a club member's restaurant (the trails are out back).

NINE MILE COUNTRY FOREST/SYLVAN HILL PARK SKI CENTER
(P. 54, C-3, #59) 500 Forest St., Wausau
715-847-5267
FACILITIES: 27 groomed km (with skating lane); rentals; lessons; restaurant.

OLD WORLD WISCONSIN
(P. 54, E-4, #60) 5103 W. 37890 Highway 67, Eagle

414-594-2116
FACILITIES: 13 groomed km; rentals; lessons; restaurant.
 During the summer, this restored 19th century house operates as a historic museum with costumed docents. In winter (weekends only), it opens the trails out back to all comers, and organizes special events and banquets.

PALMQUIST'S "THE FARM"
(P. 54, B-3, #61) 5136 River Rd., Brantwood
715-564-2558
FACILITIES: 35 groomed km, 10 ungroomed; rentals; lessons; sleigh rides; lodging and restaurant.

PAUST'S WOOD LAKE RESORT
(P. 54, C-4, #62) Rural Route 3, Crivitz
715-757-3722
FACILITIES: 30 groomed km (with skating lane); rentals; lessons; snowmobiling; sledding; ice skating; lodging and restaurant.
 Mostly beginner and intermediate trails at this popular resort, winding through woods and fields and past lakes and streams.

PERKINSTOWN TRAIL/SITZ MARK
(P. 54, C-3, #63) 850 N. 8th St., Highway 13, Medford
715-748-4875
FACILITIES: 21 groomed km; rentals; restaurant.

QUIT QUI OC GOLF COURSE
(P. 54, D-4, #64) 500 Quit Qui Oc Lane, Elkhart Lake
414-876-2833
FACILITIES: 8 groomed km; rentals; restaurant.

THE SPRINGS GOLF CLUB RESORT
(P. 54, D-3, #65) 5857 Golf Course Rd., Spring Green
608-588-7000
FACILITIES: 40 groomed km; rentals; lessons; restaurant.

TRAIL FARM
(P. 54, C-3, #66) N9110 Meyer Drive, Westboro
800-872-4594
FACILITIES: 25 groomed km (with skating lane); lessons; ice skating; snowshoeing; tubing; lodging and restaurant.

TREES FOR TOMORROW NATURAL RESOURCES EDUCATION CENTER
(P. 54, B-4, #67) 611 Sheridan St., Eagle River

715-479-6456
FACILITIES: 1 groomed km; rentals; lessons.
 Though the trail is just a training loop, it offers both flat and hilly wooded sections, and the center provides pamphlets and displays on forest conservation.

WAGON TRAIL RESORT
(P. 54, C-5, #68) 1041 Highway 22, Ellison Bay
414-854-2385
FACILITIES: 5 groomed km; rentals; snowshoeing; child care; lodging and restaurant.
 This charming retreat on Rowleys Bay abuts state park lands, linking it to thousands of backcountry acres, a wildlife preserve, and a waterfowl sanctuary.

WHITNALL PARK
(P. 54, D-5, #69) 5879 S. 92 St., Milwaukee
414-257-5100
FACILITIES: 6 groomed km (with skating lane); rentals; restaurant.

WILD WOLF INN CROSS-COUNTRY TRAILS
(P. 54, C-4, #70) N2580 Highway 55, White Lake
715-882-8611
FACILITIES: 20 groomed km; rentals; lessons; snowshoeing; lodging and restaurant.

WILLOW CREEK PARKS
(P. 54, D-4, #71) Wautoma
414-787-4631
FACILITIES: 2.5 groomed km; rentals; restaurant.

WOODLAND DUNES NATURE CENTER
(P. 54, D-5, #72) Manitowoc
414-793-4007
FACILITIES: 13.5 groomed km; rentals; restaurant.
 The trails are nicely varied; the nature center itself offers displays on conservation and the environment.

WYOMING

Wyoming, the USA's least populated state, is nature's workshop, a savagely beautiful tribute to its creative—and destructive—powers. Yellowstone National Park dominates the Cowboy State, attracting the bear's share of tourism. Yet Yellowstone sits in the shadow of an equally impressive sight: the soaring, jagged peaks of the Grand Teton range (also a national park). Not only can you ski the majestic mountains, you can also skate, glide, or snowmobile throughout the region along designated roads, visiting such legendary sites as Old Faithful, the rainbow-hued limestone staircase of Mammoth Hot Springs, and Yellowstone Falls. ❄ Wildlife sightings here are the rule, rather than the exception. While in the Jackson area, be sure to visit the National Elk Refuge, where the USA's largest herd resides. Horse-drawn sleigh rides are available. Skiers also can stay at various working cattle ranches that access thousands of acres of pristine wilderness. And High Mountains Heli-skiing (307-733-3274) drops you right in the middle of the lonesome, awe-inspiring Teton range. ❄ If you find yourself craving some urban excitement, Jackson is a rollicking, rough-and-ready cowboy town. Saunter into the Million Dollar Cowboy Bar and set yourself down on one of the saddle stools. Cody offers the rich legacy of Western legends like Calamity Jane, and Wild Bill himself.

ALPINE

ANTELOPE BUTTE/BIG HORN
(P. 55, A-4, #1) 26 Kleiber Rd., Dayton
307-655-9530
TRAILS, 5; LIFTS, 3; VERTICAL, 1,000'.
▶NORDIC: 5 groomed km.
A nice mix of cruisers (Whitetail is the most popular run) and sharper headwalls.

GRAND TARGHEE RESORT
(P. 55, B-2, #2) Ski Hill Road, Alta
307-355-2300; 353-2304; 800-TARGHEE
SEASON: Nov. 20-April 30
ANNUAL SNOWFALL: 504"
TERRAIN: 42 trails over 1,500 acres; longest run, 2.5 mi.; ◆ 20%; ■ 70%; ● 10%.
LIFTS: 4 (3 doubles, 1 surface); capacity, 3,600 per hour.
SUMMIT: 10,200'
VERTICAL: 2,200'
ACTIVITIES: Snowboarding; NASTAR; snowcat skiing; dog sledding; sleigh rides.
FEATURES: Ski school; restaurants; child care; rentals.
▶NORDIC: 15 groomed km. (with skating lane); rentals; lessons; telemarking.
Targhee is the best place to learn powder skiing in the West (rivaled only by Colorado's Irwin Lodge). It also offers some of the finest intermediate terrain anywhere. Most of the trails are above tree line bowls and ridge runs, with plenty of elbow room. If your confidence requires building after a tough day, the mountain grooms about 300 acres of runs. And despite its growing reputation, Targhee remains both down-to-earth and blissfully uncrowded, since experts usually opt for the terrain at Utah's Alta or Snowbird. Locals call this the "sunny side of the Tetons": When it isn't snowing, the sun is out full force, adding almost an hour of good light and creating a majestic alpenglow display at dusk. If you think you've skied the whole area, Targhee runs snowcat tours of Peaked Mountain, which boasts over 1,500 additional acres of pristine terrain (there is talk of installing three lifts). One of the friendliest areas around, Targhee is even developing a quietly arty reputation, thanks to dynamic owners Carol and Mory Bergmeyer. Escapees from the city rat race, they ensure that development takes a back seat to the surroundings. Talk about natural splendour: The Tetons seem to hover right in your face. Nordic trails wind through meadows and aspen glades, with stunning views of the Yellowstone area.

HIGH PARK SKI AREA
(P. 55, B-3, #3) U.S. 36, Worland
307-347-4480
TRAILS, 6; LIFTS, 2; VERTICAL, 600'.

HOGADON SKI AREA
(P. 55, C-4, #4) State Route 251, 11 mi. S of Casper
307-235-8499
TRAILS, 17; LIFTS, 3; VERTICAL, 650'.
There's something for everyone at this agreeable gladed area, from narrow fearsome steeps to wider cruisers. Some fine cross-country trails groomed by the county wind right to the mountain.

JACKSON HOLE/TETON VILLAGE
(P. 55, B-2, #5) 7658 N. Teewinot Chairlift Rd., Teton Village
307-733-2292
SEASON: Dec. 1-April 15
ANNUAL SNOWFALL: 356"
TERRAIN: 62 trails and bowls over 3,000 acres; ◆ 50%; ■ 40%; ● 10%.
LIFTS: 9 (1 tram, 1 quad, 1 triple, 5 doubles, 1 surface); capacity, 9,700 per hour.
SUMMIT: 10,450'
VERTICAL: 4,139'
ACTIVITIES: Snowboarding; NASTAR; snowmobiling.
FEATURES: Snowmaking 5%; ski school; restaurants; rentals.
▶NORDIC: 22 groomed km (with skating lane); rentals; lessons; telemarking.
Black, blacker, blackest. An ornery mountain. That's Jackson Hole's rep—especially among those who haven't skied it. Recreational types look at that incredible vertical (the USA's highest) and whopping 50% advanced rating (much of it sending chills down the spines of mere experts) and think, this ain't for me. But helpful ski hosts answer questions and lead familiarization tours of the area every morning. And needless to say, Jackson has a tremendous ski school, headed by the legendary Austrian Olympic-medalist Pepi Stiegler. If you're smart, you'll invest in a lesson, no matter what your ability. With 3,000 skiable acres, there are 1,500 acres of intermediate and beginner trails. Granted, many of the blue runs present a challenge. And though only 300 acres are rated green—these sit at the base of Après Vous Mountain—they make up a safely novice area. Only those about to graduate to low intermediate status, may feel left out of the equation—and the fun. Après Vous has miles of groomed cruisers (try Werner and Moran), with Casper Bowl and the soft moguls of St. Johns awaiting those ready for a taste of the steeper and deeper. Everyone else heads for the tram to the top of Rendezvous Mountain (grumbling about paying the extra two bucks for tram privileges). The great ones (or those whose brains were scrambled by one too many falls) head for their beloved chutes and gullies, like Alta and Expert. The most famous, the 600-foot 45-degree Corbet's Couloir (nicknamed "Lemming's Leap" by locals) can seem like bungee-jumping without the cord. It takes a 15-foot freefall just to hit ground. Then there are the wondrously precipitous bowls, like Laramie, Cheyenne, and Rendezvous. Their moguls are practice runs for The Hobacks, blissful powder magnets that are the stuff of extreme dreams. Intermediates can hazard the 3,000-vertical foot drop on Gros Ventre. The views are sensational everywhere you look, which accounts for the lure of Jackson's Nordic center. It also runs excursions into Grand Teton National Park. Teton Village is yet another mountain development, but Jackson itself, 12 miles away, is a genuine, swaggering Western town. Its ambiance carries over to the laid-back, down-home ski area, where the only style that counts is how you carve those turns.

PINE CREEK SKI AREA
(P. 55, C-2, #6) Off State Route 232, Pine Creek Canyon, 6 mi. NE of Cokeville
307-279-3201
TRAILS, 13; LIFTS, 2,; VERTICAL, 1,150'.

SLEEPING GIANT SKI AREA

(P. 55, A-2, #7) U.S. 14, 16 & 20, 48 mi. W of Cody
307-587-4044
TRAILS, 20; LIFTS, 3; VERTICAL, 500'.

▶NORDIC: 25 groomed km.
Sleeping Giant has several criss-crossing runs with rolling pitches that offer good challenge and variety. Locals appreciate the steady sunshine and lack of wind, too.

SNOW KING RESORT

(P. 55, B-2, #8) 400 E. Snow King Ave., Jackson
307-733-5200
SEASON: Dec. 5-April 4
ANNUAL SNOWFALL: 150"
TERRAIN: trails over 400 acres; longest run, 1 mile; ◆ 60%; ■ 25%; ● 15%.
LIFTS: 3 (2 doubles, 1 surface); capacity, 2,700 per hour.
SUMMIT: 7,781'
VERTICAL: 1,571'
ACTIVITIES: Snowboarding; ice skating; sleigh rides; night skiing.
FEATURES: Snowmaking 10%; ski school; restaurants; rentals.
Skiers dazzled by Jackson Hole or Grand Targhee often overlook Snow King, a locals' area in the best sense of the word, since no one else ever seems to ski it. They affectionately call it "Town Hill." What a hill! Snow King looms above Jackson. It's usually empty and offers lots of steeps, most of them ungroomed, like the S chutes and Belly Roll. Mogul runs and great powder skiing through trees are bountiful. The bottom half of the mountain is mostly intermediate—but many of those runs are navy blue, such as Elk and Exhibition. Beware: The only green run is a twisty catwalk; and since the area is usually shaded, it's sometimes icy or hardpacked.

SNOWSHOE HOLLOW SKI AREA

(P. 55, C-2, #9) Afton
307-886-9831
TRAILS, 1; LIFTS, 1; VERTICAL, 100'.

SNOWY RANGE SKI AREA

(P. 55, D-4, #10) 1414 Thomas, Centennial, on State Route 130, 32 mi. W of Laramie
307-745-5750
SEASON: Nov. 25-April 15 (open Wed.-Sun., holidays)
ANNUAL SNOWFALL: 240"
TERRAIN: 24 trails over 150 acres; longest run, 1.75 mi.; ◆ 30%; ■ 40%; ● 30%.
LIFTS: 4 (1 triple, 2 doubles, 1 surface); capacity, 3,000 per hour.
SUMMIT: 9,990'
VERTICAL: 990'
ACTIVITIES: Snowboarding.

Courtesy: Ski The Summit (see Colorado, p. 96).

FEATURES: Snowmaking 40%; ski school; restaurant; rentals.
Snowy Range appeals primarily to novices and intermediates, who enjoy wide cruisers with lots of rolls like Rawhide. Experts can check out bump runs like Crazy Horse and Overland.

NORDIC

BIG HORN MOUNTAIN SPORTS

(P. 55, A-4, #11) 334 N. Main, Sheridan
307-672-6866
FACILITIES: 50 groomed km; unlimited backcountry; rentals; lessons.
Big Horn operates trail systems in both Buffalo and Sheridan, with a vast range of terrain that includes rolling meadows and chutes (for those who want them).

DORNAN'S SPUR RANCH

(P. 55, B-2, #12) Moose
307-733-2522
FACILITIES: Unlimited backcountry; rentals; lodging and restaurant.
Founders and owners, the Dornan family homesteaded in Grand Teton National Park before it was declared a protected area. So you're right in the middle of the wilderness at this 1919 lodge. The ungroomed trails snake around the park's many gorgeous, alpine lakes.

PAHASKA TEPEE RESORT

(P. 55, A-3, #13) 183

Yellowstone Highway, Cody
307-527-7701
FACILITIES: 20 groomed km; rentals; lessons; snowmobiling; lodging and restaurant.
The resort occupies Buffalo Bill's original hunting lodge, and the area remains wild and unspoiled, with trails for all levels of ability.

SPRING CREEK RESORT

(P. 55, B-2, #14) Jackson
307-733-8833; 800-443-6139
FACILITIES: 10 groomed km (with skating lane); rentals; lessons; lodging and restaurant; night skiing (2 km lit).

SQUAW CREEK RANCH

(P. 55, A-3, #15) 4059 Crandall Rd., Cody
307-587-6178
FACILITIES: 8 groomed km; rentals (by prior arrangement); lessons; lodging and restaurant.

TETON PINES CROSS-COUNTRY

(P. 55, B-2, #16) Star Route, Jackson
307-733-1005
FACILITIES: 13 groomed km; rentals; lessons; restaurant.
The course covers the relatively flat Arnold Palmer-designed golf course, a beauty that snakes around aspens, willows and ponds; the ski school is particularly adept at working with children, making this a prime family destination.

TOGWOTEE MOUNTAIN LODGE TOURING CENTER

(P. 55, B-2, #17) U.S. 26, Moran
307-543-2847
FACILITIES: 15 groomed km; rentals; lessons; snowmobiling; dog sledding; lodging and restaurant.
The lodge opens onto magnificent terrain in the Bridger-Teton National Forest, with thrilling mountain views. Guided tours venture into the 2 million acres of surrounding wilderness.

WOOD RIVER X-C SKI PARK

(P. 55, B-3, #18) Meeteetse
307-868-2603
FACILITIES: 22 groomed km, 10 ungroomed; rentals; lodging and restaurant.

YELLOWSTONE NATIONAL PARK TW RECREATIONAL SERVICES

(P. 55, A-2, #19) Yellowstone National Park
307-344-7311
FACILITIES: 24 groomed km; unlimited backcountry touring; rentals; lessons; ice skating; lodging and restaurant.
Not only do trails wind through some of the USA's most extraordinary scenery, but the venerable Mammoth Hot Springs Hotel and Old Faithful Snow Lodge offer winter wildlife tours and a true getaway-from-it-all experience.

LOW SNOW STATES

Once upon a time local folk in Alabama and Georgia would drag a lawn chair to the neighborhood area to watch the shenanigans of the first-timers falling off lifts, then snowballing down the slopes. Yes, it may seem as though the Great Plains, Mid-Atlantic Coast and Deep South offer little for skiers. And true, what venues exist are small affairs, subject to the whims of the weather. Yet they serve a vital purpose as learning hills and in spreading a contagious enthusiasm for the sport. Folks in Georgia, Florida, Texas, Oklahoma and the like are avid skiers, driving hundreds of miles to the nearest lifts. Their ski clubs are among the most active in the USA, constantly organizing trips, and their retail shops carry the latest merchandise, holding frequent sales and special events (we have included representative examples of each for non-ski states). And you never know when Mother Nature will blanket state parks and forests with a glistening layer of snow, prompting locals to break out their skinny skis. All of which makes the following Low Snow States (the title refers to skiable snow, with an emphasis on Alpine) high-performance indeed.

ALABAMA

TOURISM: 800-ALABAMA

CLOUDMONT SKI RESORT
(P. 8, A-4, #1) Route 117, Mentone
205-634-4344
SEASON: Dec. 15-March 1
ANNUAL SNOWFALL: 15"
TERRAIN: 2 slopes over 3 acres; longest run 1,000'; ▪ 50%; ● 50%.
LIFTS: 2 (2 surface); capacity, 1,000 per hour.
SUMMIT: 1,870'
VERTICAL: 150'
ACTIVITIES: Snowboarding; night skiing.
FEATURES: Snowmaking 100%; professional ski patrol; ski school; restaurant; rentals.
A day area for Atlanta, Birmingham, Chattanooga, and Huntsville residents, where many kids cut their teeth on the gentle slopes, Cloudmont's main distinction is as one of the USA's southernmost ski venues. If conditions don't permit skiing, the owners take groups to their dude ranch for horseback riding.

ARKANSAS

TOURISM: 800-NATURAL

RETAIL: Ozark Mountain Sports (Siloam Spring, 501-524-6948).

CLUB: Little Rock Ski Club, c/o Mike Graves, 1009 N. Polk, Little Rock, AR 72205.

DELAWARE

TOURISM: 800-441-8846

RETAIL: Ski Bum (Newark, 302-454-9829).

FLORIDA

TOURISM: 904-487-1462

RETAIL: Breidenbach's Ski & Sport (Tampa, 813-960-7663); Peter Glenn of Vermont (Ft. Lauderdale, 305-484-7800); Ski World of Orlando (407-894-5012).

CLUB: Florida Ski Council, c/o Dr. Len Indianer, 501 Plaza Blvd., Daytona Beach, FL 32018.

GEORGIA

TOURISM: 800-847-4842

SKY VALLEY SKI RESORT
(P. 18, A-3, #1) Route 115, Dillard
706-746-5302
SEASON: Dec. 15-March 1
ANNUAL SNOWFALL: 30"
TERRAIN: 5 trails over 16 acres; longest run 2,200'; ▪ 40%; ● 60%.
LIFTS: 2 (1 double, 1 surface); capacity, 1,400 per hour.
SUMMIT: 3,325'
VERTICAL: 210'
ACTIVITIES: Hiking; snowshoeing; horseback riding.
FEATURES: Snowmaking 100%; professional ski patrol; ski school; restaurant; repair and rentals.
A full-service, four-season resort, Sky Valley offers golf, horseback riding, and tennis most of the year as well as skiing, and serves as a training ground for many Atlantan youngsters.

HAWAII

TOURISM: 808-923-1811

Believe it or not, there is skiing in Aloha-land, albeit for the intrepid. Adventure outfitters run trips to ski down Mauna Kea and cross-country on Mauna Loa. After all, they're both over 14,000 feet and eternally snow-capped. Unfortunately, the effects of El Nino have made skiing spotty: Call the Tourist Board for more information. When tours are offered, the experience is memorable: Warm weather, dazzling ocean views and consistent corn snow. The Nordic trails follow old lava rivers; the downhill runs include bowls, cinder cones and cornices up top averaging 35 to 45 degrees in pitch, with gentler rolling terrain for intermediates further down. Vertical ranges from 400 to 1,000 feet.

RETAIL: Choice International (Honolulu, 808-488-6903); Ice Cubes (Honolulu, 808-579-8634).

CLUB: Ski Association of Hawaii, c/o Gary Oda, 409 Mamaki St., Honolulu, HI 96821.

KANSAS

TOURISM: 800-2KANSAS

CLUB: Flatland Ski Association, P.O. Box 19131, Oklahoma City, OK 73144.

KENTUCKY

TOURISM: 800-225-TRIP

SKI BUTLER
(P. 27, A-6, #1) Route 42 (in General Butler State Park), Carrollton
502-732-4231 (res.); 800-456-3284 (snow)
SEASON: Dec. 15-March 15
ANNUAL SNOWFALL: 14"
TERRAIN: 8 trails over 25 acres; longest run 3,300'; ◆ 20%; ▪ 75%; ● 20%.
LIFTS: 7 (1 triple, 2 doubles, 4 surface); capacity, 4,400 per hour.
SUMMIT: 900'
VERTICAL: 300'
ACTIVITIES: Snowboarding; night skiing.
FEATURES: Snowmaking 100%; professional ski patrol; ski school; restaurants; repair and rentals.
This small family area is convenient for visits to the state capital of Frankfort, the thoroughbred farms of the Bluegrass Country, and the many attractions of fast-growing Lexington and Louisville. There is an adequate variety of terrain, given the area's size and vertical drop, as well as a half pipe for snowboarders. Spectacular Bid (yes, the runs are named for Derby winners) is satisfyingly steep. The party-hearty crowd can indulge in night skiing until 6 A.M. on Fridays and Saturdays. There is fine, ungroomed cross-country terrain in the state park.

LOUISIANA

TOURISM: 800-33-GUMBO

RETAIL: Security Sporting Goods (Alexandria, 318-445-6246); Sporthaus (Shreveport, 318-869-4468).

CLUB: Crescent Ski Council (see Mississippi).

MARYLAND

TOURISM: 800-MD-IS-FUN

ALPINE

WISP SKI AREA
(P. 17, C-6, #1) Marsh Hill Road, McHenry
301-387-4911
SEASON: Nov. 25-March 20
ANNUAL SNOWFALL: 90"
TERRAIN: 23 trails on 80 acres; longest run 1.75 mi.; ◆ 30%; ▪ 50%; ● 20%.
LIFTS: 7 (3 doubles, 2 triples, 2 surface); capacity 9,120 per hour.
SUMMIT: 3,080'
VERTICAL: 610'
ACTIVITIES: Snowboarding; NASTAR; night skiing.
FEATURES: Snowmaking 90%; child care; ski school; restaurants; rentals.
Wisp's respectable, 610-foot vertical means some gratifyingly steep, if short, runs for experts, such as Main Street (on the new East Ridge section), The Face, and Squirrel Cage. All have potential to develop big bumps; the rest of the area has

predominantly moderate difficulty—ideal for working on form. There are some thrilling views of surrounding mountains and farms, as well as glimpses of Deep Creek Lake.

NORDIC

HERRINGTON MANOR
(P. 17, C-6, #2) Route 5, Oakland
301-334-9180
FACILITIES: 16 groomed km; rentals; lessons; restaurant.
 One of the most scenic spots in the Appalachians, Herrington Manor draws skinny skaters from several states who enjoy gliding by the lake on gentle terrain.

NEW GERMANY CROSS-COUNTRY
(P. 17, B-6, #3) Route 2, Grantsville
301-895-5453
FACILITIES: 17 groomed km; restaurant.
 Another highly regarded track system with a good mix of terrain for all abilities; despite the lack of facilities, this state park is one of the preeminent Nordic centers in the South.

MISSISSIPPI

TOURISM: 601-875-0705

CLUB: Contact the Crescent Ski Council, P.O. Box 19131, Greenville, SC 29606, which represents seven Southern states.

MISSOURI

TOURISM: 800-877-1234

HIDDEN VALLEY SKI AREA
(P. 35, C-4, #1) Highway 109, 4 mi. north of Eureka
314-938-5373; 314-938-6999 (snow)
SEASON: Dec. 15-March 8
ANNUAL SNOWFALL: 18"
TERRAIN: 5 trails over 8 acres; longest run 1,600'; ■ 60%; ● 40%.
LIFTS: 6 (2 triples, 4 surface); capacity, 2,500 per hour.
SUMMIT: 775'
VERTICAL: 282'
ACTIVITIES: Night skiing.
FEATURES: Snowmaking 100%; ski school; restaurant; rentals.
 Hidden Valley attracts a large crowd of first-timers from St. Louis (just 20 mi. away).

SNOW BLUFF SKI & FUN AREA
(P. 35, D-2, #2) Highway 13, Brighton
417-756-2201
SEASON: Dec. 15-Feb. 28 (week-

ends only)
ANNUAL SNOWFALL: 17"
TERRAIN: 9 trails over 25 acres; longest run 1,750'; ◆ 11%; ■ 22%; ● 67%.
LIFTS: 5 (1 double, 4 surface); capacity, 2,200 per hour.
SUMMIT: 300'
VERTICAL: 150'
ACTIVITIES: Snowboarding; tubing; night skiing.
FEATURES: Snowmaking 100%; ski school; restaurant; rentals.
 A pleasant little family area nestled amid the gentle beauty of the Ozarks.

NEBRASKA

TOURISM: 800-228-4307

NEBRASKI AREA COMPLEX
(P. 36, C-6, #1) 19001 Fishery Rd., Gretna
402-332-3313
SEASON: Nov. 15-April 1
ANNUAL SNOWFALL: 50"
TERRAIN: 15 trails over 80 acres; longest run, 1,800 feet
LIFTS: 5 (1 double, 4 surface); capacity, 3,500 per hour.
SUMMIT: 1,250'
VERTICAL: 200'
ACTIVITIES: Night skiing.
FEATURES: Snowmaking 100%; ski school; restaurant; rentals.
 This area's tree-lined slopes are fairly basic, but surprisingly pleasant for advanced beginners looking to sharpen their skills. It may close, so call ahead.

NEVADA

TOURISM: 800-NEVADA8

ALPINE

DIAMOND PEAK SKI RESORT

(P. 37, C-1, #1) 1210 Ski Way, Incline Village
702-832-1177; 702-832-1132 (snow)
SEASON: Nov. 15-April 15
ANNUAL SNOWFALL: 300"
TERRAIN: 35 trails over 655 acres; longest run, 2.5 mi.; ◆ 33%; ■ 49%; ● 18%.
LIFTS: 7 (1 quad, 6 doubles); capacity, 7,628 per hour.
SUMMIT: 8,540'
VERTICAL: 1,800'
ACTIVITIES: Snowboarding; NASTAR.
FEATURES: Snowmaking 80%; ski school; restaurant; rentals.
▶NORDIC: 35 groomed km; rentals; lessons.
 Friendly and service-oriented: two reasons why Diamond Peak is one of the premier family areas in the Tahoe basin. The area has improved virtually every aspect of customer service the past several years, including increasing rentals and snowmaking capacity, (the highest in Tahoe). A major expansion doubled existing terrain and vertical a few years back, adding Diamond Peak, but skiers seem not to have caught on as it remains relatively uncrowded. The ski school is as sizable as that of resorts twice its size; instructors are particularly good with kids, incorporating bits of local lore and natural history into their lessons. The skiing is solidly intermediate off The Ridge. Crystal Ridge and Solitude Canyon offer a few chutes and ungroomed steeps to keep experts happy. The Nordic system's high elevation guarantees superb snow, with some rousing lake views as a bonus.

LEE CANYON SKI AREA
(P. 37, E-4, #2) State Route 156, 47 mi. from Las Vegas
702-872-5462; 702-593-9500 (snow)
SEASON: Nov. 25-April 8
ANNUAL SNOWFALL: 150"

USA SNAPSHOTS®

A look at statistics that shape the sports world

Where ski dollars go

About $5.5 billion is spent annually at ski areas. Where the money goes:

Ski-lift tickets 54%
Food/beverage 11%
Non-skiing recreation 8%
Ski lessons 7%
Ski equipment/clothing 4%
Equipment rental 4%
Miscellaneous 12%

Source: Economic Analysis of North American Ski Areas

By Suzy Parker, USA TODAY

TERRAIN: 10 trails over 200 acres; longest run, 5,000'; ◆ 10%; ■ 80%; ● 10%.
LIFTS: 3 (3 doubles); capacity, 3,500 per hour.
SUMMIT: 9,340'
VERTICAL: 1,020'
ACTIVITIES: Night skiing.
FEATURES: Snowmaking 65%; ski school; restaurant; rentals.
 People who think of Vegas as a desert town haven't seen the imposing mountains circling the Strip. Lee Canyon offers empty slopes and wide cruisers, enough to warrant the 50-minute drive if you get the ski bug.

MOUNT ROSE SKI AREA
(P. 37, C-1, #3) 22222 Mt. Rose Highway, Route 431, 22 mi. SW of Reno
800-SKI-ROSE
SEASON: Nov. 15-April 25
ANNUAL SNOWFALL: 400"
TERRAIN: 41 trails over 900 acres; longest run, 2.5 mi.; ◆ 35%; ■ 35%; ● 30%.
LIFTS: 5 (1 quad, 3 triples, 1 double); capacity, 8,600 per hour.
SUMMIT: 9,700'
VERTICAL: 1,440'
ACTIVITIES: Snowboarding.
FEATURES: Professional ski patrol; ski school; restaurant; rentals.
 In an effort to keep up with the big boys, Mt. Rose has recontoured trails to provide more challenging drops as well as gentler beginner terrain. It's also beefed up rental selection and food services to attract the serious skiing crowd. The deserted slopes, great snow and proximity to Reno should be sufficient.

NORDIC

SPOONER LAKE CROSS-COUNTRY
(P. 37, C-1, #4) Glenbrook
702-749-5349
FACILITIES: 20 groomed km; rentals; lessons; restaurant.
 A nice blend of terrain with some smashing desert views.

NORTH DAKOTA

TOURISM: 800-435-5663

BOTTINEAU WINTER PARK
(P. 44, B-3, #1) Highway 5 East, Bottineau
701-263-4556
SEASON: Nov. 15-May 15
ANNUAL SNOWFALL: 70"
TERRAIN: 9 trails over 50 acres; longest run, 1,250'; ◆ 30%; ■ 30%; ● 40%.
LIFTS: 5 (5 surface); capacity, 4,800 per hour.
SUMMIT: NA
VERTICAL: 200'

ACTIVITIES: Snowboarding; night skiing.
FEATURES: Snowmaking 100%; ski school; restaurant; rentals. Nothing very challenging here, although it's popular with local snowboarders (it just installed a half pipe) and the newly added Raceway attracts downhillers from Manitoba.

FROSTFIRE MOUNTAIN
(P. 44, B-5, #2) Highway 55, 6 mi. W of Walhalla
701-549-3600
SEASON: Nov. 15-March 31
ANNUAL SNOWFALL: 40″
TERRAIN: 9 trails over 25 acres; longest run, 2,600'; ♦ 60; ▪ 30%; ● 10%.
LIFTS: 3 (2 doubles, 1 surface); capacity, 1,800 per hour.
SUMMIT: 1,350'
VERTICAL: 350'
ACTIVITIES: Snowboarding.
FEATURES: Snowmaking 100%; ski school; restaurant; rentals. Frostfire offers a mix of open bowls and tight glades, making the skiing better than you'd think for such a small area. Prairie Smoke has varied terrain and several steep pitches; the narrower, twisty Columbine attracts experts.

SKYLINE SKIWAY
(P. 44, B-4, #3) Devils Lake
701-766-4035; 701-662-5618 (snow)
SEASON: Dec. 15-March 15
ANNUAL SNOWFALL: 90″
TERRAIN: 5 trails over 40 acres; longest run, 2,200'; ♦ 40%; ▪ 30%; ● 30%.
LIFTS: 3 (3 surface); capacity, 1,200 per hour.
SUMMIT: 1,740'
VERTICAL: 310'
ACTIVITIES: Sledding; tubing.
FEATURES: Snowmaking; restaurant; rentals. Although it offers fewer amenities, Skyline is noted for its consistently steep runs (Schuss is left bumped up). A half pipe will be installed for boarders.

OKLAHOMA

TOURISM: 800-652-6552

RETAIL: Chalet Sports (Oklahoma City, 405-840-1616); Skier's Choice (Tulsa, 918-494-5656).

CLUB: Flatlands Ski Association, P.O. Box 19131, Oklahoma City, OK 73144.

RHODE ISLAND

TOURISM: 800-556-2484

YAWGOO VALLEY
(P. 30, D-4, #1) Off Route 2, Exeter
401-294-3802; 401-295-5366 (snow)
SEASON: Dec. 1-March 31
ANNUAL SNOWFALL: 65″
TERRAIN: 11 trails over 28 acres; longest run, 2,200'; ♦ 20%; ▪ 30%; ● 50%.
LIFTS: 3 (2 doubles, 1 surface); capacity, 2,700 per hour.
SUMMIT: 315'
VERTICAL: 245'
ACTIVITIES: Snowboarding; tubing; night skiing.
FEATURES: Snowmaking 100%; ski school; restaurant; rentals. This locals' area boasts an excellent ski school and mostly gentle slopes. It's adding both an advanced trail and a snowboard park to please the hotshots in the family. Yawgoo's primary interest for out-of-towners is the proximity to Newport, one of the fabled haunts of the rich and famous.

SOUTH CAROLINA

TOURISM: 800-346-3634

RETAIL: The Ski Shop (Columbia, 803-750-5200); Sailing and Ski Connection (Myrtle Beach, 803-626-7245).

CLUB: Crescent Ski Council, P.O. Box 19131, Greenville, SC 29606.

SOUTH DAKOTA

TOURISM: 800-SDAKOTA

ALPINE

DEER MOUNTAIN SKI AREA
(P.49, C-1, #1) 81 Sherman, off Highway 85, Deadwood
605-584-3230
SEASON: Nov. 25-April 15
ANNUAL SNOWFALL: 150″
TERRAIN: 25 trails over 200 acres; longest run, 1 mi.; ♦ 25%; ▪ 50%; ● 25%.
LIFTS: 4 (1 triple, 3 surface); capacity, 2,300 per hour.
SUMMIT: 6,600'
VERTICAL: 600'
ACTIVITIES: Snowboarding; night skiing.
FEATURES: Snowmaking 50%; ski school; restaurant; rentals.
▶NORDIC: NA groomed km; rentals; lessons. Deer Mountain offers a surprising variety of terrain, including open areas and tree-lined slopes. There are stupendous views of the tortured landscape of the Black Hills. For a change of pace, find glimpses of the Old West in Deadwood, stomping grounds of legendary characters Wild Bill Hickok and Calamity Jane.

TERRY PEAK SKI AREA
(P. 49, C-1, #2) Nevada Gulch, 3 mi. W of Lead
605-584-2165; 800-456-0524 (snow)
SEASON: Nov. 25-April 8
ANNUAL SNOWFALL: 150″
TERRAIN: 20 trails over 120 acres; longest run, 2 mi.; ♦ 30%; ▪ 50%; ● 20%.
LIFTS: 5 (1 quad, 1 triple, 3 doubles); capacity, 5,400 per hour.
SUMMIT: 7,064'
VERTICAL: 1,052'
ACTIVITIES: Snowboarding.
FEATURES: Snowmaking 50%; ski school; restaurants; rentals. The area profile is similar to neighboring Deer Mountain's, with the advantage of a greater vertical and longer runs (they average 1.25 miles). Kussy is an enjoyable cruiser; the aptly-named Holy Terror develops some nasty bumps. Children under 6 ski free.

NORDIC

RIVERVIEW CROSS-COUNTRY-SKI CENTER
(P. 49, D-6, #3) Rural Route 3, Canton
605-987-5171
Facilities: 25 groomed km, 5 ungroomed; rentals; lessons; restaurant.

SKI CROSS-COUNTRY
(P. 49, C-1, #4) Spearfish
605-642-3851
FACILITIES: 26 groomed km; rentals; lessons. Actually a shop, but the owners are the best source of information on the area and are full of helpful suggestions. Excellent instructors are also available here. The store occasionally runs tours into the Black Hills National Forest (the 26-km system).

TENNESSEE

TOURISM: 615-741-2158

OBER GATLINBURG
(P. 27, D-8, #1) 1001 Parkway St., off Route 441 S, Gatlinburg
615-436-5423
SEASON: Dec. 1-March 1
ANNUAL SNOWFALL: 50″
TERRAIN: 8 trails over 38 acres; longest run, 5,000'; ♦ 25%; ▪ 50%; ● 25%.
LIFTS: 6 (1 tram, 2 quads, 2 doubles, 1 surface); capacity, 6,000 per hour.
SUMMIT: 3,300'
VERTICAL: 600'
ACTIVITIES: Snowboarding; ice skating; bungee tower; alpine slide; night skiing.
FEATURES: Snowmaking 100%; ski school; restaurants; rentals.

The skiing at Ober Gatlinburg offers acceptable variety, with a sizable beginner's area, cruisers like Castle Run and the tougher Ober Chute, and Mogul Ridge for the show-offs. A 5-acre Astroturf slope even permits skiing in summer. And when snow cover permits, there is unrivalled ski touring in Great Smokies National Park. But the real reasons to ski here are the fine resort facilities, ravishing Smokies vistas and quaint town (the tram rises 1,000 scenic feet right from the main street to the slopes of Mount Harrison). Non-skiers will love the variety of attractions in town, including regional crafts shops, a wax museum and Ripley's Believe It or Not museum. Moreover, C&W fans can cavort through nearby Pigeon Forge and Dollywood, a theme park as charmingly boisterous as Ms. Parton herself.

TEXAS

TOURISM: 800-888-8TEX

RETAIL: Sports Express (Houston, 713-537-8669); The Warming Hut (Dallas, 214-2334-6088); Zen 'n Boards (Austin, 512-448-4516).

CLUB: Texas Ski Council, c/o Jerry Montgomery, 2830 Lakeview Dr., Missouri City, TX 77459.

In many respects, the ski conditions and weather patterns of the Great White North mimic those of the Lower 48. ❄ Quebec and the Maritime Provinces in the East offer the same below-treeline skiing, through thick stands of spruce and pine, many of the trails classically narrow and winding. Yes, it's cold, and yes, there's ice. But for many skiers that's the ultimate challenge, just you against the mountain and the elements. These provinces also boast an equally rich architectural legacy of the French and British colonials in classic white steepled churches, weathered stone farmhouses, covered bridges, and picturesque fishing villages that cling stubbornly to the steep, highland cliffs and rugged fjords. Throughout the East, Nordic clubs maintain trails, many of them free of charge (and lacking facilities), as do National and Provincial Parks and Forests. ❄ Much of central Canada, Ontario and Manitoba, is covered by the Canadian shield, ancient eroded ranges whose highest peaks barely attain summits of 2,000 feet. Many of Ontario's areas are exceptionally scenic, affording stunning Lake Superior views, while Manitoba's dense woodlands and craggy hills are ideal for gliding. The rolling wheat fields of Saskatchewan give way to the foothills of the Rockies, blanketed with towering stands of spruce and lodge pole pine, and featuring surprisingly varied terrain, including tawny sand dunes as curvaceous as Rubens' nudes. Canada's own Old West heritage comes alive here, replete with Native American villages and frontier towns like Maple Ridge. ❄ Alberta's jagged Rockies, even younger than the USA's, are a wild tangle of glaciers, granite and evergreen so heart-stoppingly beautiful UNESCO accorded them World Heritage Site status. Add to that eiderdown-soft powder and challenging slopes and you have skier's heaven. Alberta is also legendary among cross-country skiers for its many isolated guest ranches and backcountry lodges like Mt. Assiniboine, Skoki, Lake O' Hara, and Mt. Engadine, all of which provide the ultimate ski touring adventure. ❄ More adventure is on tap in British Columbia, famed for its heliskiing. Conditions here range from dry and bountiful powder in the East to heavy, wet snow near the Pacific Coast, similar to Cascade Crud and Sierra Cement in the USA. The scenery is equally varied, from the spindly spires and glowering glaciers of the Rockies to the fjords and inlets of the western shore. ❄ Wherever you are, take time to explore Canada's cosmopolitan cities, from the walled Disneyesque Quebec City (another UNESCO World Heritage Site) to gleaming Toronto, to Calgary and Edmonton where the Wild West of ranchers and gold miners comes to life in a series of special events throughout the year. And for a break, share in the excitement of the ardent Canadian hockey fans the country over, taking in a Nordiques, Canadiens, Oilers, Flames, Canucks, Jets, Senators, or Maple Leafs game.

ALBERTA

ALPINE

CANADA OLYMPIC PARK
(P. 59, E-9, #1) West city limits on Bowfort Road NW, Calgary
403-286-2632; 403-288-4112 (snow)
SEASON: Nov. 15-March 31
ANNUAL SNOWFALL: 150"
TERRAIN: 5 trails over 80 acres; longest run, 2,200'; ■ 20%; ● 80%.
LIFTS: 5 (2 triples, 1 double, 2 surface); capacity, 3,000 per hour.
SUMMIT: 4,000'
VERTICAL: 400'
ACTIVITIES: Snowboarding; ski jumps; bobsled; luge; ice skating; night skiing.
FEATURES: Snowmaking 100%; ski school; restaurant; rentals.
▶NORDIC: 2 groomed km; lessons; rentals; night skiing.
A marvelous learner's area, with enough activities (left over from the 1988 Olympics) to suit daredevils in the family, including a spanking new snowboard park.

CANYON SKI AREA
(P. 59, D-9, #2) Red Deer
403-346-5580; 403-346-5588 (snow)
TRAILS, 12; LIFTS, 5; VERTICAL, 550'.
Ski jumps; luge.

EDMONTON SKI CLUB
(P. 59, B-9, #3) 96th Avenue, River Valley, Edmonton
403-465-0852
TRAILS, 6; LIFTS, 4; VERTICAL 120'.
Ski jump.

FORTRESS MOUNTAIN
(P. 59, E-8, #4) Kananaskis Trail, Kananaskis Village
403-591-7108; 403-243-7533 (snow)
SEASON: Nov. 15-May 15
ANNUAL SNOWFALL: 200"
TERRAIN: 31 trails over 320 acres; longest run, 1.25 mi.; ◆ 25%; ■ 55%; ● 20%.
LIFTS: 7 (1 triple, 2 doubles, 4 surface); capacity, 6,800 per hour.
SUMMIT: 7,700'
VERTICAL: 1,100'
ACTIVITIES: Snowboarding.

FEATURES: Snowmaking 30%; ski school; restaurants; child care; rentals.
This friendly, affordable area is divided into three sections. The Far Side is most popular for its lengthy cruisers and constant sunshine. Trails range from tight glades to wide-open boulevards. Fortress Mountain sees a lot of late season snow, making it a great spring skiing bet. Children under 6 ski free.

KINOSOO RIDGE
(P. 60, A-1, #5) Southern shore of Cold Lake, 9 mi. E of Grand Centre
403-594-5564
TRAILS, 10; LIFTS, 2; VERTICAL 380'.

LAKE LOUISE SKI AREA
(P. 59, E-8, #6) 1550 Eighth St. SW, Lake Louise
403-522-3555; 403-244-6665 (snow)
SEASON: Nov. 7-May 5
ANNUAL SNOWFALL: 142"
TERRAIN: 50 runs over 4,000 acres; longest run, 5 mi.; ◆ 30%; ■ 45%; ● 25%.
LIFTS: 11 (2 high-speed quads, 1 quad, 2 triples, 3 doubles, 3 surface); capacity, 21,164 per hour.
SUMMIT: 8,765'
VERTICAL: 3,257'
ACTIVITIES: Snowboarding; ice skating; sleigh rides; tobogganing; dog sledding.
FEATURES: Snowmaking 40%; ski school; restaurants; child care; rentals.
▶NORDIC: Chateau Lake Louise; 403-522-3511; 100 groomed km; rentals; lessons.
One of North America's preeminent resorts, Lake Louise consistently reigns atop most surveys in numerous categories. Nestled amid Banff National Park, the scenery is unparalleled, with Victoria Glacier casting a bullying shadow over the vast lake that gives the area its name. The development is bookended by the sumptuous Chateau Lake Louise and the Post Hotel, creating one of the most elegant, refined resorts in skidom. The terrain is wonderfully varied, with particularly superb bowls crowning the top third of the two mountains, and four faces. The layout also wins kudos, as each lift, save the Summit platter, accesses runs for all abilities. The Friends of Louise, a volunteer outfit, lead familiarization tours of the moun-

tain three times daily. Once beginners get their ski legs, they have their choice of long, winding roads home like Wiwaxy, Pika, and Deer Run. Intermediates face a wide array of temptations, with scenic cruisers like Eagle Meadows, Juniper, and Saddleback. The Front Face looks south and basks in daylong sun, making it a recreational skier's nirvana. Experts should head immediately for the vast Back Bowls (especially early, while they still have sun), where they'll find Paradise. Remember that a great deal of terrain on the backside is unmarked; the so-called Elevator Shaft bowl off the Larch Chair is a perfect example, providing rollercoaster thrills. The Larch area abounds in glades. The Summit Platter accesses gorgeous, above-tree line skiing for those who prefer a bumpy ride. Snowboarders have a large half pipe. Gliders will love both the groomed and trails the virtually unlimited backcountry opportunities, with incredible views at each turn.

MARMOT BASIN

(P. 59, C-7, #7) Off Highway 93, Jasper
403-852-3816
SEASON: Dec. 1-April 30
ANNUAL SNOWFALL: 160″
TERRAIN: 52 trails over 1,000 acres; longest run, 3.5 mi.; ♦ 30%; ▪ 35%; ● 35%.
LIFTS: 7 (1 high-speed quad, 1 triple, 3 doubles, 2 surface); capacity, 10,080 per hour.
SUMMIT: 7,940′
VERTICAL: 2,300′
ACTIVITIES: Snowboarding; ice skating; sleigh rides; snowshoeing.
FEATURES: Snowmaking 15%; ski school; restaurant; rentals.
▶NORDIC: 100 groomed km; rentals; lessons.
  This is Alberta's lesser-known beauty. Lake Louise grabs most of the headlines, thanks to its proximity to Calgary. Yet Marmot Basin boasts equally stunning scenery in Jasper National Park, comparatively deserted slopes, and splendid terrain for all abilities. The lower peak, Caribou Ridge, is mostly below tree line, and offers both wider cruisers and powder glades (some of the best tree skiing in Canada can be found off the Kiefer T-bar and triple chair; try the Milk Run area). The higher Marmot Peak is a series of rugged chutes and bowls. Charlie's Bowl is waterfall-steep and powderhound heaven. Mogulmashers can dive down the runs to the right of the Knob Chair. Recreational skiers have plenty of terrain throughout, though they'll be happiest on the lower half. Paradise is just that for intermediates and the meandering Old Road allows novices to toodle along enjoying the scenery for 1.5 miles. The town of Jasper, with a working-class ethic, stands in effective contrast to the posher Banff and Lake

Louise. The Icefields Parkway north from Banff is one of the world's most beautiful drives. Park along one of the scenic overlooks, then venture out onto the glaciers on the short hiking trails for a not-to-be-missed thrill.

MYSTIC RIDGE/MT. NORQUAY SKI AREA

(P. 59, D-8, #8) Off Highway 1, Banff
403-762-4421
SEASON: Nov. 1-April 15
ANNUAL SNOWFALL: 140″
TERRAIN: 25 trails over 162 acres; longest run, 5,350′; ♦♦ 16%; ♦ 28%; ▪ 45%; ● 11%.
LIFTS: 6 (1 high-speed quad, 1 quad, 2 doubles, 2 surface); capacity, 6,300 per hour.
SUMMIT: 7,000′
VERTICAL: 1,650′
ACTIVITIES: Snowboarding; night skiing.
FEATURES: Snowmaking 90%; ski school; restaurant; rentals.
  Mystic Ridge has shed its experts-only reputation with the addition of extensive cruising terrain in the '90s. Now options range from Lone Pine, a pogoing mogul run, to satiny cruisers like Illusion, Knight Flight, and Excalibur. An unrelenting sea of bumps is visible from the base; and, alas, the most sensational views in the Canadian Rockies can be had from the chair which heads straight for this mogul minefield, the North American. Intermediates can handle the unseen territory off the Mystic Express, where even the black runs are well-groomed. This area poses some of the ultimate challenges in Canada; the intrepid can steel themselves to shoot the chutes, like Gun Run, or take the freefall down Memorial Bowl or Valley of the Ten.

NAKISKA

(P. 59, E-8, #9) 54 mi. SW of Calgary, Kananaskis Village
403-591-7777
SEASON: Dec. 1-April 15
ANNUAL SNOWFALL: 150″
TERRAIN: 28 trails over 285 acres; longest run, 2 mi.; ♦ 14%; ▪ 70%; ● 16%.
LIFTS: 5 (2 high-speed quads, 1 triple, 1 double, 1 surface); capacity, 8,620 per hour.
SUMMIT: 7,415′
VERTICAL: 2,411′
ACTIVITIES: Snowboarding; tobogganing; sleigh rides; ice skating.
FEATURES: Snowmaking 85%; ski school; restaurants; child care; rentals.
▶NORDIC: 14 groomed km (not run by ski area).
  The closest—and newest (opened 1986)—major area to Calgary, Nakiska is as high-tech as Alberta gets. It was site of the slalom (Red Crow) and giant slalom (Whoop-Up) in the 1988 Olympics; both

boast a consistent pitch with deceptive rolls that will please stronger skiers. Experts can also attack the fearsome plunges and bumps of Eagle Tail and Black Tail. Nearly all the terrain is fall-line fast, making cruising runs off the Gold and Olympic chairs like Mighty Peace and Eyeopener ideal for intermediates. Beginners have a sizable segregated area off the Bronze chair. If there is a criticism of Nakiska, it's that the area is constantly plagued by chinooks, warm winds that cause the temperature to rise as high as 60 degrees in the dead of winter. Hence, Nakiska's snow is unreliable, though it's augmented by a state-of-the-art snowmaking system.

NITEHAWK SKI HILL

(P. 59, A-6, #10) Off Highway 40, Grande Prairie
403-532-6637
TRAILS, 9; LIFTS, 3; VERTICAL, 460′.

SNOW VALLEY SKI CLUB

(P. 59, C-9, #11) 122 Street south off Whitemind Drive, Edmonton
403-434-3991
TRAILS, 6; LIFTS, 3; VERTICAL, 128′.

SUNSHINE VILLAGE

(P. 59, D-8, #12) TransCanada Highway 1, 10 mi. W of Banff
403-762-6500
SEASON: Nov. 20-May 15
ANNUAL SNOWFALL: 360″
TERRAIN: 62 trails over 780 acres; longest run, 5 mi.; ♦ 20%; ▪ 60%; ● 20%.
LIFTS: 12 (1 gondola, 1 high-speed quad, 1 triple, 4 doubles, 5 surface); capacity, 15,200 per hour.
SUMMIT: 8,954′
VERTICAL: 3,514′
ACTIVITIES: Snowboarding.
FEATURES: Ski school; restaurant; rentals.
  Located right on the Continental Divide, Sunshine Village receives the lightest snow in the Canadian Rockies, enabling skiers to romp into June. Much of the skiing is above tree line on swooping bowls and gnarly chutes, everything from wild and woolly rides to auto-pilot jaunts. But with one or two exceptions (like The Shoulder), there's nothing really extreme. The hairiest stretches are Paris Basin off the WaWa T and the big bumps off Teepee Town. Strong intermediates will love the thrilling Great Divide views from the top of Angel Express almost as much as the runs like Ecstasy. Beginners even have their own sinuous 3-mile run from the summit. Everyone should marvel at the gondola that accesses the village itself: it actually takes several turns as it snakes up the tortuous canyon! Problems? Be prepared to pole on several sections.

Occasional storms may make skiing above timberline an adventure. A new mountain—Goat's Eye—is under construction and should open by 1996, adding a high-speed quad and six tightly gladed advanced runs.

SUNRIDGE SKI AREA

(P. 59, C-9, #13) Off 17th Street, 4 blocks S of Yellowhead Trail, Edmonton
403-449-6555
TRAILS, 10; LIFTS, 4; VERTICAL, 233′.

WESTCASTLE PARK

(P. 59, F-9, #14) Route 744, Pincher Creek
403-627-2605
SEASON: Dec. 15-April 15
ANNUAL SNOWFALL: 180″
TERRAIN: 25 trails over 250 acres; longest run, 1.5 mi.; ♦ 48%; ▪ 35%; ● 17%.
LIFTS: 3 (3 surface); capacity, 1,800 per hour.
SUMMIT: 6,500′
VERTICAL: 1,700′
ACTIVITIES: Snowboarding.
FEATURES: Ski school; restaurant; rentals.
  Westcastle Park offers a fine blend of bowls, glades and open runs, including two standouts: The Burn is wide, steep and bumpy, while North Road is cruising nirvana.

WINTERGREEN

(P. 59, E-8, #15) Bragg Creek
403-949-3333
TRAILS, 9; LIFTS, 6; VERTICAL, 620′.
Tubing.

NORDIC

CANMORE NORDIC CENTRE

(P. 59, D-8, #16) Canmore
403-678-2400
FACILITIES; 56 groomed km (with skating lane); rentals; lessons; biathlon range; restaurant; night skiing (2 km lit).
  The site of most 1988 Olympic Nordic events, Canmore offers trails for all levels.

COUNTRY CORRAL LODGE/PANTHER VALLEY WILDERNESS RETREAT

(P. 59, D-9, #17) Rural Route 1, Elmora
403-773-2442
FACILITIES; 31 groomed km; lessons; tobogganing; ice skating; sleigh rides; lodging and restaurant.

HOMEPLACE RANCH

(P. 59, E-9, #18) RR1, Priddis
403-931-3245
FACILITIES; 14 groomed km; rentals; sleigh rides; lodging and restaurant.

JASPER PARK LODGE

(P. 59, C-6, #19) Jasper
403-852-3301
FACILITIES: 25 groomed km;
rentals; lessons; ice skating;
tobogganing; sleigh rides; lodging and restaurant.
This elegant resort accesses a mix of open fields and moderately hilly woods in the national parks.

LAC LA BICHE NORDIC

(P. 59, B-10, #20) Lac La Biche
403-623-2490
FACILITIES: 20 groomed km, 20 ungroomed; rentals; lessons; restaurant.

LAKE O'HARA LODGE

(P. 59, D-7, #21) Off Highway
1, Lake Louise
403-762-2118
FACILITIES: unlimited backcountry; rentals; lessons; lodging and restaurant.
Lake O'Hara is fairly deluxe as Alberta's backcountry lodges go. The location in Yoho National Park is extraordinary.

MOUNT ASSINIBOINE LODGE

(P. 59, D-8, #22) Canmore
403-678-2883
FACILITIES; 100 ungroomed km, backcountry; rentals; lessons; lodging and restaurant.

STRATHCONA WILDERNESS

(P. 59, C-9, #23) 2025 Oak St.,
Sherwood Park
403-922-3939
FACILITIES; 17 groomed km (2.5 skating); rentals; lessons; snowshoeing; restaurant.

TECUMSEH MOUNTAIN GUEST RANCH

(P. 59, F-8, #24) Coleman
403-563-3900
FACILITIES: 25 groomed km; rentals; lessons; ice skating; lodging and restaurant.

BRITISH COLUMBIA

ALPINE

APEX ALPINE

(P. 59, F-6, #1) Okanagan
Valley, 20 mi. W of Penticton
604-292-8222; 604-493-3606
(snow)
SEASON: Nov. 25-April 10
ANNUAL SNOWFALL: 224″
TERRAIN: 45 trails over 900 acres; longest run, 3 mi.; ◆
38%; ▪ 48%; ● 14%.
LIFTS: 5 (1 triple, 1 double, 3 surface); capacity, 4,600 per hour.
SUMMIT: 7,450′
VERTICAL: 2000′
ACTIVITIES: Ice skating; sleigh

rides; night skiing.
FEATURES: Snowmaking 1%; ski school; restaurants; child care; rentals.
►NORDIC: 52 groomed km; rentals; lessons; night skiing.
Fair-weather skiers consider this the apex of resorts for its bountiful sunshine. For a good orientation take the complimentary "Mountain Magic" tours held daily. Novices and lower intermediates will enjoy cruising the velvety wide boulevards off the Triple Stocks chair. They'll warm navy blue intermediates up for the steeper silk of Juniper and Ridge Run. Experts should take the Alpine Shuttle poma to the top of Mt. Beaconsfield for the meadows of The Bowls and The Pet. They can also take the runs squiggling down the north face like the narrow chute called Gunbarrel, or the only slightly less steep mogul runs on its flanks.

BEAR MOUNTAIN SKI HILL

(P. 58, A-5, #2) Dawson Creek
604-782-4988
TRAILS, 10; LIFTS, 1; VERTICAL, 500′.

BIG BARN SKI HILL

(P. 58, A-5, #3) Fort St. John
604-785-7544
TRAILS, 11; LIFTS, 2; VERTICAL, 750′.

BIG WHITE SKI RESORT

(P. 59, E-6, #4) Big White,
Kelowna
604-765-3101
SEASON: Nov. 24-April 15
ANNUAL SNOWFALL: 223″
TERRAIN: 51 trails over 1,010 acres; longest run, 3 mi.; ◆◆
8%; ◆ 19%; ▪ 41%; ● 32%.
LIFTS: 9 (3 high-speed quads, 1 quad, 1 triple, 1 double, 3 surface); capacity, 14,100 per hour.
SUMMIT: 7,606′
VERTICAL: 2,050′
ACTIVITIES: Snowboarding; night skiing.
FEATURES: Ski school; restaurants; child care; rentals.
►NORDIC: 25 groomed km; rentals; lessons.
The name doesn't deceive. Big White is known for providing superb powder conditions and a tremendous variety of terrain (roughly half its acreage is open bowls and glades for powder fanatics and shredheads, the other half groomed cruisers for more recreational types). It added its third detachable quad for 1995, eliminating the few waits and dispersing skiers all over the mountain. This is a terrific family mountain, with miles of groomed cruisers like Enchanted Forest, Paradise, and Perfection, which fulfill the promise of their names. Poofter's Puff and Easy Out will please the novices. But experts needn't despair. They

can head toward the new Whitefoot double and its series of wide bowls punctuated by tight gullies. And the 45-degree face of The Cliff poses the ultimate challenge off the Alpine T-bar.

CLEARWATER SKI CLUB

(P. 58, D-5, #5) Clearwater
604-674-3848
TRAILS, 5; LIFTS, 2; VERTICAL, 1,000′.

CRYSTAL MOUNTAIN

(P. 58, F-5, #6) Westbank
604-768-5189; 604-768-3753
(snow)
TRAILS, 20; LIFTS, 4; VERTICAL, 600′.

CYPRESS BOWL

(P. 58, F-3, #7) Off Highway
99, 16 mi. W of Vancouver
604-926-5612
SEASON: Dec. 1-April 15
ANNUAL SNOWFALL: 197″
TERRAIN: 24 trails over NA acres; longest run, 2.5 mi.; ◆
40%; ▪ 37%; ● 23%.
LIFTS: 5 (4 doubles, 1 surface); capacity, 5,000 per hour.
SUMMIT: 4,750′
VERTICAL: 1,752′
ACTIVITIES: Snowboarding; tobogganing; night skiing.
FEATURES: Ski school; restaurants; child care; rentals.
►NORDIC: 16 groomed km; rentals; lessons; night skiing (5 km lit).
Only 20 minutes from downtown Vancouver, Cypress offers the most challenging skiing in the metropolitan area. Intermediates can check out the long cruisers of Black Mountain, while advanced skiers will enjoy the steep fall-line beauties on Mt. Strachan like Top Gun and Ripcord. Snowboarders have a half pipe. Gliders can climb the to the 4,350-foot summit of Hollyburn Peak.

FAIRMONT HOT SPRINGS RESORT

(P. 59, E-8, #8) Fairmont Hot
Springs
604-345-6311
SEASON: Dec. 15-March 31
ANNUAL SNOWFALL: 90′
TERRAIN: 14 trails over 60 acres; longest run, 1.5 mi.; ◆
20%; ▪ 60%; ● 20%.
LIFTS: 2 (1 triple, 1 surface); capacity, 2,400 per hour.
SUMMIT: 5,200′
VERTICAL: 1,000′
ACTIVITIES: Snowboarding; hot springs; night skiing.
FEATURES: Snowmaking 70%; ski school; restaurant; child care; rentals.
►NORDIC: 20 groomed km; rentals; lessons.
Fairmont is noted for its gentle beginner and intermediate terrain and sweeping vistas. One of the

best reasons to ski here is that the revivifying springs are included in the lift ticket price.

FERNIE SNOW VALLEY

(P. 59, F-8, #9) Off Southern
TransCanada Highway 3,
Fernie
604-423-4655; 604-423-3555
(snow)
SEASON: Nov. 30-April 28
ANNUAL SNOWFALL: 287″
TERRAIN: 47 trails over 800 acres; longest run, 3 mi.; ◆
30%; ▪ 40%; ● 30%.
LIFTS: 7 (1 quad, 2 triples, 2 doubles, 2 surface); capacity, 7,000 per hour.
SUMMIT: 5,900′
VERTICAL: 2,400′
ACTIVITIES: Snowboarding; sleigh rides.
FEATURES: Snowmaking 1%; ski school; restaurants; child care; rentals.
►NORDIC: 10 groomed km.
Essentially two vast bowls separated and ringed by ridges, Fernie offers the same fine bowl- and tree-skiing and feathery powder as many larger B.C. areas. The terrain is admirably balanced. The new Deer triple accesses novice runs like Meadow. Intermediates can frolic on the runs off the Griz chair. Experts gallop through the powder of Cedar (with its own new T-bar) and Lizard Bowls. Fernie is committed to further expansion of both its skiable acreage and snowmaking capabilities. Complimentary mountain tours are given daily.

FORBIDDEN MOUNTAIN

(P. 58, E-3, #10) Courtenay
604-334-4744; 604-338-1919
(snow)
SEASON: Dec. 1-April 1
ANNUAL SNOWFALL: 130″
TERRAIN: 21 trails over NA acres; longest run, 2 mi.; ◆
15%; ▪ 35%; ● 50%.
LIFTS: 4 (1 double, 3 surface); capacity, 3,400 per hour.
SUMMIT: 3,300′
VERTICAL: 1,150′
ACTIVITIES: Snowboarding; luge; snowshoeing; tobogganing.
FEATURES: Snowmaking 10%; ski school; restaurant; child care; rentals.
This small affordable family ski hill on Vancouver Island boasts breathtaking views of the Komack Valley and Georgian Straits. The blue boulevard Kandahar and wide green Logging Road are typical of its cruising trails. Boarders have a half pipe.

GROUSE MOUNTAIN

(P. 58, F-4, #11) 6400 Nancy
Greene Way, North Vancouver
604-984-0661
SEASON: Nov. 25-April 15
ANNUAL SNOWFALL: 120″

TERRAIN: 13 trails over 120 acres; longest run, 1.5 mi.; ◆ 20%; ▪ 50%; ● 30%.
LIFTS: 10 (4 doubles, 6 surface); capacity, 10,800 per hour.
SUMMIT: 4,100'
VERTICAL: 1,200'
ACTIVITIES: Snowboarding; sleigh rides; night skiing.
FEATURES: Snowmaking 75%; ski school; restaurants; rentals.
 You won't find better panoramic views of Vancouver than at this family-oriented learning mountain. In fact, skiers make up only 50% of the traffic. The rest are tourists coming for the view and for diversions like the 35-minute presentation on the city and its history. Skiing may be an afterthought, but advanced beginners will enjoy runs like The Cut, and shredders can cavort in the snowboard park.

HARPER MOUNTAIN
(P. 58, E-5, #12) 15 mi. E of Kamloops off Yellowhead Highway
604-573-5115; 604-372-2119 (snow)
TRAILS, 15; LIFTS, 3; VERTICAL, 1,475'.
▶NORDIC:10 groomed km.

HEMLOCK RESORT
(P. 58, F-4, #13) Off Highway 7, Agassiz
604-797-4411; 604-520-6222 (snow)
SEASON: Dec. 15-March 31
ANNUAL SNOWFALL: 600"
TERRAIN: 34 trails over 350 acres; longest run, 7,460'; ◆ 20%; ▪ 60%; ● 20%.
LIFTS: 4 (1 triple, 2 doubles, 1 surface); capacity, 4,000 per hour.
SUMMIT: 4,400'
VERTICAL: 1,200'
ACTIVITIES: Snowboarding; night skiing.
FEATURES: Ski school; restaurants; child care; rentals.
▶NORDIC: 13 groomed km; rentals; lessons.
 Hemlock is a great place for intermediates to sow their powder oats. Snowboarding is huge, and the area responded by building a half pipe; next up will be expanding the Nordic system.

KIMBERLEY SKI RESORT
(P. 59, F-8, #14) Off Route 95A, Kimberley
604-427-4881
SEASON: Dec. 1-April 15
ANNUAL SNOWFALL: 108"
TERRAIN: 44 trails over 550 acres; longest run, 4 mi.; ◆ 20%; ▪ 60%; ● 20%.
LIFTS: 7 (2 triples, 1 double, 4 surface); capacity, 6,000 per hour.
SUMMIT: 6,500'
VERTICAL: 2,300'

ACTIVITIES: Snowboarding; ice skating; night skiing.
FEATURES: Snowmaking 10%; ski school; restaurants; child care; rentals.
▶NORDIC: 26 groomed km; rentals; lessons; night skiing (3 km lit).
 Kimberley is nestled in a region nicknamed the "Bavaria of the Rockies." Indeed, the laid-back town itself is a kitschy yet endearing architectural tribute to the Black Forest (it even owns the world's largest cuckoo clock). The ski area takes full advantage of the splendid surroundings, offering scenic cruising and superb grooming from top to bottom on runs such as Buckhorn, Rosa and North Star Main (North America's largest illuminated run). Advanced skiers will want to check out the narrow tree-lined bump runs corkscrewing off the backside like Dean's Left Fork and Easter. Kimberley is a pioneer in the field of instruction of the physically challenged; the Canadian Association for Disabled Skiing is based here.

MANNING PARK RESORT
(P. 58, F-5, #15) Highway 3, Manning Park
604-840-8822
SEASON: Dec. 2-April 2
ANNUAL SNOWFALL: 250"
TERRAIN: 24 trails over NA acres; longest run, 1.3 mi.; ◆ 30%; ▪ 40%; ● 30%.
LIFTS: 4 (2 doubles, 2 surface); capacity, 4,171 per hour.
SUMMIT: 5,868'
VERTICAL: 1,388'
ACTIVITIES: Snowboarding; snowshoeing; ice skating.
FEATURES: Ski school; restaurant; childcare; rentals.
▶NORDIC: 30 groomed km (with skating lane); rentals; lessons;
 Development is limited as the ski area sits in the provincial park of the same name. The skiing is solidly beginner and intermediate, but the area is best known as a Nordic Mecca, accessing an additional 190 km of touring trails in the park.

MT. ARROWSMITH
(P. 58, F-3, #16) Port Alberni
604-723-7899
SEASON: Dec. 1-April 15
ANNUAL SNOWFALL: 85"
TERRAIN: 12 trails over NA acres; longest run, 1.5 mi.; ◆ 20%; ▪ 60%; ● 20%.
LIFTS: 3 (3 surface); capacity, 1,000 per hour.
SUMMIT: 5,240'
VERTICAL: 1,040'
ACTIVITIES: Snowboarding.
FEATURES: Ski school; restaurant; rentals.
▶NORDIC: 4 groomed km.
 Arrowsmith is revered by shredders for its prodigious 1,500-foot half pipe; tree-skiers will delight in

finding little shots through the glades.

MT. BALDY SKI AREA
(P. 59, F-6, #17) McKinney Road, 25 mi. E of Oliver
604-498-2262
SEASON: Dec. 1-April 1 (open Fri.-Mon.)
ANNUAL SNOWFALL: 88"
TERRAIN: 15 trails over 150 acres; longest run, 1.5 mi.; ◆ 33%; ▪ 42%; ● 25%.
LIFTS: 2 (2 surface); capacity, 700 per hour.
SUMMIT: 7,050'
VERTICAL: 1,460'
ACTIVITIES: Snowboarding.
FEATURES: Ski school; restaurant; rentals.
▶NORDIC: 47 groomed km (with skating lane); lessons.
 Mt. Baldy is a perfect example of the little known B.C. jewels. It looks down on Canada's only bona-fide desert, hence the snow is light as can be. Though small, it's a magnet for tree-skiers, with over 100 acres of steep glades and powder chutes. Beginners beware: The green runs tend to be forest green. Snowboarders will enjoy the terrain park, including half pipe; gliders and telemarkers have a vast backcountry to explore.

MT. CAIN
(P. 58, E-1, #18) Port McNeill
604-949-9496; 604-956-2226 (snow)
TRAILS, 18; LIFTS, 3; VERTICAL, 1,500'.

MT. MACKENZIE
(P. 59, E-7, #19) Revelstoke
604-837-5268
TRAILS, 26; LIFTS, 4; VERTICAL, 2,000'.
▶NORDIC: 20 groomed km.

MT. TIMOTHY SKI HILL
(P. 58, D-5, #20) 100 Mile House
604-395-3772; 604-395-4008 (snow)
TRAILS, 25; LIFTS, 3; VERTICAL, 850'.

MT. WASHINGTON SKI RESORT
(P. 58, E-3, #21) Courtenay
604-338-1386
SEASON: Dec. 1-May 1
ANNUAL SNOWFALL: 315'
TERRAIN: 41 trails over 970 acres; longest run, 1.2 mi.; ◆ 36%; ▪ 42%%; ● 22%.
LIFTS: 6 (1 quad, 2 triples, 2 doubles, 1 surface); capacity, 8,520 per hour.
SUMMIT: 5,215'
VERTICAL: 1,575'
ACTIVITIES: Snowboarding; tobogganing.
FEATURES: Ski school; restaurants; child care; rentals.

▶NORDIC: 35.5 groomed km (with skating lane); rentals; lessons; biathlon range.
 Located in Strathcona Provincial Park (B.C.'s largest), Mt. Washington overlooks the brilliantly green Comox Valley on Vancouver Island. True blue skiers love the superlative cruising on runs like Fantastic, Westerly and Linton's Loop. Bumpsters will enjoy the not-so-smooth ride on Schum's Delight, Fletcher's Challenge, and Sunrise (which leads to some mighty fine glades off its flanks). Expansive bowls and still more tree skiing lure experts to the Blue Chair area. The Nordic area offers primarily intermediate and advanced skiing.

MURRAY RIDGE SKI AREA
(P. 58, B-4, #22) Fort St. James
604-996-8515; 604-996-8513 (snow)
TRAILS, 21; LIFTS, 2; VERTICAL, 1,740'.
▶NORDIC: 18 groomed km.

PANORAMA RESORT
(P. 59, E-8, #23) Panorama
604-342-6941
SEASON: Dec. 1-April 15
ANNUAL SNOWFALL: 110"
TERRAIN: 43 trails over 400 acres; longest run, 2.5 mi.; ◆ 25%; ▪% 55%; ● 20%.
LIFTS: 8 (1 high-speed quad, 1 triple, 2 doubles, 4 surface); capacity, 7,602 per hour.
SUMMIT: 7,500'
VERTICAL: 4,300'
ACTIVITIES: Snowboarding; heli-skiing; ice skating; sleigh rides; dog sledding.
FEATURES: Snowmaking 50%; ski school; restaurants; child care; rentals.
▶NORDIC: 22 groomed km; rentals; lessons.
 Panorama is one of Canada's best family resorts, a reputation enhanced by the top-rated Heather and Don Bilodeau Ski School. They specialize in teaching powder techniques, so nearly everyone can take advantage of the heliskiing offered by the area. Of course, with a new T-bar increasing the vertical to 4,300 feet (second highest in North America after Whistler/ Blackcomb), the in-bounds area is hardly puny. Shredders enjoy the terrain park.

PHOENIX MOUNTAIN
(P. 59, F-6, #24) Phoenix Mountain Road, Grand Forks
604-442-2813
TRAILS, 9; LIFTS, 2; VERTICAL, 800'.

POWDER KING SKI VILLAGE
(P. 58, A-4, #25) Hart Highway 97, Mackenzie
604-997-6323

SEASON: Nov. 15-April 15
ANNUAL SNOWFALL: 495"
TERRAIN: 18 trails over 160 acres; longest run, 8,691'; ◆ 15%; ▪ 70%; ● 15%.
LIFTS: 3 (1 triple, 2 surface); capacity, 2,500 per hour.
SUMMIT: 5,000'
VERTICAL: 2,100'
ACTIVITIES: Snowboarding; snowmobiling.
FEATURES: Ski school; restaurants; child care; rentals.
  Another great secret, perfect for intermediates looking to work on their powder form through stately stands of fir and spruce on runs like Let It Be and No. 9. Novices will hum happily down Strawberry Fields and Penny Lane.

PURDEN SKI VILLAGE
(P. 58, B-4, #26) Prince George
604-565-7777; 604-564-7669 (snow)
TRAILS, 13; LIFTS, 2; VERTICAL, 1,090'.

RED MOUNTAIN RESORT
(P. 59, F-7, #27) Off Highway 3B, Rossland
604-362-7700
SEASON: Dec. 1-April 7
ANNUAL SNOWFALL: 300"
TERRAIN: 77 trails over NA acres; longest run, 4.5 mi.; ◆◆ 30%; ◆ 30%; ▪ 30%; ● 10%.
LIFTS: 4 (1 triple, 2 doubles, 1 surface); capacity, 4,000 per hour.
SUMMIT: 6,699'
VERTICAL: 2,800'
ACTIVITIES: Snowboarding.
FEATURES: Ski school; restaurant; child care; rentals.
▶NORDIC: 40 groomed km; rentals; lessons.
  Red Mountain is another powder keg for dynamite skiing. A number of world-class racers have trained here, including Canadian gold medalists Nancy Greene (1968) and Kerrin Lee Gartner (1992). The trail map doesn't bother indicating boundaries and half the terrain remains unnamed—this is an area where skiers can go off in search of adventure. There are two mountains. Granite is the choice of novices and intermediates, who enjoy the 360-degree wraparound runs. Beginners can amble for five miles on Long Squaw and Easy Street. Intermediates should head to Paradise for obliging cruisers like Southern Comfort and Southern Belle. But 60% of Red is rated single or double black diamond, befitting its gritty origins as a place for local miners to raise hell. Both Granite and Red Mountain offer a maze of glades and gullies. Experts flock here for the amazing tree skiing, picking dozens of lines through the woods. Favorite steeps include Short Squaw, the Slides, Roots, and the Couloir area. Gliders can take a special lift to access miles of trails from Granite's summit. They

Courtesy: Telluride Ski Resort (see Colorado, p. 100).

can also head cross the street to the Blackjack Cross-Country Ski Club Trails, which include a skating lane.

SALMO SKI AREA
(P. 59, F-7, #28) Salmo
604-357-2406; 604-357-2323 (snow)
TRAILS, 4; LIFTS, 2; VERTICAL, 1,050'.
▶NORDIC: 5 groomed km.

SEYMOUR SKI COUNTRY
(P. 58, F-4, #29) Mount Seymour Parkway, North Vancouver
604-986-2261
TRAILS, 25; LIFTS, 5; VERTICAL, 1,320'.
2 snowboard terrain parks; tobogganing.

SHAMES MOUNTAIN
(P. 58, A-1, #30) 22 mi. outside Terrace
604-635-3773
SEASON: Nov. 14-April 15
ANNUAL SNOWFALL: 590"
TERRAIN: 18 trails over 183 acres; longest run, 9,000'; ◆ 19%; ▪ 60%; ● 21%.
LIFTS: 3 (1 double, 2 surface); capacity, 2,500 per hour.
SUMMIT: 3,930'
VERTICAL: 1,630'
ACTIVITIES: Snowboarding.
FEATURES: Ski school; restaurant; child care; rentals.
  The newest area in B.C., Shames puts many larger mountains to shame with its unbeatable combination of deep fluffy snow and 50-50 mix of open bowls and tight glades.

SILVER STAR MOUNTAIN
(P. 59, E-6, #31) Off Highway 97, Silver Star
604-542-0224
SEASON: Nov. 15-April 15
ANNUAL SNOWFALL: 250"
TERRAIN: 65 trails over 1,600 acres; longest run, 5 mi.; ◆ 30%; ▪ 50%; ● 20%.

LIFTS: 8 (1 high-speed quad, 2 quads, 2 doubles, 3 surface); capacity, 11,800 per hour.
SUMMIT: 6,280'
VERTICAL: 2,500'
ACTIVITIES: Snowboarding; tobogganing; ice skating; night skiing.
FEATURES: Ski school; restaurants; child care; rentals.
▶NORDIC: 100 groomed km (with 20 skating); rentals; lessons; biathlon range; night skiing (7 km lit).
  Silver Star is a rising star in Canadian skiing, with something for everyone. Its two mountains roughly divide the terrain. Most of Vance Creek is the province of novices and intermediates. They can go on cruise control down runs like Exhibition, Milky Way, and Sundance; stronger skiers can test their mettle on Moonbeam or The Chute. Experts now have their own playground, Putnam Creek, the north side of the mountain. Canada's longest high-speed quad services cruel jewels like Holy Smoke and the Back Bowl, with drops like Black Pine, Freefall, and the Where's Bob? Intermediates can try the sustained pitch of Sunny Ridge and Gypsy Queen here; even beginners can take the rambling Bergerstrasse and Aunt Gladys from the summit. Shredders enjoy the extensive terrain garden. Nordic types will be in heaven; Silver Star is home of the national and provincial Cross-Country and Biathlon ski teams, and the terrain is wonderfully varied both at the mountain and in the adjacent provincial park. People of all ages delight in the 1890's Gaslight Era architecture of the mountain village and its friendly atmosphere.

SKI SMITHERS
(P. 58, A-2, #32) Off Yellowhead Highway, 14 mi. outside Smithers
604-847-2058
TRAILS, 18; LIFTS, 3; VERTICAL, 1,750'.

SNOWPATCH SKI HILL
(P. 58, F-5, #33) Princeton
604-295-6626
TRAILS, 8; LIFTS, 3; VERTICAL, 450'.
▶NORDIC: 30 groomed km. Tobogganing.

SUMMIT LAKE SKI AREA
(P. 59, E-7, #34) Off Route 1, Nakusp
604-265-3312
TRAILS, 8; LIFTS, 1; VERTICAL, 450'.
▶NORDIC: 5 groomed km.

SUN PEAKS AT TOD MOUNTAIN
(P. 59, E-5, #35) Heffley Creek Road, Kamloops
604-578-7222
SEASON: Nov. 15-April 15
ANNUAL SNOWFALL: 177"
TERRAIN: 61 trails over 1,075 acres; longest run, 5 mi.; ◆ 22%; ▪ 54%; ● 24%.
LIFTS: 6 (1 high-speed quad, 1 quad, 1 triple, 1 double, 2 surface); capacity, 6,371 per hour.
SUMMIT: 6,824'
VERTICAL: 2,854'
ACTIVITIES: Snowboarding; telemarking; snowmobiling.
FEATURES: Ski school; restaurants; child care; rentals.
▶NORDIC: 20 ungroomed km.
  Sun Peaks is renowned for its dry powder and wide open, uncrowded runs. The enormous bowls comprise nearly 300 acres, with Crystal and Headwall prized for their steepness and consistent conditions. But Sun Peaks also claims to groom more continuous advanced runs than any other area. Intermediates love the sustained pitch on The Sting, while greenhorns can enjoy the steady grade, with neither flats nor steep pitches, on the marvelous Five Mile Run.

TABOR MOUNTAIN SKI RESORT
(P. 58, B-4, #36) Yellowhead Highway, 8 mi. W of Prince George
604-963-7542
TRAILS, 10; LIFTS, 3; VERTICAL, 800'.

TROLL SKI RESORT
(P. 58, C-4, #37) Quesnel
604-994-3200
TRAILS, 14; LIFTS, 4; VERTICAL, 1,500'.

WHISTLER/BLACKCOMB SKI RESORT
(P. 58, E-3, #38) Off Highway 99, Whistler
604-932-3434 (Whistler); 604-932-3141 (Blackcomb)
SEASON: Nov. 25-May 10
ANNUAL SNOWFALL: 385"
TERRAIN: 214 trails over 6,698 acres (3,657 Whistler, 3,341

Blackcomb); longest run, 7 mi.; ◆ 20%; ▪ 55%: ● 25%.
LIFTS: 30 (2 gondolas, 9 high-speed quads, 8 triples, 3 doubles, 8 surface); capacity, 22,295 (Whistler), 28,800 (Blackcomb).
SUMMIT: 7,494' (7,160' Whistler)
VERTICAL: 5,280' (5,020' Whistler)
ACTIVITIES: Snowboarding; ice skating; sleigh rides; snowmobiling; snowshoeing.
FEATURES: Snowmaking 28% (Blackcomb), 7% (Whistler); ski school; restaurants; child care; rentals.
▶NORDIC: 21 groomed km; rentals; lessons.
 As far as many skiers are concerned, Whistler/Blackcomb is the best. It even beats out Vail regularly in skier surveys. Between the two mountains, the mega-resort can claim a number of superlatives, including North America's largest acreage and highest vertical by far (1 mile to be exact). Not surprisingly there's an astonishing variety of terrain. Recent expansion has softened Whistler's tough guy image while hardening the old smoothie, Blackcomb. The areas are separately owned and operated but linked by a brilliantly designed base village, which scores high ratings for convenience, lodging, dining, and nightlife. They also are skied on the same lift ticket. One of skiing's great thrills is to conquer one mountain and stare across the valley, salivating at the thought that there's another yet to come. Whistler is renowned for the expansive bowls crowning the mountain. It's exhilarating to step out from the gondola—which accesses 3,800 vertical feet—and realize your journey's only just begun. West Bowl is the choice for experts but Harmony, Glacier, Whistler, and Symphony Bowls aren't far behind. Intermediates also can experience the heady sensation, taking the incomparable cruiser Burnt Stew. Other blue beauties are Porcupine and the five-mile Franz's Run. Bumpsters will joyfully view mogulfields like Chunky's Choice and Shale Slope. Though novices can't access the summit, don't forget there's nearly 4,000 feet of vertical from the gondola's Roundhouse Station. Fantastic and Foxy Hollow will have them feeling on top of the world. Blackcomb counters with superlative cruising below the tree line (and another series of gorgeous bowls) on fall-line runs like Springboard and Cruiser and the milky trails off the Jersey Cream chair. These were Blackcomb's bread and butter for years. But the recently added Seventh Heaven superchair opened up 22 mostly advanced runs. A free tour of the terrain is available daily at 11 a.m. Xhiggy's Meadow is a perfect example of the steep wide-open skiing up here. But

intermediates will find blue streaks, and extremists can check out the fearsome, vertigo-inducing gashes called Saudan Couloir, Cougar Chute, and Pakalolo. The first was named for Sylvain Saudan, a French extreme skier who fatally crashed several years ago in Europe. It makes you wonder but never fear. There's Easiest Route that wends and winds its merry way all the way down the mountain. Beginners never had it so good. Few skiers have—even with the occasional weekend lift line and frequently wet weather.

WHITETOOTH SKI AREA
(P. 59, D-7, #39) TransCanada Highway & Highway 95, Golden
604-344-6114
TRAILS, 8; LIFTS, 2; VERTICAL, 1,740'.
▶NORDIC: 17.5 ungroomed km.

WHITEWATER SKI AREA
(P. 59, F-7, #40) 12 mi. outside Nelson
604-354-4944; 604-352-7669 (snow)
SEASON: Dec. 15-April 1
ANNUAL SNOWFALL: 265"
TERRAIN: 24 trails over 400 acres; longest run, 1.2 mi.; ◆ 40%; ▪ 40%; ● 20%.
LIFTS: 3 (3 doubles); capacity, 3,400 per hour.
SUMMIT: 6,700'
VERTICAL: 1,300'
ACTIVITIES: Snowboarding; telemarking.
FEATURES: Ski school; res-

taurant; child care; rentals.
▶NORDIC: 7 groomed km.
 Locals love this undiscovered area and its steep, steeper, steepest runs like Catch Basin, Blast, Dynamite, and Glory Basin.

NORDIC

BIG BAR GUEST RANCH
(P. 58, D-5, #41) Jesmond Clinton
604-459-2333
FACILITIES: 25 groomed km, unlimited ungroomed; rentals; lessons; child care; ice skating; sleigh rides; winter horseback riding; lodging and restaurant.
 A delightfully rustic retreat, Big Bar's trails wind through open meadows and woods, following old logging routes.

EMERALD LAKE LODGE
(P. 59, D-8, #42) Field
604-343-6321
FACILITIES: 15 groomed km; rentals; lessons; snowshoeing; dog sledding; lodging and restaurant.

HAMILTON FALLS LODGE
(P. 58, D-5, #43) Clearwater
604-674-2646
FACILITIES: 35 groomed km, unlimited ungroomed; rentals; lessons; tobogganing; dog sledding; snowshoeing; ice skating; lodging and restaurant.
 Located in the magnificent Wells Gray National Park, the lodge offers mostly intermediate gliding through hilly woods, with several

scenic lookout points.

THE HILLS HEALTH & GUEST RANCH
(P. 58, D-5, #44) 108 Ranch Rural Route 1, C26, 100 Mile House
604-791-5225
FACILITIES: 200 groomed km (with 20 skating); rentals; lessons; tobogganing; sleigh rides; ice skating; lodging and restaurant.
 Not only does the ranch access miles of rolling wooded trails, best suited to novices and intermediates, it operates a first-rate spa that offers body treatments like herbal wraps and facials, daily wellness workshops, and a fitness center that attracts big-name athletes.

LARCH HILLS SKI AREA
(P. 59, E-6, #45) Salmon Arm
604-832-7505
FACILITIES: 30 groomed km (8 skating), 120 ungroomed; lessons; lodging and restaurant.

MCBRIDE YELLOWHEAD SKI CLUB
(P. 58, C-5, #46) McBride
604-569-2738
FACILITIES: 26.5 groomed km; rentals.

NATURE HILLS RESORT
(P. 58, D-5, #47) Rural Route 1, Lone Butte
604-593-4659
FACILITIES: 15 groomed km; rentals; lessons; lodging and restaurant.

108 RESORT BEST WESTERN
(P. 58, D-5, #48) Rural Route 1, 100 Mile House
604-791-5211
FACILITIES: 150 groomed km (skating 50); rentals; lessons; dog sledding; sleigh rides; ice skating; snowmobiling; lodging and restaurant.
 Several international Nordic events have been held on this system, which offers everything from flat open trails to steep forestland, and links up with several other networks. The resort is a full-service property highly popular with families and couples looking to get away from it all.

MANITOBA

ALPINE

AGASSIZ SKI RESORT
(P. 61, D-7, #1) PTH 5, Riding Mtn. National Park, 9 mi. W of McCreary
204-835-2246
TRAILS, 10; LIFTS, 4; VERTICAL, 500'.

HELISKIING

If British Columbians didn't invent heliskiing, they certainly perfected it. Since the 1960s, skiers have raved about the deep untracked powder of the Bugaboos. If there was any bugaboo at all, it was about the expense and the perception that only hot-shots could tame the exacting terrain. But the experience is no longer just for the wealthy, wild, and woolly. It's accessible even to strong recreational skiers, thanks to innovative powder-skiing instructional programs and the advent of fat skis, whose revolutionary design transforms powder poodles into pit bulls.

Heliskiing is not confined to the Bugaboos, a small sub-division of the Purcells. The bulk of chopper expeditions take place in the Columbias, which include the equally popular Cariboo mountains in the north and the Monashees, Selkirks, and Purcells further south. Their average annual snowfall exceeds that of the Rockies to the east and the Coastal range to the west—the Monashees alone get more than 800 inches some years.

Among the best outfits are R.K. Heli-Ski Panorama (604-342-3889), Tyax Lodge Heliskiing (604-238-2446) and Kootenay Helicopter Skiing (604-265-3121). A less expensive, albeit less glamorous, alternative is snowcat skiing. Selkirk Wilderness Skiing (604-366-4424) is a leader in the field. All of the above will enable you to ski 10,000-20,000 vertical feet daily, on a series of shimmering snowfields and glaciers.

►Nordic: 65 groomed km.

FALCON SKI AREA
(P. 61, E-9, #2) Off Highway 1, Falcon Beach
204-349-2201
Trails, 14; lifts, 4; vertical, 145'.
►Nordic: 33 groomed km.
Tobogganing; tubing.

HOLIDAY MOUNTAIN
(P. 61, E-7, #3) PTH 3, La Riviere
204-242-2172
Season: Nov. 15-March 15
Annual snowfall: 90"
Terrain: 10 trails over NA acres; longest run, 2,500'; ◆ 50%; ▪ 30%; ● 20%.
Lifts: 5 (1 double, 4 surface); capacity, 4,000 per hour.
Summit: NA
Vertical: 300'
Activities: Snowmobiling; ice skating; night skiing.
Features: Snowmaking 90%; ski school; restaurant; rentals.
►Nordic: Unlimited ungroomed km.
Holiday is typical of Manitoba's downhill areas; it caters entirely to families, with a fine ski school, and offers mostly rolling terrain with a few steep pitches for downhillers (as well as gliders) on wide groomed slopes.

MYSTERY MOUNTAIN
(P. 61, A-7, #4) Split Lake Road, 4 mi. N of Thompson
204-778-7434
Season: Nov. 25-April 7
Annual snowfall: 120"
Terrain: 17 trails over NA acres; longest run, 2,200'; NA
Lifts: 4 (4 surface); capacity, 2,500 per hour.
Summit: NA
Vertical: 250'
Activities: Snowboarding.
Features: Snowmaking 80%; ski school; restaurant; rentals.
►Nordic: NA groomed km; rentals; lessons.

NORDIC

SKI VALLEY
(P. 61, E-7, #5) Minnedosa
204-867-3509
Facilities: NA groomed km; rentals; lessons; restaurant.

SPRINGHILL WINTER PARK
(P. 61, E-8, #6) Birds Hill
204-224-3051
Facilities: NA groomed km; rentals; lessons; restaurant.

THUNDER HILL SKI CLUB
(P. 61, C-6, #7) Swan River
204-539-2626
Facilities: NA groomed km;

rentals; lessons; restaurant.

ALPINE

CRABBE MOUNTAIN WINTER PARK
(P. 64, B-2, #1) Route 104, Millville
506-463-8311; 506-463-2688 (snow)
Season: Dec. 15-April 15
Annual snowfall: 120"
Terrain: 14 trails over 85 acres; longest run, 1.5 mi.; ◆ 35%; ▪ 45%; ● 20%.
Lifts: 4 (1 quad, 3 surface); capacity, 4,000 per hour.
Summit: 1,325'
Vertical: 853'
Activities: Snowboarding; night skiing.
Features: Snowmaking 30%; ski school; restaurant; child care; rentals.
Crabbe offers extremely wide open trails, save for one short glade run, that are a magnet for local families. Hume's Flume, a silky intermediate cruiser, is typical of the area profile; although King's Horn has satisfying pitch for racing types and Elgee's builds up some nasty bumps.

MONT FARLAGNE
(P. 64, B-1, #2) Off TransCanada Highway, 2 mi. N of Edmundston
506-735-8401; 506-735-6617 (snow)
Trails, 17; lifts, 4; vertical, 600'.
Tubing.

POLEY MOUNTAIN
(P. 64, C-3, #3) Waterford
506-433-3230
Trails, 14; lifts, 4; vertical, 660'.

SILVERWOOD WINTER PARK
(P. 64, B-2, #4) TransCanada Highway 2, 5 mi. W of Fredericton
506-450-3399
Trails, 4; lifts, 2; vertical, 305'.
►Nordic: 32 groomed km.
Tobogganing.

SUGARLOAF PROVINCIAL PARK
(P. 64, A-2, #5) 2 mi. outside Atholville
506-789-2366; 506-789-2392 (snow)
Trails, 8; lifts, 4; vertical, 507'.
►Nordic: 32 groomed km.

NORDIC

ROCKWOOD PARK GOLF

COURSE
(P. 64, C-2, #6) Saint John
506-658-2883
Facilities: 25 groomed km., 2,200 ungroomed acres of parkland; rentals; lessons; ice skating; snowshoeing; restaurant.
The only verifiable Nordic center offering full facilities in the province, Rockwood Park offers trails for all levels though open meadows and hilly woods. Only open weekends.

ALPINE

MARBLE MOUNTAIN
(P. 64, A-4, #1) TransCanada Highway, 6 mi. E of Corner Brook
709-639-8531
Season: January 1-April 15
Annual snowfall: 200"
Terrain: 26 trails over 126 acres; longest run, 3 mi.; ◆ 38%; ▪ 44%; ● 18%.
Lifts: 5 (2 quads, 1 double, 2 surface); capacity, 5,800 per hour.
Summit: 1,877'
Vertical: 1,600'
Activities: Snowboarding.
Features: Snowmaking 62%; ski school; restaurant; rentals.
Marble is acquiring a reputation among Canadian skiers for its demanding yet empty slopes, scenic location, and attention to detail. It appeals equally to families, couples and swinging singles—a $3.5 million day lodge, new in 1995, demonstrates the area's commitment to providing the best amenities for its clientele. It's located a short drive from both the charming town of Corner Brook and the stunning wilderness and extensive cross-country trail system of Gros Morne National Park.

NORTHERN LIGHTS SKI CLUB
Churchill Falls River Valley, Churchill Falls
709-925-3742
Trails, 4; lifts, 1; vertical, 720'.
►Nordic: 7 groomed km.

SKI WHITE HILLS
(P. 64, A-5, #2)
Off TransCanada Highway, 2 mi. W of Clarenville
709-466-7773; 800-563-SNOW (snow)
Trails, 15; lifts, 3; vertical, 750'.
►Nordic: 25 groomed km.

SMOKEY MOUNTAIN SKI CLUB
Labrador City
709-944-3505
Trails, 18; lifts, 4; vertical,

1,000'.
►Nordic: Menihick Nord Ski Club; 65 groomed km; rentals; lessons.

SNOW GOOSE MOUNTAIN SKI CLUB
Goose Bay
709-896-5923
Trails, 6; lifts, 2; vertical, 560'.

NORDIC

CLARENVILLE SKI CENTER
(P. 64, A-5, #3) Clarenville
709-466-7807
Facilities: 26 groomed km; rentals; lessons.

DEEP COVE
(P. 64, A-4, #4) Flowers Cove
709-456-2522
Facilities: 10 groomed km; rentals; lessons; restaurant.

NOTRE DAME SKI CLUB
(P. 64, A-4, #5) Lewisporte
709-535-8172
Facilities: 7.5 groomed km (with skating lane); rentals; lessons; restaurant.

WHALEBACK NORDIC
(P. 64, A-4, #6) 20 Juniper Ave., Stephenville
709-643-2486
Facilities: 22 groomed km; rentals; lessons; restaurant; night skiing (2.2 km lit).
Typically scenic area, the most developed in the province, with predominantly hilly woods ideal for all levels.

ALPINE

CAPE SMOKEY SKI LODGE
(P. 64, B-4, #1) Off Route 312, Ingonish Ferry
902-285-2778
Season: Dec. 1-April 1
Annual snowfall: 120"
Terrain: 15 trails over 85 acres; longest run, 1 mi.; ◆ 25%; ▪ 60%; ● 15%.
Lifts: 2 (1 double, 1 surface); capacity, 1,200 per hour.
Summit: 1,800'
Vertical: 1,000'
Activities: Snowboarding; ice skating; snowmobiling; tobogganing.
Features: Snowmaking 60%; ski school; restaurant; rentals.
Cape Smokey is located near breathtaking Cape Breton National Park, which offers miles of scenic Nordic trails and utter solitude. The downhill area easily presents the most difficult terrain in the province, with some gnarly bump

runs and others notable for their steep pitch. A friendly, laid-back area, the marketing people warn, "No lobster souffles, just the place to ski some challenging runs and have a few beers."

SKI BEN EOIN
(P. 64, B-5, #2) Highway 4, 17 mi. outside Sydney
902-828-2804; 902-828-2222 (snow)
TRAILS, 7; LIFTS, 4; VERTICAL, 500'.

SKI MARTOCK
(P. 64, C-4, #3) Route 14, 4 mi. outside Windsor
902-798-9501; 902-798-3000 (snow)
TRAILS, 14; LIFTS, 5; VERTICAL, 610'.
▶NORDIC: NA groomed km.

SKI WENTWORTH
(P. 64, C-3, #4) Off Highway 104, Wentworth Valley
902-548-2089; 902-548-2808 (snow)
SEASON: Dec. 15-March 31
ANNUAL SNOWFALL: 100"
TERRAIN: 21 trails over 150 acres; longest run, 1.75 mi.; ◆ 20%; ■ 50%; ● 30%.
LIFTS: 6 (2 quads, 4 surface); capacity, 5,600 per hour.
SUMMIT: 990'
VERTICAL: 816'
ACTIVITIES: Snowboarding; night skiing.
FEATURES: snowmaking 67%; ski school; restaurant; child care; rentals.
▶NORDIC: 10 groomed km; rentals; lessons.
In operation nearly a half century, Ski Wentworth offers the largest skiable acreage in the Maritime Provinces. Family-oriented, it boasts strong instructional and racing programs. The trails are mostly wide, groomed boulevards.

NORDIC

OLD ORCHARD HOTEL NORDIC CENTER
(P. 64, C-2, #5) Wolfville
902-542-5751
FACILITIES: 20 groomed km; rentals; lessons; sleigh rides; lodging and restaurant.
A picturesque blend of open meadows and woods at this popular resort.

ONTARIO

ALPINE

ADANAC SKI CENTRE
(P. 62, D-4, #1) Beatrice Crescent, 2 mi. NE of Sudbury off Highway 17
705-566-9911
TRAILS, 3; LIFTS, 1: VERTICAL,

200'.
Tobogganing; ice skating.

ALICE HILL PARK SKI AREA
(P. 62, B-5, #2) Off Highway 62, 14 mi. SW of Pembroke
613-732-2776
TRAILS, 5; LIFTS, 2; VERTICAL, 210'.

ATITOKAN SKI CLUB
(P. 62, A-2, #3) Highway 622, 8 mi. N of Atitokan
807-597-6594
TRAILS, 6; LIFTS, 2; VERTICAL, 250'.

BEAVER VALLEY SKI CLUB
(P. 62, B-5, #4) Highway 4, 5 mi. E of Markdale
519-986-2520
TRAILS, 21; LIFTS, 7; VERTICAL, 500'.

BIG BEN SKI CENTRE
(P. 62, B-6, #5) Brookdale & 7th Street West, Cornwall
613-932-4422
TRAILS, 1; LIFTS, 1; VERTICAL, 165'.

BIG THUNDER NATIONAL SKI TRAINING CENTRE
(P. 62, A-3, #6) 428 E. Victoria Ave., Thunder Bay
807-475-1673
SEASON: Dec. 1-April 15
ANNUAL SNOWFALL: 200"
TERRAIN: 7 trails over NA acres; longest run, 3,900'; ◆ 30%; ■ 40%; ● 30%.
LIFTS: 5 (1 double, 4 surface); capacity, 3,500 per hour.
SUMMIT: NA
VERTICAL: 650'
ACTIVITIES: Snowboarding; ski jumping; luge.
FEATURES: Ski school; restaurants; rentals.
▶NORDIC: 50 groomed km (with skating lane); rentals; lessons; night skiing (5 km lit).
This is a world-class training facility that has something to offer nearly everyone. The alpine facility, while small, boasts impressive steepness, wide slopes, and specially designed freestyle and slalom areas for would-be Olympians of all ages. But Big Thunder really smiles on Nordic types. The superb layout and challenging terrain earned it hosting honors for the 1995 Nordic World Ski Championships. Beginners and intermediates have more than 20 km of varied terrain. Advanced skiers will enjoy the climbs on the upper section of the system.

BLUE MOUNTAIN RESORTS
(P. 63, F-4, #7) Blue Mountain Road, 8 mi. W of Collingwood

705-445-0231
SEASON: Dec. 1-March 31
ANNUAL SNOWFALL: 110"
TERRAIN: 33 trails over 310 acres; longest run, 4,000'; ◆ 40%; ■ 40%; ● 20%.
LIFTS: 15 (1 high-speed quad, 3 triples, 3 doubles, 3 surface); capacity, 17,209 per hour.
SUMMIT: 1,475'
VERTICAL: 720'
ACTIVITIES: Snowboarding; night skiing.
FEATURES: Snowmaking 96%; ski school; restaurants; child care; rentals.
▶NORDIC: 5 groomed km; rentals; lessons.
The largest area in Ontario, Blue Mountain appeals strongly to families. Beginners have two segregated "learn-to-ski" areas. Recreational skiers love the miles of wide-open, satiny cruisers like Smart Aleck and Tranquility that afford glorious views of Georgian Bay. Experts can tackle the steeps of Spectacular. If you're not happy with conditions, you can exchange your lift ticket within 45 minutes for a voucher. But with the $3 million invested in improving the snowmaking, satisfaction is likely.

BUTTERMILK ALPINE SKI VILLAGE
(P. 62, C-1, #8) Robertson Lake Road, Goulais River
705-649-3124
TRAILS, 4; LIFTS, 3; VERTICAL, 300'.

CALEDON SKI CLUB
(P. 63, G-4, #9) 4th Line West, Belfountain
519-927-5221
TRAILS, 18; LIFTS, 8; VERTICAL, 260'.

CANDY MOUNTAIN SKI AREA
(P. 62, A-3, #10) Highway 130, 16 mi. SW of Thunder Bay
807-475-5633
SEASON: Dec. 1-March 31
ANNUAL SNOWFALL: 200"
TERRAIN: 21 trails over NA acres; longest run, 9,800'; ◆ 20%; ■ 60%; ● 20%.
LIFTS: 4 (2 doubles, 2 surface); capacity, 3,500 per hour.
SUMMIT: 1,550'
VERTICAL: 750'
ACTIVITIES: Snowboarding.
FEATURES: Ski school; restaurants; rentals.
Candy Mountain offers an interchangeable lift ticket with Loch Lomond. Between the two, they form the most complete ski mountain in Ontario. Candy offers milder trails, wide groomed cruisers that mellow out after a steep initial drop from the summit.

CAPREOL SKI CLUB
(P. 62, C-4, #11) Lakeshore Drive, Capreol
705-858-1432
TRAILS, 5; LIFTS, 1; VERTICAL, 160'.
▶NORDIC: 65 groomed km.

CARIBOU MOUNTAIN SKI CLUB
(P. 62, C-5, #12) O'Connor Drive, Temagami
705-569-3421
TRAILS, 3; LIFTS, 1; VERTICAL, 200'.

CASWELL RESORT HOTEL
(P. 62, E-5, #13) Main Street, Lake Bernard, Sundridge
705-384-5371
TRAILS, 4; LIFTS, 2; VERTICAL, 200'.
▶NORDIC: 18 groomed km. Sleigh rides.

CHAPLEAU SKI CLUB
(P. 62, A-4, #14) Martel Road, Chapleau
705-864-0707
TRAILS, 2; LIFTS, 1; VERTICAL, 180'.
▶NORDIC: 6 groomed km.

CHEDOKE WINTER SPORTS PARK
(P. 63, H-5, #15) 563 Aberdeen Ave., Hamilton
905-528-1613
TRAILS, 7; LIFTS, 4; VERTICAL, 330'.

CHICOPEE SKI CLUB
(P. 63, H-4, #16) 396 Morrison Rd., Kitchener
519-894-5610
TRAILS, 19; LIFTS, 6; VERTICAL, 195'.

DEVIL'S ELBOW SKI AREA
(P. 63, G-6, #17) 3 mi. N off Highway 7A, Bethany
705-277-2012
TRAILS, 10; LIFTS, 6; VERTICAL, 350'.
▶NORDIC: 8 groomed km.

DIVINE LAKE RESORT
(P. 62, E-5, #18) Highway 11, Port Sydney
705-385-1212
TRAILS, 2; LIFTS, 1; VERTICAL, 165'.
▶NORDIC: 5 groomed km.

DRYDEN SKI CLUB
(P. 62, A-2, #19) Highway 601, 9 mi. N of Dryden
No telephone
TRAILS, 4; LIFTS, 4; VERTICAL, 170'.
▶NORDIC: 22 groomed km.

EAGLE RIDGE
(P. 62, A-2, #20) Uchi Lake Road, Ear Falls

807-222-3716
TRAILS, 3; LIFTS, 1; VERTICAL, 200'.
►NORDIC: 10 groomed km.

ESPANOLA SKI CLUB
(P. 63, D-3, #21) Highway 6, Espanola
705-869-4333
TRAILS, 10; LIFTS, 2; VERTICAL, 200'.

ETOBICOKE CENTENNIAL PARK SKI HILL
(P. 63, G-5, #22) 256 Centennial Park Rd., Etobicoke
416-394-8754
TRAILS, 3; LIFTS, 2; VERTICAL, 130'.

GLEN EDEN SKI AREA
(P. 63, H-4, #23) 2596 Britannia Rd., Milton
905-878-5011
TRAILS, 10; LIFTS, 5; VERTICAL, 240'.

HIDDEN VALLEY HIGHLANDS
(P. 62, E-5, #24) Highway 60, Huntsville
705-789-1773
TRAILS, 8; LIFTS, 4; VERTICAL, 330'.

HOCKLEY VALLEY RESORT
(P. 63, G-4, #25) RR1, Orangeville
519-942-0754
TRAILS, 10; LIFTS, 4; VERTICAL, 312'.
Sleigh rides.

HORSESHOE RESORT
(P. 63, F-5, #26) Horseshoe Valley Road, Barrie
705-835-2790
SEASON: Nov. 15-April 15
ANNUAL SNOWFALL: 100"
TERRAIN: 22 trails over 60 acres; longest run, 2,200'; ◆ 30%; ■ 50%; ● 20%.
LIFTS: 7 (1 high-speed quad, 2 triples, 3 doubles, 1 surface); capacity, 17,450 per hour.
SUMMIT: 1,332'
VERTICAL: 309'
ACTIVITIES: Snowboarding; ice skating; night skiing.
FEATURES: Snowmaking 100%; ski school; restaurants; child care; rentals.
►NORDIC: 36 groomed km (16 skating); rentals; lessons.
One of the premier resorts in the Toronto area, Horseshoe offers top-notch, tree-lined cruising throughout the area, as well as varied cross-country terrain. Roundup is the preeminent cruiser; the steep Racing Hill and bumped-up Flying Mare appeal to stronger skiers. Snowboarders have two half pipes. State-of-the-art snowmaking and grooming allows Horseshoe to provide a "Snow Guarantee"—your money back if you're not satisfied with the conditions. There is a second mountain, The Heights at Horseshoe, open to club members only (and their guests or prospective members), which doubles the skiable terrain (to 44 trails). The Inn at Horseshoe is one of Ontario's finest deluxe properties, equally popular with families and convention groups.

KAMISKOTIA SKI RESORTS
(P. 62, A-4, #27) Highway 576, 12 mi. W of Timmins
705-268-9057
TRAILS, 12; LIFTS, 4; VERTICAL, 400'.
►NORDIC: 7 groomed km

KINGSTON SKI HILLS
(P. 62, B-6, #28) 951 Newcastle St., Kingston
613-378-6203
TRAILS, 7; LIFTS, 5; VERTICAL, 135'.

LAKERIDGE RESORT
(P. 63, G-5, #29) 790 Chalk Lake Rd., Uxbridge
905-649-2058
TRAILS, 12; LIFTS, 3; VERTICAL, 300'.

LANDSLIDE SKI HILL
(P. 62, C-1, #30) 1076 Great Northern Rd., Sault Ste. Marie
705-946-0190
TRAILS, 3; LIFTS, 1; VERTICAL, 150'.

LARDER SKI CLUB
(P. 62, A-5, #31) Highway 624, 1 mi. S of Larder Lake
705-643-2596
TRAILS, 4; LIFTS, 1; VERTICAL, 175'.
►NORDIC: 10 groomed km.

LOCH LOMOND SKI AREA
(P. 62, A-3, #32) Loch Lomond Road, 5 mi. S of Thunder Bay
807-475-7787; 807-475-8135 (snow)
SEASON: Nov. 15-March 31
ANNUAL SNOWFALL: 200"
TERRAIN: 15 trails over NA acres; longest run, 6,000'; ◆ 35%; ■ 40%; ● 25%.
LIFTS: 3 (1 quad, 2 doubles); capacity, 5,200 per hour.
SUMMIT: 1,450'
VERTICAL: 750'
ACTIVITIES: Snowboarding; night skiing.
FEATURES: Snowmaking 95%; ski school; restaurant; rentals.
Spread out over two mountains, Loch Lomond's trails plunge down heavily forested bluffs typical of the Lake Superior area. They're fairly narrow, quite steep and often bumped up, providing some of the most challenging skiing in the Midwest/Ontario area. Interchangeable lift ticket with Candy Mountain.

LONDON SKI CLUB
(P. 63, H-3, #33) 431 Boler Rd., London
519-657-8822; 519-657-8295 (snow)
TRAILS, 8; LIFTS, 4; VERTICAL, 150'.

LONDON/THAMESFORD COBBLE HILLS GOLF & SKI CLUB
(P. 63, H-3, #34) Skee-Hi Road, Thamesford
519-461-1720
TRAILS, 6; LIFTS, 4; VERTICAL, 150'.

LORETTO SKI RESORT
(P. 63, G-4, #35) Off Highway 50, Loretto
905-729-2385
TRAILS, 5; LIFTS, 4; VERTICAL, 185'.
►NORDIC: 8 groomed km.

MANSFIELD SKI CLUB
(P. 63, G-4, #36) Dufferin County Road 18, 6 mi. N of Mansfield
705-435-3838
TRAILS, 14; LIFTS, 6; VERTICAL, 440'.

MINTO GLEN SPORTS CENTRE
(P. 63, G-4, #37) County Road 2, 6 mi. N of Harriston
519-338-2782
TRAILS, 6; LIFTS, 1; VERTICAL, 185'.
►NORDIC: 25 groomed km (10 skating).
Tobogganing.

MT. ANTOINE
(P. 62, D-5, #38) Highway 533, 4 mi. NE of North Bay
705-744-2844
TRAILS, 11; LIFTS, 3; VERTICAL, 630'.
►NORDIC: 3 groomed km.
Ice skating.

MOUNT BALDY
(P. 62, A-3, #39) 322 Hartviksen St., 4 mi. N of Thunder Bay
807-683-8441
TRAILS, NA; LIFTS, 3; VERTICAL, 650'.

MOUNT CHINGUACOUSY
(P. 63, G-5, #40) Central Park Drive, Brampton
905-458-6649
TRAILS, 3; LIFTS, 2; VERTICAL, 115'.

MOUNT MADAWASKA
(P. 62, B-5, #41) Highway 62, 3 mi. S of Barry's Bay
613-756-2931
TRAILS, 9; LIFTS, 2; VERTICAL, 400'.
►NORDIC: 30 groomed km.
Ice skating.

MOUNT MARTIN SKI CLUB
(P. 62, B-5, #42) Highway 1, 1 mi. W of Deep River
613-584-2809
TRAILS, 6; LIFTS, 2; VERTICAL, 150'.

MOUNT PAKENHAM
(P. 62, B-6, #43) Highway 15, 2 mi. SW of Pakenham
613-624-5290
TRAILS, 7; LIFTS, 5; VERTICAL, 300'.
►NORDIC: 30 groomed km.

MT. ST. LOUIS/ MOONSTONE
(P. 63, F-5, #44) Highway 400 N., exit 131 right, Coldwater
705-835-2112
SEASON: Nov. 20-April 1
ANNUAL SNOWFALL: 100"
TERRAIN: 33 trails over 175 acres; longest run, 1 mi.; ◆ 15%; ■ 55%; ● 30%.
LIFTS: 13 (1 high-speed quad, 3 quads, 3 triples, 4 doubles, 2 surface); capacity, 20,000 per hour.
SUMMIT: NA
VERTICAL: 500'
ACTIVITIES: Snowboarding.
FEATURES: Snowmaking 100%; ski school; restaurant; rentals.
Another superior mountain in the Toronto area, whose trails sprawl over three peaks. The substantial beginners' area is off to the left as you face the slopes, although there is a good mix of terrain throughout the area, allowing skiers of all abilities to access the summit. Mt. St. Louis/Moonstone is primarily notable for its smooth cruisers for all levels, like Turkey Shoot, Sundance and Gentle Ben.

MOUNT WAWA SKI HILL
(P. 62, A-4, #45) Highway 17, 2 mi. S of Wawa
705-856-2086
TRAILS, 3; LIFTS, 2; VERTICAL, 150'.
►NORDIC: 20 groomed km.

MOUNTAIN VIEW SKI HILLS
(P. 63, F-5, #46) Foster's Road, Midland
705-526-8149
TRAILS, 7; LIFTS, 2; VERTICAL, 150'.
►NORDIC: 20 groomed km.

NORTH BAY LAURENTIAN SKI CLUB
(P. 62, D-5, #47) Ski Club Road, North Bay
705-474-9950

TRAILS, 7; LIFTS, 3; VERTICAL, 310'.

NORTH YORK SKI CENTRE
(P. 63, G-5, #48) 4169 Bathurst Rd., North York
416-395-7934
TRAILS, 4; LIFTS, 3; VERTICAL, 130'.

ONAPING SKI HILLS
(P. 62, D-3, #49) Regional Road 8, Onaping
705-966-3939
TRAILS, 10; LIFTS, 3; VERTICAL, 300'.

OSHAWA SKI CLUB
(P. 63, G-6, #50) City Road 9 off Highway 35, Kirby
905-983-5983
SEASON: Dec. 15-March 31
ANNUAL SNOWFALL: 85"
TERRAIN: 26 trails over NA acres; longest run, 2,500'; ◆ 25%; ▪ 40%; ● 35%.
LIFTS: 11 (2 quads, 9 surface); capacity, 9,000 per hour.
SUMMIT: 1,175'
VERTICAL: 300'
ACTIVITIES: Snowboarding; ski jumping; night skiing.
FEATURES: Snowmaking 100%; ski school; restaurant; rentals.
Oshawa offers primarily cruising through fairly narrow tree-lined slopes and one bowl; it's more significant for its ski jumping programs.

RAVEN MOUNTAIN
(P. 62, A-5, #51) Highway 66, 26 mi. E of Kirkland Lake
705-634-2676; 705-642-3319 (snow)
TRAILS, 11; LIFTS, 2; VERTICAL, 520'.
▶NORDIC: 7 groomed km.

RENÉ BRUNELLE WINTER RECREATION AREA
(P. 62, A-4, #52) Remi Lake Ski Area Road, Kapuskasing
705-367-2442
TRAILS, 2; LIFTS, 2; VERTICAL, 145'.
▶NORDIC: 10 groomed km.

SEARCHMONT RESORT
(P. 62, C-1, #53) Highway 556, Sault Ste. Marie
705-781-2340
SEASON: Dec. 1-April 10
ANNUAL SNOWFALL: 130"
TERRAIN: 18 trails over 65 acres; longest run, 7,200'; ◆ 20%; ▪ 60%; ● 20%.
LIFTS: 4 (1 quad, 1 triple, 1 double, 1 surface); capacity, 4,800 per hour.
SUMMIT: 1,600'
VERTICAL: 700'
ACTIVITIES: Snowboarding; night skiing.
FEATURES: Snowmaking 95%; ski school; restaurants; rentals.
▶NORDIC: 50 groomed km (with skating lane); rentals; lessons.
Searchmont has spent $15 million over the past few years in an effort to draw skiers from the USA. Its vertical dwarfs that of most Midwestern resorts and its runs are satisfyingly long. The skiing is scenic, with some smashing Lake Superior views, and even more strongly intermediate than the breakdown suggests. Novices have a bunny hill, then must graduate to some advanced beginner slopes. The black runs, rated advanced more for the steepness than terrain, are really more challenging cruisers. Boarders have a half pipe. The Nordic system is ranked one of the toughest in the region, with either flat, wooded trails or hilly terrain necessitating a great deal of climbing.

SILVER FOX SKI RESORT
(P. 63, G-6, #54) County Road 38, Bethany
705-277-3699
TRAILS, 7; LIFTS, 3; VERTICAL, 410'.

SIR SAM'S SKI AREA
(P. 63, F-5, #55) County Road 14, Eagle Lake
705-754-2298
TRAILS, 11; LIFTS, 5; VERTICAL, 400'.

SKI DAGMAR
(P. 63, G-5, #56) Lakeridge Road, Ashburn
905-649-2002
TRAILS, 11; LIFTS, 8; VERTICAL, 200'.
▶NORDIC: 22 groomed km.

SNOW VALLEY SKI RESORT
(P. 63, G-5, #57) Snow Valley Road, Barrie
705-721-7669
TRAILS, 18; LIFTS, 7; VERTICAL, 280'.

SUPERIOR SLOPES
(P. 62, A-3, #58) Highway 17, Marathon
807-229-3360
TRAILS, 11; LIFTS, 2; VERTICAL, 325'.
▶NORDIC: 10 groomed km.

TALISMAN MOUNTAIN RESORT
(P. 63, F-4, #59) Grey Road 13, Kimberley
519-599-2520
SEASON: Dec. 1-April 1
ANNUAL SNOWFALL: 100"
TERRAIN: 15 trails over 75 acres; longest run, 4,000'; ◆ 25%; ▪ 50%; ● 25%.
LIFTS: 7 (1 quad, 3 doubles, 3 surface); capacity, 4,500 per hour.
SUMMIT: 1,375'
VERTICAL: 600'
ACTIVITIES: Snowboarding; tobogganing; sleigh rides; ice skating.
FEATURES: Snowmaking 100%; ski school; restaurants; rentals.
▶NORDIC: 24 groomed km; rentals; lessons.
Talisman provides miles of cruising down pretty tree-lined trails, a half pipe, popular terrain garden for kids and pleasant gliding in a warm family atmosphere. Children under 10 ski, stay and eat for free if adults purchase certain packages. Talisman added three runs, a beginner lift and snowboard park in 1994.

TRI-TOWN SKI VILLAGE
(P. 62, A-5, #60) Highway 567, Lorrain Valley
705-672-3888
TRAILS, 10; LIFTS, 2; VERTICAL, 320'.
▶NORDIC: 30 groomed km.

NORDIC

ALBION HILLS CONSERVATION AREA
(P. 63, G-4, #61) Highway 50, Bolton
905-880-0227
FACILITIES: 26 groomed km (12 skating); rentals; tobogganing; restaurant.

ALGONQUIN CROSS-COUNTRY SKI CENTRE
(P. 62, E-6, #62) Highway 60, Whitney
613-637-2699
FACILITIES: 80 groomed km; rentals; lessons; dog sledding; snowshoeing; lodging and restaurant.

THE BALDWINS
(P. 63, F-5, #63) Muskoka Road 4, Windermere
705-769-3371
FACILITIES: 17 groomed km (4 skating); rentals; lessons; ice skating; snowshoeing; lodging and restaurant.

BAYVIEW-WILDWOOD RESORTS
(P. 63, F-5, #64) Port Stanton, Severn Bridge
705-689-2338
FACILITIES: 16 groomed km; rentals; lessons (clinic weekends); snowmobiling; sleigh rides; ice skating; lodging and restaurant.

BEACHWOOD RESORT
(P. 63, F-6, #65) RR1, Lakefield
705-657-3481
FACILITIES: 10 groomed km (with skating lane); rentals; lodging and restaurant.
For guests only.

BEAR TRAIL INN RESORT
(P. 62, E-6, #66) Galeairy Lake Road, Whitney
613-637-2662
FACILITIES: 50 groomed km; rentals; ice skating; lodging and restaurant.

BINGEMAN PARK
(P. 63, H-4, #67) 1380 Victoria St., Kitchener
519-744-1555
FACILITIES: 8 groomed km; rentals; lessons; restaurant.

BLUE WATER ACRES
(P. 63, E-5, #68) Muskoka Road 9, Huntsville
705-635-2880
FACILITIES: 12 groomed km; rentals; snowmobiling; tobogganing; tubing; ice skating; lodging and restaurant.
For guests only.

THE BRIARS RESORT
(P. 63, G-5, #69) 55 Hedge Rd., Jackson's Point
905-722-3271
FACILITIES: 10 groomed km; rentals; lessons; tobogganing; snow golf; ice skating; lodging and restaurant.

BRUCE'S MILL CONSERVATION AREA
(P. 63, G-5, #70) Stouffville Road, Gormley
905-887-5273
FACILITIES: 16.5 groomed km; rentals (weekends only); tobogganing; ice skating; restaurant.

CIRCLE R RANCH TOURING CENTRE
(P. 63, H-3, #71) Off Highway 2, Delaware
519-471-3799
FACILITIES: 15 groomed km (5 skating); rentals; lessons; sleigh rides; lodging and restaurant.

DEER LODGE RESORT
(P. 63, F-6, #72) RR2, Haliburton
705-457-2281
FACILITIES: 150 groomed km (with skating lane); rentals; snowmobiling; ice skating; lodging and restaurant.
The trails are actually maintained by the Haliburton Nordic Club and lie just across the road from the resort.

DEERHURST RESORT TRAIL SYSTEM
(P. 62, E-5, #73) Muskoka Road 23, Huntsville
705-789-6411
FACILITIES: 20 groomed km (3 skating); rentals; lessons;

snowmobiling; tobogganing; dog sledding; sleigh rides; winter horseback riding; ice skating; lodging and restaurant. This upscale, full-service resort offers a plethora of activities to tempt the family, as well as mixed but very hilly, mostly intermediate-advanced terrain.

DOMAIN OF KILLIEN RESORT

(P. 63, F-6, #74) Caroll Road, Haliburton
705-457-1100
FACILITIES: 26 groomed km; rentals; ice skating; lodging and restaurant.
For guests only.

DUNTROON HIGHLANDS RESORT

(P. 63, G-4, #75) Highway 24, Duntroon
705-444-5017
FACILITIES: 16 groomed km (with skating lane); rentals; lessons; tobogganing; lodging and restaurant.

ELMHIRST'S RESORT

(P. 63, G-6, #76) 1045 Settlers Line, Keene
705-295-4591
FACILITIES: 18 groomed km; rentals; lessons; snowmobiling; sleigh rides; ice skating; lodging and restaurant.

FERN RESORT

(P. 63, F-5, #77) Rama Road, Orillia
705-325-2256
FACILITIES: 12 groomed km; rentals; curling; ice skating; lodging and restaurant.

GEORGIAN SKI & CANOE CLUB

(P. 62, B-2, #78) Highway 124, Parry Sound
705-746-9277
FACILITIES: 30 groomed km (10 skating); rentals; lessons; restaurant.

GRANDVIEW INN

(P. 62, E-5, #79) RR4, Huntsville
705-789-4417
FACILITIES: 15 groomed km; rentals; snowshoeing; ice skating; lodging and restaurant.

GRAVENHURST NORDIC TRAILS

(P. 63, F-5, #80) Gravenhurst
705-687-2333
FACILITIES: 17 groomed km (with skating lane); rentals; lessons; restaurant.

HALIMAR LODGE

(P. 63, F-6, #81) RR2, Haliburton

705-457-1300
FACILITIES: 150 groomed km; rentals; tobogganing; ice skating; lodging and restaurant.

HARDWOOD HILLS

(P. 63, F-5, #82) Doran Road, Oro Station
705-487-3775
FACILITIES: 30 groomed km (with skating lane); rentals; lessons; restaurant.

HEARST CROSS-COUNTRY SKI CLUB

(P. 62, A-4, #83) Off Highway 583, Hearst
705-362-5529
FACILITIES: 40 groomed km; rentals; lessons; restaurant.

HIAWATHA HIGHLANDS

(P. 62, C-1, #84) 99 Foster Dr., Sault Ste. Marie
705-759-5310
FACILITIES: 35 groomed km (12.5 skating); rentals; lessons; restaurant.

IRWIN INN

(P. 63, F-6, #85) RR2, Lakefield
705-877-2240
FACILITIES: 7 groomed km; rentals; lessons; snowmobiling; snowshoeing; sleigh rides; winter horseback; ice skating; lodging and restaurant.

KAMVIEW NORDIC CENTRE

(P. 62, A-3, #86) #20 Side Rd., Thunder Bay
807-475-7081
FACILITIES: 24 groomed km (with skating lane); lessons; child care; restaurant.
Varied terrain, mostly beginner and intermediate, with sensational views of the Kaministiquia River and Nor'wester peaks.

LAURENTIAN LODGE AND OUTDOOR CENTRE

(P. 62, E-5, #87) Dorset
705-766-9320
FACILITIES: 10 groomed km (7 skating); rentals; lessons; dog sledding; ice skating; lodging and restaurant.

LOCARNO RESORT

(P. 63, F-6, #88) RR2, Haliburton
705-457-2012
FACILITIES: 150 groomed km; rentals; lodging and restaurant.

LOCHAVEN INN

(P. 63, F-6, #89) RR1, Haliburton
705-754-3531
FACILITIES: 2 groomed km; rentals; snowshoeing; sleigh rides; ice skating; restaurant.
Lochaven has only one short

beginner trail, but links into the 150 km Haliburton Nordic Trails System.

MANSFIELD OUTDOOR CENTRE

(P. 63, G-4, #90) Airport Road, Mansfield
705-435-4479
FACILITIES: 32 groomed km (6 skating); rentals; lessons; snowshoeing; restaurant.

MAPLE SANDS RESORT

(P. 63, F-6, #91) RR1, Haliburton
705-454-2800
FACILITIES: No groomed km; rentals; lessons; restaurant.

MATTAWA GOLF & SKI RESORT

(P. 62, D-6, #92) Mattawa
705-744-5818
FACILITIES: 20 groomed km; rentals; snowmobiling; ice skating; lodging and restaurant.

MOUNTSBERG CONSERVATION AREA

(P. 63, H-4, #93) 2596 Britannia Rd., Milton
905-336-1158
FACILITIES: 13.5 groomed km; rentals; ice skating; restaurant.

MUSKOKA FLAG INN

(P. 62, E-5, #94) Off Highway 11 at Muskoka Road 10, Utterson
705-385-2624
FACILITIES: 30 groomed km; rentals; lessons; snowmobiling; snowshoeing; lodging and restaurant.

MUSKOKA SANDS RESORT

(P. 63, F-5, #95) Muskoka Beach Road, Gravenhurst
705-687-2233
FACILITIES: 12 groomed km; rentals; ice skating; lodging and restaurant.

NANGOR RESORT

(P. 62, B-6, #96) Highway 17, Westmeath
613-587-4455
FACILITIES: 30 groomed km; rentals; lessons; ice skating; lodging and restaurant.

NOTTAWASAGA INN

(P. 63, G-4, #97) 1110 Highway 89, Alliston
705-435-5501
FACILITIES: 10 groomed km, 350 acres backcountry; rentals; tobogganing; ice skating; lodging and restaurant.

PICKEREL LAKE LODGE

(P. 62, E-5, #98) Pickerel Lake

Road, Burks Falls
705-382-2025
FACILITIES: 40 groomed km; rentals; lessons; snowmobiling; snowshoeing; tobogganing; lodging and restaurant.

PINESTONE INN

(P. 63, F-6, #99) Haliburton
800-461-0357
FACILITIES: 150 groomed km; rentals; lessons; ice skating; lodging and restaurant.
These extremely varied trails run right through the resort's property, but are operated by Haliburton Highlands Nordic Trail Association. They access several other top properties, like Willow Beach Cottages, Locarno Resort, Halimar Lodge and Lochaven Inn.

PLEASURE VALLEY

(P. 63, G-5, #100) 2499 Brock Rd., Uxbridge
905-649-3334
FACILITIES: 26 groomed km (8 skating); rentals; lessons; tobogganing; ice skating; restaurant.

POW-WOW POINT LODGE

(P. 62, E-5, #101) Highway 60, 6 mi. W of Huntsville
705-789-4951
FACILITIES: 12 groomed km; rentals; tobogganing; sleigh rides; ice skating; lodging and restaurant.
For guests only.

RED BAY LODGE

(P. 63, F-3, #102) Shore Road, Mar
519-534-1027
FACILITIES: 40 groomed km; rentals; snowmobiling; lodging and restaurant.

ROCKY CREST RESORT

(P. 63, E-5, #103) Hamer Bay Road, Hamer Bay
705-375-2240
FACILITIES: 10 groomed km; rentals; snowshoeing; ice skating; lodging and restaurant.

SHAMROCK LODGE

(P. 63, F-5, #104) Shamrock Road, Port Carling
705-765-3177
FACILITIES: 14 groomed km; rentals; lessons; tubing; ice skating; lodging and restaurant.

SHERWOOD INN

(P. 63, F-5, #105) Sherwood Road, Port Carling
705-765-3131
FACILITIES: 16 groomed km; rentals; snowshoeing; dog sledding; tobogganing; ice skating; lodging and restaurant.

SILENT LAKE PROVINCIAL PARK
(P. 63, F-6, #106) Off Highway 28, Bancroft
613-339-2807
FACILITIES: 40 groomed km; rentals; lessons.

SMOOTHWATER OUTDOOR CENTRE
(P. 62, C-5, #107) Temagami
705-569-3539
FACILITIES: 15 groomed km; rentals; lessons; dog sledding; lodging and restaurant (reserve meals in advance).

SOUTH SHORE RIM LAURENTIAN UNIVERSITY CROSS-COUNTRY TRAILS
(P. 62, D-4, #108) Ramsey Lake Road, Sudbury
705-675-1151, x1002
FACILITIES: 35 groomed km; rentals; lessons; restaurant (snacks weekends).

SPORTSMAN'S LODGE, RESORT & CONFERENCE CENTRE
(P. 62, D-4, #109) Kukagami Road, Garson
705-853-4434
FACILITIES: 50 groomed km; rentals; lodging and restaurant.

STOKELY CREEK LODGE
(P. 62, C-1, #110) RR1, Karalash Corners, Goulais River
705-649-3421
FACILITIES: 120 groomed km; lessons; lodging and restaurant.

TERRA COTTA CONSERVATION AREA
(P. 63, G-4, #111) Winston Churchill Blvd., Terra Cotta
905-877-9832
FACILITIES: 14 groomed km; rentals; lessons; restaurant.

TRILLIUM TRAILS
(P. 63, G-5, #112) 57 Snowridge Court, Oshawa
905-655-3754
FACILITIES: 23.5 groomed km (with skating lane); rentals; lessons; restaurant.

VIAMEDE RESORT & CONFERENCE CENTER
(P. 63, F-6, #113) Viamede Road, Woodview
705-654-3344
FACILITIES: 15 groomed km; rentals; lessons; snowmobiling; snowshoeing; tobogganing; ice skating; lodging and restaurant.

WASAGA BEACH PROVINCIAL PARK
(P. 63, F-4, #114) River Road, Wasaga Beach
705-429-2516
FACILITIES: 27 groomed km; rentals; lessons; snowmobiling.

WESTWIND INN
(P. 63, F-6. #115) Buckhorn
705-657-8095
FACILITIES: 10 groomed km; rentals; lessons; snowmobiling; ice skating; lodging and restaurant.

WHITEFISH LODGE
(P. 63, A-4, #116) Wawa
705-889-2054
FACILITIES: 20 groomed km; rentals; lodging and restaurant.

WIGAMOG INN
(P. 63, F-6, #117) N. Kashagawigamog Lake Road, Haliburton
800-661-2010
FACILITIES: 150 groomed km (with skating lane); rentals; lessons; snowmobiling; snowshoeing; dog sledding; ice skating; lodging and restaurant.
One of the top centers in Canada, Wigamog has trails for all levels weaving mostly through hilly woods on the Haliburton system.

WYE MARSH WILDLIFE CENTRE
(P. 63, F-5, #118) Highway 1, 3 mi. E of Midland
705-526-7809
FACILITIES: 20 groomed km; rentals; lessons; snowshoeing; restaurant.

Y.M.C.A GENEVA PARK VACATION & CONFERENCE CENTER
(P. 63, F-5, #119) RR6, Orillia
705-325-2253
FACILITIES: 5 groomed km; rentals; snowshoeing; sleigh rides; ice skating; lodging and restaurant.

PRINCE EDWARD ISLAND

ALPINE

BROOKVALE PROVINCIAL PARK SKI CENTER
(P. 64, B-4, #1) Highway 13, 15 mi. W of Charlottetown
902-368-4277
SEASON: Dec. 15-March 31
ANNUAL SNOWFALL: 90"
TERRAIN: 6 trails over NA acres; longest run, 1,400'; NA
LIFTS: 3 (3 surface); capacity, 1,800 per hour.
SUMMIT: 300'
VERTICAL: 180'
ACTIVITIES: Snowboarding; ice skating; tobogganing.
FEATURES: Snowmaking 100%; ski school; restaurant; rentals.
►NORDIC: 17.5 groomed km; rentals.
The only ski area with facilities to speak of on the island, Brookvale is very pretty and popular with families, but skiers shouldn't make a special trip.

QUEBEC

ALPINE

BELLE NEIGE
(P. 64, D-4, #1) 6832 boulevard Labelle, Route 117, Val Morin
514-476-9915
TRAILS, 14; LIFTS, 3; VERTICAL, 507'.

BELLEVUE SKI CENTER
(P. 64, D-4, #2) 81 chemin du Lac Echo, Morin Heights
514-226-2003
TRAILS, 5; LIFTS, 2; VERTICAL 300'.
►NORDIC: 100 groomed km.

BROMONT
(P. 64, E-5, #3) 150 rue Champlain, Bromont
514-534-2200
SEASON: Nov, 15-April 30
ANNUAL SNOWFALL: 190"
TERRAIN: 22 trails over 140 acres; longest run, 2.5 mi.; ◆◆ 20%; ◆ 32.6%; ■ 19.6%; ● 27.8%
LIFTS: 6 (1 high-speed quad, 2 doubles, 3 surface); capacity, 7,800 per hour.
SUMMIT: 1,879'
VERTICAL: 1,300'
ACTIVITIES: Snowboarding; sleigh rides; winter horseback riding; tubing; night skiing.
FEATURES: Snowmaking 80%; ski school; restaurants; child care; rentals.
►NORDIC: 32 groomed km; rentals; lessons.
There's always something brewing at Bromont, the nearest major area to Montreal and as close to a party-hearty place as you'll find in the traditional, family-oriented Eastern Townships. While the skiing lacks true challenge, it's perfect for families who descend here in droves, taking advantage of special package rates and the occasional, fun theme weekend. Beginners have plenty of perfectly pitched trails like the meandering delight, Brome. Intemediates have their pick of velvety cruisers like Knowlton. And stronger skiers will find a few steep runs, like Waterloo, to keep things interesting.

CAMP FORTUNE
(P. 64, D-1, #4) Old Chelsea
819-827-1717
TRAILS, 16; LIFTS, 5; VERTICAL, 595'.

CLUB DE SKI MONT VILLA SANGUENAY
(P. 65, A-6, #5) 140 St. Joseph, Alma
418-669-3473
TRAILS, 3; LIFTS, 1; VERTICAL, 175'.

CLUB DE SKI PLESSIS
(P. 65, C-6, #6) 1361 route Bellemare, Plessisville
418-453-2357
TRAILS, 10; LIFTS, 2; VERTICAL, 264'.

CLUB TOBO-SKI
(P. 65, A-5, #7) St. Félicien
418-679-5243
TRAILS, 6; LIFTS, 2; VERTICAL, 215'.

CÔTE DES CHATS CENTRE DE PLEIN AIR
(P. 65, B-8, #8) 35 rue Caron, St. Pacome
418-852-2430
TRAILS, 4; LIFTS, 2; VERTICAL, 440'.

CÔTES 40-80
(P. 64, D-4, #9) 1381 boulevard Sainte-Adèle, Sainte-Adèle
514-229-2921
TRAILS, 5; LIFTS, 3; VERTICAL, 360'.

EDELWEISS VALLÉE SKI CENTRE
(P. 64, D-2, #10) RR2, Wakefield
819-459-2328
TRAILS, 19; LIFTS, 3; VERTICAL, 660'.
►NORDIC: 30 groomed km.

GRAND COULÉE
(P. 65, C-7, #11) 1 chemin de la Coulée, off Route 283, Saint-Paul de Montminy
418-469-3453
TRAILS, 28; LIFTS, 3; VERTICAL, 1,160'.
►NORDIC: 5 groomed km.

GRAY ROCKS
(P. 64, D-4, #12) Off Route 327, Saint-Jovite
819-425-2771
SEASON: Nov. 24-May 8
ANNUAL SNOWFALL: 100"
TERRAIN: 20 trails over 60 acres; longest run, 1 mi.; ◆◆ 4%; ◆ 32%; ■ 32%; ● 32%.
LIFTS: 4 (1 quad, 3 doubles); capacity, 5,300 per hour.
SUMMIT: 935'
VERTICAL: 620'
ACTIVITIES: Sleigh rides.
FEATURES: Snowmaking 90%; ski school; restaurants; child care; rentals.
►NORDIC: 40 groomed km, 80 ungroomed; rentals; lessons.
It may seem small fry compared to its Laurentian neighbors, but Gray

Rocks is an institution. For one, it practically invented the concept of packaged, all-inclusive ski weeks. For another, its Snow Eagle Ski School is perennially rated tops in Canada, if not North America. Add to that a complete fitness center and a cozy inn that defines the après ski experience for many. The hosts adroitly match families with families and direct singles toward singles, so everyone whoops it up. No other resort in the Quebec area offers such variety of diversions once the sun goes down, from fashion shows to moonlight cross-country jaunts. So how's the skiing? It runs the gamut from bunny hill to the steeps of Devil's Dip and Bon Voyage. The grooming and snowmaking are top-of-the-line. (And so is the food). And if you want more variety, your lift ticket is good at Mont Blanc, the second highest mountain in the Laurentians.

L'AVALANCHE
(P. 64, D-4, #13) 1657 chemin l'Avalanche, St.-Adolphe d'Howard
819-327-3232
TRAILS, 9; LIFTS, 2; VERTICAL, 495'.
►NORDIC: NA groomed km.

LA CRAPAUDIERE
(P. 65, C-7, #14) 244 chemin de la Station, St. Malachie
418-642-5171
TRAILS, 11; LIFTS, 2; VERTICAL, 957'.
►NORDIC: 8 groomed km.

LA TUQUE CENTRE DE SKI
(P. 65, B-5, #15) 530 rue Kitchener, La Tuque
819-523-2204
TRAILS, 10; LIFTS, 2; VERTICAL, 555'

LE MASSIF
(P. 65, B-7, #16) 1350, rue Principale, Petite-Rivière-Saint-Francois
418-632-5876
SEASON: Dec. 18-April 4
ANNUAL SNOWFALL: 240"
TERRAIN: 15 trails over 144 acres; longest run, 2.36 mi.; ◆◆ 5%; ◆ 62%; ■ 33%.
LIFTS: 2 (1 high-speed quad, 1 double); capacity, 4,000 per hour.
SUMMIT: 2,750'
VERTICAL: 2,640'
ACTIVITIES: Snowboarding.
FEATURES: Snowmaking 42%; ski school; restaurant; rentals.
Before Le Massif installed two lifts, it was one of only two resorts in North America to ferry skiers to the slopes via heated buses. Ah, for the good old days and the camaraderie of jostling together up the slopes. Still, they haven't tinkered with the skiing, which boasts the greatest

Courtesy: Telluride Ski Resort (see Colorado, p. 100).

vertical in Eastern Canada. These are world-class steeps, led by the vicious plunges of Pioche and Cabaret. But intermediates can enjoy the sustained pitch (and marvelous views of the St. Lawrence) on runs like Petite-Rivière and Desjardins; although there are no green runs, advanced beginners can tackle the flatter Desjardins, Grande Pointe, Combe and Ancienne. The ambitious master plan calls for this diamond in the rough to exceed the acreage of Killington by the new millennium.

LE RELAIS CENTRE DE SKI
(P. 65, C-6, #17) 1084 boulevard du Lac, off Highway 73, Lac Beauport
418-849-1851
TRAILS, 25; LIFTS, 6; VERTICAL, 738'.

LE VALINOUET
(P. 65, A-7, #18) Route L201, chemin Levesque, Falardeau
418-673-3455
TRAILS, 25; LIFTS, 4; VERTICAL, 1,155'.
►NORDIC: 55 groomed km.

MASSIF DU SUD
(P. 65, C-7, #19) 1989 route du Massif, St. Philemon
418-469-3676
TRAILS, 11; LIFTS, 2; VERTICAL, 1,170'.
►NORDIC: 25 groomed km.

MONT-ALTA
(P. 64, D-4, #20) 2114 route 117, Val-David
819-322-3206
TRAILS, 22; LIFTS, 2; VERTICAL, 585'.

MONT BECHERVAISE
(P. 64, A-3, #21) 54 rue Eden, Gaspé
418-368-1457
TRAILS, 11; LIFTS, 4; VERTICAL, 920'.

MONT BELLEVUE
(P. 65, E-6, #22) 1300 rue Jogues, Sherbrooke
819-821-5872
TRAILS, 6; LIFTS, 3; VERTICAL, 265'.
►NORDIC: 9 groomed km.

MONT BELU CENTRE DE SKI
(P. 65, A-7, #23) 4855 boulevard Grande Baie sud, La Baie
418-544-6833
TRAILS, 7; LIFTS, 2; VERTICAL, 565'.

MONT-BLANC CENTRE DE SKI
(P. 64, D-4, #24) Route 117, Saint-Faustin
819-688-2444
TRAILS, 35; LIFTS, 8; VERTICAL, 990'.
►NORDIC: 4 groomed km.

MONT CASTOR
(P. 64, A-2, #25) 238 route du Centre de Ski, Matane
418-562-1513
TRAILS, 12; LIFTS, 3; VERTICAL, 610'.

MONT CHALCO
Route 167, Chibougamau
418-748-7162
TRAILS, 11; LIFTS, 2; VERTICAL, 290'.
►NORDIC: 25 groomed km.

MONT-CHRISTIE SKI AREA
(P. 64, D-4, #26) 699 Cote Saint-Gabriel Est, Christieville
514-226-2412
TRAILS, 12; LIFTS, 3; VERTICAL, 560'.
►NORDIC: 30 groomed km. Tobogganing.

MONT CITADELLE
(P. 65, B-7, #27) Rivière-du-Loup
418-497-2431
TRAILS, 5; LIFTS, 1; VERTICAL 395'.
►NORDIC: NA groomed km.

MONT DANIEL
(P. 64, D-3, #28) Route 309, Chemin Presqu'ile, Lac des Iles
819-597-2388
TRAILS, 16; LIFTS 2; VERTICAL, 475'.

MONT EDOUARD
(P. 65, A-7, #29) 67 rue Dallaire, Anse-St. Jean
418-272-2112
TRAILS, 21; LIFTS, 3; VERTICAL, 1,485'.
►NORDIC: 13 groomed km.

MONT FORTIN CENTRE DE SKI
(P. 65, A-6, #30) 3492 rue Radin, Jonquiere
418-695-7707
TRAILS, 11; LIFTS, 4; VERTICAL, 312'.

MONT GABRIEL
(P. 64, D-4, #31) Mont Rolland
514-229-3547
SEASON: Nov. 15-April 15
ANNUAL SNOWFALL: 140"
TERRAIN: 21 trails over NA acres; longest run, NA; ◆◆ 14%; ◆ 24%; ■ 28%; ● 34%.
LIFTS: 9 (2 quads, 1 triple, 6 surface); capacity, 10,000 per hour.
SUMMIT: NA
VERTICAL: 660'
ACTIVITIES: Snowboarding; night skiing.
FEATURES: Snowmaking 85%; ski school; restaurant; rentals.
The runs at this often forgotten area plunge down four sides of the mountain, offering a wide variety, but best known for two premier bump runs, O'Connell and Tamarack.

MONT GARCEAU
(P.64, D-4, #32) 190 chemin du Lac Blanc, Saint-Donat
819-424-2784
TRAILS, 17; LIFTS, 3; VERTICAL, 1,005'.
►NORDIC: 16 groomed km; rentals; lessons.

MONT GRAND FONDS
(P. 65, B-7, #33) 1000 chemin des Loisirs, La Malbaie
418-665-4405
SEASON: Dec. 18-April 4
ANNUAL SNOWFALL: 225"
TERRAIN: 14 trails over NA acres; longest run, 7,500'; ♦ 29%; ▪ 36%; ● 35%
LIFTS: 4 (1 quad, 1 double, 2 surface); capacity, 3,600 per hour.
SUMMIT: 2,420'
VERTICAL: 1,105'
ACTIVITIES: Snowboarding.
FEATURES: Snowmaking 50%; ski school; restaurant; rentals.
▶NORDIC: 141 groomed km; rentals; lessons.
Here's an appealing little family area, with both the Alpine and Nordic areas offering a fine balance of terrain. Beginners will love the gentle roll of Ti-Be, intermediates have their choice of wide boulevards like Mary Grace or delightful glades like Des Bouleaux, and experts can cascade down the narrow precipitous La Cascadeuse and La Chouenneuse.

MONT HABITANT
(P. 65, D-4, #34) 12 Boulevard des Skieurs, St. Sauveur des Monts
514-227-2637
TRAILS, 9; LIFTS, 3; VERTICAL, 710'.

MONT JOYE
(P. 65, E-6, #35) 4785 Capelton, Route 108, North Hatley
819-842-2447
TRAILS, 18; LIFTS, 3; VERTICAL, 633'.
Sleigh rides; ice skating.

MONT LABELLE
(P. 64, D-4, #36) Labelle
819-686-2626
TRAILS, 11; LIFTS, 2; VERTICAL, 541'.
▶NORDIC: NA groomed km.

MONT LAC VERT
(P. 65, A-6, #37) 265 rang Lac Vert, Hebertville
418-344-1870
TRAILS, 14; LIFTS, 2; VERTICAL, 790'.
Tubing.

MONT OLYMPIA
(P. 64, D-4, #38) 330 chemin de la Montagne, Piedmont
514-227-3523
SEASON: Dec. 1-April 1
ANNUAL SNOWFALL: 140"
TERRAIN: 21 acres over NA acres; longest run, 4,000'; ♦ 40%; ▪ 40%; ● 20%.
LIFTS: 6 (1 quad, 1 triple, 4 surface); capacity, 6,000 per hour.
SUMMIT: NA
VERTICAL: 646'
ACTIVITIES: Snowboarding; night skiing.
FEATURES: Snowmaking 90%; ski school; restaurant; rentals.
The original mountain offers lots of wide, groomed boulevard for novices and lower intermediates, but the newer mountain provides some hair-raising steeps for stronger skiers.

MONT ORFORD INTERNATIONAL TOURIST AREA
(P. 65, E-6, #39) 4380 chemin du Parc, off Highway 10 (exit 118), Orford
819-843-6548
SEASON: Nov. 15-April 15
ANNUAL SNOWFALL: 200"
TERRAIN: 39 trails over 180 acres; longest run, 2.5 mi.; ♦ 30%; ▪ 32%; ● 38%.
LIFTS: 6 (1 quad, 1 triple, 3 doubles, 1 surface); capacity, 11,400 per hour.
SUMMIT: 2,800'
VERTICAL: 1,780'
ACTIVITIES: Snowboarding.
FEATURES: Snowmaking 85%; ski school; restaurants; child care; rentals.
▶NORDIC: 35 groomed km; rentals; lessons.
The one, true peak in the Eastern Townships, Mont Orford's summit yields stunning panoramic views, especially south toward Lake Memphremagog and Vermont. Skiing covers three peaks. The shortest runs, many of them ideal for novices looking to improve, are on Mont Giroux. Mont Alfred Desroches is the purlieu of intermediates, a series of narrow tree-lined avenues with moderate pitch, usually sheltered on windy days (a chronic problem here). Mont Orford itself offers the greatest vertical and variety, ranging from cruisers like Grande Coulee and Trois Ruisseaux to the bullish bumps of Maxi and the steep spiral of Contour. Over 69 and under 6 ski free.

MONT ORIGNAL
(P. 65, C-7, #40) 160 rang Grande Rivière, Lac Etchemin
418-625-1551
TRAILS, 15; LIFTS, 4; VERTICAL, 975'.
▶NORDIC: 50 groomed km.
Tubing.

MONT PONTBRIAND
(P. 64, D-4, #41) 4567 rue de Mont Pontbriand, Rawdon
514-834-6660
TRAILS, 10; LIFTS, 5; VERTICAL, 445'.
▶NORDIC: 15 groomed km.

MONT RIGAUD
(P. 64, E-4, #42) 321 des Erables, Rigaud
514-451-5316
TRAILS, 8; LIFTS, 2; VERTICAL, 395'.

MONT ST. BRUNO
(P. 65, A-6. #43) 55 chemin des Vingt-Cinq, St. Bruno
514-653-3441
TRAILS, 14; LIFTS, 7; VERTICAL, 395'.
▶NORDIC: 27 groomed km.

MONT ST. CASTIN
(P. 65, C-6, #44) 82 chemin la Tour du Lac, off Route 73, Lac Beauport
418-849-1893
TRAILS, 14; LIFTS, 5; VERTICAL, 575'.

MONT ST. SAUVEUR/AVILA
(P. 65, D-4, #45) 350 rue St. Denis, St.-Sauveur-des-Monts
514-227-4671
SEASON: Oct. 31-May 1
ANNUAL SNOWFALL: 150"
TERRAIN: 39 trails over 175 acres; longest run, 4,900'; ♦ 50%; ▪ 32%; ● 18%.
LIFTS: 9 (3 high-speed quads, 1 quad, 2 triples, 2 doubles, 1 surface); capacity, 14,000 per hour.
SUMMIT: 1,365'
VERTICAL: 700'
ACTIVITIES: Snowboarding; tubing; night skiing.
FEATURES: Snowmaking 100%; ski school; restaurants; child care; rentals.
These neighboring areas are under the same ownership; Avila can be skied on the higher-priced St. Sauveur ticket (Morin Heights participates in an interchangeable program). Several trails connect the two. The high-speed quads efficiently disperse the hordes of happy skiers all over the mountains. This is the most popular resort in the Laurentians (although Tremblant is bidding to recapture its share of the market), not so much for its pleasant skiing as for the raft of clever promotions and its high-powered clientele. It's the place to do the scene, where movie stars learn to ski and politicians grab a power croissant and discuss affairs of state on the lifts.

MONT-STE.-MARIE
(P. 64, D-2, #46) Lac Sainte-Marie
819-467-5200
TRAILS, 17; LIFTS, 3; VERTICAL, 1,257'.

MONT SAUVAGE
(P. 64, D-4, #47) 1169 Second Ave., Val-Morin
819-322-2337
TRAILS, 9; LIFTS, 3; VERTICAL, 570'.

MONT SHEFFORD
(P. 64, E-5, #48) 1300 Denison East, off Route 112, Granby
514-372-1550
TRAILS, 12; LIFTS, 3; VERTICAL, 1,005'.

MONT SUTTON
(P. 65, E-6, #49) 671 Maple, Sutton
514-538-2545
SEASON: Nov. 15-April 15
ANNUAL SNOWFALL: 190"
TERRAIN: 53 trails over 174 acres; longest run, 3 mi.; ♦ 30%; ▪ 40%; ● 40%.
LIFTS: 9 (1 high-speed quad, 2 quads, 6 doubles); capacity, 11,800 per hour.
SUMMIT: 3,125'
VERTICAL: 1,515'
ACTIVITIES: Snowboarding.
FEATURES: Snowmaking 60%; ski school; restaurants; child care; rentals.
▶NORDIC: 40 groomed km; rentals; lessons.
Mont Sutton offers the most tree skiing in the East; fully 40% of its trails are gladed. Skiers also love the endless variety of terrain, with humps, rolls and pitches galore. The layout is easy to follow. Chairs 1 and 2 service primarily intermediate terrain, sinuous cruisers like Alouette and Capucine, surrounded on three sides by extensive green slopes. Advanced skiers should head left and down from the detachable quad to reach Chairs 4, 5, 6 and 7. These lifts increase the vertical by 500 feet and access the bulk of those lovely twisting glades. The meanest steeps—Emotion, Intrepide and Bou Bou—are off Chair 7. Sutton has instituted optional skiing by the hour.

MONT TIBASSE
(P. 64, A-2, #50) 70 Michel Hemon, Baie Comeau
418-296-8311
TRAILS, 11; LIFTS, 3; VERTICAL, 412'.

MONT TREMBLANT LODGE
(P. 64, D-4, #51) 3005 chemin Principal, Mont-Tremblant
819-425-8711
SEASON: Nov. 15-April 30
ANNUAL SNOWFALL: 140"
TERRAIN: 57 trails over 455 acres; longest run, 3.75 mi.; ♦♦ 15%; ♦ 35%; ▪ 30%; ● 20%.
LIFTS: 9 (4 high-speed quads, 1 quad, 2 triples, 2 surface); capacity, 18,800 per hour.
SUMMIT: 3,001'
VERTICAL: 2,131'
ACTIVITIES: Snowboarding; snowshoeing; dog sledding; tobogganing; ice skating.
FEATURES: Snowmaking 74%; ski school; restaurants; child care; rentals.
▶NORDIC: 90 groomed km; rentals; lessons.
Once the dowager empress of Quebec resorts (it even installed the second chair lift in North America back in 1939), Mont Tremblant had fallen on hard times until it was purchased by Intrawest, the folks

behind Blackcomb. They've invested $53 million in improvements in the past two years alone, with more to come. No aspect of the resort has gone untouched. Four high-speed quads were installed. Snowmaking and grooming were vastly improved. Runs were redesigned and widened. A sparkling new mountaintop lodge, Grand Manitou, and base hotel were built. And 18 runs were added, including an entire peak, The Edge. Oldtimers may miss the original narrow steep, Trails, but on the South Side, the new Taschereau, Vertigo and Zig Zag will remind them of those halcyon days. They may not feel so nostalgic gazing on Dynamite, added to the North Side, and its steady 42-degree drop. And old standbys like those knees-of-steel bump runs Expo and Flying Mile remain. Native Americans called it the "trembling mountain," and "mountain of the dread Manitou," a fierce spirit believed to reside on the craggy peak, and in many ways it still deserves its name. Fortunately for novices and intermediates though, many of the original trails twisting through thickets of frozen dwarf pines were modernized and they can frolic on wonderful cruisers like Beauchemin, McCullough, and the three-mile green Nansen. Now other resorts may quiver: Tremblant is back.

MONT VIDEO

Barraute
819-734-3193
TRAILS, 12; LIFTS, 4; VERTICAL, 352'.
▶NORDIC: 40 groomed km. Tobogganing; tubing.

OWL'S HEAD

(P. 65, E-6, #52) Mansonville
514-292-3342
SEASON: Dec. 1-April 15
ANNUAL SNOWFALL: 180"
TERRAIN: 27 trails over NA acres; longest run, 2.25 mi.; ◆ 30%; ▪ 40%; ● 30%.
LIFTS: 7 (1 high-speed quad, 6 doubles); capacity, 8,200 per hour.
SUMMIT: 2,450'
VERTICAL: 1,780'
ACTIVITIES: Snowboarding.
FEATURES: Snowmaking 85%; ski school; restaurants; child care; rentals.
Owl's Head boasts stunning views of Lake Memphremagog from nearly every vantage point. Along with Mont Sutton, this mellow, family-oriented area offers some of the most demanding skiing in the Eastern Townships, on classically steep, narrow trails slashing through the evergreen. The newer section off the Lake Chair offers the wider, gentler runs common in 1970s trail design. Over 65 and under 6 ski free.

PARC DU MONT COMI

(P. 64, A-2, #53) Saint-Donat de Rimouski
418-739-4858
TRAILS, 19; LIFTS, 4; VERTICAL, 1,101'.
▶NORDIC: 25 groomed km.

PARC DU MONT-STE.-ANNE

(P. 65, C-7, #54) Route 360, Beaupré
418-827-4561
SEASON: Nov. 26-April 10
ANNUAL SNOWFALL: 150"
TERRAIN: 50 trails over 400 acres; longest run, 3 mi.; ◆◆ 10%; ◆ 20%; ▪ 50%; ● 20%
LIFTS: 12 (1 gondola, 2 high-speed quads, 1 quad, 1 triple, 2 doubles, 5 surface); capacity, 17,760 per hour.
SUMMIT: 2,625'
VERTICAL: 2,060'
ACTIVITIES: Snowboarding; ski jumping; tobogganing; ice skating; night skiing.
FEATURES: Snowmaking 85%; ski school; restaurants; child care; rentals.
▶NORDIC: 240 groomed km. (136 skating); rentals; lessons.
During the 1980s, Mont Ste. Anne usurped Tremblant's throne as Canada's King of the East; now that Tremblant has launched its counterattack, it's unlikely this marvelous area will abdicate gracefully. Mont Ste. Anne has consistently been in the vanguard when it comes to innovations and improvements, having installed an eight-passenger gondola, built a model children's center, radically increased snowmaking, and developed a Ski Data system that enables skiers to pay by the hour or by vertical feet. The views of the St. Lawrence River are smashing at every turn. Best of all, the skiing is marvelously varied from the flattop summit, though nothing here will strike fear in an expert's heart. Solid intermediates can negotiate almost everything on the mountain, thanks to state-of-the-art grooming. Novice territory stretches over most of the lower south side to the right of the gondola, with the 3.6 mile Chemin du Roy making them feel like kings indeed. Intermediates will find miles of cruisers on the north and west sides, with standouts being La Beaupre and Le Gros Vallon. Advanced skiers should point their skis to the left of the gondola on the south side, where La Crete and L'Espoir (with breathtaking prospects of Quebec City in the distance) are perfect warm-up steeps, before the experts graduate to the mega-moguls of La Gondoleuse, S, and Super S. Gliders and skaters will find an exciting range of terrain and superb snow cover on the top-ranked Nordic system. Wilderness tours are available.

ST. GEORGES CENTRE DE SKI

(P. 65, D-7, #55) 2800 rue 107e, St.Georges-de-Beauce
418-228-8151
TRAILS, 8; LIFTS, 2; VERTICAL, 283'.

ST. MATHIEU

(P. 64, C-5, #56) 359 chemin du Lac, St. Mathieu
418-738-2335
TRAILS, 11; LIFTS, 2; VERTICAL, 660'.
▶NORDIC: 19.5 groomed km.

ST. RAYMOND CENTRE DE SKI

(P. 65, C-6, #57) 1226 rang Notre Dame, St. Raymond
418-337-2866
TRAILS, 7; LIFTS, 3; VERTICAL, 312'.

SKI CHANTECLER

(P. 64, D-4, #58) 1474 chemin Chantecler, Sainte-Adele
514-229-3555
TRAILS, 22; LIFTS, 8; VERTICAL, 663'.

SKI GALLIX

Sept-Iles
418-766-5900
TRAILS, 22; LIFTS, 4; VERTICAL, 610'.

SKI MONT GLEN

(P. 65, E-6, #59) Knowlton
514-243-6142
SEASON: Dec. 1-April 15
ANNUAL SNOWFALL: 135"
TERRAIN: 26 trails over 110 acres; longest run, 7,000'; ◆◆ 10%; ◆ 20%; ▪ 35%; ● 35%.
LIFTS: 4 (2 doubles, 2 surface); capacity, 3,000 per hour.
SUMMIT: 3,400'
VERTICAL: 1,155'
ACTIVITIES: Snowboarding.
FEATURES: Ski school; restaurant; rentals.
▶NORDIC: 4 groomed km.
When crowds overwhelm the "Big Four" of Estrie (Bromont, Owl's Head, Sutton, and Orford), head to this often forgotten charmer popular with local families. The upper half of the mountain offers some sneaky terrain; the lower half is pure, feel-good, auto-pilot cruising.

SKI MONT-CASCADES

(P. 64, E-3, #60) Chemin Mont Cascades, Cantley
819-827-0301
TRAILS, 16; LIFTS, 4; VERTICAL, 525'.

SKI MONT KANASUTA

Rouyn-Noranda
819-279-2331
TRAILS, 10; LIFTS, 3; VERTICAL, 485'.

SKI MONTCALM

(P. 64, D-5, #61) 3294 chemin

Park, Rawdon
514-834-3139
TRAILS, 20; LIFTS, 8; VERTICAL, 460'.
▶NORDIC: 20 groomed km.

SKI MORIN HEIGHTS

(P. 64, D-4, #62) Off Route 15, Morin Heights
514-226-1333
TRAILS, 22; LIFTS, 6; VERTICAL, 660'.

SKI STONEHAM

(P. 65, C-6, #63) 1420 Avenue du Hibou, Stoneham
418-848-2411
SEASON: Nov. 15-April 15
ANNUAL SNOWFALL: 150"
TERRAIN: 25 trails over 295 acres; longest run, 2 mi.; ◆◆ 5%; ◆ 25%; ▪ 40%; ● 30%.
LIFTS: 10 (1 high-speed quad, 3 quads, 2 doubles, 4 surface); capacity, 14,200 per hour.
SUMMIT: 2,075'
VERTICAL: 1,385'
ACTIVITIES: Snowboarding; sleigh rides; ice skating; night skiing.
FEATURES: Snowmaking 92%; ski school; restaurants; child care; rentals.
▶NORDIC: 10 groomed km; lessons.
Stoneham has developed a reputation for quiet pampering and warm ambiance; thoughtful little extras include tissue dispensers at the lift lines and a teen lounge with rock videos, ski films and video games. It offers a good range of terrain for all abilities; trails are numbered rather than named. Novices stick to a small learning area to the left of the mountain until they're ready to try the winding runs from the summit. Intermediates will strike it rich no matter what number they call, with perhaps only runs 45 and 46—the racers' runs—outside their abilities. A large portion of the mountain is lit for skiing after the sun goes down, affording dazzling views of glittering Quebec City by night.

STATION DE SKI DES BOIS-FRANCS

(P. 65, D-6, #64) 332 chemin du Mont Gleason, Warwick
819-359-2301
TRAILS, 14; LIFTS, 3; VERTICAL, 620'.

VAL D'IRÈNE

(P. 64, A-3, #65) 115 route Val d'Irene, Ste. Irène
418-629-3450
SEASON: Nov. 26-April 24
ANNUAL SNOWFALL: 220"
TERRAIN: 13 trails over 336 acres; longest run, 1 mi.; ◆◆ 15%; ◆ 23%; ▪ 39%; ● 23%
LIFTS: 4 (1 double, 3 surface); capacity, 3,000 per hour.
SUMMIT: NA

VERTICAL: 900'
ACTIVITIES: Snowboarding.
FEATURES: Ski school; restaurant; child care; rentals.
▶NORDIC: 15 groomed km.
This friendly local area is located in the awe-inspiring Gaspé peninsula.

VAL MAURICIE
(P. 64, C-5, #66) 1093 rue Shawnigan-Sud, Shawnigan-Sud
819-537-8732
TRAILS, 6; LIFTS, 2; VERTICAL, 330'.

VAL NEIGETTE CENTRE DE SKI
(P. 65, A-9, #67) 25 du Givre, Ste. Blandine
418-735-2800
TRAILS, 16; LIFTS, 4; VERTICAL, 582'.
▶NORDIC: 30 groomed km.

VAL ST.-CÔME
(P. 64, D-4, #68) Off Route 343, Saint-Côme
514-883-0701
TRAILS, 20; LIFTS, 4; VERTICAL, 990'.
▶NORDIC: 5 groomed km.

VALLÉE BLEUE SKI CENTRE
(P. 64, D-4, #69) 1418 Vallée Bleue, Route 117, Val-David
819-322-3427
TRAILS, 15; LIFTS, 3; VERTICAL, 475'.

VALLÉE DU PARC
(P. 64, C-5, #70) 10000 boulevard Vallée du Parc, Grand Mere
819-538-1639
TRAILS, 15; LIFTS, 5; VERTICAL, 555'.
▶NORDIC: 65 groomed km (36 lit).

VORLAGE
(P. 64, D-2, #71) Off Routes 5 & 105, Wakefield
819-459-2301
TRAILS, 15; LIFTS, 7; VERTICAL, 454'.

NORDIC

BEC SCIE OUTDOOR CENTRE
(P. 65, A-7, #72) 990 chemin des Chutes, La Baie
418-544-5433
FACILITIES: 35 groomed km; rentals; lessons; restaurant.
The heavily wooded, balanced trails are incredibly scenic, skirting a deep gorge and waterfall.

CAMP MERCIER
(P. 65, C-7, #73) 3000 Rue Alexandre, Beauport
418-848-2422
FACILITIES: 192 groomed km

(25 skating); rentals; lessons; restaurant.
This wildlife reserve offers miles of secluded gliding for all levels.

CENTRE DE NEIGE
(P. 65, C-7, #74) 1 Chemin de l'Eperon, Lac Beauport
418-849-2778
FACILITIES: 250 groomed km (5 skating); rentals; lessons; snowshoeing; snowmobiling; restaurant.

CROSS-COUNTRY SKI CENTRE
(P. 65, C-7, #75) 8 Rue de la Patinoire, Ste.-Brigitte de Laval
418-825-2603
FACILITIES: 30 groomed km; rentals; lessons; restaurant.

CROSS-COUNTRY SKI TRAILS
(P. 65, E-6, #76) 297 Rue Maple, Sutton
514-538-2271
FACILITIES: 25 groomed km; rentals; lessons; restaurant.

FAR HILLS
(P. 64, D-4, #77) Val-Morin
819-322-2014
FACILITIES: 109 groomed km (50 skating); rentals; lessons; sleigh rides; lodging and restaurant.
The trail system winds through several villages and a blend of fields and woods.

FARMER'S REST
(P. 65, E-6, #78) 2641 chemin Mont Echo, Knowlton
514-243-6843
FACILITIES: 56 groomed km (3.2 skating); rentals; lodging and restaurant.

GATINEAU PARK
(P. 64, D-1, #79) Meech Lake Road, Old Chelsea
819-827-2020
FACILITIES: 190 groomed km (70 skating), unlimited ungroomed; rentals; lessons.
This nature park provides trails for all abilities, more than half through flat meadows ideal for novices.

HOTEL LA SAPINIÈRE
(P. 64, D-4, #80) 1244 chemin La Sapinière, Val-David
819-322-2020
FACILITIES: 50 groomed km; rentals; lessons; snowshoeing; ice skating; lodging and restaurant.

HOTEL L'ESTEREL
(P. 64, D-4, #81) 39 Fridolin Simard, Ville de l'Esterel
514-228-2571
FACILITIES: 85 groomed km (with skating lane); rentals;

lessons; snowmobiling; dog sledding; sleigh rides; ice skating; lodging and restaurant.
This luxurious resort offers a wide range of terrain on its golf course, across a lake and through woods. The system connects with the 200-km Trans-Laurentian network.

HOVEY MANOR
(P. 65, E-6, #82) 575 chemin Havey, North Hatley
819-842-2421
FACILITIES: 50 groomed km; lessons; snowshoeing; ice skating; lodging and restaurant.

LA MONTAGNE COUPÉE
(P. 64, D-5, #83) 1000 Montagne Coupée, St.-Jean de Matha
514-886-3845
FACILITIES: 85 groomed km (40 skating); rentals; lessons; dog sledding; snowshoeing; ice skating; lodging and restaurant.
One of the finest Nordic centers in Canada, with a superior mix of woods and meadows and a charming, old-fashioned inn.

LA VIGIE OUTDOOR CENTER
(P. 64, E-4, #84) 550 boulevard Thomas-Maher, Lac Saint-Joseph
418-875-1844
FACILITIES: 40 groomed km; rentals; lessons; restaurant.

LAC BOUCHETTE OUTDOOR CENTER
(P. 64, D-2, #85) Lac Bouchette
418-348-6832
FACILITIES: 30 groomed km; rentals; lessons; restaurant.

LE CHATEAU MONTEBELLO
(P. 64, E-3, #86) 392 Notre Dame, Montebello
819-423-6341
FACILITIES: 100 groomed km (30 skating); rentals; lessons; tobogganing; snowshoeing; tubing; ice skating; lodging and restaurant.

LE PARC D'OKA
(P. 64, E-4, #87) 2020 chemin Oka, Oka
514-479-8337
FACILITIES: 53 groomed km (8 skating); rentals; lessons; snowshoeing; ice skating; restaurant.

LE PETIT BONHEUR
(P. 64, D-4, #88) 1400 chemin du Lac Quenouille, Lac Superieur
819-326-4281
FACILITIES: 50 groomed km; rentals; lessons; tubing; ice

skating; lodging and restaurant.

RIPPLECOVE INN
(P. 65, E-6, #89) 700 chemin Ripplecove, Ayer's Cliff
819-838-4296
FACILITIES: 50 groomed km; lessons; lodging and restaurant.

STE.-ANNE-DES-PLAINES CENTRE DE SKI DE FOND
(P. 64, D-4, #90) 1st Avenue S. (1re Ave. Sud), Ste.-Anne des Plaines
514-478-0211
FACILITIES: 50 groomed km; rentals; lessons; restaurant.

SASKATCHEWAN

ALPINE

MISSION RIDGE
(P. 60, D-5, #1) 1 mi. SE of Fort Qu'appelle
306-332-5479
TRAILS, NA; LIFTS, 4; VERTICAL, 292'.
▶NORDIC: NA groomed km.
Tobogganing; ice skating; sleigh rides.

OCHAPOWACE SKI AREA
(P. 60, E-5, #2) Highway 201, 18 mi. N and E of Broadview
306-696-2522
SEASON: Dec. 1-March 31
ANNUAL SNOWFALL: 80"
TERRAIN: 21 trails over 100 acres; longest run, 4,000'; ◆ 20%; ▪ 30%; ● 50%.
LIFTS: 4 (4 surface); capacity, 2,000 per hour.
SUMMIT: NA
VERTICAL: 585'
ACTIVITIES: Snowboarding; snowmobiling; night skiing.
FEATURES: Snowmaking 75%; ski school; restaurant; rentals.
This amiable family area offers the most varied skiing in Saskatchewan and by far the heftiest vertical. This translates into a series of smooth cruisers perfect for learning and improving, with one hellacious advanced run, Waterfall.

TABLE MOUNTAIN
(P. 60, C-2, #3) Highway 40; 18 mi. W of Battleford
306-937-2920; 306-937-7715 (snow)
TRAILS, 9; LIFTS, 3; VERTICAL, 370'.

TWIN TOWERS SKI RESORT
(P. 60, C-2, #4) 2 mi. S of Stanraer
306-377-4551
TRAILS, NA; LIFTS, 3; VERTICAL, 300'.

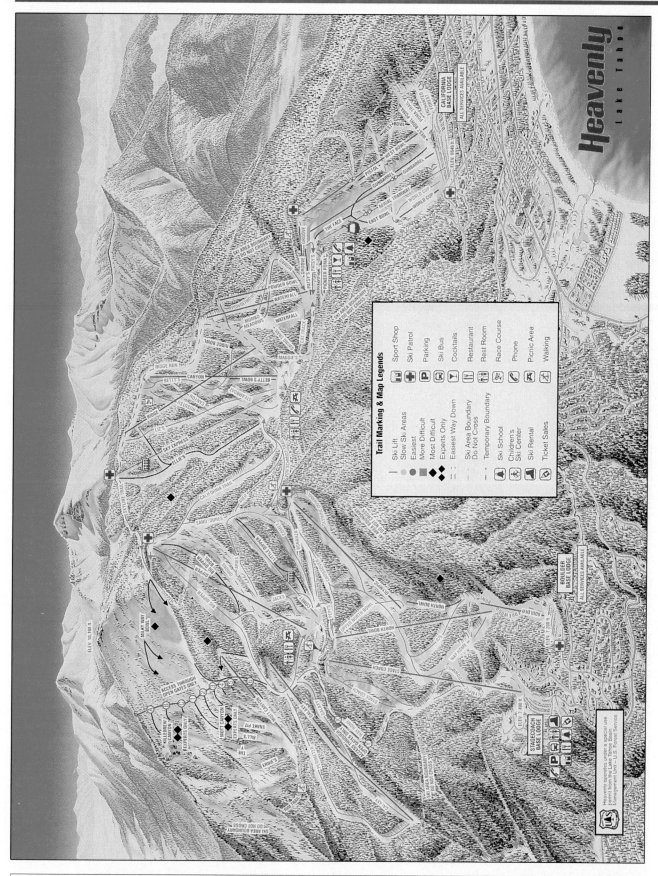

HEAVENLY SKI RESORT, SOUTH LAKE TAHOE, CALIF.

NOTICE: As ski trails may change, these trail maps are not intended for specific use, but are included here to give skiers an overview of the layouts of several top ski areas. It is recommended that skiers rely only on the latest trail information, provided by ski areas to skiers at the time of their visit. All trail maps provided courtesy of the respective ski areas.

GRANITE CHIEF
9,050 ft.

EMIGRANT
8,700 ft.

EL. 8200

BROKEN
ARROW
8,020 ft.

SQUAW PEAK
8,900 ft.

EL. 6200

KT-22
8,200 ft.

SNOW KING
7,550 ft.

SQUAW VALLEY USA, Olympic Valley, Calif.

ASPEN MOUNTAIN

HELP US RECYCLE!
Aspen Skiing Company encourages you to help us recycle all glass, aluminum and any other waste in collection centers at our ski areas.

ASPEN MOUNTAIN
TRAIL MAP AND SKIER GUIDE

■ More Difficult	✚ Ski Patrol	🎟 Tickets
◆ Most Difficult	🎿 Ski School	🎟 Ticket Information Office
◆◆ Expert Only	📞 Emergency Phones	🎿 Ski Rental
— Lifts	👁 Caution Blind Skier	🍴 Restaurant
═ Gondola	△ Danger	🪑 Picnic Tables
⌐ Quad SuperChair	Ⓝ Nastar Race Trail	🚌 Buses
High Traffic Area Ski Courteously	🕐 Self Timer Course	Powder Tours Registration
Ⓢ Closed Do Not Enter		

SYMBOLS AND COLOR CODES INDICATE THE RELATIVE SKIING DIFFICULTY FOR SLOPES AND TRAILS ON ASPEN MOUNTAIN ONLY. FOR YOUR OWN PROTECTION, DO NOT START DOWN A TRAIL OR SLOPE UNTIL YOU KNOW ITS DEGREE OF DIFFICULTY AND NEVER SKI A CLOSED TRAIL.

ASPEN MOUNTAIN, ASPEN, COLO.

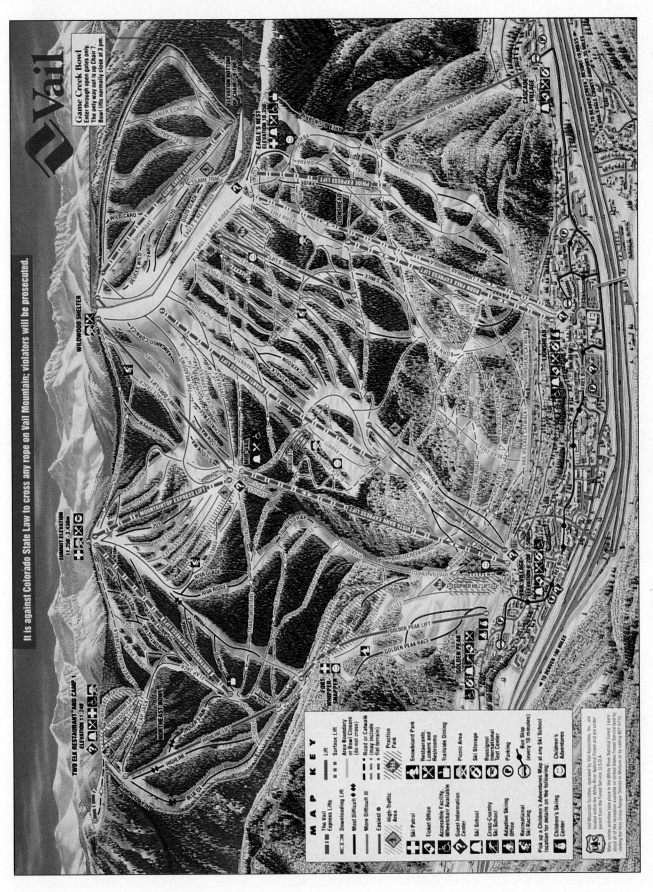

sugarloaf/usa
TRAIL GUIDE

SKIERS AND SNOWBOARDERS RESPONSIBILITY CODE

There are elements of risk in skiing that common sense and personal awareness can reduce.

1. Ski under control or in such a manner that you can stop or avoid other skiers or objects.
2. When skiing downhill or overtaking another skier you must avoid the skier below you.
3. You must not stop where you obstruct a trail or are not visible from above.
4. When entering a trail or starting downhill, yield to other skiers.
5. All skiers shall wear retention straps or ski brakes to prevent runaway skis.
6. You shall keep off closed trails and posted areas and observe all posted signs.
7. You shall not ski while under the influence of alchohol or drugs.
8. If you are involved in a collision with another skier resulting in injury, it is your responsibility to remain at the scene until the ski patrol arrives.
9. You shall observe all posted slow skiing trails and areas.
10. Do not ski trails that are too difficult for your ability.

ANY VIOLATION OF THIS CODE CAN RESULT IN THE LOSS OF LIFT TICKET WITHOUT WARNING AND WITHOUT REFUND.

A. SPILLWAY X-CUT
B. OLD WINTER'S WAY
C. MOSTATION X-CUT
D. SLUICE CHUTE

E. CRIBWORKS
F. BIRCH HOOK
G. WINDROW EXT.
H. BUCKSAW X-CUT

SUGARLOAF/USA, CARRABASSETT VALLEY, MAINE

185

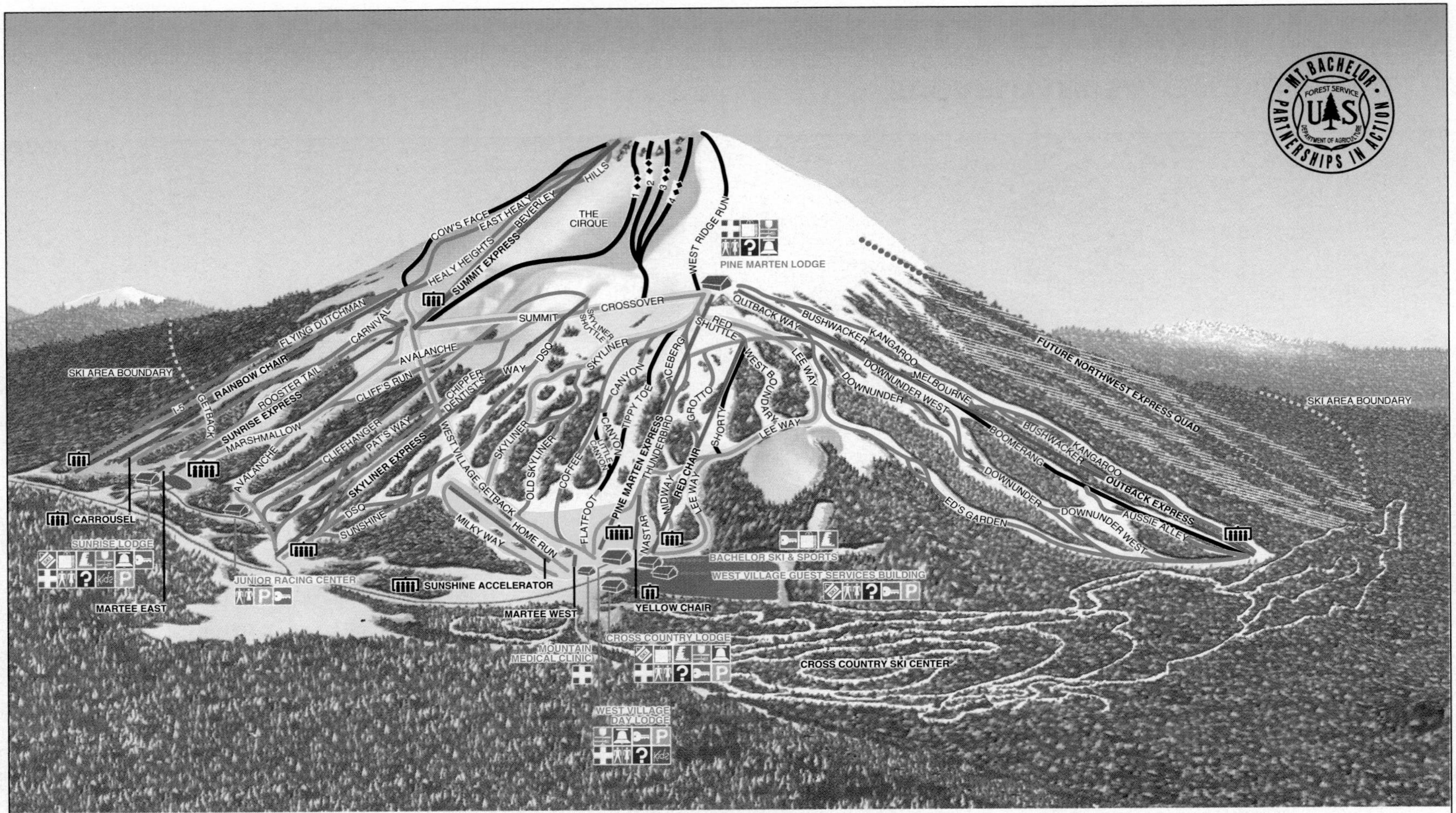

SERVICES

TICKETS	SHOPS
SKI SCHOOL	DAY CARE
FOOD	FIRST AID
RESTROOMS	INFORMATION
RENTALS/REPAIR	LOCKERS
SLOW/FAMILY AREA	PARKING

TRAILS

● GREEN Easiest   ■ BLUE More Difficult   ◆ BLACK Most Difficult   ◆◆ BLACK Experts Only

EASIEST DESCENTS

Outback—Kangaroo/Bushwacker
Yellow—Flatfoot
Pine Marten—Skyliner
Sunrise—Marshmallow
Rainbow—Carnival

Red—Last Chance
Sunshine—Home Run
Skyliner—Avalanche
Summit—Beverley Hills
Carrousel—Carnival

EXPRESS QUAD   TRIPLE   DOUBLE

LIFTS

	VERTICAL RISE
OUTBACK EXPRESS	1,780'
RED CHAIR	1,158'
YELLOW CHAIR	357'
PINE MARTEN EXPRESS	1,360'
SKYLINER EXPRESS	1,316'
SUNRISE EXPRESS	808'
SUMMIT EXPRESS	1,725'
RAINBOW CHAIR	1,215'
MARTEE EAST	50'
MARTEE WEST	50'
CARROUSEL	171'
SUNSHINE ACCELERATOR	257'

FOR MORE INFORMATION

1-800-829-2442 or 503-382-2442
On-mountain service information and reservations including
Skier Development Center, Day Care, Banquet/Group
Events.
503-382-7888
Ski report and summer events.
1-800-800-8334
Vacation planning assistance and reservations.

MT. BACHELOR, CASCADE LAKES HIGHWAY, ORE.

PARK CITY SKI AREA, PARK CITY, UTAH

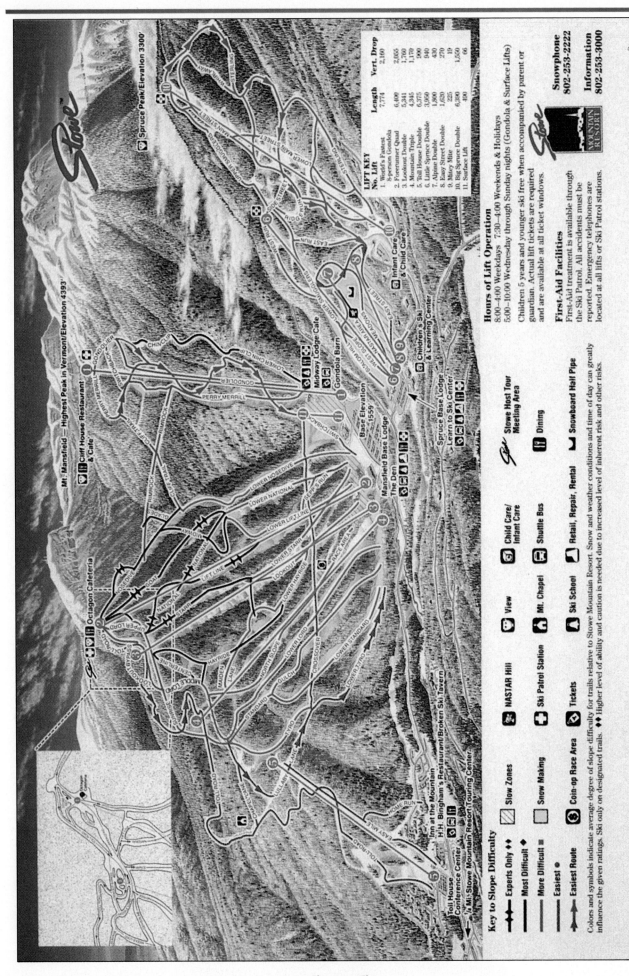

STOWE MOUNTAIN RESORT, Stowe, Vt.

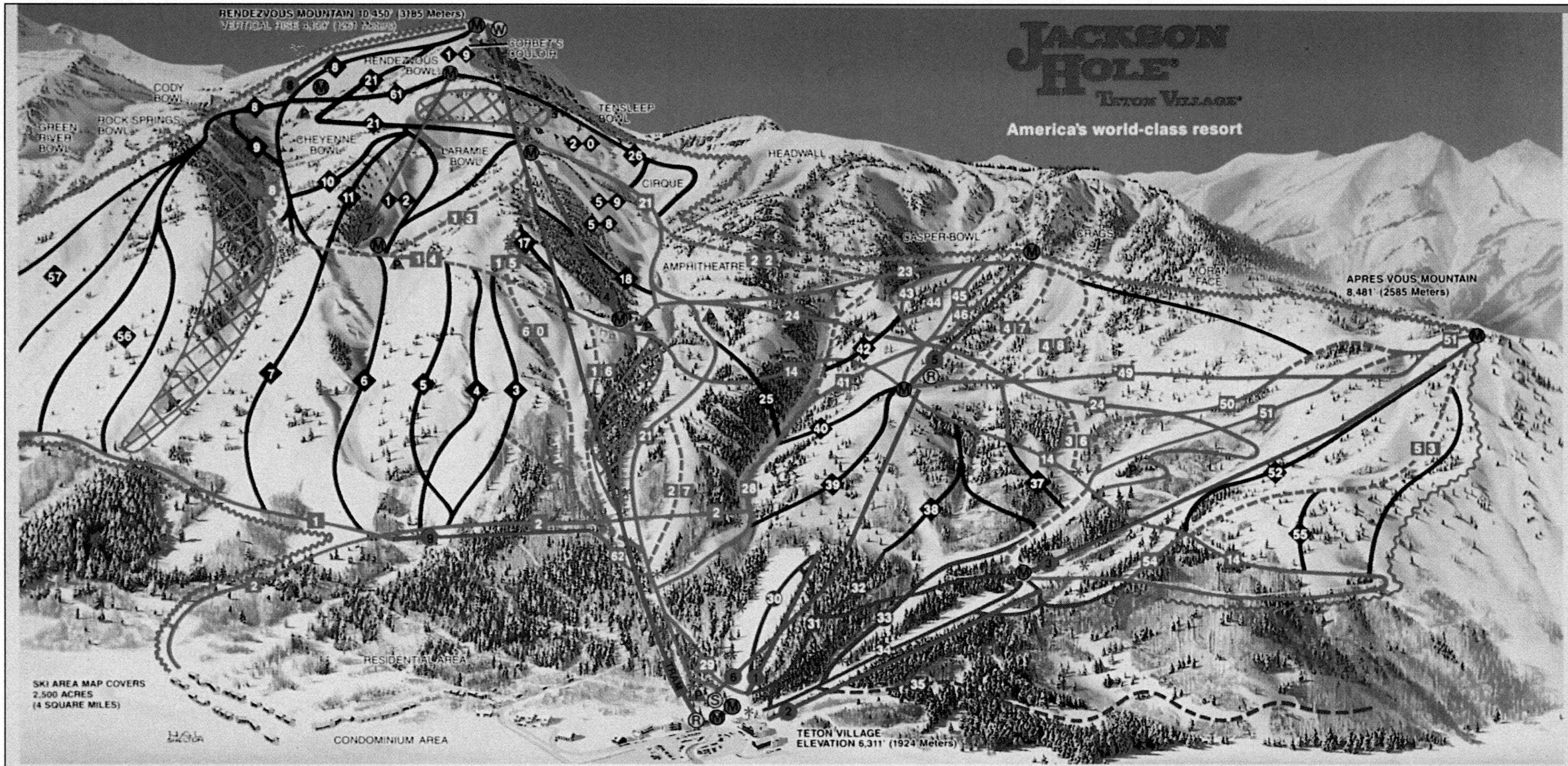

RENDEZVOUS MOUNTAIN 10,450' (3185 Meters)
VERTICAL RISE 4,139' (1259 Meters)

APRES VOUS MOUNTAIN 8,481' (2585 Meters)

TETON VILLAGE ELEVATION 6,311' (1924 Meters)

SKI AREA MAP COVERS 2,500 ACRES (4 SQUARE MILES)

CONDOMINIUM AREA

America's world-class resort

MAP KEY

- (M) MOUNTAIN MAPS
- PATROL PHONE
- LIFTS
- (R) RESTAURANT
- (W) WARMING HUT (FOOD)
- (S) SKI SCHOOL MEETING PLACE
- * SNOWMAKING
- PATROLLED AREA BOUNDARY—DO NOT CROSS
- CLOSED AREAS—SEVERE AVALANCHE HAZARD AREA
- CAUTION
- YOU ARE HERE

TRAIL DIFFICULTY SYMBOLS

- ● EASIEST
- ■ MODERATELY DIFFICULT
- ▪ MORE DIFFICULT— VARIED TERRAIN PLUS SNOW CONDITIONS FOR THE BETTER THAN AVERAGE SKIER
- ♦ MOST DIFFICULT— EXPERT
- ♦♦ MOST DIFFICULT— EXPERT USE EXTRA CAUTION

TRAIL NAMES

1. Union Pass Traverse	21. Gros Ventre	42. Sunrise
2. Way Home	22. Nez Perce Traverse	43. Camp Ground
3. North Colter Ridge	23. Amphitheatre Traverse	44. Timbered Island
4. Buffalo Bowl	24. Solitude Traverse	45. Easy Does It
5. South Colter Ridge	25. Avalanche	46. Lift Line
6. Rawlins Bowl	26. Downhill	47. Sleeping Indian
7. Lower Sublette Ridge	27. Slalom	48. Wide Open
8. Rendezvous Trail	28. Sundance Gully	49. Togwotee Pass Traverse
9. Bivouac	29. Eagle's Rest Cutoff	50. Moran
10. Bird In The Hand	30. Eagle's Rest	51. Upper Werner
11. Pepi's Run	31. Pooh Bear	52. Upper Teewinot
12. Alta Chutes	32. Antelope Flats	53. St. Johns
13. Grand	33. St. Johns	54. Teewinot Gully
14. Lower Teewinot	34. Lower Werner	55. Secret Slice
15. Gannett	35. South Pass Traverse	56. North Hobback
16. Lower Tram Line	36. Solitude Cutoff	57. South Hobback
17. Riverton Bowl	37. Ashley Ridge	58. Tower Three Chute
18. Thunder	38. Beaver Tooth	59. Paint Brush
19. East Ridge Traverse	39. Jackson Bowl	60. Lander Bowl
20. Expert Chutes	40. Nez Perce	61. Hanging Rock
	41. Blacktail	62. U.P. Connection

LIFTS

Lift	Length	Vertical Rise	Time
AERIAL TRAM	2.4 Miles Long	4,139' Vertical Rise	12 Minutes
1. EAGLE'S REST DOUBLE CHAIR	2,260' Long	330' Vertical Rise	5 Minutes
2. TEEWINOT DOUBLE CHAIR	3,060' Long	425' Vertical Rise	7 Minutes
3. APRES VOUS DOUBLE CHAIR	5,000' Long	1,745' Vertical Rise	10 Minutes
4. THUNDER DOUBLE CHAIR	3,770' Long	1,466' Vertical Rise	8 Minutes
5. CASPER BOWL TRIPLE CHAIR	3,450' Long	1,046' Vertical Rise	8 Minutes
6. CRYSTAL SPRINGS DOUBLE CHAIR	4,113' Long	1,196' Vertical Rise	9 Minutes
7. UPPER SUBLETTE RIDGE QUAD CHAIR	4,108' Long	1,630' Vertical Rise	
*8. RENDEZVOUS BOWL SURFACE LIFT	2,714' Long	824' Vertical Rise	5 Minutes
9. UNION PASS SURFACE LIFT	1,360' Long	150' Vertical Rise	2 Minutes

* This lift does not operate during periods of adverse wind, weather or snow conditions.

IMPORTANT NOTICE

FOR SKI PATROL ASSISTANCE.
DIAL 150 ON ANY SKI PATROL TELEPHONE, OR CONTACT NEAREST LIFT OPERATOR.

This trail map is conceptual in nature and generally represents the location and difficulty of ski trails. The classification of ski runs is based on good weather and snow conditions. During periods of low visibility or other inclement weather and snow conditions, the degree of difficulty of the ski runs may change. For specific trail conditions, ask ski patrol or ski host.

Be aware of changing conditions. Natural and man-made obstacles exist. Grooming activities are routinely in progress on slopes and trails. Use caution, ski in control, and ski only on designated slopes or trails.

Skiing closed areas is a misdemeanor and subject to a fine of up to $100.00.

THE JACKSON HOLE SKI RESORT IS OPERATED IN COOPERATION WITH THE BRIDGER-TETON NATIONAL FOREST

JACKSON HOLE/TETON VILLAGE, TETON VILLAGE, WYO.

BOYNE HIGHLANDS, Harbor Springs, Mich.

Vernon Valley   Great Gorge North   Great Gorge South

Trail Map Key
- ✳ **BEGINNER**
- ● **EASIEST** (Novice)
- ■ **MORE DIFFICULT** (Intermediate)
- ◆ **MOST DIFFICULT** (Expert)
- ✚ **FIRST AID** – SKI PATROL

VERNON VALLEY/GREAT GORGE, Vernon, N. J.

● 33% *EASIEST*   ■ 32% *MORE DIFFICULT*   ◆ 35% *MOST DIFFICULT*

Slow Ski Areas   Slope Access Walking Trails   Caution

⊘ Skier Traffic Controlled
Access to these trails limited at times

Safe On Skis

SNOWSHOE MOUNTAIN RESORT, Snowshoe, W. Va.
(Silver Creek, not shown, is operated by the same owners.)

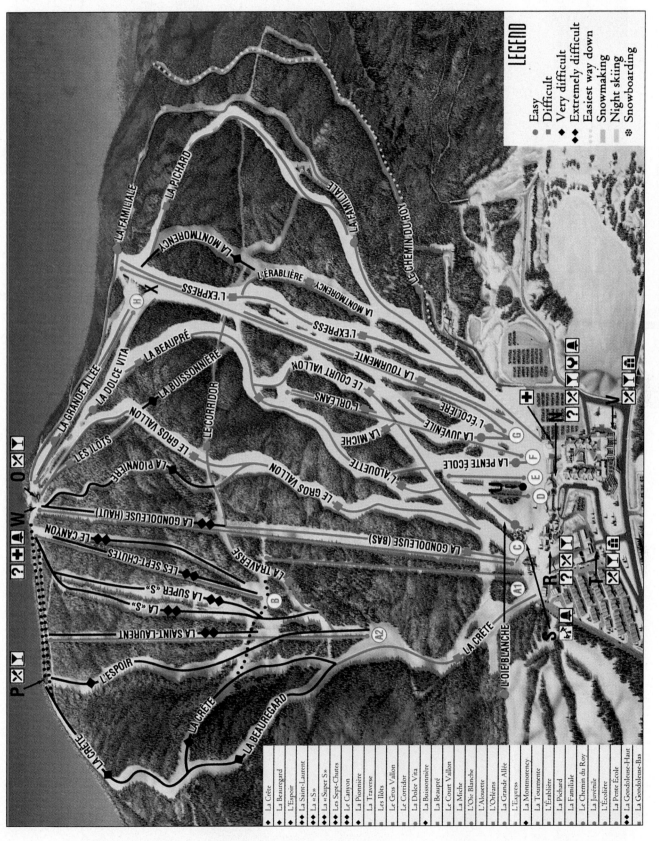

PARC DU MONT-SAINTE-ANNE, BEAUPRE, QUEBEC

LEGEND

●	Easy	
■	Difficult	
◆	Very difficult	
◆◆	Extremely difficult	
◆	Easiest way down	
∷	Snowmaking	
▬	Night skiing	
❈	Snowboarding	

La Crête	◆
La Beaurgard	◆
L'Espoir	◆
La Saint-Laurent	◆
La «S»	◆◆
La «Super S»	◆◆
Les Sept-Chutes	◆
Le Canyon	◆
La Pionnière	◆
La Traverse	●
Les Îlôts	●
Le Gros Vallon	■
Le Corridor	■
La Dolce Vita	■
La Buissonnière	◆
La Beaupré	■
Le Court Vallon	■
La Miche	■
L'Oie Blanche	●
L'Alouette	●
L'Orléans	■
La Grande Allée	■
L'Express	●
La Montmorency	■
La Tourmente	◆
L'Érablière	●
La Pichard	■
La Familiale	●
Le Chemin du Roy	●
La Juvénile	●
L'École	●
La Pente École	●
La Gondoleuse-Haut	◆
La Gondoleuse-Bas	●

MT. PATTISON

HELM

MCBRIDE RANGE

MT. BAKER

CHEAKAMUS GLACIER

WHIRLWIND

WHISTLER MOUNTAIN
PEAK LOOKOUT 2,182M/7,160'

BAGEL BOWL

WEST BOWL

OVERLORD

FISSILE

SINGING PASS

PICCOLO

GLACIER BOWL

WHISTLER BOWL

OVERLORD GLACIER

FLUTE

SYMPHONY BOWL

HARMONY BOWL

THE ROUNDHOUSE & PIKA'S

RAVEN'S NEST

The Spearhead &
Spearhead Glacier

BLACKCOMB PEAK

SEVENTH HEAVEN

RENDEZVOUS LODGE

OLYMPIC STATION

FITZSIMMONS CREEK

WHISTLER CREEK BASE
QUICKSILVER CAFE
DUSTY'S

ALTA LAKE

ARNOLD PALMER 18 HOLE GOLF COURSE

WHISTLER VILLAGE GONDOLA BASE

WHISTLER VILLAGE
ELEVATION 675M/2,214'

BLACKCOMB MOUNTAIN
2,284M/7,494'
HORSTMAN HUT

BLACKCOMB GLACIER

HORSTMAN GLACIER

SAUDAN COULOIR

BLACKCOMB BOWL

GLACIER BITE

HORSTMAN CREEK

BLACKCOMB BASES

ROBERT TRENT JONES JR.
18 HOLE GOLF COURSE

RUBY BOWL

CRYSTAL RIDGE

CRYSTAL HUT

WHISTLER/BLACKCOMB SKI RESORT, WHISTLER, BRITISH COLUMBIA